THE

QUESTIONS

OF

JESUS

Don C Harris

The Questions of Jesus (2007 Second Printing) (2015 Third Printing)
 By Don C Harris

Printed in the United States of America

ISBN 978-0-9792829-0-4

Unless otherwise indicated, Scripture quotations are taken from the King
James Version of the Bible

AREOPAGUS PUBLISHING

www.AreopagusPublishing.com

*To my mother,
who taught me the power and
beauty of words, from a very
young age.*

Thanks Mom.

Introduction

The questions in red letters became a curiosity to me because of their depth and scope, but more so, because of who asked them. Albeit some of the questions asked by Jesus Christ were rhetorical, that is, asked for effect, or asked more to provoke thought than to solicit an answer, some questions Christ posed were asked merely because He wanted an answer. For some, it makes them uneasy to think that Jesus did not know the answer in advance. We have been taught that "Jesus knew everything" as if He were some sort of mind reader or telepathic. The Scriptures do not support this idea; it is therefore only conjecture. Poor conjecture, in my opinion. When the Scriptures state, "...Jesus knew their thoughts..." (Luke 6:8 – Matthew 12:25) they simply speak of perception. Jesus was infinitely wise and extraordinarily perceptive and He knew mankind better than they knew themselves. As John states so perfectly, "But Jesus ... knew all men... for he knew what was in man." (John 2:24-25)

It is Christ's keen perception and His unique wisdom that shines from His questions. Sometimes, with His questions, He exposed hypocrites to the world. Once, He asked the sanctimonious Pharisees, "The Baptism of John, was it commissioned from heaven or of men?" knowing they could not answer and remain veiled to the people. Sometimes His questions quietly and discretely exposed the inner thoughts and motives of His own disciples so that their intentions would become apparent to themselves, as when He queried them about their motivation for attending John the Baptist's meetings in the wilderness, "What went ye out to see?" But, sometimes He asked a question simply because He did not know the answer and wanted one, as when He asked Mary about the burial place of her brother, Lazarus, "Where have ye laid him?"

Whatever the reason Jesus asks His questions, in all our conversational encounters with the Savior, it will be His wisdom that beams, His glory that shines, and His Heart of love and compassion that is laid before us. Your answers to His questions will sometimes make you uncomfortable and lay your heart open to Him in return, but to whom, save Christ, could you trust your candid answers and confessions, and before whom could you lay your condition in forthright display in full assurance of acceptance? Who is able to open your life for examination in pure love and unfeigned truth as Jesus can? What a Preacher He was, what a Teacher, and what a Friend we have in Him.

As you hear His questions and consider your own answers, you are thrust into His time and He into yours. By quiet contemplation, words on a page become a live conversation. In meditation, ink and paper can become living words in your ears, and it is then that the words of God become The Word of God. It is then that you will experience more than the mere reading of history; you will become part of a verbal exchange, a part of the repartee, banter, and even argument with our Lord Jesus Christ! If you will only answer His questions honestly and with sincerity, you may well peer into depths of your own soul and purpose, heretofore undiscovered and unknown.

Ours is a quest to learn of our Messiah and His Father, YHVH. Jesus asked questions of the people in the Bible's stories to fulfill the will of God, and that was (as it remains with us) to bring the chosen ones closer to His Father. With this devotional, you can experience a daily exchange of thought with the Christ of the Bible, leading you closer to Him, revealing His ways, His thoughts and eventually, if He wills it so, His Father. As He said in Matthew 11:27-28, "All things are delivered unto me of my Father: and no man knoweth the Son, but the Father; neither knoweth any man the Father, save the Son, and he to whomsoever the Son will reveal him."

I have been frustrated with books that assume that I, the reader, have the same literary background as the author. I want you to feel no such annoyance. There will be no quotes from Greek poetry here, but you will find an abundance of Scripture. May I assume you have a familiarity with the Gospel accounts of the life of Christ? The questions, in some cases, are composites from all Gospel accounts containing the same question. For clarity, all Scriptures where the question appears are noted. If you doubt your level of familiarity and want to re-read the Gospels, this devotional will make a good companion for such an endeavor. The text references are in chronological order (as much as is possible) so you can follow the events in the life of Jesus if you want to. However, there is no necessity to follow my order if you are not inclined to do so. My advice is to read this book in the same manner it was written to help you appreciate (and hopefully, experience) the power in which it was received.

Over a period of four years of morning devotional time and meditation, life experience and revelation was this book created and edited into the form you have in your hand. Time cannot be a factor in revelation of truth, dispensation of grace, or receiving of solace from our God.

Take one question at a time. Read it and contemplate it quietly for a while; allow time for the Lord to speak to you. Resist the temptation to push through to the next question. Each question takes only approximately ten minutes to read, take again as long to sit quietly and then perhaps add notes of your own impressions. Trying to read several questions one after the other or an attempt to quickly finish the book will not prove to be satisfactory. You may be prompted to worship or pray afterward, so time allotted for this will be very valuable. Sometimes the message of one question will be on your mind all day. These are times when Truth is to be revealed many hours after devotional time has ended. Take your time.

The context and background of each story will prove to be a rich source as well. Have your Bible handy to establish context and read the references and footnotes given. In my personal devotions, I would read the verses before and after the referenced Scripture to understand the timeframe of Christ's life and to get a feel for the mood of the hearers before I would meditate on each question. I also recommend reading the "Author's Notes" below before beginning the devotional material. There you will find my reasoning about the "mechanics" of the writing, i.e. capitalization, emphasis in quotation, etc.

What a wondrous journey writing this was for me. Each devotional was written during and after my early morning hours of meditation as the Lord opened them to me, one question at a time. It was always a joy to discover a new question and explore it. When the end of the Gospels was drawing near I felt a sadness, as if I was losing a magnificent opportunity to visit with the Savior each morning. As I edited the work, going back through it and reading it as you will, I was pleased to find my experiences repeated and yet, somehow, were richer than before.

I am happy to share these devotionals with you. I would love to know that you received them in the same richness of Spirit that I did.

Author's Notes

View of Scripture:

Your author has the highest respect for the Bible as a document miraculously given from God to contemporary man. It is not, however, prudent to elevate it to the status, rank, or position belonging to our living Savior as our Teacher and Guide. His promise was to send a Comforter who will lead and guide us to all Truth. That Guide is none other than His own Spirit, the Spirit of God.

The Bible is a true and accurate record of men experiencing that selfsame guidance. However, the record of this guidance in the lives of others is merely that – a record. A glorious and markedly valuable record indeed, but this record should never replace the personal experience of sitting at the Master's feet. Jesus Christ is alive again from the dead and fully capable of opening[1] the Scriptures to His followers. We know that God spoke in time past to the fathers by the prophets. Has He in these last days spoken unto us by ink and pen? No! He has spoken unto us by his Son. So says Hebrews 1:1-2.

It is our Father's intention to teach us directly through a living relationship with His Son Jesus Christ. In times past, He used men as prophets; it is mistakenly assumed that today He uses only a book. The verse in Hebrews, cited above, makes no such assertion nor does it defend such an idea. From this Scripture it is clear that Jehovah speaks to us by His Son.

Discussions on the infallibility of Scripture, contradictions found therein, dubious inspiration of modern Bibles, etc., I will leave to some other forum. These views are usually traditional, typically personal, frequently inflammatory, and have proven to be useless deliberations that put man no closer to his goal of reconciliation to God. Regrettably, it is also observable that those who enjoy engagement in these disputes are usually the worst violators of their own Bible's clearest doctrines.

The Bible is an inestimable gift of God to lost and lawless mankind. Without it, in our modern sinful and separated condition, living so far from our ancestral family in God, I fear it would be nearly impossible (especially in our short lifetimes) to gain such instruction from our Father directly. Even so, to merely learn it or read it is not the same as hearing it. Remember, Jesus' words were not, he who has eyes let him read, but he who has ears, let him hear. To mistake one for the other, results in deficiency and confusion, harm and loss. For this singular reason, churches, supposedly built upon unambiguous teachings of an infallible Bible are diverse, contradictory, and dissimilar rivals. Hear the voice of the living Savior. He will guide you.

---

[1] Luke 24:32, "And they said one to another, Did not our heart burn within us, while he talked with us by the way, and while he opened to us the scriptures?"

Scripture Text Quotation:

All Scripture text, capitalization, punctuation, and spelling within quotes are copied directly from the King James Version of the Bible and referenced. Ellipses represent text deleted for brevity or clarity. Individual words in a text may be bolded, to emphasize its connection to a subject, or italicized to bring the readers attention to a particular word. Words in brackets are inserted to assist definition but do not appear in the text cited. In all such cases, the references are noted if the reader feels confirmation necessary. There is no intention to change the meaning of any passage.

The title of each devotional is derived from Scripture, but in some cases is transliterated for clarity. Some questions appear several times throughout the Gospels. These texts are usually combined into one all-inclusive idea and every attempt is made to faithfully include all the descriptive terms in each Scripture. From that idea, one representative question is used as title. References for these are given as well.

Footnotes:

There are undoubtedly some to whom the Bible and other literary references will be well known and obvious. Others will appreciate the footnotes referencing the texts themselves or the locations of texts drawn upon. Many references are parenthetically added to the end of the quotation while others are footnoted so as not to clutter the reading. I hope this arrangement will provide smooth reading for both those familiar with each reference and those inclined to research all of them.

Capitalization of Terms:

Many words in our language are used to portray our indescribable God. When differing descriptions are floating around in the reader's head, sentences can become confusing and sometimes significance and meaning are sacrificed. Even the meaning of Scripture can be lost or misunderstood when improper definitions are attached to words. Capitalizing these words can help to clear some of this confusion. Capitalization was considered carefully when writing this document. Care and thought was given to the definition and application of a word when considering whether it should be capitalized.

For example, the words, "Way, Truth, and Life,"[2] when capitalized, denote a personage of divinity -- Christ in particular. Any word referring to deity will be capitalized.

"Church," when capitalized, refers to Christ's faithful, gathered, yet invisible, body of obedient servants and children of God. When not capitalized, it is intentional. The Quaker (Religious Society of Friends) term for what conventional Christianity calls "church" is "Meeting." It is capitalized only to

---

[2] John 14:6, "Jesus saith unto him, I am the way, the truth, and the life: no man cometh unto the Father, but by me."

9

set it apart from the usual understanding of the word. "Friend" is capitalized for the same reason.

The word "Truth" is capitalized when it refers to Christ or the Truth of God, (the powerful, eternal Truth that is revealed supernaturally to the heart of man) also known as the Truth of the Gospel. It is also the universal, yet supernatural, understanding of what is right, holy, honest and true or the "...light that lighteth every man that cometh into the world"[3] (the Truth Paul mentions in Romans 1:18-20). The lower case form of "truth" is what is accurate, factual and correct no matter its consequences or its effect upon righteousness. For example: $2+2 = 4$ is a mathematical truth.

"Spirit" is capitalized when referring to the Spirit of God. Whether it be the selfsame Spirit found in Christ during His incarnation or His Spirit found in the heart of a believer. There are spirits foreign to the kingdom of God that most assuredly are not capitalized, but there is a spirit in man as well that, while not deserving denotation of evil, does not attain the level or distinction of divine origin. This is the yearning spirit of man to attain what is good and decent, not the fleshly lust of shortcutting righteousness, or the desire to gain beyond his design. School spirit, true patriotism, and desire for justice are all from the spirit of man. Although these are vestiges of the One who created us, over the sinful eons it has degraded to become an untrustworthy replacement for God's Holy Spirit promised to rejuvenate and restore us.

The word "Prophet" is capitalized when referring to Christ, or as part of a particular person's title, or the all inclusive term "Prophets" referring to the collection of writings of the prophets of old. Reference made merely to the office itself is lower case.

The word "Law" is capitalized in admiration of its Author, origin, permanence and immutability.

"Bible" is capitalized somewhat because of tradition, but primarily because of my personal respect for our miraculously preserved and wonderful gift from God, purchased and repurchased over the centuries with the blood of His faithful servants.

Many personal and other pronouns are capitalized when they refer to deity.

The King James made no such distinction and no capitalization changes are made when it is quoted.

Denominational Sensitivity:
None. You will undoubtedly find ideas and views in this writing that are, in varying degrees, difficult for you no matter which denomination you find most comfortable. My own umbrage for the denominations that hold so many Christians back from a personal communion with Christ could easily be blamed for my lack of consideration for their protests with this writing.

---

[3] John 1:9, "That was the true Light, which lighteth every man that cometh into the world."

Many of the ideas that disquiet denominational Christianity presented in this text were new to me at the time of writing, as most everything here is a record of my personal devotions. Although abrasive and perhaps condemning at times to conventional views of doctrines, no revelation of the Lord Jesus has ever disappointed me. His revelations of the Scriptures have always surprised me and delighted me, sometimes shamed me and not a few times, startled me.

The Lord still reveals things to me that startle me at first, then, as I look at it from other angles, view other Scriptures from my new vantage point, I become amazed that I have not seen it this way all of my life. Revelation is like that. Don't rush. Don't condemn out-of-hand simply because your denomination's vocabulary is not found here or familiar axioms or clichés of your church are not used. I make no pretense to follow any denominational guidelines, not even of my beloved Society of Friends. I learned years ago, to have a mind that is not hemmed in by prejudice, stifled by tradition, fenced by preconception is to have all knowledge at least within reach. It is a daily fight to keep these encroachers at bay, but is well worth the struggle.

To see something that is so familiar to you a little differently because the God of the universe took time to illuminate you, will change you forever. I am different than when I started this book four years ago. I hope you will be, too.

Contents

I Early Ministry

II Days of Popularity

III Days of Opposition

IV Last Days

V After the Resurrection

Introduction

From time to time you may hear someone say, "That's a good question." This can mean a variety of things to the one who says it and to those who hear it. Usually it means, "I'll have to think of an answer." As I read the questions of Christ in the Gospels, I was constantly saying to myself, "That's a good question..." and almost immediately I would add, "... and it deserves an honest answer."

Then I endeavored to gather and examine all the recorded questions Jesus asked throughout His life and ministry and honestly attempted to answer them, or to apply their rhetorical truth, one by one, for myself. The idea of this guide is for you, the reader, to do the same. You will find here, riches yet untapped, available by a simple honest approach to the questions of Christ. Answers to these questions provide a sound basis to answer questions of life. A foundation of solid understanding awaits an honest seeker.

Much of our time and consideration is given to the questions that we ask God. These questions often go unanswered and leave us in a state of confusion worse than before we asked. Is it that they have no answer? As C. S. Lewis asked, "Can a mortal ask questions which God finds unanswerable? Quite easily, I should think. All nonsense questions are unanswerable."[4] But what about the questions He asked us? Because they were formulated in the mind of the Son of God they must be answerable and of inestimable value as well.

At the end of each devotional meditation the question is presented to the reader for consideration in new light. Let an answer formulate within and ponder it and its implications. It is unfortunate, but the reader will find that today, many of the questions Jesus asked are never posed and certainly never honestly answered. What a waste of resource this is! Jesus was a master communicator. In this day, we chase to and fro to find someone to help us, to motivate us, to guide us. Communicators we may have among us, but one with such a message, one with such pure motivation, one with pure caring and love for His audience, is more difficult to find. To whom but Jesus could we ascribe our unrestrained trust with our very lives? Unfortunately, His Bible, though still a best seller, remains least read. Alas, Bibles bought, but not owned; stories read but not heard; questions asked but not answered.

---

[4] C. S. Lewis (1898–1963), British author. *A Grief Observed,* pt. 4 (1961).

I Early Ministry

"He who begins by loving Christianity better than truth, will proceed by loving his own sect or church better than Christianity, and end in loving himself better than all."

Samuel Taylor Coleridge
(1772–1834), English poet, critic.

1. *How is it that ye sought me?*

Luke 2:49, "And he said unto them, How is it that ye sought me? Wist ye not that I must be about my Father's business?"

There are many seeking Christ today. This book will likely share a shelf with many others, the presence of which testifies to the fact that man seeks a relationship with God. But are we seeking God or are we seeking a way into God's favor? Though subtle, there is a difference.

As the feast drew to a close, the families that ate and played and worshiped together prepared for the long trek home. Assuming Jesus was with other family members of Joseph son of Jacob, they set upon their journey. Then, Jesus was nowhere to be found among the family! His parents sought Him desperately for three days; sorrowing all the while they were searching. They finally found Him conversing with the doctors of the Law in the Temple. He was so assured that they knew where to find Him, He asked, nearly surprised, "How is it that ye sought me? [Didn't you know]…that I must be about my Father's business?"

When we are outside of Christ and we determine to find Him, we seek Him frantically, panicking and sorrowing that He is not found in the places we look for Him. We put our trust in others or in ideas that seem to point us to Christ, but as time goes by, we find that things were not as we supposed. People disappoint us, the authors of our books turn out to be profiteers, pastors prove to be only hirelings, and friends are only as actors in a play, we find no truth, no substance, no reality, no answers.

We do not find the true Christ in the experience of the people around us or their leadership, we do not find Him in churches or seminaries, we do not find Him in books or lectures, sermons or songs, He is neither to be found in philosophies new nor old. We finally collapse in discouragement and despair and can feel it is no use to search any longer.

We even entertain thoughts of conspiracy and sinister plots of illusion, or perhaps we surmise that God is not real at all; it is all fakery and a crutch to the hopeless and fearful, not for a thinking man or one who demands truth! This couldn't be more mistaken. Just because the real Jesus is not where you look for Him does not mean He does not exist. What you, my friend, need to identify is "The Father's business."

One Sabbath day, not much different than any other, everyone gathered at the synagogue to hear the scrolls of Moses and the Prophets read. Men above the age of thirty were given, in turn, the opportunity to read from the Law and or Prophets, with the rest of the rabbis. This Sabbath was different only in that this week, it fell to Jesus, the son of Joseph, to read. He read from Isaiah, "The Spirit of the Lord is upon me, because he hath anointed me to preach the gospel to the poor; he hath sent me to heal the brokenhearted, to preach deliverance to the captives, and recovering of sight to the blind, to set at liberty them that are bruised, To preach the acceptable year of the Lord." (Luke 4:18-19) Then He closed the book and said, "This day this Scripture is fulfilled in your ears." Jesus, by reading this and confirming it, here shows us the prophesied and fulfilled mission of Messiah. We may find here, "The Father's Business."

The Father's Business

In our day, it is a little more difficult to "follow" Christ as He asked the disciples to do in Scripture. They simply had to physically follow Him around. By doing so they were shown His work and ministry and made familiar with His way. We must find His way and get in it. This is not difficult to do if we are not "helped" by well-meaning, but misguided persons who tell us what Christ requires of us in no uncertain terms. The problem is that they have no idea either what God expects of them, or us. You must depend rather on the Spirit of God to show you this way and when you find it, you will find Christ. His ministry is to be about the Father's business.

The Father's business is opening eyes blinded by hatred and sin, to heal the broken hearted, the life-trodden souls that are only "chess pieces" to the power brokers of the "real" world. The Father's business is to justify, rectify and set in fair and proper order the heart of desperate man and to make him acceptable in the sight of God. The Father's business is to preach the Jubilee of the Lord! The year that all is set right!

You will not find on Isaiah's prophetic list of Messiah's accomplishments, from which Jesus read, the erecting of church buildings, or the organization of denominations. You will find that God's business has little to do with conventional Christianity and even less to do with doctrines, creeds, and liturgies. He is not interested in developing philosophies or trite maxims to live by, or in publishing "Seven Easy Steps to Salvation." He is not wringing His hands over the latest and greatest preacher or songwriter, author or singer, hoping that they will do well and "touch many lives."

The Father's business is to seek and to save those who are lost and out of the way, those who seek Him and repent, and those who live without offense to their conscience and know the taste of humility. Why do we search for God in the new and clean buildings when His interest is in alleys and suburbs and wherever His called ones are coming to the light of Christ? When you associate yourself with those who "have," you are farther from Christ than ever. When you get involved with those who "have not" and feeding the hungry, and helping the helpless, you will be closer to the ministry of Christ than ever before. You must come out of the convention, come out of the ordinary, do something for the one in prison, the one in bed with illness, and empty your closets for those who have needs. In doing so, you will find Christ.

Both of the examples in the story below were surprised when they found Christ was embodied in the poor, the sick, and the hungry ones. There is sadness in the realization that Christ was in their own community and they did not know it. *"Then shall the righteous answer him, saying, Lord, when saw we thee an hungred, and fed thee? or thirsty, and gave thee drink? When saw we*

19

thee a stranger, and took thee in? or naked, and clothed thee? Or when saw we thee sick, or in prison, and came unto thee? And the King shall answer and say unto them, "Verily I say unto you, Inasmuch as ye have done it unto one of the least of these my brethren, ye have done it unto me."

Jesus was not found in the religions of the world, nor was He found in some deep meditative state; He was found by those simply doing the Father's business. You can easily be cheated of His presence and power by running after the schemes concocted by modern teachers and preachers. All the while He may be easily found, in all His fullness, in repulsive places that these fancy, slick talkers and "spiritual guides" will not dare to go.

But fear not. When you do find the real Jesus, the true Messiah, the Son of God, He will comfort you and welcome you as though you had come from a long journey. You will tell Him of your horrible escapades, your close encounters with false prophets and liars of all sorts who told you where to search for Him. You will expound in detail how you almost gave up and thought He was dead! You will feel silly and ashamed when He looks at you and asks, "How is it ye sought for me? Didn't you know I would be about my Father's business?"

2. *What good is it to love those who love you?*

The question comes from Matthew 5:46-47 and its parallel in Luke 6:32-34 (Combined)

For if ye love them which love you, what reward have ye, what thank have ye? Do not even the publicans the same, for sinners also love those that love them? And if ye salute your brethren only, if ye do good to them which do good to you, what thank have ye, what do ye more than others? Do not even the publicans and sinners so? If ye lend to them of whom ye hope to receive, what thank have ye? for sinners also lend to sinners, to receive as much again. But love ye your enemies, and do good, and lend, hoping for nothing again; and your reward shall be great, and ye shall be the children of the Highest: for he is kind unto the unthankful and to the evil.

This Scripture has had many applications, most of which have been applied to the duty of Christians to feed the poor and clothe the naked and destitute. The dedicated Christian has done well in these areas, but, however applicable these Scriptures may be, let's look at it another way.

It must be admitted that we Christians like to play in our own backyard. We hang around those who don't challenge us, we cling to those who accept us as we are, and we give a wide berth to those who are willing to criticize us. We claim we avoid those who find fault in us, because they do not love us. The truth is that we simply don't love them. We can't seem to love an enemy; we can only love our friends. We don't love them enough to like them, nor like them enough to love them.

This deficiency is sometimes camouflaged as an enviable character trait. We pride ourselves on being easygoing, non-controversial, or a person who opposes confrontational issues, when in reality we lack an ability to love those who don't readily agree with us, so we overlook the differences, redefine words and assume the kindest of motives on the part of our detractors. We cannot love someone who doesn't agree with us so we don't bring up certain subjects, or say that "it doesn't matter" or that the disagreement is "majoring on minors." We know within ourselves that we can't love those who are different than us so we make efforts to avoid them. It that goodness? Is that kindness? Is that honest?

We must expand our circle of inclusion to take in the uncomplimentary, the uncouth, the unlovely, and yes, even the unclean, if we are to live to honor the words from Christ's sermon. We must be honest and admit that the level of love under which we operate is insufficient to include those who don't like us, or those who won't tolerate us, or those who don't hold us in the high esteem that we have developed in our spheres of familiarity.

You should ask yourself, "Do I like only those who like me? Am I willing to take social risks only with those who are familiar with my accomplishments or my social status? Do I have what it takes to hold my own in the world that doesn't know 'who' I am?" Do you have within you the love required to love those who are not impressed by you – to love those who do not rate you above them?

Sometimes this character flaw shows in our speech, our manner of dress, our deportment or even more subtle behavior seen by others and not readily recognizable to us.

The refining of this behavior will not come easily, as so much of it is below the level of conscience thought. It may help you to think of the differences that God was willing to overlook in order to create and maintain a relationship with you. You are admonished in the Scriptures to love and forgive even as you are loved and forgiven of God.[5] What good is it to love those who think you are great? Or, as Jesus put it, "What good is it to love those who love you?"

It is interesting that Jesus asks, "What good is it?" What good does it do; what good does it bring about? Then He adds, "Do not even the publicans and sinners the same?" When we find ourselves unable to love those who do not love us, we are discovering one of the dreaded attributes to our unregenerate heart and, perhaps, a soul yet in sin. When we can only love white, Anglo-Saxon, heterosexual, republicans, we advertise to the world that we have not known Christ.

When we only associate with those who have graduated from college, have a job on a certain pay scale, watch only public television, and only vote the democratic ticket, we are shallow and hollow and have little to offer the world. When we only socialize with those hold to our articles of faith, attain a certain level of righteousness, anti-smoking, anti-drinking, anti rock and roll, types that insist on saying, "Amen" instead of, "I agree" at the conclusion of everything we say, we are purposefully closing our world into a tighter and tighter circle because our affection toward the men and women whom Jesus loved, is diminishing.

What good is it to love those who love you? It really does not matter with whom you choose to identify and whom you avoid; it is the fact that you cannot love that condemns you and renders your faith in Christ a pretense. John 13:35, "By this shall all men know that ye are my disciples, if ye have love one to another."

Tolerance – The New "Love"

Many have made love an act of their will. Masquerading as loving, caring Christians, they are only tolerant of others. Tolerance is the new "love" among Christians. It is touted as a wonderful attribute, when in reality, it is a sinister replacement for the love that could be shed abroad in our hearts by the Holy Spirit if we would only let go of our pride. Tolerance is peddled as a

---

[5] Ephesians 4:32, "And be ye kind one to another, tenderhearted, forgiving one another, **even as** God for Christ's sake hath forgiven you."

superlative capacity, available only to those on a higher spiritual plane, when, in truth, it is a baleful substitute for the love of God.

Who among us wishes to be tolerated? Who would not rather be loved? When we tolerate the homosexual we do him no service, we only appease our own prejudices and render the guilt we feel, innocuous to our conscience. When we tolerate the obnoxious sinner we lead him no closer to Christ, we bring Christ no closer to him. When we tolerate opposition to our view we will find ourselves no closer to understanding our adversary than before. But, if we love them…what power! If we love them…what witness! If we love them…what reward! Alas, but how?

The answer may be simpler than you think. If we can remember that we pity those below us, we aspire to those above us, but we love those beside us. It can be our pride and ego that make true love so elusive. For whatever reason you convince yourself that you are avoiding the "unlovable," you must first judge the person as unlovable. This is done by classifying him as different from you. (Whether we judge them above us or below us is of little moment in this analysis.) The truth we avoid is that we are but a few facts (and even fewer secrets) from being deemed as unlovable as any, as obnoxious as any, and as repulsive as anyone else. Again, think of the person that God sees.

It is when you see yourself in this light that you begin to understand that all you are doing, when you offer true love to those who do not like you, is providing them what you so desperately need yourself. You do not want to be tolerated… you want to be loved. Love suffers long, and is kind, love envies not, love does not boast, love does not behave improperly, love will not allow you to seek your own way, love repels anger, love thinks no evil toward anyone, love never allows rejoicing when wrong is done but only when truth and justice are accomplished. Love "Beareth all things, believeth all things, hopeth all things, endureth all things." Love never fails. (1 Corinthians 13)

> *He drew a circle that shut me out—*
> *Heretic, rebel, a thing to flout.*
> *But love and I had the wit to win:*
> *We drew a circle that took him in.*[6]

The difference between the unregenerate one and you who knows Christ is that you have a capacity to truly love the unlovable. You have that ability because He first loved you.

When you love only those who love you, you deceive yourself into believing that you really love people. How do you respond to those who do not love you? How do you react to the unlovely or your would-be enemies?

If you exemplify the love of Christ, you bring hope to your community. Your supernatural love for those who do not love you is light – Light borne to a dark world, but…. "What good is it to love those who love you?"

---

[6] Author :Edwin Markham

3.   *Which of you by taking thought can add one cubit unto his stature?*

Matthew 6:27, Luke 12:24-38 (Combined) Therefore I say unto you, Take no thought for your life, what ye shall eat, or what ye shall drink; nor yet for your body, what ye shall put on. Is not the life more than meat, and the body more than raiment? Behold the ravens and fowls of the air: for they sow not, neither do they reap, nor gather into barns; yet your heavenly Father feedeth them. Are ye not much better than they? Which of you by taking thought can add one cubit unto his stature? If ye then be not able to do that thing which is least, why take ye thought for the rest? And why take ye thought for raiment? Consider the lilies of the field, how they grow; they toil not, neither do they spin: And yet I say unto you, That even Solomon in all his glory was not arrayed like one of these. Wherefore, if God so clothe the grass of the field, which to day is, and to morrow is cast into the oven, shall he not much more clothe you, O ye of little faith? Therefore take no thought, saying, What shall we eat? or, What shall we drink? or, Wherewithal shall we be clothed? (For after all these things do the Gentiles seek) for your heavenly Father knoweth that ye have need of all these things.

Without a doubt, to carry out the advice in this passage is difficult. If you are like me, you feel a sense of disobedience as you read these words. I want to live in that elusive place of love and plentitude and pick the fruit of God's providence as I stroll through this life without a care, yet, in defiance of YHVH's command, I fall dreadfully short of my desire.

What will we do with this feeling of defiance? We can add sobriety to our decision-making by answering the question: "Which of you by taking thought can add one cubit unto his stature?" The obvious answer is that none of us can. The truth is, when we do "take thought" for the things of this world, we are doing for ourselves what our God wants to do for us.

It is His desire to be in daily communion with His children. Since the beginning, when He walked with Adam in the cool of the day, He has missed this fellowship with man. Listen, as He speaks in Isaiah 1:2-3, "I have nourished and brought up children, and they have rebelled against me. The ox knoweth his owner, and the ass his master's crib: but Israel doth not know, my people doth not consider." The owner and crib are symbols of care and feeding, the very things of which we are admonished to beware not to become the agents of acquisition.

Notice that this particular Scripture is not speaking of preparation for disaster or disease or mayhem, it is speaking only of the daily things – those things that demand our attention three times a day. Three times a day we could be reminded to commune with God and three times a day we could thank Him truly for the food provided. Unfortunately however, because we provide our own food, our "thanks" or "blessing" said at mealtime has become a hollow act of ritual if compared to one that we would offer over food known to be provided by God alone. We can almost hear in the song of the birds every morning, "Give us day by day our daily bread" and "Thank you" as they find and gather for themselves and their young.

We must live in God's pleasure to be able to have this kind of confidence in His provision. Most of us provide our own food as surely as we guide our own lives. We know within ourselves that God's provision comes to us as we are submissive to Him as our Lord provider, and we rightfully link the action of our submission to His supply. We know that we must strive to be in His pleasure to enjoy His provision. This is borne upon other Scripture that immediately follows the one we are examining now. "No man can serve two masters: for either he will hate the one, and love the other; or else he will hold to the one, and despise the other. Ye cannot serve God and mammon."

Beware Of Ambition

We have a streak of God-like ambition in us that must be curbed. This desire to "increase our stature" by taking thought, by taking our life into our own hands, is a most dangerous one. It can only lead to self-exaltation no matter how much we pretend to dress it up in humble clothes and insist that we "thank God" for our self-gotten increase.

Your exaltation or advancement (if you are to have any at all) or your debasement must occur only by God's divine providence. This is the only way you may be assured that you are not out-running your guide, or taking a seat higher than you deserve. This point is clear in the parable from Luke 14:8-11,

"When thou art bidden of any man to a wedding, sit not down in the highest room; lest a more honourable man than thou be bidden of him; And he that bade thee and him come and say to thee, Give this man place; and thou begin with shame to take the lowest room. But when thou art bidden, go and sit down in the lowest room; that when he that bade thee cometh, he may say unto thee, Friend, go up higher: then shalt thou have worship in the presence of them that sit at meat with thee. For whosoever exalteth himself shall be abased; and he that humbleth himself shall be exalted."
Jesus would ask again, "Which of you by taking thought can add one cubit unto his stature?"

Some have translated this Scripture to read, "Who, by taking thought, can add one hour to his life span?" If this translation were true, we would have, in our century, an opportunity to challenge this Scripture. (Or do we?[7])

Some claim to be alive and well only because a doctor, somewhere in their past intervened with the natural progression of death. Doctors today are praised for adding, not only an hour, but possibly years to their life span. Some will credit their health and years to a regimen of exercise and vitamin supplements.

---

[7] Although, contrary to the explanation offered about increasing man's life span, statistics indicate the apparent increase is due mostly to the improvements in birth viability and not length of years.

Unfortunately, the years added are, in most cases, lived out in nursing homes, attached to machines, or with umbilicals of drugs, hospitals, and doctors, all parasitically draining their savings from them, along with the quality of their lives, till both are gone. The effort of immortality is a futile one. The sober consideration of this proposition as an impossibility is to be our impetus to accept the futility of trying to take thought in order to advance our lives as well. We must not push, we must not strive, and we must be content.

So how do we accomplish this idea of living for now, with no care for the inevitable needs of our future? It is clear in this advice, "… seek ye first the kingdom of God… and all these things shall be added unto you." Relax your hand on the wheel that steers your life. Hold the course He set for you. As you find yourself making your own provisions, let go. Make an opportunity for life to take another course. When you set your mind on gaining something, relax your effort and risk losing it. Let it come from another source, or let it not come at all.

Do we really want to live an hour longer than God's plan provides? Do you really want an inch more stature than He sees fit for you? How much of what you have now was gained only as a result of your efforts and not His?

Remember, the saying, "The Lord helps those who help themselves" is *not* Scripture, nor can the idea be supported by Scripture. Little by little you can let go of your way and fasten to His way. How fast you go should be none of your concern. If you are moving at all, no matter how little, you need only make sure of your direction. For, "Which of you by taking thought can add one cubit unto his stature?"

4. *How do you make salt, salty again?*

Matthew 5:13, "Ye are the salt of the earth: but if the salt have lost his savour, wherewith shall it be salted? it is thenceforth good for nothing, but to be cast out, and to be trodden under foot of men."

How do you make salt, salty again? Our fallen nature causes us to turn our ear from this statement because there is a sound of impossibility in these words of Christ. It is, in fact, quite impossible to make salt that has lost its savor, salty again. How many of us have opened a new package of salt and, with it, over-salted our food? "WOW, that is salty!" we say. Actually, the salt we had used before had lost its savor. We used more and more of it as it became less and less effective. How can you make old salt salty again? You can't – it is, from then on, good for nothing. In Jesus' question there is a sound of futility – in His answer there is negativity, finality, permanence, and condemnation.

Modern-day man wants options. Go to any store, any car dealer, or anywhere that caters to mankind's self-indulgence and you will find lists of options. We like options. Contrarily, impossibilities, narrowed choices, vanishing opportunities, and immutable consequences cause us to shrink and fear. The sober person must admit, though, that all opportunities do not stand permanently open and that some consequences cannot be avoided.

Christ's teaching was popular with the desperate and destitute. It is the man who has everything, who has never befriended Christ – nor will he. A man in charge of his life wants options, not dead ends; he wants a wide range of broad avenues, not a straight, constricted path through a narrow, unrelenting gate. A man in control wants more control, not to relinquish control to someone else. A man in control does not want to hear anything about finality and everlasting, unchangeable damnation.

Not only have options been made plenteous in our society, the risk of loss and unavoidable penalties have been nearly eliminated as well. With insurance, and 24-hour police, 24-hour emergency care, warranties, guarantees, contracts, safety equipment, lawyers begging in advertisements for lawsuits, the list of "consequence eliminators" could go on and on. We have become near strangers to harm and loss. (Consider the first questions asked when someone's house burns down?)

There is even a modern Gospel message that "guarantees" us an eternal home. But our Lord Jesus spoke of impossibilities and narrow ways, unchangeable outcomes and desperate consequences. Dangerous situations exist on this way we have joined, situations that can cost men their souls. Jesus taught to fear God's judgment and to live as though judgment was swift and sure and soon. He calls us the salt of the earth then asks us to seriously consider, "Once salt loses its flavor, how do you make it, salty again?"

Many theories have been put forth on the idea of Christians being the salt of the earth and exactly what this means. By the context (as the concept of us being the "salt of the earth" appears only in Matthew) our "salt" is our witness, or how we appear to the world. (Matthew 5:10-16) Other passages connect the idea of "having salt" with character and fortitude. The salt mentioned in Luke 14:34 and Mark 9:50 is tied to our "cross" that we must bear after Christ and the persecution of the righteous.

However, the broad and obvious message is clear in all of the passages, that this salt is within our control, that we will stand judgment for the retention of its savor, and that the consequences are unchangeable and everlasting. We should earnestly seek God for an understanding of this salt, what it is, and what our responsibilities are to the world as a witness. We should pray that we retain the savor left to us.

In our world of options and choices, we have become spoiled children who think that there are always options. If we go this way or that, if we make this choice or that, we will always be able to make a fresh start, or get a second chance or that we will all come out at the same place no matter which way we go. After all, "it's never too late," God is infinitely merciful and He will always forgive…right?

Your Salt Is Your Reputation

We have become careless in our lifestyles because of risk reducers like insurance and lawsuits. Who among us fear losing our possessions by theft or fire? Do we not rather think to ourselves, "I'm insured" when we wonder about whether we left a heater plugged in or a door unlocked? Now that loss has been placed under control, and options abound, it is difficult for the American mind to grasp, in totality, the warnings of Christ about permanent, irreparable, unchangeable damage and loss.

This example (the impossibility of replacing the savor of salt) is used by Christ to describe the immutability and permanence of the damage done to ones character, ones witness, and ones life from bad choices and wrong roads taken. You must take great care in your choosing. You must exercise caution in developing your lifestyle and character. You are capable of wasting the precious and irreplaceable savor given to you, leaving you only to lament the foolish choices of your past.

Don't overlook your opportunity to suffer. To place your life in God's hands is a frightening choice to be sure, but how else will the world around you see that this world is not your home – that the comforts of this life hold little sway in your enjoyment of life – that you need not have an abundance of goods to give to others – that death does not end your life – that your hope is not in this life but in life everlasting – that you need not live constantly in sunshine to smile and continue your life of faith in God? How else will they taste the "salt" in you if your calamity is always arrested, your loss always insured, and your health and happiness held in highest regard? You may be shortcutting your opportunity to witness and test your faith for yourself.

Christ's message is that options do not always exist. Our sovereign God offers THE way, not A way. Christ Jesus described that way as "straight" and the gate at the end of it as "narrow." There are consequences that love and grace and kindness and mercy will not erase. The boundless love of God, the mercy that endures forever, the kindness and compassion of an infinite heavenly Father full of grace and forgiveness will not step over and ignore your stubborn and rebellious heart to save you. When you fall down, He picks you up in loving arms till you get your footing again. When you sit down He waits with His mighty arms folded and head slightly turned to the side, not looking at you, but listening for your repentant cries.

The pliability of your temperament, the humility in your character, the accepting nature of your will, is the briny flavor the world "tastes" in you. The conformity to mistreatment, the suffering of undeserved contempt, and the daily bearing of this "cross" of Christ's is the salt that you need to protect and retain.

You should know from Christ's admonition that once it is gone, once it loses it savor it cannot be restored. You will be trodden under the foot of men, held in disrepute, scorned, and lampooned. Be careful. Be cautious of your reputation. Once it is gone…it is gone forever…for how can you make salt, salty again?

5.   *Is not life more than food?*

Matthew 6:25, "Therefore I say unto you, Take no thought for your life, what
ye shall eat, or what ye shall drink; nor yet for your body, what ye shall put
on. Is not the life more than meat, and the body than raiment?"

The ad says, "Eat all you want and lose weight." We should be ashamed that we are so willing to lay aside common sense (not to mention unchangeable laws of physics) to embrace a lie conceived in avarice, propagated by greed and believed only by the selfish and foolish. Why do we do this? In an interview with a confidence man convicted of bilking older people out of their fortunes by wild investment promises, he was asked how he could convince his victims of such ridiculous schemes. He stated, "We all believe in what we want to be true." It could be added that if the plan involves indulgences, count us in; if it involves abstinence, count us out.

We are willing to do anything that adds to us, whether to our bank account, our indulgent lifestyle, or our circle of friends. We are awash in advice and counsel on how to live longer and have more and we take it into our heads, our homes, our Meetings, and our hearts. We have become obsessed with the prospect of having all we want to eat and still looking thin. We are fascinated with schemes of being paid more and more for less and less work. We are sold toys and gadgets making impossible promises of less work and more enjoyment.

Because of this philosophy, the average American is manacled to credit card debt. The mail, delivers monthly the tenacious reminders of reality left over from the accumulation of things he was convinced he wanted and needed (or the things he convinced himself) that he "could not live" without. The fact that our spiritual subsistence and our physical proliferation are at opposite ends of the scale of our care, our attention, and importance, seems to elude our thinking. We know it; we just can't seem to remember it when we see something we want. We need to reassess our condition and consider the question Jesus asked here, "Is not the life more than meat, and the body than raiment?"

Granted, some of our sloth in these areas is due to weakness but some is due to plain inattentiveness. You would likely be surprised at the difference in the portion of your fortune that is given toward the advancement of the Kingdom of God and what portion is allotted to restaurants. What is the difference in time devoted to preparing the soul and mind by meditation, worship, and prayer, and the time devoted to dressing, preparing, and feeding the body? An evening with a calculator and your credit card statements can be very enlightening. (These figures more than surprised me— I was ashamed.) We simply have not paid attention. Where a man's treasure is (or is spent) there is where you will find his heart. This is elementary, but a lesson from which many seem to have never graduated. "Is not the life more than food, and the body than clothes?"

Aahhh... This Is The Life!

It is interesting to note that Jesus asks, "Is not *THE* life... more than food...etc. I like the way He asks us about *the* life. Not life – but *the* life. In our vernacular we use this same term when things are as we think they should be. When all is in place, and life is working well, when we are comfortable and happy, we sigh and look to our companion and say, "This is the life!" Contrarily, when things are not so great, when our toys and machines break down, when we hear our neighbor or our companion complain about the way things are, we answer with futility and say, "Well, that's life!"

Somehow, there is a message in the words of Jesus here for us Americans. "Is not the life more than food?" Sure, life, subsistence, survival, basic biological propagation is hardly more than the acquisition of food, but the life is a different question altogether. Life in its basic and biological form is continued by what we can add to it, food, water, shelter, all the basic necessities, but, the life, where all is as it should be, I am convinced, is obtained by what we can leave out of it.

This may be the most difficult of all paradoxes in life to apprehend. I have seen the idea pass through the minds of many, but I have seen it take root in few. I have seen envy on the face of men worth millions when they meet a man with nothing more than basic necessities, but it was just a fleeting notion. I am sure this idea of simplicity and minimalism was being considered by the rich young man who came to Jesus and asked Him, "What must I do to inherit eternal life?"[8] Jesus said, "If thou wilt be perfect, go and sell that thou hast, and give to the poor, and thou shalt have treasure in heaven... But when the young man heard that saying, he went away sorrowful: for he had great possessions." Many days in this young man's life, he likely said, "Aahhh... this is the life!" – but, he knew it wasn't.

The saddest part of the question posed by Jesus, too, is the answer. When we consider in full, our lives, how they are spent, the things over which we worry and complain, we must answer His question with a resounding, "No." He asks, "Is not the life more than meat, and the body than raiment?" "No, dear Savior, it is not," our answer must come back. "Our life is no more than an opportunity to acquire our delicacies and our body, only a hollow mannequin with no other purpose than to display our fashionable clothes. Our bank accounts are there only to hold in store for us our treasures and to serve our wants and desires at our beck and call. Our pantries store goods for many days and as in the Bible story[9] we say to our soul, 'Soul, eat drink and be merry!'" Indeed, an honest answer would be shameful one.

---

[8] Matthew 19:16-22, "... Good Master, what good thing shall I do, that I may have eternal life? And he said unto him ...if thou wilt enter into life, keep the commandments. ...The young man saith unto him, All these things have I kept from my youth up: what lack I yet?"
[9] Luke 12:16

Jesus taught that taking thought for these things will hinder your ability to let go of your life, a necessary action for true conversion. This focused concern for your belly causes you to be able to see no further than the plate of food in front of you, and when it is gone your thoughts can extend no further than the source of your next morsel. It causes difficulties for faith as related in Luke 12:29, "And seek not ye what ye shall eat, or what ye shall drink, neither be ye of doubtful mind." The stories of Jesus mention an activity common among the unjust, the faithless, the doubtful, and the wicked. Can you guess what it was?

Drunkenness And Gluttony

They were nearly always eating and drinking. Matthew 24:49, "And shall begin ...to eat and drink with the drunken."

Luke 12:19-45 "And I will say to my soul...take thine ease, eat, drink, and be merry."... "But and if that servant say in his heart, My lord delayeth his coming; and shall begin...to eat and drink, and to be drunken;"

The Church has done poorly at keeping the words eating and drinking linked together as equally wicked sin. Eating (or better called gluttony) is a favorite pastime of those who profess Christ. It is a behavior accepted by the conventional church while emphatically condemned by the Scriptures! It is no different than drunkenness. You will be hard pressed to find many Scriptures that do not show these two horses in the same harness.

A staggering alcoholic and a body laden with fat are as near kin as are thieves and liars. The religious say nearly nothing when the health of a friend is taxed from excessive eating and if something were said, it certainly would never equal the stir that would come from a churchman with alcohol on his breath.

A drug addict, whose health stands in jeopardy and whose wellbeing is set aside as he purchases and prepares another fix, is not a whit different than anyone who ignores their palpitating heart, their shortness of breath and their ever-increasing size to sidle up to the table and swallow another mouthful of unnecessary food. Although they are equally wicked, and equally dangerous to body as well as the soul, the fact that they are both blatant sins against God and good sense, has somehow escaped us.

Jesus taught that overeating could cause the day of Christ to overtake you while you are "unaware." It is the "unawareness" that is so dangerous. When you understand that it is the "unawareness" that you seek when overeating and it is the "unconsciousness" provided by indulgence that you are looking for, you will treat overeating with the same disdain as drunkenness. Perhaps you will avoid overeating as you avoid intoxication in other forms. "And take heed to yourselves, lest at any time your hearts be overcharged with surfeiting, and drunkenness, and cares of this life, and so that day come upon you unawares." (Luke 21:34)

32

Have you a problem with dullness of mind? Do you anguish over your indifference to spiritual things? Surfeiting (overeating) is the main cause of apathy and ennui.

When was the last time a fast of several days found its way into your schedule? You know that your heart, your spirit, even your very soul is affected by indulgence in any form, yet, as helpless as any alcoholic or drug addict the behavior continues. Perhaps you may gain strength in contemplation of the question of Jesus, "Is not the life more than food?"

6.   *Why take ye thought for raiment?*

Matthew 6:28, "And why take ye thought for raiment? Consider the lilies of the field, how they grow; they toil not, neither do they spin..."

If we are going to answer this question honestly, we must first accept the premise that we do take thought for raiment. Could there be anyone who does not agree with this? Clothes are some of the most important things we use in judging status in our society. Clothing is a major visual clue we use to decide "who" we are talking to, what place in society he or she holds, what they may do for a living, and into what financial bracket they fall.

These clues are apparent to us, whether consciously or unconsciously; by the clothes we see them wear. Secondly we may look to the face and expression, third to the conversation and deportment, and fourth to the claims they make with their words, but for the most part, we judge and decide, criticize and condemn, or justify and idolize by the clothes a person wears. With objective consideration, we would discover this behavior to be shameful at least, and at worst, insane.

The Clothes Make The Man.
Or so it is said. We are all subjected to this "Dress for Success" mentality in one form or another. Any of us will feel different, and indeed, be different to one degree or another, if given a different outfit of clothes.

We all look for the clothes to be, at least congruent to the station in life to which that person lays claim. Imagine a policeman with no emblem of authority, no uniform, without anything to separate him from the crowd and nothing to show his authority? What could he accomplish? Imagine what respect a stockbroker would get at an investment strategy meeting who was dressed in tatters. Or conversely, wouldn't an employee who dressed better than all his peers be considered first for promotion? Consider what changes would come over even a homeless man with a new suit of clothes. We must concede – there is power in appearance.

In our society, we are trained to look at the cloth with which a person is wrapped, from Barbie dolls to CEO's. Life and society has taught us that we are no greater than how we appear, we are no more noble, no richer, no more intelligent, no better, than the clothes on our back. Although nearly all of society judges and is judged by dress, is a Christian to participate in this masquerade party? Opinions are many on this subject, so let us defer to the Scriptures.

"My brethren, have not the faith of our Lord Jesus Christ, the Lord of glory, with respect of persons. For if there come unto your assembly a man with a gold ring, in goodly apparel, and there come in also a poor man in vile raiment; And ye have respect to him that weareth the gay clothing, and say unto him, Sit thou here in a good place; and say to the poor, Stand thou

there, or sit here under my footstool: Are ye not then partial in yourselves, and are become judges of evil thoughts? Hearken, my beloved brethren, Hath not God chosen the poor of this world rich in faith, and heirs of the kingdom which he hath promised to them that love him? ...If ye fulfil the royal law according to the scripture, Thou shalt love thy neighbour as thyself, ye do well: But if ye have respect to persons, ye commit sin, and are convinced of the law as transgressors." (James 2:1-9)

Some may argue that this Scripture only deals with our attitude toward the way someone is dressed and says nothing about whether we should give so much care to the way we dress ourselves. But consider this: When we dress ourselves in clothing finer than our peers are we not respecting a person's outer appearance? Albeit, we are respecting ourselves, are we not expecting others to have respect toward us and hold us in higher esteem because of our clothing? Are we not guilty of creating in others, the very sin we are admonished to reject in ourselves? A few moments of consideration will reveal the convoluted reasoning we have used to dress according to our pride and avarice while simultaneously condemning "respect of persons" as sin. When we expect others to respect us, or form opinions about us, by the way we dress, we are cultivating characteristics in others that are unwelcome in ourselves.

Another consideration is mockery. When we drape our body with garnish, gold, and finery, do we not mock God? After all, clothes are only a necessary part of our life because of mankind's sin. Can you see the connection in sin and clothing? These elements, present at the fall of man in the Garden of Eden, are consistently appearing in our list of present-day struggles with righteousness. Clothes, food, pride, and every lust of the eye, are all present in our daily quest to avoid sin and please God. To take pride in our covering, indeed in our atonement, is a strange (if not evil) behavior, is it not? None put it better than did the Quaker apologist, Robert Barclay speaking on simplicity in dress...

"In the first place, the use of clothes originally came from the fall of Adam, and otherwise man would apparently have had no use for them. But his miserable state made them necessary to cover his nakedness and keep him from becoming cold. Both are good and sufficient reasons for wearing clothes, and the principal reason we do so. But it can in no way be lawful for a man to delight himself with the fruit of his iniquity and the consequences of his sin. Any superfluous additions or extensions beyond their real use are clear abuses of the creation and therefore they are not lawful for Christians. Those who love gaudy and ostentatious clothing demonstrate little concern for mortification or self-denial. They apply themselves more to beautifying their bodies than to improving their souls. Those who have so little regard for their mortal condition are more nominal than real Christians."[10]

---

[10] From *Barclay's Apology in Modern English* edited by Dean Freiday p. 406 ©1991 Barclay Press

"…let it not be that outward…"

What waste we would avoid and what equality we would enjoy if we were to gain mastery over this insidious flaw in the character of man. What thrift, what humility, what reality would we be brought to if only we evaluated each other as God does?

"…for the LORD seeth not as man seeth; for man looketh on the outward appearance, but the LORD looketh on the heart." (1 Samuel 16:7b)

"Whose adorning let it not be that outward adorning of plaiting the hair, and of wearing of gold, or of putting on of apparel; But let it be the hidden man of the heart, in that which is not corruptible, even the ornament of a meek and quiet spirit, which is in the sight of God of great price." (1 Peter 3:3-4)

Jesus said, Behold, [for example, let me present] the flowers. They don't work until they're weary so they can wear the best fashions. They wear what is provided and eat what is provided. What outstanding examples of faith in their God, and what great examples of health and beauty. If our lives reflected such health, beauty, and faith, what excellent examples we would be to behold.

Clothes have a power far beyond their basic and intrinsic ability for weather protection and obscuration of nakedness. This power must be respected and held in check. Do you place more value upon clothes than is just and right? Do you judge God's children by the cut and price of the mere cloth draped over their shoulders? Are you more concerned with a garment's fashion than its function? You should consider, the question of Christ, "Why take ye thought for raiment?"

7.   *If a son shall ask bread...will a father give him a stone?*

Luke 11:11, "If a son shall ask bread of any of you that is a father, will he give him a stone? or if he ask a fish, will he for a fish give him a serpent?"

We are often reluctant to pray "Thy will be done." It is even taught today that it is a sure sign of a lack of faith to pray, "Not my will but as thou wilt" although that is a quote from the Son of God, Christ Jesus. Many use this phrase out of obligation to the commandment or fear of rejection. After giving God the list of needs and wants, "Thy will be done" is added to offset any disappointment of not receiving our selfish petition. More thought must be given to prayer than this. If we have no assurance that the things we desire are the will of God for our lives, we have no business asking for them. It is a basic distrust of God as a "good father" that causes us to hold aloof the words, "Thy will be done." "If a son shall ask bread of any of you that is a father, will he give him a stone?"

Prior to this question in Matthew 7, Jesus was teaching that we are to ask for God's will to be done, here, just as it is done in heaven; and that an honest, seeking person will not go away empty-handed. He was assuring us that we need not fear asking for God's will to be done. To make the point clear He asked the following question:

"...what man is there of you, whom if his son ask bread, will he give him a stone? Or if he ask a fish, will he give him a serpent? If ye then, being evil, know how to give good gifts unto your children, how much more shall your Father which is in heaven give good things to them that ask him?"

When Luke recorded this, he added, "Or if he shall ask an egg, will he offer him a scorpion?" (Luke 11:10-13) This further makes the point that this is a rhetorical question, because it evokes the response, "Of course we would not do that!" He wants us to know that praying for God's will and our good are not crossed purposes.

A Part of Our Model

Jesus places this concept into the model prayer and therefore puts it into a category of richness beyond the first glance. As with all of the Lord's model prayer, it demands we make personal changes. To make the prayer comfortable or natural, you must either change it, or you are forced change yourself. When you see your life not conforming to the words of the prayer, it shows that you are out of sync with the life that Christ intended for you. Who, but a few, could honestly pray for "daily bread" with a week's supply of food on hand? Who can say, "Forgive me because I forgive everyone who sins against me?" You must therefore make your life fit the prayer.

We have, rather, attempted to change the prayer, or at least made it impotent. We set aside the power of this prayer by teaching it as a nursery rhyme and saying it with the cadence of a limerick. But for this prayer to truly have its intended effect, we must make "Thy will be done" as easy to pray earnestly, and in truth, as it is to say from memory.

When you say the first words "Our Father," these words should truly reflect your feelings of community with other believers and your place in family of God. "Thy Kingdom come" should roll from lips truly desirous to see the His Kingdom established. "Forgive us our debts," ought to be said in full assurance of being granted because no grudge or debt is being held by you toward anyone. Then, "Thy will be done" can be said and felt sincerely, clearly, and confidently. After all, "...what man is there of you, whom if his son ask bread, will he give him a stone?"

The imagery in the words used by Jesus is astounding. Notice all the desired articles mentioned: bread, an egg, a fish – all items of sustenance and nourishment. Notice the articles we assumed to receive from God were a stone, a scorpion, or a serpent – items that are common, useless, dangerous, and even deadly. Is this how we consider His will for us? Are these the "gifts" we presume to avoid by evading the prayer, "Thy will be done?" Shame on us for thinking our God to be such a father.

As you become increasingly aware of the goodness of God, and understand that His demands are not unfair, that His commandments are not grievous, and that His way is not arduous, you will accept (and soon even desire) His will above your own. Yes, you will wonder why you avoided His will before.

You will find that it was your idea of bread that should be considered a stone when compared to His bread; much like a hungry child may want cake over potatoes or candy over vegetables, your desire for the poison of your own will is only a misunderstood hunger for true sustenance. From God's viewpoint, the eggs you ask for may in fact be scorpions, and although you ask for fish with your mouth your fingers are pointing at serpents. Let our loving heavenly Father feed you from the table of His will and you will never reach for serpents, stones, or scorpions, while hungry for bread.

Good Things

In Luke, we find that the author replaced the words "good things" with "the Holy Spirit." "If ye then, being evil, know how to give good gifts unto your children: how much more shall your heavenly Father give the Holy Spirit to them that ask him?" (Luke 11:13) Many who interpret this to mean a "gift" of the Holy Spirit, seem to miss the point. "...to them that ask Him"... ask Him for what? The Holy Spirit? No, the Holy Spirit is not a gift given to anyone who simply asks for it as a gift. It is a state of being, an indwelling, set aside for those who surrender their will to Him and those who can honestly pray "Thy will be done" without reservation, without hypocrisy, and with a sincere heart. Can you say, "Lord, don't give me what I want...give me what you want me to have, no matter what"? It is then that you are able to be indwelled. It is then that you are qualified to receive the "gift." As you make an inhabitable home for the Holy Spirit, by humility and surrender, you become capable of receiving the good things that He desires you to have. The Holy Spirit of God would not, indeed could not, be in harmony with simultaneous distrust of YHVH as a good Father.

When you doubt His will and disbelieve His good intentions, when you are skeptical and distrusting about praying, "Thy will be done," and when you think that your desires are honorable and His are suspect, you make an antagonistic environment for the Holy Spirit. For the Spirit of God knows God only as thoroughly good[11] and appreciates no will other than His. In this condition of doubt and fear of an untrustworthy God, you can expect never to experience in fullness the indwelling Christ, nor the warmth of the Comforter, nor the uninhibited fellowship of the Father. The Holy Spirit, spoken of by Jesus, will never be a gift to you.

Why do we distrust Him so? Why do we fear to say, "Thy will be done?" Why, in our deepest distress, when loss of life or a loved one is before us, when life's tragedies are imminent and sorrow seemingly unavoidable, can we not cry out to God in full assurance that our good and ultimate joy is considered when we pray "Thy will be done?" Do we really think that what He offers is more grief, more sorrow, and more heartache? If His will is so far from ours, should we not make the changes necessary to reconcile the two?

He loves you more than you can know. You can only trust Him as much as you love Him and love Him as much as you trust Him. As you inch your way by faith to more love and more trust, isn't it a lovely thought to contemplate the question, "If a son shall ask bread...will a father give him a stone?"

---

[11] 1 Corinthians 2:10-11, "But God hath revealed them unto us by his Spirit: for the Spirit searcheth all things, yea, the deep things of God. For what man knoweth the things of a man, save the spirit of man which is in him? **even so the things of God knoweth no man, but the Spirit of God.**"

8. *Why reason ye in your hearts?*

The Pharisees overheard Jesus say, "Thy sins be forgiven thee" and asked among themselves, "Who is this that speaks blasphemies?" "And immediately when Jesus perceived in his spirit that they so reasoned within themselves, he said unto them, Why reason ye these things in your hearts?" (Mark 2:8, Luke 5:22)

As Jesus went about doing good He perceived from time to time that someone would tune in to His mission or purpose and indeed start to realize who He was. This time, with the Pharisees, was different than the others. Usually when the scribes or Pharisees mumbled to themselves, Jesus blasted them for being treacherous to the Kingdom of God. But this time He was pleasant, as if He saw in them a glimmer of hope. For a moment they asked within themselves, "Who can forgive sins but God alone?" ... They thought, "Maybe this is Messiah."

Jesus perceived this and was willing to take them a little farther, and so to accomplish this, He showed them a miracle. The Mark 2 account records no negative reaction, but rather a response as "...insomuch that they were all amazed, and glorified God, saying, We never saw it on this fashion."

Why reason ye in your hearts? Do you have an opinion about the motivations of Jesus? Was He a performing a true miracle? Was it just hypnotism? Was it fraud or deception? Why have you formed that opinion? You must never underestimate the power of the Scriptures on this regard. When these stories are read, they demand an opinion. Information creates an opinion. You must decide whether to believe or not. Jesus perceived they were approaching faith as they watched Him. He gave them more information to process as He asked, "What are you thinking?"

We must ask ourselves what are we thinking as we listen to Christ make assertions, such as, "I am the door... anyone climbing up some other way is a thief." (John 10:1) When we hear Him plainly say that He is the ONLY way, what reason ye in your hearts? What about when He says, "I and my Father are one." (John 10:30) When Jesus makes Himself equal with God, what reason ye in your hearts? Do you search for or invent ways for His message to be different than it is written, or do you accept it as an accurate record? Why are you reasoning in your heart?

When our Lord makes demands like, "Take no thought for your life," why reason you in your heart? What about when He says, "No man can serve two masters," or "Judge not, that ye be not judged" or "...depart from me, ye that work iniquity, I never knew you" Consider to yourself what Christ asks, "Why reason ye in your hearts?"

Listen closely as you study your Bible, or as you meditate, or as you listen in prayer, or as you listen to others minister the Word of God. Listen to what you reason in your heart. We may be dismissing God's Word, His revelation, or His miracle by lack of sound reasoning. Is your reasoning carrying you toward Christ or away from Him? Is your inclination to believe and follow, or doubt and prove in order to hold to your own way? "What reason ye in your hearts?" "Why reason ye in your hearts?"

When demand is made on us by way of the Scriptures, ministry, or revelation, or even by life's burdens, we may be prone to excuse our behavior. For some reason of incompatibility between the source of this demand and our "peculiar" circumstances we dismiss it as impertinent. We must be very careful with conviction. Our consciences are the ONLY natural sense that can keep us along the way and recover us when we falter. We must consider the care of our convictions and promptings as important or more so, than the care of our sight or hearing, knowing that when it's gone there is no second chance[12].

Sometimes in traumatic situations the human psyche has the ability to block out facts seen and heard, skew them into fantastic illusion and believe them. We have all disbelieved what we saw or heard in some painful or frightening situation.

Disregarding Our Consciences

We know it is possible to DISREGARD what we take into our five senses. We also know that a constant disregard can lead to a numbing or in some cases an atrophied condition of the senses that can cause a dangerous situation. So it is with our consciences. If we disregard or explain away our discomfort, we run a risk of losing the most valuable sense we have – the sense of right and wrong – the sense that our acts are hurting our God, thwarting His purposes, short-circuiting His plan, or breaking His Commandments.

The conscience is more than knowing. The word is a Latin cognate *(com- + scire)* that means exactly that – *more than knowing*. The Scripture mentions it, using the Greek word suneidesis {soon-i'-day-sis} to know within. I am convinced that it is "the light" John spoke of. "That was the true Light, which lighteth every man that cometh into the world." (John 1:9) It is the lamp to our path – the Word of God to our heart to lead us to Christ. John recognized it, Paul protected it, and Peter saw it as a guide toward righteousness.

And they which heard it, being convicted by their own conscience, went out one by one, beginning at the eldest, even unto the last: and Jesus was left alone, and the woman standing in the midst. (John 8:9)

And Paul, earnestly beholding the council, said, Men and brethren, I have lived in all good conscience before God until this day. ...And herein do I exercise myself, to have always a conscience void of offence toward God, and toward men. Acts 23:1 - Acts 24:16

Holding faith, and a good conscience; which some having put away concerning faith have made shipwreck: (1 Timothy 1:19)

---

[12] Question #4 Can you make salt... salty again?

41

For this is thankworthy, if a man for conscience toward God endure grief, suffering wrongfully. (1 Peter 2:19)

Your conscience is protected by your sensitivity to the Holy Spirit. You protect it by never grieving your guide (the Holy Spirit), by remaining pliable, willing, and subject to the subtlest movement of the Spirit of God. The Holy Spirit is the force by which you are sealed unto the day of redemption.[13] To interfere with, frustrate, or grieve Him is a dangerous action.

The apostle warns in Ephesians 4:30, "And grieve not the Holy Spirit of God, whereby ye are sealed unto the day of redemption." It would behoove us to cultivate this sense, attempt to increase our sensitivity to that which displeases God so that our actions would be more in line with His will and way.

As this sensitivity improves, it starts to merge with our other physical senses and soon we can know good and evil by sight, by touch, and intuition. The writer of Hebrews claims this intuition is the mark of one who has come to full age in Christ. "… even those who by reason of use have their senses exercised to discern both good and evil." (Hebrews 5:14)

The Pharisees in the story were on the verge of recognizing Messiah and possibly believing on Him and changing their entire destiny. They were playing games of rationalization, justification and in their own minds, they finally decided that if someone was wrong, they reasoned, it had to be this carpenter's boy. Alas, they reasoned – they reasoned incorrectly. They toyed with their better judgment – their conscience. They ignored the truth that was becoming apparent to them. They turned from the light given them that day. They shunned their conscience and in doing so, they shunned the God of the whole earth. Maybe the Spirit would deal with them again, possibly once more, twice perhaps – who's to say?

You must protect your conscience. It is your only defense against an insincere conformity to religious codes. It is your first defense against sin. It is your lifesaver when you stumble. Remember 1Timothy 4:2, and the use of the phrase"… having their conscience seared with a hot iron." A sinful man with no conscience is in a condition of little hope – a religious man without one is likely a hypocrite.

The Pharisees moved, slowly but surely, through this time of reasoning to final and total rejection of the Messiah. Although total apostasy may be remote for you, you may find yourself with severe gaps in theology, understanding, or comprehension of spiritual concepts and values. When you encounter pricks in your conscience, don't reason it away. When you feel leadings of the Spirit, convictions of displeasing behavior, you must be quick to respond.

When at the crossroads of decision, see clearly in your mind the Lord Jesus, perceiving the movement of the Spirit in you, looking your way, and asking, "Why reason ye in your hearts?"

---

[13] Ephesians 4:30, "And grieve not the holy Spirit of God, whereby ye are sealed unto the day of redemption."

9. *Why do you call attention to splinters in your brother's eye?*

Matthew 7:3-5, "And why beholdest thou the mote that is in thy brother's eye, but considerest not the beam that is in thine own eye? Or how wilt thou say to thy brother, Let me pull out the mote out of thine eye; and, behold, a beam is in thine own eye?

Sometimes we direct this reprimand of Christ toward the Pharisees, but this particular reproof was a general one. Let us accept the question as though it was directed to us. We have no good answer to His question. We cannot even claim concern for our neighbor as motivation for this behavior. He constructs an idea with this question that makes the operation of "mote removal" a dangerous one. His metaphor implies that we are performing eye surgery while blinded.

This question begins with the statement, "Judge not, that ye be not judged." (Matthew 7:1) Whenever I hear this verse quoted by the ungodly I envision one of those little "promise boxes" on their breakfast table. Every morning they open it and remove a card and read the verse for today, only, in their box, it is the same Scripture everyday. For people who live their own way, it is the Scripture of choice! It is tirelessly quoted by everyone from the heroine addict in the alley to the deacon called before the church board, but is it truly understood by any of us?

Are we really never to call into question the behavior of anyone? Are we never to voice God's displeasure about the sinful acts of anyone? How will those who never their lives in the light of righteousness understand the judgment that is upon them? How will they ever come to know forgiveness? Furthermore, if our duty is to reprove or correct one another, as the Scripture plainly teaches, how do we honor the clear command to "judge not?"

As in the days of Christ, we are occasionally found in the company of those who judge us unfairly. In Luke it is written this way, "Judge not, and ye shall not be judged: condemn not, and ye shall not be condemned: forgive, and ye shall be forgiven..." (Luke 6:37) This is more complete in thought than the Matthew account.

This verse teaches that we must keep in mind our own condition as we help or guide others on their way. We should judge like we want to be judged, condemn as we wish condemnation for ourselves and forgive as we desire forgiveness to be granted us. That should take the edge off of our high and mighty tone.

It Is Love That Is Lacking

In harsh judgment, it is the love that is lacking. The purity of empathetic love can enable a counselor to say, without reprisal, things that no one else would dare even approach. When I was involved in the children's home ministry, I instructed my teachers and staff in this concept: a child is only to be disciplined or corrected if he is absolutely sure that he is loved by the one who disciplines him. A great test for loving involvement in the child's life was questions like, "Do you know the child's middle name? Do you know his best friend? Do they have brothers and sisters?" If they are sure you love them, you can say nearly anything, but if they doubt your love at all, you can offend with the most delicate of correction.

Love is not the only thing missing in counsel to our brethren; it should also be noted that the standard by which we judge is deficient. We can only speak from our own perspective. As much as we would like to be the holders of all truth, we are not. Things change, people change, and situations are viewed assorted ways by different people at various times. We cannot know all, to finally and completely judge anyone. After all, are you the same person today you were 10 years ago? Did you have an opinion then? Did you offer it to others? Did you not demand that you were right? Are there things you understand today that you didn't understand then? All these things should be considered when you find yourself offering differing or judgmental opinions. Humility will serve well in this situation. Love will present common ground.

As you live, you learn. As you look back, you may see that you had a "beam" in your eye, or actions that displeased God, which were never revealed to you. As they came to light and you dealt with them, you were amazed that God had tolerated them (and you) for all those years! Have you come to realize that you should do the same for your brothers and sisters in Christ? Let God reveal the faults of your brethren to them. We can count on Him to do so clearly, distinctly and mercifully. Meanwhile, if you have not created a situation of enmity between you and those with whom God is dealing, they may come to you for guidance.

Also, consider that if you have recognizably grown in the Lord, it is probable that you will continue to do so. Ten years from now you may have "beams" removed, that today, you are not even aware that you have. As these beams are removed, you become a better Christian, a better person, and a better counselor. You may then see clearly and be in a better position to help your brother with his "mote." Remember the Scripture didn't tell you to be unconcerned with your neighbor's mote, it asks why you are attempting to remove it while blinded by a "beam." As the verses continue:

"…first cast out the beam out of thine own eye; and then shalt thou see clearly to cast out the mote out of thy brother's eye."

Notice how the language has changed from "beholdest the mote" to "cast out the mote." To "behold" is an Elizabethan term (King James) used to call attention to something. To behold is not simply to notice or to know of its existence. It is to expose, to uncover, or bring to the fore. It is obvious the person who is only beholding the mote is more interested in framing the flaw for exposition than in helping to make positive changes.

It goes without saying that when the flaw is put on display, it is an attempt to compare –to make someone look better (or worse) than someone else. Our responsibility is clear that we must not judge, condemn, or neglect forgiveness. But, as things are discovered in our brother that will eventually condemn him, if we are keeping vigilant watch over our own life and remaining clear before God we must, in humility, help him to remove it, but only as the need for its removal is revealed to him and he seeks our assistance. As we find there, things for which we feel God's judgment will be incurred, we are obliged to keep our own life free of that which blinds us and hinders our helping him.

Judgment that is beneficial, and that is not condemned in Scripture, is done in **love** and **humility** and **order**. You must love those you evaluate. If you do not love them, they will know it – whether consciously or sub-consciously and they will despise your assessment and suggestions. You cannot fake it, so don't try it.

The humility factor is made plain by the apostle in the book of Galatians (6:1), "Brethren, if a man be overtaken in a fault, ye which are spiritual, restore such an one in the spirit of meekness; considering thyself, lest thou also be tempted." We are never far from possessing the very same fault we find in another; we are indeed all in the same precarious condition. The order, that is so necessary, is clear in the words of Jesus Christ, "…first cast out the beam out of thine own eye; and then shalt thou see clearly to cast out the mote out of thy brother's eye." The words "first" and "then" show the order. It would seem simple but it is easily forgotten. Many hours of self-examination, prayer and comparison of *your* life to the examples in Scripture and to the yardstick of the Spirit need to take place before you reach for the splinter in your brother's eye.

You must remember that you are the salt of the earth, and the light of the world, not the x-ray machine. You are to add and enhance – to enlighten what is *already* visible. Not discover and reveal what is hidden. When you judge, you are assuming an office that is to be occupied by God alone. As Christ was leaving this world, He told of the Holy Spirit's ministry. He will lead and guide and He convinces the world of sin. It is simply not your job.

Jesus asks, "Why do you call attention to your brother's problem?" If you are doing this you need to examine why. It may be that you are becoming aware of a shortfall in your own life. The revealer of men's hearts may be convincing you, at this moment, of a problem. If you are to fulfill Christ's order to "see clearly" so you can help your brother, you will have to remove your ocular barrier. Perhaps this is why Jesus called the Pharisees "blind guides" and "blind leaders of the blind."

Your brother's splinter is aggravating him. It hurts and hinders his ability to see. He only thinks it is normal by comparing his tiny sliver to other's two by four boards.

There is no good answer to Christ's question. It is your board you are trying to conceal when you make your brother's splinter known. A confession of this is the only honest answer to Christ's question, "Why do you call attention to splinters in your brother's eye?"

10. Do men gather grapes from thorns?

Matthew 7:16, "Ye shall know them by their fruits. Do men gather grapes of thorns, or figs of thistles?"

An immutable law of nature is that all life brings forth of its kind. Thus the question, do men gather grapes of thorns, or figs of thistles? The answer is no, they do not, and Jesus implied, they cannot. This Scripture is often misunderstood through misapplication. It does not instruct us how to discover "true Christians" nor provide a touchstone for self-evaluation. Also, it is often erroneously tied to Galatians 5:22-23, "But the fruit of the Spirit is love, joy, peace, longsuffering, gentleness, goodness, faith, Meekness, temperance: against such there is no law." Well-meaning teachers have led us through the evaluation of our Christian walk and made claims that the absence of this listed fruit in our lives is an indicator of not being converted (or completely converted). Absence proves nothing. It is the PRESENCE of fruit that determines the family of the vine.

Foe example, you may walk through a garden and see a vine with no fruit on it. Discounting the ability to identify by foliage, can you accurately say this is not a pumpkin vine because you see no pumpkins? Of course not. It may be fully under way growing pumpkins at that very minute, but perhaps it's diseased or malnourished, or at that moment it's too young, or hindered in some other way to bear fruit. The presence of a watermelon, however, proves it is not a pumpkin vine.

The question remains, to whom does this Scripture apply? In context, the Lord was warning us of false prophets. He says that we will know false prophets by their fruit,

"Even so every good tree bringeth forth good fruit; but a corrupt tree bringeth forth evil fruit. A good tree cannot bring forth evil fruit, neither can a corrupt tree bring forth good fruit. Every tree that bringeth not forth good fruit is hewn down, and cast into the fire. Wherefore by their fruits ye shall know them." (Matthew 7:17-20)

Jesus was telling those who would hear, "These men are thorns, not vines." If you find a grape on a thorn it is because it was stuck there, it did not grow there. How it got stuck there is a matter for consideration.

A false prophet is a deceiver. This is a person falsely speaking for God (without authority) or a person speaking falsely for God (saying things that are not true). The difference is subtle, but important. The latter speaks lies in the name of God. These are usually not a threat to biblically sound people. The words of a false prophet are weighed and found in error by way of the axiomatic truth that the Spirit of God will not contradict Himself. Neither will the Spirit within us nor will the Spirit who brought forth the Scriptures, allow the lie to be believed. But, the other is more deceptive. The person falsely speaking for God however, may be saying very nice things, Scriptural things, and things without the least contradiction; they are being said, however, without unction, without compulsion, without authority to speak. Through this kind of false prophet we are led into creaturely activity (fleshly motivated good works) and this subsequently causes an erosion of active communion with God to take place.

The Clothing of a Shepherd

All that being said, we are warned to beware of the false prophets because they wear the "clothing of a shepherd" (sheep's clothing) and are inwardly starving, and desperate wolves. Sometimes "sheep's clothing" is misunderstood to mean that these starving wolves dress themselves up like sheep, but it is, more correctly, the clothing of a shepherd that they don in order to deceive. They don't try to look like sheep; they try to look like a shepherd, which is an office awarded to only one, our Christ Jesus. It is the intention of these wicked "shepherds" not to feed, but to fleece and flay, and the first step, toward that end, is deception.

A person intending to deceive must work first at appearances. With the warning that we will "know them by their fruits," the deceiver must surround himself with fruit. This is why we may find grapes on thorns but must realize they didn't grow there. There are many who tout their accomplishments – not to gloat, but to deceive.

Jesus said, "Abide in me, and I [will] in you. As the branch cannot bear fruit of itself, except it abide in the vine; no more can ye, except ye abide in me." (John 15:4) From this verse, you must realize that any fruit borne OUTSIDE of Christ is corrupt fruit. This is not as easy to prove as it is to sense. If you are born of the incorruptible seed, you have within you the Holy Spirit who will witness to this, and therefore, you must maintain a clear conscience and contrite heart in order to hear the slightest whisper of His warning.

These issues of life from your heart are the only true defense against the false prophets, the endless parade of literature, books, movies, preachers, Bible translations and close dear friends and family who mean well, but are in error. "Keep thy heart with all diligence; for out of it are the issues of life." (Proverbs 4:23)

You must be vigilant and even suspicious to every twitch within you as you read, hear, and see things from all sources, accepting only that which the Lord reveals to you as true and worthy. The Scriptures secondarily, are never to be compromised as they were penned by men under the unction and authority of the Holy Spirit of God.

It would never insult a true prophet for someone to doubt, then check, and wait for confirmation from God on any revelation given them. Paul commended the Bereans for this. "These were nobler than those in Thessalonica, in that they received the word with all readiness of mind, and searched the scriptures daily, whether those things were so." (Acts 17:11) It is only the false prophet that leads people away from Christ's witness within, and the Scripture's witness without.

There are many fruits which are ascribed only to the children of God, and many which are found only on the withered and diseased branch of the false prophet. These fruits are well worth your attention and study.

When you determine a man to be truthful and faithful by the fruit abounding around him, you must be careful that you are not ascribing fruit to his ministry that did not grow there. I have seen whole churches full of proselytes.

A grape stuck on a thorn is not abiding in the vine. Although you may find a bramble bush loaded with grapes, Jesus wants us to know that they did not grow there. You should ask yourself, "Do men gather grapes from thorns?"

11.   *Why would Satan cast out Satan?*

Matthew 12:26 And if Satan cast out Satan, he is divided against himself; how shall then his kingdom stand?

Mark 3:23 ... How can Satan cast out Satan?

Luke 11:18 If Satan also be divided against himself, how shall his kingdom stand?

Anyone remotely familiar with spiritual things has heard about the doctrine of the unpardonable sin. It has made its way into nearly every discussion, and usually it is never dealt with in a final way, settling the issue. What is it? How can someone commit such a sin? Is there no hope afterward?

Jesus had just performed a miracle of unmistakable credit. A lunatic that was mute and blind was brought to Jesus. This man was known in the area and it was obvious that there was a spirit on this man that had bound him physically. Jesus healed him so that the man could both speak and see. The religious leaders who witnessed this event could not attribute it to God for this confession would convict them. If they were to remain segregated from Christ, and they were to continue to teach that He was not who He said He was, they must condemn what He did and attribute it to some other power. So they said, "By the Lord of the Flies, (Beelzebub)[14] this man casts out Satan, not by YHVH." Jesus looked at them and said, "My Father will forgive anyone...of anything...but that."

Many of the charlatans involved in "miracle" ministries today use this ploy. The idea of doubting their credibility is considered "blasphemy of the Holy Spirit" and they warn those who do, of committing an unforgivable sin. Some others, playing on words, say that, "not accepting Christ" is the unforgivable sin. It has also been attached to specific sins such as using the name of God in vain. What exactly is "blasphemy of the Holy Spirit?"

Matthew 12:31-32, "Wherefore I say unto you, All manner of sin and blasphemy shall be forgiven unto men: but the blasphemy against the Holy Ghost shall not be forgiven unto men. And whosoever speaketh a word against the Son of man, it shall be forgiven him: but whosoever speaketh against the Holy Ghost, it shall not be forgiven him, neither in this world, neither in the world to come."

It is clear that anyone who watched this miracle take place could not doubt that the source of the miracle was none other than YHVH the Creator. It was only stubborn pride and arrogance and a filthy heart that would conceive Christ's collaboration with demons and let such an accusation spew out of their mouth.

---

[14] See Question 64, "What do they call you?"

When these men who were steeped in religion purposefully turned their eyes from the evidence and determined to harden their heart against accepting the clear witness of the Messiah, Jesus said that they had sealed their fate. Their rejection of the Father, who graciously sent them an irrefutable sign to believe in Messiah, was not only rejected and ignored, but then attributed to the archenemy of all mankind, the first rebel and hardener of hearts. The glory of God's grace and power that was lovingly sent to us to help us and save us was sullied and ascribed, as though given by Satan to deceive us. It was the ultimate insult, done by intent, done by rebellion.

The miracle was incontrovertible. This was no parlor trick that could be done by slight of hand or mirrors. This miracle was unquestionably genuine, an attribute to which the "miracles" of today would have difficulty laying claim. When this miracle occurred, look at the reaction from the religious people there. It divided them into two. "But some of them said, He casteth out devils through Beelzebub the chief of the devils. And others, tempting [testing] him, sought of him a sign from heaven." (Luke 11:15-16) In another place the Scriptures say, "And many of the people believed on him, and said, When Christ cometh, will he do more miracles than these which this man hath done?" (John 7:31) One group dismissed Him out-of-hand and rejected Him as a deceiver, the other's attitude showed interest in more spectacular signs.

The group that is not mentioned is the family and friends of this poor man who was no longer dumb and blind. As the commotion rose from the religious leaders, some condemning Jesus and some urging Him on to do other miracles, there was a man looking at the world around him for the first time in his life.

He looked into the faces of his brothers and friends and was able for the first time to speak to them. The din of the crowd lessened to give way to the thoughts now rushing through His mind. He stood thoroughly fascinated with the world he beheld. There was opening before him, in full color, a world that, before today, he had only heard. Satan had been cast out. Darkness was replaced by light; abundant life was now in the stead of misery. Jesus, ignoring the selfish requests for miracles, looks back over his shoulder at this man who now sees for the first time his own way home and his friends flocking around him, patting him and shaking his hand, wonders how anyone could see such a deliverance as the work of Satan. "The thief cometh not, but for to steal, and to kill, and to destroy: I am come that they might have life, and that they might have it more abundantly." (John 10:10) He looks at the religious leadership and wonders to Himself, 'Why would this miracle cause them to blaspheme God...How can they think this is the work of Satan?' Then Jesus looks at them, holds His hand up and asks them out loud, "Why would Satan cast out Satan?"

Us Four...And No More

Sometimes we become so group oriented that we start to think that our group is the only one through which God moves and works. We are dangerously close to blasphemy when we attribute the wonderful work of God that occurs in circles we do not frequent, to forces that are considered to be at enmity with Heaven. We should thank God for the fruit no matter at which end of the vine it grows.

The deliverance from sins, the freedom in Christ, the healing of bodies and lives are reason enough to thank God, no matter from whose camp it came. None of us are the possessors of all truth; we walk in obedience (at least that is our goal) and take the path He lays before us. As Paul says, "Who art thou that judgest another man's servant? to his own master he standeth or falleth..." (Romans 14:4) We should rejoice and follow Christ. We are not to chase miracles we deem proper, nor are we to condemn those we determine are not. We are to follow.

Once when John, one of Jesus' disciples, found another ministering in Christ's name he came to Jesus and said, "...Master, we saw one casting out devils in thy name, and he followeth not us: and we forbad him, because he followeth not us. But Jesus said, "Forbid him not: for there is no man which shall do a miracle in my name, that can lightly speak evil of me. For he that is not against us is on our part." (Mark 9:38-40)

Jesus feels no threat when someone outside your denomination does a wonderful work in His name. You should not either. If good is being accomplished then so be it, and thank God for it. When you see Satan's kingdom suffer, no matter at whose hands, you can rest assured that our God has commissioned someone to do the job. When you think that the Devil is in the one who "followeth not us" you can easily determine the source by asking the same question Jesus asked of the doubting Pharisees, "Why would Satan cast out Satan?"

12.   How can ye, being evil, speak good things?

*Matthew 12:33-37, "Either make the tree good, and his fruit good; or else make the tree corrupt, and his fruit corrupt: for the tree is known by his fruit. O generation of vipers, **how can ye, being evil, speak good things?** for out of the abundance of the heart the mouth speaketh. A good man out of the good treasure of the heart bringeth forth good things: and an evil man out of the evil treasure bringeth forth evil things...For by thy words thou shalt be justified, and by thy words thou shalt be condemned."*

Among us there are those who have a propensity for kindness when considering man's fallen state. Some think that mankind is in a totally depraved condition and lacks no ability to fully develop any evil thought, word, or deed. Then, the contradistinctive position is assumed that we are good beings that are getting a bad deal through no fault of our own (Adam) and God has since apologized by sending His son to die for us and we are all eventually going to live forever with God in bliss. In the mean time, the world is rampant with sin and not getting better.

In our day we are overrun with books and tapes explaining the question, "Why do bad things happen to good people?" We must admit that unpleasant things happen all the time to people who appear undeserving. Contrariwise we must admit that pleasant things happen to people who appear undeserving, unappreciative and unthankful and even unaware of any heavenly Father of lights from whom the good and perfect gifts come.[15] Ecclesiastes 8:14 says that this is an empty, or vain thought, "There is a vanity [waste of time] which is done upon the earth; [to consider] that there be just men, unto whom it happeneth according to the work of the wicked; again, there be wicked men, to whom it happeneth according to the work of the righteous: I said that this also is [a waste of time] vanity."

There are a couple of points to keep in mind when considering these hard questions about the good and bad happening to all, that don't seem to surface in the discussions on "why." One point is that bad things don't happen to good people. There are no good people. "ALL we like sheep have gone astray, EVERY one of us has turned to his own way." (Isaiah 53:6) All have sinned and come short, all have missed the mark. Jesus Himself said, There is none good – but God. Is this a technicality? Is this inapplicable when considering whether man is good or not, whether he deserves bad things or not? We must not look at the "bad things" as getting what we deserve as much as fruit that has come to the tree. We must make either the tree corrupt and its fruit corrupt or make the tree good and the fruit good, but we cannot say that a good tree is bringing forth corrupt fruit.

In Matthew 5:45, Jesus taught that we should bless and give gifts as God does, revealing that God gives the good things of life to all – without

---

[15] James 1:17

partiality. Life is indeed a gift from God. What if the rain only fell on the crops of those who love Him? "That ye may be the children of your Father which is in heaven: for he maketh his sun to rise on the evil and on the good, and sendeth rain on the just and on the unjust."

Here we see the impartial loving favor of God, but what about the unpleasant things? In Ecclesiastes 2:14, where he was considering the fate of fools and wise he said, "… I myself perceived also that one event happeneth to them all." The only thing that separates God's people from the rest is how the disaster is handled, not whether or not it comes. "For a just man falleth seven times, and riseth up again: but the wicked shall fall into mischief." (Proverbs 24:16)

After the initial point (that there are no good people) is accepted, some will alter the question and ask, "Why do bad things happen to God's people?" The question is yet moot, for just as there are no "good" people, we must consider that there are no "bad" things. The things that we insist on calling bad, really, are unwanted, unpleasant, painful, or costly. Who would call a new baby a bad thing? Yet no one would look forward to hours of painful labor; or, if a man suddenly came into a great deal of money and it eventually caused him to turn from God and lose out on the eternal reward laid up for him, who could call the windfall a "good thing?" Jesus asked, "What would it profit a man to gain the whole world and lose his own soul?" Just because things are unpleasant and painful, we cannot label them "bad" until we see their effect on us in the long run. Just because we gain what we want, we cannot call the experiences "good" until we see how these things effect us long term.

From where do these things come? How are these pleasant and unpleasant things set into motion and suddenly appear in our lives? Jesus said that they come from our hearts and our mouths. We, who dwell on the wickedness in us and in this world, cause this wickedness to manifest and eventually (in the form of unpleasantness) appear in our lives. They do not necessarily appear as unpleasant items mind you, but our reaction to ANYTHING – pleasant or unpleasant, good or bad, welcome or unwelcome, riches or poverty, sickness or health, causes our downfall, failure, hardship, or it brings about deliverance, joy, and accomplishment. We have the ability to make castles from sand or make sand of our castles. All this creative power comes from the ABUNDANCE of our heart.

…how can ye, being evil, speak good things? For out of the abundance of the heart the mouth speaketh. A good man out of the good treasure of the heart bringeth forth good things: and an evil man out of the evil treasure bringeth forth evil things…For by thy words thou shalt be justified, and by thy words thou shalt be condemned."

Realization of this idea (that you have the power within you to make any situation a stumbling block or a stepping stone) has caused an erroneous teaching. The error is that the abundance is in your control, namely in the words you speak. This is not a matter of learning to speak right, avoiding certain words or making good confessions of faith, nor is it control of your own will. You cannot decide to fill your heart with good things so your life will be better. You must lay down your life filled with evil, your heart filled with evil things, and exchange them for the abundant life and a heart full of good things.

This exchange is only accomplished through repentance and conversion. Cry out to God for His mercy, and surrender your will to His. He will fill your heart with good things so that your reaction to the evil things, the "bad" and unpleasant things, will bring about goodness and blessing in your life.

Out of the Abundance of Your Heart

The abundance of your heart will cause you to speak good things. These words will not be a forced or wooden parroting of positive thinking verses; they will be true and genuine representations of the contents of your heart. There will be heard from your mouth the most gracious words of acceptance and goodwill. You will bless, and not curse, the things seemingly invading your life. ANY thing, good or bad will have the same effect of blessing. You will be surprised how the things that ruined you before will encourage and strengthen you now. From the abundance of your heart your mouth will speak. Job 8:20-21 says, "Behold, God will not cast away a perfect man, neither will he help the evil doers: Till he fill thy mouth with laughing, and thy lips with rejoicing."

Your own wickedness causes your grief. As soon as you realize that, you will be well on your way to repairing it. God waits for you to change your evil and selfish way. When you go His way, He will change your heart. That will change your acceptance of His will and your attitude toward your own life and the "good" and "bad" things that happen in it. This change will be heard in your speech. Complaints, condemnation, and confusion will disappear, and be replaced with blessing.

Your speech should sound as if God were in control. You need to smile and bless, and not condemn and not complain. It is true, your words need to change, but "How can ye, being evil, speak good things?"

13.   What were you looking for?

"And as they departed, Jesus began to say unto the multitudes concerning John [the Baptist], What went ye out into the wilderness to see? A reed shaken with the wind? But what went ye out for to see? A man clothed in soft raiment? Behold, they which are gorgeously apparelled in soft clothing, and live delicately, are in kings' courts and houses. But what went ye out for to see? A prophet? yea, I say unto you, and much more than a prophet." Luke 7:24-26 Matthew 11:7-9 (Combined)

All Israel was awaiting the return and ministry of the Prophet Elijah. This was misunderstood to mean a visitation from a man who would call himself Elijah (something John did not do) and would introduce the Messiah (something John did do). John, for whatever reason, went unnoticed as the fulfillment of the ancient prophecy, "Behold, I will send my messenger, and he shall prepare the way before me: and the Lord, whom ye seek, shall suddenly come to his temple, even the messenger of the covenant, whom ye delight in: behold, he shall come, saith the LORD of hosts." (Malachi 3:1)

John did not fill the description that they had developed (or had been developed for them) in their mind. They were convinced he could not be "that Prophet." The fact that John did not consider himself to be "that Prophet" did not help matters either. He was once asked, "...Who art thou? And he confessed, and denied not; but confessed, I am not the Christ. And they asked him, What then? Art thou Elias [Elijah]? And he saith, I am not. Art thou that prophet? And he answered, No. Then said they unto him, Who art thou? That we may give an answer to them that sent us. What sayest thou of thyself? He said, I am the voice of one crying in the wilderness, Make straight the way of the Lord, as said the prophet Esaias [Isaiah]." (John 1:19-23)

The disciples had no better understanding of the prophecy. Peter, James and John, after witnessing the transfiguration, seeing and recognizing Elijah with Christ, decided that this event that they witnessed must be the coming of Elijah for which all Israel had been waiting. Jesus corrected their thinking, *"...Elias truly shall first come, and restore all things. But I say unto you, That Elias is come already, and they knew him not, but have done unto him whatsoever they listed [pleased]. Likewise shall also the Son of man suffer of them. Then the disciples understood that he spake unto them of John the Baptist."* (Matthew 17:11-13)

The coming of Elijah was a monumental event in the lives of all Israel and they waited for it with anticipation and delight. They set a place for the Prophet Elijah at every Passover meal and looked out the door to see if he was coming. They knew that he was the forerunner to Christ. They had, unfortunately, created an idea in their mind that the prophet for whom they waited would be much different than John the Baptist actually was. Consequently, they missed the prophet for which they waited for centuries.

In our imagination we may see Jesus with his hands out at His sides, palms up, with a slight shrug in His shoulders as he asks, "When you came out here to see John, what were you looking for? Did you come out here to enjoy nature (a reed in the wind)? Were you disappointed that He was not finely dressed and did not represent the epitome of all your own earthly desires? Those who have the things you desire to see are Kings, not prophets. Is that what you wanted to see? A prophet? John was much more than a prophet. But what did you expect to see? You are looking for signs and wonders, prophets, and mighty men, and are disappointed with all who are sent to you. What are you looking for?"

This is a good question. What are we looking for? What would get us out of our houses and down to the riverbank? What would get our attention? We all have in our mind our own description of what a proper person, a prophet, a church, or a philosophy would be. The descriptions we have in our minds need to be brought out and analyzed. It could reveal what we seek and why. Jesus listed a few of the motivations that men may seek and these may help us categorize our own.

What Are We Looking For?

A Naturist? He is someone with answers that fit into the natural scheme of things but are, in a sense, benign, ineffectual, and undemanding of change. A reed, shaking in the wind. He is sought by those who can see God in a sunset, but have trouble with His presence in the Commandments.

A Representative of our Humanity? This man will satisfy those who look for someone who has the answers, or has conquered the trials of life, who has overcome, a winner, one who has raised above the norm, a man in fine clothes, handsome and successful.

A Man of God? This is the man sought by those who are looking for a prophet, a Seer, or preacher who has the ear of God, and was commissioned or empowered by God. Someone above the average man. Those seeking this, feel that their quest is more noble than that of others; that they are seeking higher or "spiritual" things. They are often taken in by tricks, lofty language, goose bumps, platitudes, flattery, and promised acceptance by God.

Which one of these could take you in? Perhaps a combination of two, or all three? What would you go out to see? We all need to examine our motivations and desires and make sure they are as they should be. Which leads to the query, how should they be?

Your answer is not around you; it is in you. "To whom God would make known ... Christ in you, the hope of glory." (Colossians 1:27) Not surprisingly, Christ perfectly satisfies all three of the attributes He listed. His ministry and His very life teach that you are not to look for answers in the creation (sunsets and nature); you are to look to the Creator.

Jesus was the "Representative of our humanity." He was the "Man of God" there is no other. Yet the one who waited for Messiah missed Him, too.

You will not be able to recognize fulfillment of prophecy by comparing what you see to your Bible's pages, recognition will come from the Spirit within you. Nowhere in the Scripture does it say that when Messiah comes He will tell you how many husbands you have had, but some how the woman at the well knew.

She ran to her friends and said, "Come, see a man, which told me all things that ever I did: is not this the Christ?" (John 4:29) Do not forget that He warned that deception was a possibility and even a probability. Remember His admonitions from Matthew 24, "Many will come... and will deceive many. Pay attention so you won't be deceived. ... when they say, 'look, He is in the desert,' go not forth." Who are these "many" who are being deceived? Don't they own Bibles? Don't they know prophecy? It is not enough to know the book, you must know *Him*.

He knows that you have a tendency to look around before you look within. If you consider in advance, what you like and what you are like, you will be fore-armed against deception. The history of man shows that false teachers are sought and true prophets are killed. Even the Son of God Himself was not safe among us. One of the most dangerous deceptions is the one that convinces you that you are immune from deception.

If you feel that you cannot be deceived, you are presently in the throes of the worst deception of all. You needn't think that deception always leads to communes, poison Kool-Aid, space ships and suicide pacts. Sometimes it just subtlety corrodes a person's faith till there is nothing left in him but questions and doubt and fear of the unknown. Sometimes deception takes the form of knowledge.

Heaps of education can console and comfort those who once searched for Truth -- becoming a bulwark of defense against simple and uncomplicated faith in God. In every case, deception replaces Truth – the Truth that sets men free. Once it is gone nothing remains but a hollow shell where there once was a budding, burgeoning faith in God. What are you looking for?

14.   *You believe because of what I said? – You will see greater things.*

"Now Phillip ... findeth Nathanael, and saith unto him, We have found him, of whom Moses in the law, and the prophets, did write, Jesus of Nazareth, the son of Joseph ...and saith unto him, Come and see. Jesus saw Nathanael coming to him, and saith of him, Behold an Israelite indeed, in whom is no guile! Nathanael saith unto him, Whence knowest thou me? Jesus answered and said unto him, Before that Philip called thee, when thou wast under the fig tree, I saw thee. Nathanael answered and saith unto him, Rabbi, thou art the Son of God; thou art the King of Israel. Jesus answered and said unto him, Because I said unto thee, I saw thee under the fig tree, believest thou? thou shalt see greater things than these." John 1:44-51 (Condensed)

Jesus was impressed with the simple and ready faith of Nathanael. There are those who are ready to believe, and there are those, like Thomas, who need to see the "holes in His hands" before they can believe. We should feel sorrow for those who need such confirmation, for their skepticism is misdirected. Almost without exception, upon interview we will find that those who have no faith in what they cannot see (where spiritual things are concerned) seem to place all faith in what others claim to see (where the natural and temporal is concerned). It is as if they trust other's vision more than their own in science and psychology, but trust only their own sight, feel, reason and understanding in religion and theology.

It seems that we place our trust first in the world's philosophy and science. That misplaced priority is exposed when we say things like, "We've done all we can do. All we can do now is pray." Faith in God's provision and love could only do us good, but it is with doubt and with demand of proof that we reluctantly carry out His plan, place faith in His way, or trust Him with our lives. Jesus was amazed that Nathanael was so willing to do this. The response He was expecting was more like Thomas' reaction to the news of His resurrection.

"But Thomas, one of the twelve, called Didymus, was not with them when Jesus came. The other disciples therefore said unto him, We have seen the Lord. But he said unto them, Except I shall see in his hands the print of the nails, and put my finger into the print of the nails, and thrust my hand into his side, I will not believe." (John 20)

It makes me sad to read this story. Think of the sorrow and hurt the Lord must have felt when He held out His hands and said, "Thomas, Reach hither thy finger, and behold my hands; and reach hither thy hand, and thrust it into my side." The point to note here is that Jesus did accommodate Thomas – even in his unbelief. Though we may not arbitrarily apply this promise of meeting a person halfway to every searcher lacking in faith, it is cause for great hope, and shows the heart of Christ was with this disciple.

He then said, "Thomas, because thou hast seen me, thou hast believed: blessed are they that have not seen, and yet have believed." (This story can be found in John 20.) That blessing Jesus mentioned is directed toward us – we who believe, having not seen. We hold the entire Gospel story by faith. There are great measures afoot to "prove" the Gospel is true and there are equal strides to "prove" that it is adulterated, exaggerated, or false.

These measures simply do not apply to us of unfeigned faith. What scientists, preachers, or mystics say does not move us. No matter what life itself tells us, we are men and women of faith in Christ. We do not believe because "the facts" line up and declare we should believe; we believe because He is alive in us and His Spirit is working in us, sustaining our very lives. As Paul said, "I am crucified with Christ: nevertheless I live; yet not I, but Christ liveth in me: and the life which I now live in the flesh I live by the faith of the Son of God, who loved me, and gave himself for me." (Galatians 2:20)

True faith in God is rarer than you might deduce by polls taken in the United States. To say that we believe in God is much different than saying we live by faith in God. Yet, the Scriptures say, "…the just shall live by his faith." (Habakkuk 2:4) If you are waiting for science to prove God to you, or you are waiting for men of faith to prove that scientific theories are wrong, you are waiting in vain. You must now believe from your heart in Christ. You must hold to whatever shred of belief still remains in you and cultivate it into a life based in faith. The Scriptures give little hope to those who ignore the inner promptings of God within them, claiming that the Spirit will not always work in man.[16]

The Faith Perspective

If you are one who doubts the existence of God, consider this. Perhaps your focus is too narrow. Maybe you secretly want God to do parlor tricks, or maybe it is that your focus is upon yourself. In the Psalms, the writer, having a keen sense of the immense nature of God, had an opposite notion. He was amazed that the God of all creation would have anything to do with him at all! He asked, "When I consider thy heavens, the work of thy fingers, the moon and the stars, which thou hast ordained; What is man, that thou art mindful of him? and the son of man, that thou visitest him?" (Psalms 8:3-4) Yet selfishly we may ask, "Why don't you do something for me?" It may be that life, society or those around you have taught you to be too self-centered and self-important. If that is the case you may never see God as the Psalmist did.

Testimony of the Christian faith is not to be based upon scientific consultation, or theological perfection, but it is to be one of experience. The internal witness and life within, by the presence of the Holy Spirit, is how we know that He is risen and is seated at the right hand of God. We need not visually see Him there to proclaim it. C. S. Lewis, a former atheist said, "I

---

[16] Genesis 6:3, "And the LORD said, My spirit shall not always strive with man, for that he also is flesh: yet his days shall be an hundred and twenty years."

know that the sun is risen, not because I see it, but because by it, I see everything else."

Nevertheless, when your focus shifts from the mundane and temporal, when your goal becomes getting to know your God instead of proving His existence, and your life become less egocentric, new realms of faith and Spirituality await you. Not an ethereal, non-existent, ignorant faith, but one of depth and reality known by the power of God extended to us on our behalf.

Our Savior knows that this does not come easy for some. He knows it has its difficulties. Nathaniel took Him by surprise when he so readily and quickly believed. The story of Nathaniel is not told us to set him apart from us, but for us to covet his faith. To believe simply because Christ said so is a wonderful trait and full of promise.

You, as a Christian, should require no more than the word of Christ to believe. If you do, it will be said of you that "you will see greater things" but first, you must stop putting God to the test. You desire "great" faith, when what you need is "easy" faith – faith that comes quickly and easily. The greatest things will only be seen as your faith becomes easier and easier to exercise. To act on His word to your heart alone is the greatest faith.

When Christ speaks words to your heart, be quick to receive them, without doubt. Surprise the Lord when He requires faith of you. What joy you will feel when He says, "Do you believe because of what I said? You will see greater things than these."

15.   *Have you not so much as read?*

Luke 6:3, Mark 2:28, Matthew 12:3-8, John 7:23 (Combined) "But he answering said unto them, Have ye never read so much as this, what David did, when he had need, and was an hungred, he, and they that were with him? How he entered into the house of God, and did eat the shewbread, which was not lawful for him to eat, neither for them which were with him, but only for the priests? Or have ye not read in the law, how that on the sabbath days the priests in the temple profane the sabbath, and are blameless? ... But if ye had known what this meaneth, I will have mercy, and not sacrifice, ye would not have condemned the guiltless. And he said unto them, The sabbath was made for man, and not man for the sabbath: For the Son of man is Lord even of the sabbath day."

This is one of few accounts that appears in all four Gospels and is a lesson often lost in the mire of arguments about the Sabbath day. Let us focus on Jesus' question, "Have you not so much as read...?" Notice that He uses this question to preface the references to the Law of Moses and David the Prophet.[17] Christ almost has a tone of surprise in His voice, wondering how this concept had eluded their reading and study. Let's look at the Scripture Jesus quoted:

Hosea 6:6, "For I desired mercy, and not sacrifice; and the knowledge of God more than burnt offerings."

The "knowledge of God" is more desirable than offerings and sacrifice. Hebrew prose had poetic values; to repeat a thought in the next phrase with different words of the same meaning was common when the writer was trying to emphasize a point. There are many examples of repetition for emphasis throughout the Old Testament to demonstrate this. By pairing up the repeated thoughts synonyms can be found. Here we see the word "sacrifice" used as a synonym to "offering" and "knowledge of God" in synoptic position with "mercy."

By this verse we may learn that revelation of the knowledge of God will not only reveal Him as merciful; it also places demand upon us to be merciful in order to live in concord with Him.

It is fascinating how often this "New Testament" concept appears in the "Old Testament." Psalms 40:6 says, "Sacrifice and offering thou didst not desire..." Psalms 51:16-17 repeats, "For thou desirest not sacrifice; else would I give it: thou delightest not in burnt offering. The sacrifices of God are a broken spirit: a broken and a contrite heart, O God, thou wilt not despise." God's desire for mercy and not sacrifice is an ancient one. We must not think that God desires sacrifice – His desire is mercy, submission and a contrite and obedient heart. Once, this same concept of sacrifice being second to righteousness, condemned and deposed a King with almost the same words that Jesus quoted from Hosea: "And Samuel said, Hath the LORD as great delight

---

[17] Acts 2:30

61

in burnt offerings and sacrifices, as in obeying the voice of the LORD? Behold, to obey is better than sacrifice, and to hearken than the fat of rams." (1 Samuel 15:22)

David: An Example for Us

David was so intimately familiar with Jehovah that he saw no conflict (and certainly no sin) in eating the forbidden shewbread in the temple. Jesus somehow applied this example of familiarity with the Lawgiver to His disciples who were gathering corn to eat on Sabbath. There is a mystery here that has not been revealed. David knew something to which we have not been made privy; there is something here like a back door or a peek into the Spirit circumnavigating the letter of Law without breaking it. Though it is elusive and difficult to know it in its fullest sense, its truth is contained in the verse:

"The Sabbath was made for man, and not man for the Sabbath: For the Son of man is Lord even of the Sabbath day."

Those who hear in this verse that we can do whatever we want on the Sabbath Day because it was made for us, or those who think Jesus said that He can do whatever He wants because He is Lord of the Sabbath, somehow giving Himself permission to break the Commandment, simply don't understand this verse. It is deeper than this.

There is more to this than wholesale negation of the Law. We cannot do whatever we want yet we are called and compelled to seek God and learn of Him and gain the knowledge of Him and seek Him with our whole heart. This is so we can live, move, and have our being[18] in Him, without fear, without condemnation and still live a life free from sin (not freedom to sin.)

The simple application to this is that, possibly, what we think is sin …may not be – and what we think is not sin…is. Our difficulty comes from the fact that we don't know God! As much as we may delight in our experience of Him, as proud as we may be of the road we have traveled, as far as we think we may have come, we may still go outside on a starry night and look up and know that this saying is true: "For my thoughts are not your thoughts, neither are your ways my ways, saith the LORD. For as the heavens are higher than the earth, so are my ways higher than your ways, and my thoughts than your thoughts." (Isaiah 55:8-9) Why do we not know Him? Jesus said it may be because we have not so much as read His Scriptures.

We must make ourselves familiar with our God. How are we to do that if not by reading His Scriptures? We must learn of His ways and make them our ways. We cannot continue as marginally obedient children, or part-time doers of the Law. Nor can we consider ourselves sinless solely by virtue of what some would claim to be an "abolished" Law. We must learn of Him. We must read His Law, His Prophets, and the testimony of Jesus Christ.

The Scriptures provide insight beyond anyone's years; they contain the intelligence that created the world, the heart of love that gave up to death an

---

[18] Acts 17:28

62

obedient Son to save the rebellious ones. We may no longer blamelessly saunter through Christian bookstores hungrily begging for scraps. We cannot continue expecting tradition, and ceremony to satisfy the eternal need for true and meaningful communion.

We may sit no longer at the feet of mere men asking advice, seeking direction, or attempting to gain some second-hand guidance. How can we ask our most gracious God, who gave the Scriptures, preserved them, and freely dispersed them throughout the world, to speak to us, give us guidance, and day to day leading if we refuse to read, the gift of all earthly gifts, the Scriptures? Do you expect God to tell you something twice, or three times? Or do you demand that He write a letter, mail it, deliver it, open it, and read it to you? What must our heavenly Father do to teach you?

The Bible is the book of all books. It contains answers to questions with which you are struggling right now. It has insight to impart to you that could make next week into a miracle instead of a massacre. By writing a Bible, our God has lifted the requirements of holiness to hear a word from Him. Anyone can read it. Anyone can hear the words He spoke and spark within them the light of understanding to begin the journey toward peace with God. What a gift! To be given, without prerequisite, a window into the mind and heart of God.

You may be ignoring the most wonderful love letter ever written, all the while pleading for intimacy and "the knowledge of God"; all the while living in unnecessary sin and ignorance. To what extent must He go to make His way known to you? How will you stand before Him and plead ignorance of His ways, knowing He could look at you and ask, "Have ye not so much as read?"

16. Why are ye so fearful?

Matthew 8:26, "And when he was entered into a ship, his disciples followed him. And, behold, there arose a great tempest in the sea, insomuch that the ship was covered with the waves: but he was asleep. And his disciples came to him, and awoke him, saying, Lord, save us: we perish. And he saith unto them, Why are ye fearful, O ye of little faith? Then he arose, and rebuked the winds and the sea; and there was a great calm. But the men marvelled, saying, What manner of man is this, that even the winds and the sea obey him!" Also refer to: Mark 4:40, Luke 8:25

One of the beautiful things about having four Gospels is reading the same account from three or four perspectives. This account of Jesus calming the storm is no exception. In one he asks, "Why are ye fearful, O ye of little faith?" in another, "Why are ye so fearful? How is it that ye have no faith?" and then finally (as this story only appears in only three of the Gospels) He asks, "Where is your faith?"

From this story, take notice that the lack of faith is an indicator to Jesus that they are full of fear, or vice versa if you prefer, but it is obvious that faith and fear are mutually exclusive forces. More so than a discussion of faith, we want to consider the question that brought about the self-examination, "Why are you so fearful?"

Many of the answers to the questions Jesus asked were for our information not His. Even if we do not hold to the idea that Jesus "knew everything" or could "read minds," we must agree that His wisdom far surpassed mankind's. He asked, "Why are ye so fearful?" not because He did not know; He asked in order to initiate an internal and self-questioning process within the disciples. He was saying, "Stop, wait a minute and think! Why are you so fearful?"

This self-examining process is an essential part of the Christian faith that is lacking in most of our personal lives and certainly in conventional congregational worship. This process cannot be bypassed, done in haste or hurry, nor can it be accomplished in formulaic steps or procedures. It is a meeting of minds, so to speak, a meeting of reality within us that can only be accomplished through honest questions and honest answers.

In silent contemplation, we listen to the Word of God (the living Christ) within us, as He evaluates our condition and queries us, we answer Him and our answers may candidly determine our shortcomings and expose the necessary changes. But it is the waiting; the silent waiting upon Him that will present light to our souls and refresh our innermost being. The noise of our lives and noise of our churches attest to the lack of quietness within our spirits. Quietness is uncomfortable to most, because it naturally reveals the noise in our souls. We try to avoid this candid meeting with Christ from occurring within us, for we dread it may make our fears of our Father's displeasure a reality. Noise is necessary to keep this honest, internal conversation from happening, lest we find ourselves convicted in our favorite lifestyle and then obliged to change it.

Peace with Our God

It is the lack of our Father's approval that deprives of serenity; we want to feel His hand of salvation on us so that we can feel peace, but we avoid feeling His hand of correction. How can we have one and not the other? Do not both touches of His hand come at once? The writer in Hebrews 12 says, "For whom the Lord loveth he chasteneth, and scourgeth every son whom he receiveth. If ye endure chastening, God dealeth with you as with sons... Furthermore we have had fathers of our flesh which corrected us, and we gave them reverence: shall we not much rather be in subjection unto the Father of spirits, and live? ...that we might be partakers of his holiness. Now no chastening for the present seemeth to be joyous, but grievous: nevertheless afterward it yieldeth the peaceable fruit of righteousness..." (Verses 6-11 abridged, emphasis added) It is the pain of correction that brings about the feeling of being true children of your Father in heaven, as well as effecting lasting changes in our lifestyle that please Him.

But we avoid this pain. Sometimes we mistakenly think that the absence of discomfort we feel resulting from the singing or orchestrated harmony with others when we are making "joyful noise," is His approving hand on our lives. But relief is not remedy. Our temporary comfort is no more a sign of healing than drug-induced pain alleviation is an evidence of a medical cure.

We are fearful because we do not know our future; we do not know our future because we do not have faith in God. We do not have faith in God because we are not in communication with Him; we are not in communication with Him because our sins have created a painful barrier between us. Sadly, what has been forgotten are the words of the Old Testament Prophet Isaiah: "Behold, the LORD'S hand is not shortened, that it cannot save; neither his ear heavy, that it cannot hear: But your iniquities have separated between you and your God, and your sins have hid his face from you, that he will not hear." (Isaiah 59:1-2)

Now that we know the answer, let us hear the question again, "Why are ye so fearful?" When faced with a trial of our faith we naturally think of ways we have displeased our God. It is as though we have a delinquent debt to the local hospital and we find ourselves in need of their services again. Though they may treat us through mercy, we know, because of our debt, we do not deserve it. You should live in such a way so that no debt, no sin or shortcoming should be outstanding, as you approach the Father in prayer.

Why are you so fearful? It is likely that you feel afraid in your trials because your disobedience and your recent failures give you no assurance that God is in control or will help in time of need. Selfish acts and concerns are often responsible for faithlessness and fear. Don't live in a manner where only your interests are preponderant. In doing so, you will surely consider the storms that rise as obtrusive impositions into your world or even punishment for your sin.

Notice that Jesus did not ask, "Why are you afraid of storms?" That would be a silly question as it is well established that storms are dangerous. He asked, "Why are ye *so* fearful?" Jesus was awakened by His disciples asking, "Master, carest thou not that we perish?" Not only had they become fearful of the tempest, but they had also surmised, in their fear, that Jesus did not care if they died. They did not doubt His ability to act as much they now doubted His willingness to act on their behalf.

Jesus asked them about their *fearfulness*. They were not only afraid of the storm (which was normal); He asked them why they were full of fear. "Why are ye so fearful?" "Where is your faith?" "How is it ye have no faith?" These questions would sober any honest Christian, and initiate self-examination. You may feel that fear is out of your control. However, you should remember that the fear you feel is in inverse proportion to your faith in God. Your works exemplify and give evidence of your faith in God... and your works are within our control.

When weather, out of your control, pitches and tosses your boat, you can bravely steer ahead on into the waves and remain afloat only if you know that you are going where you were told to go, doing what you were told to do, and serving your Master and not your own interests. Steer, go, do, and serve! All are works within your control. It is only the one who seeks the easy way, or who looks for the loopholes, who fears when the way grows dark and ominous. Those who dodge responsibility and perform only the least that is expected are uncertain that God cares, or doubt that He would use His power to save.

You are not to be cowardly and worthless, trembling and unsure. You are to hold in high regard your commission and the Commissioner. You may only exemplify that respect by your servile attitude and selflessness. Then you can function in true and trusting faith. You can live in full assurance that if He says to *go*, you'll *go* until you arrive. If He says to *do*, you'll *do* until you are done. You will fear nothing because you are not your own, you are bought with a price. You have nothing to fear as you live day to day doing only that which pleases Him. So then, "Why are ye so fearful?"

17.   Where is your faith?

Luke 8:24-25, "And they came to him, and awoke him, saying, Master, master, we perish. Then he arose, and rebuked the wind and the raging of the water: and they ceased, and there was a calm. And he said unto them, Where is your faith? And they being afraid wondered, saying one to another, What manner of man is this! for he commandeth even the winds and water, and they obey him."

A story is told about a circus performer who walks among the crowd after successfully walking across the high wire suspended above a gorge, and asked, "Do you believe I can go across pushing a wheel barrow?" The crowd chanted, "Yes! Yes!" Then stone silence fell as he prepared the wheelbarrow for the narrow journey and not a word in answer came when he asked, "Now, who would like to ride?" Corresponding action is the ONLY indicator of unfeigned faith.

The Bible records a question that is often quoted, but seldom answered. "What doth it profit, my brethren, though a man say he hath faith, and have not works? Can faith save him? It is most uncomfortable to answer the question because it shows us to be faithless in many cases. We must admit, however, that faith without actions that corresponds to the faith is not faith at all. And, "Ye see then how that by works a man is justified, and not by faith only." (James 2:14-24)

The action that corresponds to faith (or the lack of action) is not only a marker of absent faith, it can also provide clues to us indicating in what or where we have placed our faith. Jesus made the same point this way, "For where your treasure is, there will your heart be also." (Matthew 6:21) Behind the words is the principle that we live what we believe. Or as a Mississippi preacher friend of mine says, "We be livin' what we believin'." If what Jesus and my friend say is true (and I believe it is) then we may look into our own lives and easily see where our faith lies. "Where is your faith?" becomes more than a rhetorical question. It becomes a question of introspection. Your faith is somewhere, where is it?

Sometimes the action that exposes our misplaced faith is only a mental process. When trouble arises we may look for help. The process of looking starts with a mental inventory of useful items, people, and resources. When faced with a problem we might immediately think of a friend to help us who has expertise or political power. When faced with a loss we may think of our insurance policy or our savings account. When a health issue appears we may want to consult with a doctor of reputation among his peers. Where our thoughts go is to our treasure, and where your treasure is, there is where you will find your heart of faith.

When King David was faced with trouble he said, "I will lift up mine eyes unto the hills, from whence cometh my help. My help cometh from the LORD, which made heaven and earth." (Psalms 121:1-2) Could it be said that

David had misplaced faith? Never a man had chariots and horses, armies and men so devoted to him as David had. He was truly a man of resources, but his attitude was, "Some trust in chariots, and some in horses: but we will remember the name of the LORD our God." (Psalms 20:7) Can anyone see a man here who doubts God? Do we have to ask David, "Where is your faith?"

I believe that God enjoyed the faith of Job, Noah and Daniel, and I believe that YHVH enjoyed David's faith. David's faith was different. It had a humble and unassuming quality. Although it was a no nonsense faith, it never even encroached disrespect. Jesus even mentions (I believe with a smile on His face) a time when David ate the shewbread in the Temple, which is unlawful for any man who is not a Priest to eat, and asked the Pharisees what they thought of that. It is no wonder that David was known as a man after God's own heart.[19] The eternal reign of Christ in the new Kingdom has been prophesied for years as the "the throne of David." David's relationship to Jehovah was so close that he once circumvented the office of the priest and a man was killed in the process. David grieved for Uzzah and believed it was his fault that he died.[20] With all these ideas in our head, we are left with this mystery pertaining to David's relationship to God. But a day came in the life of David where his actions would show, loud and clear, where his faith was. This was a day that grieved the Lord and things were never the same after this event.

"And Satan stood up against Israel, and provoked David to number Israel." (1 Chronicles 21:1) What could be so bad about taking a census? Look at the figures that were given to David. "And Joab gave the sum of the number of the people unto David. And all they of Israel were a thousand thousand and an hundred thousand [1,100,000] men that drew sword: and Judah was four hundred threescore and ten thousand [470,000] men that drew sword."(Verse 5) These statistics were to verify the POWER available to David as king. It was obvious that the object in which David placed his faith was changing, and it was deplorable to God. David's action showed where his faith was. He no longer looked unto the hills as in the days of his youth. He no longer was saying that some trust in chariots and horses, for his actions are now speaking louder than any words of his past. But why did he falter?

Always Enough

I remember going away to school and, for the first time, I was in charge of my finances. In some homes Dad keeps the wallet and balances the checkbook, in my home, my Mother was the one. She taught me how to spend money and how to save it. I remember setting up an account at the school for needs and supplies that would eventually crop up as the year progressed. "How much money are you going to put in there?" I asked my mother. She told me that there would always be enough, as long as I only bought what I needed. I lived by the faith that what my mother told me was true. For many months I

---

[19] 1 Samuel 13:14, "...the LORD hath sought him a man after his own heart, and the LORD hath commanded him to be captain over his people..."
[20] 2 Samuel 6

never looked into that account or even cared how much was there and, just as she said, whenever I needed something I could go to the clerk and ask for an amount and there was always enough.

But the day came when I wanted to buy MORE than I needed. What do you think was my first thought? My faith in Mom was instantly transformed. I could not count on what was out of my control, namely the will and ability of my mother; I had to rely on what was within my power and possession. My actions showed where my faith was. It was in me.

The Disciples were skilled boatmen. This was not their first time at sea. David was a man of war skilled in every area of battle. When it came time to take inventory of assets it should come as no surprise that these men counted on their own power. David realized what he had done and repented. After the ordeal was over David likely heard within himself the words, "Where is your faith?"

That thought never occurred to the disciples, however. They rowed and rowed. They used every trick in the book. After all hope was gone and their resources were exhausted, and they worked hard to no avail, they went to Jesus. Asking Him why He did not care if they perished, Jesus looked around at the panting men who were totally spent trying to recover themselves, and asked, "Where is your faith?"

18. How is it that ye have no faith?

Mark 4:38-40, "And he was in the hinder part of the ship, asleep on a pillow: and they awake him, and say unto him, Master, carest thou not that we perish? And he arose, and rebuked the wind, and said unto the sea, Peace, be still. And the wind ceased, and there was a great calm. And he said unto them, Why are ye so fearful? how is it that ye have no faith?"

Have you ever wondered what the Lord wanted the disciples to do? I have. Did He want them to speak to the storm like He did? Did He expect them to stand on the bow of that boat and say, "Peace, be still? The Lord Jesus Christ is on this vessel and has commissioned us to go to the other side!" Is that what Jesus expected them to do? I think He did.

Faith – true faith – requires a word from God directly to us. It is imperative that we hear from God, personally, the word, the commission, or the orders to go or to do or to speak. Not just some vague Scripture reference to an action or unction of centuries past, but a fresh word from God. This personal word was present in the command, "Let us go over to the other side of the lake." When the snag in life comes, (in this case a storm) the authority and commission of those who are called should come to the fore. Remember Jesus' words to his disciples,

"And he said unto them, I beheld Satan as lightning fall from heaven. Behold, I give unto you power to tread on serpents and scorpions, and over all the power of the enemy: and nothing shall by any means hurt you." (Luke 10:18-19)

The problem was that these men were fishers. They were well acquainted with the destructive power of the sea. They had known of lives being claimed out there on that water. They would have to change their minds and habits about very familiar things – a task very difficult indeed. The ingredient missing here was faith. "How is it that ye have no faith?"

The Lord wants and even commands us to have faith saying in Mark 11:22b, "Have faith in God." This is rendered in Greek, "Have the faith of God." Unswerving, confident, and assured faith that what God promised He is able to perform. This is why Jesus could, without flinching, place the two adjectives, faithless and perverse in the description of His disciples. In Matthew 17:17 the Lord chided the disciples for not having faith enough to cast out the demon in a boy who was brought to them, "Then Jesus answered and said, O faithless and perverse generation, how long shall I be with you?"

How Important Is Faith?

We should place as much importance on faith as the Lord did. Our concern for ourselves and doubting God can put us in the category of perverse. Look who is included in the list of the damned in Revelation 21:8, "But the fearful, and unbelieving, and the abominable, and murderers, and whoremongers, and sorcerers, and idolaters, and all liars, shall have their part in the lake which burneth with fire and brimstone: which is the second death." What a list on which to have an attribute of your personality included!

When Jesus tells His disciples the reason they could not cast the devil out He used the phrase, "because of your unbelief." He did not say they didn't have enough faith or that their faith was not large enough, He said that it was not there. "How is it that ye have NO faith?" The disciples must have wondered in themselves, "Do we need a greater faith?" But Jesus told them, "I say to you that if your faith were the size of the smallest seed it would have been enough. The problem was that faith wasn't there at all.

Jesus' words and actions said clearly, "You doubted my word. I gave you power and authority over unclean spirits and you doubted it." This tenacious demon played the same role as the contrary wind and sea was to the prior mission. They had opportunity to learn this earlier. Had they learned the lesson from the Sea of Galilee they would have spoken to this demon and cast it out. Alas, they had no faith in this situation either. They did not speak to the wind in faith and they likely did not speak to this demon either. They had the command, the word, they knew what action to take, but they did not have the faith.[21]

Do we disappoint God when we doubt and fear? I believe, for the most part, we do. Especially when it comes to everyday provisions. We hear Jesus say, "...for your heavenly Father knoweth that ye have need of all these things"[22] we can hear a sadness in His voice that we do not comprehend this in reality.

However, many times, in order to keep from disappointing God, we err in the other direction – *presumption*. We presume God's favor or blessing when, though we have no word from God, we capriciously take from the Bible someone else's' promise or prior record of God's provision and arbitrarily claim it for ourselves. Claiming that we are practicing faith, we mock the God we allege to glorify for our provision.

How is it that we have no faith? I submit it is because we have not *heard* from God. We have not sought commission by Him to live, work, or play, nor have we heard His voice in any matters of our life. How can we have faith, or live by faith if we have never heard the Word of God in any area of our lives? We are not living by faith... we are living by hope. Hope is good, but it is not faith. We hope God is in control. We hope He will bless us in next week's business. We hope He will expand our borders and make our way prosperous, but we have no real word from God upon which we may lay claim and no promise upon which we may rest our full assurance of faith.

We know what to do, but we have not been told to do it. We know the job to be done, but we have not been commanded. When we are working under our own power and the storm looms overhead and we hear the thunder roll and

---

[21] Excerpt from the audio book "*On Faith*" by this author.
[22] Matthew 6:32

the see the seas swell, our faith is exposed as only hope because we have no commission to call upon.

Faith Comes By Hearing

All we need to hear from our God is to go and do this or that and we would be strong in our faith. We would know our commission. No one in a right frame of mind wonders whether God is ABLE. We wonder if He is willing. We wonder if He is willing because we do not know His will! We must hear a word from God. We must hear the Word of God. Here is one of the most misunderstood principles in Christendom today. It is misunderstood mainly because the most misunderstood Scripture is so often used to teach in this situation.

"So then faith cometh by hearing, and hearing by the word of God."
Romans 10:17

If you mistakenly define "the Word of God" as "the Scriptures," you have rendered the power of this truth impotent. You will not receive faith from reading, nor will faith come by study, faith comes by HEARING. It is when you receive your commission to "go to the other side of the lake" that you have the faith to say, "Peace, be still." But you have to HEAR it. We cannot presume it, we may not read the promise made to someone else two centuries ago, but you must hear for yourself.

Many of us are living our lives having never consulted God about the direction that they are to go. You may assume He wants you to do this or that, you may presume He will bless your efforts if you do the best you can, but if you want to claim to live by faith, you must hear from Him about your direction and purpose in life.

If you want to have faith you must hear that voice that authorizes you to overcome any obstacle. If you want to have faith – true faith – you must HEAR the Word of God. "So then faith cometh by hearing, and hearing by the word of God." We cannot group the whole Church into this category of faithlessness nor blame them for not exercising faith.

There are some who have heard the Word of God, who know the direction and purpose for their lives. They have been commissioned and told where to go and how to get there.

Like the disciples were told to go to the other side, some have received their orders. It is to those who know their instructions that Jesus addresses His question. "I gave you orders, I empowered you to overcome all obstacles, how is that ye have no faith?"

19.   Why do you think evil in your hearts?

Matthew 9:4, "And Jesus knowing their thoughts said, Wherefore think ye evil in your hearts?"

Jesus approached a man suffering from palsy and said "...Son, be of good cheer; thy sins be forgiven thee." Then He asked some of the scribes who were watching Him, "Why did they think evil thoughts?" Here is a curiosity. God is about to do a wonderful thing and the religious leaders are on the outside looking in. They feel that they are outsiders and respond by finding fault. They comment, "This man blasphemes." This comment was what caused Jesus to turn to them and ask the question, "Why do you think evil thoughts in your heart?"

It would be good practice to answer Jesus when He asks a question (especially when we find ourselves exemplifying the traits of the one being questioned.) If we find ourselves thinking evil thoughts, it would do us good to answer the query, "Why?" We should feel shame for the similarities in the thoughts we have about our brethren in Christ and the judgment poured upon Christ by the Pharisees and scribes. Even the worst examples of Christianity, in theology, in doctrine, or in practice, do not deserve our criticism. We must ask, "Why do I think evil thoughts?"

What are these "evil thoughts?" Evil thoughts are clearly identified in Scripture. From Luke 6:45 and Matthew 12: 35,

"...an evil man out of the evil treasure of his heart bringeth forth that which is evil: for of the abundance of a man's heart his mouth speaketh."

From Matthew 15:18-19 and Mark 7:20-23 "But those things which proceed out of the mouth come forth from the heart; and they defile the man. For out of the heart proceed evil thoughts, false witness, adulteries, fornications, murders, thefts, covetousness, wickedness, deceit, lasciviousness, an evil eye, blasphemy, pride, foolishness: All these evil things come from within, and defile the man."

We also know that, though this is an impressive list, this is not an exhaustive one. Although the heart of a "faith pretender" likely won't lead him to practice all of the worst ones mentioned here, their thoughts can be as dangerous. After we read this list, we must then ask, "Why do evil thoughts arise in our hearts – thoughts of pride, foolishness, suspicion and even blasphemy? Perhaps it would be easier to consider this objectively by looking at the example given in the story above. Why did the scribe engage suspicion and accuse Christ of blasphemy? Simply because the scribe did not believe that the man he saw in front of him was the Messiah. Why did he not believe it? It was because Jesus did not fit the mold that the scribe (and tradition) made for Him.

Human nature is to avoid responsibility. Also, this nature avoids servitude. The knowledge of Christ and the subsequent acceptance of Him as Messiah will require both. He thinks, "If I only search for the Christ, I am counted among the faithful and not compelled to obey Christ." This convoluted thinking is practiced by many. Not only the scribe, but also modern seekers who look into Christianity and discover that finding Jesus as Messiah means to take Him as Lord. Not wanting to do the latter, they stay in "search mode" and determine never to find anything for sure. Because they are searching they assume an air of sincerity.

However, the day we find Christ, the search is over. At that time we must either give up or give over to Christ, or we must reject Him. Those who do not wish to reject Him (because they indeed know He is Lord and Christ), nor wish to serve Him (because they want their own way and yet do not want to appear as infidels) can purposefully remain in that state of uncertainty, remaining skeptical, objective, undecided. We enjoy these words being attributed to us, as they tend to lend to the bearer an air of intelligence, sobriety and cerebral superiority. It makes us seem as if we use analysis instead of some silly faith and so we will appear not to "jump to conclusions."

The scribes were not much different. However, these men who saw Christ Jesus were not intelligent; they were blinded by closed eyes. They were not being analytical so they could believe; they were being critical so they would not have to. We who have Christ revealed to us and hold out for "proof" or who choose to remain "open minded" are literally playing with fire.

Those who turn their heads, close their eyes, or stop their ears, are only making provision for more self-indulgence and more self-rule. They only avoid the "giving up." The "surrender" is the threshold over which they cannot seem to step. All lives, before surrender, are lives of evil thought, evil surmising, doubt, fear, and skepticism. All the while, they ride the fence, socializing with God's people; they pretend to be intelligent and open-minded Christians. They pick apart and criticize; they try to hold others back to avoid "fanaticism." They fancy themselves as those who keep organization and order.

Christ is asking, "Why do you doubt everything you read in the Scriptures? Why do you criticize the deeper brethren who don't see things the way you do? Why is it you call dedication "going overboard," call sober Christians "stuffy," and sanctified persons, "fanatics"? "Why do evil thoughts arise in your heart?"

How Would You Answer?

Our answer will not be much different than the scribe's would have been. The scribe was looking at total humiliation at the first sign of accepting this Galilean carpenter's boy as Messiah. All that this scribe ever said would have to be retracted. All he ever believed would have to be changed. He would likely be put out of the synagogue, and rejected by his own family. All of his future aspirations would be put into jeopardy. So he decided to find fault and back it up with Scripture. After Jesus said to this man, "Thy sins be forgiven thee." The scribe says, "Who can forgive sins but God alone?" He was reasoning to himself, "He can't be Messiah if He is a blasphemer!"

He holds Jesus up to perfection to see if He measures up. Jesus fails his test. Jesus always fails tests designed by man. He always will. You will never prove that He is God. He will have to prove it to you.

You must learn the origin of "evil thoughts" and why they appear. You must learn that good and proper theological arguments are sometimes used to justify a lifestyle or to get your own way. Debate and skepticism accomplish nothing if surrender does not follow when truth is discovered. Some enjoy the search, but searching is useless if the seeker refuses to find.

God lovingly guides us to the Savior by people and events entering and exiting our life all the time. Information, evidences, internal witnesses, all appear to bring us along the way that leads to eternal life. Care should be exercised to weigh everything, examine everything, and look for our Guide's signature in it. If you reject what He sends there is no assurance that He will send it again. Examine rather, why you are rejecting what you really feel compelled to believe. Ask yourself, why do you think evil in your hearts?

20. *Whether is easier to say, Thy sins be forgiven thee; or Rise up and walk?*

Matthew 9:5 Mark 2:9 Luke 5:23 (Combined) For whether is easier, to say to the sick of the palsy, Thy sins be forgiven thee; or to say, Arise, and take up thy bed, and walk?

To convince the scribe in this story that his theory on identifying Messiah may be flawed, Jesus offered a question, "Whether is easier, to say, Thy sins be forgiven thee; or to say, Rise up and walk?"

The answer to this question is difficult for we know He is not speaking of merely saying either of the choices given, but is asking, which is easier to do. For with Jesus, to say or to do was the same thing. (It should be that way for us as well.) In this case however, the question was, "If I am who I claim to be, I can forgive sin. If I am who I say I am, I can heal diseases as well." To which the scribe, as a scholar of the Old Testament, must attest. It was clear in the Scriptures that Messiah would be able to do these things. Then Jesus says,

"But that ye may know that the Son of man hath power on earth to forgive sins, (then saith he to the sick of the palsy) I say unto thee, Arise, take up thy couch bed, and go unto thine house. And immediately he rose up before them, and took up that whereon he lay, and went forth before them all and departed to his own house glorifying God. And they were all amazed, and they glorified God, and were filled with fear, saying, "We never saw it on this fashion. We have seen strange things to day." (Matthew 9:6-7 - Mark 2:10-12 - Luke 5:24-26 Combined)

Now what will the poor scribe do? The man has just seen Messiah's prophecies come to pass before his own eyes and he is left with no other alternative but to believe. The record here says they glorified God and were filled with fear. This was a reaction any of us would have had.

Messiah came with a long and detailed list of prophecies that he would fulfill. These prophecies were misunderstood and misapplied and caused nearly a whole nation to miss the Messiah. Jesus was not averse to proclaiming his familiarity with these prophecies and attaching His life and works as fulfillment. Read this story recorded in Luke 4:16-22,

"And he came to Nazareth, where he had been brought up: and, as his custom was, he went into the synagogue on the sabbath day, and stood up for to read. And there was delivered unto him the book of the prophet Esaias. And when he had opened the book, he found the place where it was written, The Spirit of the Lord is upon me, because he hath anointed me to preach the gospel to the poor; he hath sent me to heal the brokenhearted, to preach deliverance to the captives, and recovering of sight to the blind, to set at liberty them that are bruised, To preach the acceptable year of the Lord. And he closed the book, and he gave it again to the minister, and sat

down. And the eyes of all them that were in the synagogue were fastened on him. And he began to say unto them, This day is this scripture fulfilled in your ears. And all bare him witness, and wondered at the gracious words which proceeded out of his mouth. And they said, 'Is not this Joseph's son?' "[23]

As He traveled, He never missed genuine opportunity to use this anointing. Through this He was seen by those of open heart as the Messiah and to those of closed mind as a blasphemer, lawbreaker, a man gluttonous and drunken. The honest folk received him gladly under this premise: "…When Christ cometh, will he do more miracles than these which this man hath done?" (John 7:31) The miracles showed them (and us) that His power exceeded the norm, but what is that to us today? Today Jesus, the Messiah, is still the ONLY healer and He is the only one who forgives sin. When Jesus asked the question, "Whether is easier, to say arise and walk or thy sins be forgiven thee?" we can see His objective was to demonstrate His authority to do either or both at will.

True Grace

There is more to glean from this question of Jesus. What we must draw from this story is that the one who has power to heal, has power to save. What we can draw from His question is that one will be as easy to accomplish as the other. Jesus is uniquely qualified to effect conversion of the soul, proven by His ability to heal. It is He alone who has this power and the sovereign will to use it on our behalf. We are to learn that we are desperately helpless in both of these situations. We can save our soul from destruction as easily as we can make a lame man walk again. Both of these are so far from our level of ability it is ludicrous to attempt either one.

Today, it is commonly taught to play games of forgiveness in our mind. It is not uncommon to hear that we can make ourselves better through "inner healing" or by "forgiving" ourselves, unfortunately, neither is possible. Our guilty conscience before God does indeed wreak havoc with our health and well-being, but forgiveness and healing are gifts from God given to those who seek forgiveness from Him. It is, after all, His Law that is broken. It would be foolish to tell people to "forgive themselves" when they transgress against their fellow man, but it is borderline blasphemy to instruct them to do so when they sin against their Creator. Forgiveness is appropriate only from the one who was offended, what good can come from someone trying to alleviate the condemnation of God by "forgiving himself?" If you are under the

---

23 The gracious words were not great oratory; they were words of meaning. It was as if Shakespeare were reading Hamlet's soliloquy to you, or as if you were transported in time to hear Lincoln himself give the Gettysburg address – not to hear the best reader, or the best actor, or orator, but to hear the author himself. Jesus was reading a prophecy that the entire synagogue knew could only be speaking of Messiah. Then with more audacity of any prophet or priest ever known, He said, "Isaiah's prophecy of Messiah is fulfilled…today… in your ears!" Is it not amazing that in our day we have theologians going to and fro telling us that Jesus never claimed divinity?

condemnation of the Judge of all the earth, you need to seek the forgiveness in His court alone.

To attempt to speak to your own paralyzed legs to cause them to leap and lift you from the floor will likely prove to be a disappointment. (Unless, of course, you are told to do so by Christ.) It is with that futility in mind that you should approach the idea of effecting your own salvation or forgiveness. It should seem as impossible to you, to forgive your own sin as to infuse strength into an inert limb. Forgiveness is a gift of God in the person of His Son Jesus Christ. Christ, sought and found, will answer all the questions of sin, forgiveness and guilt. To attempt to remove guilt by the pretense of "forgiving" yourself will never have lasting results, to say nothing of eternal value.

When you attempt to "better" yourself, "forgive" yourself, or in any way attempt to bring about your own salvation, it would behoove you to ponder this question of Jesus, if only for a few minutes, "Whether is easier to say, Thy sins be forgiven thee; or to say, Rise up and walk?"

21.   Is it lawful on the Sabbath days to do good?

Luke 6:9, "Then said Jesus unto them, I will ask you one thing; Is it lawful on the sabbath days to do good, or to do evil? to save life, or to destroy it?"

When a person decides to keep God's Sabbath Day, seemingly out of the woodwork comes everyone to offer opinion, criticize, scrutinize, or in some cases, open their denomination to you for membership. If the subject of Sabbath comes up in discussions, we are apt to hear stories about how impossible it is to keep the Sabbath and how "Jesus changed all that Sabbath keeping stuff." It is not a subject for the unprepared as the passions are deep and various.

Some have chosen to avoid the subject altogether. I cannot blame them. It is unfortunate that such a pleasant thing as Jehovah's ordained rest should be so tiresome. It is equally unfortunate that God's gift of the Sabbath Day should become a matter of debate and division. But so it is when men confuse and convolute the simplicity that is to be found in Christ.[24]

Let us begin with the apostle's words in 1 John 5:2-3, "By this we know that we love the children of God, when we love God, and keep his commandments. For this is the love of God, that we keep his commandments: and his commandments are not grievous." How sad that the Commandments of God are grievous to many who claim to be Christ's.

To some, giving God one day of their seven is as though they are being asked to give up something to which they are entitled, something that they own, or something that is owed them. How can those who seek communion with Christ neglect the time He has set aside for that communion? How can we consider it a grievous task to come aside and rest awhile? It is because man has added to the Commandment and made it into a chore of duty and drudgery. He has done this OUTSIDE of the Scriptures, yet we still consider man's words over the Scriptures of truth.

The Jews created documents that, with the intention of keeping the Commandments, made them more difficult to keep. The "Sabbath day's journey" is a good example. The Sabbath day's journey was intended to place an explanatory, or definitive framework around the Scripture. The Law they refer to only says, "See, for that the LORD hath given you the sabbath… abide ye every man in his place, let no man go out of his place on the seventh day." (Exodus 16:29) Somehow, Jewish leadership decided how far it should be that a man can wander "from his place" without breaking the Commandment. They came up with 2000 paces or yards, how they arrived at this distance is unclear.

---

[24] The observance of Sabbath is not a part of traditional Quaker faith and practice, neither on the first day (their day of worship) nor on the true Sabbath. Your author departs from Quaker tradition at this point, compelled to esteem the fourth Commandment, the life and practice of Jesus, the life and practice of the Apostles, and recorded early church history above Quaker understanding as examples of proper Christian behavior and righteous living.

Nevertheless, we find that many think to travel farther than "a Sabbath day's journey" on the Sabbath is a violation of the Commandment and therefore, sin. But, the Scriptures make no such assertion. When we read the Scriptures pertaining to Sabbath we will find that Sabbath is not a grievous restriction, nor a calculated observance, but a day set aside, sanctified, and made holy by voluntarily ceasing from our labor and honoring God's request to remember Him.

The Sabbath Is a Gift

When you read, for yourself, the Scriptures that pertain to Sabbath, you will find that the Commandment is not a grievous one, nor one that requires more than you can do, but a Commandment of love and promise. It is a Commandment that bears a gift from God.

In the days of old, the Bible records an execution associated with the breaking of this Law. A man was found gathering sticks on the Sabbath and for that, he lost his life. Without understanding, we may find it hard to take comfort in a gift that we are forced to receive. But it was not the lack of acceptance of this gift that caused his death; it was his despite of God's Commandment.

The gift is not the Commandment and the Commandment is not the gift. The gift is to be found in *obedience* to the Commandment. When we place our own interests above the Commandment, are we not placing ourselves above our Lord? As says the Lord Jesus, "Verily, verily, I say unto you, The servant is not greater than his lord; neither he that is sent greater than he that sent him. If ye know these things, happy are ye if ye do them." (John 13:16-17) The operational phrase is, "Happy are ye if ye do them." The happiness, blessedness, and the gift are to be found in the doing.

When we submit to God's Law we will find, in our obedience, that the Law is not grievous. When we go only to the Scriptures, we will find that the Commandments are not difficult either. The Jews of Jesus' day (and the naysayers in our day) made the walk of faith into difficulty and impossibility. "We can't do this on Sabbath day and we can't do that" say they, while the blessed Scriptures may be completely silent on that particular subject.

We need to take our cues from the words God has spoken in our heart, and our conscience, and forget the traditions of men. We make living by our faith impossible when we add to or take away from what God has plainly said. When you ignore the Word of God within you, your conscience and Guide, and hold to traditions of men, you make "the word of God of none effect through your tradition." (Mark 7:13) When you ignore the Commandment and hold to tradition you bring to life the word of warning Jesus gave to the Pharisees, "Thus have ye made the commandment of God of none effect by your tradition." (Matthew 15:6)

Jesus was astounded that these well-learned men, these scribes and Pharisees, could not see the clear intent of Sabbath day. These men, along with everyone in their tow, had ceased to worship ON the Sabbath and had begun to worship the Sabbath itself! They were accusing Him of violating and desecrating their "god sabbath" by healing a blind man!

There are those who struggle with Sabbath worship even today. Mankind always seems to teeter and totter back and forth across lines and boundaries, words and laws, definitions and excuses. He never seems to get it right; he never seems to be able to balance himself. Should we go for a walk? Should we make a sandwich, should we feed the homeless on Sabbath? Should we use electricity, city water or phone service? Because, by using these services we are causing others to work on our behalf on Sabbath day (neither thy manservant nor maidservant). The arguments and explanations are seemingly endless.

The sad fact is that this Commandment can be easily kept and held in reverence, perfectly and completely by anyone wishing to simply honor God's will over their own. There is no need to wonder if you are breaking the Commandment if you are getting your information from the Scriptures and living in such a way as not to grieve the Holy Spirit or violate your conscience. The Holy Spirit will guide you; He will not allow you to break God's Commandment, even in ignorance. No one is better equipped to keep God's Commandments better than the "New Testament" believer.

There is no need to create rules, set up boundaries, write down lists of acceptable unacceptable behavior; you have within you the Author of the Commandment, promising to lead you and guide you into all Truth. He will not let you violate the Scriptures, He will not let you sin against God, but you must obey Him.

I recently met someone who felt there was a conflict with the Sabbath when they worked in a homeless shelter feeding the indigent. They spoke of all the work they had to do, cooking, cleaning, washing up, and wondered why God would hold them accountable for breaking His Commandment. I submit that they were letting the commandments of men take the place of the Commandment of God. No Commandment forbids doing good on Sabbath. Contrarily, it is a wonderful day for it, a wonderful day indeed!

"Then said Jesus unto them, I will ask you one thing; Is it lawful on the sabbath days to do good, or to do evil? to save life, or to destroy it?"

22.   Can the blind lead the blind?

"Then came his disciples, and said unto him, Knowest thou that the Pharisees were offended, after they heard this saying? But he answered and said, Every plant, which my heavenly Father hath not planted, shall be rooted up. Let them alone: they be blind leaders of the blind...Can the blind lead the blind? shall they not both fall into the ditch?" Luke 6:39, Matthew 15:12-14 (Combined)

It is interesting that this analogy of the blind appears in two places and spans two separate subjects. In one place (Luke 6), our Lord is showing how we are blind leaders of the blind when we attempt to remove specks from our brother's eye while blinded by a beam. (Ref. Question 9)

The Matthew account presents to us the hypocritical Pharisees as blind leaders that will eventually cause themselves, and those they are leading, to fall into a ditch. Jesus asks, "Can the blind lead the blind?" He did not ask, should they, could they, or may they, He asked, "Can they?" The implication is that they cannot. Any of us would agree that it is an impossibility, and we will study this impossibility.

In the age in which we live, education has become a necessity. Unfortunately, it has become common to look to education, teachers, institutions, and books whenever a field, an idea or an endeavor unfamiliar to us, presents itself. I say "unfortunately" because this habit transfers to the spiritual realm all too easily.

When we find a passage of Scripture that is hard to understand, we may reach for a commentary to explain it. When we have difficulty in life and find ourselves tangled in emotion and unable to think objectively, we sit before counselors, ask opinions, and take advice. We scour books to deepen our spiritual understanding, when all we can gain from these things are the opinions our fellows. As well intentioned as it may be, and as good as it may be, when man offers his solutions, it is just one degree of blindness helping another. It is like someone with cataracts helping another with myopia. Jesus would ask, "Can the blind lead the blind?"

Blindness is an excellent analogy. Jesus used it often to describe the condition of the religious teachers of His day. The Matthew 23 account, where Jesus chides the Pharisees, He uses the word "blind" five times. In John 9:39-41 Jesus states, "... For judgment I am come into this world, that they which see not might see; and that they which see might be made blind. And some of the Pharisees which were with him heard these words, and said unto him, Are we blind also? Jesus said unto them, If ye were blind, ye should have no sin: but now ye say, We see; therefore your sin remaineth." Here, and many other places, there are examples of blindness depicting the spiritual condition of man. Being healed of blindness can stand as a parallel and metaphor to our first encounter with Christ. The thought of blindness and our state of sinfulness being allegorically equal offers something very special when it is carried over to other Scriptures like John 9:32, "Since the world began was it not heard that any man opened the eyes of one that was born blind."

The blindness, however, that we examine here is the blindness of humanistic leadership. The "help" of our modern Christian leadership can be engaged at nearly every level of spiritual growth. There are those on academic levels from so-called Sunday school teachers to seminary professors. There are counselors offering help to those who need emotional stability or help dealing with tragedy or loss. There are those who claim special powers of healing and deliverance from every bondage – mental, physical and spiritual.

Actually, not unlike the other modern specialist fields, the modern "minister's" domain is becoming more and more specific and professional. If anyone, in our country today, felt a desire to become more spiritual, or to attain peace with God, they could find thousands of books, thousands of tapes; they could attend hundreds of seminars all across the country, churches, study groups, Bible studies, sermons, and lectures. Yet, with all this help and knowledge at our disposal, our hearts are in turmoil, our minds are troubled, our churches fragmented, our families torn. A church starts on one side of town and another loses longtime members in a bitter split. Pastors, once held in high esteem, leave their towns in disgrace of sin.

How Did This Happen?

Why is the body of Christ so divided and diverse when we all use the same Scriptures, worship the same God, and all supposedly share the same goal? Are all these sources of help doling out faulty information? Are they false prophets, or are they simply "blind leading the blind"? We can come to no other conclusion when we look at the results of 2000 years of "Christianity" purportedly under the leadership of the same Spirit of God, for the outcome blatantly betrays us. We are not traveling the straight and narrow path, we are not even on the broad way; we are hardly moving.

Sometimes, when we read of the power that early Church had in Jerusalem, in the writings of the apostles, and even the writings of Josephus, the martyrs recorded by Foxe and such; it looks as though we are going backwards. We are not moving… we are not in the road… we are in the ditch.

What has gone wrong? Where did we miss the mark? Many different people have many different answers to that question. I submit that we went wrong on guidance.[25] We looked to man to help us along our way not knowing that he was as lost as we, as blind as we, and in need of the selfsame guidance that we were seeking. John 16:13, "Howbeit when HE, the Spirit of truth, is come, HE will guide you into all truth… and HE will shew you things to come."

If we cannot rely on the Holy Spirit to guide us, how can we rely on Him to keep us, seal us, and ultimately save us? If we do claim to rely fully upon Him, why do we run to man and seek his opinion? Why do we depend

---

[25] More information can be found in the booklet or audio CD "On Guidance" by this author.

upon the honor of man to tell us the truth? If he knows the truth, where did he find it? If your teacher learned truth from other men, it is worthless to you, even if he learned at the feet of Christ Himself, what prevents you from doing the same thing? We have tripped at the same stumbling stone as our fathers; we have placed our trust in men. Galatians 1:11-12, "But I certify you, brethren, that the gospel which was preached of me is not after man. For I neither received it of man, neither was I taught it, but by the revelation of Jesus Christ."

Other than Christ Himself, our guides are blind, our books are foolishness, and our lives are destined for the ditch. We must look to Christ. He has come, by the Spirit of God, to teach His people Himself. Nothing is more important to our Christian walk than to be in fellowship and communion with those with whom we are supposed to be walking. Since the apostles, all of us have the SAME access to God. No one has secured some special heavenly communication and later been commissioned to share their "special wisdom" with the "less fortunate." Whether people claim this divinity or not, they certainly do imply their superiority by hawking their wares and selling their "Gospel" to those who are seeking and unsuspecting.

The Truth of God, filtered through man, is no truth at all. There is truth and righteousness, grace and the knowledge of God waiting for those who seek them. The answers to your life long questions are waiting in God and in you. Look to Jesus alone for the knowledge you seek. Go to Him and learn of Him, and you will find rest for your soul. The source of Solomon's wisdom awaits your bowed knee.

The Creator of the universe is willing to infuse your contrite heart with His power. The Son of God is again willing to open eyes, blind from birth, and replace your teachers, your books, your pastors and counselors. Your Guide is not blind. He can see from here to eternity and back. Do you waste your time with these earthly and temporal helps? Jesus asks, "Can the blind lead the blind? Shall they not both fall into the ditch?"

23. *Whereunto then shall I liken the men of this generation?*

(Luke 7:31-35 - Matthew 11:16-19), "And the Lord said, Whereunto then shall I liken the men of this generation? and to what are they like? They are like unto children sitting in the marketplace, and calling one to another, and saying, We have piped unto you, and ye have not danced; we have mourned to you, and ye have not wept."

Have children always claimed to be bored? I have trouble remembering being bored as a child, but many children today, complain constantly that they are unstimulated if they find themselves idle for over three minutes. Perhaps it is a selective memory on my part, maybe things have changed somewhat, but I suspect that we all become "bored" when we do not have what we want, or want what we have.

Jesus used the example of "little children" to illustrate His point about the men of the generation He then occupied. It was, as if they wanted what they did not have and, what they were given, they did not want. They were given John the Baptist and although, in the estimation of Jesus, he was the greatest prophet ever born, he was rejected as a lunatic. They were given the very Son of God and they said that He was not what they expected. By their rejection they said, "He is not holy, He is not mighty, He is not sympathetic to our religion, He does not fulfill prophecies or our expectations."

It is a pity, really, for He was all that and much, much more. Jesus saw the men of that generation as impudent children selfishly demanding more than what was given to them. Their actions spoke volumes, their words dripped with venom toward the Son of God. Their hearts, callused over with rebellion, were indifferent to the designs and desires of God; neither could their eyes see the gift of God who stood before them.

As we complain about the degree to which our God has decided to reveal himself to us, or we cry and beg Him to be more real, more available or more willing to use His power on our behalf, we are acting as bored, spoiled children. Perhaps we do not perceive, like the Pharisees, that it is we who though we see, are not seeing, we who though we hear, do not understand, and perhaps it is we who cannot see what is plainly shown to us.

The pleasures, as well as the heartaches of this world, tend to create in us an evaluation of good and evil, right and wrong, sin and righteousness and so forth. This evaluation system, over the years, creeps into everything we do and think about. It forms our policies and politics. This basis of good and evil becomes the foundation of teaching our children and learning from life. If we do not receive this foundation from Jesus Christ, the living Word of God within our souls, we risk the danger of making molds into which we expect even our God to fit. We create doctrines from our minds and experiences that we expect Him to sanction. The lifestyles we *predict* will please Him, repulse Him and

85

ultimately condemn us. Worst of all, because of our warped and selfish views, we stand still in the streets while He plays music that, to Him, is lively and attractive, compelling and gay, but to our insensitive ears is dull and lifeless. We heard it before, it's not our favorite tune, or for whatever reason we care not to dance.

For centuries, Our God has given many prophecies about His sheep, His people, and their plight of sin and their subsequent separation from Him. He has voiced His displeasure with sin, and on several occasions, He named what grieves Him most. He has listed in Scripture the seven things He hates, things that are an abomination to Him and that He despises.[26] Most people cannot list these things. How many can you name? Do you know what grieves the God you claim to love and serve? Can you name the things He hates? Has it become a part of your nature to hate what God hates? How can you love as He loves if you do not know what He hates and why? His nature is foreign to most and little or no effort is made to discover His temperament.

How Well Do You Know Him?

The Father weeps over Israel. Do you weep with Him? YHVH cries out in anguish for the lost of His people who will not repent and turn to Him. Do you? He stands in fiery displeasure of those who lie in His name and falsely speak for Him and misrepresent the Gospel of the Lord Jesus Christ; do you investigate the validity and origin of what is taught you as doctrine? He weeps and laments and His Church does not mourn. "Whereunto then, shall I liken the men of this generation? They are like unto children."

It looks as though not much has changed from the men of that generation to the men of this one. We need, as they did, to see the gap between our desires and His, between our evaluation criteria and His, between our tastes and His. The gap is large, but it is not so large that it cannot be spanned.

There are many changes to be made in our thinking, many pauses to be inserted into our speech, many of His concerns added to our list and many of ours to be dropped. What will you do if you find that God cares not a whit about recycling? What will you do if His concern is for those in your life you have heretofore avoided? What will you do if your life in no way resembles the life that He has designed for you? Are you willing to acquire His taste in social order, charity and government? Are you willing to make changes in your doctrines, faith and lifestyle? Are you willing to dance to His music?

The troubles and trials of life create sorrow in us. Relief from the sorrow or oppression that presently possesses us creates in us a false understanding of good and evil. What releases us from oppression is not necessarily "good" and what eliminates or hinders comfort is not necessarily "bad." Any reader of the Scriptures can tell story after story exemplifying

---

[26] Proverbs 6:16-19, "These six things doth the LORD hate: yea, seven are an abomination unto him: A proud look, a lying tongue, and hands that shed innocent blood, An heart that deviseth wicked imaginations, feet that be swift in running to mischief, A false witness that speaketh lies, and he that soweth discord among brethren."

deliverance made possible through personal tragedy. Nations were sold into slavery because someone sought their own "good."

We must get our understanding of "good" and "bad" from the Lord and from the Scriptures. The Scriptures were given for that very reason – to learn the expectations, disposition and personality of our God. Jesus begged, "Learn of me!"[27] YHVH lamented, "I have nourished and brought up children, and they have rebelled against me. The ox knoweth his owner, and the ass his master's crib: but Israel doth not know, my people doth not consider." "And they bend their tongues like their bow for lies: but they are not valiant for the truth upon the earth; for they proceed from evil to evil, and they know not me...."[28]

When we tune into our own understanding of tragedy, we can be standing amidst worldwide wreck and ruin and not see beyond our own pain. When we hurt, our compassion is cut short, our eyes become nearsighted and our ears are dull to hear what is beyond our own grief. We stand in the streets as a funeral dirge is played by none other than Jehovah Himself and we stand silent – no mourning, no care, no tenderness for what does not concern our immediate need. He mourns unto us and we do not lament.

The "men of our generation" are emotionally retarded, psychologically damaged, sinfully advanced – a frightening combination indeed. The Church of Jesus Christ reflects this as well. We have buildings full of people who only compare themselves to others worse than they and therefore are pleased with the results. Their thinking is so far from God's thinking that they cannot hear the music, much less dance to it. They cannot dance to music they do not like, nor can they mourn to lamentations that only speak sorrowfully of things about which they feel no grief.

Have we become spoiled children who only want what they do not have and have what they do not want? Have we become so bored with the things that enthuse our Father that we sit still and refuse to dance waiting with crossed legs and crossed arms until we hear our favorite tune? Does the news from across town that breaks His heart fall upon our ears as unimportant and mundane?

Seek fresh revelation from the Father about His concerns, His loves. Search the Scriptures to discover the personality and heart of the Creator, for only His music is worthy of your dancing, and it is to His sorrowful lamentation you should mourn.

Determine to reject what He hates and embrace what He loves; for if you continue to expect the God of the whole earth to conform to your thinking, instead of pursuing your conformity to His, you will be no closer to sympathy with the concerns of God than those whom Jesus asked, "Whereunto then shall I liken the men of this generation? They are like unto children... sitting in the marketplace..."

---

[27] Matthew 11:29
[28] Isaiah 1:2-4, Jeremiah 9:3

24. *Who has such a friend?*

Luke 11:5-10, "Which of you shall have a friend, and shall go unto him at midnight, and say unto him, Friend, lend me three loaves; For a friend of mine in his journey is come to me, and I have nothing to set before him? And he from within shall answer and say, Trouble me not: the door is now shut, and my children are with me in bed; I cannot rise and give thee. I say unto you, Though he will not rise and give him, because he is his friend, yet because of his importunity he will rise and give him as many as he needeth. And I say unto you, Ask, and it shall be given you; seek, and ye shall find; knock, and it shall be opened unto you. For every one that asketh receiveth; and he that seeketh findeth; and to him that knocketh it shall be opened."

I can remember hearing, when I was a youth, that a true friend was a rare thing, and that if I had more than one in my life, I would be most blessed. I have always desired a close companion, one with whom I could enjoy a similar sense of honor, right, humor, and one who would improve my personality, as Proverbs 27:17 promises, "Iron sharpeneth iron; so a man sharpeneth the countenance of his friend."

I found such a friend in my wife. We share all the best that can come from friendship and closeness. However, a fellow man would be a different thing altogether. I cannot help but feel that great power and strength would come from such a true friendship.

Perhaps I place friendship into a lofty and an unattainable category. It may be that friendship is potentially present in all relationships or present in a relationship merely when enmity is absent. Perhaps a friend is simply someone who is not an enemy. We tend, in modern vernacular, to differentiate between friends and acquaintances in that way.

Maybe I make too much of it, maybe not. I cannot speak from experience. Proverbs 18:24 says, "A man that hath friends must shew himself friendly: and there is a friend that sticketh closer than a brother." It is this friend that sticks close, of whom I wish to speak now. As we reflect upon our lives and ponder the stream of people whom have entered and exited our life, touched, helped, or supported us, can we find a friend that has stuck closer than a brother? The question becomes even more poignant, "Who has such a friend?"

In the story above, Jesus asks us if any of us have a friend to whom we may go at midnight and ask for food. It is obvious that He is making the situation as awkward as it can be, as inconvenient for the friend, and as frivolous a request, as possible, to make the point. Bread, though essential for life, is not necessary at midnight; it could just as well be placed before his traveling friend in the morning if his arrival was late. His friend, upon whom he has laid his burden of hospitality, is in bed and likely was asleep when this man called.

Jesus has set up a scenario of unnecessary aggravation to test this friendship and push kindness to its limits. He does this for a reason. He wishes to show us the value of a friendship that has no limitations, a friendship that has identical values and importance.

Many times we find our friendships strained when one of the two parties considers something important that the other does not. It is obvious in this story that the man in bed did not care that his friend had no bread to set before his traveler, for his friend pleads with him, "… lend me three loaves. For a friend of mine in his journey is come to me, and I have nothing to set before him. And he from within shall answer and say, Trouble me not: the door is now shut, and my children are with me in bed; I cannot rise and give thee." (Luke 11:5-7) Here Jesus shows that one friend has a problem that the other does not evaluate as important.

It is when we put friendship to these kinds of tests that it proves to be worthy or not. Let us go from this understanding to what a friend we have in Christ. It is Christ who proves time and time again to be a true friend of those who follow Him. It is well established what a friend we have in Christ, but what kind of friend has He in you? As we follow, we should make those things that are important to Him, important to us. We are to show ourselves "friendly." For if we are to have a friend, even if it is Christ with whom we wish to be friends, we must show ourselves friendly. We do this by making His concerns, our concerns.

Who is At the Door?

If it is occurring to you that the friend in bed is not Christ, but us, you are starting to see the picture.

Many times this story is told that Christ is the friend in bed with whom we plead to help us. We are told that, although He really does not care about our needs, if we make enough noise, if we pray long enough, if don't give up, He will eventually come to the door and give us whatever we are whining about, and send us on our way.

What a sorry example of a friend! Christ is **not** that kind of friend at all! It is He who calls upon us and is given excuse after excuse. It is when He calls us in the small hours that we are too tired to spend thirty minutes in quiet devotion. We are the ones who say, "Trouble me not, the door is now shut, I cannot rise and give thee." It is only for Christ's importunity that we act at all. It is because He does not give up that we finally obey.

He goes on to make clear that when there is a mutual friendship, when we pray, He will respond, "And I say unto you, Ask, and it shall be given you; seek, and ye shall find; knock, and it shall be opened unto you. For every one that asketh receiveth; and he that seeketh findeth; and to him that knocketh it shall be opened." (Luke 11:9-10) He shows us that His part of the friendship will be carried out without delay, but will ours?

If we were true servants of Christ we have to respond to His every wish. If it were a servant in bed on that cold night of request, a servant would have pushed his children into the floor to rise and give his master all he asked, but he was not his servant, he was his so-called friend. Therefore, he felt that he had a choice… he chose, as many of us do… he chose wrong.

I will say something that may sound strange to you at first. Jesus does not desire to be our Lord forever, though that is surely the beginning of our relationship to Him. We cannot come to Christ without surrendering our will to Him and accepting His Lordship. But, His ultimate goal for us is to be His Friends. Listen to Him talking to His disciples in John 15:15, "Henceforth I call you not servants; for the servant knoweth not what his lord doeth: but I have called you friends; for all things that I have heard of my Father I have made known unto you." These words stand out to me, "for the servant knoweth not what his lord doeth." When I hear the man on the outside of the house confess, "For a friend of mine in his journey is come to me, and I have nothing to set before him," I hear Christ telling us what servants would never be told. Take a moment and think about this.

But, what could Christ ever "need" from you? As Christ receives men who come to Him, He must receive physical men into a spiritual Kingdom. This is undoubtedly a difficult process that, to make the transition easier, can require help from someone here, someone entering in themselves, someone who has the "Bread" to give the new friend of Christ. Jesus could command you at any time to make your bread available to such a one. In the midnight hour, someone may find Christ, as their long journey comes to an end. You may be needed to make available real and tangible assistance to this one, and welcome him into this glorious Kingdom of our Father. Now, can you hear these words of Christ in new light? "Friend, lend me three loaves. For a friend of mine, in his journey is come to me, and I have nothing to set before him."

Christ is looking for a Friend that sticks closer than a brother. One upon whom He can depend, one who feels the importance of the moment, one with whom He can share intimate details and purposes. The mutuality of dependability marks the sort of friendship Christ is seeking. He makes it plain that He will be there for your needs. He says, "Ask, and it shall be given you; seek, and ye shall find; knock, and it shall be opened unto you" but, will you be there for Him? Are you that friend who would rise at midnight, or must He become importunate and aggravate you into obedience? Hear His longing, when He asks, "Who has such a friend?"

25. *How much then is a man better than a sheep?*

Luke 13:15-16 – 14:5 Matthew 12:11-12 (Combined- abridged),

"... Which of you shall have an ass or an ox fallen into a pit, and will not straightway pull him out on the sabbath day ... Thou hypocrite, doth not each one of you on the sabbath loose his ox or his ass from the stall, and lead him away to watering? ... What man shall there be among you, that shall have one sheep, and if it fall into a pit on the sabbath day, will he not lay hold on it, and lift it out? How much then is a man better than a sheep?

There is a wonderful truth here that is hidden under the arguments on Sabbath keeping and interpretation of the Law. It is a simple question that is more difficult to answer today than it was in days in which it was asked. The society of today places great value on animal life of all sorts with the exception of human life. We live in a world where, every year, we're told 1.5 million [29] children are killed in the womb of its mother and at the same time, a person who mistakenly spayed a cat that was newly pregnant was in danger being incarcerated for animal cruelty.

We are taught to feel guilt for our position at the top of the food chain and humility is defined as boasting of our being at the bottom of the world's priority list. All of this modern foolishness aside, we must, if only for a moment, look at the world as our Father sees it. (In truth nothing matters more.) We must see life as His creation and His design in order to implement His plan.

On the eve of the end of the perfect will of God, the day that sin found its way into the heart of Adam, God made a statement when He chose the death of a lamb to facilitate the atonement of sin. Although we do not find blood sacrifices performed for atonement, we do find that the Scriptures mention that God made Adam and his wife [30]clothes of skins to cover their nakedness that was now causing shame. We have no way of knowing it was a lamb from which these skins were obtained, but perhaps it was, as it was a lamb that later became the symbol of atonement (covering). Granted these conjectures, we could say that God took the life of a lamb to cover the sins of man.

All of the references to the Lamb, from Genesis through Revelation, take on some form and character found in the sacrificial death of Christ. It requires no theological degree to readily see the metaphor, parallel, and symbolism that are to be found throughout the Testaments, Old, and New. From the Lamb skins provided for the first sin in Genesis, to the Passover Lamb of Exodus, to the Lamb that John the Baptist claimed was to "take away the sin of the world", to the Lamb that was slain from the foundation of the world found in the Revelation, Jesus is, was, and shall be our Pesach, our

---

[29] Figures like this are often ignored for lack of an understanding of numbers of this magnitude. An example of the number, 1,000,000 (one million) is that this whole book has slightly less that 1 million typed characters in it.
[30] Genesis 3:21, "Unto Adam also and to his wife did the LORD God make coats of skins, and clothed them."

Passover, our atoning sacrificial lamb. Because He loves us, He gave His life for ours; the Lamb dearly beloved, slain by divine Commandment, for the sin of the world.

The Passover is a wonderful example of the love that God has for man. The lamb that was to be slain was not to be brought in from the fields on the day of the slaughter, nor was it to be purchased at the stockyard and slain, the lamb was to be brought from the fields and into the home of each of the families of Israel, as if it were a pet, for three days prior to its being killed[31]. This lamb would likely become endeared to each family member as they were forced to see it and feed it day after day, probably from their own table. It is as though God never wanted the Passover Lamb to go unnoticed, unappreciated, or valued as nothing.

Why A Lamb?

The lamb is the epitome of servitude; it has no other purpose than to give. No reason but to serve, the lamb always provides food and clothing and neither offers resistance to the one who shears it, nor to the one who slaughters it. It is this innocent animal that becomes the symbol of redemption, the innocent lamb, that did no wrong, that never strayed from its Creator's way or disobeyed; the lamb that submits to any, rebels against none, the symbol of purity and gentleness was to suffer for no cause of its own making, it was to die for our sin.

I think that the account in 2 Samuel 12:3 is Nathan's remembrance of the emotions he felt for the Passover lambs from his youth. It is an account that illustrates the Passover lamb and describes the practice, "But the poor man had nothing, save one little ewe lamb, which he had bought and nourished up: and it grew up together with him, and with his children; it did eat of his own meat, and drank of his own cup, and lay in his bosom, and was unto him as a daughter." The value of this lamb was to be well understood at Passover. The lamb was to be loved, its slaying dreaded, and its consumption made distasteful for sorrow. But why?

Again a message is found in Jesus' question, "How much then is a man better than a sheep?" We can make no mistake about the love God has for us if we understand the value He places on sheep. Knowing this, Jesus Christ came and took on Himself the "form of a servant." He took on Himself the form of a lamb – the Lamb of God that taketh away the sin of the world. So when Jesus asks, "How much then is a man better than a sheep," He places your life in great esteem, and deems His own as expendable. These words are prophecy of His own death and make clear to us His intent – to give Himself "the lesser" for us "the greater." By these words we see His evaluation of Himself as our servant.

---

[31] Exodus 12:5-6, "Your lamb shall be without blemish, a male of the first year: ye shall take it out from the sheep, or from the goats: And ye shall keep it up until the fourteenth day of the same month: and the whole assembly of the congregation of Israel shall kill it in the evening."

92

Our Father God places great value upon us as well and loves us very much. The parallel continues in the Passover ordinance and the sacrifice made inside the Family of God. Our Father took His Lamb; raised in His own house and that ate from his own table and offered it in our place. Then, He went even further, this Lamb was not simply the best of His flock, or just His pet, or even His best friend … it was His only son. His beloved Son willingly took this position, as less than man… as a servant of man, in order to accomplish this task of ultimate and total selflessness.

Knowing that He was to be the sacrificial Lamb of God; knowing that he had willingly placed Himself in this category of expendable livestock, He had the love and grace to ask the question, "How much then is a man better than a sheep?"

II Days of Popularity

"I have never wished to cater to the crowd; for what I know they do not approve, and what they approve I do not know."

Epicurus
(341–270 B.C.)
Greek philosopher. Fragments, no. 187

26. What seek ye?

John 1:34-40, "And I saw, and bare record that this is the Son of God. Again the next day after John [the Baptist] stood, and two of his disciples; And looking upon Jesus as he walked, he saith, Behold the Lamb of God! And the two disciples heard him speak, and they followed Jesus. Then Jesus turned, and saw them following, and saith unto them, What seek ye? They said unto him, Rabbi, (which is to say, being interpreted, Master) where dwellest thou? He saith unto them, Come and see. They came and saw where he dwelt, and abode with him that day: for it was about the tenth hour. One of the two which heard John speak, and followed him, was Andrew, Simon Peter's brother."

Here we are made privy to the meeting of the Christ and His first disciples. Perhaps, the unnamed person here was the author, John (the beloved), as this testimony begins "...and I saw and bare record." At the beginning, John and Andrew were disciples of John the Baptist, and the day after overhearing John identify Jesus as the Lamb of God, they went after Him. As they pursued Him, Jesus turned and asked, "What seek ye?"

It is a shame that they did not answer His question, for I would like to know their answer. If these men were disciples of John, they were not zealots looking for a warrior to free them from Roman oppression. As disciples of John, they were likely out of fellowship in the synagogue and, therefore, were not taught what to expect. Their motivation had to be from the simple message of John. Which was, to clean up their lives and build a smooth path for the Messiah, for He is coming. This message could only appeal to men of faith; to dedicated men who desired to see Israel gain again its rightful place as the beloved state it once was, and men who desire to redeem themselves to YHVH. These were religious men, if you will, men whose desires were spiritual.

Jesus called His other disciples from the place they occupied in the world. Their occupations were as diverse as tax collecting is from commercial fishing, but these two men found Jesus and made their place with Him. These two were looking for Him. This makes His question even more interesting. He asked, "What seek ye ... What are you looking for?"

In the beginning of the book of John, the author points out that, "...He (Christ) came unto his own, and his own received him not." This is an interesting situation. The zealots were looking for a soldier (political impetus), the church was looking for a deliverer like Moses or Elijah (religious impetus), the church leaders were looking for signs and wonders to be performed to add supernatural confirmation to their theories and studies (intellectual/ego impetus), and the men of commerce were not looking at all. This is very similar to the situation today.

The conventional Christian church of today is again looking for Jesus to return and set all things right. We must remember that the church totally missed Him the first time. They not only missed Him, they were instrumental in His execution. They had thoughts regarding, who He must be, whence He must come, who His parents must be, what He must do, and what He must not do! With all these criteria set up in the religious minds of the day, the "script" Messiah would have to follow was written; the stage was set for an execution.

Day after day, these two men who sought Jesus heard the message from John the Baptist, "Prepare the way of the Lord, make His path "straight." Look at the concept of making "straight the path." John was preaching what had been prophesied hundreds of years before, as recorded in Isaiah 40:3-5,

"The voice of him that crieth in the wilderness, Prepare ye the way of the LORD, make straight in the desert a highway for our God. Every valley shall be exalted, and every mountain and hill shall be made low: and the crooked shall be made straight, and the rough places plain: And the glory of the LORD shall be revealed, and all flesh shall see it together: for the mouth of the LORD hath spoken it."

Highway Construction:

One day my wife, Pamela, and I were driving through the mountains, and I was explaining how the interstate construction crews dynamite the tops off of the hills and let the rubble fill the valleys on either side creating a more even roadbed. I explained that this is why there are cuts in the tops of each hill.

As I said this, I remembered the above Scripture, "Every valley shall be lifted, and every mountain and hill shall be made low" and I realized that this is how we are to make the "highway" for our God. Not by creating doctrinal "mountains" for Him to step over, not with Scriptural tests and hurdles to prove He is who He says, but by letting Him be who He is, and not who we think He must be!

If we create and hold to doctrinal ideas that are "mountain tops" that *He* must surmount, and "valleys" of testing *He* must pass through, we are making His path crooked and difficult. If we are to know Him when He appears, we must know Him in Spirit and not the letter. We must make His path an easy one, a smooth one, one of His choosing. Luke 17:20 says, *"And when he was demanded of the Pharisees, when the kingdom of God should come, he answered them and said, The kingdom of God cometh not with observation* [calculations, signs and wonders]." Later, Luke 19:11 records Christ's motivation for saying this, *"...because they thought that the kingdom of God should immediately appear."*

There are many examples of mankind misunderstanding who Christ should be and what He should do. Jesus demonstrated that there was a delusion in the minds of these who could not understand. When Jesus was asked, *"Why speakest thou unto them in parables?"* He answered, *"Because it is given unto you to know the mysteries of the kingdom of heaven, but to them it is not given."* (Matthew 13:10-11)

On this subject Paul confirmed the prophet when he repeated, *"Well spake the Holy Ghost by Esaias the prophet unto our fathers, Saying, Go unto this people, and say, Hearing ye shall hear, and shall not understand; and seeing ye shall see, and not perceive:"* (Acts 28:25-26) There was a purposefully placed "veil" over His first coming. Whatever this veil of delusion was, it was God's doing and it accomplished His purpose.

Knowing that deception is possible, we must use caution, for the event of Christ's return according to Scripture, will be concurrent with a "strong delusion"[32] sent by God. This delusion is designed for the damnation of all of those who do not love Truth and have pleasure in unrighteousness. That can include scores of people in the world and many in churches. Our only defense is to love Truth and to "prepare the way of the Lord." We must make His path straight and smooth. We must not build up criteria with which the signs of His coming must comply nor should we establish proof texts to acid test the returning Christ or we may find ourselves caused to experience the strong delusion that is coming.

As we consider the mental image of our Messiah and the "script" we have created in our minds of His return, and how it will be, are we sure that the "facts" we have gathered over the years are trustworthy? Where did your eschatology originate? Where did you get your understanding of last things?

It would shock many today to find that the most widely held beliefs in regard to what moderns call "the rapture" is only about 150 years old; it was never preached by the Apostles and never believed by the early Church. Even though it is lacking Scriptural support and it is deficient in historical evidence, it is believed by many and taught prominently in churches, seminaries, and over the airwaves daily. What do you believe? …What are you seeking?" Have you set in your mind exactly what Messiah's appearance is to be? The Pharisees looked for a miracle worker. The Sadducees looked for a King. You should be open and pliable to His Spirit. You should research what you hold as true and be willing to change in conformity to Truth. The delusion that is sent is based in incorrect information, it is founded in lies, and only those who love Truth will see through it.

Notice that, according to the Scripture in 2 Thessalonians 2, it is not required of you to know the Truth. Notice that this protection from the delusion is not based on knowledge, but it is required that you love Truth.

Do you love Truth? Those who are familiar with, recognize, and promote Truth, are those who love Truth. Matthew 24 is replete with warnings that you should beware of being deceived, "Let no man deceive you," and, "Take heed that ye be not deceived." We do not know what this strong delusion will be, but it will involve a false Christ[33] and this false Christ will be exactly who some people are seeking. "What seek ye?"

---

[32] 2 Thessalonians 2:10-12, "And with all deceivableness of unrighteousness in them that perish; because they received not the love of the truth, that they might be saved. And for this cause God shall send them strong delusion, that they should believe a lie: That they all might be damned who believed not the truth, but had pleasure in unrighteousness."

[33] Matthew 24:23-25, "Then if any man shall say unto you, Lo, here is Christ, or there; believe it not. For there shall arise false Christs, and false prophets, and shall shew great signs and wonders; insomuch that, if it were possible, they shall deceive the very elect. Behold, I have told you before."

27.   Have ye understood all these things?

Matthew 13:51, "Jesus saith unto them, Have ye understood all these things? They say unto him, Yea, Lord."

Jesus was always speaking in parables. This was to the dismay of His disciples for they were unfamiliar with this idea and asked Him, when they were alone, "Why do you do this?" Jesus explained, "Because it is given unto you to know the mysteries of the kingdom of heaven, but to them it is not given." (Matthew 13:11) For those who hold to the ideas of universalism (the eventual saving of all mankind) and similar doctrines contrary to Biblical election and foreordination, speaking in parables is an irritation, and a stumbling block.

However parables are received, Christ never budged from His modus operandi. There is understanding available for those to whom the parables are given, but to the rest, they will be considered foolishness, be misunderstood, or forever remain a mystery. (It is interesting to note that, with few exceptions, most people think that they do understand the parables of Jesus. I think I understand, and you think you do, but do we?)

Jesus was teaching on the end and final judgment of all mankind. He taught that there was coming a day when all injustice will be overridden, all inequity balanced, and all things set right. On this day, there will be a selection and separation that takes place. He terminated the lesson with this analogy:

*"Again, the kingdom of heaven is like unto a net, that was cast into the sea, and gathered of every kind: Which, when it was full, they drew to shore, and sat down, and gathered the good into vessels, but cast the bad away. **So shall it be at the end of the world**: the angels shall come forth, and sever the wicked from among the just, And shall cast them into the furnace of fire: there shall be wailing and gnashing of teeth." (Matthew 13:47-50)*

Then he looked into the unblinking and wide eyes of His disciples and as they shook themselves back into this world they heard Him ask, perhaps for the second or third time, "Have you understood all these things?" They nod their head slowly and automatically and say, "Yes, Lord."

Friend, have YOU understood all these things? Do you understand that one day you will stand before a judgment bar and give an account? The analogies, parables, metaphors, all interpreted any way you like – will lead even the slightly motivated to understand that one day, we will stand before the One who made us and face judgment for how we conducted ourselves while here on this earth. The fish in the net, the sheep in the cote, the ready and waiting bridesmaids, all are to be applied to mankind standing judgment. By all accounts we will not be asked what we believed, what doctrine we held to or what Bible we read. We will not be asked questions to which there are right or wrong answers. There is no quiz requiring a passing grade. We will give an account of our works – what we did – what we did not do, and that alone will prove what we believed while living on this earth.

Have You Understood All These Things?

Do you know that there is an irreversible day in your future? A day in which you will be determined to be chaff or wheat (Luke 3:17), a sheep or a goat (Matthew 25:32), faithful or unfaithful (Matthew 24:45). A day in which you will be found ready or not ready (Luke 12:40), wise or unwise (Matthew 25), walking on the straight path that ends at a narrow gate entering life, or walking the broad road terminating at the wide gate which leads to your destruction? A day when all the choices you made in life, all the paths you may have chosen in your journey, will be held in the piercing light of pure and holy judgment.

It will be then that it occurs to you it was not a string of choices that directed your life, but you will find that they all were the same choice made over and over again. It is the choice of life and death, the choice of your way or His way, made over and over and over. Soon it will be shown that the little, daily choices you made add up and divide out to be the great choice of your eternity! For it will culminate into one last great choice that you will find has already been made – by you. It will be shown that you have already chosen, by your very life, one of two roads, one of the two destinations, one of two eternities, between two rewards, and between two Lords.

You cannot expect to be granted the reward of those who always chose His way in life, if your record is that you have consistently chosen mammon over your God in the whole of your life. Do you think that if you choose Him at the end of your life and the beginning of eternity, that it will erase the evidence of a misspent life? No, this choice, your choice, you will find, has been made, before this great day, in every choice you made while in this life. Have you understood all these things?

We need to re-read the text recording what Christ said concerning the end, our judgment, and eternity. He was very prolific. He minced no words. He left no room for doubt on matters of judgment. The clarity of our understanding on that day, the inane excuses that we will never bother to offer, the futility of our lives, the uselessness of our influence, the stupidity of political power, the helplessness and hopelessness of the damned, are all too clear as we read the words of Christ. The very life that we have striven to keep – will be forever lost. The money we gained will be in another's hand. The barns and bank accounts, filled by us, will be emptied by another. At the dawn of judgment, our vaporous life we nurtured and cherished so much will, at the first peek of the red hot sun's appearing, vanish away into a dreamlike story whose insipid and meaningless plot will then determine our eternity. Jesus warned as no one else ever has. Have you understood all these things?

Our lives are only as good as their end. When we chase temporal things in life, we become dull to eternity. When we seek God's will and search out His way in all we do, we find real life – a life with a purpose, a life with no end. We cannot avoid life's final chapter. It is more sure than the sunrise, more dependable than gravity, as much a part of life as birth; yet we do not live for its end. Read the words of William Penn.[34]

> The great business of man's life is to answer the end for which he lives; and that is, to glorify God, and save his own soul: this is the decree of heaven as old as the world. But so it is, that man minds nothing less than what he should mind most; and despises to inquire into his own being, its original duty and end; choosing rather to dedicate his days to gratify the pride, avarice, and luxury of his heart; as if he had been born for himself, or rather given himself being. And so, not subject himself to the reckoning and judgment of a superior power. To this wild and lamentable condition has poor man brought himself, by his disobedience to the law of God in his heart, by doing that which he knows he should not do, and leaving undone what he knows he should do. And as long as this disease continues upon man, he will make his God his enemy and himself incapable of the love and salvation that He has made real to us by His son, Jesus Christ, to the world.

Have you understood all these things? Christ Jesus has an answer. He has an answer for any who call on Him. You need not dread the end; you can face it with the confidence that you will face not an enemy, but a Friend, if you do what He commands. You need not pay for your selfish life with your eternal life, for He laid His life down in your stead. (Reference John 15:13-14) Christ can redeem and sanctify you, make you clean and He can secure your eternity if you will trust Him with your life. "Have you understood all these things?"

---

[34] William Penn, (1644-1718), English Quaker and the founder of the colony of Pennsylvania. Written while confined in the Tower of London, at the age of twenty-four, it is the introductory paragraph in the literary work _No Cross, No Crown_.

28. *Who is my mother?*

Matthew 12:48, "But he answered and said unto him that told him, Who is my mother? and who are my brethren?"

Mark 3:33, "And he answered them, saying, Who is my mother, or my brethren?"

The idea of being "born again" has received a pretty thorough battering in recent years. This status has been claimed by everyone from Presidents to pornographers. Not only the words have been abused; the concept has been made cliché. The experience of being "born again" has been reduced to such benign statements as "turning over a new leaf" or is referred to only in an innocuous, poetic sense, such as the outcome of a "Rocky Mountain High." Its definition has even plumbed the depths of ecstatic feelings derived from sex or drugs. But is there a real experience of being made over, being fashioned again, or recreated in the image of our new Father? The words of Christ communicate clearly that being born again is a real experience and that "Except a man be born again, he cannot see the kingdom of God." (John 3:3)

How are we born again? Let's look at the first time the incorruptible seed of God conceived life. Lost in the Christmas traditions is the story of the birth of Christ as recorded in Luke 1. You may wish to read it again to make yourself familiar with it in order to recognize the excerpts below.

The story of the birth of Christ is not given to us to make a celebration or a day of giving gifts. It is given as a glimpse of the marvelous work of God as He joins us, in this life. It is a picture of the birth that is to occur in all of us. Emmanuel – meaning God with US!

When the angel appeared and made his salutation to Mary, his greeting contained a declaration of favor: "...Hail, thou that art highly favoured, the Lord is with thee: blessed art thou among women." The awareness of being favored accorded to those who are visited by the Holy Spirit, is nearly absent today.

Somewhere among the dialogue of "whosoever will" and indiscriminate "Jesus Loves You" bumper stickers, we have laid aside the glorious doctrine of election and adulterated the sovereignty of our God. We have come to expect our God to promptly answer when we call, but when the Creator of the universe visits you, it is a wonderful day, and you are highly favored "...for thou hast found favour with God." (Luke 1) "[We] were born, not of blood, nor of the will of the flesh, nor of the will of man, but of God." (John 1:13)

"Christmas" Has Hidden the Story of the New Birth

Then the angel explained to Mary what was about to happen: "And the angel answered and said unto her, The Holy Ghost shall come upon thee, and the power of the Highest shall overshadow thee: therefore also that holy thing which shall be born of thee shall be called the Son of God." (Luke 1:35)

We see here that the "holy thing" is Christ. After questioning the impossibility of such a proposal and being assured that it would be as God said, Mary submitted to the will of God and surrendered herself totally to Him. "And Mary said, Behold the handmaid of the Lord; be it unto me according to thy word. And the angel departed from her." (Luke 1:38)

In this story we can begin to see a parallel to the experience we call being born again. We see the overshadowing or visitation, the expectation of an impossibility, the questioning within, and finally the submission to the higher One. When we reach this point of submission we have the seed of God implanted in us.

This seed has within it the DNA structure of a new you in Christ. As Mary was to carry Christ within her for the next nine months and then give birth, it is our responsibility to care for and nurture that seed to birth and finally, maturity.

Paul spoke of this mystery. "To whom God would make known ... this mystery among the Gentiles; which is Christ in you..." (Colossians 1:27) In Ephesians 4:15, Paul spoke also of our growing up into Christ, "But speaking the truth in love, [we] may grow up into him in all things, which is the head, even Christ."

As you submit to God in this process of the new birth, He places His seed within you. The new birth is not an instantaneous one that takes place the second you pray a "sinner's prayer" as is commonly taught today. First, there is a visitation, a yielding, and then a pregnancy, which you are expected to nurture and care for, till it comes to the time of birth. If you do not cherish the new Seed of Christ you could miscarry, and lose this "holy thing" within. The doctrine of instantaneous "new birth on demand" is faulty and misleading.

There are scores of people still struggling with sin and trying to reconcile their present wretched lives with their past experience of being "born again." When, in reality, their visitation only planted a seed that they must bring to the birth by responsible and caring behavior. Remember that the Scripture says, "But as many as received him, to them gave he power to become the sons of God." (John 1:12) We have been given the "power to become" just as a woman impregnated has been given the potential to bring forth life.

The care and nurture necessary to bring about this new birth successfully is to be guided by Christ, to be a disciple, and carrying ones own "cross" – to do the will of the Father. In fact, being a disciple is living under the discipline that creates the proper environment for the new birth.

No one can successfully bring new life into an environment hostile to the nature of the life conceived in them. You cannot force the lips of Christ in us, to tell lies, nor force His hands to strike, His mouth to curse or His heart to worship idols and yet expect this holy Seed to thrive.

102

You must first learn to obey His Commandments and do His will to successfully bring about a live birth of the Seed within. Luke 14:27, "And whosoever doth not bear his cross, and come after me, cannot be my disciple." You must DO the will of God to care for, and not miscarry, the seed within. After you have been "mother" to this holy life within you, it is then that you are born into the family of Christ, and have become brothers and sisters of His.

Second, after prenatal development, comes the birth, and "mothering" of this new "Christ in you" and is a matter of feeding, protecting and maturing. As Peter says, "As newborn babes, desire the sincere milk of the word, that ye may grow thereby..." (1 Peter 2:2) Being born again consists of the Spirit and Life of Christ being born in you. "Marvel not that I said unto thee, Ye must be born again." (John 3:7)

"Being born again, not of corruptible seed, but of incorruptible, by the word of God, which liveth and abideth for ever." (1 Peter 1:23)

On this particular day when Jesus was teaching and ministering to His followers, His mother Mary and His brothers were standing outside the place and were calling to Him. For what cause He was ignoring them, is unknown. Whether it was for this lesson alone or for other reasons, we don't know. The crowd told him that His mother and brothers were outside and wanted to see Him, and Jesus asked a profound thing. "Who is my mother?"

As you consider the holy child that you are carrying and birthing as raising the seed of God, "Christ in you," you may now see new depth to the question of Christ, "Who is my Mother?" This is a question you need not answer, as the answer is given quickly afterward, "And he looked round about on them which sat about him, and he stretched forth his hand toward his disciples said, Behold my mother and my brethren! For whosoever shall do the will of God my Father the same is my brother, and my sister, and mother."

29. *Art thou a master of Israel and knowest not these things?*

John 3:10, "Jesus answered and said unto him, Art thou a master of Israel, and knowest not these things?"

Nicodemus, a teacher of all Israel, recognized that Jesus was a different sort. He was troubled by Messiah's insistence that a man must undergo some transformation in himself beyond his power to do so. He decides to go see Jesus and ask Him about it. He goes at night, so as not to be seen, and attempts to flatter Jesus by acknowledging Him as a worthy teacher, "Rabbi, we know that thou art a teacher come from God: for no man can do these miracles that thou doest, except God be with him."

Upon hearing this, we would expect Jesus to thank Him and exchange the admiring comment with Nicodemus. "Oh thank you," We might expect Him to say, "and you, too, are a wonderful teacher and well respected. What can I do for you?" Actually, Jesus did not accept the compliment nor make any verbal exchange in kind, Jesus answered and said to him, "Verily, verily, I say unto thee, Except a man be born again, he cannot see the kingdom of God."

What a strange answer. Jesus knew that this man could not see the Kingdom of God. Something in the salutation of Nicodemus evidenced his blindness. The Pharisees, perhaps even Nicodemus himself, witnessed Jesus casting out devils and the miracle was explained to them this way, "But if I cast out devils by the Spirit of God, then the kingdom of God is come unto you." (Matthew 12:28) Again in Luke 11:20, "But if I with the finger of God cast out devils, no doubt the kingdom of God is come upon you." Jesus taught His disciples to say when they healed the sick; "The kingdom of God is come nigh unto you." And when the disciples were not accepted in their journeys and ministry, they were to say, "Even the very dust of your city, which cleaveth on us, we do wipe off against you: notwithstanding be ye sure of this, that the kingdom of God is come nigh unto you." But, as Jesus said, unless a man is born again… he cannot see the Kingdom of God.

According to Luke 10, John the Baptist, Jesus and His disciples preached the "Kingdom of God." It was their focus and their theme, so much so that Nicodemus had to confess he could distinguish Jesus as part of that invisible Kingdom. His salutation (we know that thou art a teacher come from God) was nothing less than a profession of his faith in Christ as Messiah. Perhaps what the man conveyed to Christ was, "We see you do things we cannot explain, so you must be operating within the Kingdom of God." He was saying that he could not disprove Jesus was Messiah. Many of the Christian population use the same analysis and deduction as Nicodemus. They default to faith in Christ. As opposed to believing in Him – they cannot disprove Him. It is only because they cannot disprove Christ that they believe in Him. Their faith is placed on the safer side of the equation, but they have not seen the Kingdom of God. Are you simply on the "safe side" or have you seen the Kingdom of God?

The profession of Nicodemus was not enough. Jesus answered him by pointing out that though he may have seen evidence of the Kingdom, he did not see the Kingdom itself. In order to see the Kingdom we must be born from above. He said, "Except a man be born again, he cannot SEE the kingdom of God." Jesus becomes incredulous and asks him, "Art thou a teacher of all Israel? And knowest not these things?"

He goes on to explain the difference between seeing the Kingdom and only seeing evidence of it, "The wind bloweth where it listeth, and thou hearest the sound thereof, but canst not tell whence it cometh, and whither it goeth: so is every one that is born of the Spirit." (John 3) Just as we can see the evidence of the wind and not see the wind itself, Nicodemus could see the evidence of the Kingdom being close to him but he could not see the Kingdom itself. We must be born again and become a part of the same Spirit in order to see, to witness from within, to belong to, the Kingdom of God.

The Gospel of the Kingdom

Mark 1:14-15, "Now after that John was put in prison, Jesus came into Galilee, preaching the gospel of the kingdom of God, And saying, The time is fulfilled, and the kingdom of God is at hand: repent ye, and believe the gospel." The Kingdom of God and the Kingdom of heaven were both mentioned by the gospel writers as Jesus' sermon and parable subjects during his ministry. This subject in general was known as the "Gospel of the Kingdom." Matthew 4:23, "And Jesus went about all Galilee, teaching in their synagogues, and preaching the gospel of the kingdom...." And elsewhere, "And Jesus went about all the cities and villages, teaching in their synagogues, and preaching the gospel of the kingdom..." (Matthew 9:35)

The Gospel of the Kingdom was preached by John the Baptist as well. The power of God was transferred from the Law and Prophets to the Gospel of the Kingdom according to Luke 16:16, "The law and the prophets were until John: since that time the kingdom of God is preached, and every man presseth into it." Examples of the Gospel of the Kingdom of God in the Scriptures are too numerous to mention. It is curious that the term is hardly used today. Does it make you wonder if its existence is as much a mystery to our modern church leaders as it was to poor Nicodemus?

If we stand in question as to what the definition of the Gospel of the Kingdom is, or we yet lack an understanding of the true Kingdom of God, we are admitting we have not seen it. Even if we can define the Kingdom of God, we are in no better condition than our friend Nicodemus, who had to say that he was only a believer by default; not as an eyewitness to the Kingdom, but only unable to disprove its existence.

We must also take notice that Jesus did not say thee must be born again using the singular form. He said ye (plural) must be born again. All of us, like Nicodemus, need our eyes opened and our Spirits quickened from above. If we are to preach the Gospel of Kingdom of God,[35] we must speak from a familiarity of that Kingdom; we must be able to see the Kingdom of God to be familiar with it, and to see the Kingdom we must be born again.

Why is practically nothing said about the Gospel of the Kingdom? Why is the Kingdom of God such a mystery to the prominent Bible teachers of today? Do you hear teaching in Bible classes, or over pulpits, or in prophecy, lessons or lectures pertaining to the Kingdom of God? Could it be that it remains a mystery because few have been born from above; few have actually seen the Kingdom to tell us about it?

Even our Christian institutions have lost ground to the secular-thinking majority. The Nehemiah Institute's[36] survey of Christian Schools reveals that even those students who are in Christian environs and under the tutelage of the best our Christian society has to offer are barely more than secular humanists with scores in this area steadily dropping every year. These faithless ones, whether preacher or churchgoer, pastor or parishioner, teacher or student, do not – cannot – see the Kingdom, many of them are as pitiable Nicodemus and surrender only to Christ from an inability to disprove His authority or an intense desire to believe Him. He must – we must – you must be born again!

In the capitol of Judaism among the best of the best, stands Nicodemus as the source of guidance and knowledge, yet he could not see the Kingdom evidenced before him. The people in Israel looked to Nicodemus as a teacher for answers about a Kingdom, which he himself had never seen. Should we not wonder about the answers we receive from men who are in that same condition today?

If Jesus were to interview the men from whom we obtain our Spiritual guidance, and inquire about their intimate knowledge of the Kingdom of God, would He look at them and ask, "Are you a teacher, [author, lecturer, seminary professor, elder, pastor...] and you don't know these things?"

---

[35] Matthew 24:14, "And this gospel of the kingdom shall be preached in all the world for a witness unto all nations; and then shall the end come."
[36] Source: American Family Policy Institute

30. *How shall ye believe, if I tell you of heavenly things?*

John 3:12, "If I have told you earthly things, and ye believe not, how shall ye believe, if I tell you of heavenly things?"

Recently, secular scientists are becoming divided and polarized on the creation issue. A few short years ago, the scientific community was monolithically purporting an earth that is millions of years old, and the fossil record stood as an irrefutable witness. The "facts" proved the evolution theory as "truth" and consequently, the Bible's Genesis story, as a myth.

This is not so today. With dubious carbon dating, and the fossil record's interpretation revealing itself flawed, the previously insurmountable evidence can be easily set aside by logic, common sense and basic scientific reason. For those who withheld believing the Bible in deference to science...good news! You can believe the Bible now! Science gives you permission to believe the Scriptures – at least until they can disprove it another way.

Actually, there were many of us who believed the Bible account of creation all the while science was saying that it was impossible. Now, the fact that the scientific community is taking another look at instant creation makes not a whit of difference to our faith in God's Bible account. If God said six days, then six days it is.

The excavation of Nineveh revealed an interesting example of faith in the Scriptures in the face of opposing science. The book of Jonah stated that Nineveh was a "great city." When the ancient city could not be found, it was thought that the story of Jonah was an allegory, just a big "fish story," (pardon the quip) and not indeed the truth. However, even when the city was discovered, archeologists still maintained that it must be an exaggerated tale because Nineveh was discovered to be a small town not a "great city" as the Bible story declared. As the scientists dug a little deeper, they found that the city into which they dug was built upon the ruins of a bigger city, an older Nineveh. Upon investigation the city of Nineveh was found to be as "great" as sixty miles wide!

Also, there were those who considered the New Testament unreliable because of references made to Pontius Pilate, a ruler for whom no record could be found. Just recently his name was discovered carved in stone, naming him as ruler of the area. Again, science catches up to the Bible record.

Another example is the modern idea that crucifixion by nails was not a common form of Roman execution. Archaeology again catches up to the Scriptures when, just recently, an anklebone was found with an iron nail through it.

The Bible is a trustworthy book. Reason, directed inaccurately by outside influences, may cause us to strongly doubt. Evidence is only as good as is its interpretation. We must admit that the only reason we doubt it is because some man causes us to do so. We are not to trust in flesh for many reasons. One reason is that the heart of man is desperately wicked and no one knows the depths of his own depravity. Jeremiah 17:9, "The heart is deceitful above all things, and desperately wicked: who can know it?" Another reason is, "Because the carnal mind is enmity against God: for it is not subject to the law of God, neither indeed can be." (Romans 8:7)

An untrustworthy heart conceives, and a carnal mind reasons that the earth is billions of years old, hence, we choose against the Scriptures. A scientist with a wicked heart and a mind at enmity with God conjures up a theory that the Bible is a fairy tale, and we choose to believe him over the testimony of the Creator. This speaks ill of us and reveals how willing we are to let slip the things we accepted readily as faithful children. We would sooner be offended if our earthly father were called a liar than if our heavenly Father were.

Man's Influence on Faith

The fact is that if we eliminated man's input, if we took extra-Biblical sources out of the equation, we would have no reason to doubt the Scriptural account of creation, history, or prophecy. Only as science is forced to do so, it admits, bit by bit that the Biblical account stands undaunted as an accurate record.

However, we are not to believe the Bible account simply because it cannot be disproved. We should believe the Bible account because it has been revealed to us as true. We are not to believe the history of the Bible because science says it is undeniable. We are to believe it, only as the Spirit of God shows it to us. Otherwise, ours is a sort of reversed faith in science and not a genuine faith in God.

Even to have faith in the Bible is unacceptable. The Bible is a book of words. The Word of God is not a book; The Word of God is Jesus Christ.[37] We are to have faith in God and His Word, Jesus Christ.

You are not to have faith in the words you read, for even if every word were inscribed by God Himself, interpretation is inescapable. Every word you read is interpreted by a human mind – yours! You are only to have faith in what is supernaturally revealed to you as you read or study or pray and meditate.

As the Bible is read, God reveals its truth and accuracy. What is revealed becomes an immutable, internal fact forever. For example, your author believes that the earth was created in six 24-hour days. I always felt that God was perfectly capable of saying and writing the words "billions of years" if that was the accurate term to describe the time it took to create the earth. Further, if it took billions of years and God said that it took a day, I would consider that a

---

[37] John 1:1-2, "In the beginning was the Word, and the Word was with God, and the Word was God. The same was in the beginning with God."
Revelation 19:13, "...and his name is called The Word of God."

deception on His part; therefore God, and His Scriptures would be untrustworthy. I will wait for science to catch up with Bible – not vice versa.

Let's face it, when the Bible is deemed to be on a level with Aesop's fables or Mother Goose, it puts us in precarious straights. Those of us who found our way to Christ through the Scriptures are on shaky ground. At the same time, we are to be careful not to cling to the Scriptures through desperation – as if they are our only hope. Remember, Jesus is the Word of God; the Bible is a record of that word. Faith placed in Christ is never unrewarded.

Your Father reveals His Word through the Bible, through Nature, through truth in all forms – even science! You need not ignore true science in deference to the Bible – it is unnecessary to do so. Neither science, nor scientists are enemies of the Christian faith. True science shows the Bible to be true. It, as well as nature, will enhance your understanding of the Scriptures. But when some new theory goes against the Bible record, you need to be careful, be wary, and be discriminating. The accuracy of the Bible has proven to be sound, but most of all, its Author has proven to be your trustworthy Friend. When you discount the record He left, the words He spoke, the prophecies He gave, you are setting yourself up as a discerner of truth about a time in which you did not live, and about a land to which you have never traveled.

Trust Him when He speaks, whatever He says. He had the ability to write whatever He wanted. He could have conveyed to the writers of the Bible whatever He wanted to say, or used whatever words He wanted to use. He could have used indefinable words, (which He has on occasion) and left us all totally baffled as to the origin of man, or the history of Christ, or the plan of redemption, etc. His choice, though, was a loving one. You possess a wonderful record.

Have confidence in His words found in your Bible. You cannot expect Christ to tell you the truth in one area while lying to you in another. If you do not trust His science and biology, if you do not trust His story of creation, how will you rely upon His guidance and navigation to a world you have never seen? He states it best, "If I have told you earthly things, and ye believe not, how shall ye believe, if I tell you of heavenly things?"

31.   *Wherefore didst thou doubt?*

Matthew 14:26-31, "And when the disciples saw him walking on the sea...
Peter answered him and said, Lord, if it be thou, bid me come unto thee on the
water. And he said, Come. And when Peter was come down out of the ship, he
walked on the water, to go to Jesus. But when he saw the wind boisterous, he
was afraid; and beginning to sink, he cried, saying, Lord, save me. And
immediately Jesus stretched forth his hand, and caught him, and said unto
him, O thou of little faith, wherefore didst thou doubt?"

Faith is a favorite subject in Christian circles. It has a "genie of the lamp" quality to it that is hard to resist. If it works, it is as though we have broken through and become "special" in the eyes of the Father of Lights, or have been deemed worthy of gifts from God. If it does not work, we can always claim that the lamp was not rubbed correctly to keep the legend intact. Keeping the legend going is easy to do and requires only superstition to keep it alive in most circles of faith. It has a gaming or lottery feel to it and the mystery sells it over and over again. "You are so close. You just need to buy this book or go to this church or join this group and it will all come together for you. Don't give up… it may just be this time you will get lucky."

If I sound cynical, you are correct, for the injustices and superstitions in "faith" teaching abound. Sold as magic, practiced like slight of hand, used in self-promotion, the charlatans peddle faith like snake oil elixir to Christians who have lost the joy of their newly found life in Christ. The luster of holiness and a soul free from sin is gradually replaced with a self-centered magic act. We are convinced that "miracles" prove a solid relationship to God. Our position in the family of God is "special" and is evidenced by the power He uses on our behalf. This kind of faith takes a person farther and farther from "Thy will be done," and eventually tosses the practitioner into despair, as inevitable failure undeniably presents itself. No lasting good comes from forsaking the pursuit of holiness or waging the battle of self-promotion – nothing except despair awaits those who bend God's arm and demand that He do as they wish. We are better off to forsake what we have been taught by these who are no less than mountebanks and rediscover in the real faith of the Scriptures how to receive from God.

All this being said, we must not impose our preconceptions onto the story of Jesus bidding Peter to walk on the water. This was not a magic lesson. It was a story of a man, any man, compelled and called by Christ, and how these ingredients can make that calling a prelude to the miraculous. When we are called of Christ to do the impossible, or the unusual, or even when we are called to do the customary, we may doubt and cause ourselves to fail. When we do, Christ gives us a question to get us back on track, *"Why Did You Doubt?"*

When He Looked About

For Peter the answer was that he looked about him and saw the storm. Usually, what makes us doubt is just raw fear and is not based in reason. Though reason can cause us to doubt, especially when accomplishing what is well above our ability, this was not the case in Peter's sinking. When he saw the wind and the waves, he doubted. What has the weather to do with walking on the water? Could someone walk on the water if it were still enough? Could someone step out of his boat into the sea if there was no wind?

Peter's proximity had something to do with his doubt as well. This happened when he looked around. When he looked about, what did he see? He saw the wind and the waves, but more so he saw that he was between his boat and his Savior. He had left one for the other and now was without either. This moment in time is a dramatic representation of where we are as Christians. We, who have given up our way and our abilities and now are come to Jesus "on the water" (so to speak), find that we have not quite reached our destination where safety is assured nor have we the support of our previous life of which we were in full charge. This can be overwhelming for those who look about them. Some choose not to look. Some trust Christ when they start to sink and are saved. Some, I really believe, try to make it back to their boat – but they do not walk back – they swim.

Peter, in this instance, was not to be blamed for having no faith. Jesus did not chide him for having NO faith, but for doubting. Like a father reaching for the tottering bicycle while teaching his child to ride, Jesus asks, "Why did you doubt? You were doing fine!" Sometimes we criticize Peter for his "little faith" causing him to sink and elevate this event of walking on water to an act of deity alone, but consider for a moment that Peter did walk on the water – even with his "little faith" that some impugn – He did walk on the water – an enterprise I would not recommend to the greatest men of faith I know.

Jesus is good to us. He stands waiting for His called ones to step out of the boat, He waits for us to walk, and when He sees us look around, He starts toward us knowing we will need Him shortly. Like a friend, not a judge Jesus asks, "Why did you doubt?"

Is it not a great comfort to know Christ is there when you fail, and that He encourages you to continue and loves you through it all? He gives you the key to regain your position and footing when you start to sink. "Wherefore didst thou doubt?" Or "Why did you doubt?" If you can determine the cause of your doubt, you can find the root of your hindrance to faith. Perhaps, you are just used to being in control. Maybe you know that what you want in life is not the will of God and therefore you are sure that you cannot rely on Him to accomplish it. Whatever the cause, you can at anytime forsake it, look into the face of Jesus, and cry out, "save me!" You can feel the iron grip of His hand around yours, setting your feet on what feels to be concrete to you that appears to be water to everyone else, and continue the mission of faith.

Failures, setbacks, or just the stagnant and nonproductive life in the "boat" can be overcome. Look past the seas rising and falling. Brave the wind and spray in your face, and see Christ out there standing still on the water. If He says to you, "come," you should go – no matter if you die in the attempt. Remember that life is not a sink or swim proposition. In Christ, we have another option. On the ocean of life in Christ it is sink, swim or WALK!

Many of us have many reasons to doubt. Honest, self-evaluation will reveal to you your needs and weaknesses. You will come to an understanding of your flaws and overcome them. You can rise above your own fears only when you keep your eyes on your Savior and fear only things that He says are dangerous. With faith in Him to keep you afloat you walk upon the infirm water to the destination to which you are called. Called to do the impossible and faith in your heart fully ablaze, you obey, you walk. It is only doubt that will sink you.

Perhaps you spend too much time examining your faith and neglect to examine your doubt. Your doubts will reveal the weaknesses heretofore obscured by the "busy-ness" of your life. Time spent in solitude, meditation and silence will facilitate your search. Set aside some time to examine the failures in your life, let Christ show you clearly where and why you doubted, where and why you started to sink. It is then that you will walk as you are commanded.

If walking is difficult or your steps seem insecure, cry out to the Savoir, "Save me!" While you are being called and His hand draws you out of the cold sea, perhaps even for the third or fourth time, and you are made to stand again, learn from your sinking. Don't be discouraged. Hear Jesus' question and consider, "Wherefore didst thou doubt?"

32. Why do you transgress the Commandment of God by your tradition?

Matthew 15:1-14 - Mark 7:1-9, "Then came to Jesus scribes and Pharisees, which came from Jerusalem, and when they saw some of his disciples eat bread with defiled, that is to say, with unwashen, hands, they found fault, saying, Why do thy disciples transgress the tradition of the elders? for they wash not their hands when they eat bread. For the Pharisees, and all the Jews, except they wash their hands oft, eat not, holding the tradition of the elders. And when they come from the market, except they wash, they eat not. And many other things there be, which they have received to hold, as the washing of cups, and pots, brasen vessels, and of tables. Then the Pharisees and scribes asked him, Why walk not thy disciples according to the tradition of the elders, but eat bread with unwashen hands? He answered and said, "Why do you transgress the commandment of God by your tradition?"

Jesus made a distinction between tradition and Commandment. Over the years the leaders of the synagogue added to the Law, rules to "help" people obey it. Jesus called these additions "burdens."[38] God spoke about these additions in no uncertain terms,

"Now therefore hearken, O Israel, unto the statutes and unto the judgments, which I teach you, for to do them, that ye may live, and go in and possess the land which the LORD God of your fathers giveth you. Ye shall not add unto the word which I command you, neither shall ye diminish ought from it, that ye may keep the commandments of the LORD your God which I command you." (Deuteronomy 4:1-2)

From the beginning, in the Garden of Eden,[39] when Eve added "neither may we touch it" to the Commandment "thou shalt not eat of it," the practice of adding rules continues today. As the rules of man become over time "the way we've always done it," they are firmer and more ensconced as tradition. Later in the Scripture, Jesus called these added traditions, "the commandments of men."

"Ye hypocrites, well did Esaias prophesy of you, saying, This people draweth nigh unto me with their mouth, and honoureth me with their lips; but their heart is far from me. But in vain they do worship me, teaching for doctrines the commandments of men." (Matthew 15:7) Here Jesus labeled those who make and teach these traditions as hypocrites. Knowing He does not use words unwisely, why did He consider them to be hypocrites?

---

[38] Matthew 23:4, "For they bind heavy burdens and grievous to be borne, and lay them on men's shoulders; but they themselves will not move them with one of their fingers."

[39] Genesis 3:3, "But of the fruit of the tree which is in the midst of the garden, God hath said, **Ye shall not eat of it, neither shall ye touch it**, lest ye die." God said nothing about touching it. Genesis 2:17, "But of the tree of the knowledge of good and evil, **thou shalt not eat of it**: for in the day that thou eatest thereof thou shalt surely die."

Why Hypocrites?

The definition of hypocrite is actor, pretender, or phony. What then is the pretence they made? What is the pretence we make when we change God's Law, even the slightest bit? The pretence is *whom* we serve. When we obey our law, we serve ourselves; we only pretend to serve God and obey His Law. Authorship must be intact for the Commandments of God to be pure.

We must be obeying our heavenly Father when we do whatever we do. Not only do we find it self-gratifying to serve under our own set of laws, but these laws of our own making obscure to ourselves and others our disobedience to the Spirit of the Law of God. As Jesus went on to give examples, He showed how the tradition only appeared to serve the Laws of God, but in truth it bypassed them. Are there any traditions you keep and hold dear that the Spirit of God has prompted you to investigate?

The authorship of the Commandments is an important aspect. The apostle James said, "For whosoever shall keep the whole law, and yet offend in one point, he is guilty of all." (James 2:10) Why is this so? Because, as he says later, "There is ONE lawgiver." John said, "... sin is the transgression of the law." Transgression against the Law is sin only because the Law is the Commandment OF GOD. Obedience is a tribute to the Lawgiver. When the author of the Law changes, the tribute of obedience changes as well. Just as disobedience to the law is accounted as disobedience to the author of the Law (sin), obedience to the law can only be accounted as obedience to the author of that law. If our traditions ARE the commandments by which we live, we, as authors, are obeying our own Law; we therefore serve only ourselves. No matter how honorable our actions are, we are only pretending to serve God, but in reality, we are hypocrites; we serve ourselves.

This sin compounds itself when we lay guilt upon those around us for violating our traditions and yet feel totally at ease while the Commandments of God are broken. We herald the virtues of doing things our way while God's way is neither known, nor followed, nor taught. We claim to be God's children all the while we obey only our own law, "...this is a rebellious people, lying children, children that will not hear the law of the LORD" (Isaiah 30:9)

Now, the hypocrisy that Jesus saw becomes clearer to us. We are only pretending to do God's will when we are, in reality, doing our own will. What we want to do is appear to be followers of God as His dear children. In truth, we are but doing what our family wants, doing what our denomination wants, or worse yet, doing only what we want. All the while we shame others for not doing as we do.

We should not write law, or tradition, nor should we trust our own desire to serve God. "The heart is deceitful above all things, and desperately wicked: who can know it?" (Jeremiah 17:9) We cannot make and follow our own ways or traditions (however noble they may be) and please God. When these elders condemned the disciples of Jesus for not washing their hands Jesus could not care less. He knew two things, this was only a tradition of man's making and this tradition had covered up a greater sin that lay beneath the façade. Transgression against the Law often hides beneath obedience to our own traditions. Jesus saw through this convoluted web and exposed it and the spiders that had spun it. "Then came his disciples, and said unto him, 'Knowest thou that the Pharisees were offended, after they heard this saying?' But he answered and said, 'Every plant, which my heavenly Father hath not planted, shall be rooted up. Let them alone: they be blind leaders of the blind. And if the blind lead the blind, both shall fall into the ditch.'"

Traditions have a place but they are never to occupy the allegiance of your heart. Traditions are never to obscure the pure Word of God, the living voice of your Savior within. If you find yourself in transgression because of traditions, no matter how old or honorable they may be, drop them like they were hot iron. Immediately lay aside the hindering traditions that blind you, for you are most assuredly bound for the ditch with others in your tow.

It is not always easy to identify the traditions that transgress. They are sometimes discovered only after damage has been done, or by seeing objectively, others snarled in them. Sometimes they originate from the most well meaning people and even "fathers of the faith," but nevertheless, they will blind your understanding, undermine God's purpose and plan for you, or just entangle, hinder and ultimately discourage you.

Take great care to examine and analyze the things you do and why you do them, especially the things about which you make harsh judgments about others and yourself. Take care that you are not twisting the Bible's words and wringing your traditions out of the Scriptures, and then ignoring the messages which flow from the Scriptures plainly, so plainly as to be understood by a twelve-year old. You need to listen to the author of the Scriptures and wait for the sweet witness of His Spirit. It is your only assurance to avoid the painful answer to His question, "Why do you transgress the Commandment of God by your traditions?"

33.   *What will a man give in exchange for his soul?*

*Mark 8:37- Matthew 16:25-26 "For whosoever will save his life shall lose it:
and whosoever will lose his life for my sake shall find it. For what is a man
profited, if he shall gain the whole world, and lose his own soul? or what shall
a man give in exchange for his soul?"*

Confidence men believe and therefore say, "Everyone has a price." If
we can believe for a moment that this motto is accurate, that everyone has a
price, (and there is little evidence to the contrary) a responsible person must be
somewhat curious about what his price is. All of us must wonder within
ourselves, and individually ask ourselves, "What is my price?" We must also
pray that we do not find out the hard way.

There is a story of a man approaching a woman to escort him on a date,
he asked, "If I gave you a million dollars, would you go out with me?" Even
after he made it clear that she was to favor him afterwards, she replied, "Yes, I
would." The man then asked, "How about twenty dollars?" The woman,
incensed, exclaimed, "What do you think I am?" To which the man answered,
"We've already established what you are, now we're negotiating price."

The high price tag on moral compromise, that we place there, is often
mistaken for high personal character. As we go through life improving our
character, we raise the price of our compromising with the world higher and
higher while others around us (with lower prices) admire us and reinforce our
false character and ego, encouraging us to raise the price higher still. Then we
may find that we have undergone no real changes in our character; it is just that
the cost of embarrassment or social standing outweighs whatever pleasure the
moral compromise offers us.

This can fool a person into thinking he has progressed toward morality
when indeed he has only become proud. The fear of "getting caught" is another
deterrent to bad behavior that has no virtue or character in and of itself, but only
fools those of us who are fearful into thinking we are morally accomplished,
when in reality, we are merely cowards with unsatisfied desires. With ego and
cowardice removed from the equation we may find our true price shockingly
lower than we thought at first.

Once the labels and price tags are torn from any merchandise, the value
must stand on the item's own merit and intrinsic value – good or bad. Similarly,
once we remove our price tags and evaluate ourselves, we stand only on our
internal values and true characters. This may be depressing to some, but it must
be part of the consideration of the question, "What will a man give in exchange
for his soul?"

There are those who believe that we are truly no better than we are at
our worst; and there are those who think we are no worse than we are at our
best. The truth is that we are composite beings with complicated lives and
social pressures that influence us hourly. We cannot evaluate our mental health

or our spiritual state with trite sayings nor even with time-honored maxims. We must give these ideas time to season within us without immediately adding to them excuses and permissions, and give the Holy Spirit opportunity to speak. If we find that we have fault (and we will) let's summon the faith and strength to deal with it squarely.

We must be vigilant, as the Scriptures admonish, and this vigilance includes deciding for ourselves the cost of this way of Truth, and resolving to pay it. We must decide exactly WHAT we will GIVE in exchange for our soul... then GIVE it! "What will a man give in exchange for his soul?"

The Exchange

An interesting angle of this question is that there is an exchange that takes place. Many questions arise from this idea. If there is an exchange, when does it occur? Has it occurred yet? How does it happen? There is, prevalent in the Christian world, an idea that Christ is ADDED to our life. It is said that we accept Christ into our lives or hearts. However, the Scriptures teach that the Christian experience is not addition, it is EXCHANGE. What is this exchange? You may hear some lament that they gave up certain habits they enjoyed, or fame and fortune. Some boast of foregoing position or prestige.

Let's look at how Jesus defines this exchange. "And when he had called the people unto him with his disciples also, he said unto them, If any man will come after me, let him deny himself, and take up his cross, and follow me. For whosoever will save his life shall lose it: and whosoever will lose his life for my sake and the gospel's shall find and save it. For what is a man profited, if he shall gain the whole world, and lose his own soul? or what shall a man give in exchange for his soul?" (Mark 8:34-37- Matthew 16:24-26 Combined)

It is clear that the exchange is not any part or portion of our lives. It is not our money or fame, our good habits or bad ones; the exchange is for our life itself. We are to exchange life for life. This was so real to the apostle Paul that he unequivocally wrote that he accredited even his physical life to his faith in Christ. He tells us that he is actually dead and the reason he doesn't appear so is because of Christ. Galatians 2:20, "I am crucified [dead] with Christ: nevertheless I live; yet not I, but Christ liveth in me: and the life which I now live in the flesh I live by the faith of the Son of God, who loved me, and gave himself for me."

This life exchange is the goal for which we must strive, knowing that Christ will settle for nothing less. This price is difficult because of the affinity we have for our own life. We love the life we live, no matter what it is – because we have control. Many would not readily exchange their lives for anyone else's, no matter what social or economic advancement it would bring. We feel we have a handle on our own lives, and that we are in control. Most who do covet fame and fortune do not want the life of those who have riches. What they desired is their beauty, or their fame and fortune added to the life they now possess. We love our lives because of the control we feel we have

117

over it. As illusory as our control may be, we won't give it up easily...even for the new life offered in Christ.

It is the control of our life that determines the owner and source. It is at the wheel of the ship you will find the Captain. It is the Pilot who determines course. The decision-maker is the one in possession of the life. This is why the line from "Paradise Lost" rings in our ears and haunts our mind as a true warning to all of us about our ego and pride that demands that we control our lives, it reminds us that most would "rather rule in Hell than serve in Heaven." This is why we will easily find more people willing to die for Christ than are willing to live for Him.

The only thing that was ever asked, as a price for your soul, was your life. Many preachers and teachers have told you this, and you may read it in your Bible but who can tell you how to do it? It is not merely your money, but the control of your finances, income and outgo; it is not merely your time He demands, but your right to schedule your work, play and worship.

You may not be asked for your life to be given in physical death, but only through the daily death of which Paul spoke (surrendering to Christ's control, Lordship, and rule) can you truly give your life to the Savior, making Him your Lord. The world stands ready to make a bid for your life. What will you have to give up in order to keep the control in your hands? The Lord asks, "What will a man give in exchange for his soul?" Are you willing to give it?

34. *What have I to do with thee?*

John 2:2-4, "And both Jesus was called, and his disciples, to the marriage. And when they wanted wine, the mother of Jesus saith unto him, They have no wine. Jesus saith unto her, Woman, what have I to do with thee? mine hour is not yet come."

Along the way, we tend to get diverted and tangled in business that is not ours. Sometimes we find things suddenly to be important, and even critical, that would not be important at all if we were on the proper task, moving in the right direction, and more concerned with the destination toward which we know God wants us to go. Have you ever wondered about the broken lives around you that are seemingly forsaken of God, lives you cannot seem to help no matter what you do or say?

It may be a surprise to some, but our Father God has a ministry. He is ministering to His lost sheep. When they call out in panic, when they find themselves away from the flock and the sun going down, they cry out and He hears. He may send us to these lost sheep if we were in position to listen to Him. We could be deeply involved in this ministry of God searching out His sheep, but due to our self-concern, fear, or pride, we therefore, will not, or cannot hear His instructions. Wanting to do His will (but only on our terms) we become restless and we may take a stroll into the world on our own, and should we find any of the Father's sheep we will gladly witness to them! This is not necessarily an excursion into sin or disobedience; it is just going about our business (instead of His), just a little diversion, or even just a little fun.

On our way we meet sheep in dire situations, who have nearly no awareness of the Shepherd, His purpose, or plan. We try to "minister" to them or witness to them and they seem unresponsive and in some cases hostile. We forgot momentarily that God has assigned Jesus as the Great Shepherd and it is His business to minister to those who the Father draws to Him. Then we find ourselves enmeshed in situations that are in desperate need of repair and we find our lives entangled in lives that are little more than webs spun of the rebellious and of little or no importance to the immediate purposes of God. We are concerned with problems that were years in the making, or even clearly caused at the fault or negligence of those involved. We can find ourselves grieved and praying for the betterment of people that don't care a whit about their own estate. All because we have strayed from the path that God has assigned us. Our hearts go out to them, we cry out for God to help. He must ask, "What Have I to do with thee?" Whether praying for someone who doesn't care, or asking for God's power to fill with His presence a life that cares nothing for Him, we will hear Him say, "What have I to do with thee?" He is asking, "Why are you asking me to involve myself here where I am not wanted?"

In the story of the water and wine, Jesus conceded to his mother's wishes and performed a miracle that He would not have done otherwise. This is an example of concession to the will of a believer like the importunate prayer in Luke 11. In both of these stories, it is obvious that He of whom the request was made had no desire to do the action requested, and, minus the request, would have done nothing on His own.

We definitely have the ability to ask what we will and He will grant and give us these desires even outside of His own desire, but is it the best way to minister? In the story of the importunate prayer, found in Luke 11:8, we read, "I say unto you, Though he will not rise and give him, because he is his friend, yet because of his importunity he will rise and give him as many as he needeth." It is as if to avoid aggravation that the friend conceded. Again in Luke 18:5 the parable of the importunate woman, she constantly comes and asks to be avenged of her adversary, something of no concern to the judge. We read the judge's words, *"Though I fear not God, nor regard man; Yet because this widow troubleth me, I will avenge her, lest by her continual coming she weary me."* Though He cared not at all, He answered her request. To avoid this, we need to remain close to the Father's work and be ready to work on His behalf and not our own.

The Scriptures say, "The steps of a good man are ordered by the LORD: and he delighteth in his way." (Psalms 37:23) Are we not supposed to be in the "way" He directs? Doesn't He expect us to go in His direction? Though we may see needs that we feel should be met we need to realize that God is not following us around to see if we need Him, we are to follow him, and wait till we are called upon to minister. Romans 12:7, "… let us wait on our ministering…" When Christ was on the earth He was questioned about how He performed miracles and He answered, "My Father worketh hitherto, and I work." (John 5:17) As He walked in God's way, and watched, and listened to His Father, He would do the works of His Father. He is our example.

Sometimes we get ourselves tangled in affairs that do not pertain to us, nor do they have the immediate interest of God. Sometimes we wonder why He doesn't answer our prayers, why He seemingly ignores situations and even people who need Him. This is why it is essential that we commune with God, learn His way, and get in it. When we make requests of God on behalf of the people in these situations, we may be missing His purpose. James 4:3 says, "Ye ask, and receive not, because ye ask amiss..." The model prayer and numerous parables mention the idea of being led along as we go. This is an essential part of living in His will. It is imperative to know the will of God in order to do the will of God.

But when it's Right…

To hear His voice in whispers we must be near the task. We must not wander. When we are close to His work we may even anticipate His next move, but we dare not make it till He nods.

It is a beautiful thing, when a need arises, and all things are right between you and God – to know you are "on task," and know are in the center of God's will, and can see the "Father work hitherto" (have seen Him work up to this point) and are ready to hear the slightest whisper of His wish! The joy and anticipation you feel even now as you read this is no match for the reality of doing the right thing at the right time, saying the given word to the right person, or having the needed item ready to give to the person of God's choosing. There is nothing like working within His will, and being used by the Creator of the universe to minister to His loved ones here on earth.

God has given great latitude in life for recreation and entertainment, but you need to be aware of your duty as you engage even in good diversion. When you go your own way, constantly seeking something or someone to entertain you, going when you should not go and doing more than you should, you sacrifice the blessing of being a vessel "meet for the Master's use." Paul said, "Although all things are lawful, all things are not necessary, all things don't make me a better person." (1 Corinthians 10:23 author's paraphrase).

Care needs to be taken that you don't attach yourself to things and even people with whom the Lord is not presently working. Although He may answer your request, is your desire the Lord's desire? Do you care for things for which He shows no concern? Are you asking amiss that you may consume it upon your lusts? Are you asking for wine for your own consumption?

How sad it is, after you have poured out your heart, and laid the petition of your desire at the feet of your God only to hear Him say, "What have I to do with thee?" Even if He answers and makes your water wine, what have you gained but your own drunkenness?

35.   *How many loaves have ye?*

Mark 8:5, "And he asked them, How many loaves have ye? And they said, Seven."

Matthew 15:34, "And Jesus saith unto them, How many loaves have ye? And they said, Seven, and a few little fishes."

Mark 6:38, "He saith unto them, How many loaves have ye? go and see. And when they knew, they say, Five, and two fishes."

There is a lovely story told in Acts 3 about a man, lame from birth, who was laid at the gate and asked alms of those who passed by. Peter and John going into the Temple passed by him and said, "Silver and gold have I none; but such as I have give I thee: In the name of Jesus Christ of Nazareth rise up and walk." (Acts 3:6) We can only give what we have.

In the story from which comes our question, the Lord is putting forth a query regarding inventory. As the masses approach, all know that it is many miles back to the town. It is likely these came out unprepared to stay, but the Master taught, and preached, and healed all day and time has now escaped them. There is a crisis. The body clocks have ticked through suppertime and beyond.

Jesus saw an opportunity to teach a lesson of faith and show Himself as the sustenance of life. He asks, "How many loaves have ye?" Their answer makes it glaringly apparent that there is not enough. A mild, but increasing panic presents itself to the disciples. Jesus continues to search their silent faces for ideas. The empty expressions and glances back and forth are halted by Jesus' next instruction. "Command them to sit down," He said (now that it is established that they can do nothing to alleviate the problem).

Why would Jesus ask everyone to sit down? It is because, in a crowd, when all are standing, it is very difficult to see anything except the one in front of you. It is obvious that He wants all to see Him supply the need. He blessed, then broke the bread and the disciples handed it out to the people… there was more than enough.

Do you believe that Jesus is the very Son of God, the redeemer of all mankind, and the bread of life? He claims to be the bread that comes from heaven. He also claimed that if we eat from His table we will gain eternal life. "I am the living bread which came down from heaven: if any man eat of this bread, he shall live forever…" (John 6:51) Now let me ask you, concerning this Bread from heaven, "How many loaves have ye?"

The Bread of Life

In your trek on this earth you may never be in such a place of responsibility to feed as many as did the disciples. Even spiritually speaking, you may never find yourself as someone to whom many might look to find the

Bread of Life. But you should still ask yourself and answer the question, "How many loaves have ye?" If someone came to you spiritually malnourished and begging for a right relationship to God, do you have the Bread of Life for which they so desperately seek; and if you do, do you have it to spare?

You may have read books and done your homework. You may listen attentively to teachers who claim to know, but when it comes down to showing the logistics and realities of a life in Christ, when it comes down to effecting Christ as real to someone who needs Him, as bread is to a starving man, can you do it?

When talking of the Christian life to someone who knows the jargon, or with someone familiar with your faith and practice, many things can go unsaid and yet understood. But what does your faith, your Meeting, church or denomination have to offer those on the streets – the vagrants, the drunks, the destitute? How many loaves have ye? Do you hold in your possession the Bread of Life that can take away forever the gnawing hunger in the soul of the man you may meet downtown, on the job, or in the mission?

When the realization comes, of your impoverished cupboards where the Bread of Life is to be in store, you may panic and seek out those who seem to have an abundance. There are many who claim to have plenty bread for the hungry of soul and are willing to teach us and thus supply this "bread." But, should you trust these merchants to fill in the gaps of your lacking relationship? Is this food of the soul to be found in education, or preparation or held in store by mental or mechanical processes?

If you are not sure of the supply, nor the source, you must then suspect that perhaps, you may not have enough for yourself. In any case, you should realize that the ability to share the wonderful life in Christ is yours only because you possess and enjoy the wonderful life in Christ. The realization becomes more painful when you recognize that your reluctance to share Christ, or your inability to do so, may be because you have no such life experience of your own.

Evangelism takes on a sadistic tone if we are showing only images of bread we do not possess. We create appetites for which we ourselves have no satisfaction. We can tell the hungry about the bread our forefathers possessed. We can recite Scriptures telling about the bread the apostles had, but when it comes down to actually offering true grace, true power, true life changing baptism by fire, we are as poor as those we have coaxed to our cupboard. Does our ministry only tantalize and create hunger then leave them hopeless for a sample of this Bread of Life? We will find that many teachers who claim the ability to win souls can only mime and parrot, creating converts who enjoy no true or lasting effect. They sell books and tapes and lectures… they give advice and counsel… they enthuse and excite… but they have no bread. How many loaves have ye?

Once, in the life of George Fox, founder of the Quaker faith, he challenged a group of religious people stating that they were well trained in the Scriptures and could repeat, with little difficulty, what the apostles said, and they could recite what Christ said, but, he asked the crowd, "What canst thou say?" Many may quote Scripture, but who can hear and reproduce the words of God from his own heart?

Many have such a mechanical relationship with Christ that the Word of God, to them is a book to be memorized. Many know the words, but don't know the Word. How many realize that the Word of God is to flow from the mouths of Christians? No, not recitation of Scripture, but the living Word of God, God's message to His people is to come from us -- the Bread of life, the Word of God, by which we are to live. Consider these Scriptures in this new light:

> *Matthew 4:4, "...Man shall not live by bread alone, but by every word that proceedeth out of the mouth of God."*
> *Exodus 13:9, "...that the LORD'S law may be in thy mouth...."*
> *Deuteronomy 30:14, "But the word is very nigh unto thee, in thy mouth...."*
> *Isaiah 59:21, "...and my words which I have put in thy mouth, shall not depart out of thy mouth, nor out of the mouth of thy seed, nor out of the mouth of thy seed's seed, saith the LORD, from henceforth and for ever."*
> *Jeremiah 1:9, "... Behold, I have put my words in thy mouth."*
> *Romans 10:8, "But what saith it? The word is nigh thee, even in thy mouth, and in thy heart: that is, the word of faith, which we preach;"*

The world has gone into starvation lacking the Bread of Life. Our towns, our villages, our homes, even we ourselves are starved for this Bread of Life of eternal life. How many loaves have ye? Though it may be that you can only give what you have, the good news is that what you have can be made enough by Christ Jesus if it is given to Him. You need not go through this life fearing that someone may ask of the hope that is in you, you can prepare yourself by dedication and study, by consecration and holy living, by meditation and worship.

Christ is able to take what you have and multiply it to the masses, to the group, the family, the friend, and the neighbor. Place what you have in His hands and make yourself ready to get it back in bounty! He is the Bread of Life! "How many loaves have ye?"

36. Are we children of the kings of the earth or strangers?

Matthew 17:24-25, "...they that received tribute money came to Peter, and said, Doth not your master pay tribute? He saith, Yes. And when he was come into the house, Jesus prevented him [anticipated his questions], saying, What thinkest thou, Simon? of whom do the kings of the earth take custom or tribute? of their own children, or of strangers?"

Peter was asked if his Lord paid tribute and he thoughtfully answered, "Yes." Later, Jesus asked him the question, "Do the children of a kingdom pay taxes to that kingdom?" To which Peter attested that only those who are strangers to the kingdom pay such taxes. Here the Lord evokes thoughts never before considered by this disciple, or many of us for that matter.

We are in an ambiguous state of citizenship here on this earth. We, who are seeking redemption, are amphibians on the shoreline between the terrestrial and the celestial. Since our conversion, are equally able to swim the depths of the spiritual Kingdom of God as well as walk in this temporal world. We must perform a balancing act between putting bread on the table and gathering manna in the field. Jesus was not untouched by this same paradox of dual citizenship in exclusive realms. He asked this question to focus Peter's thoughts on this matter.

When tax time comes around, the payment of these taxes can have an effect worse than that of merely depleting our finances, they can artificially knit us to the world in which we physically live. Taxes, world crises, voting obligations, selective service requirements, draft, disputes and alliances (both state and municipal) all bring our focus down to the soil beneath our feet and obscure the blessed hope of our redemption and induction into the Kingdom of God.

Hebrews 11:13-17, "These all died in faith, not having received the promises, but having seen them afar off, and were persuaded of them, and embraced them, and confessed that they were strangers and pilgrims on the earth. For they that say such things declare plainly that they seek a country. And truly, if they had been mindful of that country from whence they came out, they might have had opportunity to have returned. But now they desire a better country, that is, an heavenly: wherefore God is not ashamed to be called their God: for he hath prepared for them a city."

Then later in Hebrews 13:14, *"For here have we no continuing city, but we seek one to come."*

We have not only a city but also an entire country to call our own. We are to consider ourselves as pilgrims and strangers here. "Of whom do the kings of the earth take custom or tribute...of their own children or of strangers?" Are we children of the kings of the earth, or strangers?

After questioning His own and Peter's citizenship, Jesus added the statement, "... Notwithstanding, lest we should offend them..." "[We will pay the tax.]" It is obvious that, as long as it is understood exactly with which kingdom the citizenship lies, and with whom allegiance was pledged, there was no need to struggle or complain under the payment of taxes. Jesus was probably thinking of the Exodus 30 requirement to pay such a temple tax and felt no contradiction in paying it. He went on in other Gospel accounts to teach that we should give the government what belongs to the government. We should, as well-balanced Christians hold all things loosely.

Children of the Earth?

But more importantly, as we wait for the country that Abraham sought,[40] we should hold our citizenship here loosely as well. Better to be found a traitor to any country on earth than to betray the Kingdom of God. Normally the collusion within us is more subtle than that. It is not a simple matter of betraying one country for the other; it is our impaired orientation that causes the wrestling in our minds when action is demanded by either.

When we make decisions – life changing or financial, domestic or political – the duplicity of our loyalty comes to the fore. Are we children of this country or are we children of the parallel and simultaneous Kingdom of God? Decisions that advance ourselves physically (longer life), or advance us financially (less work - more money), or advance us politically, will demand of us the same energies (and many times opposite energies) that effect advancement in the reciprocal Kingdom. This is not always true, but when this is true, it is tragic when we choose the way that only advances us in our temporal, tangible and temporary lives.

When life makes its demands of your time and money, or when you are told that your stand on political issues is not a "patriotic" one, you need to ask, "Of whom do the Kings of the earth take custom or tribute?" Remember that Jesus said that His Kingdom was not of this world[41] and that you are not of this world either.[42]

Jesus also taught an uncompromising stand on serving two masters. Applied to this situation of allegiance little latitude can be given. Matthew 6:24 and Luke 16:13 say that no man, no servant, can serve two masters "for either he will hate the one, and love the other; or else he will hold to the one, and despise the other. Ye cannot serve God and mammon."

---

[40] Hebrews 11:8, "By faith Abraham, when he was called to go out into a place which he should after receive for an inheritance, obeyed; and he went out, not knowing whither he went."

[41] John 18:36, "Jesus answered, My kingdom is not of this world: if my kingdom were of this world, then would my servants fight, that I should not be delivered to the Jews: but now is my kingdom not from hence."

[42] John 15:19, "If ye were of the world, the world would love his own: but because ye are not of the world, but I have chosen you out of the world, therefore the world hateth you."

Mammon

Unfortunately, "mammon" is commonly mistaken to mean "money" in this scripture. The whole thought however, is much more than money, wealth or even avarice. It describes the whole earthly system of "getting along." Other than being the object of misdirected worship, money itself has little to do with the concept of mammon. Money becomes mammon when it seems to be the answer to all the problems of life. When faced with difficulty, do you tend to calculate the amount that will be needed to solve your problem? If so, you may be becoming the servant of mammon.

Recently, I found myself in a legal/political dispute. Having been politically active with town governments in the past, I was well aware of the money and influence (mammon) that is necessary to bring about changes in politics. When I was about to appear before the powers of the city I was surprised when the familiar thoughts of "how to get things done in politics," did not come into mind. This time was different. I felt as though I was an outsider, a foreigner, an alien ambassador from another world, just speaking to the powers that are in control here. All I was doing was voicing a complaint and making a friendly suggestion. No bravado, no preaching about my rights as an American. No threats of legal actions and political pressure, just a take it or leave it attitude. Frankly, I did not expect them to understand or care about my position nor did I expect a remedy to be effected. I almost didn't care how it turned out, but I felt compelled to go and speak my grievance and let come what may. I am a citizen of another country.

When we consider ourselves as children of this world more than we consider ourselves to be children of the Kingdom of God, mammon seems the right way to get things done. But when we walk in the Spirit and want only God's will – it seems ridiculous.

We know experientially that these two kingdoms are as water and oil. Their irreconcilable views have proved combative on nearly every subject. We know instinctively that allegiance to one will mean denial of the other. We also know it is fear that draws us toward the counsel of mammon and faith that welcomes the counsel of God. Yet, often we look to mammon first.

It is a compliment when the world makes its demand on your property or your purse. You should gladly give it because kingdoms demand taxes and tariffs only from strangers. When it demands your allegiance or your loyalty, you must take a stand for the country to which you belong, remembering your ambassador status as a stranger and pilgrim with faithful Abraham.

When you attempt to advantage yourself in this world, or look to mammon for answers, you approach treason – treason most foul toward the Kingdom of Heaven. After all, "...are we children of the kings of the earth, or strangers?"

37.   How can ye believe?

John 5:44, "How can ye believe, which receive honour one of another, and seek not the honour that cometh from God only?

There is an unmistakable tone of impossibility in the words of the Savior here. He says that those who seek acceptance and honor of men could never have true faith in God. Honor received from God precludes honor of men and honor received from men makes impossible the honor of God. Jesus once used the term "leaven" to describe the philosophy of the scribes and Pharisees. When cautioning His disciples about this philosophy of hypocrisy, He said in Mark 8:15, "Take heed, beware of the leaven of the Pharisees, and of the leaven of Herod." What is the leaven of Pharisees? What is the leaven of the Herod? In Luke 12:1-4 He explains and defines this "leaven," "...Beware ye of the leaven of the Pharisees, which is hypocrisy."

The Pharisees and Sadducees and Herod all had a common philosophy. The Scriptures call it a "doctrine." Note Matthew 16:6-12, "Then Jesus said unto them, Take heed and beware of the leaven of the Pharisees and of the Sadducees...Then understood they how that he bade them not beware of the leaven of bread, but of the doctrine of the Pharisees and of the Sadducees.

What was this common philosophy, or doctrine that Jesus called leaven? First, we will look at the Pharisees and Sadducees. Jesus was always calling to their attention the fact that they cared what men thought of them. Luke 20:46-47, "Beware of the scribes, which desire to walk in long robes, and love greetings in the markets, and the highest seats in the synagogues, and the chief rooms at feasts; Which devour widows' houses, and for a shew make long prayers."

Matthew 23:5-7, "But all their works they do for to be seen of men: they make broad their phylacteries, and enlarge the borders of their garments, And love the uppermost rooms at feasts, and the chief seats in the synagogues, And greetings in the markets, and to be called of men, Rabbi, Rabbi."

Jesus was forever in violation of the Pharisees' man-made laws and on occasion they "went about to kill Him." At several opportunities they desired to take Him, stone Him, and even murder Him, but they feared the people. Mark 11:32, "...they feared the people" Mark 12:12 "...but feared the people" Luke 20:19, "... they feared the people" Luke 22:2, "... they feared the people" Later, in Acts 5:26, they showed that they learned nothing when they sought to lay hands on the newly empowered disciples, again, "...they feared the people"

"But all their works they do for to be seen of men" From our spiritual infancy we have understood false pride and the problems associated with it. The fact that pride is repugnant is not peculiar to Christianity. Arrogance and hypocrisy are repulsive even to the common man who holds no faith in God at all. We understand this and avoid the blatant warning and examples we see in Scripture, but the doctrine goes deeper than mere pride of appearance. The doctrine is a philosophy that is deeper than looking our best to those around us, or casting the best light on our works. Achieving the honor of men becomes the root of our decision-making, deceiving even those who hold such philosophy, and worse yet, it precludes the honor of God. To see this let us look at Herod.

Herod was steeped in this doctrine/philosophy as well. Though Herod was not a religious man, he operated under the same philosophy as the religious leaders of his day. Actually, his philosophy was not a religious doctrine at all but one common to all mankind even today, i.e. hypocrisy, or acting, if you will. Herod had built, in his own mind, a persona he wished others would see when they looked at him. The man in his mind was a powerful man of integrity who took orders from no one and did as he pleased – a king.

Herod was intrigued with John the Baptist and did not hate him at all. He actually used to go and listen to him[43] (whether in the wilderness or when he was in Herod's prison, we don't know) and showed signs of affection toward John when he was scheduled to be beheaded[44] and "...Herod feared John, knowing that he was a just man and an holy, and observed him; and when he heard him, he did many things, and heard him gladly." (Mark 6:20) Why then did he kill him?

The Hatred of Herodias

The hatred that Herod's wife, Herodias, had for John, caused her to conspire with her daughter to trick Herod into giving her John's head on plate. Herod made an unconscionable, lust-driven promise to a tawdry, whorish girl during a party, and because he feared the people, John was killed. Matthew 14:9-10, "And the king was sorry: nevertheless for the oath's sake, and them which sat with him at meat, he commanded it [John's head] to be given her. And he sent, and beheaded John in the prison."

Acting and performing for people will get us nowhere. It makes us useless to the Kingdom of God. We cannot hide our true self forever, or pretend we are better than we are; neither should we want to. The very nature of grace, forgiveness, and salvation demands honesty with ourselves, with God, and with others. "For there is nothing covered, that shall not be revealed; neither hid, that shall not be known. Therefore whatsoever ye have spoken in darkness shall be heard in the light; and that which ye have spoken in the ear in closets shall be proclaimed upon the housetops."

It will all come to light one day; there is no reason to pretend. Neither should we fear what men may think of us, or do to us. "And I say unto you my friends, Be not afraid of them that kill the body, and after that have no more that they can do. But I will forewarn you whom ye shall fear: Fear him, which after he hath killed hath power to cast into hell; yea, I say unto you, Fear him." (Luke 12:4-5) We as believers have an obligation to be honest in everything we do and say. True faith is living in this state of purity and honesty.

---

[43] Mark 6:20, "For Herod feared John, knowing that he was a just man and an holy, and observed him; and when he heard him, he did many things, and heard him gladly."
[44] Mark 6:26, "And the king was exceeding sorry..."

If we are constantly and continually concerned with our appearance to others, our status in life, and what the majority thinks, Christ gives us a slim chance of recovering ourselves by faith in God. You are constrained to earnestly seek acceptance in the eyes of God alone. Otherwise your confidence is misplaced and a life of faith is impossible. If you seek the favor of people you will not find yourself on a narrow path, where few are found, but upon the broad road with many people, and a road with wide gates.

Unfortunately, the Scriptures describe those gates as the ones that lead these back-slappers to their destruction. Away they all happily go, praising, promoting, and congratulating each other. To follow your God in faith will separate you and, in some cases, isolate you and can cause your persecution. The Savior gives you little hope of salvation if you go the broad way of hypocrisy. This is why He asks, "How can ye believe, which receive honour one of another, and seek not the honour that cometh from God only?"

38.   Can ye fast, while the bridegroom is here?

Luke 5:34, "And he said unto them, Can ye make the children of the bridechamber fast, while the bridegroom is with them?"

Matthew 9:14-17, "Then came to him the disciples of John, saying, Why do we and the Pharisees fast oft, but thy disciples fast not? And Jesus said unto them, Can the children of the bridechamber mourn, as long as the bridegroom is with them? but the days will come, when the bridegroom shall be taken from them, and then shall they fast. No man putteth a piece of new cloth unto an old garment, for that which is put in to fill it up taketh from the garment, and the rent is made worse. Neither do men put new wine into old bottles: else the bottles break, and the wine runneth out, and the bottles perish: but they put new wine into new bottles, and both are preserved."

The Quaker idea of the reality of Christ within is most fascinating. Other denominations include some aspects of the idea, and accept most of the idea in word, but few people (even while including some Quakers) have come to the reality of Christ in us as our counselor, our advocate, our Savior and Lord. As the apostle says, the indwelling Christ is a mystery, "Even the mystery which hath been hid from ages and from generations, but now is made manifest to his saints: To whom God would make known ... which is Christ in you..." (Colossians 1:26-27)

From the ages past, from creation till now, since the original sin, our Father God has wanted to have communion with His own children; not a communion of grape juice and crackers, but one of purity and truth; not one of timely ceremony and pomp, but one of intimacy and love. This unbroken communion with God is the goal of everyone who has truly come to know their condition before their Judge, and it is the goal of the One who is Judge of their condition. Yes, our God wants to commune with His obedient children.

Jesus taught also that there is a Kingdom within. There is a Kingdom of God that is not apparent to those outwardly observing it. "...The kingdom of God cometh not with observation: Neither shall they say, Lo here! or, lo there! for, behold, the kingdom of God is within you." (Luke 17:20-21) It was Jesus' message that His Kingdom is different than any other in that it is not upon the earth. John 18:36, "Jesus answered, My kingdom is not of this world: if my kingdom were of this world, then would my servants fight... but now is my kingdom not from hence." It can be firmly established in Scripture that the Kingdom of God is a "Kingdom within," with a divine ruler establishing His throne upon the center of our being; a Kingdom, a retreat, a tranquil home of comfort and acceptance to which we may resort at any time.

For lack of this peaceable Kingdom within us, or the ignorance of it, we may suffer turmoil and unrest in our hearts. What comfort and peace we forfeit. What nobility we trade for pottage. How often we digress to our own strength and trust in our arms of flesh when we could enjoy the courage and confidence that comes from living within a Kingdom occupied and protected by Christ our King. Why do we mourn and plead, why do we beg and cry? How "can the children of the bridechamber fast while the bridegroom is with them?"

We must admit that the benefits of this glorious Kingdom are not a vivid reality. Although we may know of the Kingdom's existence, or at least its mention in Scripture, most of us have been taught little about it and we have done even less to enter it. Wanting it is not enough. Jesus taught that it must be entered by work. Speaking of the Kingdom, He said, "Strive [work] to enter in at the strait gate: for many, I say unto you, will seek [want] to enter in, and shall not be able." (Luke 13:24) We must know about it, we must want it, and we must strive to enter it.

Jesus used the question, "Can the children of the bridegroom fast...?" for several reasons. It was to start their thinking in a new direction. He wanted them to know that we are not putting new wine into old bottles. We are not sewing new cloth onto old garments. He is saying, "This is something you have never seen before, built upon a totally new premise!" The Jews made it a common practice to fast. Fasting has its place, even in the life of Christians today, but there was no reason to fast when the disciples were enjoying the presence of the Messiah Himself. Notice that the two analogies above (wine in new bottles and new cloth sewn to old garments) were signifying the addition of a new thing into an older, weaker host. An old bottle cannot contain new wine, nor can an old shrunken garment be repaired properly by new, unshrunken cloth. The old things cannot utilize the new neither can the new repair the old; the new can only prove the old to be even more ancient, unusable, and inadequate.

Not a Patch Job – It's Something New

The addition of the residing Holy Spirit of God into the equation of man's redemption is a new thing, unable to be contained in ordinances and unable to repair, by patchwork, the inadequacies of the Law. This Comforter, who will lead us and guide us into the Kingdom of God, is something completely new.

The other reason Jesus asked the question, "Can the bridegroom fast?" is for the rhetorical response and the subsequent deduction that when we mourn and fast we demonstrate His separation from us. Contrarily, the joy and blessedness that comes from living daily in His Kingdom is shown in our eating and drinking and dispositions of cheer and gladness. This occurs to us naturally when we hear His question, "Can the children of the bridechamber mourn, as long as the bridegroom is with them?" His question forces us to admit that we mourn because we do not have a real sense of the Bridegroom with us.

No one can give you a ten-step plan to enter the Kingdom of God. For some to enter, I am sure, it will be two or three steps, for some others, it may take many steps. The wonderful thing about the Kingdom is that it is not ruled, kept, or governed by silly, impulsive men. The Father calls whom He wills, the Son admits whom He wills. We are but mere answerers of His call.

132

If you are one who cries and complains or who fasts and afflicts his soul, perhaps the very present Kingdom of God has eluded you. Maybe the "Kingdom without" has failed to materialize and has left you empty and feeling alone. Could it be that you have been looking for the Kingdom to appear in the physical realm – in the healing of your body or the restoration of your outward life – while all along, the "Kingdom within" has escaped you? Do you long for the presence of the Lord? Do you wonder how it must have been for the Disciples to have Christ immediate and present with them at all times? How could the Lord have said that it is better (expedient) for you that I go away; how could it be better?

"Nevertheless I tell you the truth; It is expedient for you that I go away: for if I go not away, the Comforter will not come unto you; but if I depart, I will send him unto you... when he, the Spirit of truth, is come, he will guide you into all truth...your sorrow shall be turned into joy. ... I will see you again, and your heart shall rejoice, and your joy no man taketh from you. ... ask, and ye shall receive, that your joy may be full. ... Jesus answered them, Do ye now believe? ...be of good cheer; I have overcome the world."
(John 16:7-33 Abridged)

Now I ask you, "Can ye make the children of the bridechamber fast, while the bridegroom is with them?"

39.   How is it that ye do not understand?

During a trip the disciples realized that they had brought no bread along for their journey. They were considering this blunder when Jesus made a statement of warning to them about the "leaven" of the Pharisees. They said among themselves, "We're in trouble now! He knows we forgot the bread!"

Which when Jesus perceived, he said unto them, O ye of little faith, why reason ye among yourselves, because ye have no bread? perceive ye not yet, neither understand? have ye your heart yet hardened? Having eyes, see ye not? and having ears, hear ye not? and do ye not remember? Do ye not yet understand, neither remember when I brake the five loaves among five thousand, how many baskets full of fragments took ye up? They say unto him, Twelve. And when the seven loaves of the four thousand, how many baskets took ye up? And they said, Seven. How is it that ye do not understand that I spake it not to you concerning bread, that ye should beware of the leaven of the Pharisees and of the Sadducees? Then they understood how that he bade them not beware of the leaven of bread, but of the doctrine of the Pharisees and of the Sadducees. Matthew 16:8-12 Mark 8:17-21, (Combined)

Sometimes our shortcomings cause us to narrow our focus. We mentally center on our own weaknesses and apply anything said to us as meant specifically to spotlight our faults. This makes us nearly unteachable and frustrating to our Master as seen in this example of Scripture. This impairment of our understanding can be easily remedied, but it will require courage and persistence.

Here again we find Jesus asking questions for the benefit of us hearing our own answers. In this passage He asks many questions to which He knows the answers. He certainly knew the answer to the question, "How is it that ye do not understand?" He was, and is yet, well aware of the reasons we cannot understand. The idea of asking is for us to consider why we are missing what He is saying. This is a question we should ask ourselves when we hear even the simplest of His commands. Even when we think we understand, we need to consider the possibility that we do not. Perhaps the message is clearer than it seems. Maybe the message lies beneath the question and our feeble understanding obscures it.

In this Scripture, Jesus gave us a great way to consider our thought processes. As the disciples heard what Jesus said, they first thought that they were being reprimanded for not fulfilling their responsibilities for the trip. He had to call to their remembrance the miracles of the past to put their concern for no bread into proper perspective. He said that with which they were concerned was a small thing – there were far more important things to think about. He was trying to give them a dire warning about a menacing and destructive doctrine that could impair their ability to follow Him, and all they could think of was their own skin.

We do this too. As we hear God's voice within our hearts trying to guide and direct us, we misapply His instructions or warnings to our petty missteps about which He has little or no concern. Our mind reels as we attempt to construct and utilize a condemnation/guilt/blame procedure to justify ourselves and we miss the message He intended for us. We seek absolution from sins He has not mentioned while missing solemn warnings that could destroy us.

He unsuccessfully tries to give us the instruction to carry us through the next big trial in our lives, He tries in vain to tell us exactly what we need to know to be an example to others, to be triumphant in the temptation around the next corner, to be prepared for the disaster that awaits next week or next year, but alas, we are bogged down and cannot understand what He said because we try desperately to apply what He said to the sin of yesterday, the shortcoming of last week or the petty habit that plagues us. He tries to warn us... He tries to prepare us... He tries to communicate... but is left with only the frustrating question, "How is it that ye do not understand?"

Holiness is the Key

The first and most important thing we can do to avoid this hindrance is to cease to commit these sins. This is a simplistic answer to be sure, but if carried out, will go a long way to cure this problem. We simply need to be better stewards of time and talent and pursue our given lots in life with honest efforts and due diligence. We need to keep our lives clean and give no reason for the world to speak reproachfully of us. This covers everything from dealing justly in business to properly taking care of our garbage cans. (Need we add here that no Christian should be dealing with transgression on a Commandment level?)

We do well if we understand this aspect of sin and avoid it. It is for this reason we are perplexed when our judgment and understanding is impaired. "We don't habitually sin," we wonder to ourselves, "so what is the problem?" In the quiet time, in the still hours before sleep and before rising, the Lord has His way of making your shortcomings known to you. In the quiet time of listening and worship your level of discomfort is directly proportional to the level of spiritual imbalance and dishonesty you have allowed into your demeanor. Shortcomings are no secret to those who listen.

Although we may not have flagrant sin, most of us have lives full of inequities, hypocrisies and small injustices to our fellow man. Not the blatant wicked sort that we appall, but the subtler sort – the face change upon arrival of guests, the language that becomes more saint-like at the sight of a Friend from Meeting or fellow Christian, the difference in how we handle disputes among friends and how we handle disputes at our family table.

These "little sins" are the barriers to hearing Christ's instructions when they come to our mind as He approaches us in worship or prayer. These problems must be worked out of our lives with much effort and endurance or we will never be able to see past them. We know that we displease God with these habits and flaws in our character, and they stand as barriers to a deeper understanding of His way.

If you confess and place these problems upon an altar of honest repentance they will lose their power to influence and impair your judgment. You need to give an honest try to overcome these things and confess them as faults to one another. You need to look to Jesus who can cite example after example of people who overcame such obstacles and the abounding grace that covers those who are repentant and honest. You will be asked to count the baskets of overabundance and confess that His grace is indeed sufficient.

Many things you found hard to understand will become clear as you make these changes in your living and look to Christ for encouragement. You should not be afraid to question what you think you understand to be fact. The disciples could easily have continued on the trip thinking that Jesus was angry with them for forgetting bread, and making excuses for themselves while mumbling and murmuring about how hard it was to be a Christian, but Jesus was kind to them; and so that they could go on to perfection, so they did not have to continue in their ignorance, so that they would be prepared for the future, He asked them to stop and consider for just a moment, "How is it that ye do not understand?

40. What is a man advantaged, if he gains the whole world, and is cast away?

Luke 9:25, "For what is a man advantaged, if he gain the whole world, and lose himself, or be cast away?"

To be cast away… What a thought! It seems the Scriptures give us two modes of damnation. One of which is to never be found or recovered from the sinful state into which we unalterably placed ourselves in our youth. Many continue in this way of carnality, seeking gain and betterment of themselves and their estates, but never dealing with the question of their basic depravity.

Ironically, their inherent knowledge of this depravity, or lacking, is the basis for the psychological need to advance, improve, and gain wealth, etc. Yet, this root cause is never dealt with, it is never even addressed. To consider this situation, is sad from Christian's viewpoint. We are amazed that some people never find, nor even search for, the wonderful gift of being touched by God's grace, thereby experiencing new birth by which old things are gone and "all things are become new!"

Job 8:20, "Behold, God will not cast away a perfect man." The other mode of damnation is the one mentioned here in Job and in our subject, and is termed being "cast away." In modern vernacular it would be termed "thrown away," like throwing away trash. In this case, the object in question has been examined and deemed worthless and tossed aside as useless, unusable, of no redemptive value. To apply this, look at the mental processes used for determining trash. For example: We find a magazine as we are cleaning. We pick it up to throw it away and we mentally sort through its pages remembering the information we read in it, and perhaps the pictures we saw in it. We wonder if it is worth saving as a reference, or for enjoying again, or giving to someone else that may enjoy it. At last we determine it has no use, no value, and we throw it away. It becomes trash.

To determine an old magazine to be trash is one thing, to apply that process to a human being is another. One decision is inconsequential; the other is tragic. For God to look through a life and see nothing worth saving or even of interest to Him, to see no sign of loyalty or true affection toward Him is sad on His behalf, but upon ours, it is frightening. How does a person find himself or herself in this state? How can we avoid such an event?

Jesus taught that those who seek to preserve the lower life would lose the higher life. He said in Luke 17:33, "Whosoever shall seek to save his life shall lose it; and whosoever shall lose his life shall preserve it." This concept is peculiar in regard to its appearance in all four of the Gospel records, as if it were a hallmark of His preaching. The concept appears in four different topics of Christ's teaching as well. It appears when He speaks of the risk of being killed as followers of Him, in Matthew 10:39, "He that findeth his life shall lose it: and he that loseth his life for my sake shall find it." It appears when He speaks of His own crucifixion in John 12:25, "He that loveth his life shall lose it; and he that hateth his life in this world shall keep it unto life eternal." When explaining that a person must deny himself, take up the cross and follow Him, He ends with, "For whosoever will save his life shall lose it: but whosoever will lose his life for my sake, the same shall save it." (Luke 9:24) And finally, after He rebukes Peter for suggesting the carnal way of making Christ king (by avoiding the cross), He explains, "For whosoever will save his life shall lose it; but whosoever shall lose his life for my sake and the gospel's, the same shall save it." (Mark 8:35)

A Closer Examination

Seeks, finds, saves, and loves: Notice the four transitive verbs used in these examples to describe preserving our life. Seeking, finding, and saving our lives are all acts of desperation because of the intrinsic knowledge that our lives are transitory, illusive, and fleeting. These three are acts we perform to make ourselves feel alive by evoking emotions. This often takes the form of entertainment of all sorts, watching sports, gossip, high-energy music; the list is too long and embarrassing to enumerate. The fact is, we are in a dying mode because of our sin. We don't like to face this and therefore we seek... and hope to find... and hope to save... ourselves.

The lesson we must learn is that we are dying. We must admit why and make preparation. Our lives are like an old pocket watch with a broken winding stem you would find in a musty old drawer. Unable to wind it, we helplessly only shake it...it ticks for a while...it stops. We shake it again. It's useless! It may run, but not long and never accurately.

If the worldly man reaches "success" in his attempts to save himself, the eventuality of his redemption becomes even more hopeless and less likely. For this causes in him the fourth condition Jesus described; he begins to love this life. If a man, yet in his sins, becomes successful in the world he becomes harder to win – if for no other reason, that he is seemingly "winning the game" and it is hard to convince him that he will ultimately lose everything. It is like trying to convince a gambler, as he drags his winnings across the table toward his chest, that the deck is marked or the dice are loaded. This delusion of winning is one of the reasons why Jesus said; "... Verily I say unto you, That a rich man shall hardly enter into the kingdom of heaven." (Matthew 19:23) When we are dealt into this game we need to realize, no one walks away a winner. The deck is marked; the dice are loaded. Note that all four of the acts – seeking, finding, saving, and loving our life in this world – all end with the same statement. Those seeking, finding, saving, and loving life... "shall lose it." All of these attempts to win, preserve, promote, and gain, end in loss.

This fourth condition (loving this life) is the most insidious one, as it affects the Christian as well. Even though you are well aware of your state of being, and after having committed your life to Christ, you may still fall into this trap. If you, as a Christian, find yourself seeking "life" (pleasure, entertainment, diversion) and find what you are looking for outside of the Christian experience, or you attempt to preserve, empower, lengthen, or enhance this lower life, you need to re-evaluate your Christian experience.

You must be vigilant and suspicious of all your motives and actions. You should, as a Christian, find Christ to be all-sufficient in the areas of pleasure and entertainment, and if you do, diversion will become ridiculous. Loving the lower (ego – animal) life affects Christians more so than the lives of the people of the world. (For it is the ONLY life the worldly man knows!) The apostle Paul said in 1 Corinthians 9:27, "But I keep under my body, and bring it into subjection: lest that by any means, when I have preached to others, I myself should be a castaway." Again we find the concept of being cast away.

Paul's concern in this area and his motivation for keeping his physical body under control was his fear of being cast away. There are prevalent in our Christian society, those who teach that there is nothing to fear in this area; but we cannot find that unconditional assurance in the Scriptures, nor in the Spirit within us.

The Scriptures and the Holy Spirit both witness to the necessity of a sober and diligent approach to the Christian life to enable us to have and hold this confidence steadfast unto the end.[45] Affection for the world makes us worthless to God, and His final evaluation will find in us no love for Him. "Love not the world, neither the things that are in the world. If any man love the world, the love of the Father is not in him." (1 John 2:15)

The Lord warned that you are not to give this life any consideration – even unto death. You are not to fear them who kill the body, "But I will forewarn you whom ye shall fear: Fear him, which after he hath killed hath power to cast into hell; yea, I say unto you, Fear him." (Luke 12:5) For what is a man advantaged, if he gain the whole world, and lose himself, or be cast away?

---

[45] Hebrews 3:14, "For we are made partakers of Christ, if we hold the beginning of our confidence stedfast unto the end;"

41.   Which of them would love him most?

Luke 7:40-42, "And Jesus answering said unto him, Simon, I have somewhat to say unto thee. And he saith, Master, say on. There was a certain creditor which had two debtors: the one owed five hundred pence, and the other fifty. And when they had nothing to pay, he frankly forgave them both. Tell me therefore, which of them will love him most?"

It is inevitable that our personal experiences with Christ will vary from person to person. Sometimes, especially when someone is trying to build a monolithic religion, it becomes a problem that all who come to Christ do not experience Him the same way. It cannot be avoided that those having full revelation of their wretched condition before their Judge will appreciate His forgiveness more than those who consider themselves to be relatively clean in His sight. In this story, Christ asks, "Which of them will love him most?" Both of the men in the story were absolved of their indebtedness to the King. Both received the same gift, but the value of the gift was different because of the assessment of debt owed by the recipient. Simon was struggling with comparisons. We all struggle with comparisons.

Let us digress to the incident that started all this comparing and doubt. "And one of the Pharisees desired him that he would eat with him. And he went into the Pharisee's house, and sat down to meat. And, behold, a woman in the city, which was a sinner, when she knew that Jesus sat at meat in the Pharisee's house, brought an alabaster box of ointment, And stood at his feet behind him weeping, and began to wash his feet with tears, and did wipe them with the hairs of her head, and kissed his feet, and anointed them with the ointment." (Luke 7:36-38)

This afternoon, Jesus was to eat with Simon the Pharisee. It is obvious that Jesus had won this Pharisee, and caring not for his reputation, Simon invited his Lord Christ to dinner. Prior to visiting Simon's house, we can safely assume that Jesus had met this woman before and imparted to her, forgiveness. It is not known for certain who she was. Some say that Simon the Pharisee was also a leper and that this account and the story of Simon the leper[46] coincide. Some say this woman was Mary Magdalene. Some say Mary the sister of Lazarus;[47] some say an unknown local girl. One thing is for sure, she certainly made a mark upon history[48] that will never be erased.

If we consider for a moment she *was* Mary of Magdala, or a woman very much like her, there was much to be forgiven, for out of Mary had come

---

[46] Matthew 26:6-7, Mark 14:3, "Now when Jesus was in Bethany, in the house of Simon the leper, There came unto him a woman having an alabaster box of very precious ointment, and poured it on his head, as he sat at meat."

[47] John 11:2, "(It was that Mary which anointed the Lord with ointment, and wiped his feet with her hair, whose brother Lazarus was sick)"

[48] Matthew 26:13, "Verily I say unto you, Wheresoever this gospel shall be preached in the whole world, there shall also this, that this woman hath done, be told for a memorial of her."

seven demons.[49] Her life was led in such a way as to finally become shattered by forces not understood; habits and compulsions untamed, and sin uncontrolled.

The Way Mary Saw It

Can we even imagine the quiet hours in this woman's life? Can we, for an instant, set aside our lives of ease, peace and plenty, and mentally place ourselves into her living torment? Can we imagine her waking in the middle of the night, when all was quiet and the hustle of life could no longer quell the voices and turmoil within her heart, when her conscience is at full volume and her mind races listing and re-listing all her wickedness and enumerating her sins? The hopelessness and helplessness of such a person, so far from her redeemer, would be more than we could endure. In a moment of unimaginable internal distress, we can easily imagine her looking heavenward, and crying, unable to even ask, and for what, she does not even know. One day, our Father heard her unspeakable prayer and guided Jesus to meet her. The rest, as they say, is history.

The scene changes to the house of Simon the Pharisee, a man of impeccable character, and high in the community. "…when she knew that Jesus sat at meat in the Pharisee's house, [she] brought an alabaster box of ointment…" Here she was, an uninvited woman, of no good reputation, approaching Jesus from behind. Jesus was obviously kneeling, as His feet were behind Him and out of His own sight. Simon sees her and rages within himself and even begins to doubt the Messiah's ability to perceive wickedness in the worst of people, because our Lord makes no mention of her, nor does He condemn her. Simon squirms and fidgets.

The tension is broken for a moment by Christ's statement, "Simon, I have something to say to you." He began, "There was a certain creditor which had two debtors…" Simon's mind reeled as he wondered what this parable could mean. As Jesus finished, Simon heard the question, "Which of them would love him most?" He answered almost without thinking, for the answer was so obvious. Simon answered and said, "I suppose that he, to whom he forgave most." Jesus said unto him, "Thou hast rightly judged." "Whew!" Simon thought, "That was close," but then the application of his answer started to become real to him.

Sometimes we are too quick to judge those who do not "do it the way we do," as less than we. Sometimes we are too quick to label those less animated than we are, as stodgy, stiff, or uncaring. We also call those, whose excitement and volume may exceed ours, as fanatical or superficial. Though we received the same grace and power from the same God, perhaps He found us at different stages of our degradation and sin. Or, it may be that we have never fully realized our true condition of sin. After all, from God's perspective, was

---

[49] Luke 8:2, Mark 16:9, "… Mary Magdalene, out of whom he had cast seven devils."

there really much difference in Simon the Pharisee and this woman of ill repute?

Awareness of the sin of which you have been forgiven, obviously, will make a great difference in your level of devotion. You should realize by now that this revelation of your condition before Christ found you, is highly valuable and could greatly effect your excitement, dedication, and commitment. Seek your Father for that revelation. Compare yourself to men like Job, Daniel, Noah, Moses, David, and others with whom your Father was pleased.

You will also begin to understand your true condition when you evaluate yourself in the light of the holiness, righteousness, and purity of the God you serve. After you have filled your mind and spirit with these Scriptural examples, you must turn to the Father and ask Him to make this fact real to you. As your heart opens to receive this revelation, you will change. You will change into another person. You will become a person who cannot look at others and condemn for you will be one who love loves much, because you now realize you were forgiven of much.

It is possible to be unaware of the total work of Christ in you; and it is possible to forget what Christ has done, but it is *impossible* to be fully aware of your condition and yet despise your fellow man who loves the Lord.

If you must make comparisons, here is one to make: After you are supernaturally enlightened to your previous condition, and after you realize the self-righteous delusion under which you have lived, you may then compare yourself to the way you were, to the former person you were – sanctimonious and blind – and ask, "Which of them... would love him most?"

42. *Seest thou this woman?*

Luke 7:44-48, "And he turned to the woman, and said unto Simon, Seest thou this woman? I entered into thine house, thou gavest me no water for my feet: but she hath washed my feet with tears, and wiped them with the hairs of her head. Thou gavest me no kiss: but this woman since the time I came in hath not ceased to kiss my feet. My head with oil thou didst not anoint: but this woman hath anointed my feet with ointment. Wherefore I say unto thee, Her sins, which are many, are forgiven; for she loved much: but to whom little is forgiven, the same loveth little. And he said unto her, Thy sins are forgiven."

Jesus visited the house of a Pharisee named Simon. While they sat there, a woman was found washing Jesus' feet and obviously weeping as she did so. She was despised in the eyes of the host and his contempt immediately caused him to question whether Jesus was who He claimed to be. "If He were a prophet," the Pharisee reasoned, "He would see what I see when He looks at this woman." Jesus could have answered, "I not only see what you see, I know what you can't see." Then Jesus looked to Simon and asked, "Do you see this woman?" Jesus then told a little story about two people being forgiven a debt that they could not pay, one of whom owed ten times more than the other. After the story, Jesus asked, "Which of them loved the creditor most?" Simon answers rightly, "The one that was forgiven most."

Sometimes we need to step out of our situation and be objective in judgment. We get so close to a situation that we become emotionally, or personally involved, and when people are close to us, we become border conscious, jealous, or comparative. Like otherwise friendly pups when at play, we may growl or snap at the feeding dish. Jesus asked, do you really see the person you condemn?

Do we see the *person* in the one whom we feel is an enemy, or a threat to us, the person we don't like, or avoid? "And as Jesus passed forth from thence, he saw a man, named Matthew, sitting at the receipt of custom: and he saith unto him, Follow me. And he arose, and followed him." Jesus saw a man – everyone else saw a tax collector. He saw a man – all of Israel saw nothing but a traitor. Christ saw a man – the Jews saw a thief. Jesus saw a man.

There is also a personal touch to this story that may escape us if we read it too quickly. As we look at the passage we are considering, notice the reference: (Matthew 9:9) the author of this passage is the man in the story. He knew personally the joy of being considered and evaluated without prejudice. Matthew was rejoicing, and here he is exclaiming, "He saw me!"

The practice of seeing without regard to political status or outward appearance is an attribute of God. Remember the story in 1 Samuel 16, "But the LORD said unto Samuel... for the LORD seeth not as man seeth; for man looketh on the outward appearance, but the LORD looketh on the heart." From the days of the Law that forbade the practice[50], all through the Scriptures, and even now within our own hearts, we know that it is wrong to judge a man by what we see on the outside. There are two main reasons for this. If read together, these reasons may sound contradictory; obviously they will require deeper thought than at first glance.

Deceitful men *can* control what you see on the outside. If a person wants to deceive you, he may be able to do so by showing you what he wants you to see. This deceit ranges from the way he dresses to showcasing his possessions. In this case, we should refer to the advice found in James 2:1-4, "My brethren, have not the faith of our Lord Jesus Christ, the Lord of glory, with respect of persons. For if there come unto your assembly a man with a gold ring, in goodly apparel, and there come in also a poor man in vile raiment; And ye have respect to him that weareth the gay clothing, and say unto him, Sit thou here in a good place; and say to the poor, Stand thou there, or sit here under my footstool: are ye not then partial in yourselves?" We actually reveal ourselves when we respect persons. We must admit, we only respect traits and features that we wish to be ascribed to ourselves.

Sinful men *cannot* control what you see on the outside. When a person is in sin or under the burden of disobedience to God, he is in bondage. He is in that condition because he has no control. We would be more likely to tolerate the drunk that stumbled into one of our Meetings and would extend compassion toward him (if only for the day), but the one with a sour disposition, or those who do not agree with us readily, are avoided. What about those who dress differently?

Most of the judgment we feel comes from a notion within us that says that they act this way or do something *purposefully*. We reason that it is their fault, but, we do so incorrectly, unjustly, and without the compassion that Christ has shown to us. Again we reveal ourselves in this.

We despise in others, the sins over which we gained control within our own strength and we feel it is reasonable to expect the same from them. When we feel this resentment, it is unjust and cruel; it should be a signal to us that we are operating on our own conation and within our own strength. It is then that our love is held in reserve and our judgment is freely dispensed. When a person has been fully delivered by the power of God, granted forgiveness for their sin, this person does not despise sin in others. It is then that our judgment is held in check and our love is dispensed.

So whether we respect what we see in the deceptive rich man, or despise what we see in the sinful ragged one, our response is apt to be influenced by our own greed, deliberate misleadings, or our own self-righteousness. Without the Lord Jesus' example, this revelation could be very

---

[50] Deuteronomy 1:17, "Ye shall not respect persons in judgment; but ye shall hear the small as well as the great; ye shall not be afraid of the face of man; for the judgment is God's: and the cause that is too hard for you, bring it unto me, and I will hear it."

depressing. The key is to operate only by true compassion -- not respect, but compassion for those who feign riches. Not judgment, but, compassion for those bound by sin – for both are qualities of which we have great need.

We can see the compassion in the Lord's actions on this day at Simon's house. Notice the reference says, He turned to her and said to Simon. He was not looking for a reaction from Simon. He was not testing him to see what expressions he may show. He was not really quizzing Simon, as much as He was expressing His sorrow for the lack of compassion Simon showed. Christ showed the same compassion toward both the rich and the rejected that day. He saw that both of them needed the same thing.

Forgiving one and teaching the other He reached out to both. We can see Jesus with one hand out to her and the other toward the Pharisee as He tries to connect the unsympathetic churchman to the one who needed the Church so desperately. Though Jesus' face was turned away, Simon can plainly hear the question that rung in his ears for the rest of the evening, "Can't your eyes see this poor woman?"

To see a person is not a gift to pray for, or an endowment to obtain supernaturally. It is an ability that lies within you if have truly experienced repentance, forgiveness, and justification. It requires only an accurate memory. "But call to remembrance the former days…"[51] and remember, "such were some of you: but ye are washed, but ye are sanctified, but ye are justified in the name of the Lord Jesus, and by the Spirit of our God."[52]

When you find yourself praying about your despite toward a brother who is not what you think he should be, you need to hear the Lord, who was able to see you through your sin, say, "Look deeper." When you encounter a woman who exemplifies, practices or even promotes, everything you stand against and you feel self-righteousness well up inside you, hear your Master ask within, "Do you see this woman?"

---

[51] Hebrews 10:32
[52] 1 Corinthians 6:11

43.   *What is written in the law? How readest thou?*

Luke 10:25-26, "And, behold, a certain lawyer stood up, and tempted him, saying, Master, what shall I do to inherit eternal life? He said unto him, What is written in the law? how readest thou?"

When Jesus was approached and asked a question about obtaining eternal life He always directed the seeker to the Law. This point is not palatable to the modern "saved by faith" preachers – they would rather quote "Ye must be born again." Although being born again, or more correctly "born from above," is a practical concept and a reality to the Christian, it was not the response to any question about obtaining eternal life. Jesus always directed those who sought eternal life to the Commandments of God. Why did He do that?

If someone came to you and asked, "How may I obtain eternal life," how would you answer? Jesus told such a person, "If thou wilt enter into life, keep the commandments." Mark 10:19, Matthew 19:17, Luke 18:20, all agree that His answer pointed the seeker in the direction of the Commandments, and promised, "Do this and you shall live" But where does grace and faith enter the equation? Paul states, "I do not frustrate the grace of God: for if righteousness come by the law, then Christ is dead in vain" (Galatians 2:21). How do we reconcile the two seemingly opposing concepts?

If a child came to you and expressed a desire to buy a house and support himself and asked how to accomplish this, your answer may be something like, "stay in school and get an education." If the same child came to you and asked the same question 15 years later your answer may be, "get a job and save your money." And later, as an adult, if asked how to buy a house, your advice would be quite different yet again. You could insist that these advices are contradictory and even wrong; after all, what in the world could going to school have to do with buying a house? But we all know how life consists of one thing that is built upon another, that is built upon another. We know the boy's dream and we know all the problems associated with it. We know the costs and responsibilities; and we know the joy of owning a home will only happen in its fullness when all of his experience, character, talents, and assets will eventually allow him the home he desired from his youth.

Simply put, Jesus was sending His young inquirer to school. Paul said, "Wherefore the law was our schoolmaster to bring us unto Christ, that we might be justified by faith." (Galatians 3:24) Jesus knew what steps were first, and then second, and so on. Knowing the man had need of what the law taught, He directed him there to learn it. The man responded, "I have already been to school and am ready to graduate!" Jesus said, "Okay, here is your final exam, go and sell all that you have and give it to the poor, then you may graduate from the Law." The man walked away – failing his exam.

Paul taught that faith is the proper end result of tutelage under the schoolmaster Law. He says, "But after that faith is come, we are no longer under a schoolmaster." (Galatians 3:25) Jesus taught us by this story that when we have graduated from this course in Law we would understand and obey the command to sell all we have and give it to the poor. On these grounds, most of us cannot claim to have learned all that the Law has to teach. Do you understand and obey the Commandments? Many Christians today don't even know the Commandments. How can you be sure you obey rules that you do not know?

Some think that the Law is impertinent to the "New Testament Christian." They say that Jesus taught that we are to only love God and our neighbor and thus did away with the Law. Some don't realize that Jesus quoted the Law when He said, "…thou shalt love thy neighbour as thyself…" (Leviticus 19:18) Paul continues this idea in Galatians 5:14, "For all the law is fulfilled in one word, even in this; Thou shalt love thy neighbour as thyself." What did he say was fulfilled? The Law. James learned this truth, for He wrote, "If ye fulfil the royal law according to the scripture, Thou shalt love thy neighbour as thyself, ye do well." (James 2:8) Paul confirms again, "Owe no man any thing, but to love one another: for he that loveth another hath fulfilled the law." (Romans 13:8) Has fulfilled what? What did he say was fulfilled when love was prime?

All through the Commandments of God we can see that the Schoolmaster, Law, has a wonderful lesson for us. The Law is not, and never has been, an enemy to Christ. Although some may feel that the Gospel offers no room to Commandment keeping, the opposite is true.

The Law, Our Schoolmaster

The schoolmaster, Law, is no more an enemy of faith than phonics is an enemy to reading. It is true that there may be no use in drilling in phonics after someone is proficient in reading, but the proficient reader would never set them aside. He would not withhold phonics from one who cannot read, nor would he have any reason to put phonics into disuse in his own life, and he certainly has no reason to despise them. Rather, you would think that they would be held in high esteem as a fundamental building block to his entire education!

Just so, Law should hold such a place in the heart of the Christian. The place that the Law of God has had to assume in the life of the modern believer is appalling. We have been given our diplomas by sinful, greedy men who have bypassed the Schoolmaster. We do not respect the Law of God because we did not come through the Law. We do not know what our God expects from us because we are unfamiliar with what He plainly asked of His people in the past.

The Law is not an enemy to the true Christian; it is an enemy to those who wish to do his own will. It has value and is due a respect that it does not receive in modern churches. The modern Christian wrings his hands in prayer asking God to reveal His will to him, give him instruction, or guide him in his everyday life, all the while his heavenly Father's will is plainly written in the book that he carries with him, and yet ignored, put into disuse, and in some cases even despised. We act as foolish as an educated man, fully graduated, who now despises the teachers who taught him, when we turn our backs on the holy Commandments of God and say they are no longer applicable, useful, or binding.

How is it that we despise our Schoolmaster who brought us to Christ? It is because many of us did not come to Christ through the Law, we came another way. We came through the school that did not teach phonics. We leaned by rote and sight and memory. We cannot read any word we see; we only know what we were taught; we cannot learn for ourselves. We learned the names for every word; we learned from men who supposedly knew. We did not come the way Jesus taught; we came via the shortcut. We have no respect for the Law because it was never our Schoolmaster! Out of the hundreds listed, how many Laws of God do we know? Granted, that may be unfair. That would be like asking a graduate to copy out the periodic table from his chemistry class, but can we even recall the Ten Commandments? Many modern Christians do not even read the Old Testament, thinking its words irrelevant.

The trouble is that most of us are not 4.0 graduates. I submit that we need not be straight-A students of the Law to respect it, but I find it hard to believe that we possess a foundational faith if we cannot even pass a basic exam of fundamentals. We may not have misgiving about a man's education because he cannot remember the atomic number of uranium, but we may well hold his education in doubt if he cannot recite his ABC's.

If you cannot pass the basic exam that Jesus gave this rich young ruler, you must surmise that your education has suffered gaps, came from the wrong source, or was altogether faulty. Perhaps you dropped out early, shortcut or cheated the system, or it may be that you were "socially promoted" by unscrupulous teachers. It may be that you have never even enrolled, but it is certain that you didn't graduate with honors if you cannot pass the exam. Maybe you need to look at the curriculum again and do some lessons.

Do you obey the Law in your everyday life or do you count on "grace" to cover for you? Have you done your duty or are you depending on the love of God to overlook your shortcomings? Do you really love your neighbor as much as you love yourself? Do you love the Lord with all your heart, soul, mind and strength? Was the Law ever your schoolmaster, or did you come to graduate another way?

Are you ready? Here is your exam: "What is written in the law? How readest thou?"

44. *Doth he not leave the ninety and nine?*

How think ye? What man of you, having an hundred sheep, if he lose one of them or one of them be gone astray, doth he not leave the ninety and nine in the wilderness, and goeth into the mountains, and seeketh after that which is lost, or that which is gone astray until he find it? Matthew 18:12 Luke 15:4 (Combined)

This Scripture is often used to show the love Christ has for the lost (and rightfully so for He truly does), but, let's look at a part of the question that is usually overlooked: "Doth he not leave the ninety and nine?"

Can you see the disparity of the ministry of modern Christianity in its relation to the ministry of the Christ of whom we read in Scripture? That difference is, namely, the interest in the ninety and nine. Contrary to the ministry of Christ, we tend to build our Meetings and churches by focusing our attention upon the fold, neglecting the strays.

Look at the words Jesus used to describe the characters in this example. It is an interesting study. The one sheep, for which the shepherd is searching, is described in Luke as "lost" as if the herdsman lost track of him. Whether by negligence or exercising less than due diligence, one of them is missing. The other description given is that the sheep has "gone astray," as if it has wandered against the advice or leading of the shepherd. So whether the wandering and subsequent separation are by choice, ignorance, or enticement, the sheep is outside the security of the fold, the protection of the shepherd, and it is likely that its life is in danger.

On this side of the metaphor (in the assembly of believers) there are plenty of discouraged, hurt, disenchanted, and dismayed "lost sheep" that have been left to the wolves while we focus our attention on our ninety and nine. This practice is against all we find in the Scriptures pertaining to our commission and duty. We might claim that Jesus taught that He was the Shepherd and that He "has lost none" that came to Him, and we would be right. Referring to John 18:9 we find, "That the saying might be fulfilled, which he spake, Of them which thou gavest me have I lost none."

Consider for a moment the concept taught in this story, *"What man of you, having an hundred sheep, if he lose one of them, doth not leave the ninety and nine in the wilderness, and go after that which is lost, until he find it?"* We know that Jesus is the Good Shepherd and that we are **not** the shepherds of His flock, but the concept applies to good stewardship as well as good shepherding. As stewards and keepers of our fellow man we must ask, which is better, a large congregation of sheep that have no tendency to wander, or a sheepfold, no matter how small, about which we may claim, "We have lost none"?

When we focus inwardly, toward ourselves, it becomes a problem globally as well. Bible schools are pouring out preachers, pastors and counselors, music ministers, song leaders, Bible teachers and theologians onto the already saturated soil of the United States and neglecting the parched lands abroad. We have become "intro-nutritive," (if you will accept this word) and by doing so we are making mockery of the question, "Doth not he leave the ninety and nine?" We must answer truthfully, "No, he does not." We must answer, "He stays with the ninety and nine, feeds them and forgets the one." For, (their actions say) "There are more where that came from."

Why is this tragedy so? Because we have twisted our theology and made no room for love. We do not feel responsibility for the single one who has strayed because we have conveniently transferred that obligation, either to the Lord, (and expect Him to convince and caution and comfort the lost lambs of our Meetings) or we have transferred the responsibility to the lost lamb itself, with a "serves them right" attitude. May God have mercy on us.

The only indicators that Christ has commenced our conversion were that we would know by the love we have for God, the Holy Spirit witnessing in us and that we keep his Commandments[53] – and that the world would know by the love we have, one for another. "... By this shall all men know that ye are my disciples, if ye have love one to another." (John 13:35)

We need to be blameless in this area and stop this reprehensible practice. The only way to do so is to love these lost ones of our fold. 1 Thessalonians 3:12-13 says, "... abound in love one toward another...To the end he may stablish your hearts unblameable in holiness before God, even our Father, at the coming of our Lord Jesus Christ..."

Again our assurance of indeed being in Christ is coupled with the love we have for the brethren and the Holy Spirit within. In the Scripture 1 John 4:11-13, "Beloved, if God so loved us, we ought also to love one another...If we love one another, God dwelleth in us, and his love is perfected in us. Hereby know we that we dwell in him, and he in us, because he hath given us of his Spirit."

Again we are asked the important question by James, "If a brother or sister be naked, and destitute of daily food and ...ye give them not those things which are needful to the body, what doth it profit, my brethren, though a man say he hath faith, and have not works? Can faith save him?" (James 2:14-16, Arranged by thought)

Again, Paul, teaching on the restoration of lost or fallen lambs does so with this advice: "Brethren, if a man be overtaken in a fault, ye which are spiritual, restore such an one in the spirit of meekness; considering thyself, lest thou also be tempted." (Galatians 6:1)

Again a question by John, "But whoso hath this world's good, and seeth his brother have need, and shutteth up his bowels of compassion from him, how dwelleth the love of God in him?" (1 John 3:17)

---

[53] 1 John 2:3, "And hereby we do know that we know him, if we keep his commandments."
1 John 5:2, "By this we know that we love the children of God, when we love God, and keep his commandments."

Our Brethren

The conventional church tries to apply the Scriptures above to the homeless, the poor and the indigent, attempting to show ourselves as obedient servants, thinking the paucity of relief we have offered the poor would somehow justify us.

We must note however, that all these Scriptures, and many others, are plainly speaking of a brother or sister. It is not the wayfarer or the stranger who has tumbled into the crevasse; it is our brother or sister who has fallen. It is not the drunk or drug addict for whose life we will be held responsible as hirelings in Christ's flock, it is our fellows, our friends, our neighbors, who have fallen and were never attended who will sully our faces in the judgment. If we took our Christian family more seriously and felt the sorrow that the Shepherd feels, our attitude would change toward those who are out of the way.

As the evening falls the Shepherd counts his flock. Ninety-eight... ninety-nine... ... ... he starts to panic and counts again. Ninety-nine! He runs toward the canyon and between the howls of the wolf he hears a faint bleating. He glances at the flock that is bedding down for the night and looks into the dark canyon.

This is exactly where you stand when you see an empty place beside you in your Meetings for worship where your brother in Christ used to be. Friend, hear the bleating for help echo through the canyons of sin, and leave the ninety and nine. Take the risk and venture out to save your brother.

If you only could feel the fear and loneliness of these lost ones who look around to find no one who cares, it would bring about in your mind an altered list of priorities, a wholly different agenda by which your life would be scheduled, and you would certainly suffer less shame when you read Scriptures as the ones above.

More importantly, you would have a much less embarrassing answer to offer the Lord when asked, "Doth not a man leave the ninety and nine and search till he finds the stray?"

45. Know ye not this parable? How then will ye know all parables?

Mark 4:13, "And he said unto them, and how then will ye know all parables?"

Jesus had just finished teaching the parable of the sower. This parable teaches that the word is like broadcast seed and that its production is commensurate with the soil in which it is sewn. The parable is found in several of the Gospels – Matthew 13:1-53, Mark 4:1-34, Luke 8:4-18. This is a good amount of reading but well worth the reader's time. Jesus warned us that if we did not know this parable we were not likely to know any. This is a dire warning to be sure. From His statement, we can logically conclude that this would be the place to start to understand all parables, but, unfortunately, it seldom is. What is the lesson we are to learn so that we will know "how to hear"?

"Keep" the Word

In His explanation of the parable of the sower, Jesus points out certain foibles in our life that corrupt the communication of Spiritual truths through parables, such as "keeping" the word that was sown. We must not let Satan take away the word that was sown in our heart. Keeping the Word of God need not be considered some dramatic or drastic measure; neither should it be necessarily a supernatural occurrence. It may be simply taking the time and application of diligence in reading the Scriptures and spending time in quiet before the Lord. Sometimes we simply forget what the Lord impressed upon us at a particular time; and because we were too busy, we did not meditate upon it and hear it in its fullest. Neither did we simply write it down.

Sometimes the Lord speaks to us (the true Word of God) when we are busy going about life. Answers for which we have sought His wisdom may come to us at any time, and we must therefore, at all times, be ready to receive the Word of God. If we forget, or we do not take the time to receive the Word in its fullest, our slothful and disorganized lives may be the cause of our own digression. Diligence must be used here to retain the word.

Persecution

Arguments are sometimes brought against revelation. God may reveal truth to someone, and another may argue that it goes against tradition or his understanding. Your revelation may be put to the test at this point. You may be asked hard (and sometimes cruel) questions, like "Do you think that all of the forefathers were wrong and you are right?" Or, your detractors may ask if you think that God has changed. They may make arguments about remaining true to tradition or family. They may even "prove" their point with misapplied

Scripture, or they say in so many words, "Well, you can believe what you want but I'm not going to change."

In effect they are ostracizing you, setting you aside and you now face a choice of loneliness with your revelation or fellowship without it. The hot sun is coming up on your new seed. Let your root of revelation run deep, where it can find water from below. Know your God, know His voice, and know His Scriptures. "Yet hath he not root in himself, but dureth for a while: for when tribulation or persecution ariseth because of the word, by and by he is offended." (Matthew 13:21) To avoid these arguments is most beneficial. If we give it up – if we give in – that word will be scorched, and it will wither and die. Which brings us to the second point in learning – How to hear.

Dealing with persecution and temptation has taken many forms over the years. Our forefathers would likely laugh (or perhaps cry) at what makes us knuckle-under today. The slightest social persecution, even among friends, causes us to become mumbling, stuttering cowards. Few of us stand for what we believe and; therefore, many good ideas, answers for today's questions, and perfectly sound doctrines are lost forever. Do we really believe in continuing revelation or do we not. Do we really believe that God speaks to us today or don't we? Can it be that we believe our forefathers were infallible... and possessed all of the knowledge of God... and that they were incapable of being wrong... on any and all matters?

The apostles had the ability and commission to write Scripture, we do not. However, if we have had revealed to us ideas within the framework of honestly interpreted Scripture, we should not cower and tremble before our peers. Great men of reformation, from apostolic times until now, stood upon their revelation, against ALL their peers, against EVERY church and ALL conventional thinking.

The Scriptures witnessed to what was revealed to them, and though it may be widely accepted today, it was NOT then. Their insistence on their revelation brought many reformers to the point of death and abandonment. We should not fear what man will say or do; we should quake at the prospect of answering to a living God for our reluctance to obey, preach and be willing to die for Truth.

The Cares of the World

The third point is, resisting the cares of this world. We become so busy and concerned with making a living we find ourselves doing so at the cost of life itself. We readily see the ebbing of happiness and health as we push our way through this world, but I wonder if we are aware of the dulling of our ears and the cataracts of care that impairs our spiritual vision? We are absorbed in a world that constantly offers us things – and shames those who do not have them. We are bombarded by gifts and rewards and compelled to give them in return for nearly any and every occasion. We are compelled to be intrigued with great bargains and with getting something for nothing, lotteries, gaming, raffles, door prizes, awards, rebates, discounts, refunds, coupons, sales, giveaways, offers, etc.

All these snares are based in an importance of money and the possession of things. This is the most influential yet of the dangers about which Christ warned us in the parable of the sower. It is a claim on our soul that we will not easily shake. As a dieter cannot quit eating altogether, but must daily deal with food truly, and honestly, even so must all of us deal with money.

There are those who try to distinguish money from the love of money. They do this to justify their greed that they think they have under control. They call money "good" but only the love of it they call "bad." I ask you, how can the love of something that is wholly good, be evil? If we choose to be wary of it altogether we will be much safer. Money is an evil that must be used everyday in order to live. It will take supernatural talent and ability to maintain your balance. Do not take this for granted or count it a light thing.

Money will try you every time you have to use it. You must take it one instance at a time, seeking God's help to deal with this "necessary" evil. Or as Jesus put it, "[What is] sufficient unto the day is the evil thereof." Jesus taught that what you need to live everyday is all the "evil" you can deal with on daily basis. After He taught not to be concerned with what you will eat and what you will wear, He said, "Take therefore no thought for the morrow: for the morrow shall take thought for the things of itself." (Matthew 6:34)

How you hear the Word of God has little to do with your physical ears. It really has more to do with the life and body to which these ears are attached. Those who fail in any areas outlined by Christ in the parable of the sower have prepared themselves to misunderstand, misapply, and misconstrue His teaching – not only in this parable but in ALL parables.

You may be viewing here a main cause of the anemic church we all witness in the twenty-first century. Modern society majors in the lust of the eye, lust of the flesh, and pride of life. Advertising is ineffectual without being able to play upon all of these flaws in human character. The pride some take in being a part of the crowd, coupled with the fear of being alone, was introduced and enforced from a young age, and the idea is refreshed daily in the media.

Selfishness and pride are played upon in marketing and focused upon our children and encouraged throughout their school years. How will they learn to stand for their individual thought if being one of the crowd is made so important to them?

Much is owed to the men and women of the past for whom adherence to their revelation was a matter of honor and character and truth. These are things that hinder understanding of God's voice within. Failure in the three areas just discussed is a prime cause for misunderstanding of doctrine, of Scripture, and one another.

You must have properly prepared soil for the seed of the Word of God to take root and grow. To do that, you must take heed "how you hear," because if we miss these points of warning outlined in the parable of the sower... "How then will ye know all parables?"

154

46.   *Why callest thou me good?*

Matthew 19:17, Mark 10:18, Luke 18:19 "...one came and said unto him, Good Master, what good thing shall I do, that I may have eternal life? And he said unto him, Why callest thou me good? there is none good but one, that is, God: but if thou wilt enter into life, keep the commandments..."

Many theories have been applied to this text to explain Christ's question. It puzzles many that Jesus did not claim goodness to describe Himself; for by any definition of "good" we could certainly say that Jesus could declare the attribute for Himself. Why then did He reject the description?

There are some who claim that He was making a statement of divinity. Some say that because He said that He is good proves that He is God. So the question, "Why callest thou me good, there is none good but God?" is, in other words, the statement, "You call me good because I am good and none is good but God, therefore I am God." However, this approach is more like a riddle than the forthright statement usually heard from our Savior. It is not congruent with the "woman at the well" experience where Jesus plainly said, "I am He"[54] and the event with Bartimaeus where He claimed outright to be Messiah, "It is He that talketh with thee."[55] He was not shy, fearing to say exactly what He meant. The words Jesus heard, and what He thought, and what He subsequently said that day, was more intricate than mere riddles that make furtive claims of divinity.

The subject at hand was perfection, not the goodness (or Divinity) of Christ. Jesus was not showing humility or admitting imperfection. He was catching and exposing a preconceived notion with which this man was fascinated. The conversation in today's vernacular might be like this: "Reverend, what perfect deed must I do to be saved?" Jesus would answer, "Why do you call me reverend? There is none worthy of reverence except God. And do you think perfect deeds will save you? You cannot do perfect deeds." The man would say, "I have kept all the Commandments from my youth!" Jesus would respond, "Yes, but perfection requires that you deny yourself the things you want, and do only the things I want." And then, realizing that he was not willing to do this, the rich man would leave, sorrowfully regretting his lack of character.

This story appears in three Gospels and does not read identically in Greek or in English. Luke and Mark's account say the ruler asked after Christ calling Him "Good Master," but Matthews' Greek text does not call Him "Good Master" at all. Obviously, the King James translators (and others)

---

[54] John 4:25-26, "The woman saith unto him, I know that Messias cometh, which is called Christ: when he is come, he will tell us all things. Jesus saith unto her, I that speak unto thee am he."

[55] John 9:35-38, "Jesus heard that they had cast him out; and when he had found him, he said unto him, Dost thou believe on the Son of God? He answered and said, Who is he, Lord, that I might believe on him? And Jesus said unto him, Thou hast both seen him, and it is he that talketh with thee. And he said, Lord, I believe. And he worshipped him."

conferring with each other, added the word "good" anyway. Also, Matthews' account attributes the word "good" to the thing to be done rather than to "teacher", and asks, "What good thing must I do?" The Amplified Bible gives a rendition true to the Greek. It reads, "...Teacher, what excellent and perfectly and essentially good deed must I do to possess eternal life?" To which Jesus responded, "Why do you ask after the perfect and essentially good? There is none that is perfectly and essentially good except the one God."[56] This translation makes it easy to understand why He later said to the man, "If thou wilt be perfect, sell all you have and give it to the poor."

We must be careful to listen to what we say. Sometimes our speech gives us away. We may hear someone ask, "How can I improve my prayer-life," or "What project can our group take on," or "What can we do to increase the attendance of Meeting?" Just as Jesus asked why are you inquiring about doing good, we need to ask ourselves, "Why are we asking about good deeds?" What do we want from a good prayer-life, a good deed project, or a larger Meeting? Perhaps we are concerned that our relationship to God is not as it should be.

Do-goodism

It may be that we Quakers may suffer with this desire to "do good" more than most. We have less hoopla and noise to cover up the voids and gaps in our personal spirituality. When there are no songs, sermons, services and programs present to keep our minds off of our personal condition, our appearance before God becomes glaringly apparent in quiet meditation. The distance we feel from God in times of our spiritual dryness should only cause us to lean toward Him and wait for Him. However, sometimes we reason that some action is in order. We may think that if we do some good thing we will grow more spiritual or less worldly, thus alleviating our "dryness."

When this search begins for something to do, we often give away our inmost fear and concern when we ask, "What can we do..." We must be careful not to expect ourselves to be accepted because of good works – for that will never happen. Acceptance only is achieved when we respond to God's call to Himself in faith. We must, as all Christians, be careful to expect our sanctification to come only from our baptism in the Spirit and never from a change of dress or language. The forgiveness of God comes at His gracious declaration, in response to our empty-handed plea and is never meted out according to our catalogue of good deeds. Do these things really need to be said? Perhaps we need to hear them from time to time – just as a reminder.

We should remind ourselves of these things in periods of dryness and put a guard on our mouth, so that we do not insult the grace of God by asking what "good thing" we can do. We should weigh everything we say and consider the good works as complimenting rather than providing our sanctification, forgiveness, and acceptance.

---

[56] Amplified Bible –Zondervan – Copyright 1987

Our speech gives us away when we speak of Christ, too. He asked, "Why callest thou me good?" There is a tendency to transfer attributes to people we admire or dislike intensely. These attributes can include qualities to which we aspire, or faults of which we are ashamed, respectively. Jesus noticed the word "good" was attributed to Him and asked the man about it. He found, by inquiry, that this man had a hang-up about doing good deeds and that he was mistaken about the power of good works to bring about eternal life. We often hear people describe the Christ who they know, with attributes that are important to them.

Some attribute qualities like mercy or kindness to Christ because they have none within themselves, or they consider it a desirable trait. People, yet in sin, who despise Christ, consider Him to be unfair only because of the flaws and unfairness in themselves. There are those who have trouble controlling their tempers, who love to recite the cat-o-nine-tails incident in the Temple.[57] We can tell a lot about ourselves by listening to our own prayers, our conversations with each other, and by noting the qualities we attribute to those we admire and the faults we find in our enemies.

Jesus used this kind of psychology (though it was not called that) in several instances. We may learn a great deal by taking time and asking ourselves simple questions like, "Why do I feel this way? Why do I like this person and not that one? What am I desiring and why?" While in prayer and meditation, your mind can aggravate you by carrying you away to undesired thoughts. These "rabbit trails" however, are deserving of your deliberate consideration. Your quiet hours are the perfect time to honestly investigate your interests. You should leave no thought uninvestigated, but bring all under scrutiny "...bringing into captivity every thought to the obedience of Christ." (2 Corinthians 10) One of these excursions into your thoughts may bring to light a solution to a problem you have wrestled with for years. Answers to your basic psychological needs, exposure of your inmost wicked condition, and revelation into your inner self can all be known from a simple question asked at the right time!

How can Christ speak to your condition if you don't take time to know what your condition is? Realization and revelation occur to you about problems you didn't even know that you had ten minutes before! How does Jesus do that? This same delicious thought may have occurred to a rich young man 2000 years ago, somewhere in the Middle East, as he walked home with his head down and considered, probably for the first time in his life, that he had a problem with money, things, security, and pride – all because a teacher from Galilee asked, "Why callest thou me good?"

---

[57] John 2:13-21

47. How is it that ye do not discern this time?

Luke 12:54-56, "When ye see a cloud rise out of the west, straightway ye say, There cometh a shower; and so it is. And when ye see the south wind blow, ye say, There will be heat; and it cometh to pass. Ye hypocrites, ye can discern the face of the sky and of the earth; but how is it that ye do not discern this time?"

Matthew 16:2-3, "He answered and said unto them, When it is evening, ye say, It will be fair weather: for the sky is red. And in the morning, It will be foul weather to day: for the sky is red and lowring. O ye hypocrites, ye can discern the face of the sky; but can ye not discern the signs of the times?"

Meteorology is an interesting science but not an exact one. I hear that a forecaster's accuracy, on a national average, is somewhere around 40 percent. In the days of Jesus, a one-day forecast was all that was expected. It was experience that taught them that if the sky was red and getting lower that it meant foul weather was coming. Earlier generations would teach the signs of the heavens to the newer ones. Also, they would predict seasons through signs of nature. Have we not all marveled as we listened to the older generation predict a colder than normal winter, or a dryer than normal summer by looking at birds, squirrels and wooly worms? Jesus' question still has merit and is well worth answering. Why don't we discern the signs of the times like we do the weather?

Prediction and forecasts are based upon the premise that we must look backward to accurately look forward. Weather prediction is anchored in a simple fact: that the laws of physics are immutable and the same conditions that caused certain effects in the past will cause the same effects in the future. These unchangeable laws are the basis of prediction. If, for example, water froze at 32 degrees today and at 45 degrees tomorrow, weather forecasting would be difficult, to say the least.

Because our God has said, "I am the LORD, I change not"[58] we can, in like manner, predict His responses to our actions and conditions. God's Law is also immutable, even more so than the laws of physics, for the laws of physics are subject to Him and His Law is not subject to anything. We serve an unchangeable God who feels the same way today about mankind as He did in the past, with one exception: now, the sin of man has caused the undeserved death of His son. As Paul the apostle said, about the times in mankind's unenlightened past, "...the times of this ignorance God winked at; but now [He] commandeth all men every where to repent: Because he hath appointed a day, in the which he will judge the world in righteousness by [Jesus Christ]." (Acts 17:30-31 Emphasis added). Judgment is surer today than ever.

---

[58] Malachi 3:6

On Any Street

"Looks like rain," a passer-by says to you as you meet by chance and you answer, "Yep, looks like a gully-washer!" No argument between you exists because the signs are obvious to anyone. Now, at the end of this sultry day, you feel the river of cool air that rushes past as the warm moist sky is boiling with low, blue-gray clouds. Lightening can be seen beneath them in the distance and low rumblings of thunder are felt more than heard. The wind elevates debris all around that had been perfectly content to lie in their places for days before. Folks who saw a flash out of a corner of their eye are now walking in a half-run, head down, only glancing upward to see the threatening sky over their heads. Now, with their shoulders raised to their ears, they reach for their collars instinctively as a second later a clap of nearby thunder is heard and the pelting rain is heard on nearby hot tin roofs. The dusty streets are cleared of unprepared people and doors and windows slam as the sun-parched concrete prepares to drink the first drops that appear.

We cannot look at the sky and see it red and lowering and not think of rain. Yet, we look at the world around us and pay no mind to our imminent future. We see the clouds gather, but we make no preparations. We see we are unprepared for judgment, but we make no changes. The system to bring about the surest of destruction is being put into place, but we do not warn our children. We read our Scripture's warning, but we continue living as we feel is best. What do you need to see to believe that the time is short? Matthew 24 reads like a checklist: wars, famine, earthquakes, false prophets, etc. What will it take for the urgency of this hour to overtake you?

Look at some of the events in our day:

o The God and Creator of the earth is impugned and ridiculed daily in every media form, and in our institutes of higher learning. In the schools that teach our tiny, precious ones they are taught to worship the earth while forbidden to mention God as the creator of it. We who worship God are considered unbalanced and scrutinized for aberrant conduct. Children are encouraged to report this behavior in their parents.

o So-called Christians complain that the Ten Commandments are not allowed on the walls of our schools or in our courtrooms, but they do not teach them in their churches or in their homes. The right to discipline our children hangs delicately upon the judgment of ungodly persons and our children's very presence in our home is only at the authorities' capricious wills.

o Churches are considered social clubs and tax shelters in the eyes of most of the world and as "threats to democracy" to the rest. Pornography is freedom of speech. Feces spread on canvas is art. War is peacekeeping. Peace is compromise.

o For many, the safest place to be is under the care of the US government, and the womb of today's mothers is the most dangerous. After a person is born, this physical life is considered supreme and its preservation and prolongation is most important over all we do. Therefore, "right" and "good" are defined only by whatever makes our lives on this earth prosperous, better, happier, healthier, and longer.

o Only that which has monetary value is precious. Our only societal improvements over the last half-century are technological ones. (viz. the paint on our houses now lasts longer than the families inside them.)

o The world now totters on nuclear or biological disaster held in check only by the conscience of terrorists and the leadership worldwide is migrating to the ungodly, the militant, the inhumane, and the insane.

o "Character" has degraded to an indefinable political buzzword. "Loyalty" has been demoted to being true to your school, football team, or favorite brand names or labels. Being "ethnically sensitive" is more important than being sensitive to what is ethical. Truth is relative.

o Education holds all the promises. All hope seems to be in our good health. The psychologist and pharmacist have replaced the prophet and apostle. Chemicals and lies are preferred over repentance and faith to answer to life's problems.

o Spirituality and the glorious new life in Christ have been reduced to occupy the same appraisal, in the minds of the world, as voodoo, astrology, tarot cards, mind games or party tricks.

How is it you can discern the signs in the sky, but you do not discern the signs of the times?

III Days of Opposition

"The Christian ideal has not been tried and found wanting. It has been found difficult; and left untried."

G. K. Chesterton
(1874–1936)
British author.
What's Wrong with the World

48. *Suppose ye that I am come to give peace on earth?*

Matthew 10:34, "Think not that I am come to send peace on earth: I came not to send peace, but a sword."

Luke 12:51, "Suppose ye that I am come to give peace on earth? I tell you, Nay; but rather division:"

This statement could probably stand as one of the most disappointing of all Jesus ever said. All of us want the presence of Christ to solve the turmoil in our lives, and in our families, not create more of it. We want the reign of Christ to bring peace to our lives and indeed to the whole earth, not create division. We are always surprised at these words no matter how familiar they are to us. There is, in all of us who know Christ, a longing for the day when all will be put right; when there will be no inequities, no evil, no turmoil, no heartache, or sorrow. Jesus sensed this in the disciples of his day and wanted them to know that day had not come – not yet. We are to strive toward that goal now. We are to stand in the gap between wickedness and justice, but most of all, it will be the day of Christ that will usher into the earth a time that all inequities will be set straight, fairness will become the norm, and goodness – commonplace.

Jesus wanted us to be under no delusions that His presence in the world (or in us) would bring about any external peace. Contrariwise, He taught in no uncertain terms that life would become more difficult as we represent Christ's presence here. "You will be hated of all men" He told us. He made it clear that, "The world will hate you because you are not of the world." Words like "persecution," "hate" and "tribulation" were common when forecasting how the world would treat us; and words like "love," "kindness," and "forgiveness," followed by orders to do good were the words used to describe our relation and response to the world.

Knowing this fact, we should not be depressed when our relation to the world becomes rocky, uncomfortable, or even combative. Rather, we should feel great concern when enmity with the world does not exist. The world's philosophy is similar to ours insofar as it desires peace and harmony. However, these two philosophies, these two worldviews are so entirely different they cannot exist together except by short acquaintance. They have different origins, plans of execution, and although they may resemble each other at the beginning, they ultimately end at different goals. Sometimes we are fooled by the talk coming from the world that sounds like solid and sound theology and we may briefly think we are brothers, later, we find that our two ways just momentarily met on the same road only to part again at the next fork. We must make sure we don't follow them at the fork in the road, but make certain our path is the one on which we were instructed to walk.

We must remain true to our Pilot, focus upon His goal, and keep it clearly in mind. Though they may briefly appear to be similar, the world's objective of peace and our goal are not the same. Remember, we have not been given a goal to achieve – but a path to walk, a Savior to follow, a narrow road. Jesus emphasized the "the way" not the goal. As a matter of fact His words were clear, "He that... climbeth up some other way, the same is a thief and a robber." (John 10:1)

Whose Job Is It?

Peace is not our goal. This may shock some, but it is true nonetheless. Peace is *our Lord's* goal and it is *He* who will bring it to pass. Remember, peace, as well as it is understood, is essentially everyone's desire. Excepting the insane or mercenary, the idea of war is repulsive to any thinking person. But the responsibility of peace lies with the Prince of Peace alone.

When we try to cause peace we may easily confuse the presence of peace with the absence of an armed conflict. We must, as slaves of Christ, be more humble in our understanding of what peace is and how it is accomplished. Also, we should be careful when we join hands with those who employ an anti-war mentality yet show no submission to God. The viewpoint of those who honor life and limb is not to be considered the same philosophy as those who honor God. From a distance they look as though they are the same but it comes down to a matter of authority. We will be disappointed if we try to use the anti-war strategy as a common chord to harmonize the ministry of a holy, sovereign God with the efforts of a sinful, selfish world.

What is the main difference? Many anti-war proponents feel peace is accomplished by never addressing the line of controversy. This line marks the point at which either, or both, will abandon the peace effort and resort to force. This line, either ignored or purposefully avoided, will frustrate and exacerbate the tension between antagonists. The enterprise then becomes a matter of effort upon the peacemaker to maintain talks and diplomacy to keep in check ever-increasing anger and hostility – an impossible task. All opponents stare at the line they have drawn and diplomatically try to avoid speaking of it and may even consent to moving it forward and backward from time to time, but the line remains.

Everyone has these lines; they are just drawn at different places. As servants of God we are not to pretend these lines do not exist but are to erase such lines. We are to teach that all men should work toward his brother's welfare, to allow himself to be cheated, to give more than is expected, and lay down his life for his friend. The ministry of Jesus is not verified in His people by peace and harmony left in their wake, but Christ's ministry is accomplished by the love His people show for their enemies and in those who unselfishly do exactly as they are led.

Some are willing to kill for peace – they are easy to find – the standard "warmonger." There is a better sort who is willing to live for peace. Though misguided in many areas of endeavor, their goal is admirable, but usually, their efforts are disappointing and less than effective. There are too few of these. Then there are those who are willing to die for peace. A man willing to die for you will not quibble if you steal his stuff, or take his land. If it is our sincere goal to be a minister to every man, to give more than we are asked, all we have is essentially theirs anyway. True peace is absence of war, not in a man's country, but in a man's heart.

Jesus said, "I came not to bring peace, but a sword." Though it would be difficult and highly argumentative to show examples, it cannot be said that all war is wrong. We may witness within our Spirit that this specific war is wrong or we may intuit by the Spirit of God that that particular military action is wrong, but we cannot attach a judgment of God upon all war by calling all war "wrong." We must live moment to moment and let opinions develop through fellowship with Christ. Thereby, we can only say that warring is wrong for us personally and that we cannot participate. We make decisions, consult our innermost feelings, and through fellowship with Christ and from these conversations we develop opinions.

Many of us make determinations before we know anything to be fact, and often before we have consulted our Lord. To be true to Christ as head of the Church, we cannot make a general, sweeping statement like "All war is wrong." One day, according to Scripture there will be a massive war confronting evil. The Commander in Chief of which will be Christ. If Christ has revealed to you that war is wrong then by all means speak it as your vision, understanding that your revelation was not given to all nor is there a favorable reference to unilateral disarmament recorded in Scripture.

Politics make strange bedfellows. If you push an idea of peace you may ally yourself with persons of no Spirit, persons of dubious character, perhaps persons not humbly submitted to the Lord Jesus Christ at all. Since the tragic terrorist strike on the World Trade Center many have espoused newfound patriotism. Young men have, as in wars past, enthusiastically declared their willingness to fight for their country. In days like these, those of us who know what Spirit we are of[59] can be hastily called cowards. Those who oppose us are ungraciously called warmongers. People of both opinions have a tendency to polarize in time of war.

Hatriotism has often been mistaken for patriotism. We as Christians need to steer clear of "hatriotism" (willingness to kill for their country). Similarly, some of the "peaceniks" among us need to learn patriotism (willingness to die for their country). In any case, we all need to stand on revelation, and upon the reality of Christ within us. He is fully able and willing to lead you. And all you need to be is willing to go with Him to the death. Are you following His goal of peace, or yours? Are you committed to peace, or to

---

[59] Luke 9:52-56, "And sent messengers before his face: and they went, and entered into a village of the Samaritans, to make ready for him. And they did not receive him… And when his disciples James and John saw this, they said, Lord, wilt thou that we command fire to come down from heaven, and consume them…? But he turned, and rebuked them, and said, Ye know not what manner of spirit ye are of. For the Son of man is not come to destroy men's lives, but to save them."

164

Him? May He lead you anywhere, tell you anything, and change your mind, or your tradition?

Will Christ lead you into His Kingdom? Or do you intend on just meeting Him there? Could He lead you into war or have you drawn a line of your own? Have you presupposed His mission and His method of executing it? The disciples did. That is why He asked, "Suppose ye that I am come to give peace on earth?"

49.   *What wilt thou?*

Matthew 20:32, "And Jesus stood still, and called them, and said, What will ye that I shall do unto you?"

Mark 10:51, "And Jesus answered and said unto him, What wilt thou that I should do unto thee? The blind man said unto him, Lord, that I might receive my sight."

Luke 18:41, "Saying, What wilt thou that I shall do unto thee? And he said, Lord, that I may receive my sight."

Mark 10:36, "And he said unto them, What would ye that I should do for you?"

Matthew 20:21, "And he said unto her, What wilt thou? She saith unto him, Grant that these my two sons may sit, the one on thy right hand, and the other on the left, in thy kingdom."

Imagine you are a first century Israelite. You have heard of Jesus traveling throughout all Judea healing and causing miracles that free people from physical illness and demonic forces. You have made your way to Him because you know that if you see Him, He will answer your greatest need. You are nearer to Him now; He is only ahead in the crowd by a few feet. You can hear His words and are drawn in as you listen to His stories that intrigue the crowd. You hear His riddles that perplex the religious leadership and perhaps a parable conveying deep significance and you wonder what it could mean and you find yourself pondering the gracious words that come from Him.

Finally, He shifts through the crowd and you realize He will come right past you if you only stand still and let the crowd pass. He gets nearer and notices you. You look at Him and now you are wondering if a great man as He will do what you ask. Thoughts of unworthiness flood your mind as you try to maintain hope that He will even listen to you. He looks to you... No! He is looking through you and beyond. And He asks... "What do you want?"

There are several cases where Jesus asked someone in a crowd or someone alone, "What wilt thou?" Once He asked two blind men, "What do you want me to do for you?" (Matthew 20:32-Mark 10:51-Luke 18:41[60]) This seemed a strange question to ask them. Would we really have to ask a blind man, "What do you want"? What, besides his sight, would he want from a man like Jesus? But Jesus asked.

In one case where the Lord asked, "What wilt thou?" He received a disturbing answer. It is not clear from the Gospels whether it was the mother of

---

[60] Though Matthew adds another blind man, Mark and Luke insist there was only one. The discrepancy notwithstanding, these three accounts are of the same story. Mark and Luke were not eyewitnesses and Matthew perhaps remembered that there were indeed two men that day.

James and John or they themselves, but a request was made for them both to sit in positions of power when Christ's Kingdom was established. This not only prompted a corrective discourse from the Savior about humility and servitude, but caused the other ten disciples to despise them for it as well.[61]

Our literary background exposes that we are lust-driven creatures with desires for things that are out of our reach and we are people who wish for impossible things. Even our children's books contain stories of genies and lamps that grant wishes. Our culture is replete with novels and plays that depict the "local boy" who gets his big break or makes good or somehow gets what he "wants." Are you lifted into thoughts of magically being given all you desire? Are you lust-driven, motivated by gain, or enlivened by the possibility of a miraculous granting of your inmost wish? What do you want?

In the days when screenplay and novel writers felt an obligation to teach a moral lesson they always included the pitfall that invariably follows the receipt of our unchecked appetites. Not so today. Not unless it offers comic relief, do we see the undesired consequence of getting what we "want." It is a consequence hidden from our view because it is becoming part of our culture to promote wishing and lusting for that which we do not have. We are encouraged from childhood to aspire to higher levels of "achievement." Ambition is touted as a worthy character trait, while those who are content, are deemed lazy and non-productive.

There was a charlatan preacher in our recent times who used to declare, "You can be what you want to be, and have what you want to have." All this was supposedly done in the name of Jesus Christ, and was purported to be unquestionably the will of God.

Modern "Christianity" offers this same rubbish in a different wrapper. The modern gospels of prosperity are plenteous and proliferate. Unfortunately, the modern gospel messages sound credible only to those who do not know who it is they worship. We all are vulnerable to this "Genie of the lamp" mentality if we are animated by what we want out of life, or our life contains much sorrow or lack. What do you want?

Analyzing Our Desires

Even if your desires are honorable ones, care must be taken to wait for clearness to approach the Father with your request. This is the main reason behind Christ's admonition to add the proviso, "...if it be thy will." This statement should remind you of your submission to your King and places your desires in proper perspective. No request should be heard from the lips of God's children without including this verbal surrender of will. Remember, the highest and most noble prayer ever heard came from a sinless Man, asking to be spared a punishment that He did not deserve, yet He prayed, "Not my will, but thine be done."

---

[61] Mark 10:36, Matthew 20:21

Some who pray fancy their requests more noble than most when contemplating a wish to be granted. They have visions of world peace or food for hungry children or some "unselfish" desire for "others." Just as the blind man wanted his sight health is a most desirable thing. All desires, no matter how noble, are subject to lusts. No one is above and beyond our ever-present, ever-encroaching flesh. Remember, the poor need a little more than they presently have and want what they cannot buy; the rich want a little more than they presently have and need what they cannot buy. What do you want?

When you exercise the most valuable privilege ever granted, when you pray to your listening Father in heaven, do you fully realize the scope of your petition and the depravity of your position? Do you consider the price that was necessary to purchase you? Perhaps, with modern Bible teachers calling you a "King's kid" and telling you that you "deserve the best," it is easy to become a spoiled child. Remember that true promotion and exaltation comes from God. It is attained not by prayer and asking but as the apostle in 1 Peter 5:6 said, "Humble yourselves therefore under the mighty hand of God and HE will exalt you... in due time."

In the two cases cited in today's Scripture, Jesus asked, "What wilt thou?" Two answers, diametrically opposed, were given. For the blind man, his whole world revolved around being a burden to society and himself. He had never had the satisfaction of doing for himself but always depended on others to do for him. His inmost desire was to see and be a whole man, a valuable citizen, and a complete person. Jesus granted his request.

The idea of James and John, however, was based in selfishness and pride. It revealed things better left hidden about the secret desires of these men. It also serves today as an example of the depravity of man even in the presence of God. These men walked with Jesus Christ. Does familiarity breed contempt even when Jesus is concerned? How could they ask, or be privy to a plan, to exalt themselves to an authoritative position?

As we grow more and more familiar with Christ do we also grow more impertinent and feel we can say anything, do anything, or ask anything we want? James and John knew Jesus and He called them His friends. Do you grow more cavalier as you gain familiarity with Christ? Does self-interest protrude into your requests during prayer? Does the Lord only hear words generated from wickedness, selfishness, or fatuous flesh when He is petitioned? What will you answer when your King, the Word, the Creator, The Messiah, the Son of God asks you, "What wilt thou – What do you want?"

50. Can ye drink of the cup?

Mark 10:38, "But Jesus said unto them, Ye know not what ye ask: can ye drink of the cup that I drink of? and be baptized with the baptism that I am baptized with?"

Matthew 20:22... "They say unto him, We are able."

James and John and their Mother approached Jesus to request that He exalt them to power in the Kingdom He was to establish. They had no idea what this Kingdom was, where it was to be, or the political structure of it, yet they knew that they wanted to be heads of state in it. (This behavior is more typical of children than adults.) Jesus was quick to point out that there is a price tag attached to this seat of office. This price tag lists two items. Jesus called them "the cup" and "the baptism." These two may be viewed as that which is served to us and we take into ourselves (the cup) and that into which we are immersed, overwhelmed, and ultimately overcome (the baptism).

The cup of the Lord is mentioned throughout the Old Testament. "For in the hand of the LORD there is a cup, and the wine is red; it is full of mixture; and he poureth out of the same: but the dregs thereof, all the wicked of the earth shall wring them out, and drink them." Psalms 75:8

Even until the revelation of Christ, this cup of wrath is mentioned. It says in Revelation 14:10, "The same shall drink of the wine of the wrath of God, which is poured out without mixture into the cup of his indignation." This cup is judgment. It is the fury of God felt by those who ignore, disobey, and reject the reign of God in their lives. The stiff-necked and rebellious, the proud and haughty, will all taste of the cup of God's wrath. Jesus was expecting the service of this cup the night He prayed in the garden. He was about to take onto Himself the very thing that would separate Him from God, His Father.

This cup of Judgment was prepared for us, and then set aside for Jesus as Messiah and Redeemer to lift and drink for us. Jesus also knew that the deliverer of this cup would be the ancient enemy of God. He always is. He, working through his sons on the earth, crucified Christ and thereby made a way for us to enter the Kingdom of God, a mystery, and plan not then revealed to these sons of Belial. "Which none of the princes of this world knew: for had they known it, they would not have crucified the Lord of glory." (1 Corinthians 2:8) Unknowingly, the prince of this world also opens the gates of splendor for Christ's followers as well, through death, persecution, and martyrdom. A delicious irony indeed! Jesus also knew that this cup of hatred and loathing, handed to Him by the princes of this world, would be waiting for those professing His name afterward. He warned, "If the world hate you, ye know that it hated me before it hated you." (John 15:18) And, "If they have called the master of the house Beelzebub, how much more shall they call them of his household?" (Matthew 10:25b) This is why Jesus had no reservation in saying that they would surely drink His cup.

The "baptism" is the same contents of the cup – only it is total immersion – the flooding over and overcoming. Not all of us experience this. This is, in short, severe persecution, or martyr's death. There was a time when this was nearly unavoidable and proved to be inescapable to nearly all of Christ's disciples. So Jesus was not just loosely warning them, He was promising them it would be a factor in their future.

Loving Our Lives

Martyrdom is considered the height of spiritual achievement, but only by those who treasure their lives on this earth. The martyr's loyalty lies elsewhere. The martyr's value of his life is skewed by his view of eternity. Those who do not have goals beyond the life in which they presently find themselves, do not hold to their faith through martyrdom. They usually escape death through compromise. But the faith of martyrs is precious in God's sight. As their appearance at the fifth seal shows in Revelation 6, the martyrs will play an important role in the key events of the apocalypse.

All this notwithstanding, we need to ask ourselves, "Can we drink of the cup?" If there were a threat outside our Meetinghouse doors of torture and death, this question would carry a heavier meaning. The threat is not there, and because it is not there it makes the thought a hypothetical one and, unfortunately, easier to answer in the affirmative. However, we need to consider our walk with God, and our relationship's value to us. Are you willing to drink of that cup? Are you willing to go down under the fiery baptism of a martyr's death?

The other question we should ask ourselves is if we are living in such a way so as to cause this cup of hatred, of which Jesus spoke, to be served to us? Persecution does wait at the door, but not for everyone. Persecution, segregation, banishment, and hatred await all who live godly in Christ Jesus, so says II Timothy 3:12. Many of us, however, cannot be distinguished from anyone else, and therefore do not feel persecution at at all. Our lives should be loudspeakers that proclaim our allegiance and loyalty.

This is not accomplished by making ourselves conspicuous spectacles or oddities but by the pure testimony and conduct of our lives. Unfortunately, as it is said, "If being Christian was illegal, many of us would be acquitted for lack of evidence."

You need not consider IF you will be asked for that ultimate sacrifice – the question the Lord asks is, "can you," or "are you able?" Your ability is not established by determination, but in preparation. A life lived for Christ, with few reservations for the flesh, few considerations for self and comfort, brings a life into a state of ultimate preparedness. It is by small, nearly invisible sutures that stitches your life and hopes to the world under your feet. Reserving yourself, holding back for comforts and desires, making provision for fears, making provisos, and caveats to protect yourself, will eventually transform you

170

into a coward. You may find it ever increasingly difficult to let go of your self-made protections and become stymied when your dependence upon God becomes more difficult.

You may have thought that if you worked a little more, or had a few more things, or made yourself a little more comfortable, you could be in better shape to serve God. But, sadly you will find that the opposite is true. You are no closer to full surrender now than you ever were. Though you might be a little richer, perhaps more secure, you may find that you have spent a miserable life only pursuing a miserable life and have gained little ground inside the Kingdom of God.

Many cannot even imagine the death of martyrdom. Even of those who may consider it a noble way to die, few are prepared. Though it is not your desire to seek a martyr's death, if your life were lived in a way that is pleasing to God, martyrdom could become a part of the equation of your life as easily as any other facet of Christian service. The problem is preparation. For as distasteful as martyrdom is, it is much easier to find those willing to die for Christ than it is to find those willing to live for Him. "Can ye drink of the cup?"

51. *What is thy name?*

Mark 5:9, "And he asked him, What is thy name? And he answered, saying, My name is Legion: for we are many."

Luke 8:30, "And Jesus asked him, saying, What is thy name? And he said, Legion: because many devils were entered into him."

A person's name means a good deal in most cultures. In the United States though, we have adulterated the naming process, until there is nearly nothing of essence left. Here, we name our children names that only sound good or names that conjure up feelings of familiarity or happiness. We scour books or ask opinions of others until we hear a name that strikes us as pleasant and then we hang that moniker on our unsuspecting child for life.

Anyone who has been in a gift store has seen the obtuse plaques, bookmarks and trinkets with ridiculous "meanings" of names emblazoned on them. They all contain nonsensical platitudes of wonderful character (mostly fabricated in the mind of the publisher) intending to tell us what an infinitely great and noble people we all are – all because of what our parents unwittingly named us. They totally disregard the fact that we were named before anyone knew anything about us – as if we grew into these wonderful names and now, somehow, exemplify their exquisite meanings.

There was a time, however, when names did have real meaning. They were not necessarily names meaning good things. For example, there was a boy in the Bible who was named Ichabod. He was named at a time of severe grief felt by his mother. She heard news of the deaths of her husband and brother-in-law, killed in war, and that her father-in-law fell dead at receiving the same news, and that the Ark of the Covenant (considered by all to be the very presence of God) was stolen from Israel just as she was giving birth. Upon hearing all this, and feeling very much forsaken, and very afraid, she named her child, Ichabod, which means, "God has departed."[62]

There was also a child who was named "laughter," (Isaac) because the news of pregnancy at 90-plus years of age made both his parents laugh.[63]

Many do not know that when God created man He said, "Let us create Adam in our image." Adam was named before he was created. Any reader of the Bible will attest that names had deep and meaningful significance in those days.

Our thin and superficial American culture robs us of many things we would instinctively understand otherwise. One of the things we have missed is a meaningful name. In Jesus' day, we find men named for how they were known. Simon, one of the disciples, was known as a zealot; thus his name, Simon Zelotes. When a given (first) name was common, it was customary to

---

[62] I Samuel 4
[63] Genesis 17 & 18

add an outstanding characteristic to the name. Simon the tanner was obviously a ·hide tanner or leatherworker. There was Simon Barjona (Son of Jonas), Simon the Canaanite, Simon the leper, etc.

Many names used today in our culture and many others were derivations from occupations. Taylor, Fuller, Mason, Carpenter, Farmer, Smith, Sawyer, are only a few. Reputation was also a way to name someone. Names ending in "man" were likely names of reputation. Goodman or Truman would be a coveted name in those days!

Some traditions, as this one of naming a child or family with real meaning, find their roots in God's way of doing things. His names are true representations of who we are. We may remember how YHVH changed Jacob's name (trickster) to Israel (prevailer). Jesus changed Simon's name to Peter (rock). Names are important to God and we can be sure we are not now fully aware of the reasons why.

"My name is Legion FOR we are many." If we can realign our thinking to the days when names had meaning, we can understand the word "FOR." He was saying that, because we are many, my name is Legion. This spirit entity was given the name Legion – because it was many spirits. We can only assume it was named in some other world – a world with which Jesus and this demon spirit were familiar. Jesus was often recognized and identified by beings from an existence outside our own.[64] Jesus asked the demon's name – not so He could call it by name or because it is proper etiquette, but to KNOW with whom He was dealing. A name from the other world would give Him that information, as He obviously knew that names there have true meaning.

There are many things we do not know about this situation. One of which is, did Jesus recognize this name when He heard it? Some say of course He did know, asserting that "Jesus knew everything" but if this is so, why did He ask his name? We cannot help but to believe He asked because He did not know it, and wanted to. He asked and was answered and from that information, He made His decisions.

Although names in our time may be given for superficial reasons, or come from frivolous motives, in the world where these two once knew each other, names had meaning. In our world, we say that a man has a "good name" when he has a good reputation. Perhaps with this connection we can see how a name and a reputation can be inseparable.

"A good name is rather to be chosen than great riches..." (Proverbs 22:1) If your name ACTUALLY reflected your character, what would your name be? If others knew the significance of that name, how would that affect your life? Example: If your name were a number and that number was known to everyone to be equal to your net worth... how would that affect your life... your acquaintances... your pride? Or, what if your name were a true and accurate reflection of your unvarnished character, your true, but heretofore

---

[64] Luke 4:34, Mark 1:24.

unseen self, how would that affect your relationship with the world... your family... your church or Meeting?

A New Name

There is a true name that belongs to you, that reflects you, as you really are – a name that upon hearing it tells exactly what you are – who you are – and displays your genuine character. One day you will hear that name for the first time as you enter the Kingdom of God which will be physically established on this earth. Though hearing it for the first time, you will know it. It will be a recollection of sorts – it will be much like a woman, married for many years, remembering herself as a youth, upon hearing her maiden name used by an old friend from her past.

Revelation 2:17, "He that hath an ear, let him hear what the Spirit saith unto the churches; To him that overcometh... [Jesus] will give him a white stone, and in the stone a new name written, which no man knoweth saving he that receiveth it." You will recognize that name and realize that it fits you perfectly. You will find that you have grown into the name He gave you. As you become more and more like the person God wants you to be, you are taking on the character that your name describes. You are growing into that name and becoming worthy of it as you advance toward Christ. Do you wonder what it will be?

Just as Jesus asked the fallen spirit, "What is thy name?" conversation in the Kingdom of God on the earth will begin with introductions. We will know with whom we are talking as soon as we hear the name. Perhaps in the reign of Christ, we will hear names given to folks we only thought we knew, and we will be surprised that they were not who we thought they were at all!

This new name, carved in the white stone, will accurately depict and display your service to God, your character and your value to the Kingdom. How will you answer Christ when He sees you and inquires of your name? Will your name reflect the honor and dignity of a faithful and wise steward or the shame and remorse of a misspent life? Will you say your name in confidence and delight because it shows that you stood as a faithful friend of Truth, or will you have to bow your head in shame knowing your name reflects lukewarm or cowardly service to God? How will you answer when He asks, "What is your name?"

52.   Who touched me?

Mark 5:30 - Luke 8:45, "And Jesus, immediately knowing in himself that virtue had gone out of him, turned him about in the press, and said, Who touched my clothes...who touched me? When all denied, Peter and they that were with him said, Master, the multitude throng thee and press thee, and sayest thou, Who touched me?"

Here is a curious event. Jesus is plodding along as best He can through the streets of Jerusalem, He is being thronged by folks making demands on Him, asking for healing, asking for guidance, asking questions to gain His attendance. The crowds are pressing hard against Him and suddenly He asks, "Who touched me?" Jesus taught that His works, His miracles and ministry, were not His but were the works of the Father who dwells in Him. (John 14:9-10, John 5:17) He insisted that His method of doing miracles was not an act of His own will but was only His Father's will set into motion. (This was the defense He offered as the reason He healed on the Sabbath day.)

Power to do miracles was obviously in His control. His mother was well aware of it as she looked to Him to rectify the wine shortage at the wedding of Cana. At the request of His mother, He reluctantly did this miracle as an act of His own will. Many other instances showed our Christ Jesus doing miracles by request. "If you will, you can heal me," they would say. Then Jesus would answer, "I will." Working as the Father wills or working as He Himself wills was understandable, but what happed here, when Jesus asked "Who touched me?"?

Jesus was on His way to heal Jairus' daughter. As He moved through the street the crowds grew to the point that they pushed Jesus along and from side to side. A woman came, unseen from the crowd, and reached out and touched the garment of Christ. This act drew "virtue" (power to be healed) from Him. Jesus stopped. He asked, "Who touched me?" He asked again, "Who touched my clothes?" Jesus knew that He was speaking only to the one who touched Him, for only that person would know why He asked. His disciples said, "Master, everyone is touching you, what do you mean, 'Who touched me?'" Silence must have held for a while, as the crowd rumbled to a stop. As the dust was just about to settle, a woman, moments earlier electrified with the excitement of being healed of a horrible plague that had taken all of her life and money, was enjoying the moment within herself. She felt in her body that she had been healed. She received what she came for and her life was to be different from then on.

When she came to herself, she heard the deafening silence of the heretofore maddening crowd. She heard whispers racing through the crowd, "Who touched Him?" "Who was it?" Then the voice of Jesus came booming over the others in clear authority and undeniable request. "Who touched me?" The scriptures say,

"And when the woman knowing what was done in her, saw that she was not hid, she came fearing and trembling, immediately and told him all the truth. Falling down before him, she declared unto him, before all the people, for what cause she had touched him, and how she was healed" (Mark 5:33 - Luke 8:47 Combined)

This touch was different than all the rest. In it lies some secret, unknown to the theologian and the pious. Yet it was a very natural act to the woman in need. This touch got the attention of Christ, not because the request was odd, or profound, or out of the ordinary, but because it drew from Christ what He usually had to exude as an act of His will – or as an act of obedience to His Father's will. This woman took from Christ that for which others begged. It impressed Him. It may have even disturbed Him a little. We are certain that it surprised Him, and, at last, pleased Him. You can almost hear a lilt in His response as He comforts her and assures her that she has done well.

"But Jesus turned him about, and when he saw her, he said unto her, Daughter, be of good comfort: thy faith hath made thee whole; go in peace, and be whole of thy plague. And the woman was made whole from that hour." (Luke 8:48 - Mark 5:34 - Matthew 9:22 Combined)

Touching Jesus

This kind of faith is rare. A faith that doesn't beg or coerce just makes effective contact. A sort of "Thy will be done" attitude that touches and goes about its business knowing that if God is aware, it is enough – a soul satisfied in knowing that God knows. No begging or pleading a case to prove whether it is a worthy cause, no deals made, no bargains struck, just plain contact. She said, "If I can just touch Him – just His garment, I'll be healed."

For her, it was a matter of only getting near Him. Some teach that "getting near Him" is a way to be healed, delivered from trouble, or a way of receiving blessing. Some would entice the selfish to pursue "touching Jesus" in order to receive from God – a genie's lamp or magic wand sort of thing – as if it is something you can decide to do. Perhaps rather, it should just be a way of life. Maybe it is a way for us to live everyday, make our requests known, and let the answers, or the lack of an answer, speak for themselves – to seek out Christ, remain near Him, in our need – and if we receive from Him we are favored and blessed and thankful. This kind of faith brought about healing. It could have as well brought a surprised smile to the face of Jesus. It *was* different.

Jesus is touched, fondled, and handled by the crowd even today. We hear His name used and abused on the television and radio. We see His name on billboards, bumper stickers, and hear it vainly used by empty preachers gathering to themselves lambs for shearing. Jesus is being thronged by the irreverent crowds even today as His presence is evoked, coerced and conjured in our filthy society. But as the dust settles – as the crowd dies down and listens – wouldn't it be nice to be the one who made the genuine contact? Wouldn't it

176

be great to be the one out of all, who got what you came for; the one who surprised Christ by your faith?

You must live expecting God to care for you. You come, without begging, importunity, or coercion, just with a simple faith that God will supply your needs. Faith that if He does not, you will go your way knowing you touched, you made contact and it was not to be. All you must do is touch. One day you may be privileged to raise your hand in response when He asks, "Who touched me?"

53. Do ye not remember?

Mark 8:18, "Having eyes, see ye not? and having ears, hear ye not? and do ye not remember?"

There are many different kinds of flaws in character that make people difficult. One of the worst is moodiness. Upon seeing moody people in the morning, instead of asking, "How are you today?" we might be more compelled to ask, "Who are you today?" We find no such flaw in our heavenly Father. This fact constructs for us an interesting support to faith. We may simply remember His previous works and take comfort, knowing that the future will duplicate the past.

The disciples presumed they were in trouble with Jesus for not making provision for a journey by taking bread. Jesus scolded them for not being able to pull themselves above the temporal, physical existence and view the spiritual battle that was at hand. He was trying to warn them that they could not hear because their heads were cluttered with concern for food, social climbing and petty mistakes. He chided them and asked, "Having eyes, see ye not? and having ears, hear ye not? and do ye not remember?"

There are actually two separate thoughts going through the mind of Christ here. The first of His questions was to call to their minds the writings of the Prophet Isaiah, "And he said, Go, and tell this people, Hear ye indeed, but understand not; and see ye indeed, but perceive not." (Isaiah 6:9) He wondered in Himself if these men were indeed still closed to understanding.

The second was the question; "Do ye not remember?" It was as if He were saying that even if we lay aside spiritual understanding for a moment, our memories should suffice as record of His way of doing things and His provision. A large portion of our discouragement, worries, and lack of understanding, come from having no basis for our memory. We cannot remember what we have never experienced, never heard, or never read. Looking back plays a great role in going forward. God commanded the children of Israel to teach their children Israel's history to form this kind of basis for their memory.

Deuteronomy 6:6-12, "And these words, which I command thee this day, shall be in thine heart: [memorized] And thou shalt teach them diligently unto thy children, and shalt talk of them when thou sittest in thine house, and when thou walkest by the way, and when thou liest down, and when thou risest up. And thou shalt bind them for a sign upon thine hand, and they shall be as frontlets between thine eyes. And thou shalt write them upon the posts of thy house, and on thy gates. ...beware lest thou forget the LORD, which brought thee forth out of the land of Egypt, from the house of bondage."

The first important task in order to remember as we should is to place in our hearts the wonderful works of God. We cannot remember what we never knew. We cannot gain comfort or direction from what we do not remember. We must learn of Him…and find rest for our souls. (Matthew 11:29) God has given us a gift of forgetting the unpleasant and remembering the good. This "gift" can work to our detriment if we forget the unpleasant consequences of disobedience. This is why we need to make ourselves familiar with the stories of God's deliverance and His chastisement. Many foolish and hurtful acts may be avoided if we simply remember.

Jesus continually called upon the Scriptures to prove, corroborate, and witness to what He said and did. He quoted the Prophets and the Law to the amazement of those around Him. They would say, "How knoweth this man letters, having never learned?" (John 7:15). Perhaps Jesus read and learned on His own. Maybe He could recall from the former glory He had with the Father. No matter, He knew the Scriptures and from them and their recollection He gained strength, battled Satan, put to flight the naysayers and doubters, declared the Scriptures as a witness, and fulfilled them all perfectly. He is our fine example.

Our Call to Remember

We need to know the Scriptures as personally and as clearly as He did. Then we can call to remembrance, at the moment we need them, the wonderful acts, the deep revealing prophecies, and the unchangeable law of God. Many problems and heartaches would be dissolved at the first glimpse of precious memories collected from the Scriptures. Hebrews 10:32, "But call to remembrance the former days, in which, after ye were illuminated, ye endured a great fight of afflictions."

Trustworthy sources are essential to gain lasting strength from memory. Even remembrance of your own experiences will change in your mind over time. We need to recognize that our own mental record is untrustworthy in this regard. A journal can minimize the danger of a "selective memory." A journal need not be daily nor detailed to be useful as a memory aide, but it does need to be accurate. Personal journals are coming back into vogue, but, unfortunately, emphasis is placed on recording "thoughts" instead of facts. Thoughts are fine to enlighten, but facts will inform and remind.

Care should be taken also with the so-called experiences offered to us as examples by well-meaning friends or counselors. Remember that their memories are selective as well and facts forgotten or altered would show their circumstances to be an entirely different situation than what they remember. Advice, no matter how well intentioned, may be harmful.

The Spirit of God was commissioned by Christ to call to our remembrance what we need in times of persecution. John 14:26, But the Comforter, [will] bring all things to your remembrance, whatsoever I have said unto you." Note that He would "call to our remembrance." These are things that are experienced and later forgotten. We must experience them first.

Once these things are experienced, we need to remind ourselves of them and keep them "in front of our eyes" so that we won't be caught in doubt and fear. If we doubt because we were uneducated, or because we were disadvantaged in our youth, we could offer excuses for our fear. Comfort, however, is to found in the most convenient place of all – in our own memories!

The trouble is that we are not as familiar with the stories of Scripture as we should be, nor do we live a life rich in blessing, in order to create a history of God's provision. If our lives were as focused, as they should be, if we were as dedicated, as we should be, we would have a rich history of provision and deliverance from which we could draw comfort and assurance.

When these times do exist, and you have experiences to draw upon you must not fail to do so. God is so good to prove Himself and fight our battles; it is a shame when cries are made again and again, as if He changes daily, as if you have no confidence in Him. When you call on Him to do what He has done time and time again, are you not embarrassed when the Lord says, "Do you not remember?"

54. Why make ye this ado, and weep?

Mark 5:39, "And when he was come in, he saith unto them, Why make ye this ado, and weep? the damsel is not dead, but sleepeth."

Professionalism makes all ministries into hypocrisy. There was a time when schoolteachers, doctors, men who worked in government and even lawyers held their occupations because they felt a divine calling to do it, not for monetary reasons. Then, there were no money motivations involved, just a desire to what was right and fulfill a commission of God in service to their fellow man in need.

In the little town in the story, from which our verse comes, Jairus' daughter lay dead. At first, as we read Jesus' comments, it looks as if He is insensitive and uncaring and perhaps even a fool. Why would anyone walk in to a death-room and ask, "Why make ye this ado and weep?" To find the answer to that puzzling behavior we need to understand who Jesus addressed as He walked in. These were not truly grieved persons; they were professionals. They were hired mourners. But, who would hire mourners?

It is said that it was so shameful to have a funeral at which no one wept that folks were compensated to take time from their work to come and mourn at a funeral. It was just part of funeral expenses. As the idea became commonplace, the poor or indigent would show up at the house of the sick and dying and mourn aloud at their death hoping to receive some coin or gift. This "hired" weeping was apparently false, and later was shown to be so by their actions. They were as willing and ready to lament as to laugh. They could switch from sobbing to snickering as though it was nothing. Without knowledge of this custom, we may wonder at the verse in Luke 8:53, "And they laughed him to scorn, knowing that she was dead." They switched to laughter easily, because they were only pretending to grieve. True sorrow makes no room for humor. Rather, it despises it.

These mercenary mourners were there for selfish reasons; there was no genuine care for the family of the dying. Think of how the truly mournful family must have felt, to hear outside these falsetto cries go up at one minute and laughter break from the same crowd the next moment. How can they be so insensitive? Such behavior is effortless for those who make a ministry into a profession. When we bypass "cause" for "effect" we are nothing short of hypocrites. When we want the benefits of a virtue without cost, we are no better than thieves.

Jesus had no sympathy for hypocrisy. He knew exactly what was going on that day which is why He felt no sorrow for the crying mob. They likely stood outside and waited to hear the news of this precious daughter's impending death. As the parents of the little girl pled to God for mercy and the recovery of their darling, the crowd, just outside the window, was waiting for those requests to go unanswered.

Then, suddenly it happened. The life slipped from the girl and a cry goes out from a mother destroyed by grief. The word is passed to the professional "vultures" circling outside the window, and their cries are added to the din. The crescendo was heard in the town, and beggars and thieves from all over come to feast on the sorrow of this saddened family, hiring themselves out as mourners. Jesus walked up on this crowd of avaricious actors and said, "You received bad information folks, she's not dead." He said, "Why make ye this ado, and weep? The damsel is not dead, but sleepeth." Then they laughed at Him.

Of course we know the rest of the story. The little girl is raised from the dead and restored to the family. However, from this story we must learn that we all have a little of this hypocritical "actor" in us. There may be any number of causes that trigger this hypocrisy. Sometimes we give over to emotions because we are ashamed that we are not moved as everyone else is. There is also a "drunkenness" in sorrow into which we may escape. We may even voluntarily offer ourselves to grief to extract the benefit of remoteness, or departure from reality or responsibility. This is often mistaken for feeling sorry for oneself. We must honestly evaluate, "Why make we this ado, and weep?"

Getting Used To Grief

Some are not as sad today as they were about things they experienced 5, 10, 20, or 50 years ago because we all naturally forget grief. It becomes a problem when we feel a bit guilty for "forgetting." We mistakenly transpose our forgetting grief to forgetting the loved one we lost. This is not the case at all. We must look at our selective memory. The ability to lay grief aside and continue is a wonderful gift of God.

Another motivation for sorrow is our condition of sinfulness. We may mentally apply our sorrow and grief to unforgiven sins to gain thereby some sort of absolution from being sad. This is usually evidenced by feeling as though someone is being "paid back" or by questioning "Why me, God?" Some will take time during the day to conjure up past grief and loss for this very purpose.

The truth is, we feel no genuine sadness for our sin, and we latch on to sadness whenever it does occur, thereby (in our mind anyway) paying for our sin. This is the worst deception of all, because it replaces the true forgiveness that comes from repentance, faith in Jesus Christ and responsible living by His Commands. Only by doing this can we make sure that our lives are clean and forgiven. Then we will feel no need to manufacture grief or cultivate old sorrows to make ourselves feel normal, alive, or "like everybody else."

The problem is exacerbated when we expect others to keep this grief alive as well and mourn with us, thus separating friends and family for our twisted need of grief. The Apocryphal book, Sirach states this bit of wisdom, "Do not give yourself over to sorrow, and do not afflict yourself deliberately." (30:21 RSV) Paul spoke of a godly sorrow (as opposed to an emotional one)

182

that leads to repentance.[65] This Godly sorrow is what comes from heaven when we ask for God to convict us and make us, as we should be.

Today, much is made of demonstrating grief and sorrow. We are told how it is necessary for mental health and well being, but we, as Christians, should be aware of the spiritual implications of purposely indulging in, or manufacturing emotions. We know that acting (which is hypocrisy) or drunkenness (escape of any kind) is NEVER good. We must seek for the real, the true, and the genuine. We must seek God both when a "natural" reaction is absent, when we feel no sorrow, or when our reaction is overreaction.

Our emotions, or lack of them, can indicate our spiritual condition. We must be willing to be honest and upright and not succumb either way to pressure to be what we are not. We must trust God to make us what we should be. The absence of care and love for our fellow man is a sign of a deeper spiritual problem.

On the other hand, purposely enhanced sorrow, feigned love, or pretended grief for our brethren only covers up problems just like painkillers may mask cancer. You need to be very careful of how you manipulate your emotions and be aware of the reasons you suppress or engage them. It would do you well to ask and answer, "Why do we make this ado and weep?"

---

[65] 2 Corinthians 7:10, "For godly sorrow worketh repentance to salvation not to be repented of: but the sorrow of the world worketh death."

55. By whom do your sons cast out devils?

Luke 11:18-20, "If Satan also be divided against himself, how shall his kingdom stand? because ye say that I cast out devils through Beelzebub. And if I by Beelzebub cast out devils, by whom do your sons cast them out? therefore shall they be your judges. But if I with the finger of God cast out devils, no doubt the kingdom of God is come upon you."

It is obvious that Jesus was not the only person to cast out devils. Whatever the act of casting out devils was, it must have been a practice of the Priesthood and commonly known among the people of Jesus' time.

However, ignorance still abounds in this area today, as a brief scan of religious publications and broadcasts will attest. (I say ignorance because there are just as many people who say that it is one thing as there are others who say that it is something else.)

Be that situation as it may, the people of Jesus' time were confirming His goodness and genuineness by these acts of the supernatural. They were recorded as saying, "When Christ cometh, will he do more miracles than these which this man hath done?" (John 7:31) The generous attitude toward Jesus aggravated the religious leaders of the day and they sought ways to discredit Him. The Pharisees would say, "This man is not of God." The people would argue and say, "But He casts out devils just like you do." Then they said, "He casts out demons by the prince of demons." If that did not produce the desired effect they would use a name detested by the Jews. It was an epithet given to the local god of the Egyptians. It was a play on words that meant "Lord of the Flies." They attributed His works to "Beelzebub" and not YHVH in order to frighten the people and cast doubt as to His validity.

Undaunted by this accusation, Jesus asked them, "If I, by Satan, cast out Satan, by whom do your sons cast them out?" "Therefore their actions condemn your condemnation of me." Or more accurately quoted, "therefore they shall be your judges."

Whenever we encounter something that is new to us, we are left with an exercise in ego to be performed. When this is in the area of religion, it is complicated by our insecurity. When the new way or idea leads us away from the community of those who see things the way we do, it further complicates the decision to follow Truth with the threat of loneliness, defensiveness and fear of failure.

All these emotions and fears add up to folks saying and doing things that are destructive and damning to themselves and those they love (and/or those upon whom they depend). This was, no doubt, the case with these Pharisees. Their whole world was coming to an end. No doubt there were those who spoke against their religion before, but opposition, coupled with such power with God, had never been seen!

The Pharisees knew how to set the people at variance with those who opposed them and explain the supernatural acts Christ performed, they simply said, "He is demon possessed."[66] This made the people, who feared the Pharisees as leaders, give Jesus a wide berth, which was just what the Pharisees wanted. In this we see that the epithet "vipers" given the Pharisees by John the Baptist was well deserved. They could counter any who came against their system by this stratagem of intimidation.

These vipers could see that Jesus was different. He had power with God. He had persuasive ways because He spoke truth and was all God wanted Him to be. He spoke with Truth and Wisdom. When He touched, He healed. When He spoke, His words caused action. What will the Pharisees do with such a man? They took the course that the religious leaders today take most often. First they make sure their own authority in the minds of their followers, then they tell these people under their authority to avoid this "new way" by discrediting it as heretical, unsound, unscriptural, or, if the supernatural is displayed, empowered by demons. Nothing much has changed among the religious of that time and ours… nothing *except…*

The Council at Nicea.

The council of Nicea provided the religious leaders of its day (and ours) ammunition to strike down anything they do not wish to undertake to understand or incorporate into their denominations. Every "new thing" is held to scrutiny, not an examination by the Scriptures, nor an examination through someone's own regenerated Spirit, nor are "new things" simply held up to God in submission, but rather held to the scrutiny of the Nicene council.

These self appointed judges of doctrine will ask, "Do they hold to the trinity?" Or, "How do they explain the essence of Christ? Was He all God or all man?" All of which is unintelligible gobbledygook of man's own mental undertaking, none of which was important enough to God to clearly outline in Scripture. These tests were created by men trying to hold to their own authority by discrediting any thought that arose outside their own school of thinking. How did the essential criterion of "Trinity" become the test of orthodoxy? How did that become the standard by which we judge all men and their doctrines? Or how did the essence of Christ become a criterion?

Did the thief being tortured with Christ have a full understanding of the essence of Christ? Did the apostle Paul? For that matter, did the apostle Paul ever mention the Father, Son and Holy Spirit in the same sentence? Did he not rather refer only to one God, the Father, and one mediator, His Son, our Lord Jesus Christ?[67]

The Holy Spirit is consistently left out of Paul's understanding of the Godhead. This trait in his writings, if written today, would exclude his epistles

---

[66] Matthew 11:18, "For John came neither eating nor drinking, and they say, He hath a devil."

[67] 1 Corinthians 8:6, "But to us there is but **one** God, the Father, of whom are all things, and we in him; **and one** Lord Jesus Christ, by whom are all things, and we by him."

1 Timothy 2:5, "For there is **one** God, **and one** mediator between God and men, the man Christ Jesus;"

from many modern theologians' shelves. And John, too, rebuts this supposed basis for condemning non-Trinitarians when he says, "He is antichrist, that denieth the Father and the Son."[68] Again, confirming there are only two members of the Godhead. By the modern concept of "Trinity," and the Holy Spirit's indispensable inclusion as a "third person," these men would have been considered heretics.

A New Doctrine?

We must be careful not to condemn new or foreign ideas too readily. We may find they are not new at all, but old ideas rediscovered. Jesus was accused of teaching "new" doctrine by teaching, "…that which was from the beginning." Paul arrived at Mars Hill and was greeted by those who wished to hear a "new thing" but was told rather that their own altars were inscribed years ago to the unknown God who created them.[69] John said he had a "new Commandment" for the recipients of his letter and later confessed it was not a new, but an old one.[70]

Man's judgment of other men, doctrines, and religious matters is almost always tainted with selfishness, pride, and empowered or enforced by fear and intimidation. Man's judgment is never to be trusted to bring about confidence in the salvation found in YHVH, or to a lasting, saving faith in His Son Jesus Christ. Only God's Spirit can lead us into Truth and proper doctrine, wisdom and understanding.

We must not become entangled in how or whether someone baptizes, or how or whether the "Lord's Supper" is served, or any other such matters. We should look for the works of God being done. When we realize Satan does not come against his own house to destroy it, we will recognize the works of God being done as an indication we are indeed near the Kingdom of God.[71]

When we see "our sons" meaning those among us, our brethren, cast out devils, (doing the works of God) and we condemn them for it, saying it is a work of the devil because they don't do it our way, we need to ask ourselves, by whom did Jesus cast out devils?

Is it so hard for you to imagine that those who do not hold to your doctrine, creed, or vocabulary could carry on the work of God? The fruit of the act should be enough evidence to convince you of its source and validity.

None of us need think we know it all, nor that God and all His glory will fit into our inane doctrines, formulaic equations of the Godhead, or so-called Apostolic creeds.

We all need to be less judgmental and exacting, and more seeking and open to the living Spirit of God. I am sure it was the first time these well-educated Pharisees ever considered the question when Jesus asked, "If I by Beelzebub cast out devils, by whom do your sons cast them out?"

---

[68] 1 John 2:22
[69] Acts 17:21-33
[70] 2 John 1:5-6, 1 John 2:7
[71] Matthew 12:28, "But if I cast out devils by the Spirit of God, then the kingdom of God is come unto you."

186

56. Did not God make what's inside as well as outside?

Luke 11:40, "Ye fools, did not he that made that which is without make that which is within also?" Ref. Mark 7, Matthew 15

Tradition, symbolism, and custom are enemies to faith, truth, and things spiritual. Jesus found Himself living in a culture steeped in tradition and custom. He was constantly fighting it, and His actions were usually mistaken for breaking the Law of God. Still today, many think that Jesus broke the fourth Commandment (Remember the Sabbath Day) and in doing so set a precedent for us to do likewise. But we must distinguish between tradition and Commandment.

Try as you might, you will not find a Commandment to wash your hands before you eat. It was only a "tradition of the elders" – as was their ambiguous enforcement of Sabbath. Here Jesus attempted to change their thinking. He was in the house of a "certain Pharisee" and again found Himself in violation of one of their traditions – hand washing. You may ask, what could it hurt to wash our hands before we eat? Why needlessly offend? Similarly, some ask, "Why *not* baptize, why *not* partake in communion? What could it hurt? Why needlessly offend?" I would answer that there is an offense of **Truth** that outweighs the offense of *others*.

In the above reference, this story takes on other dimensions. We can assume that after this meal the news was spread that this Jesus fellow does not wash before He eats, nor does He teach His disciples to do so! He was cornered by some synagogue leaders and asked; "Why walk not thy disciples according to the tradition of the elders, but eat bread with unwashen hands? (Mark 7) Jesus answered them citing several reasons. He said, "Well hath Esaias prophesied of you hypocrites, as it is written, this people honoureth me with their lips, but their heart is far from me." By this He was pointing out the hypocrisy of the act. Then He said, "Howbeit in vain do they worship me, teaching for doctrines the commandments of men." Here He points out their replacement of the true Commandment with tradition. He continues, "Full well ye reject the commandment of God, that ye may keep your own tradition."

When dealing with symbolism and traditions, two factors present themselves as evidence that these are to be avoided: 1) the hypocrisy of performing these commandments of men while ignoring the Commandment of God, and 2) the fact that these symbols and traditions take the place of the Truth and the reality which they are intended to illustrate. In the light in which Jesus placed this "harmless" act of hand washing, we can see that it is not harmless at all. He asks, "Ye fools, did not he that made that which is without make that which is within also?" He is asking, why do you care for and nurture the outside and NEGLECT the inside? He said later in one of His public tirades, "Woe unto you, scribes and Pharisees, hypocrites! for ye make clean

187

the outside of the cup and of the platter, but within they are full of extortion and excess. Thou blind Pharisee, cleanse first that which is within the cup and platter, that the outside of them may be clean also." (Matthew 23:25-26)

All their washing was for no other reason than to be seen of men. Jesus shows that hand washing had no basis in hygiene when He said, "…whatsoever entereth in at the mouth goeth into the belly, and is cast out into the draught" (Matthew 15) He goes on to say that if anyone really cared to keep himself free of all defilement, that he would keep himself from the things that truly defile a man. (He continues listing them in no uncertain terms.) Also, it may not set well with the nutritionist crowd, but Jesus made a statement that is pretty bold. He said, "There is NOTHING from without a man, that entering into him can defile him: but the things which come out of him, those are they that defile the man." (Mark 7:15)

So much for hygiene reasons. So much for health reasons. There must be another reason that they washed those bowls and cups and utensils and tables and hands and feet. It is clear that they had no Commandment from God to do it. So why did Jesus view it as wrong? It was wrong because it was done for no other reason than to be seen of men.

The Show Must Go On

Many traditions in the church world today have this same purpose at their core. That is not said to be only critical but as a signal to proceed with care. We should do nothing that is based in pride or ego. This is one of the reasons why things that are ornate and showy are popular in religious society. This is one of the reasons the so-called "sacrament" of communion is something in which we are not to engage ourselves. It is a symbol only. And by the very definition it is something that represents a quality or condition that the person displaying the symbol may or may not have. It can be a deceitful label – fooling not only those reading it, but those wearing it. Just because you take communion does not mean you have communion. By definition, it is hypocrisy.

Still another other reason is the most detrimental. The symbol occupies the place of the true article. If someone asks you, "When was the last time you had communion?" Your mind races back to the time when you were last served the bread and cup. If you are a Quaker of many years you may answer, "I cannot remember." But even the birthright Quaker that answers "never" falls prey to the deception. If we understood the true definition of communion we should answer the question, "Just this morning," or "last evening," or whenever it was that the true communion (to which we are all called) took place.

The true communion of the blood and body of the Savior takes place as we consider His gift and sacrifice and through that sacrifice we commune and gain strength and find our nourishment from Him. We sup with Him and, He with us.[72] The bread and wine replace the true communion. The singular act of

---

[72] Revelation 3:20, "Behold, I stand at the door, and knock: if any man hear my voice, and open the door, I will come in to him, and will sup with him, and he with me."

water baptism *replaces* the act of daily death and burial of ourselves and resurrection of Christ within us. The baptism in water is not to be a replacement for the baptism in the Holy Spirit to which we are all truly called. Baptism in water is nothing more than the baptism of John, inquired of by Paul in Acts 19:2-4, "Unto what then were ye baptized? And they said, Unto John's baptism." Our baptism is to be a Spiritual one, without which we are not baptized at all.

The body and reputation (that which is without) is nurtured and cared for, and every effort is made to see that it has every label and decoration of achievement. At the same time, that which is within goes unnourished with no adornments of heart, no enhancements of beauty. Some would never miss the "Lord's supper" at church, but miss nearly every opportunity to commune with the living Christ. "Ye fools, did not he that made that which is without make that which is within also?"

This was the basis for Peter's admonition in 1 Peter 3:3-4, "Whose adorning let it not be that outward adorning of plaiting the hair, and of wearing of gold, or of putting on of apparel; But let it be the hidden man of the heart, in that which is not corruptible, even the ornament of a meek and quiet spirit, which is in the sight of God of great price."

Jesus advised, "… cleanse first that which is within the cup and platter, that the outside of them may be clean also." (Matthew 23:26)

Society, Meetings, churches and perhaps you place too much emphasis upon the outside, to the neglect of the inside. If you purchased a shiny used car from a man who placed "too much emphasis on the outside" to the neglect of the inside, you would accuse him of fraud – and rightly so. If you bought a home with plumbing and electrical problems from someone who made it look good on the surface only, you would say you were cheated. What can be said about those who endeavor to shortcut the process of true beauty? What would describe those who have only symbols, labels, emblems, or tokens outside, to indicate their spiritual conditions inside?

Jesus was not kind to those who had spent more time and effort on the outside than the inside. He said, "…for you are like unto painted tombs, which indeed appear beautiful outwardly, but within, are full of dead men's bones, and corruption."[73] Have you been baptized? When was your last communion? Before today, communion may have been appraised as participation in ceremony and sharing of temporal bread and wine.

Perhaps before considering these things, baptism was held as a singular occasion of accomplishment. Now, seeing it all as Christ saw it, consider why He asked the Pharisees to take into account more than the liturgical acts of dogma, more than the traditional, more than the physical. One may not be neglected for the other anymore. He asked, "Did not God make what's inside as well as outside?"

---

[73] Matthew 23:27 (Author's paraphrase)

57. How long must I suffer you?

Luke 9:38-41, "And, behold, a man of the company cried out, saying, Master, I beseech thee, look upon my son: for he is mine only child. And, lo, a spirit taketh him, and he suddenly crieth out; and it teareth him that he foameth again, and bruising him hardly departeth from him. And I besought thy disciples to cast him out; and they could not. And Jesus answering said, O faithless and perverse generation, how long shall I be with you, and suffer you? Bring thy son hither."

The disciples' lack of faith and their fears were very trying to the Lord when He was here. I suppose it still is. The disciples, not many days earlier than this incident, were commissioned to go out and preach the Gospel of the Kingdom. They were given power over unclean spirits and power to heal the sick and raise the dead. (Matthew 10) The man mentioned in the story above obviously traveled far to find the one about whom the disciples spoke and then begged Him to cast out the demon in his son. Jesus did so.

In other Gospels this story turns to a conversation with the disciples. They ask later, "Why could we not cast him out?" The answer must have rung in their ears, "Because of your unbelief."

The Lord wants (and even commands) us to have faith, saying in Mark 11:22b, "Have faith in God." This is rendered in Greek "Have the faith of God." The faith of God could be defined as unswerving, confident, and assured faith that what God promised He is able to perform. This is why He could, without flinching place the two adjectives "faithless" and "perverse" in the same sentence.

We should place as much importance on this as the Lord did. Concern for ourselves, and our doubting of God's promises, can put us in the category of "perverse." Look at the list of the damned in Revelation 21:8, "But the fearful, and unbelieving, and the abominable, and murderers, and whoremongers, and sorcerers, and idolaters, and all liars, shall have their part in the lake which burneth with fire and brimstone: which is the second death." (Author's emphasis)

As He considered His short stay here on this earth, Jesus became more concerned that the Gospel would soon be placed into the hands of the disciples. His question was "How long shall I be with you?"

When Jesus tells His disciples the reason they could not cast the devil out, He used the phrase, "…because of your unbelief." He did not say they didn't have enough faith, or their faith was not large enough, it was not there. In Matthew's account of this, it was almost as if the disciples asked him, "Did we need a greater faith?" to which He replied, "I say to you that if your faith were the size of the smallest seed it would have been enough." The problem was – it wasn't there at all. You doubted my word. I gave you power and authority over unclean spirits and you doubted it. Howbeit [although] this kind goeth not out but by prayer and fasting." [74]

Dedication to Our Faith.

It is not enough to have faith; the faith must be a real and viable part of our life. The prophet said that it is the very life of a righteous man. "… the just shall live by his faith." (Habakkuk 2:4) It is subsequently quoted in the New Testament three times more:

In Romans 1:17, "For therein is the righteousness of God revealed from faith to faith: as it is written, The just shall live by faith."

In Galatians 3:11, "But that no man is justified by the law in the sight of God, it is evident: for, The just shall live by faith."

And in Hebrews 10:38, "Now the just shall live by faith: but if any man draw back, my soul shall have no pleasure in him."

When a man "lives" by his faith, fasting is but a small thing. Fasting does not increase our faith, but it does inform us of its importance and its progress in growth. When Jesus fasted He did not come to the conclusion that He was hungry, He came to the conclusion that man does not live by bread alone. Jesus did not tell them that lack of fasting or lack of prayer was their problem. He said that, because those things were absent it was evidence of a lack of faith. Perhaps a better rendition of the Scripture would be, "This kind goeth not out but by the prayed and fasted man of faith."

To be faithless…is that perverse? Can belief and unbelief exist in the same spirit of man? It probably can, but it would be worth little. It is described well in James 1:8, "A double minded man is unstable in all his ways." James goes on to say that this man will not receive anything from God. It is poorly worded in translation when we read what the man with the demon possessed son said to Jesus – "I believe, help thou mine unbelief." In the Aramaic Peshitta[75] it is stated, "I do believe, help my little faith." He recognized his own fledgling faith and admitting that to Christ, asked for help. Fledgling faith is enough initially, but not for forever. He expects us to mature and come to the fullness of the knowledge of God and unity of faith.[76]

Now we should see the perverseness of our fear and understand the frustration Christ felt when He asked, "How long shall I be with you? How long shall I suffer you?" When you feel the same as Christ does about the perversion that fear and lack of faith causes in your life, you may not tarry as long around the thought of "what if" or toy with worst-case scenarios. You should have courage to go and do as the Lord commanded – fearless and undoubting, pledging your very life.

---

[74] Paragraph excerpt from "On Faith"

[75] The Peshitta is a translation to English directly from the Aramaic. The peculiarity of which is that the Peshitta is supposedly in the original language of the Prophets, Apostles and, of course, our Lord Jesus. Consequently, it is considered a direct translation, per author, George Lamsa.

[76] Ephesians 4:13, "Till we all come in the unity of the faith, and of the knowledge of the Son of God, unto a perfect man, unto the measure of the stature of the fulness of Christ:"

When you pray for Him to give you supernatural confirmations about things you are already sure that are to be done, and like poor fearful Gideon,[77] when you ask Him to wet and dry the fleece over and over again, you might well be ashamed. The weariness you may cause your Friend Jesus Christ, when you are so weak in faith, is heard in His question, "How long must I suffer you?" A little longer, please, dear Savior… a little longer.

---

[77] Judges 6

58.   *What shall the Lord do?*

Mark 12:9 - Luke 20:15 - Matthew 21:40 (Combined), "When the lord therefore of the vineyard cometh, what shall therefore he do unto those husbandmen?"

The role of judge is one that modern man seems to have difficulty attributing to the character of God, as if a judge needed to be cruel, unsympathetic or hard to execute proper judgment. Few seem to understand how fairness and love, kindness and impartiality, honor and equity are necessary for just judgment and nowhere are these characteristics to be found completely, but in God. Even fewer persons grasp how these characteristics, held in perfection, not only enable judgment, but also demand that judgment be done.

In this parable we are made familiar with the "Lord of the vineyard." Although God the Father of our Lord Jesus cannot be equated with all lords mentioned in all parables, we may safely assume that it is He of whom Jesus speaks in this one. Let's look at the character "The Lord of the Vineyard."

Every provision was made for the subsistence and existence of the vineyard. Even protection was provided. "A certain man planted a vineyard, and set an hedge about it, and digged a place for the winefat, and built a tower, and let it out to husbandmen, and went into a far country." (Mark 12:1)

All that the lord of the vineyard asked was that he receive the gain of His investment. "And when the time of the fruit drew near, he sent his servants to the husbandmen, that they might receive the fruits of it." (Matthew 21:34)

Not only was he refused but his messenger was rejected and despised as well. "And they caught him, and beat him, and sent him away empty. And again he sent unto them another servant; and at him they cast stones, and wounded him in the head, and sent him away shamefully handled. And again he sent another; and him they killed, and many others; beating some, and killing some."

"Then said the lord of the vineyard, What shall I do? I will send my beloved son: it may be they will reverence him when they see him. Having yet therefore one son, his well-beloved, he sent him also last unto them. But when the husbandmen saw him, they reasoned among themselves, saying, This is the heir: come, let us kill him, that the inheritance may be ours."(Luke 20:13-14, Mark 12:3-6 Combined).

And so they did just that, they killed the Lord's Son. Which brings us to the question, "What shall the Lord do?" "What would you do?" Jesus had no qualm in asking this question because He knew that those with whom He was talking had a clear and lucid understanding of lordship. Lords did what they wanted to do. They were not sassed or disobeyed. No one rebelled openly toward a lord. Lords ruled the economy and government, and there were few

193

places to hide. The disciples' answer was swift and sure and it was without equivocation or enigma. "He will miserably destroy those wicked men," they said looking among themselves and nodding to one another as if to confirm that there was no other answer.

The onlookers, as well as the disciples, well knew the wrath of a ruler scorned, and to just imagine the killing of the ruler's son sent cold chills through them as they thought of it. They did not realize that they were hearing prophecy of the very actions they themselves would carry out not many days hence, nor did they realize they were hearing this from the lips of the scorned Son Himself.

The other side of this coin is equally rich. Notice that Jesus placed this judgment call into our hands for us to evaluate. When He asked, "What shall the Lord do?" In essence He asked, "What do you think?" As if to tell us that judgment will not be a surprise nor will it be a strange judgment that we are incapable of understanding. We know how we would react, and Jesus is saying that we should not expect God to feel any differently.

We are conscious of our sins and we are fully aware (if we search within) of exactly when we displease God in our everyday lives and what we are to do to rectify it. We will not be surprised at judgment, we will know beyond all doubt that we are being judged fairly, (for we will know it within ourselves) and we will have no excuses to offer. In today's vernacular Jesus would have asked, "What do you expect the Lord to do?" Indicating that judgment will be an instinctive, intrinsic, or natural reaction on God's part. After we have rejected His son what would we expect His reaction to be?

The parable Jesus shared caused anguish in the heart of anyone truly listening. For we all can see ourselves in this selfish and sinful act. Have we not all rejected God when He makes His demands upon us? No matter how fair and equal, no matter that we owe Him every minute, every penny, and every breath, have we not all rebelled and fallen short? The apostle Paul said,

> "And the times of this ignorance [before Christ came and died] God winked at; but now commandeth all men every where to repent: Because he hath appointed a day, in the which he will judge the world in righteousness by that man whom he hath ordained [Christ] ... in that he hath raised him from the dead." (Acts 17:30-31)

The Stone

Jesus always seems to offer hope in our times of despair and when we find ourselves under the convicting power of the Father's spirit. After portraying Himself as the great cornerstone rejected by the builders, He said, "Whosoever shall fall upon that stone shall be broken; but on whomsoever it shall fall, it will grind him to powder." (Luke 20:18)

We all need to fall upon that stone. Hope can be found nowhere else but at the feet of the Judge himself. With His vineyard commandeered, His ambassadors thrust out, and finally, the Lord's own Son spurned, scorned and rejected, Jesus would ask, "What do you expect the lord of the vineyard to do?" You must fall upon the rejected Son and become broken. To become broken and contrite before God is the only hope of all mankind, it your only hope as well. Have you rejected His guidance and His conviction, have you lived your life as if only for yourself? If regard for Him or our fellow man has not been a part of your life, when judgment comes, "What shall the Lord do?"

Judgment is sure and, in comparison of eternity to a man's lifetime, swift. There is coming a day, as sure as sunrise, when everyone will stand before a fair and pure God that will make the division between clean and unclean, holy and unholy, just and unjust. Judgment is not a mystery to those who deal in Truth. You know exactly what judgment will reveal. You know exactly where you will stand. It is not a mystery to you if you are honest and open to what you have read in Scripture. Jesus told an easily understandable story and then He asked a question. You know how you would react if your son were disrespected, beaten and murdered by people employed and supported by you. You know that YHVH is just and fair, you know He will "…by no means clear the guilty…."[78] You know He will not overlook, or turn away, or forget. When considering the day of His return, Jesus asks, "What will the Lord do?"

---

[78] Exodus 34:7

59.   Why tempt ye me?

Matthew 22:18 - Luke 20:23 - Mark 12:15 (Combined), [The Pharisees asked,] "Shall we give, or shall we not give [to Caesar]? But Jesus perceived their wickedness, their hypocrisy and their craftiness, and said unto them, Why tempt ye me, ye hypocrites? bring me a penny, that I may see it."

If only treason could be proved, the Romans would deal with Jesus and the men of the synagogue would be clear in the matter. So they conspired to entrap Jesus by having Him declare the tribute to Caesar as unlawful in the eyes of God, and thus making Him guilty of insurrection. All of the Jews felt the heavy and burdensome hand of Roman rule. They knew that their offerings were to go to the temple and not to Caesar, but no one dared to speak it. Those who did were considered "zealots" and spent their share of time in jail. Those who spoke it or taught it were considered traitors and could likely lose their lives.

"Is it Lawful to give tribute unto Caesar or not?" They knew that any God-fearing man would certainly have a problem with the financing of the Roman Empire. More so, the tithe was a method of worship as well as a financial plan of support for the Temple. This gift given to Caesar did not set well with the Jews. Notice that they did not say "pay taxes." They asked if it was lawful to "give tribute" – as if the offering was a tribute of respect or worship. Jesus could not answer well without either slighting God or Caesar... or could He? Here our Lord Jesus opened a wholly new way of thinking. If His message is properly received, we may never look at money in the same way again.

"Shall we give, or shall we not give? But he, knowing their hypocrisy, said unto them, Why tempt ye me? bring me a penny, that I may see it. And they brought it. And he saith unto them, Whose is this image and superscription? And they said unto him, Caesar's. And Jesus answering said unto them, Render to Caesar the things that are Caesar's, and to God the things that are God's. And they marvelled at him." (Mark 12:15-17)

"Why tempt ye me?" Jesus asked, "Why are you testing me?" An honest answer from this group would be, "Because if you fail the test, the pressure on us is alleviated and we will feel no obligation to listen to what you say." No one will hear this answer except deep within their own hearts. For we all know that if Jesus was not, yea rather, is not who He said He is, the pressure is off to believe anything He said.

There is today a contemporary "testing" of Jesus. The words of Jesus in the New Testament are being scrutinized today by the "educated," thinking men of colleges, universities and even seminaries. In these so-called searches for the historical Jesus, men decide whether or not Jesus actually said what He said, whether He was quoted incorrectly, or whether the writing was purely fantasy. I predicted that they would eventually find among themselves that there is little, if anything, to take seriously about Christ or that He was a myth altogether. I was right. If the "panel of experts" could hear Christ He would ask them, "Why do you test me?

Christ is still tested daily. Those who feel that His way is difficult, discover contradictions in His words for the purpose of alleviating the compulsion to do as He says. Anyone who squirms under His authority *will* test Him. Satan himself felt it a matter of first priority to test Him, hoping for a failure that would alleviate his obligation to serve Him as Lord. Jesus appeared to the world as Messiah at His baptism by John. Once a mystery, now widely known to all, as the words came from heaven, "This is my beloved Son," Jesus is revealed as the Messiah.

Satan lost no time. He set up a test for Him. We are struck by the word "immediately" in Mark 1:12, "And immediately the Spirit driveth him into the wilderness." If Jesus fails this test, He fails all. The three-fold power of sin and rebellion, the lust of the eye, flesh, and the pride of life are all to be vanquished and overcome by our Savior. As Jesus passes the tests it marks the last of Satan's tests in the spirit. He seems to have learned what man seems to never learn, for the testing of Christ by man continues to this very day.

He Is Still Tested Today

Tests that come from man grieve the heart of God, as they are unwarranted and foolish. Why would we want to be free from the "burden" of obedience to Christ? His is a light burden, one for which we should gladly trade our own loads of laden. We can hear sorrow in Christ's question, "Why are you testing me?" He must wonder why we want to be free from Him.

The familiar fury Christ displayed in the presence of hypocrisy can also be heard behind this sadness. "Why do you try to entrap me? You hypocrites are pretending to be friends of Caesar all the while, you are hating Him." They pretended to love Caesar to get what they wanted. Recalling John 19:15, "But they cried out, Away with him, away with him, crucify him. Pilate saith unto them, Shall I crucify your King?" The chief priests answered, "We have no king but Caesar."

Soon the "Jesus Seminar," attempting to find the historical Jesus, will be finished. All who have wanted a reason to eliminate the words of Christ will soon have in their hand paper "proof" that they need not heed this figment of imagination and superstition, this religious figure called Jesus who has no basis in fact. Soon they will be free to pursue their lives of pleasure with no convictions, no condemnation, not having to answer to Jesus for anything. Or will they?

The nagging question of Christ's legitimacy and relevance will continue upon the moral sense of man as long as man is capable of hearing his own conscience. Man will forever try to escape the voice of his disobedient heart answering in the silence to a just and holy God. This is why we hear more and more noise in the lifestyle of man. Man avoids silence when his heart is bursting to repent – a TV left on in every room, a radio turned to nearly its loudest volume, while the world at large feels the need to supply music in every public place, from holding on telephones to loud speakers at gas pumps, we are inundated with noise to mask our soul's cry for help.

Those who do not try to avoid hearing the still small voice and yet wish to continue their own way must seek an alternative route to peace with God that bypasses repentance. Their disquieted souls seek to be rectified and justified, but the price of losing oneself, of giving oneself totally to God, is too high a price to pay. So they attempt to debunk the source of all their conviction. The idea is: test the history of Jesus by science, logic or deduction, in order to fail Him as unworthy to be our example, thereby rendering the Bible inaccurate and unreliable thereby making God an unbelievable fairy tale. No God, no Bible, no Jesus, no conviction, no problem!

When we do this, Jesus asks, "Why do you test me?" Our sad answer is: "If you fail, we have a cloak for our sin." All testing of Christ is born of rebellion and sin. You must be honest about your intent when you test what you are to know only by faith. You must be ever so careful when you find yourself holding the Scriptures under scrutiny. You must ask yourself, "Am I learning of Christ as He asked me to do, or am I tempting Him, testing Him to empower myself in wrongdoing?"

The only way to be sure of your motivation is to live above reproach, to live in obedience and humility and then you may interrogate any subject, ask any question, investigate every word of the Scriptures, and never violate His will for you. But, if you lead an unregenerate lifestyle or participate in selfish and lawless conduct, customs, and behavior with which you have no desire to part, you will never have the assurance of a pure motive. Be honest; answer Christ's question, "Why tempt ye me?"

60. *Whose image is this and whose name is written here?*

Luke 20:22-25, "Is it lawful for us to give tribute unto Caesar, or no? But he perceived their craftiness, and said unto them, Why tempt ye me? Shew me a penny. Whose image and superscription hath it? They answered and said, Caesar's. And he said unto them, Render therefore unto Caesar the things which be Caesar's, and unto God the things which be God's."

Many, who read this passage, are apt to apply it to taxes, money and such. It has been used to alleviate guilt for not paying taxes, or perhaps to dampen the pride of being a faithful taxpayer. Both are topics worthy of interesting discussions. However, "rendering unto Caesar" is only half of Christ's Commandment. The other, more neglected part, is giving to God, "the things that be God's." Which should lead us to ask, "Which things are God's?"

Tithes, offerings, and sacrifices have traditionally been a part of man's worship from the beginning. Not only did God accept an offering from Abel at the beginning of the world, but accepted the tithe and offerings throughout the days of Abraham and later He commanded the tithe, in the written Law, in the days of Moses. More so, it is the heart of man that commands him to give to that which he loves. He cannot help but to make and send gifts to his friends, his lovers, his God. What kind of offering does our God anticipate from us?

We must admit we can add nothing to the God who created all things. For, at one time, all was His. Any gift for Him would be anti-climactic for He possesses all. Likewise, Rome, in the days of Christ, seemed to own all. Roman oversight and presence was felt and seen everywhere. They could take by force anything they wanted, but to avoid insurrection and mutiny they would extract a tax, or "tribute" to Caesar. These taxes would amount to as much as they could feasibly exact without revolt.

The government under which money is issued has always determined its value. Both in denomination and true value, the "realm of the coin" has always proven to be more important in determining value than the "coin of the realm." This system has proven to be best, for when people and trends determine value; emotion and greed may cause inflation or recession to wildly occur, destabilizing trade and market values. When money is used, and its value manipulated, to satisfy the avarice of the few in whose hands this power has been placed, it eventually becomes worthless and must be replaced. Caesar put his image and name on each coin to denominate and identify the coin as to which kingdom it belonged and to assure its value. This would give the seller and purchaser confidence in the value of the funds used.

The Kingdom of God has a currency as well, a coin of great value. The value of this coin is determined by the King and is never subjected to private evaluation by anyone. Though we have arbitrarily valued and devalued it from time to time, its true worth has remained constant. It still brings joy and

199

pleasure to God when this coin is given in offering, and anyone wishing to offer it must discover it, possess it, and then give it in tribute.

In Matthew 13:46, Jesus told a story about a man finding such a thing of great value. "A pearl of great price" it was called. He "went and sold all that he had, and bought it." If we could discover such a valuable "coin" of the Kingdom of God, it would be worth everything we presently own to possess it, for it is the only genuine tribute we may truly offer as a gift to the Kingdom, with which our Father would be pleased.

Jesus also told of a field, "Again, the kingdom of heaven is like unto treasure hid in a field; the which when a man hath found, he hideth, and for joy thereof goeth and selleth all that he hath, and buyeth that field." When we find and identify the gift that God wants from us – the only gift that will bring pleasure to God – we will have found an object of great price, an irreplaceable and rare gift to bestow upon the Creator of all things. We will be able, for the first time, to give to Him what He will not take for Himself, though He possesses all things. (Matthew 13:44)

These men in the parables who found the treasure and the pearl were able to find what others missed. They were able to identify what no one else could. How can we be sure not to walk over the gift, like everyone else did for all those years, as it lay just beneath the soil? How will we find and identify the only gift of tribute that God desires? When Jesus says to, "render to God the things that are God's," we must first find the things that are God's.

Jesus identified Caesar's property. He asked, "Whose image and superscription hath it?" It therefore became obvious who owned and controlled it by the image and superscription that it bore upon it. The coin had a profile image of Caesar and his name was boldly inscribed around its perimeter to make its owner and evaluator unequivocal. It was, unmistakably, the property of Caesar.

When we look in to the Scriptures we may find some clues like these to identify the property of God. In Genesis 1:26-27, we can see the image of God was impressed upon the form of man himself. The creation story tells us we have His image. Where will we find His superscription? The promise of Revelation 3:12 states, "Him that overcometh ... I will write upon him the name of my God..."

Minted By YHVH

From beginning to end the Bible declares us to be the property of God; minted, if you will, by His hands. Coined in His mind, and valued by His love, guaranteed by His grace, we are His most valued possession. He spoke of His own heart of compassion when, in the story in Luke 15, He told of the woman who had ten pieces of silver. He asks, *"...if she lose one piece, doth [she] not light a candle, and sweep the house, and seek diligently till she find it? And when she hath found it, she calleth her friends and her neighbours together, saying, Rejoice with me; for I have found the piece which I had lost."* Then to *make the parable unmistakable, He adds, "Likewise, I say unto you, there is joy in the presence of the angels of God over one sinner that repenteth."*

Your service to Him, your overcoming the world, your relinquishment of selfish control, inscribes His name upon you making Him alone the determiner of your value. Your tribute to Him can be no less than to "render unto God the things that are God's."

You are God's own creation and He demands no less than you and your service as the only reasonable tribute "I beseech you therefore, brethren, by the mercies of God, that ye present your bodies a living sacrifice, holy, acceptable unto God, which is your reasonable service."[79] Look in the mirror and consider what you owe to God. Look at your life and service, and ask, "Whose image is this and whose name is written here?"

---

[79] Romans 12:1

61.   How shall ye believe my words?

John 5:45-47, Do not think that I will accuse you to the Father: there is one that accuseth you, even Moses, in whom ye trust. For had ye believed Moses, ye would have believed me: for he wrote of me. But if ye believe not his writings, how shall ye believe my words?"

All the Gospel accounts of Jesus agree that Moses testified to the ministry of Christ. From the transfiguration to the resurrection and beyond, we can find the name of Moses and the testimony of the Law confirming the acts and words of Jesus Christ. To the Jew, the Law and Prophets were ample testimony. When an event, doctrine, or idea was found contained in the Law, little argument was posed against it. To have the testimony of the Prophets was also corroboration. When Jesus rose from the dead He took time with the disciples and taught them these testimonies. *"And beginning at Moses and all the prophets, he expounded unto them in all the scriptures the things concerning himself."* (Luke 24:27)

Note, in this instance, that when Jesus showed these men Himself revealed in the Scriptures, not one word of the New Testament was yet written. Can we find Christ in the Prophets? Have we seen Christ revealed in the Law? Perhaps a better question would be, "Has Christ revealed to us the Old Testament Scriptures concerning Himself?" Unfortunately many "New Testament" Christians seem to have an aversion to even reading the Old Testament. Many see the Law as damaging to their faith or as a threat of dangerous legalism or justification by works.

In reality, the Law never taught justification by works. By Abraham's covenant with God, all were justified by faith. Paul taught that the Law came about because people continued to sin. "The Law was added because of transgression," Paul says. (Galatians 3:19) The Law showed them that they were sinning. For we who are Christians, this is now the ministry of the Holy Spirit. "And when he [the Holy Spirit] is come, he will reprove the world of sin, and of righteousness, and of judgment." (John 16:8) This ministry, operating in full capacity, renders the Law unnecessary in this regard, but who among us would claim to have the Spirit of God working in us at full capacity? Therefore the Law still has its uses among us imperfect ones.

This is good news, however. The Law is not a threat to faith. As Jesus has told us, it has within it testimonies of Him.[80] This quality, in itself, is interesting. Jesus was constantly referring to the Law as He describes His ministry and mission. A good example is John 3:14, "And as Moses lifted up the serpent in the wilderness, even so must the Son of man be lifted up." Here Jesus compares His death on a tree comparable to the brass serpent on a pole

---

[80] John 5:38-39, "And ye have not his word abiding in you: for whom he hath sent, him ye believe not. Search the scriptures; for in them ye think ye have eternal life: and they are they which testify of me."

that healed the Hebrews of deadly snakebites. (Numbers 21) The parallels are striking.

We should be more familiar with the riches of the Old Testament. It is a treasure trove of ideas, prophecy, and symbolism that facilitates a better understanding and appreciation for Christ Jesus. As we read it, we feel like we are there with God as He works, thinks, and emotes. We feel like, off stage observers; we were privy to the script from the beginning to end, while we see it played out before us.

Our Unique Prospect

This privilege is a remarkable opportunity. We, as Spirit filled believers, may read the Old Testament with the understanding that even the WRITERS did not have! Read Jesus' words from Matthew 13:17, "For verily I say unto you, That many prophets and righteous men have desired to see those things which ye see, and have not seen them; and to hear those things which ye hear, and have not heard them." The Holy Spirit makes this insight possible. The comforter leads, guides, and expounds every letter of the Scriptures as we read of Christ in the Law and the Prophets and Psalms.[81]

Time would fail to show even a small sampling of finding Jesus in the Old Testament. Did you know that Jesus was named for Joshua (Jesus is a Greek rendition) who led the Children of Israel out of the wilderness and into the Promised Land? (Matthew 1:21) Do we hear the Lord Jesus' voice in creation, "Let us make man?" Are we aware that His is the "heel" mentioned in Genesis 3:15? Do we see Him in the scarlet cord of Rahab or the manna[82] in the wilderness? Have we met him in Melchisedec[83] or see His parallel in the only begotten son of Abraham that lay upon the altar?[84] Do we hear the familiar jingle of silver paid for the patriarch Joseph as was paid to Judas for Jesus? Does not our heart melt in humble acceptance of His love as He declares Himself to us in the Song of Solomon? Can anyone read the Psalms and not hear the heart of the Savior cry for His people? Can we see His figure in Ruth's kinsman redeemer,[85] the Lamb of substitution for Isaac,[86] the Passover lamb,[87] the fire of guidance in the wilderness,[88] or the scapegoat sacrifice?[89] Is He not

---

[81] Luke 24:44, "And he said unto them, These are the words which I spake unto you, while I was yet with you, that all things must be fulfilled, which were written in the law of Moses, and in the prophets, and in the psalms, concerning me."

[82] John 6:32, "Then Jesus said unto them, Verily, verily, I say unto you, Moses gave you not that bread from heaven; but my Father giveth you the true bread from heaven."

[83] Hebrews 7, Genesis 14, "...he gave him tithes of all."

[84] Genesis 22:2, "Take now thy son, thine only son Isaac, whom thou lovest ... and offer him...."

[85] Ruth 3:13, "Tarry this night, and it shall be in the morning, that if he will perform unto thee the part of a kinsman, well; let him do the kinsman's part: but if he will not do the part of a kinsman to thee, then will I do the part of a kinsman to thee, as the LORD liveth: lie down until the morning."

[86] Genesis 22, "...And Abraham said, My son, God will provide himself a lamb for a burnt offering: so they went both of them together."

[87] Exodus 12:3, "Speak ye unto all the congregation of Israel, saying, In the tenth day of this month they shall take to them every man a lamb, according to the house of their fathers, a lamb for an house:"

[88] Exodus 13:21, "And the LORD went before them by day in a pillar of a cloud, to lead them the way; and by night in a pillar of fire, to give them light; to go by day and night:"

the power in the voice of all the prophets, and the lesson in all the Laws? If we do not read (and therefore believe) the Law and Prophets, How shall we believe His words? They are one, and the same.

The Old Testament Law speaks of sin and death only to the sinful and dying. From it, those born from above may receive life and insight into the heart of Jehovah and His son, Joshua the Messiah. The redemption of man, the love of God toward His people, the plan of salvation, all these can be found there! It is not a book that threatens faith; it is, in fact, a book that records the very beginnings of faith.

The Jews of Jesus' day knew all the words yet missed the Word Himself. (John 1:1) They fancied themselves as students of the Scriptures, yet Jesus told them that if they had known the Scriptures they would have recognized Him. Jesus warned those who ignored His appearance in the Old Testament that Moses [figuratively] will point a finger at them in judgment and testify that they were indeed told. Jesus did not claim to be their accuser, as Moses had already accused them.

We stand accused by Moses as well. The Old Testament is not a "take it or leave it" proposition. It is not just rhetorical or recreational reading. It is not a book of myths and legends. If we do not, can not, or worse yet, *choose* not to believe what we read of Moses, how can we believe Christ? You may *claim* to follow Christ, but how can you follow whom you cannot believe? For if you don't read and believe Moses' writings how shall you believe His words?

---

[89] Leviticus 16:8, "And Aaron shall cast lots upon the two goats; one lot for the LORD, and the other lot for the scapegoat."

62. Why do you call me Lord and not do what I say?

Luke 6:46, "And why call ye me, Lord, Lord, and do not the things which I say?"

Evangelical Christianity has warred upon this battlefield for years. Are we saved by faith alone? Are we saved by works alone? In his attempt to codify his faith and practice, man has made many false notions feasible and many feasible notions false. Balance is not to be found among those who are zealous to prove points, argue positions, and defend opinions. It is unfortunate that balance is absent in this endeavor, for it is exactly what is most necessary.

Once, I sent an electronic document to a friend for editing. The attributes of the file I sent had the title and particulars, and it also contained my name as the author's name. When I received the document back, after my friend edited it for me, the title was the same and all the particulars, but, because she edited the content, the computer changed the author's name to hers. Even if she only replaced one comma the program renamed the author of the document to the one who edited it -- and rightfully so.

Likewise there are those who believe that we should keep the Law, and, finding it difficult, they edit the Law in their minds so that compliance is more comfortable for them. They say that the Law is different today than it was yesterday, or that the Spirit of the Law teaches otherwise than the letter, or that one part is ceremonial Law and one part is moral Law and we need not keep either one part or the other.

We must be advised that when we edit the Law, the Law is made to be our document and not God's any longer. So, if we change one jot or tittle,[90] the document's author changes, too. We end up keeping our own Law – not God's Law.

Then there are those who believe that the Law is past and is ineffectual, and they think that they need not keep any of it. But either way, few people will engage and live by a faith that inconveniences them. Few people have a Lord over them. Most do as they please. The submission under which we place ourselves is false and deceiving. For we submit to God's Law changed into our own law – changed ever so slightly perhaps, but nonetheless – changed.

As an example, a woman may be proud of being submissive to her husband as the Scriptures declare; but, it just so happens that her husband never inconveniences her. This kind of husband is considered to be lord by his wife so long as no demands are made that she could consider to be unreasonable.

Some Christians fancy themselves submissive to God, but it is not YHVH, it is a god of their own making, a god who demands nothing more than they are willing to give. Similarly, some Christians think they are obedient to the Law, but it is not THE Law they are keeping, it is THEIR Law, by virtue of

---

[90] Matthew 5:18, "For verily I say unto you, Till heaven and earth pass, one jot or one tittle shall in no wise pass from the law…"

the fact that they have edited it to their liking. Others are proud of their full compliance to their denominational guidelines. The way they believe, the way they dress, the way they talk and act is all-compliant, but it is what they wish to do. Few of us do more or less than we wish to do.

Some Christians are proud of carrying out their duty to God, but their "master" just so happened to give them a duty that pleases them well. Their "god" is strained through their denomination, their understanding, their vocabulary, their wishes, their desires, and their convenience. If the modern god of "Christianity" is given the name we want Him to have, the power we want Him to have, the control, the latitude, the shape and form we want Him to have, we have fit Him into the box we have made for Him. This is not life under a Lord – this is idolatry (worshiping the god of our own making). This is NOT living under a King, this is living with an elected President whose attributes we have chosen.

In the days of Christ, the people to whom He spoke were well aware of Lordship, what it meant, and what it was. Our American culture has nearly erased this concept. With our understanding of equality and independence, it has become impossible for us to even imagine a Lord over us, and making his will ours. In the days of Christ, if a man found himself in need, for reasons of poverty or debt, he could surrender to his benefactor as a slave or a sharecropper. Everything he had was surrendered for the debt. His house was no longer his, nor was his land, his furnishings, even his own time was no longer at his discretion. He may go to his lord and say, "My mother is very sick in a nearby town, may I and my family go to see her?" To which the lord may reply, "Yes" or "No." Knowing this, Jesus asked, "Why do you call me Lord, and not do what I say?"

Savior, But … Not Lord?

There is ongoing debate among evangelical Christians about whether or not the concept called "Lordship Salvation" is right or wrong. One side maintains that a person can look to Christ for salvation while maintaining rule over his own life. In short, He is Savior, but not Lord.

The other side says that this idea is impossible. On whichever side we find ourselves, we must admit that there is a sound of perplexity and confusion in the voice of the Savior when He asks, "Why call ye me Lord, Lord, and do not the things that I say?" It is as if He asks, "How can I be Lord, yet see no evidence of it?" "How can I be a Lord, with no subjects?"

This way of thinking takes us back to the subject James and Paul disputed, and the one we started with; "Are we saved by faith alone, or are we saved by works alone?" While James says in James 2:21, "Was not Abraham our father justified by works, when he had offered Isaac his son upon the altar?" Paul disagrees and asserts, "For if Abraham were justified by works, he hath whereof to glory; but not before God." (Romans 4:2) The problem comes when we attempt to codify doctrine. Why must we insist on the inclusion of the word "alone?"

Why must we select, identify, and determine a singular absolute? Could it be that we are saved not by faith alone, nor by works alone but by both, by grace? Could it be that the difficulty in definition is because, though the terms of faithful obedience are separable, the execution of it is not? We reject it, because it will not fit into our dogma. By demanding "all or nothing at all," we reject perfectly sound ideas. Here is where the "feasible" is made "false."

What good would Abraham's actions have been if they were not done in faith? Faith is integral and indispensable. What if Abraham offered His son Isaac presumptuously, or out of hatred, or even stupidity? What if He killed his son by an accident? Would it have achieved the same resultant righteousness? It is ludicrous to think that his actions would be acceptable by God under any circumstance, done by any motive, or even at his own will.

Consider for a moment the opposite. What if he had never obeyed? What if he altered the orders slightly to make compliance more comfortable for himself? What if he had offered another boy? What if he had chosen another hilltop, or decided to do it on another day, or in a different manner? It is an inescapable fact that we must do exactly as we are told, to remain under the grace of God, as well as have faith. As we consider this, we should ask ourselves and answer the question of James, "… a man say he hath faith, and have not works? Can faith save him?" (James 2:14)

Though they are few, there are those who answer this question affirmatively, believing that Christ can and will save those who do not honor Him as Lord of their life, those who do as they wish, as long as they have faith that He will forgive them. They believe that the blood of Jesus Christ will be applied as atonement and that the forgiveness of God is granted to those who do as they please and those who feel no duty to God (as servants) or to Christ (as Lord). There are also those who dare not answer the question readily with a "Yes," yet live this way everyday, as if they fully expect Christ to overlook their disobedience, their willful ignorance, their laziness and rebellion. However if such an idea were true, why would the Lord ask the question that He did? Does He not know that we can indeed call Him "Lord" and not do what He says?

You may go through this life as free as you wish, doing only what is pleasant, claiming that you are not compelled to obey any Law, or Commandment of Christ, boasting that you are just a sinner saved by grace, and still claim Jesus as your Lord, even calling Him Lord, Lord. You may claim Him… but does He claim you? He makes it abundantly clear that, "Not every one that saith unto me, Lord, Lord, shall enter into the kingdom of heaven; but he that doeth the will of my Father which is in heaven." (Matthew 7:21, Author's emphasis)

If yours is a Lord of your choice, not one who insists on His preeminence but one who allows you to do as you please – if you feel no obligation to do what is clearly a commandment of Christ – if you do what you want, expecting forgiveness as part of a contractual agreement, you have no Lord. If you have no Lord, you must candidly ask yourself if you have a Savior.

Perhaps the answer to that question can be found in the answer to the question the Lord Jesus asks in earnest, "Why do you call me Lord, and not do the things that I say?"

63.   Have ye not read, "I am the God of Abraham, Isaac and Jacob?"

Matthew 22:31-32, "But as touching the resurrection of the dead, have ye not read that which was spoken unto you by God, saying, I am the God of Abraham, and the God of Isaac, and the God of Jacob? God is not the God of the dead, but of the living."

Probably the most inexplicable position is that of the anti-Semitic Christian. There are those who take on this ridiculous prejudice as their own and some who just mentally separate Jews and Christians as two different sects altogether. The anti-Semite is likely not a person fully familiar with the love of Christ. Unfortunately, those having segregated views or can mentally erect a wall of separation between Jew and Gentile are more common than we might think.

Paul made no such distinction. We may read in Galatians 3:26-29, "For ye are all the children of God by faith in Christ Jesus… There is neither Jew nor Greek… for ye are all one in Christ Jesus. And if ye be Christ's, then are ye Abraham's seed, and heirs according to the promise."

The book of Romans was written to folks that were ready to dispense with all Jews as enemies and raise Christianity up as founded upon Christ, forgetting the past Jewish history. This may not set well with many Christians today either, but our salvation is not founded upon some new Christian covenant, but rather founded upon the first covenant with Abraham. It is founded upon the promise made to Abraham centuries before the sacrifice that made salvation possible.

We cannot separate from Jewish culture, for we have been adopted into it. Paul asks,

"What then? are we better than they? No, in no wise: for we have before proved both Jews and Gentiles, that they are all under sin; As it is written, There is none righteous, no, not one: There is none that understandeth, there is none that seeketh after God. They are all gone out of the way, they are together become unprofitable; there is none that doeth good, no, not one." (Romans 3:9-12)

Jesus confirms the connection to Israel when talking to a Samaritan woman about salvation. He had no problem telling her,

"Ye worship ye know not what: we know what we worship: for salvation is of the Jews." (John 4:22)

Though salvation would be impossible without the Messiah Jesus, its plan is based upon a covenant made between Jehovah and Abraham. As a matter of fact, the salvation plan we cherish did not even include Gentiles initially. We are being used as a lever, a tool, an example, (if you will) to provoke the Jew to jealousy.[91] God has adopted us into His family to antagonize His Jewish children to follow Him again.

We Cannot Get This Wrong.

We are only default winners of a contest. We were given first place only because the real winner did not claim the prize. We are as stepchildren gaining the inheritance because the true children were cut out of the will. We need not boldly claim a place in this Kingdom that was never intended for us – we need to accept humbly the opportunity given us, gracefully, thankfully and not be so stupid as to say, "I will worship God as I please. All that Jewish stuff is for the Jews, we need not encumber ourselves with THEIR religion."

"For there is no difference between the Jew and the Greek: for the same Lord over all is rich unto all that call upon him." (Romans 10:12)

The entire book of Romans is an interesting read. Paul tries to convince Gentiles to take up the Law and Prophets, the forefathers and family of God, and the entire Jewish nation as a whole, as their own. He tries to convince them that they are grafted into a Jewish vine, an olive tree whose roots are planted in Jewish soil. But he even warns the Gentiles not to brag about being grafted into this tree from which branches were broken off that we might be grafted in. "Well; because of unbelief they were broken off, and thou standest by faith. Be not highminded, but fear: For if God spared not the natural branches, take heed lest he also spare not thee." (Romans 11:20-21)

Most Christians know little about the Jewish religion. The Jews are only known as those who rejected Jesus as Messiah, those who crucified the Lord, or as members of a strange, old-world religion. We must realize that the Jewish faith in God comes from the same Scriptures we carry along with us.

Most Christians today do not even read the Old Testament, considering it "a book for the Jews." Jesus never condemned the Jewish faith, but rather, He cherished it. He only condemned their traditions that were not based in Commandment. He condemned their concern for how they appeared to each other. He condemned their lack of concern for each other, their hypocrisy, their arrogance, their unbelief, but are there any Gentiles without these problems? We must not erect walls between the Jew and us like the Romans were trying to do. These attitudes and actions are based in pride, a motivation also condemned by Christ.

There are, however, thousands of years of history available through the Jews. Theirs is a culture rich in heritage and deep commitment toward the same God we serve. Why don't we want to know more about the Jew's calendar, their Holy Days, their writings, their family names?

Can we recognize names found in Scripture, as they are known today? Why do the Jews worship like they do and why do they believe what they believe? What do the Holy Days mean to them – or to us? Today Jesus would

---

[91] Romans 11:11, "... through their fall salvation is come unto the Gentiles, for to provoke them to jealousy." Romans 10:19, "...I will provoke you to jealousy by them that are no people, and by a foolish nation I will anger you."

likely look at our worship, our holidays, our songs, our teaching, all devoid of Old Testament heritage, depth and richness and say, "Ye worship ye know not what."

Please do not infer from this advice that we should follow Judaism (the religion). Although some have accepted Christ, their religion, as a whole, rejects Jesus as Messiah; and, therefore, is foundationally flawed. But, in some ways they love and follow the God of the Old Testament with a love and respect that is missing among us who have received His son as Messiah. We could learn much from the Jew. We must know what we worship, the Jew could tell us, but most of all, if these walls were not built, the Jew could gain much from us.

Israel has been made blind[92] so that God might redeem us Gentiles. In that way, we are responsible for the blindness in the Jews that causes us to distrust and even despise them. We as Gentiles need to realize that we share in the responsibility. We need not despise anyone. If we have a problem with Jews, we have a problem with Christianity. Christ was the called King of the Jews – and so He was. If we have a problem with Jews, we have a problem with salvation, for, as Jesus said, "Salvation is of the Jews." If we do not respect the Jews, how can we respect the Scriptures? "…Because that unto them were committed the oracles of God." (Romans 3:2)

Everywhere we look, the history of Christianity and the Jewish faith are identical. Does the root bear us? Or do we think we bear the root?[93] Who is this God we serve anyway? Jesus would answer, "Have ye not read, 'I am the God of Abraham, Isaac and Jacob?'"

---

[92] Romans 11:25, "For I would not, brethren, that ye should be ignorant of this mystery, lest ye should be wise in your own conceits; that blindness in part is happened to Israel, until the fulness of the Gentiles be come in." John 9:39, "And Jesus said, For judgment I am come into this world, that they which see not might see; and that they which see might be made blind."

[93] Romans 11:18, "Boast not against the branches. But if thou boast, thou bearest not the root, but the root thee."

64.   *What do they call you?*

Matthew 10:24-25, "The disciple is not above his master, nor the servant above his lord. It is enough for the disciple that he be as his master, and the servant as his lord. If they have called the master of the house Beelzebub, how much more shall they call them of his household?"

Beelzebub? Why Beelzebub? It turns out to be a name indeed most foul. Easton's Bible dictionary has this to say about that name:

Beelzebub: (Gr. form Beel'zebul), the name given to Satan, and found only in the New Testament (Matthew. 10:25; 12:24, 27; Mark 3:22). It is probably the same as Baalzebub (q.v.), the god of Ekron, meaning "the lord of flies," or, as others think, "the lord of dung," or "the dung-god."

The Jews twisted the pronunciation of the name Baalzebub to make it an epithet to anger the pagans. Their pronunciation changed it to mean Lord of flies. Since flies were prevalent in the dung heap – thus the dung-god.

Jesus endured many verbal injuries, especially during the last days of His life. Much is made of and said about the nail prints, the crown of thorns, and the lashings and such. And indeed, it is by those sufferings that we are made whole today, but consider for a moment the day-to-day insults that He must have borne.

The Jews who hated Him were not beyond callous insult. Once, even the legitimacy of His birth was called into question. It is a subtle thing, but listen closely to the Jews insult Him in John 8:39-41,

*"They answered and said unto him, Abraham is our father. Jesus saith unto them, If ye were Abraham's children, ye would do the works of Abraham. But now ye seek to kill me, a man that hath told you the truth, which I have heard of God: this did not Abraham. Ye do the deeds of your father. Then said they to him, **We be not born of fornication**; we have one Father, even God."*

Why would they mention "fornication?" There were many ways to pollute a bloodline. Adultery, marrying outside of the tribes of Israel, whoredom, and even ceremonial uncleanness and separation could cause impurity and separate a man from his Abrahamic family tree. But it was the sin of fornication that loomed over the birth of Jesus and raised the eyebrows of all who knew Mary and Joseph.[94] After all, no really good explanation could ever be given for their first child arriving in less than the usual nine months after their wedding. Many of these men knew this family for years and as they did the math on their fingers, some would shake their heads in disgust, some would smile and giggle to themselves, but none would keep the sordid story a secret. And no enemy of Christ would leave this ammunition unused when challenged

---

[94] John 6:42

by this "bastard" child about their miserable state of unrighteousness. We can almost feel the nasty underlined emphasis on the word "we" when they say, "We were not born of fornication!"

On several occasions these vicious persons also accused our Lord of being possessed of a devil.[95] There was little known about such phenomenon, but it was an easy way to discredit someone and it was needless (and indeed impossible) to qualify such an accusation. Nevertheless, it was said and though never proven, it accomplished its purpose – to vilify the spotless Son of God and provide an excuse for those who would rather not believe and continue in their own way, to ignore and reject Him on pious grounds.

He *Expected* Us to Suffer

It is obvious that Our Lord was despised and rejected. It is equally obvious that He expected that we would suffer at least the same or perhaps greater things than He did. This concept has caused some problems with the less than enlightened when following the less than honest. Sometimes persecution can be used as a cloak for sin – a condition that fools the persecuted as well any onlookers.

I recently heard of a "pastor" who was lamenting his maltreatment by the press and other governmental agencies, and was citing long and laborious examples of persecutions and even cases of martyrdom in ages past and present. His argument sounded like valid persecution until, with the slightest investigation, it was made apparent that he was indeed evolved in most heinous sexual trysts with innocent attendees of his church. It just so happened that these were the "lies" that were being told about him. To him, however, the "persecution" was proof of his being a "man of God." He had convinced himself that no wrongdoing had caused his torment, but that it was genuine persecution. We must not forget what Peter teaches – that when we suffer, we are to make sure it is always "wrongful" persecution by never deserving the punishment we receive.[96]

Persecution does not assure that we walking in God's perfect will, but the absence of persecution would signify that the opposite is likely the case. Jesus states it emphatically in John 15:18-20,

"If ye were of the world, the world would love his own: but because ye are not of the world... the world hateth you. Remember the word that I said unto you, The servant is not greater than his lord. If they have persecuted me, they will also persecute you..."

This Scripture leaves no room for doubt. Nothing in the whole of Scripture leaves any impression other than, "Yea, and all that will live godly in Christ Jesus shall suffer persecution." (2 Timothy 3:12)

---

[95] John 7:20 The people answered and said, Thou hast a devil: who goeth about to kill thee? John 8:52 Then said the Jews unto him, Now we know that thou hast a devil.
[96] I Peter chapters 2 - 3

Now here's the difficult question. How much persecution have you been required to endure? Are you living "Godly – in Christ Jesus?" The enemies of Christ called Him the god of the garbage can – the god of the sewer – the Lord of the flies… what do they call you? Some of us may have to answer that we are well respected in our circles and even in our wider secular fellowships. Some can even flash their "Christian faith" in an election campaign and garner favorable results. Some have status in their community and they suffer no ill effects from their association with the church. But Jesus would ask you a question, "The disciple is not above his master, nor the servant above his lord. If they have called the master of the house Beelzebub… [what] shall they call them of his household?"

The question remains, in a world more wicked than that in the days of Jesus, how can we attain a rank or position of higher respect than He held when He was here? How is it possible that the same hands that put Jesus to death, grasp ours in firm and warm handshakes?

Our Lord warns, "Woe unto you, when all men shall speak well of you! for so did their fathers to the false prophets." (Luke 6:26) Phillip received the SAME hatred that was accorded Jesus. Paul received the SAME treatment Jesus was given. Peter received the IDENTICAL death Jesus was given (perhaps even worse). According to His promise, all of the apostles received the SAME or worse handling than Jesus received. But, not so for many of us. Our familiarity with the false church of today has made us a brother to them. Our conformity to their doctrines has made us a colleague to them. Our compromise has made us their close companions. What is worse yet, our lifestyles have made us indistinguishable from them.

Persecution is **extraordinary** to most modern Christians. This is in direct contrast to the admonition of Peter when he says, "Beloved, think it not strange concerning the fiery trial which is to try you, as though some strange thing happened unto you."[97] This strangeness is not scarcity. Conversely, I hear in this Scripture a warning from Peter that we should think it strange when persecution DOES NOT happen. So how can it be that persecution is so rare to us?

There is a gross inequity in our faith and the faith of our fathers. There is a vast disparity in our walk of faith and the apostles of old. There is an immense difference in the life that Jesus was so sure would encounter persecution daily and the one we actually live. Why is that? Was Jesus unduly concerned about persecution? Was He too protective? Or are we just so far from what He expects us to be that we now may consider His words to be the mutterings of an anachronistic, over-reactive zealot?

They called Him blasphemer, heretic, revolutionary, criminal, reprobate, and when all else failed they even resorted to calling Him a bastard. Are you hearing this kind of viciousness that Jesus promised His disciples that they would hear, or do you find yourself enjoying a position "above" your Lord

---

[97] 1 Peter 4:12.

in respect and dignity in your sphere of influence? They called Jesus a low-life because he hung around tramps, hobos, whores and criminals. They called Him a glutton and a drunk[98] and a false prophet in league with Satan.

Could they call Jesus anything worse? They called Him the dung-god. "What do they call you?"

---

[98] Matthew 11:19, "… and they say, Behold a man gluttonous, and a winebibber, a friend of publicans and sinners…"

65.   Are not five sparrows sold for two farthings?

Luke 12:6-712:24, "Are not five sparrows sold for two farthings, and not one of them is forgotten before God? ... Fear not therefore: ye are of more value than many sparrows." "... how much more are ye better than the fowls?"

The value system, upon which God bases His evaluation of nature, mankind, life, and death, is not as different from ours as it is simply larger, all encompassing, and more complex. For example, we place a great deal of value upon the life of a man. God, for very different reasons – reasons more complex – places more value upon man's death.

Here Christ asks, "How much do you get for five sparrows... one cent?[99] Yet not one of them is forgotten or abandoned of God. To God, you are worth flocks of sparrows." There are many ways to assimilate this information. Ecologically, we could place our needs above the animal kingdom. Spiritually, we may consider ourselves the most valued in creation. Mathematically, if we take the economical data given in the Scripture and from that surmise that we are worth "many sparrows", and if a flock had, say, a thousand birds, we may deduce from this information that we are worth more than two dollars to God! (Perhaps one can *over* analyze.)

All that Jesus was saying here was that there is no reason to fear our death if we realize our death would be of great value and importance to God. Here, Christ was foretelling the persecution and death of His disciples. He was encouraging them that God was watching over them and would not forget them at their deaths. The account in Luke mentions only forgetting, but look at this same account in Matthew 10:29-31, "Are not two sparrows sold for a farthing?[100] and one of them shall not fall on the ground without your Father. But the very hairs of your head are all numbered. Fear ye not therefore, ye are of more value than many sparrows."

The term "fall on the ground" refers to their death. "Without your Father" speaks of God's knowledge. We see God witnessing and evaluating the death of man. We presuppose the acknowledgment of God at the death of a martyr, but the disciples obviously feared a lonely death, "without the Father." Dying, under the best conditions, without the Father, would be a horrible proposal. Jesus gave them comfort in this.

"God knows everything!"

When considering this concept, the idea of the "omniscience" of God becomes a factor. Some who believe that "God knows everything" could take

---

[99] farthing -- Greek assarion, which was a Roman coin equal to a tenth of a denarius or drachma, nearly equal to a halfpenny of our money.

[100] It is duly noted that Matthew's account says two sparrows while Luke says five. The disparity is purposefully evaded to avoid distraction from the subject at hand. The incongruity is irrelevant to the message that little value is placed by man upon sparrows.

little comfort in the words of Jesus here. When the subject of omniscience is debated, these Scriptures are often cited. "God knows how many hairs you have on your head!" say they, "Don't you think He knows everything?" Actually the Scripture says that the "hairs of your head are all numbered" as if the each of them has their own serial number. It is not just that God knows how many He knows which hair goes where!

However, it is not what God knows that will interest the martyr, or those being persecuted, or those who stand seemingly alone for righteousness. It is not the "fact" that God "knows everything" that gives comfort when we suffer or when we are hurt for our faith. It is the fact that the death of a faithful person gains His interest that comforts us. How can we find comfort when asking "Is God aware and concerned about my situation?" when the glib answer comes back, "Sure... God knows everything!" Jesus is not simply teaching that "God knows everything," He is comforting His disciples in the fact that God has interest in their death. He cares for the death of sparrows...and you are worth flocks of sparrows.

Again, we come to the evaluation of death, in the estimation of God. We must admit that we do not see things the same way He does. We should strive to understand the plan and strategy of life and death so that His way makes sense to us.

If you approached a table where there were competitors in a golf match arguing their scores, and you had never heard of the game (you were assuming the high score would win) you may be surprised to hear them argue about their score, insisting that it was lower than was counted. Until you understood that the idea was the lowest score wins the game of golf, you might not understand the discussion at all.

When we approach the death of a loved one for whom we have prayed (and seemingly are receiving no answer) or we read of the deaths of martyrs over history, or the holocaust, or we consider any of the deaths of those who cried out to God only to feel the cold, brassy heavens reflecting their anguish as their prayers went unheeded, we cannot understand. We cannot understand *until* we learn how the score is counted, how the evaluation is performed, *until* we see it from God's perspective.

We need to ask God to reveal His ways to us instead of expecting Him to explain to us His actions or lack of intervention on our behalf. His ways are higher than ours. So says the prophet, "For as the heavens are higher than the earth, so are my ways higher than your ways, and my thoughts than your thoughts." (Isaiah 55:9) We will gain little from fitting God into our lives and trying to make His ways understandable by reducing Him to terms such as "all knowing" or "all caring" or by tritely offering to those who are suffering sayings like, "God knows best." We should aspire to learn His ways and change our understandings and systems of evaluation so that we see things the way He sees them.

There are many things we do not know. We will feel much shame and anguish when we find that we have wasted the valuable, shunned the best, ignored the important, and traded beauty for ashes, joy for sorrow, and His highest for life's mediocre.

YHVH places value on that which we reject and sell for little. We do not understand His evaluation process or system. We prove this is true when we hold on to life with white-knuckled fervor and we claw and scratch our way into our graves while we wish for only one more moment of life. Our actions say there must be something we do not know. Why don't we realize that our deaths are our door – our lives are our prison? We are in a world that hates our God and we serve a God who views our death with hands folded but with great interest when we belong to Him.

If God places a great deal of value in places and upon things that we do not, your death would certainly be one of them. While wishing to die would be unnatural, you may, if you begin to see things God's way, live in the "straight" in which the apostle Paul found himself.

"According to my earnest expectation and my hope…whether it be by life, or by death. For to me to live is Christ, and to die is gain…For I am in a strait betwixt two, having a desire to depart, and to be with Christ; which is far better: Nevertheless to abide in the flesh is more needful for you." (Philippians 1:20-24)

The difference in the way that God sees things and the way we see them is a problem. The gap needs to close between the two paradigms. When we read the Bible or the Words of Christ or the Prophets, they should make sense to us. We should understand what God is saying and why. We should not have to ask God to explain Himself to us; we should rather ask His help to change us so that we can understand Him when He speaks or acts. He places value upon the death of a sparrow. Why?

Jehovah's Point Of View

He watched this tiny bird from its beginning; He knew its parents and watched the death of its grandparents. He knows any sparrow's lineage back to the fifth day of creation. (Which is one day before our own) He fed it every mouthful of food, according to Christ, along with all the fowls of the earth. He watched mama sparrow lay and hatch her eggs and He became aquatinted with all her young as well.

One day this sparrow, going about to find food, was taken in a snare and placed in a cage with four others and placed on a noisy street in Jerusalem to be sold, along with her four other captives for two pennies. Jesus, pointing at them flailing, flopping and trying to escape the cage, illustrates the point that we do not evaluate life *or* death the way He does.

He questions the price on His feathered friends. Do you see things they way the Father sees them? The evaluation of **death** is key. "Are not five sparrows sold for two farthings?"

218

66. Who made me a judge or divider over you?

Luke 12:13-15, "And one of the company said unto him, Master, speak to my brother, that he divide the inheritance with me. And he said unto him, Man, who made me a judge or a divider over you? And he said unto them, Take heed, and beware of covetousness: for a man's life consisteth not in the abundance of the things which he possesseth."

It is interesting that Jesus wanted no part of this squabble though they sought Him to be a fair and impartial judge. His reputation preceded Him. Jesus was known to display wisdom and justice in all He said or did. So much was the case that this man searched for Him to speak to his brother about being selfish with the inheritance.

Solomon was known to be an excellent judge of people, and after the case of the overlain baby he was also known as a divider. (See 1 Kings 3:16-28) The Scriptures say, "All Israel heard of the judgment which the king had judged; and they feared the king: for they saw that the wisdom of God was in him, to do judgment." I suppose that was the case with Christ. Anyone would not have to exemplify a great amount of right judgment before it becomes blatantly evident, for society is awkwardly lacking in the area of true wisdom.

On this day, this brother went home none the richer, none the wiser. To be sure, he probably heard little else after his request was quashed. As the Lord went on to explain that we should beware of covetousness, the man's mind whirled with possible additions to his plea to make the Savior change his mind. Perhaps he could deny covetousness and say it was for beneficent reasons he needed the money—or maybe he could say…. As his mind raced and recited retorts he realized the Master had finished speaking and that he had not heard what He had said. If he had only heard the Lord's answer he might have become a different man!

Many of us in modern Christianity make Jesus a divider of wisdom, and also a divider of doctrines and theology. We use His words to "prove" our case or way of thinking. Surely, we are all guilty of this. We use the words of Christ as a lever to add weight and moment to our ideas and pet doctrines. We should exercise great care when we do this, for in doing so, Jesus is made to be in agreement with us, instead of showing ourselves in agreement with Him. It is a fine line, to be sure, but none the less, a line we must avoid overstepping. We should have a great deal of trouble envisioning Jesus involved in our petty doctrinal debates and becoming a divider or judge. In these matters we may hear Him ask, "Who made me a judge or divider over you?" Then, as in the story, we could expect Him to expose our selfish motives and call for our repentance.

We *cause* Him to be a divider over us when we use His words to force our brethren to accept us as we are. We do this by using the Bible to "prove" our case. If we want to drink wine, we say, "Jesus drank wine!" "Tell 'em Jesus…tell 'em that its OK to drink wine."

In times like these, we need to hear Him say within us, "Who made me a judge over you?" Then we should expect to hear Him expose our motives, our real objectives just as He did to the brother that tried to use Him in this way. He may say to those wishing to drink wine with a clear conscience, "Beware of escaping into your bottle. Beware of desires that can overtake you. Beware of drunkenness."

"The Bible Proves that I Am Right!"

Sometimes when trying to prove a doctrinal point with the Bible, we may find conflicting written testimony there. If we assume that the clarity of a doctrine or Commandment is in some way proportional to its importance, and extra-biblical sources are eliminated, we will find that few of our doctrines are really important doctrines at all.

When we use the Bible or the words of Jesus to "prove" a position or idea, we make Him partake in something that He may, or may not, want to be a participant. When we make Him a judge or a divider between others and us we make Him involuntarily arbitrate and decide between brothers, not to mention the fact that all this is done through the filter of human thinking. We should not make Him a divider or judge. He conducts business on a personal level, through the ministry of the Holy Spirit, guiding, teaching, and revealing Himself. Little can be gained in the heart of your opponent by "proving" your case, other than hardness and stubborn refusal, or humiliation and reluctant submission. Jesus asks, "Who made me a judge over you?"

What can we really prove anyway? Though preponderance of evidence can lead to conclusion, can anyone factually prove that Jesus rose from the dead? Can anyone prove to you that faith in Christ will save you? Is it a matter of fact that we conduct ourselves in certain ways, on certain days, or believe certain things? Everything that is lasting about the faith we have in Christ has been given to us by revelation, by the Father, through the Holy Spirit. Even when things are proven by Scripture the time comes when they must be accepted and adopted willingly (by faith) by those to whom they were proven. When all is said and done there is little to be gained by "wresting"[101] the Scriptures to convince, convict or condemn. If we concede that Jesus wants nothing to do with this sort of thing, and that He is more concerned with the person and purpose behind the action, we have little to prove, little to teach, little to gain by calling on Christ to arbitrate our silly debates.

Jesus looks behind every question and sees the inquirer. He looks behind every action and sees the motive. He looks through man's questions… and sees through man! This is why, when Jesus was asked to, "Make my brother divide the inheritance" He answered, "Beware of covetousness." This is

---

[101] 2 Peter 3:16, "…which they that are unlearned and unstable wrest, as they do also the other scriptures, unto their own destruction."

why His answer to "...Master, we know that thou art true and teachest the way of God in truth" was "Why tempt ye me?" When the Pharisee Nicodemus said, "...Rabbi, we know that thou art a teacher come from God" Jesus answered, "Ye must be born again."

Jesus had no interest in playing word games then, nor does He now. He is interested in changing men's lives, making them whole beings and capable of acceptable service. When you arbitrarily place Him into petty and self-centered squabbles, His ministry is cheapened and his words are forced to do what they were never intended to do. Pray that your heart is mollified and made accepting of His words and that everyone in your realm of influence is as well. This is all you can do and still remain faithful to His ministry. You need not make Him a divider. You need not make Him a judge.

The next opportunity you have to "prove" to someone that you are right by taking out your Bible and pointing to Scriptures, hear Christ whisper in your ear, "Who made me a judge or divider over you?"

67.   *Why take ye thought for the rest?*

Luke 12:26, "If ye then be not able to do that thing which is least, why take ye thought for the rest?"

Life is a really big job... and it is seems to be getting bigger. Life is full of opportunities to do what makes us die. That is not as contradictory as it may sound. Everyday we have to make decisions that determine our course through the hour in which we live. Larger decisions plot our way through the day, the week, the month, and the year. The decisions that frighten us most are the ones that seal our fate and direction for our entire lives, decisions about career, education, debt and finance, marriage partners, and childbearing.

The sobriety and wisdom required for the decisions of life are only available to those whose maturity and age is far past the date that the decisions are required. When you're twenty you figure out how to handle the bully in grammar school, when you are thirty you can properly decide the direction your education and career should go, when you are forty you have the sense to pick a bride, etc. Yet all of these decisions, right or wrong, were made decades before the level of experience was available. Even the everyday decisions – take this road or that one – go to this place or that one – visit here with these folks or go there and spend some time alone, all these decisions and their consequences can grind on a person to the point of weariness.

These everyday decisions steal life away. The predicted consequences of these decisions add pressure to the moment and exacerbate anxiety so as to render the decision even harder to make, and by virtue of the fact that the decision is now made in worried haste – more than likely, the decision will be wrong. What is more, decisions extract joy from a person's life by forever dangling the nagging poser, "What if?" at every questionable juncture in life.

Life need not be so fragile and teetering that we must fear making the wrong decision. Our lives have only become fragile due to a long line of incorrect directions taken and years of bad decisions made. Our lives are sensitive to trouble because of our bad choices based in flawed and emotional human reasoning.

What are we to do? Is there a better place in life for the Christian than this – where we do not have to make difficult, life-altering decisions? Is there some secret formula that can make life decision free? No one enjoys making decisions. We even classify men and women who easily make decisions as leaders because they stand out in life and seem to "have answers." A person having answers is in the minority in our world. Should this be an attribute of a Christian?

Ambition is considered a virtue in the 21st century. Now, more is better. What is new is better than what is old. In the modern world, what is "the latest" is also the "greatest." We, who have uncoupled ourselves from this speeding train, turned off our TV's, and cancelled our newspapers, have a difficult time understanding what all the fuss is about.

When the outlook is thoroughly Christian it is different. Some turned to Christ because life quit making sense. It was not just a matter of getting old; it was a matter of being tired of the same old grind that never seemed to wear away the rough spots in life. Many of us became tired of advancing through life, yet never finding ourselves far enough ahead, tired of an ever-increasing income, yet seeing it buy even less. We became tired of the "high" life that ends in death, and we traded it for the "lower" one that ends in life eternal. For some of us who became older and wiser, ambition was easy to give up because we simply quit. Outside of the Christian world-view this life makes no sense at all.

What's The Point?

It is fun to teach a child to play Tic Tac Toe, but it is nearly impossible to find an adult who will play, because he understands the game too well. After so many games it becomes a coin flip, not a game of skill. After the game of life is understood, it is hard to continue to play.

But what about the young one who still thinks that life offers its bounty only to those who dig in and try? What of those who think that the right decisions, made at the right time, will produce all the desires of their heart? What of those who think that well supplied is well equipped and that the silver platter of life is only offered to those who work hard for it, and the brass ring is there for the one who reaches out just a little bit farther than all the rest? To merely wait and watch life swallow them would be cruel. I would rather implore them to learn from Christ the principle of being in the world and not of it.[102] Mostly, they could learn from an example that "a man's life consisteth not in the abundance of the things which he possesseth."

Ambition is a characteristic that requires foolhardy, arbitrary and uninformed decision making. Although it may be human nature to act upon your undesirable circumstances, it is never smart to move in any direction until purpose and objective are known (or at least sensed). There are some who are foolish enough to say, "As long as we're moving, we're not sitting still" – as if sitting still is the worst thing that could happen to anyone. There are some for whom ambition has become a drug. Just as advancement cannot be determined to be helpful or detrimental until a direction is ascertained, it is extremely important to learn that ambition cannot be defined as good or bad until its source is discovered. It must become apparent that decisions we make within the framework of our own capabilities and unaided reason are likely to be the wrong ones. Simply put, our desires are never a proper source of ambition; we must heed, obey, and trust the Holy Spirit of God as a faithful Guide.

---

[102] 1 John 2:15-16, "Love not the world, neither the things that are in the world. If any man love the world, the love of the Father is not in him."
John 17:15, "I pray not that thou shouldest take them out of the world, but that thou shouldest keep them from the evil."

Said before, and worthy of repetition is this, life is made of opportunities to do what makes us die. This opportunity is, namely, decision-making. We naturally fear making the wrong decision because of the consequences, but we should try to avoiding the decision itself. For when there is a decision to be made we are likely in a situation of our own making, created by a prior decision that we should not have made. We are not to make decisions; we are to follow our Guide. It is all part of being under a Lord.

When a life is free from sin, an inviolate conscience can be trusted. No matter what the outcome of our life's choice is, we have been obedient. We know when something feels right, when a direction seems the right way to go. When the direction we take costs us money, relationships, or opportunity we need not fret that it was a wrong one. The Lord may lead us wherever He desires us to go. He is our Shepherd; we shall not be in want. Our life is to be led by the Spirit of God, not by our intellect or reason. "For as many as are led by the Spirit of God, they are the sons of God." (Romans 8:14)

But, does not this line of reason (the elimination of worldly ambition) work toward laziness, poverty, and slothfulness? At worst, does it not work toward foolhardiness or even danger if we do not plan for success and make decisions that will carry us upward in life? After all, couldn't a person go broke if he was not driven to succeed? These are matters for each of us to work out inside ourselves. It is a matter of faith and trust.

There are some who readily trust Jesus with their death, and yet, have no intention of trusting Him with their life. There are those who believe that He feeds the fowls of heaven and clothes the grass of the field but cannot (or will not) believe He will take care of them. There are those who claim that God has provided them their sustenance through their own strength, will, and ambition. They fear that if they would look to Him on a daily basis, it would somehow insult Him. There are many schools of thought on this matter. Most of the formulas for success, you will note, insure that their present income is not lessened by one penny.

You need to realize that you are in the hands of a loving God, whether you are there willingly or unwillingly, whether bound or free, whether in control of your life or not, God alone can protect you. Life has its cruel ways of letting you know that there is no security, no nest egg, no reserve pantry, and no insurance policy that can alleviate the misery that can come in a night.

Life only takes on the sweetness of assurance, the fragrance of being in the arms of God when we have followed Him. Being led, not by our reasoning, but being led by the Spirit, not by vain ambition or the voices of our peers, but by obedience to His voice alone. We need to transfer our "bank accounts" to heavenly treasures, trade our "barns" for his "windows of heaven,"[103] exchange our trust in our insurance for His blessed assurance.

---

[103] Malachi 3:10, "Bring ye all the tithes into the storehouse, that there may be meat in mine house, and prove me now herewith, saith the LORD of hosts, if I will not open you the windows of heaven, and pour you out a blessing, that there shall not be room enough to receive it."

Trading the Choice for the Voice.

We need to reject decision making as a creaturely activity and a vain endeavor, and determine to do nothing till He makes the right way known to us. Ambition must be rejected as the world's way to advance though life. We are to wait for the voice behind us saying, "This is the way…walk ye in it."[104]

There are so many things we cannot fix in life. So many things are out of our control. Why do we attempt to take on even larger things, make bigger decisions, take greater risks, determining to make our lives better? We cannot prevent a common cold and yet we think we hold cancer at bay with vitamin pills and hold heart disease in check with medication. We cannot balance our checkbooks and yet we claim to know which stocks will rise in value. It is vanity to place so much reliance on our ability that blatantly, obviously, lacks in so many areas.

Ambition reveals itself as vanity, planning proves to be nothing more than gambling, protection, nothing more than guesswork, prevention of future trials and troubles – just empty wishes of the fearful. "If ye then be not able to do that thing which is least, why take ye thought for the rest?"

---

[104] Isaiah 30:21, "And thine ears shall hear a word behind thee, saying, This is the way, walk ye in it, when ye turn to the right hand, and when ye turn to the left."

68. *What will I if it already be kindled?*

Luke 12:49, "I am come to send fire on the earth; and what will I, if it be already kindled?"

The ministry of Christ Jesus is quite different from His perspective than from ours. From our view, we see a simple rescue mission, a throwing of a lifeline as it were. From His perspective, it is more than that.

His is a mission to rescue perishing sheep, dividing them from the goats, as well as the judgment of wolves who threaten them. Though He came to fulfill the Law, He came also to simultaneously nail the handwriting of the Law to the same wood upon which He was executed. His mission was replete with enigma and mystery, paradox and irony.

When He came to forgive and cleanse the repentant sinner, His coming also sealed the condemnation of the hypocrite. He came to open the eyes of the blind and to cause the blindness of those who claim to see. His was an all encompassing mission of rescue from fire and to set one. His was a mission of deliverance as well as captivity, of healing the broken hearted and to break the hearts of stone. When we preach or teach only one side of His mission, we are not preaching the whole counsel of God. The whole counsel of God includes judgment as well as blessing. Jesus came to seek, to save, and to send fire and sword.

To what was Jesus referring when He mentioned this commission of "sending fire" on the earth? In the song of Moses there is a passage that touches upon the ministry of Christ.

*"Of the Rock that begat thee thou art unmindful, and hast forgotten God that formed thee. And when the LORD saw it, he abhorred them, because of the provoking of his sons, and of his daughters. And he said, I will hide my face from them, I will see what their end shall be: for they are a very froward generation, children in whom is no faith. They have moved me to jealousy with that which is not God; they have provoked me to anger with their vanities: and I will move them to jealousy with those which are not a people; I will provoke them to anger with a foolish nation. **For a fire is kindled in mine anger, and shall burn unto the lowest hell, and shall consume the earth with her increase, and set on fire the foundations of the mountains.**"* (Deuteronomy 32:18-22)

Jesus came to set this fire. This fire is the hiding of God's face, the provoking to jealousy and anger. The fire Jesus was to set would show all Israel that nothing would ever be the same because they forgot Him, their Rock. Because they were unmindfully following laws, rules, and traditions, and not following the Creator who made them, but rather looked to gods that were not gods, they too would be left behind for a people who were "not a people." This is nothing other than the transfer of the Gospel of salvation to the Gentiles.

226

"And other sheep I have, which are not of this fold: them also I must bring, and they shall hear my voice; and there shall be one fold, and one shepherd." (John 10:16)

The fire Jesus was to set was a fire of judgment, recompense, and the breaking down of tradition's walls, to burn to cinders the framework of the "old house." The discarding of the old bottles that would break and lose the new wine, the rejection of the old garment repaired again and again to make way for the new garment sewn of a whole new cloth. This fire is a purging fire, a cleansing fire that will devour all adversaries. The writer of Hebrews warns us of such fire. In verse 10:26-27, it says, "For if we sin willfully after that we have received the knowledge of the truth, there remaineth no more sacrifice for sins, But a certain fearful looking for of judgment and fiery indignation, which shall devour the adversaries."

Judgment Has Already Begun

When Jesus taught on the last things and His coming again, He taught us to be ready. He taught that there was coming a judgmental fire in which we did not want to be caught. We need to know that this judgment has already started. "What will I...if it be already kindled?" Jesus said that His mission was to send fire on the earth, but it had already been kindled. The judgment of God had already begun in the heart of man.

Because of Jesus, mankind has condemned himself. The rejection of Christ in a man's mind sets a fire in his soul that will burn until he is ultimately consumed. Insanity, obsession, compulsive behavior, and additions of money, toys, and noise, are all signs of this desire to quench the fire in our soul.

When we sin willfully we have nothing to look forward to but more of the fiery indignation in our future. We try to silence that voice of conscience, if for only a moment, by noise and clamor, song or dance, by busying ourselves with our vocations or hobbies, and we weary ourselves so that we may sleep, then we wake to do it all over again. Some turn to drink or drugs, and many (wishing to be more socially acceptable) eat until their soul is quieted. The fire of eternity has begun in our souls and we are so unaware of its origin that we call it compulsion, obesity, alcoholism, sickness, neurosis, psychosis, or disease. The disease in our bodies is nothing less than the dis-ease of our souls. The fire of the judgment Jesus said would be sent to the earth has already been kindled.

The judgment that awaits us is not fearful because it is unfair and exacting; it is fearful because we know it will be fair and exacting. Given to us is a keen awareness of ourselves and our condition before God that causes us to fear true and fair judgment before God. We know within ourselves when we do wrong and we therefore attempt to justify our actions.

A person never feels a need to justify actions that are pure, only those that have gone against the code written in his heart. This violation of conscience is the basis for our fear of judgment and our compulsive behavior.

We know God will be fair and we know that He is aware when we are not honest with ourselves.

This consuming fire, kindled within us when we sin or violate our conscience, is the foretaste of God's judgment to come and is well known to any one who contemplates it for ten minutes. It is that silent ten minutes that we avoid. Many even fall asleep to TVs or radios playing and wake to alarms to avoid that revealing silence. The fire of judgment is already kindled and we know that one day the fire that smolders within us (the burning that merely inconveniences us now) will one day, at His appearing, be fanned into a blaze of righteous, undeniable judgment. This adds to our fear and desire for escape.

Do you live each day as if the Lord was returning to judge you that evening? Of course this is difficult while living in the contradictory power of the flesh, but you must try. If you are to avoid disease, both mental and physical, you must live in harmony and accord with your conscience. You must take responsibility and do what is within your power and understanding everyday. Jesus said it this way:

"Who then is that faithful and wise steward, whom his lord shall make ruler over his household, to give them their portion of meat in due season? Blessed is that servant, whom his lord when he cometh shall find so doing. Of a truth I say unto you, that he will make him ruler over all that he hath. But and if that servant say in his heart, My lord delayeth his coming; and shall begin to beat the menservants and maidens, and to eat and drink, and to be drunken; The lord of that servant will come in a day when he looketh not for him, and at an hour when he is not aware, and will cut him in sunder, and will appoint him his portion with the unbelievers.

And that servant, which knew his lord's will, and prepared not himself, neither did according to his will, shall be beaten with many stripes. But he that knew not, and did commit things worthy of stripes, shall be beaten with few stripes. For unto whomsoever much is given, of him shall be much required: and to whom men have committed much, of him they will ask the more."

"I am come to send fire on the earth; and what will I, if it be already kindled?"

69. *Now, how is your vision?*

Mark 8:22-25, "And he cometh to Bethsaida; and they bring a blind man unto
him, and besought him to touch him. And he took the blind man by the hand,
and led him out of the town; and when he had spit on his eyes, and put his
hands upon him, he asked him if he saw ought. And he looked up, and said, I
see men as trees, walking. After that he put his hands again upon his eyes, and
made him look up: and he was restored, and saw every man clearly."

Here, we are not given the words of Jesus. Within the Scripture is a
question of Jesus but we cannot hear His words. We are told what He asked but
not the exact words that He used. I take some license in my assertion that He
used these words. He may have used other words, but the message is clear that
He was testing the man's visual acuity and the degree of healing.

This miracle would stand as an example of an incomplete healing if it
was not understood. Jesus, knowing this event could be told and used as an
example for centuries, took this opportunity to show the value of a second
touch. We must understand that we, as frail and incomplete humans, cannot
receive all that Christ has to offer in one brush of His presence. It is folly to
assume that when we have one initial encounter with Him that we will know
all, understand all, and need no more of His grace.

It is common today to hear a "gospel" stating that we receive all we
need from Christ when we initially come to Him for forgiveness; however, I
fear that this first touch is all that most of us ever encounter. Most converts
move from this first encounter directly to submersion into the "church world"
and from there they receive teaching and guidance from men. From this first
meeting onwards, the social and spiritual gaps are filled by association with
religious people; the need for the second touch is rarely felt.

We must, after we are enlightened, go on to perfection as the apostle
admonishes us in Hebrews 6:1. Our need for perfection reaches far beyond our
immediate need of peace with God (forgiveness). We are creatures copious
with habits and problems detrimental to the well-being of ourselves and others.
We are not ready to understand, nor are we ready to see men as they are. We
came to Christ blind and in need of our sight. He opened our eyes and now we
see for the first time. We have our sight, such as it is, but we need the second
touch – the interpretation of what we now see.

Many of us became discouraged with our Christian life as we found it
did not have the power and grace as we assumed it would. We wanted more
than to see men as trees. We still struggle with our flesh and old nature. Though
we have moved into a spiritual Kingdom and been translated from the world to
which we have become accustomed, there are many things to learn that we are
not yet ready to learn. No wonder we become discouraged. No wonder we feel
alone and out of place. If we assume that all Christ has to offer us has already

been bestowed in all its fullness, we would have good reason to be dissuaded and forlorn.

The good news is that He has not done so! He asks, now that you have been given sight, "What do you see?" Are you discouraged with what you see and how you see? There is a second touch for you that will clear your eyes so that you will see all things vividly! Our perfection is of utmost importance to Christ. It is the reason we are here and the reason we struggle with our day to day trials and persecutions. Jesus said that if we become discouraged due to these things we would bear no fruit. Our fruit is our perfection. "... [These] are they, which, when they have heard, go forth, and are choked with cares and riches and pleasures of this life, and bring no fruit to perfection." (Luke 8:14)

We are not on the earth for the purpose of, trying to be saved, trying to be good, trying to be holy, or trying to become acceptable in Jehovah's sight. Because of our inability to do so, Jesus has done all of that for us. Our goal is to perfect ourselves by surmounting trials, and living in faith with full assurance of God's grace and care, never faltering, and, by remaining true to our calling, we will prosper. "Therefore, my beloved brethren, be ye stedfast, unmoveable, always abounding in the work of the Lord..." (1 Corinthians 15:58)

Striving For Perfection

I fear that our concern with being perfected is of low priority. It is our own comfort that seems to hold the place of highest regard in our lives. Our prayers are laced with pleas for deliverance, and health, gifts and blessings. We must place the attaining of our perfection high on our priority list. Our desire for perfection is to be higher than our comfort, higher than our success, higher than the preservation of our very lives.

It is when we answer His question after our decision to follow Christ that we begin this process. It is after our eyes have been opened and He asks, "Now how is your vision?" that we start down this road of being made perfect. What if the blind man, so happy to have any sight at all, said, "Oh everything is fine, I am thankful to be able to see at all." – and never mentions his inadequate eyesight. Similarly, we may be as he was, so happy to be forgiven and finally at peace with God, that we dare not be candid with Him and say, "Although I am happy to be forgiven, I still do not love my fellow man as I should." Or, "I still have trouble with forgiveness." Or, "I still find it hard to withdraw from the world." (You may insert your imperfection here.)

I can remember my struggle with pacifism. I met many who, through their faith in Christ, had become pacifists and I wondered why I felt that I have a right and duty to defend myself and my property, even at the cost of human life. I felt no qualm about killing an intruder or marauder and thought myself fully capable of doing so. I held it as my duty to defend and protect my family, and could not fit, "Do violence to no man," into my Christian understanding. (Ref Luke 3:14) Nor could I understand fully, "Dearly beloved, avenge not yourselves, but rather give place unto wrath: for it is written, Vengeance is mine; I will repay, saith the Lord." (Romans 12:19) I was in need of the second

230

touch. I had to say, "I see men...but they are as trees." Now I must confess, they are as men to me, I see every man clearly.

It is not an insult to Christ or His redeeming power to say, "I see men as trees," for in doing so we show that we wish to see clearly. It is no insult to say, "I do not love my fellow man as I should," for it shows our desire to do so. We need a second touch.

Jesus knows that a second touch is needful, and is waiting for you to honestly confess that to Him. Go to Him. Perhaps you will not like what Jesus tells you, but you must go to Him. As the rich ruler who came to Jesus was told, "If thou wilt be perfect...go and sell all that thou hast," the qualifier still today is, "if thou will be perfect..."

Again, you are faced with the responsibility for reaching for your own perfection and completion. Again and again the Scriptures show that it is your *personal* duty. What could be more glorious than to see all things clearly, to love truly, to care intuitively, and understand fully? When you contemplate the change that has occurred in you since the point of your visitation, you must be honest. The second touch requires it, and the will of God demands it. When your head raises for the first time to view the world, don't be disappointed if things aren't as you expected, you don't know everything yet.

There is another touch in your future. There may be many. You must look at your life in Christ, evaluate your shortcomings, and sincerely respond to His question when He asks, "Now... how is your vision?"

70. Is it lawful to heal on the Sabbath day?

Luke 14:3, "And Jesus answering spake unto the lawyers and Pharisees, saying, Is it lawful to heal on the sabbath day?"

For the most part, the keeping of the Sabbath Day is the forsaken Commandment. Like no other point of the Decalogue, the fourth has been misunderstood, misapplied and ignored by men, or changed, repealed, erased or revoked by religion, but in relatively few hearts has it held a place of immutability and importance as was intended. Until we decide to keep Sabbath and defend its honored place in our lives as Christians, we cannot fully comprehend this chasm between the two theologies. The division that Sabbath-keeping creates between fellow Christians, friends, and family is more than a theological one.

There is not a monolithic understanding in the community of Sabbath keepers either. Even among those who consider it to be an important factor, it has undergone many interpretations and methods of compliance. Some take their cues from the Jews, and attempt to mimic their Sabbath observance, and some make their own rules. How we comply, whether we comply, are matters of endless debate, and this has been the case for centuries.

Scholars give us information about the Scriptures that we use to interpret them. We apply our understanding of customs and manners of the day, the chronological timetables, and the "context" of the Scripture, so that we can interpret the Commandment "accurately." We find out who wrote it, when it was written, and to whom it was written. From that information, we decide whether or not it applies to us and how, or if, we should keep it.

Most of the time, we find ourselves in trouble when we decide that we know why a Commandment was written, because if we think we know why, we can deceive ourselves into complying some other (usually easier) way. We egotistically determine that we know why God said to remember the Sabbath day, and we decide to give Him what we think He wants some other way than what He specifically said to do (or not to do).

The argument is a familiar one; it is much like the one we make when we roll through a stop sign when we see no one else in an intersection. We think we know why the law was written, so we determine that there is real need to come to a complete stop. Although the law does not mention the presence of other cars in the intersection, or the pressing appointment to which we are rushing, or the pressing schedule of the driver, we factor all of that into the equation because we think we know why the law was written. We even deceive ourselves into believing that by doing so, we are obeying the spirit of the law. Note: You can receive a citation for obeying the spirit of the law in that way.

I submit that we do not "know" as much as we think we do. As a stupid and selfish man, unable to plumb the depths of my own depravity, and with an unfathomably desperate and wicked heart, I have determined not to "know" anything. I have decided to blindly and humbly follow the revealed will and words of God as if I am stupid and unlearned, unsophisticated and uneducated; as if God Himself wrote, exactly what He wrote, and gave it to me to read and obey. I am willing to believe that God wrote what He meant to write in the stone tablet that day on Mount Sinai.

Some declare that since Christ has come, things have changed. It is true that many things have been fulfilled in Christ and many things have been revealed that were kept secret since the foundation of the world.[105] Among the things that have changed is the physical location of the written Law. The words of God were written in tablets of stone, later they were in scrolls and books, and are now to be found written in the hearts of all who obey the Gospel.[106] Who among us, who truly know Christ, does not also know that we are to love our neighbor as ourselves? John said that if we do not love our brother, while saying we love God, we are liars. Why does he say that? Because, "...this commandment have we from him, That he who loveth God [is to] love his brother also." (1 John 4:21) Try as you might, you will not find that written anywhere in the Commandments. Where is that written? It is written in the heart of all who know Him.

With these Commandments written in our minds and hearts, we also are keenly aware when we violate them. Our conscience tells us when we are living in accordance with God's will and therefore we are never to violate this internal guide. We grieve this Holy Spirit both when we lay undo burden upon ourselves to stay within the bounds of Law, or live in liberality, violating it.

The Perfect Law of Liberty

We must find and maintain the balance that holds us in a life of obedience and does not hinder us and show our lives as burdens to the world. The perfect law of liberty, in Christ Jesus, will make us free from the Law of sin and death.[107] There is a place in Christ where we well know just exactly what is expected of us, exactly what we are to do to make our lives pleasing to our Father, to give us a rich and balanced life, for which no apology to the world is necessary. Our lives, lived in this perfect Law of liberty, leave us without a sense of guilt, nor have we any fear of unknowingly displeasing God.

There is a place in Christ where we can walk in full assurance of our faith, never violating any Commandment, never wondering if an action is "lawful" or not, and never displeasing Christ. This is a place of understanding that is unavailable to unregenerate people. It is a place foreign to those who look to books and regulations, education and knowledge, or tradition and religion. It is only found through communion with Jesus Christ.

---

[105] Matthew 13:35, "That it might be fulfilled which was spoken by the prophet, saying, I will open my mouth in parables; I will utter things which have been kept secret from the foundation of the world."
[106] Jeremiah 31:33, "...I will put my law in their inward parts, and write it in their hearts; and will be their God, and they shall be my people."
[107] Romans 8:2, "For the law of the Spirit of life in Christ Jesus hath made me free from the law of sin and death."

Jesus saw that religious men had no understanding of "why." They were befuddled that Jesus could walk through a field picking and eating grain on the Sabbath and have a clear conscience. They were amazed that He could do what He did, say what He said, live the way He lived and still believe that He was in compliance with the Law. This is the way we should appear to the religious as well. We, too, have this ability to know as Christ did – as David did. We can know within ourselves how to fully comply with God's will, through the ministry of the Holy Spirit.

When He approached the Pharisees this day, Jesus was asking much more than what it appears. He was asking them this question to see what understanding they had. He wanted to know how much they knew about the nature of God, the depth and purpose of the Law, and He wanted to reveal this lack to them as well.

We would do well to quiz ourselves in the same manner. If we are legalistic and pedantic it will show up when we ask ourselves the question Jesus asked them. To the Pharisee there was no middle ground. Nothing was to be done on the Sabbath. Nothing. Their eyes had closed to God's purposes and their understanding had replaced God's intention. Jesus knew that they did not have what it took to answer the question.

It must have saddened Him when they stood mute; with eyes darting back and forth searching for an answer that allowed both the laws they had made in God's name *and* the goodness and miracle of healing that could only be attributed to God. They stood knee-deep in the mud of their own religion and were dumbfounded and silent when He asked, "Is it lawful to heal on the sabbath day?"

71. *Who will commit to your trust the true riches?*

Luke 16:11, "If therefore ye have not been faithful in the unrighteous mammon, who will commit to your trust the true riches?"

Be ye wise as serpents and harmless as doves. These great words of advice come from the Lord Jesus as He anticipated the experiences that His disciples would undoubtedly encounter when He sent them out two by two. He said I am sending you "as sheep in the midst of wolves." (Matthew 10:16) He knew that they needed "hearts" not "smarts." In saying, be ye wise as serpents and harmless as doves, His message is that we need to handle the world in an unworldly manner. The world outside of Christ has an idea of survival too. It is to be as wise as doves and harmless as serpents. Not very wise… but deadly. Now that we are in the wolf pit and in need of His advice, we need not think that worldly wisdom will be enough.

Why all this about the world and its ways? It is because this question deals with money and its value. We must keep our head above the crowd and consider money in the same light as Christ did. Here He used it as an indicator of faithfulness where valuable things are concerned. Don't think that you are being considered to be a handler of God's true riches if you are unfaithful, slothful, and sloppy with money.

However, neither does this question compel us to be financially savvy, nor does it teach frugality, or austerity. Its objective is not to teach us to spend or save properly nor is it to teach us how to take care of things; it is talking about our faithfulness and character. The question presupposes that if character is present, these other values will be forthcoming and handy. It is not a matter of spending or saving, buying or selling, earning or idleness; it is a matter of management. He could as well ask, "If we can't manage our own money what major company would put their books into our care?" Would a large company hire a bookkeeper that is constantly writing bad checks from his personal account due to neglect or errors in subtraction?

Skill and character go hand in hand to insure good check writing. If you assume the bookkeeper knows how to keep books, it then becomes a matter of his character that allows bad checks to be written. If he writes checks in earnest, thinking there is sufficient funds, his bookkeeping skills are then suspect. He is therefore either a poor bookkeeper or a man of questionable character. Both traits are detractors from a bookkeeper's character – and a faithful steward's.

Good character is lacking in all phases of life and commerce. A faithful man of impeccable character and talent is nearly impossible to find, as any employer in business today would attest. But, what about we who are Christians? If your nobility and character, or your faithfulness and honesty were being judged, based upon your management of money, how would you fare? If God makes His decision as to the bestowment of the true riches based upon your management of your false and temporal ones, how are you doing?

Is that to say that the rich are spiritually wealthy and the poor are spiritually impoverished? Not so! Again, it is not the quantity of money we are speaking of – it is management of it. There are rich men who have so much that their mismanagement is hidden under piles of money. At large corporations, millions of dollars can be lost, stolen, mishandled, and may disappear without a trace of blame or sometimes even detection.

On the contrary, it is the management of meager means that makes some seem rich who have very little. They do not waste or buy impulsively; they value everything on its own merit and intrinsic value, not its price tag only. They buy what is functional, necessary, or high quality. They save part of their income, give to those in need, maintain what they have, and curb their appetites in style, excess and superfluity.

Our Finances Mirror Our Lives

Like it or not, we who are bankrupt or impoverished due to our own mismanagement of our money, are likely overdrawn, overextended, and perhaps bankrupt in other areas of life, too. We owe more than we can pay emotionally; we pay out more than we take in socially, and we depend on others to make up the deficit in our misspent lives, becoming an emotional burden on those around us. Many in this condition end up on a societal or emotional "welfare system," depending upon others to supply to them what they lack in proper relationships. They can have no friends who have needs; they may only have friends who can supply needs, because they themselves are so needy.

We can see from this that economic and social management are deeply intertwined and that the appearance of a shortfall in one may well indicate an insufficiency in the other. A man or woman who can scarcely keep up with either the economic or the social demands that the world places upon them will likely never be considered to occupy offices of responsibility or stewardship, nor are they candidates to become holders of what Jesus called the true riches.

You have an obligation to keep and spend, hold and give, earn and save as if God Himself is watching. For if "ye have not been faithful in the unrighteous mammon, who will commit to your trust the true riches?"

What is unrighteous mammon? Some say it is money. Some say it is the love of money. Mammon is more than money; it is more than the desire for it. It is the way of the world. When we see billboards, magazine ads, or television commercials, we are bombarded with mammon. Madison Avenue thrives on it, Hollywood creates it, the media promotes it, and we, unfortunately, buy it.

You may buy into mammon, not only with your money, but also by your silent consent when you see your child's eyes light up at its presentation and you say nothing. If you do not call it the poison that it is, if you do not warn those you love that mammon is deceitful, if you do not turn your own face away, you may watch your children forsake the true riches and run after mammon and you may eventually believe the lie yourself. At that point you have done worse than buying mammon with your money; you have taken it into your heart and home. We all make too little effort to counter mammon's claim that the world holds all the answers. Then, after years of the world's loud indoctrination and our consenting silence, we wonder why our children seek answers elsewhere than home, faith, and God.

When we look at our personal economy, how we spend our time, money and talent, we may be amazed how much of our life is dedicated to mammon. The worldly society is constantly telling us to take their pills, to use their psychology, and to think according to their philosophy. Much of our thinking comes from our societal environment. It is an uncommon man who develops his thinking by communion with God alone. Few people fabricate a philosophy by which to live their lives, from reading the Bible. At best we may find a man who has a life philosophy made from a mixed bag of Bible stories and other "good" books. He appreciates both Christ and Confucius; he tempers his religion with "solid" modern thinking, in other words, God and mammon.

It is the economy of your life, the use of your time, the expenditure of your money, and the occupation of your mind, that will show you the system to which you have subscribed, the source of your philosophy, and to whom your allegiance will unmistakably fall when you are in difficulty. If you are consistently falling prostrate before the mammon of the world, seeking answers, seeking sustenance, you cannot expect God to entrust His true riches into your mammon-stained fingers. For, as Jesus said, Ye cannot serve God and mammon.

Be faithful to identify mammon as mammon, something to be avoided, a god requiring worship, sacrifice, and allegiance from those who approach with requests. The gain of true riches is in jeopardy when you bow yourself to the false riches of mammon. Being faithful in unrighteous mammon is to never consider it as anything else. "And if therefore ye have not been faithful in the unrighteous mammon, who will commit to your trust the true riches?"

72.   Don't you violate your own laws?

Luke 14:5, "And [Jesus] answered them, saying, Which of you shall have an ass or an ox fallen into a pit, and will not straightway pull him out on the sabbath day?"

Many people read this (and other similar passages of Christ's words on Sabbath) and go away with a message that He did not preach. How many times, in conversations about Sabbath, have you heard someone say, "I'd prefer not to work on the Sabbath, but if you've got an ox in the ditch…?" Many think that, Christ made provision to work on the Sabbath if there is an emergency, but upon closer investigation you will find it will be a difficult thing to prove. Would Jesus have given instruction to outright violate the Law of God? The Law makes no such provision for "emergencies." Let us look at another Scripture from which this concept is taken.

(Matthew 12:11) "And he said unto them, What man shall there be among you, that shall have one sheep, and if it fall into a pit on the sabbath day, will he not lay hold on it, and lift it out?"

Notice He said that this is what they did. "What man is there among you" who does not lift out his sheep, pull out his ox and so on? He is not saying that we can do this and remain inviolate of the Law; He is just saying that these hypocrites are condemning Him for doing what they do all the time. Their Law allowed them to save an ox or rescue a sheep, but omitted kindness and rescue aimed toward mankind. God's Law sets the value of man above all.

This is why Jesus asked them, is not a man better than a sheep? Really, God's Law on Sabbath was much easier to understand and obey than the Pharisees taught. The Sabbath had become a line, over which if anyone stepped, branded them as a sinner. Then, by man's meddling, the Sabbath was made more and more difficult to obey, making the club of religious folks more and more exclusive. But, from the beginning it was not so. The Sabbath was made for man…not man for the Sabbath.

Many feel that Jesus changed the Sabbath Law and made it more livable by adding provisions for emergencies and so on. All that He really did was fulfill it by living His life and never breaking it, thereby providing us an example. Though He broke the law of the Pharisees many, many times, He never broke God's Law. He did not say I come to make the Law easier to live under, He said that He came to fulfill it. He did not change the Sabbath; He clarified it for us. He did not change the ancient purpose or regulation, He said it as though it were always so… "The Sabbath was made for man." It was a gift. (Would God take back His gift?)

Where He did find fault was with the hypocrisy of the Pharisees. Also, their lack of understanding was a frustration to Him. If they had wanted, the Pharisees could have discovered these things. They could have understood what Sabbath, and indeed all of the Laws of God were about – how to live by them, fulfill them, and please God, but they did not. He taught that this information was made available to them by simple discernment. He gave examples:

John 7:22-23, "Moses therefore gave unto you circumcision... and ye on the sabbath day circumcise a man." They saw nothing wrong with circumcising a man-child on Sabbath. Why did they not see that if the Law is perfect, the Law could not make demands that cause other Laws to be broken?

The paradox was this: A child was to be circumcised on the eighth day. If a child is born on the sixth day of the week he must be circumcised on a Sabbath. Jesus uses the situation and teaches that if Sabbath can be used to take a man apart, could it not be better used to put a man together? He says, "If a man on the sabbath day receive circumcision, that the law of Moses should not be broken; are ye angry at me, because I have made a man every whit whole on the sabbath day?"

Some work was acceptable to their tradition and some work was not. "The Lord then answered him, and said, Thou hypocrite, doth not each one of you on the sabbath loose his ox or his ass from the stall, and lead him away to watering?" (Luke 13:15) Here, He is asking, "Don't you violate your own laws?" With some, it was acceptable to water and feed livestock, but other farm work was considered abominable. I was recently told of a Sabbatarian farmer that condemned the feeding of livestock on Sabbath. Yet, he himself sat at his own table and fed himself every Sabbath. Jesus would ask, "Don't you violate your own laws?"

Although the hypocrite will be undoubtedly exposed here, it should mean more to us than just avoiding hypocrisy. We should be examples of serving God and not ourselves, of obeying God and not mindlessly following man's ideas. Many of the ideas of unregenerate man are stupid and illogical, and their motives can be easily realized by fifteen minutes thought, yet many times, they are followed without question.

There was no Law about feeding or not feeding cattle on Sabbath, watering or not watering, lifting or not lifting fallen livestock out of ditches. These were all man's additions to God's gift – transforming the lovely gift into a loathsome burden. We, as New Covenant Christians, should be led of the Spirit and not the ideas of man.

Accepted Sins

As in the days of Christ, we accept certain sins in our company and among our religious groups and other sins we shun entirely. For example, we shun those who smoke cigarettes in order to cope with life and accept with open arms those who eat to do so.

We, by example, teach that if the sinner can exchange his tobacco for chocolate and his alcohol for valium we will let him come among us and call himself by our name. We still strain out gnats and swallow camels. (And by the girth of some of those the modern church most highly respects, they look as though that is exactly what they have done!)

The apostle Paul asks in Romans 2:21-23, "Thou therefore which teachest another, teachest thou not thyself? thou that preachest a man should not steal, dost thou steal? Thou that sayest a man should not commit adultery, dost thou commit adultery? thou that abhorrest idols, dost thou commit sacrilege? Thou that makest thy boast of the law, through breaking the law dishonourest thou God?"

If Jesus were here watching us with our noses pinched when a smoker enters our congregations, or sees us shift in our seat when those we deem less than ourselves attempt to seat themselves close to us, He would be ashamed. Have ye not read? Do you not understand? Who among us does not have the same problem, just handled in a different way? Who among us is blameless? When Jesus asked these questions, He was asking us to put ourselves into the shoes of those we condemn.

The Pharisees had laws about Sabbath that they should be ashamed of, because they were found by Christ to be in hypocritical violation of them. We have laws about certain antisocial behaviors of which we, too, should be ashamed for the same reason.

When we condemn others for violating laws of our own making, are we any different that the Pharisees were? When condemned by the laws of the Pharisees, Jesus asked, "Which of you shall have an ass or an ox fallen into a pit, and will not straightway pull him out on the sabbath day?" "Don't you violate your own laws?" He asked. This condemned them where they stood.

We stand in violation as well when we condemn drinking alcohol with our medicine chests full of mood altering drugs. We too, are guilty when we exchange our cigarettes for potato chips and think that we are clean and smokers are dirty.

We, too, are hypocritical when we exclude those who break man made laws and never consider how we ourselves may be doing the same thing every day in other ways. Hear again, the searching question of Christ, "Don't you violate your own laws?"

73. *Who shall give you that which is your own?*

Luke 16:12 "And if ye have not been faithful in that which is another man's, who shall give you that which is your own?"

When raising children we watch how they handle things of their own and thereby decide how and when we will commit to them things of greater value. We reason that if they learn caution and care in dealing with their own things they will use caution and care dealing with the things committed to their trust by others. But in this Scripture Jesus seems to teach the opposite. His question is, "If ye have not been faithful in that which is another man's, who shall give you that which is your own?"

The committed Christian, he whose desire it is to please and walk with the Lord, will naturally desire himself to be considered trustworthy and his life profitable to the Kingdom of God. We all want to be considered as family members – brothers of Jesus Christ the firstborn of many, and to pray "our Father" in full assurance that He is indeed, our Father. Jesus mentioned the stages of this walk for us in John 15:15, "Henceforth I call you not servants; for the servant knoweth not what his lord doeth: but I have called you friends; for all things that I have heard of my Father I have made known unto you."

We see here that they were once considered by Christ as servants (stage 1) and later as friends (stage 2). After a person receives Christ, John says that he is given the power to become a child of God. (John 1:12) How do we become sons of God? These stages of development are clearly seen in Gospel accounts of the disciples. As they left "all" and followed Christ they were placing themselves in His care and doing so as servants to a Lord.

This is the stage in which most sincere Christians live. Some may never make it to this point at all, but if they do there is planted within them a seed of "yearning." This yearning is much like a desire for seniority in Christ or perhaps better, a familiarity with Him. Not a rank or status to lord over others, but an acquaintance with Him, a closeness like we would find between a trusted right-hand man and a supervisor. Paul puts it, "That I may know him..."[108]

As servants, the Lord said plainly, we are not made privy to plans, actions, and strategies. We just carry out orders and do as we are told. This demeans and embarrasses the servant that has not fully controlled his pride. Pride is the problematic cause of most setbacks in Spiritual matters. We have one Leader, one Lord over all, under whom falls all of the rank and file, peons, drudges, and nobodies. We need not become ambitious in this Kingdom. We need to become faithful in that which is least. It is up to the Lord to make us ruler over much. Our greatest goal should be to anticipate the return of the "Lord of the vineyard" and do as we were commissioned, faithfully to the end.

---

[108] Philippians 3:10

In our service to the King, we read from the Bible instructions that guide us along this path and its words alert us to what is and is not sin, and what pitfalls and consequences lie ahead in our path. As we read and study, learn and become more familiar with the revelations given our apostles and prophets, we soon see that God had ongoing relationships and even conversations with these men and women. This creates a desire to have such a relation in those who love their redeemer.

Headlong or short cut attempts to gain this relationship can lead some into unhealthy motivations and even obsessions. But, in others, it leaves a longing, a yearning for the relationship, and conversation, but more so, they desire acceptance into that family circle. "Behold, what manner of love the Father hath bestowed upon us, that we should be called the sons of God..." (1 John 3:1)

A verse in Isaiah 30:21 has always created desire like this in me, "And thine ears shall hear a word behind thee, saying, This is the way, walk ye in it, when ye turn to the right hand, and when ye turn to the left." To desire this communion, within itself is not wrong, to attempt to extract it, push it, or presume it, is definitely wrong and ineffectual. If we desire a walk with God, in which He directs our path, and orders our steps; we must be faithful to the light given to others before us.

The apostles were given commission to take the Gospel to every place. They did that through their writing and personal witness. We must heed and obey this witness of theirs and be faithful to their vision. If we ever expect to experience God's leadership on a personal level, we must be faithful to the light and leading of the prophets and apostles gone before us.

As it is, we need only read for a few minutes before we run across a passage we may have explained away, counted as unimportant, unnecessary, impertinent, or confusing. In truth, it was not confusing or unimportant; the reality is that we simply did not wish to comply with it. Rebellion is not an option so we feign ignorance or dismiss it on theological grounds. We fear it may ruin us socially or in our Meeting, or it may cause us to lose our job or make us appear foolish.

All these concerns are probably very real, but unconditional obedience is rare – so is friendship. To be friends with Christ, to be on the inside, to be one whom Christ can lead anywhere, reveal any truth, one to whom Jesus can tell anything, would have to be the height of glory. This level of friendship is an honorable goal. The aspiration to which can serve as motivation for surmounting any problem, conquering any habit, paying any price, or suffering any persecution. It should certainly serve as impetus for obedience.

Proving Ourselves Faithful

First we must prove faithful in obedience to the Scriptures we have before us — no more excuses, no more justifications. How can we seek a new revelation from a God whose written words we ignore? We must remember that we are seeking instruction from a God tired of speaking to a disobedient people.

How can we seek friendship from a Savior whom we will not obey? How foolish we must sound when we ask for guidance from the mouth of God all the while ignoring the words of His prophets and apostles. God has given revelation to the prophets and apostles of old.

You must evaluate your obedience to the revelation given to them. Have you been faithful to the words given to you through the Scriptures? If not, why would you think that you would receive a supernatural communication to obey? What assurance does God have that you are faithful to obey His living Word of guidance if your history shows you have not been faithful to the revelation of the Scriptures?

Jesus asks, "Why do you pray for personal guidance and revelation? If ye have not been faithful in that which is another man's, who shall give you that which is your own?"

74. How say the scribes that Christ is the Son of David?

Matthew 22:42, "Saying, What think ye of Christ? whose son is he? They say unto him, The Son of David." And Mark 12:35-37, "And Jesus answered and said, while he taught in the temple, How say the scribes that Christ is the Son of David? For David himself said by the Holy Ghost, The LORD said to my Lord, Sit thou on my right hand, till I make thine enemies thy footstool. David therefore himself calleth him Lord; and whence is he then his son?"

What a person thinks of Christ tells a lot about his faith. Most of us devote little time to this consideration. We simply believe Christ to be exactly who we have been told that He is.

Messiah and Son of David were the same words in the mind of the ancient Hebrews and in the minds of the Jews of Jesus' day. They had determined that Christ would be the son of David but they did not expect that He would be the Son of God. In Matthew alone look at the many times He was referred to as the Son of David:

9:27 ... two blind men followed him, crying ... Thou Son of David, have mercy on us. In 12:23, And all he people ... said, Is not this the son of David? In 15:22, And, behold, a woman of Canaan ... and cried unto him, Have mercy on me, O Lord, thou Son of David. And in 20:30, "And, behold, two blind ... [said] Have mercy on us, O Lord, thou Son of David." Then in 21:9, "And the multitudes ... cried, saying, Hosanna to the Son of David.

The Pharisees upon hearing the people worshiping Him at His entry into Jerusalem on that famous sixth day (Friday) admonished Him to silence His disciples and the multitudes. The reason the Pharisees did not like the people calling out, "Hosanna! ... son of David!" was not because they thought Jesus should reject their praise, it was because the crowd was proclaiming Him as Messiah.

On another occasion Jesus decided to give the churchmen a quiz on this subject of the son of David. He asked, "Just what do you mean by the term?" Matthew 22:41-46, "While the Pharisees were gathered together, Jesus asked them, Saying, What think ye of Christ? whose son is he? They say unto him, The Son of David. He saith unto them, How then doth David in spirit call him Lord, saying, The LORD said unto my Lord, Sit thou on my right hand, till I make thine enemies thy footstool? If David then call him Lord, how is he his son? And no man was able to answer him a word, neither durst any man from that day forth ask him any more questions."

All of the knowledge that the scribes and Pharisees had, they had gathered from the Scriptures. This is the main reason the Bible is an imperfect guide, because it is an imperfect means of thought and information conveyance.

If a sign is unintelligible or difficult to interpret, or written in another language, what value has it as a sign? The very reason that the apostle Paul discouraged speaking in tongues was that it was as a "trumpet that gives an uncertain sound." Paul asks in 1 Corinthians 14:8, "For if the trumpet give an uncertain sound, who shall prepare himself to the battle?" He goes on to say that unless the message is clear it has to take a lesser place in the list of gifts.

An Uncertain Sign

When driving through Mexico my wife, Pam and I were more intent than the locals when it came to reading the signs. It took longer for us to read and understand them. A rather large and looming sign appeared on the highway and it was exceptionally frightening because of its size. The fact that it had unfamiliar words – big words we had not seen on the signs before it – caused us to panic and miss what it said. "Obedizca las Señales." I wondered out loud, "What did that say?" I thought it may have said, "Bridge is Missing" or there is a large, motorhome-swallowing hole in the middle of the road ahead. Actually, we saw it later and realized it merely said, "Obey the Signs." (Which, by the way is good advice for driving *AND* life in general.)

The *uncertainty* of the sign on that hot desert highway led to needless turmoil and confusion and fear. For the sign to have its desired effect, namely safety and information, **it must be *understood*.** The Bible, without the Spirit of God to interpret it can lead the reader in the opposite direction that the author intended.

Upon the same basis the Bible must take second place to the Spirit of God. Not that the Scriptures would be contradicted by the Spirit but our interpretations and understanding MUST give way to the truths of God revealed by His Spirit. We have a tendency to label what we understand the Bible says, as indeed what the Bible says, but that is just not so.

The Scriptures can only say what they say and the Spirit reveals their truth to us. Our Bibles, our interpretations and translations and theologies must make way for, give over to, and bow before the Spirit of the living God. In this story, the Bible said plainly that the Messiah is to be the son of David, not the Son of God. Are we to reject our own understanding, or the truth revealed to us by Christ?

The question Jesus asked was, "How say the scribes that Christ is the son of David?" The question is calling for an answer in the form of an explanation. "How say?" "How do they say that?" "Upon what authority, upon what basis, how do they arrive at that conclusion?" By the Scriptures? The Scriptures say that David calls Him Lord. "If David then call him Lord, how is he his son?" Jesus has blown their source for their assumption. He told them that they missed the message, they misinterpreted, misunderstood.

There are many doctrines we believe are true and would stake our eternal life upon and indeed we do. But how did we arrive at them? You may believe that Jesus is the Messiah. How did you arrive at that? How did it come to you? Was it told you, taught to you? Did you merely read it and accept the testimony of the words on a page or was it revealed to you in your quiet moments? Have you ever considered the impossibility of untainted information?

Many will boast that they don't listen to men but only believe what the Bible says. Unless they believe that the book they hold in their hand was dictated, written, produced and published on the printing press in heaven, how could it be free of the influences of man? At every turn of the investigation of the origin of the Scriptures we must trust in man to hear, copy, print, interpret, and define the words of God. I do not say this to discredit the Bible, but to inspire you to seek the living Word – to seek Christ.

The Spirit of God will never lead you to misunderstand, misinterpret the words of God. The Spirit can open new avenues of thinking and definition that are unavailable to mere readers of the Bible. Jesus assessed the Spiritual acuity of the Pharisees. The scribes and Pharisees were convinced of the identity of Messiah as told in the infallible Scriptures. Jesus put them to the test, How say ye that Christ is the Son of David?

We are quick to claim what we believe, but until we take the time to determine the origin of what we believe, we are building on shifting sand. How say you that Christ is the Son of David? The revelation of Jesus as Messiah is one that Jesus knew came from the Father only. Even when Jesus stood before Pilate and Pilate ask him if he was indeed the Christ, "Jesus answered him, Sayest thou this thing of thyself, or did others tell it thee of me?" (John 18:34)

Have you stood before God and waited for your revelation? There is hardly a more important question. "*How* **say you** that Christ is the Son of David?"

75.   Did God commission John to baptize or not?

*Matthew 21:27, Luke 20:4, Mark 11:30 (Combined) "The baptism of John,
whence was it? From heaven, or of men? Answer me. And they reasoned with
themselves, saying, if we shall say, Of men; we fear the people; for all hold
John as a prophet. If we shall say, From heaven; he will say unto us, Why did
ye not then believe him? And they answered Jesus, and said, We cannot tell.
And he said unto them, Neither tell I you by what authority I do these things."*

Do you remember the story of the centurion that called for Christ to
heal his servant? Jesus was amazed that a Roman had such faith. What was
there about this man that showed Jesus that he had the kind of faith that was
never seen by Christ in all of Israel? The centurion understood the authority of
Christ. He knew that Christ was sent from God, and that He was authorized and
therefore commissioned, and empowered by God Himself. Authority is key to
understanding the mission and purpose, power and scope of any endeavor, even
the salvation of the world.

I refuse the silly notion that Jesus was simply tricking these men, or
cleverly manipulating them. Many who teach this idea say that Jesus was
blindsiding them with an unanswerable riddle so that He would not have to
answer their questions. Those who teach this, tell this story almost is if it is a
joke; they laugh as though Jesus then said to these men, "Ha ha! Gotcha!"

Since when do we find Jesus furtively withholding answers to
questions about His authority? Since when is He reluctant to claim to be the
Son of God? Since when does He resort to trickery to avoid the Pharisees
probing questions? There was more here than clever lines, riddles and evasions
of questions.

There are several reasons Jesus did not answer. The question that Jesus
asked was a foundational question on authority. In military terms, the question
would be, "Would an officer of an occupation *explain* his authority to someone
whom rejected the legitimacy of the occupation?" Or in civil terms, "Would a
police officer patiently *explain* his authority according to law to a person
obviously breaking that law?" What good would it do? If the basis for authority
is rejected, spurned and ridiculed, what would be the point in further placing
ones weight or authority upon it?

Christ's question was asked to establish foundation. It was asked to
find allegiances and loyalties. These men had no concerns except their
appearance to others. These Pharisees asked Jesus how He was able to do these
things and with whose authority He speaks. An answer to the Pharisees'
question would demand from them, an action to be taken, a position to be
assumed, and an opinion to be formed. They were not ready for such a
showdown. Jesus knew this.

We are responsible for what we know to be fact and we must act
accordingly or stand guilty of rebellion, sin, or disobedience. Jesus knew this

too. If Christ proclaimed Himself to these men as sent from God He could have caused their destruction and apostasy. As He said in John 9:41, "... If ye were blind, ye should have no sin: but now ye say, We see; therefore your sin remaineth."

With the question, "Did God commission John to baptize," Jesus was determining their degree of blindness. His questioning went like this in other words, "Did you recognize, accept, or understand the authority of John the Baptist?" When they answered no, He said, "Then you can't recognize, accept, or understand my authority either."

The Leaven of the Pharisees

Remember that the Pharisees cared more about what others thought than the discovery of truth. This was their whole life and religion. From the wide borders on their garments to the long robes and loud prayers in the streets, these did what they did for man's praise and adoration. Jesus called it their "doctrine" and He taught that it was as leaven spreading throughout all of God's people, and He told us to beware of it. Ref. Matthew 16:6-12. This "doctrine" caused them to swerve from recognizing and accepting John as sent from God and would soon cause them to reject Jesus as Messiah.

"By what authority do you do these things?" they asked. Jesus said, "Do you understand authority? Do you submit to authority? Do you recognize authority? Tell me, who commissioned John to baptize? Did his authority come from men or God? Answer me." They said among themselves that they feared the people stoning them if they said that John came on his own commission. Further, if they said that God sent John He will ask them why they did not believe and follow him. So they answered, "We cannot affirm his authority." Jesus then said, "Then I do not offer mine to your scrutiny. You do not understand, recognize or submit to authority I will not seal your fates this day by forcing you to rebel against God." Admittedly these are more words than written, but there was more said here than what was written.

There was no trick, no slick maneuvering, it was perfectly balanced compassion and logic, as always, that motivated Christ in this exchange. Jesus was not shy about answering questions on His authority, but He knew that to confirm in ones mind the fact that they were in the presence of God, forced acceptance or rejection to occur. As the verse in Matthew 12:28 says, "But if I cast out devils by the Spirit of God, then [undeniably] the kingdom of God is come unto you." He told Peter, when the disciple confessed, "Thou art the very Christ of God," that he tell no man that thing. Jesus depended on revelation from God to do this work of revelation, as it was the Father only that draws.

Jesus loved the Pharisees. He took time and much care with those who saw him for who He was. (John 3) He explained and reasoned with all who cared. He did not come to condemn but to redeem, to seek and to save that which was lost. Many times He reached back to the Prophets and the Law to establish in these learned men's minds who He was.

Too much consideration is given to whether Jesus was the Christ or not, whether He was the Son of God or not. There is a basis of authority, a foundation to be laid to reach such understandings. Could it be possible for someone to believe all the Law and all the Prophets and all the apostles and NOT believe in Christ? The questioning should begin there. An inquiry into the authority of Abraham, Moses, the prophets, and apostles would reveal more about a person's faith in Christ than silly questions as to whether he can walk through walls. Do we believe these ancient witnesses? Were they who they claimed to be? They all wrote and spoke of Christ.

It is this "great cloud of witnesses" that lay a proper foundation. If you accept these, you are prepared to make a mature decision about Christ. If you do not accept these servants sent to us but, as the ones of those times, reject, kill, and ignore them, chances are you will reject the Messiah too.

Take care also in nurturing the brethren. Before you lay Christ out to them and force Him down their throats, demanding that they believe in all His miracles, sayings and demands, perhaps you would do well to nurture their faith in the Scriptures, in the story of Abraham, the burning bush and walls of Jericho, and the baptism of John. I believe many converts to Christ have never come to an understanding of authority. Why ask a man about the Christ of the Bible if he has yet to believe the Bible at all? Instead of asking if they believe that Jesus is the Son of God, the Messiah and that He alone offers salvation to the world -- you could ask, "Did God commission John to baptize or not?"

76. *Why judge ye not of yourselves what is right?*

Luke 12:57, "Yea, and why even of yourselves judge ye not what is right?"

From time to time we witness Jesus' fascination with mankind's stumbling. This is just such an occasion.

Christianity's greatest strength has been rendered virtually ineffectual in our day. This has been done through the well intentioned as well as the insidious, but mostly through the clergy.

I heard a preeminent preacher/teacher giving advice to a woman whom was looking for a church to attend. He told her to make sure it stood firmly in the Faith, believed in the Trinity, administered the Sacraments, and believed that the Bible was the Word of God. He then warned her of signs of a cult (a word that has yet to be defined among evangelical Christians) and one of those sure signs of a cult was "personal revelation" or "internal witness." The teacher went on that we should never trust ourselves to judge what is right; we should get that direction only from the Bible.

It is factual that many have been led astray by following without reservation their "internal witness," but we must admit many have been led from the true Christ Jesus, and the faith of our forefathers with their Bible held firmly in hand and enthroned in their heart. We must also realize that NO ONE has EVER been led into darkness or error or even slightly askew by following the Holy Spirit. This idea of elevating the Bible to the status of Christ Himself (and even giving it His name, "Word of God") and vilifying the Holy Spirit as an untrustworthy guide is probably the most crippling doctrine in our modern world.

When we turned our lives to the service of Jesus Christ, he placed within our broken hearts the down payment of our eternal life. Paul says it this way in Ephesians 1:13-14, "In whom ye also trusted, after that ye heard the word of truth, the gospel of your salvation: in whom also after that ye believed, ye were sealed with that holy Spirit of promise, Which is the earnest of our inheritance until the redemption of the purchased possession..." The Spirit of God Himself lives within us, nay, IS our very life. Why then are we told we cannot trust or consult Him? Must we consult with a book... a pastor ... or a teacher to keep from going astray? An attempt to find motivation for this kind of doctrine could not be done without being unkind to those who promote it. For whichever it is, whether it is ego, job security, propagation of the priesthood, or combination of all, it would not be complementary.

There was a time when preaching was a tough job, done in adverse circumstances. Preachers of the Gospel brought that Gospel to a hostile world, proclaiming for God the way of righteousness to an unrighteous world. Now, preachers have come off of the streets and have taken safe refuge in churches behind pulpits preaching to those who are not hostile toward Christ. They have told us that we need these "men of God" to read our Bibles to us and tell us what they mean.

In our day we have "educated" men who stand before us and expound to us the Bible and tell us what it means properly translated from Greek, Hebrew, and Latin. All the while, they tell us to stay away from personal revelation because it will lead us astray. We should trust them, they say. Some are bold enough to say, "Go to your Bible and check up on me, make sure I am telling you the truth."[109] But alas, we are not educated as they, in Greek, Hebrew, and Latin. We have no letters behind our name. We have no idea what hermeneutics or apologetics are. How can we open and understand this book?

The True Light Within

How many of us have heard an idea, a sermon, even a song or hymn, and felt within ourselves, "Something is wrong with that"? We may not be able to put our finger on it, but we just "know" it is not right. That is the guide within us that we need to obey. That is the guide within us that we need to cultivate. That guide was put into all of us. It is the light of guidance. "That was the true Light, which lighteth every man that cometh into the world." (John 1:9) As a person heeds that light and recognizes Christ as sent from God to redeem us, and surrenders to Him as Lord, the Spirit of God accompanies, and increases that light. More light to lead guide and direct our steps is given us.

The Scriptures can be twisted and deceitful men can manipulate them, but the Spirit of God in an honest heart can be trusted. It is our only duty to remain honest and pure in heart, and listen to our Guide. He will direct you. Just as the initial light, that was given to all, led you to Christ and told you that surrender was the right thing to do, this Guide given you afterward, is a hundredfold brighter and deeper and will Guide you into ALL truth. ALL TRUTH.

Knowing that God did not create mankind without a moral compass, Jesus was astounded that men had so quickly extinguished this light given them. He must look at us the same way when we run from church to church, preacher to preacher, teacher to teacher, seeking someone to tell us what to do, how to feel, and how to find our way. He knows that within all of us there is a guide that will lead you to Him. If a man finds Him, He will fill that man with living water that springs up from inside so that going from well to well is unnecessary. He will fill Him with the Holy Spirit, the Spirit of God, and the Author of the Scriptures, the Voice of the prophets and Wisdom of the ages.

When our Christ Jesus sees us as sheep with no shepherd, He is saddened, because all provision was made for us to have comfort, guidance, and nourishment. He put within us at the expense of His own life, the Holy Spirit of God. Why don't we judge in ourselves what is right by this Spirit?

Before you read books or follow preachers around or sign up for every seminar that remotely sounds as though it will answer your questions, first

---

[109] Of all heretics I have ever investigated, all have made this statement.

listen... for the Spirit to speak. As you throw down one book and pick up another, go from one Meeting to another, and from one counselor to another, quietly listen in the depths of your soul. Can't you hear the Savior ask, "...Why judge ye not of yourselves what is right?"

77.   *What is this then that is written?*

Luke 20:17, "And he beheld them, and said, What is this then that is written, The stone which the builders rejected, the same is become the head of the corner?"

Many of us have a tendency to believe the best about ourselves. We give reasons when we explain our shortcomings and when others do, we call them excuses. When we read about the multitudes in the Bible we tend to think of ourselves as special, different, and that we stand not with the crowd, but alone and individually.

When Jesus was teaching by way of parable, He told the story of the lord of the vineyard who set up his winery, making every provision for it. He hired a staff, put them in charge, and left the country. Upon sending emissaries, the lord found that the workers had grown wicked and selfish. So he sent his son thinking they will reverence him. After telling His hearers that they killed the son and tossed his beaten body out to the birds, Jesus looks at the Pharisees and asks, "What do you think will happen now?"

He received an answer commensurate with the offense, as He expected, but at this point they had not considered that they were they of whom Jesus spake. When this occurred to them they were angry and the Bible says they sought to take Him. What was the key that made them realize that it was they whom Jesus condemned in the story? Jesus asked them a question. "What is this then that is written?"

This story brought the Pharisees to an objective state in which they could see themselves as they really were. When they were minus their selfish blinders they could see the horror in their actions. When they realized that it was themselves whom they had just condemned, they were angry.

Thou art the Man

Nathan the prophet in King David's time used this method in showing David his sin with Bathsheba. Hearing a story of a rich man taking an only lamb from a poor man, David became incensed and demanded that the man be punished severely. Nathan then told David, "Thou art the man."[110] Sometimes when we read the Scriptures we apply the blessings and good parts to ourselves and the unpleasant portions to all those people we don't know. When we read, "God so loved the world," we claim the word "world" applies to us. When it says, "He was in the world... and the world knew him not." We say that the word "world" applies to someone else.

Once when Jesus was making a point about His Lordship He asked about a certain Scripture and suffixed the question with "... and the scripture cannot be broken..." [111]making the inference that the Scripture is a reliable and

---

[110] 2 Samuel 11:1—12: 7
[111] John 10:34-36

trustworthy record and most of all – it is true. If we can assume that it is true and unbreakable then we may ask several questions about what is written there. When we couple our natural tendency to believe the best about ourselves and the fact that the Bible is a faithful record of past and future events, we find discrepancies.

Jesus speaks of a straight gate into which FEW go. He speaks of a straight way upon which FEW find the desire or ability to walk upon. He also spoke of a broad way and a wide gate that MANY find and travel that leads them to destruction. Contrariwise, we think that MOST of those we know are on the path that leads to life. And FEW are on the destructive road that leads to everlasting death. This discrepancy is hard to rectify. None of us have trouble with famous murderers being thrown to the flames but it is never anyone we know. Yet, "What is this then that is written?"

Jesus spoke of servants that were cut off, cast away, and disregarded. Who are these? If we decide that it is not us, or does not apply to us, we must ask, "What is this then that is written?" If the Scripture cannot be broken, "What is this then that is written?"

Who? Me?

Matthew 7:22-23, "Many will say to me in that day, Lord, Lord, have we not prophesied in thy name? and in thy name have cast out devils? and in thy name done many wonderful works? And then will I profess unto them, I never knew you: depart from me, ye that work iniquity." Who are these people who were well on their merry way into the reward for which they thought they were working only to be thrust out into outer darkness? If we decide that they are no one we know personally, and it certainly cannot be us, then, "What is this then that is written?" Consider:

o The *"foolish man, which built his house upon the sand:"* Matthew 7
o The *"many will say to me in that day, Lord, Lord"* Matthew 7
o The *"foolish [virgins that] took their lamps, and took no oil with them:"* Matthew 25
o The *"man, having put his hand to the plough, and looking back"* Luke 9

o The five brethren of the rich man of whom it was said, *"If they hear not Moses and the prophets, neither will they be persuaded, though one rose from the dead."* Luke 16:31
o The *"many who are called"* from which *"few are chosen."*

Who Are These People?

Are the people mentioned in these parables anyone we know? Could they be us? Or are they loose and undirected points of a sermon, hitting, and missing with no certain target? Perhaps these parables are just scare tactics to coerce our compliance. Or maybe they are dire warnings, serious messages with meaningful words and urgent notices to beware of pitfalls and traps. Perhaps they are true and as sure as the Scripture that cannot be broken.

254

If these warnings are not for your mother and father, sister and brother, son or daughter, if these warnings are not for your close neighbors and friends, if they are not for *YOU*, then, "What is this then that is written?"

78. Who is it that doesn't consider costs?

Luke 14:28, "For which of you, intending to build a tower, sitteth not down first, and counteth the cost, whether he have sufficient to finish it?"

Luke 14:31, "Or what king, going to make war against another king, sitteth not down first, and consulteth whether he be able with ten thousand to meet him that cometh against him with twenty thousand?"

It is not very popular to talk about the cost of our salvation. It becomes an argument with those who insist that it is a free gift, they feel it is blasphemy to say that works are warranted, necessary, or in anywise an integral part of salvation. Scripture references are conspicuously absent from their assertion and hymn titles like, "Jesus paid it all" usually have to suffice for "text" but they hold to the idea anyway. From this idea of a "sin debt" and its "payment" by Christ, they derive there are no works left to do. The Scriptures, however, provide no references that say that Jesus paid for anyone's sin.[112]

There are costs for salvation, one that Christ paid, and one that we must pay as well, as is taught in these examples that Jesus gave. We must ask, "If Jesus paid it all, what cost is He asking us to count in the Scripture cited above? What difference does it make if we quit in the middle of our journey, if we succumb to temptation? What does "He that endures to the end shall be saved"[113] mean if Jesus indeed "paid it all" and nothing further is required of us?

Anyone who maintains that nothing further is required, has not only been fooled by ineptly worded hymns, they are fooling themselves. For in the depths of our own spirits, we are sure that there are requirements that must be met, that there are tests of faith we must pass, and there is a cost that we choose to default upon or pay. Even before we ever met the Master and Lord Christ of the Scriptures, it was clearly known that we would have to keep this faith to the end to be saved. It is written upon our heart and remains even now. This other doctrine (that Jesus paid for the sins of the world) must be preached incessantly to counteract the gnawing in our own spirit that there is yet a price to be paid.

What then must a person do to earn His salvation? What must a person do to make himself or herself worthy of saving? What may a man or woman do to justify themselves in the sight of God and earn this love and redemption? Jesus was asked a question similar to these in John 6:28-29, "Then said they unto him, What shall we do, that we might work the works of God?" They

---

[112] William Penn, a great man in the Society of Friends and founder of Pennsylvania, was incarcerated in the Tower of London for making this very claim. Although it may be a pleasing thought (that Christ paid for the sins of the world) it is not supported by the Scriptures. The purchase, spoken of in Scripture, is Christ's purchase of mankind. He did not pay for your sins He paid for your freedom. He did not buy your sins, He bought you.

[113] Matthew 10:22, "And ye shall be hated of all men for my name's sake: but he that endureth to the end shall be saved."

256

asked, "What work can we do to make ourselves worthy, to give us value to the Kingdom of God?"

We must admit that this was a worthy notion, and an honorable goal. What would you think would be a work that could earn you a place of worthiness? Jesus answered and said unto them, "This is the work of God, that ye believe on him whom he hath sent." The fact is, there is nothing that will earn this gift. Faith in Christ alone is all that can affect the grace of God on our behalf. There is no sacrifice we can make, no good work that we can do that will accomplish redemption in our own souls or those of any other man. Are the thoughts of the last two paragraphs a contradiction?

Free Puppies?

Some labor over the question, "Why wouldn't anyone accept the FREE gift of salvation?" Perhaps it is because they understand the truth that it is not at all FREE. They know that it will cost them at least their freedom and at most, their very lives. The world sometimes has a clearer picture of the Christian life than do those who sit under preaching day after day. These who can hear their hearts, know that coming to Christ is a costly gift. Though it sounds like a contradiction in terms, salvation is a costly gift.

What is a costly gift? Example: A child and an adult see two totally different things when they see a sign that says "free puppies." The "gift" of a puppy is vastly different than a gift of a simple inanimate souvenir. A gift cannot be considered "free" based on its acquisition costs alone. The maintenance costs, the care and feeding, and responsibilities must be a factor in the cost of any gift. We acquire salvation as a gift from God, but to say salvation is free is misleading.

Who is it that doesn't consider costs? Many have signed on to Christianity as a free ride and as they become aware of the costs, they seek out and settle into faiths and denominations and teachings of no challenge to minimize demand placed upon them. But have they paid what is required? Have they endured? If we stay hidden away and remain silent about our faith are we not admitting that the price is too high? Can we say that we are willing to pay any price? Can we expect God to deliver on His promise if we do not hold to the conditions under which it was made?

You may have heard, "There are no conditional promises in the Bible." Search for promises, any promise, without a condition attached and you will not be able to find one. At least I haven't been able to do so. All of your promises come with conditions. All of my promises have conditions. All of God's promises have conditions, too. If they have no conditions they are statements of fact, not promises.

Promises presuppose trust and faith on the part of the beneficiary. Why trust and faith? Because, there is an investment to be made by those to whom the promises were given. Promises declare the future benefit regarding the investment, or an exchange made upon fulfillment of an agreement, if you will. This is like the covenant we have with God. Promissory notes are called such because they have this characteristic. Banks promise interest, but only on what you invest.

We must count the costs in order to be honest and just in our dealings with men and money and with God. Who starts to college and just waits for the bills to come in? Does he not first sit down and count the cost of a full degree to see if he has sufficient funds to finish it? Who builds a house and never asks, "How much will it cost me" and, "How much do I have?" Who is it that doesn't consider costs? Who sets out on a trip and doesn't look at a map to calculate the costs? Have you ever wondered what your faith in Christ may cost you? Jesus made lists of things on several different occasions. Let us look at them in brief.

It may cost you the peace in your home:

Matthew 10:35-39, Luke 12:53, "...And a man's foes shall be they of his own household."

It may cost you your possessions:

Matthew 19:29, "And every one that hath forsaken houses...lands, for my name's sake...."

It may cause you to have to choose between your faith and your family:

Luke 14:26, "If any man come to me, and hate not his father, and mother, and wife, and children, and brethren, and sisters... he cannot be my disciple."

It may cost you your life:

Luke 14:26, "Yea, and his own life also..."

So this "free gift" of salvation is starting to run quite a tally! Are you willing to pay it? Who is it that doesn't consider costs?

There is no way that you can make yourself aware of all the costs involved in faith in Christ, but you must at least consider the costs that Jesus outlined here. Christ's point is twofold:

1) You consider any costly endeavor fully before you commit to it or take it to yourself, why take on the most important decision of your life with no thought of its cost?

2) He makes it clear that looking back, turning back, not paying the price, is nothing short of total apostasy. What else could be inferred from, "...he is not worthy of me ...he is not fit for the Kingdom of God or ...he cannot be my disciple?"

To honestly and properly consider costs, you must not only consider what it will cost you to attain and remain in the Kingdom to come, but you must also consider the cost of default and failure. Who is it that doesn't consider costs?

79. *Wilt thou be made whole?*

John 5:6, "When Jesus saw him lie, and knew that he had been now a long time in that case, he saith unto him, Wilt thou be made whole?"

Thirty-eight years is a long time to be sick and immobile. Could it be possible that this man got used to being in his condition? Many allowances and provisions had to be made to accommodate this man in his affliction. He must have made them and many must have been made for him.

It is entirely possible that this condition came upon him at birth, (making him nearly forty years old) but if it came upon him in his youth, he may have been in his sixties. He was a mature man in any case. After many years of affliction, sickness, pain, even suffering, the aggravation wears off and an acceptance replaces it.

At the time that injury or illness strikes there is the shock of our lifestyle and schedule being interrupted and altered, then with everything that was earlier considered "important" laid aside, we take on the battle for normality. We employ doctors and specialist and consult books and knowledgeable people to help give us back our life, as we once knew it. As it settled upon us that our illness or injury is never going to be better, we resigned a little of our fighting spirit and a little of our lives to the victor.

I suffered the near amputation of my right hand as an eighteen year old. The hand I have now is scarred and dysfunctional. Because the median nerve was cut, only three fingers of the five have tactile sensitivity enough to feel anything other than extreme heat or cold. (You should see me typing!). Every effort was made to restore the hand. Many doctors were surprised that I was able to keep it at all. Dr. McCarthy was skillful and persevering and with all that was available in those days (1975) made my hand useable again.

I have now been with this impaired hand longer than I ever had the one with which I was born. I had so much pain for the years of surgery and rehabilitation, I used to wonder if my hand ever stopped hurting or I had just become accustomed to the pain. It seems impossible, but I have become so used to its deformity and pain and lack of utility, I can hardly remember what it was like to be any other way.

From time to time I may meet an orthopedic surgeon who becomes interested in my injury. I see him trace with his fingers on my already scarred skin, lines of surgical openings and talk of making further repairs. He tries to engage my enthusiasm by promising more freedom, less pain, removal of scar tissue, and restoration of sensitivity. All I can think of is the five surgeries that preceded my present condition and the pain of rehabilitation and the fact that I get along pretty well as it is. In essence, what the doctor is saying to me is, "Wilt thou be made whole?" I answer, "Nahhh! I'll be alright."

To one degree or another we all have been through this. Some were left with only scars as a reminder, some with debilitating disease. When it occurs to the strong and independent man that he will not always be so, and to the young and beautiful woman that those two terms are inseparable, the futility of struggling falls upon us.

Jesus sensed this. We can hear in His question and in John's introduction of the question a concern for the length of time that the man had struggled with his illness. When Jesus saw him lie, and knew that he had been now a long time in that case, he saith unto him, Wilt thou be made whole? It is as if Christ was asking the most ridiculous question. How could anyone in that condition for thirty-eight years NOT desire wholeness?

Comfortable With Affliction

However, it is possible he had become comfortable, cynical, pessimistic, or even content with his affliction. It had become his life, his conversation, his "condition" that set him apart, and gave him personality, notoriety, or noteworthiness. So Jesus' question had merit, "Wilt thou be made whole?"

The Amplified Bible says it this way; "There was a certain man there who had suffered with a deep-seated and lingering disorder for thirty-eight years. When Jesus noticed him lying there helpless He said to him, do you want to become well? [Are you really in earnest about getting well?]" His willingness was in question because a long period of time had passed. We have a tendency to adapt to, or accept a condition that is out of our control.

In like manner, when sin takes hold in our lives, when we find ourselves in transgression, the fight for "normality" commences. We remember the fresh anointing of the Holy Spirit and now we can feel that He is grieved with us, the doubting and the fear that has been a stranger to us recently, now makes its home in us. We struggle for a cure. We implore, ask, consult, and read till we fall on our faces before God, repent, and make it all right again. Just as our life regains its balance and the joy of our salvation has been restored – alas, it happens again.

We sometimes come through with only scars, sometimes debilitating and irrevocable harm, and loss. When it occurs to us that we are prone to wander and even likely to disappoint the Lord we love, so in the physical, the futility of struggling falls upon us.

After acceptance comes we are in danger of carrying about an attitude that says, "This is the way God made me and I can't help it." We may even enjoy it a little, the notoriety and two minutes of fame it gives us. But will you be made whole, even if it makes you like everyone else, takes away your notoriety and your secret indulgences?

Have you lost the sweet taste of being whole? Have you so soon forgotten the glory of cleanliness before God and the wonderful forgiveness that washes over a man and fills him with the very presence of God? Will you be made whole?

We all risk complacency creeping into our lives. Can I revive in you a desire to be as you were the day Christ first cleansed your soul? Do you remember the fervor with which you attacked the sin and shortcoming in your life? Can the lost and forgotten ideal, faded by time and disappointment be renewed into the fresh hope you had at the beginning?

If I cannot, you are in danger of a fatal acceptance of lukewarm mediocrity. As the years slide by, the hope of being totally free from sin will ebb away till that hope will be transformed into dream, the dream will eventually turn into wish, the wish will degrade into preference and finally preference will become nothing more than whim. Have you decided to live with your situation, with your malady, in your maimed and impaired condition?

Have you become discouraged with the prospect of living above sin? Have you forgotten the grace of God that empowers you to win over the sin in your life? You may have folded and given up, thinking that the fight is hopeless, but it is not. You do not have to sin everyday as you may have been told. You are commissioned by God to KEEP His Commandments and endure! There must be a renewal within to remember the presence of the indwelling Christ and freshly commit to living exemplary lives as children of God. Christ waits to indwell and empower you, to give you the first desire of your conversion[114] – that you may know Him and the power of His resurrection[115] – the power to become the sons of God![116]

But, first forgiveness must come with cleansing and repentance. Jesus knows that you have been in your state for quite a while. He wonders if you have settled in and grown comfortable in your lukewarm condition and asks, "Wilt thou be made whole?"

---

[114] Romans 8:19-21, "For the earnest expectation of the creature waiteth for the manifestation of the sons of God. For the creature was made subject to vanity, not willingly ... Because the creature itself also shall be delivered from the bondage of corruption into the glorious liberty of the children of God."
[115] Philippians 3:10, "That I may know him, and the power of his resurrection..."
[116] John 1:12, "But as many as received him, to them gave he power to become the sons of God, even to them that believe on his name:"

80.   Doth this offend you?

John 6:61-62, "When Jesus knew in himself that his disciples murmured at it, he said unto them, Doth this offend you? What and if ye shall see the Son of man ascend up where he was before?"

Any modern-day evangelist would have appreciated the crowds that followed Christ. Anyone trying to preach to the masses would have given anything to experience the kind of numbers that the Lord was getting to attend His meetings. What would a person have to do to get such turnouts? Perhaps feed them for free? Although that was not His purpose, after a couple of these free feedings, He was becoming popular.

When a group followed Christ across the Sea of Galilee, Jesus did something that would be considered odd to those trying for high attendance numbers. He called them freeloaders and sent them home upset and disappointed. He said that their only concern was getting food to eat. He invited those who thought He was a meal ticket to eat the real food that would provide lasting benefit; He invited them to eat His flesh and drink His blood. (An idea repulsive to anyone, and to Jews – it was blasphemous and pagan.) It seems as though the actions of Christ are the opposite of someone trying to attract crowds. He thinned the crowds of thousands back down to the original twelve.

Upon exposing these that had followed Him for food, He launches into a tirade about being the manna that was sent down from heaven to feed God's people. He makes outrageous claims. In the sixth chapter of John and elsewhere in the Scriptures we find that instead of being known simply as a good and wise teacher, we hear Him make wild claims to be the son of God, to be the bread that was sent from heaven, to be the only way to the Father, to be more than Moses, greater than Solomon, and backed by the Prophets of old. He claims to have seen the Father, and thereby claims to have an intimate knowledge of Him.

This was problem for the followers of Jesus then, and it is a problem for some now. As long as Jesus is a good and wise teacher, a rabbi, or even a prophet (in other words, human) we can tolerate Him. But when He makes claims to be more than that, He lays claim to worship; He commands obedience, He makes our opinions worthless and our compliance imperative. When He finishes the "tirade" about eating His flesh and drinking His blood He looks at His disciples and asks, "Doth this offend you?" His question was more rhetorical than interrogative, for He was sure that it did indeed offend them.

John 6:60-61, "Many therefore of his disciples, when they had heard this, said, This is an hard saying; who can hear it? When Jesus knew in himself that his disciples murmured at it, he said unto them, Doth this offend you?"

Well, twenty-first century believer, does it offend you? Does it offend you to hear that Jesus is the very Son of God? Does it set crosswise with you to hear that He is the only way to the Father; is it offensive to you to hear that the

Father draws us to Christ and that salvation itself is not within your prerogative and power? Is it offensive to you to hear that Jesus Christ is alone the one prophesied to be the redeemer of all mankind? That beside Him there is no other?

Customizing Our Theology

This idea is offensive to many. Modern theology makes provision for any and every school of thought. No one is to be left out. Seminaries apologize for their stance in years past and pledge to take a more "compassionate" perspective in the future. Preachers make provision for liberality among their congregations and the "straight and narrow" is never heard as long as the sanctuary has debt or the building program is active.

A peculiar doctrine has emerged from this fear of offending. Somehow the church has blamed YHVH for the straight-laced ideas of holiness and teaches that Jesus has changed all that. There has been a customizing of the Gospel to accommodate everyone and exclude no one. The new Gospel depicts the Father Jehovah as harsh and exacting; His Son, however, is portrayed as gentle and forgiving. In the Gospel man writes, there is no need to make uncomfortable changes or worship in fear of judgment because it is a friendlier Gospel. There is a factor modern Christianity has neglected to consider in their wonderful plan of evangelization – it is not their Gospel to edit as they will! How can we depend on the Author of the true Gospel to carry out His promise to those who believe the Gospel, if the Gospel they believe and live by is not the Gospel of the Author?

If we find that our theology is custom made we must change it. Usually we customize it to accommodate sin in ourselves or our loved ones; we make room for Grandpa's ideas or our spouse's opinion, or our own interpretations. We do this so that we can gain the "free food of indulgence" and we do so at the expense of Truth. Jesus will one day sit at the right hand of majesty on high and rule in the perfect will of Jehovah – not one jot or tittle being changed from the foundation of the world. If He is not the meek shepherd seen in portraits, with a staff in one hand and a lamb in the other, but rather turns out to be the Son of God, perfectly replicating and reflecting the God you thought retired, will it offend you?

When Jesus told of His position of authority, power and might, when He revealed His majesty and worthiness of worship, when He said I and my Father are one and the same, He asked, "Doth this offend you?"

Jesus went on to say that it would become clear to us that He has only scratched the surface of His position in the Kingdom. It will become clear that He is not only the Bread of Heaven, the only Way, the beloved Son of the Father, but He is Lord and Judge. He is to sit at the right hand of God as ruler of all and King of Kings and Lord of Lords.

If it offends you to give Him lordship over earthly rulers, and over earthly kings; if it offends you to give Him the prime position in your own heart and life, how will you feel when the Kingdom of God is given over to Him and

His power, will and purpose is made fully known? *"When Jesus knew in himself that his disciples murmured at it, he said unto them, Doth this offend you? What and if ye shall see the Son of man ascend up where he was before?"*

81.   Will ye also go away?

John 6:66-67, "From that time many of his disciples went back, and walked no more with him. Then said Jesus unto the twelve, Will ye also go away?"

Jesus found Himself in the company of those who were following Him in order to see miracles and eat free food. Jesus told them that His ministry was more than that. When Jesus finished His exclamation of deity and the commandment to eat His flesh and drink His blood He offended many and they decided He must be insane or at least they were ashamed to associate themselves with Him further. It would be comparable to hearing a person whom you trust say something that is wild and realizing you cannot, for reasons of association, ally with them anymore.

There are those of us who find no offense at these words of Christ, however crazy they may sound. We have no problem with Him as deity and welcome Him as King of Kings and Lord of Lords. We know exactly what He means when He tells us to eat His flesh and drink His blood. But remember that His disciples did not.

When Jesus looked around where crowds of thousands stood moments before and saw nothing but wind blown footprints quickly disappearing in the sand, He looked at His twelve motley disciples and asked, "Will ye also go away?" "Why are not you leaving too?"

When Jesus taught that we had to make choices in life, whether by parable or by preaching, He always taught that there were only two choices to make. There were two gates, two roads, two sons, two servants, two destinations, etc. He never made provision for the lukewarm, the fence-straddler, the indecisive, or the fearful. We, in our modern age, have made provision for all and any that cannot keep up, cannot seem to make up their mind, those who put their hand to the plow and look back, those who "have issues" and "a lot on their mind."

But Jesus made no such provision and rightfully so. You will find that it is rarely beneficial to pander to and support those who want it their way, or are waiting till "all the facts are in." This life in Christ is a life of faith and all the facts will never be in. This life in Christ is a matter of faith, a matter of the heart, a matter of doing what we know is right. It is time to make a choice.

When Jesus looked at His disciples, He asked, Will ye also go away? "Then Simon Peter answered him, Lord, to whom shall we go? thou hast the words of eternal life." (John 6:67-68) They were saying, "We have no idea what you just told this crowd or why, we do not understand why a Jew, forbidden to touch blood or dead men, would be asked to eat human flesh and drink blood but we believe that you must have a good reason. We're staying. We are convinced that you are the very Christ and we're staying." Then Jesus answered them, "Have I not chosen you twelve?" We can almost see a smile on His face as He heard the right answer come from Simon.

It was an attribute of faith for which Jesus sought when searching for the disciples. He was not looking for a man with good communication skills or good money management, but a man capable of believing and following. When we know the One in whom we believe, we trust His words – when we trust His words we must distrust our understanding within ourselves.

We must open ourselves to the understanding given of the Father. If He says something that makes no sense or is contradictory to our way of thinking, we must be willing to stop and seek God for further understanding. If need be, we should change our thinking, and align ourselves to His words. We do not have the option of aligning His Word to our understanding. We must accept or reject what He tells us. There is no option to change, no option to omit or add until we can make sense of it all.

If Christ is who He says He is, then His words should stand as truth, unaided by anyone's interpretation, or explanation. To contort words and meanings, to spiritualize or literalize verses of Scripture, or omit reading of certain passages to avoid dealing with them, or turn our reading toward extra-biblical sources, we are determining Christ as insufficient to communicate His truth to us. It is only our selfishness and sins that hinder clear communication. We would do well to take on the attitude of the disciples who said, "To whom shall we go?"

Being Taught of the Lord

It has long been a Quaker principal to listen to the Spirit within us and gain guidance from God directly. This is not a matter of sifting through ALL available information as is done by some; it is rather reading God's words and hearing God's Word. It is being "taught of the Lord,"[117] the "hearing a voice behind thee,"[118] the "law written in your heart."[119] It is sitting at His feet as Mary did.[120] What need we of teachers and books and explanations and excuses of spiritualizing the literal and literalizing the spiritual in order to understand. Why not listen, as the disciples did, not understanding at all, but trusting that the Lord has the words of eternal life? Then we are open to enjoy the moments of unfolding that await the patient and humble hearer as we witness in the Gospels. "... and when they were alone, he expounded all things to his disciples." (Mark 4:34)

---

[117] Isaiah 54:13, "And all thy children shall be taught of the LORD; and great shall be the peace of thy children."

[118] Isaiah 30:21, "And thine ears shall hear a word behind thee, saying, This is the way, walk ye in it, when ye turn to the right hand, and when ye turn to the left."

[119] Jeremiah 31:31-34, "Behold, the days come, saith the LORD, that I will make a new covenant with the house of Israel, and with the house of Judah: ... I will put my law in their inward parts, and **write it in their hearts**; and will be their God, and they shall be my people. And they **shall teach no more** every man his neighbour, and every man his brother, saying, Know the LORD: for they shall all know me, from the least of them unto the greatest of them, saith the LORD: for I will forgive their iniquity, and I will remember their sin no more."

[120] Luke 10:42, "But one thing is needful: and Mary hath chosen that good part, which shall not be taken away from her."

When you depart from Him and look for understanding elsewhere, you are like those that day who turned back and walked no more with Him. They went to seek understanding elsewhere; they went to where the words fit their understanding instead of seeking understanding of His words. Can you imagine the disbelief of the disciples as they watched the multitude of persons trekking home over the hills till all is silent; and wondering to themselves, "Where are they going? Who will tell them what Christ can tell them? Who knows what He knows? He has the words of eternal life?"

When you run across Scripture that is difficult, can you not trust that these are words of eternal life? When you hear God's word inside you bubbling up as a live spring, can you trust that it is the Lord who is dealing with you? Can you not rely upon the voice that confirms your salvation, guides you along your journey, keeps you from sin, and opens the Scriptures to you? Why go to mere and fallible man for understanding? Why seek out new ways, new interpretations, and new teachers? "One is your teacher even Christ." (Matthew 23:8)

Jesus is seeking disciples of understanding. He is seeking those who will come to Him, stay with Him, and believe His words. He desires to teach those who will look to the Holy Spirit of God when they do not understand. He does *not* tutor those who go out and seek men and others to explain, expand or adulterate God's precious words.

The next time you find Scripture or revelation hard to hear or hard to understand and you are tempted to take it before men for explanation or scrutiny, listen. For the Lord is asking, "Will ye also go away?"

82. *Have not I chosen you twelve?*

John 6:70, "Jesus answered them, Have not I chosen you twelve, and one of you is a devil?"

There is a vast difference in choosing Christ and being chosen by Christ. I recommend that you read the entire sixth chapter of John to get a grasp of this thought. The concept would be better understood yet if a foundation was first laid. In our culture the Bible is read as one devotional thought after another. We need to view a wider context in this writing of John 6. Notice, if you will, the subject. All who the Father gives me will come to me. Here we see a clear definition of election. "All – will come" shows the certainty of election. The proviso "...who the Father gives me..." shows the sovereignty of election.

Election is an avoided subject in most every religious circle. No one likes it, although if we are honest, we will admit that it is not the election of the saints with which we take umbrage it is the selection that gives us pause. Without approaching how it is done we will consider this sixth chapter of John conceding that it is done and that election is an inseparable part of the salvation process. John 6:37, "All that the Father giveth me shall come to me; and him that cometh to me I will in no wise cast out."

The miracle in the first part of the chapter of feeding thousands with a small amount of food was a sign to some that the Prophet for whom they were waiting to come and rescue them from their political distress was indeed He who stood before them.

They thought to make Him a King. When Jesus perceived this, He removed Himself by stealth to avoid a political uprising. When they followed Him over the sea they asked Him for a miracle sign to show them He was the one anointed to be King. They felt that the installation of Jesus as King would be "the works of God," (God's will, in other words). "...What shall we do, that we might work the works of God?" they asked. Jesus was disappointed because they did not believe in Him; they only deciphered that He was the Messiah. They were not sent to Him of the Father, they came because they saw Him as their King and benefactor. He wanted them to believe in Him, not make Him King. Making Him King was not "the work of God." Jesus answered, "This is the work of God, that ye believe on him whom he hath sent."

Now, with the subject clearly established, He shows that the Father has sent them all the evidence they need to believe and yet they still do not. They mention Moses (another ruler, benefactor, feeder of people). Jesus rebuts, "Moses did not give you bread, it was my Father. My Father now gives you the true bread from heaven and yet you do not believe. You want to see a sign? I am the bread sent from heaven, But I said unto you, That ye also have seen me, and believe not." (John 6:36 with author's additions and translations)

Here, Jesus explains the two-fold process of being included in the resurrection. One step is clearly within our control and one is obviously out of our control. The will of God concerning election is that He reveals Christ and we believe what has been shown us. "And this is the will of him that sent me, that every one which seeth the Son, and believeth on him, may have everlasting life: and I will raise him up at the last day." (John 6:40)

After this speech, the Jews were angered that He said that He came down from heaven. The religious leaders murmured and grumbled about what blasphemy had been committed and made it clear to all around them that they did not believe Him. Jesus said don't worry boys, you can't believe on me...unless the Father says so. He actually said, "No man can come to me, except the Father which hath sent me draw him...." (John 6:44)

Jesus goes on from here to explain the intricacies of this faith to which God has called us. This manna from heaven, this bread of life given to us is none other than Christ Himself, who has come to give life to all who take Him into themselves. This is why He says, "Whoso eateth my flesh, and drinketh my blood, hath eternal life; and I will raise him up at the last day."

Jesus Said This for The Express Purpose to Offend.

When you place your life in the hands of Jesus Christ, what can he say that would make you turn back? When Christ has been revealed to you, what choice do you have but to follow? But when it is a matter of volition, deduction, or simply following the One from whom we receive the greatest benefit, the choice remains as one to be made everyday.

We may find ourselves constantly weighing alternatives and benefits, evaluating costs and rewards, following one day then leading the next. When we are called of God to seek Christ, then subsequently chosen by Jesus, our lives are navigated from above. We are as slaves and bondservants of our own desire to follow Him who bestowed such favor and grace and power on our behalf.

We do not follow for food. We follow because we believe that He is the way. We follow because the Father has shown us the Messiah, and made us able to be partakers in such grace. There is no offense to be taken, no choice to be made, no evaluation, no balancing of sacrifice and blessing to be taken into account before we take His road or ours. We take His way because we love Him. We love Him because we see Him. We see Him because the Father draws us to Him and reveals Him to us. If we obey Him, He in turn reveals the Father to us.

As if to prove what He had been saying throughout this chapter, and as if to verify the calling and choosing of these men He asks, "Will ye also go away?" "Master," they said, "To whom shall we go? ...thou hast the words of eternal life." When individuals are called by God to go to Christ and they obey the Father and seek and find Him, and then they are chosen by Christ to follow, these believers will be different than the masses. They will be tenacious disciples that have the strength that comes from having seen, having known and will not turn back. Although, even these are to endure their time of testing, they make no decisions in ignorance for they have seen with their eyes, they have heard with their ears and their hands have handled the Word of God.[121] They know in whom they have believed.[122]

To be chosen is to live in assurance – assurance that you did not force your way into the Kingdom, but were invited… by God Himself. You obeyed that voice and sought out Christ, believed on Him and surrendered to His leadership. Your salvation does not hang in doubt, nor do you fear the day of judgment for you were called by God and chosen by His son.

After the disciples look at Him so anxiously and asked, "To whom shall we go?" Jesus answered them, "You see? This is what I was talking about. These people want to make me their King, you know me *as* King within yourselves. They want me to make them bread from heaven, you see me *as* the bread from heaven. When I say things they do not understand they turn and seek another. You know that there is no other. **Have I not chosen ye twelve?**"

---

[121] 1 John 1:1, John 12:38-41
[122] 2 Timothy 1:12, "…for I know whom I have believed, and am persuaded that he is able to keep that which I have committed unto him against that day."

83. Are ye angry at me, because I have made a man whole?

John 7:23, "Are ye angry at me, because I have made a man every whit whole?"

Jesus has been the subject of ridicule, of language most foul, the butt of jokes, and taken to be some mystical figure to whom "weak" people cling in order to get through life. To them, He is not the One who will become the powerful ruler of all the Earth, nor is He, in their minds, now at the right hand of God awaiting the commencement of the last battle over which He will reign as victor. It is difficult to find among the populace, much more than contempt for Him and hearers repugning the mention of His name.

It would be easy to blame the ridiculous preachers who have made His name repulsive by going about the country doing tricks (calling them miracles) and getting their own way by declaring His precious name over their efforts. They gathered their living from the fooled masses and the Lord was given the blame by association. You will find though, it is deeper than even that. These charlatans did (and continue to do) the Kingdom of God no good, but we cannot blame them wholly for the distaste the world has for Christ.

All nature lovers are not hikers. Some of us larger, heavier, and non-athletic types love to view nature as much as the fit and strong, young and healthy; however, we will not likely be found in hiking boots. A person sharing my physique may even mistake his distaste for hiking as distaste for nature. When asked, "Do you enjoy nature?" I may answer, "No," because I might have heard the question as, "Would you like to go on a five mile hike up into the mountains?" Just so, a person who enjoys the exercise of hiking may mistake his love of hiking for a love of nature. The point being that we have a tendency to misplace our affections and our anger.

I use the word anger because it is usually the default emotion of our fear. We fear that which we do not desire. We fear that conditions will be forced upon us in which our impotence or our inabilities will be made known. We fear failure and embarrassment. This fear is expressed basically in two ways, we either fight what we fear or we run from it. As an animal's characteristics are bent by species or breed to either fight or run from confrontation, we too may have, by personality, such propensities. Those who would rather fight will confront and openly reject or repudiate Christ on any grounds, and those who are more willing to run, remain remote from Christ (and Christians) altogether.

When we encounter those who are willing to fight what they fear, many times we mistakenly take up the fight. We equip ourselves with Scripture references and "proof texts" and scientific data to make our case. We are proud when we score a mark in God's favor (really our favor) and unfortunately find ourselves winning battle after battle while losing the war.

The basis of our fear is the enemy; the fighting is just our response. If we take on Christ's question as our own, we will defuse and disarm rather than, blade to blade, conquer them as menaces. What a wonderful thought is found in Christ's question, "Are ye angry at me, because I have made a man whole?" What is there about Christ to cause you fear? What evil thing has He done? How has He made the world worse? Who is worse for having followed Him?

Many, when they think of Christ, do not think of His goodness or His power, His love or His forgiveness. They think of the demand He places upon them, the contrast that His presence creates, the unworthiness, the sin, the difference between them as they are, and them as they should be. The thoughts create anger and this anger is misplaced and focused unjustly upon Christ. It is the thought of the *drill*, not the dentist that makes some say, "I hate dentists."

The question, "Why do men hate Christ?" is nearly a rhetorical one among the evangelical. A better one would be "Why do we not hate the world?" Why do we not hate every thing that comes from Hollywood, Madison Avenue, and the television networks? Who can say that the world is a better place for their influence? What mother can say that their child is better for having watched TV, gone to see a movie, or participated in the world's fashions? What broken hearted father can look at his son or daughter steeped in the world's mammon with no regard for God and righteousness and not despise the source of the enticement that took them away?

On the one hand there is Christ who has done nothing but good. Anything negative in Christianity can be traced to selfish and wicked men, not to our Savior. On the other hand, we have mammon that has brought about nothing but destruction. Any good to be found in the world is only from the semblance of Christianity left in it from days gone by. Will we continue to set our affection upon the world and its trinkets of distraction? The decision is plain. There is hardly a decision to make at all.

As an example, our lives should make plain the difference in the two. We should be examples of how Christ is not to be feared, but revered. To be angry with Him is much like being angry with a doctor who hurts us while setting a broken bone. The world is afraid of Christ; what He will require, what He will demand. They are afraid of the pain of the "broken bone" being set right. A lot of their fear is because we, the modern Christian population, are examples of the surgery completed. They are afraid because of what they see in us. Our contorted lives do not stand as shining examples of the doctor's art. Many times we have the same problems, indulge the same vices, and fear the same future as they.

We Are *His* Exemplars

Christians should present Christ as the restorer of men and eliminate the fear felt on the part of those who do not know Him. If we present Him as One to whom we go to be made whole and show the world that this indeed happened to us, and we are living proof of His power, we make the way for Christ to touch them and make them whole. He can use us for an example of

His power to make their lives better and therefore allay their fears. When we are examples of wholeness, we can be used of God.

There is no cause for a man to be angry at Christ. Neither is there cause to fear Him. Anger is a natural response to fear and doubt, and it is certainly a reasonable reaction to misunderstood pain. To keep anger in check it is good to keep in mind the benevolent motives of the man who sets a broken leg bone throughout the painful process. If the patient doesn't know what the healer is doing, or why, he can mistake his medical skill for needless and additional injury.

The happy and healthful results of painful processes must be kept in view in order to suffer the pain with no resentment. Perhaps if there was an example of success to which reference could be made there would be less fear in approaching Christ. Maybe a shining example of the grace of God would ally the fears and answer the doubts of those who consider Christ as a possible solution to the chaos and turmoil in their lives.

Like a dentist who displays pictures of pearly smiles to relieve the fears that come at the first appearance of the tray of shiny tools, or a doctor who catalogs testimonials to offset the pain of surgery or the tastes of medicine, you could be an exemplar to the world of men and women seeking God. When someone within your sphere of influence blames Christ for all their ills, and calls Him the source of their misery, or impugns Him as phony or non-existent, maybe our Savior can point to your life and pose the question in full assurance of a positive response, "Are ye angry at me, because I have made a man whole?"

84. Did not Moses give you the law, and yet none of you keepeth the law?

John 7:19, "Did not Moses give you the law, and yet none of you keepeth the law?

Jesus was pleading with the people around Him to understand that He was not sent, nor was He preaching, in His own name. Rather, He was sent by the Father to do the Father's will. Yet the people could not (or at least would not) see. As Jesus begs them to understand He says, "My doctrine is not mine, but his that sent me. If any man will do his will, he shall know of the doctrine, whether it be of God, or whether I speak of myself. He that speaketh of himself seeketh his own glory: but he that seeketh his glory that sent him, the same is true, and no unrighteousness is in him." (John 7:16-18)

This Scripture makes it clear that if a man will do God's will, he can know whether the doctrine he hears is of God or not. Wow! What a promise! We can live without fear of deception by living in God's will. There are those who refuse to read or even hear doctrine that has not been approved by their pastor, their denomination, or their loved ones. But here we see that we can live in such a way that we would never be deceived – that we could know by inner witness whether a Scripture, a doctrine, a word from God, or a revelation is true. The 17th verse declares, "If any man will do his will, he shall know of the doctrine, whether it be of God, or whether I speak of myself." James 1:22 bolsters this idea by asserting that we are to, "...be ye doers of the word, and not hearers only, deceiving your own selves." The deception is self-imposed when we don't DO what we are told.

There are those who have no interest in reading apocryphal texts, Gnostic Gospels, Dead Sea scrolls or even versions of the Bible other than theirs, because they fear being deceived. The people of Christ's day struggled with the same fear about Christ Himself. They questioned themselves (and Christ as well) to see if He was indeed the Messiah. Listen to some of the questions they asked among themselves. "... Is not this he, whom they seek to kill? But, lo, he speaketh boldly, and they say nothing unto him. Do the rulers know indeed that this is the very Christ?"

Then they reasoned, "Howbeit we know this man whence he is: but when Christ cometh, no man knoweth whence he is." Then they thought, "When Christ cometh, will he do more miracles than these which this man hath done?" "Many of the people... said, Of a truth this is the Prophet. Others said, This is the Christ. But some said, Shall Christ come out of Galilee?" Hath not the scripture said, That Christ cometh of the seed of David, and out of the town of Bethlehem, where David was?" So there was a division among the people because of him." (John 7:25-43)

They were vacillating back and forth in their own minds about whether or not Jesus really was the Messiah. Their quandary was not much different that ours is today. Would not our walk with Christ, our level of dedication, and our worship be deeper, richer and upon a higher plain if we settled once and for all that the Christ we know within us is indeed the Christ of the Bible and is the very Son of God?

When these basic truths are in doubt we are weak in our faith. When we are weak, we tend to cling to temporal and tangible reinforcements for our faith. This is an inroad to idolatry. We begin look to signs, symbols, we dabble in the mystical and mysterious instead of developing a faith based in reality and reason. Our blessings are more like "luck" and our tragedies become "bad Karma." Oh, we may give God the "glory" for our blessings but in truth, we have no idea how they came about.

We beg God to show Himself to us and make His way clear to us, to reveal truth, to verify doctrine, and thereby condone our behavior and our so-called "faith." His answer is sad but nonetheless true, "I have revealed things to you before and you did not listen." "I have given codes to live by, rules to judge by, and I reveal myself in all of them, but you will not DO them." "Did not Moses give you the Law, yet none of you keep the Law?"

Be Ye *Doers*

By this He reveals a key for which we have been searching. He says that the key to understanding, the way to know truth from error is to do God's will. Here is something totally within our control. If we DO what God has revealed in His Commandments, and we live in them, and by them, and do so in faith, we would recognize Christ in the doctrines we hear, or we will know them as false. He says, "If any man will do his [the Father's] will, he shall know of the doctrine, whether it be of God, or whether I speak of myself." (John 7:17)

Jesus told us these revelations of God by way of the Law (and obedience to it) would have helped us in our recognition of Christ. What an honor it would have been to have had such insight – to recognize Christ and His doctrine, to recognize God the Father and His doctrine. And how do we receive such insight? By DOING the will of God. We simply DO what He has revealed. God said, "Behold, I set before you this day a blessing and a curse; A blessing, if ye obey the commandments of the LORD your God, which I command you this day: And a curse, if ye will not obey the commandments of the LORD your God, but turn aside out of the way which I command you this day, to go after other gods, which ye have not known." (Deuteronomy 11:26-28) Here it is again; defection from truth and the beginning of idolatry brought about by discounting God's Law.

In my study of doctrines and denominations that are false there is one common thread that seems to run through most of them. Jehovah is forgotten. The God of the "Old Testament" hardly appears in the day-to-day living within their denominational guidelines. The Father of our Lord is depicted as a God who failed to redeem man His way and now His Son is going to try. The Laws of God are negated and considered condemning or ineffectual. His calendar is forgotten as unimportant, antiquated and replaced by pagan observations of times and seasons. His prophets' writings hide in obscurity and uselessness. Yet, Jesus told us these revelations of God would have helped tremendously our recognition of Jesus as Messiah.

It is futile to ask or beg God to show us whether or not doctrines are truly His or not. He made it plain in Scripture that guidance and steadfastness are products of a life lived in obedience to His Law. It is pointless to question, test, and deduce in order to arrive at a conclusion as to whether or not doctrines are true or false. Jesus said if we lived in His Father's will, we would KNOW that His doctrine was true.

Why beg God for guidance when you have proven you will not follow it? Why ignore His obvious counsel to live by His Commandments? When you live in doubt and disobedience and ask for word of affirmation, or when you pray "lead us not into temptation" [testing], His answer could only be, "Why do you not keep the Laws I gave you for that very purpose? If you ask for confirmation, guidance or even verification of doctrines that you question, Jesus must reply, "Did not Moses give you the law, and yet none of you keepeth the law?"

85. Whence shall we buy bread?

John 6:5, "When Jesus then lifted up his eyes, and saw a great company come unto him, he saith unto Philip, Whence shall we buy bread, that these may eat?"

Too often we may try to categorize and pigeon hole so that we might be able to understand or manage life and its details. It is easy to find those willing to call things that they like, "good" things, and call unpleasant things "bad" things. In the Christian world it is equally easy to find those willing to label temptation as "evil" and originating from Satan, while words inspiring "faith" are quickly attributed to God.

One of the values of Scripture is that it is a record of actions in the past that we may read objectively and apply them in our own understanding. If you look into Scripture you will find that all "good" and "evil" words may not be attributed to God and His enemy respectively. Before we do this we should have a good understanding of Scripture. Words of Scripture (read alone or out of context) that inspire faith in the heart of a believer, may come from any source and for any purpose. But, it is the purpose, not the words that identify the source. It is our reaction, and not the source that determines whether they evoke faith or fear.

If God made a promise to supply your every need, and one day in despair you doubted that promise, would it not be an inspiration to faith to hear in your own spirit the question, "Has not God promised...?" Words like these could inspire you to once again trust in God and could place you back on the road of faith! Yet, these are the very words of Satan to both Eve in the garden and Christ on the mount of temptation. The same words can bring very different results depending on your reaction to them. Not the words themselves but it is the purpose for which they are said that reveals their true source and nature. Knowing this, words that make us doubt cannot necessarily be attributed to evil sources and vise versa.

Doubt is as much an integral part of faith as fear is an inseparable part of courage and as offense is necessary for forgiveness. To see things the way they really are, and yet believe God's word to you, is honest faith. When you have a "head in the clouds," a silly, or assuming faith, it can be a weak one. The faith that requires that you remain uninformed about reality is a dishonest faith. Sometimes good honest doubt can bring about more solid, faithful, obedience than all of the "dishonest faith" in the world.

Doubt that leads to faith is an essential part of faith that pleases God. Did Abraham shed no tears on that day he offered his son? Did Joshua not tremble on the seventh day march around Jericho? What did Moses think as he saw the Egyptian armies at his back and the Red Sea in front of him? True faith reaches over doubt and grasps the promise. It does not ignore the reality; it accepts it as fact and yet embraces the promise.

277

In the instance we investigate now, the Lord had in mind to see how Phillip was thinking. The verses say, "... he saith unto Philip, Whence shall we buy bread, that these may eat? And this he said to prove him: for he himself knew what he would do." Jesus had no intention at all to buy bread for 5000 people. He was testing Phillip under fire. Philip answered him, "Two hundred pennyworth of bread is not sufficient for them, that every one of them may take a little." (John 6:5-7) When we feel in our spirit the little prods to choose faith or to find ways of human means, it very well could be our Lord inspiring us to higher or better things. When we are faced with choices of natural mundanity or supernatural excellence and we hear a word of discouragement, we may be on the verge of a miracle.

The Lord asked Phillip, "By what human means can these be fed?" "How can we buy enough to feed all these?" It was as though He was making sure that the job at hand was an impossible one before He involved Himself. He invited Phillip to consult all his resources to resolve the crisis. Phillip confessed that their resources were not sufficient. It was then that Jesus made His power known to all.

Who Said That?

You should wield the same amount of caution when hearing, "God said to me..." as when you hear, "The devil tempted me..." These kinds of statements may reveal our ignorance about spiritual things. We cannot place every thought that challenges our faith in the category of evil. It could very well be Christ Himself who is proving us. It is God's pleasure to see us act as though what He said to us is true even though the circumstances clearly show otherwise.

When you hear in your ear, "How are you going to pay that bill?" or "How will you meet that obligation?" or "You've really stuck your neck out this time," we cannot assume that these are either our own mind or Satan tempting us to doubt. It may be the pleasure of the Lord to watch us react in faith to the questions.

Remember who said, "Hast thou considered my servant Job?" Satan was invited to listen as the reaction to calamity was about to commence. Satan wagered that Job would curse God to His face, but God knew His servant. He must have found immense pleasure when Job, in the midst of all his sorrow, said, "The Lord gives and the Lord takes away... Blessed be the name of the Lord." It may be that God has asked the tempter himself to come and hear your answer of unswerving faith. I hope you answer well.

The thoughts of doubt that plague us when we are in crisis should serve to strengthen us. We should not feel offended by these thoughts nor should we attribute them to evil forces set on our destruction. We need not consider the presence of these thoughts as failure or weakness, nor should we stand up to them and fight them as if they are the "messages of Satan!"

How ridiculous would it have been for Phillip to turn to Jesus and said, "Get behind me Satan!" We need to realize it is our reaction that makes the temptation "good" or "bad." The word in your ear could be the Lord asking, "Will you depend on me? Will you trust me? Will you believe what I have promised?"

When you find yourself facing insurmountable problems that have no human answer and you know that you are following the Lord, you can depend on Him to answer His own question when He asks, "How will you do this?" When you follow the Lord, and He gives you His promises and His power, you can fold your arms in surrender and answer, "Lord thou knowest."

You can actually look forward to the time of testing when the hungry ones who seek the Bread of Life look to you; and Christ, with a trace of a grin, whispers in your ear, "Whence shall we buy bread that these may eat?"

86.   *Why go ye about to kill me?*

John 7:19b, "...Why go ye about to kill me?"

There has to be hundreds of ways to destroy the faith that mankind places in God, but there is unlikely one as effective as removing Christ from the equation. Satan has created mock churches that are totally unauthorized and boasts of having all authority. There are whole evangelical mindsets that are equilaterally deceived on certain theological points that render them impotent and illogical.

There are cults, and sects based as much in good intention as bad theology. There are some who believe their Bibles come from God and some, whose God comes from their Bibles. Some even claim to have their own church, songbook, and Bible. But how shall Satan destroy those who have genuine faith; what will be done about the true believers?

I have heard so-called Christians say that if they found that their denomination was in error they would give up completely on God. They say, that they have always been a _____ (insert almost any denomination here) and further promise to always be one. I have also met those who say that if the Bible was proven to be a fraud that their faith in God would wither away. But what is to be done about those who do not care about denomination or about how the credibility of the Bible supposedly hangs in a delicate balance with every new book that comes to the shelves?

How would you spoil the faith of a man who has faith in God alone? Or, how would you go about spoiling the faith of the man born blind that Jesus healed? How would Satan tempt Lazarus, after being raised from the dead, to give up his faith, or to believe that Jesus was a fake? These men had no church, no denomination, or Bible to back their faith.

When men place their faith in Christ alone, the plan to destroy faith must change. The strategy narrows when the faith is in God and not in a book or a doctrine or a set of denominational guidelines. The strategy must be total destruction. This answers the question, "Why go ye about to kill me?"

If we place our faith in Mom and Dad's religion or the oldest denomination, or the best known or largest church, or in those which we feel most comfortable, we are doomed to be disappointed upon any honest investigation of it. Our doctrines, if based upon good solid logic, will fail at the line of faith; and a doctrine based in faith alone, permitting reality to be ignored, is bound to step over the line of reason into foolishness. We are in trouble if our faith in God is based solely upon denominational foundations.

"Jesus Loves Me, This I Know, For The Bible Tells Me So."

That may be a nice children's song but it is a really pitiful basis of faith in God. Jesus does love me. This I do know. But, I don't need the Bible to tell me so. I am happy that it does, but if it did not, I would still know His love because of the Spirit He has put within me.

The fact is, that when we place our faith in the Bible's words alone we have bypassed this precious witness of Spirit and we lack an essential element to our faith. In order to bolster this paper witness we invented terms to add to it like, infallible and inerrant – terms of description it never took to itself.[123] Many of us unwittingly attached powers to this book subscribed only to the Son of the Almighty God. Though never instructed to do so, we entitled it the "Word of God" thereby giving a book His eternal name.[124] We are in deeper trouble than we realize if we need an infallible book to be our infallible God in order to have faith in Christ.

All these things were not a problem for the disciples or the early Church. They were under no delusion that any book was the Word of God, nor did they look to any church to give their faith credibility. They looked, where we should still look today – to Christ. This is not to say that these sources are worthless, for the pages of Scripture are one of the greatest gifts to mankind, divinely inspired and supernaturally protected and preserved. The Church in its true form, the invisible body of Christ, is of inestimable value to the believer in innumerable ways, but our relationship is to be with Jesus the living Christ.

For those who place their trust in church, I have little hope, for the conventional church is rife with failure and controversy and contradiction. For those who place their faith in the "infallibility" of the Bible, a life of denial and absurd reasoning awaits them, for anyone who claims the Bible to be free from error has either never read it or they are willing to lie to themselves.[125] Both characteristics (ignorance and dishonesty) are unbecoming as attributes gained from a source of true faith. But for those who anchor their souls in Christ, in a real relationship with the living Savior though there may be persecution in their future, doubt and fear are conspicuously absent. Theirs is an abounding and sure faith, for they have anchored themselves to the Eternal.

In Jesus' day, all this discourse about where one's faith lies was unnecessary. Men who had faith in Christ had their faith in Jesus alone. That is why He was the target... the only target. Jesus was destroying the Pharisee's understanding of Messiah.

We are not to hear God's voice through a book; we are to hear directly from Him. "God, who at sundry times and in divers manners spake in time past unto the fathers by the prophets, Hath in these last days spoken unto us by his Son, whom he hath appointed heir of all things, by whom also he made the worlds;" (Hebrews 1:1-2) It is clear that He is to speak to us, not a book.

---

[123] The infallibility of the Bible is a doctrine that ironically has no foundation in Scripture.

[124] Revelation 19:13, "...and his [Christ's] name is called The Word of God."

[125] It doesn't take long for the avid reader of the Scriptures to find errors therein, nor the honest reader, contradiction. This does not, however, make the Bible untrue or worthless. On the contrary it lends credibility to it as eyewitness and genuinely, albeit humanly, recorded history. The minor errors and inconsistencies declare in every way, "This really happened!"

The fact is that we want a religion, we want a rulebook, we want anything but a Living Lord that reigns and rules over us. We will listen to a group. We will listen to a book that we can manipulate by claiming education or intelligence, but we do not want a Lord who can speak for Himself. This is why we are told that Christ does not speak to us except by the Bible. The dead cannot speak. We preach Him to be dead if we preach that He cannot speak. Our modern attempts to kill Christ take an academic form; the attempt to prove He is dead by teaching that He cannot speak. Jesus would ask them, "Why go ye about to kill me?"

We can twist the Scriptures to say what we want them to say. We cannot control Jesus if He is a living Savior. We can make the church into anything we want, but we have no control over a risen Christ. We suffer from the same problem of pride the Pharisees had of old. We can handle what is written, we can manipulate people, but we cannot do so to a living, autonomous and sovereign Christ. So we reduce Him to pages in a book, a story, a man of history, in other words we keep Him dead, unable to speak except through a clergyman, priest, or a book. In other words, we go about to kill Him.

Let Him live! Let Him live in the hearts of all who believe on Him. If you find yourself talking about Him in the past tense, or insisting that He only speaks now through a book, you should immediately cease these actions that abolish Him. Still pertinent today, His question remains to be answered by modern man, "Why go ye about to kill me?"

87.   *Why do ye not understand my speech?*

John 8:43, "Why do ye not understand my speech? even because ye cannot hear my word."

This is one of the few questions Jesus asks that He answers directly, not waiting for a response. His quick answer indicates that it is likely we would answer incorrectly. We probably would answer Him with this reason or that, claiming that His speech is difficult and offer excuses unrelated to truth. Perhaps we would never figure it out and give up in dismay. It is hard to think about, but Christ's words are worthless without understanding. Understanding only comes from communion with God.

One the most detrimental doctrines to come from the reformation is the exaltation of the Bible. It has been given the name of Christ[126] and the office and mission of the Holy Spirit. The Scriptures were never intended to be the voice of God to mankind. "But the Comforter, which is the Holy Ghost... shall teach you all things..."[127] We neither by commandment or example are compelled to call the Bible "The Word of God." The title was given to Christ in the beginning, (John 1:1) and the name is still His in the end (Revelation 19:13) ... and his name is called The Word of God."

The misapplication of this title and office has caused great misunderstandings of the Scriptures, of both their nature and message. We must not mentally interject "the Bible" when we read the words, "Word of God." This practice causes us to err in Scriptural applications and hampers our ability to discern by the Spirit.

When Jesus said that we do not understand what He says because we cannot hear His word, He was not talking about Bible reading. He was talking about hearing God's voice within. The voice of our teacher is within us, not printed on pages. When we read Romans 10:17, "So then faith cometh by hearing, and hearing by the word of God" do we mentally substitute "the Bible" at the end of that Scripture, replacing the words, "Word of God"? Have not we shortchanged the one seeking God to hand him a book and never tell him of the precious communion between the living Lord Jesus Christ and His Church? The Scriptures, read by the hollow and shallow, offer only mysterious, inapplicable words to the dry and dusty soil of the heart. We must tell this poor one of the gift of God, the gift of the Holy Spirit, the gift of Christ within us, teaching, applying, and making every word real, thereby watering the dry

---

[126] Revelation 19:13, "...and his [Christ's] name is called The Word of God."
John 1:1, 14" In the beginning was the Word, and the Word was with God, and the Word was God." "And the Word was made flesh, and dwelt among us, (and we beheld his glory, the glory as of the only begotten of the Father) full of grace and truth."
[127] John 16:13-14, "Howbeit when he, the Spirit of truth, is come, he will guide you into all truth: ... and he will shew you things to come. He shall glorify me: for he shall receive of mine, and shall shew it unto you." John 14:26, "But the Comforter, which is the Holy Ghost, whom the Father will send in my name, he shall teach you all things, and bring all things to your remembrance, whatsoever I have said unto you."

places of our heart and causing the hot soil to bud. The gift is not a book but a promise of communion.

"Jesus answered and said unto her, If thou knewest the gift of God, and who it is that saith to thee, Give me to drink; thou wouldest have asked of him, and he would have given thee living water... whosoever drinketh of the water that I shall give him shall never thirst; but the water that I shall give him shall be in him a well of water springing up into everlasting life."
(John 4:10, 13-14)

A Wellspring of Life

It is the gift of God, this voice that leads and guides and directs us through life. It is daily communion that gives the insight needed to understand what Jesus says. His words are confusing, divisive, and even dangerous when we do not consult the Spirit of God within us.

There are Scriptures with which I wrestle and cannot understand. I wonder about translations and interpretations, customs of the day, context, grammar, transposition, syntax, chronology, corroborating extra-biblical text... nothing helps. Then, I read this Scripture, "Why do ye not understand my speech? Even because ye cannot hear my word." I close the book and sit quietly. Then I look at it again, "Why do ye not understand my speech? Even because ye cannot hear my word." I cry out, "Oh Lord draw me nearer to thee!" Nothing magical happens. As a matter of fact, the Scripture I have in mind as I write this is still not revealed to me to this day – but, I will continue to seek God. He will reveal the Scripture in time.

Let the Spirit of God teach you. The guide and teacher inside us are in the Person and Spirit of Christ. We must look there for understanding. This is our only message to the converted, seeking soul. We waste a lot of time and effort teaching each other. Turn inward. Turn to the gift of God. Turn to Christ within you. Silently wait on Him to deal with the things He considers high priority and let the other come as He wills. We will receive day by day our daily bread as the children of Israel did in the wilderness if we recognize and do not forget that the Word of God is not a book, but a person, not ink and paper but was flesh and blood and even now it is He who sits at the right hand of God.

Don't be discouraged and think you are in need of higher or specialized education or religious counsel because there are passages in the Scriptures that you do not understand. Many things are hidden and to be revealed only as they are deemed timely and right by the Father Himself. Be open to hear the voice of God within and understanding will grow as you are carried along. The Word is a living being, not to be read but to be heard. "Why do ye not understand my speech? even because ye cannot hear my word."

88.   *Which of these is your neighbor?*

Luke 10:36, "Which now of these three, thinkest thou, was neighbour unto him that fell among the thieves?"

"And, behold, a certain lawyer stood up, and tempted him, saying, Master, what shall I do to inherit eternal life? He said unto him, What is written in the law? how readest thou? And he answering said, Thou shalt love the Lord thy God with all thy heart, and with all thy soul, and with all thy strength, and with all thy mind; and thy neighbour as thyself. And he said unto him, Thou hast answered right: this do, and thou shalt live. But he, willing to justify himself, said unto Jesus, And who is my neighbour?" (Luke 10:25-29)

Jesus was teaching on the greatest Commandment. He was challenged on a point of definition. "Just who is my neighbor?" Who are the people whom I must love as myself? Jesus told a story to explain the definition of the Commandment's term "neighbor."

Many people read this parable and draw from this a commandment to love everyone, but that message is not to be found here. It is found in other Bible stories and verses to be sure, but it is not here. As a matter of fact, nearly the opposite is stated. We are to consider as neighbors only those who treat us well. Is not the message clear? Is not the answer to the man's question, "Who is my neighbor?" answered clearly, "Those who do well to you?" This parable is not about brotherly love – it is about prejudice.

*Luke 10:30-36, "And Jesus answering said, A certain man went down from Jerusalem to Jericho, and fell among thieves, which stripped him of his raiment, and wounded him, and departed, leaving him half dead. And by chance there came down a certain **priest** that way: and when he saw him, he passed by on the other side. And likewise a Levite, when he was at the place, came and looked on him, and passed by on the other side. But a certain Samaritan, as he journeyed, came where he was: and when he saw him, he had compassion on him, And went to him, and bound up his wounds, pouring in oil and wine, and set him on his own beast, and brought him to an inn, and took care of him. And on the morrow when he departed, he took out two pence, and gave them to the host, and said unto him, Take care of him; and whatsoever thou spendest more, when I come again, I will repay thee. Which now of these three, thinkest thou, was neighbour unto him that fell among the thieves?"*

In His comments about the priest Christ shows us that self-concerned churchmen who show no compassion toward those whom perhaps they see as less than themselves, unclean, or defiled are not included in the list of folks we are commanded to love as we love ourselves. It is equally obvious, by His example of the Levite, those who are "born to greatness" are not in this list as well. Jesus' message was clarion. Our goodness toward one another is the only identification we may trust. It is the badge of being the neighbor worthy of our love.

Here Jesus exposes one of the deepest of emotions felt by the fearful – bigotry. He states that we MAY NOT decide whether or not we will be a neighbor (doing good, or loving others as ourselves) based upon social, economic, ancestral, or religious grounds. We may not decide who our neighbor is by anything they profess or claim, but by their actions of love and concern. These are our neighbors. These are those we are commanded to love as ourselves. "Beloved, let us love one another: for love is of God; and every one that loveth is born of God, and knoweth God." (1 John 4:7)

The Gospels, in other places, make it equally clear that Jesus taught us to love our enemies, and to good to those who use and abuse us, but that message is not here. The Samaritan is a good example for us, to love those who don't love us, but we must not try to combine the two messages. Here He is explaining the definition of "neighbor" in the commandment, "Thou shalt not avenge, nor bear any grudge against the children of thy people, but thou shalt love thy neighbour as thyself: I am the LORD." (Leviticus 19:18) "And this is his commandment, That we should believe on the name of his Son Jesus Christ, and love one another, as he gave us commandment." (1 John 3:23)

The prejudicial Jews would dismiss their obligation to their Samaritan brothers by defining the word neighbor narrowly so as to exclude them. This prejudice was not done quietly or secretly, it was obvious and blatant. Remember the surprise of the Samaritan woman at the well? "Then saith the woman of Samaria unto him, How is it that thou, being a Jew, askest drink of me, which am a woman of Samaria? for the Jews have no dealings with the Samaritans." (John 4:9) Jesus was called a Samaritan as a disparaging epithet. "Then answered the Jews, and said unto him, Say we not well that thou art a Samaritan, and hast a devil?" (John 8:48)

Jesus knew well that the people of Judea had problems with the people of Samaria because of their mixing with their conquerors during their military occupations. They were considered unclean, and unholy. Jesus dug at the heart of the matter. The one whom the hearer of the parable was compelled to identify as a neighbor, was also Samaritan. This parable was all about prejudice – the oldest sin of mankind. It killed Abel in the beginning and it will be cause of the crime in the paper tomorrow. It still ranks high as the sin of preference among the religious.

Of One Blood

Many who profess Christ have no qualm about using inflammatory words of prejudice, exclusionary behaviors and practices within their churches. We have forgotten we are of "one blood" as says the Scripture. "And hath made of one blood all nations of men for to dwell on all the face of the earth..." (Acts 17:26)

Although Peter was likely there listening, it would be years later that it would occur to him that we are to consider all men who live peaceably among us as our neighbor, regardless of their color, pedigree or religion. Through a vision, shown three times, he finally realizes that they who God has cleansed are not to be considered as less than ourselves. *"And he said unto them, Ye know how that it is an unlawful thing for a man that is a Jew to keep company, or come unto one of another nation; but God hath shewed me that I should not call any man common or unclean... Of a truth I perceive that God is no respecter of persons: But in every nation he that feareth him, and worketh righteousness, is accepted with him."* (Acts 10:28, 34-35)

Here is the formula again. Not a blanket acceptance or universal "brotherhood," but those who fear God, and work righteousness (as the Samaritan) are to be considered our neighbors. Thus defining for us the word "neighbor" in the Commandment cited by Jesus.

Our identification to each other as brothers and neighbors is this: that we love each other. John 13:34-35, *"A new commandment I give unto you, That ye love one another; as I have loved you, that ye also love one another. By this shall all men know that ye are my disciples, if ye have love one to another."* And John 15:17, *"These things I command you, that ye love one another."* 1 John 4:11, *"Beloved, if God so loved us, we ought also to love one another."*

The religious leader could not defile himself, the religious aristocrat could not be bothered, but the one who really loved the poor injured man could not ignore him. "Which of these is your neighbor?"

89. *Whose shall those things be?*

Luke 12:19-21, "And I will say to my soul, Soul, thou hast much goods laid up for many years; take thine ease, eat, drink, and be merry. But God said unto him, Thou fool, this night thy soul shall be required of thee: then whose shall those things be, which thou hast provided? So is he that layeth up treasure for himself, and is not rich toward God."

The bequest of our earthly possessions is of universal concern, for the Christian and non-Christian alike. Their disbursement at death is a matter of paperwork, but what about the arrangement and distribution while our goods are yet in our hands? The unregenerate man has little concern here. His strategy is simple, gather all you can, spend it wherever you want, (it is, after all, yours) save at your own discretion and rate, and give to whomever seems worthy. The unfortunate part of the comparison between the Christian and the one following his own path in life is that they are so similar; they are almost identical.

If a difference were to be found between one who follows his own leadings and one who claims to be led of God toward (and eventually through) salvation it would seem that it would be most visible in the area of interface with the world's goods. Of all the differences that would stand as benchmarks in a life dedicated to God, this one would be, to say the least, profound! It was nearly a favorite subject and supplied endless parallels for Christ's teaching. It was used as sign of conversion for Zacchaeus[128], as sign of a missed conversion with the unjust steward,[129] and an insurmountable stumbling block to the rich man in the familiar story of the Gospels.[130]

Money, mammon, riches and wealth, are all problems for the man who tries to gain a world beyond this one, as their very existence bespeaks the power and authority of the world to which they are attached. Money answers every question for those yet in their sins. For them, wealth gives opportunity, opens doors, provides security and is the game piece or marker in the amusement of life to declare winners and losers. The unregenerate rich are fond of saying, "Money isn't everything, but it's a great way of keeping score." The more a man deals pleasurably with this unrighteous mammon the more he stitches his soul, day by day, thread by thread, to the system that values it.

The prospect of treating money as the root of all evil has been backpedaled and soft-soaped, diluted and lampooned as a ridiculous notion put forth by the "hyper-Christian" or the fanatic. Tirelessly these mammon soaked clergymen provide example after example of why a Christian "needs" money and how it is not money that is evil, it is the love of it. On and on the prosperity preachers go attempting to prove that it is godly to be rich and some even go so far as to say that is a sign of wickedness to be poor.

---

[128] Luke 19
[129] Matthew 18:23
[130] Matthew 19:16, Mark 10:17, Luke 18:18

Paul actually called these pearly parsons "men of corrupt minds." "Perverse disputings of men of corrupt minds, and destitute of the truth, supposing that gain is godliness: from such withdraw thyself." (1 Timothy 6:5) In reality they are only trying to stamp out the fire that burns in their soul when they hear the Savior say that it is easier for a camel to go through the eye of a needle, than for a rich man to enter into the kingdom of God. (Matthew 19:24 - Mark 10:25 - Luke 18:25)

Sometimes we make excuses for ourselves and insist that we cannot be the "rich" one being compared to a camel trying to slip through the needle's eye. We should not try to justify our wealth by saying we are "blessed" with much money like Abraham was, in order to feel better about the faithless lifestyle we enjoy. Most of us would feel that we were blessed of God if, in answer to our prayer for peace of mind, He gave us much wealth. For what could render peace of mind more surely than enough of everything we need to live?

Actually, if we had a properly developed idea of money, its volatility, its mutability and uncertainty, we would feel, to say the least, shortchanged with it as an answer to prayer. But we have so exalted it, become so dependant on it, we could receive it as an answer to prayers of security, healing, hunger, loneliness, lack of self-worth, or purpose in life and feel it sufficient for all these and more. As a matter of fact money could answer just about any of the problems we have today… or so we think.

"Money Can't Buy Happiness" … Or Can It?

At this point the Spiritual person will disagree and insist that there are many things money cannot buy, but the challenge remains to find something that it does not touch. Find something that it does not taint, discolor, skew to its viewpoint, or evaluate in its light. Find something for which no substitute can be purchased, manufactured, or imported to replace. It is difficult to the point of impossibility to find something in our world that has any value at all, unless it has monetary value. The very word value has come to have a monetary connotation.

You may ask, "Who can put a monetary value on the feeling you get while watching a sunset?" That may sound poetic and pious, but I assure you there are folks who have no clothes, no warm bed to sleep in, and no breakfast to wake them in the morning who do not feel the same contentment that you do when seeing the same sunset. That same sunset, that gives you a warm, comfortable feeling, strikes in the heart of the destitute fear and dread that the warmth of the day is passing into another cold damp night.

How do we break loose from the stronghold of riches? How do we evaluate properly, and deal justly, and become stewards instead of owners? By treating money as the imposter that it is. We must live day to day and know within us that the day is coming when we "may no longer be steward"[131] and

---

[131] Luke 16:1

289

we must be wise with the power that has been placed within us. We should do good and spend what we have, alleviating suffering and equalizing the discrepancies in rich and poor. We should be ready to distribute, willing to communicate, and thereby lay up in store for ourselves a "good foundation against the time to come, that they [we] may lay hold on eternal life." (1 Timothy 6:19) We must consider the second coat in our wardrobe as the cloak that belongs to the one who is naked. We must see the extra pair of shoes as if taken from the feet of him who has none. Someone shivers tonight because his blanket waxes moth-eaten in your cupboard.

Just as what we deem valuable in the Kingdom of God is considered worthless to the world outside, we should, in turn, consider what they deem utmost in value as but chaff with us.

The manna that fell in the wilderness had a peculiar property of being perishable. It was given for immediate use, and when stored, it rotted and stank.[132] We as modern and spiritual children of Israel have our cupboards and closets, our barns and banks full of rotten provision while the world starves, not so much for the Gospel, but for the *example* of one who lives by it.

When your soul is required of you, when your carcass is carried away from all your possessions, "Whose shall those things be?"

---

[132] Exodus 16:20

290

90.   *Who is that faithful and wise steward?*

Luke 12:42, "And the Lord said, Who then is that faithful and wise steward, whom his lord shall make ruler over his household, to give them their portion of meat in due season?"

Matthew 24:45, "Who then is a faithful and wise servant, whom his lord hath made ruler over his household, to give them meat in due season?"

What is your goal in life? What do you want above all things? It may be a monetary goal, or one of accomplishment, or simply to be known as good. It may be that you desire lofty or noble achievements such as accomplishments in benevolence or charity. Perhaps your goals are more earthy and immediate like paying off a debt or buying a house. No matter, our goals – our true goals – will likely be met.

There are stories of men and women accomplishing great feats of high achievement simply by setting a goal and making that goal a top priority. We hear of insurmountable odds being overcome, hurdles of seeming impossibility leaped, mountain peaks scaled, rivers crossed, etc. Quite inspiring it is.

Jesus just told a story that had an end unlike any ending that we have ever heard. He spoke of a time and place where all of the achievements and motives of mankind will be revisited and judged. Do we believe such a story as this? He gave an example of **good** stewardship:

Luke 12:35-40, *"Let your loins be girded about, and your lights burning; And ye yourselves like unto men who wait for their lord, when he will return from the wedding; that when he cometh and knocketh, they may open unto him immediately. Blessed are those servants, whom the lord when he cometh shall find watching: verily I say unto you, that he shall gird himself, and make them to sit down to meat, and will come forth and serve them. And if he shall come in the second watch, or come in the third watch, and find them so, blessed are those servants. And this know, that if the goodman of the house had known what hour the thief would come, he would have watched, and not have suffered his house to be broken through. Be ye therefore ready also: for the Son of man cometh at an hour when ye think not."*

He gave an example of **bad** stewardship:

Luke 12:45-48, *"But and if that servant say in his heart, My lord delayeth his coming; and shall begin to beat the menservants and maidens, and to eat and drink, and to be drunken; The lord of that servant will come in a day when he looketh not for him, and at an hour when he is not aware, and will cut him in sunder, and will appoint him his portion with the unbelievers. And that servant, which knew his lord's will, and prepared not himself, neither did according to his will, shall be beaten with many stripes. But he that knew not, and did commit things worthy of stripes, shall be beaten with few stripes. For unto whomsoever much is given, of him shall be much required: and to whom men have committed much, of him they will ask the more."*

It is not difficult to see the difference in the two. One steward waited patiently for the return of his master, which he believed was imminent; the other was convinced the return was distant, any day but today. One steward was prepared; one was not. One did the will of his master; one did not.

The Key Was Readiness.

Jesus used words like "immediately" to describe the opening of the door upon arrival, almost as though the servant's hand was upon the latch as the master touched the door knocking; as though the master could not even finish knocking before the door flew open to receive him.

It is this state of readiness that should be our ultimate goal. Above all else, our goal to be considered faithful and wise by our Master should hold priority over all goals. Who wishes to be considered unwise? Who could desire the title, "unfaithful?" Who is that faithful and wise steward? It is undoubtedly the one who, when his Master comes, shall find him watching. "And what I say unto you I say unto all, Watch." (Mark 13:37)

Jesus gave us insights into the world to come. He told of life there, domestic structures, economics and governments. He used a particular phrase over and over. *"So the last shall be first, and the first last," (Matthew 20:16)* then He said, *"But many that are first shall be last; and the last shall be first." (Matthew 19:30)* And in Mark 9:35, *"... If any man desire to be first, the same shall be last of all, and servant of all."*

Later in Mark 10:31, *"But many that are first shall be last; and the last first."* He repeats in Luke 13:30, *"And, behold, there are last which shall be first, and there are first which shall be last."*

He spoke of ideas and doctrines held here in this life affecting the rank and recognition in the life to come.

Matthew 5:19, *"Whosoever therefore shall break one of these least commandments, and shall teach men so, he shall be called the least in the kingdom of heaven: but whosoever shall do and teach them, the same shall be called great in the kingdom of heaven."*

He spoke of our willingness to stand for Him in this world and how that stand would affect His willingness to stand for us there.

"Whosoever therefore shall be ashamed of me and of my words in this adulterous and sinful generation; of him also shall the Son of man be ashamed, when he cometh in the glory of his Father with the holy angels." (Mark 8:38 - Luke 9:26).

How sad it would be to accomplish great feats of commerce, or build great edifices, or be recognized by everyone as honorable and yet be known to God as unwise, or for the King of Kings to be ashamed of you. What sadness would be felt to be known as a faithful father, faithful husband, and faithful friend and yet, known to God as an unfaithful steward?

Yes, even the loftiest and most noble goals will not supplant the satisfaction and reward of the most essential and eternal one. To be recognized here, as a great man is enjoyable, but to be recognized there -- that will be something else entirely.

It would be joy to be found among the redeemed, be favored and be counted as a friend of Christ – to be honored of Him in the new Kingdom by His recognition and reward. It would be ecstasy above all else for someone to point toward you and ask a bystander, using the same words of Christ Himself, "Who is that faithful and wise steward?"

91.   *Do you think that they were sinners?*

Luke 13:1-5, "There were present at that season some that told him of the Galilaeans, whose blood Pilate had mingled with their sacrifices. And Jesus answering said unto them, Suppose ye that these Galilaeans were sinners above all the Galilaeans, because they suffered such things? I tell you, Nay: but, except ye repent, ye shall all likewise perish. Or those eighteen, upon whom the tower in Siloam fell, and slew them, think ye that they were sinners above all men that dwelt in Jerusalem? I tell you, Nay: but, except ye repent, ye shall all likewise perish."

You may call it instinct, or intuition, or conscience, but we all have the voice within us that asks, "Why did this happen to me?" Whenever calamity strikes, we immediately think of causes in our life that may have brought about the situation. We judge ourselves and take inventory of our recent past when troubles present themselves, and the severity of the calamity is proportional to the depth of the searching. If the pain or loss is deep enough, we are willing to examine our lives back to our first recollection of sin. Dredging up every little thing we can think of, we place our sacrifice of confession at the feet of our accuser.

Are our sins the cause of our misery? Does the past have power over the fortune of the future? When tragedy crawls over the horizon to torment us, can we find the cause for its presence within our own record of sin?

There are victims of war, there are starving persons in Cambodia, Bangladesh, Calcutta, there are homeless in Chicago, New York there are victims of drive-by shootings, public bombings, raids, riots and burglary in all cities. Do you think that these were sinners because they suffered such things? Do you think that they only got what they deserved? Do you think that there was some sin in their life that caused their demise? No, (Jesus would say) there was no sin that caused it, but except you repent you will die like they did.

There is a price to disobedience. There are costs involved in living by our own devices and by our own wits, outside of the Lordship of Jesus Christ. Does living outside of Christ's Kingdom cause these calamities? No, but unless you repent you will likely perish by them.

How many of us have looked at a friend or acquaintance and upon contemplating their misfortune wondered why "everything" seems to happen to them. Have we ever listened to someone tell their story and it is populated with every kind of misfortune imaginable and wondered why they continually get the bad deal, the bad "luck" or the short end of the stick? Are these people sinners above all others? Are they worse than most of the other people who have relatively few troubles in life? No, but except you repent you will all likewise perish.

In the Scripture above, the "tower of Siloam" was a description of the garrison of soldiers that guarded that area. Pilate sent these soldiers in to slay in cold blood the worshipers who were visiting from another part of the country as they were making sacrifice. Thus it is said that their blood was mingled with sacrifices [blood].

This was a horrible tragedy and it undoubtedly caused many to wonder and doubt the sincerity and purity of the worshippers whom God watched die at the hands of wicked men, doing nothing to stop it. Jesus asked, "Were these men more wicked than all who were at Jerusalem?" He answers is own question in the negative, then adds, "but... except you repent you will all likewise perish."

What Is He Telling Us?

Is He saying that if we repent we will not suffer such things? We know this is not the case, but He IS saying that we most assuredly will suffer these things if we do not repent.

The main difference is the word "perish." When these troublesome things happen to some people they perish by the trouble, when it happens to the righteous it makes them better. Calamity follows some people around. Individuals who lie all the time, those who you cannot believe anything they say, have many troubles in their life. Just ask them! Their lives are tragedies in most every area.

Those who steal, those who cheat, those who slight men what is due, who don't follow rules, who don't obey when not being watched, and those who cannot be trusted, are usually plagued with every sorrow and calamity. This calamity and misfortune seems endless in the lives of these poor souls and they are usually blind to its cause. They convince themselves that they must cheat and/or steal to get by or to make up for their "bad luck."

When we step from the higher plain to indulge in a little cheating (just a little) or we move to a darker mode of thought, we are toying with this network of misfortune and inviting it to join itself with us. When we say that which is not true, when we exaggerate or diminish (whatever benefits us most), when we demand what is exact when it is coming to us and then pay out with a slack hand, when we are quick to collect a debt yet slow to pay one; when we refuse to suffer, refuse to give, refuse to lose; when we cheat the lengthy path and search for shortcuts, we are dabbling with the cause for all men's troubles. Our most valuable ally, our conscience, is in danger of being compromised.

The newspaper, the radio, and TV news all are replete with stories of the misfortunate innocents of coincidence. "If they had not been there at that time the train would have not hit their car." The recent sniper in Washington triggered more thoughts of intriguing coincidences "If he had not arrived at that moment he would have never encountered the gunmen."

These are speculations we all consider when senseless calamities strike the lives of the blameless. A little faster, a little slower, if they had come another night, if they hadn't come at all – how are we to defend against such a thing if there is no pattern – no plan – no justice? Because we have toyed with sin we are beleaguered with uncertainty. Because of our uncertainty we are plagued with "if" scenarios in our mind that go nowhere and accomplish nothing. We are perishing under our load not the weight of those who stalk us, or the calamities that await us.

All we need know is that when we dabble and play with ideas in our minds, encouraging the sinner that lurks in us, or even when we try it our way, it is then that we have nothing to look forward to but fearful expectation of inevitable sorrow to cross our path. We must keep our conscience clear so that when trouble comes, (and it most assuredly will) we can hold our chin up and suffer wrongfully.

If we suffer for no cause of our own making, we may bypass the soul-searching, the sin dredging, and the self-abasement and loathing. We need not wonder what we have done to deserve our fate; we can know that we've done nothing amiss. This is the secret to joy in tribulation. Who would have thought it? It is as simple as: Do right – always.

When you hear of the senseless death or trouble of seemingly innocent folks and wonder if they were involved in some sinful behavior, hear the Lord's question again, "Do you think that they were sinners, above all others? Then hear his answer, "No, but except you repent…"

92. But where are the nine?

Luke 17:17, "And Jesus answering said, Were there not ten cleansed? but where are the nine?"

According to modern polls and surveys, America and other major European countries contain over fifty percent Christian people. Even worldwide population reports 10 to 30 percent (depending on where you look.) So... when it comes to evangelism, how are we doing? If these statistics were a report card on spreading the Gospel, how do we shape up for 2000 years of work? Before we condemn ourselves as poor salespeople we must look at other attempts to spread new ideas across the globe.

Television, for example, turns out to be much more popular than Jesus and spread more rapidly. Developed in the early 1900's, a production model was ready in the early 30's and by 1960 ninety percent of the homes in the US had accepted it as lord of information and savior of the boring evening at home. Later it became friend, confidant, educator, informer, babysitter, and counselor. It has taken only thirty years to become a worldwide altar to which we daily come for comfort and counsel, entertainment and illumination. So we do know how to spread an idea.

The Gospel of Christ though, has never been received with such trust and surrender. We approach in caution the promise of a new life in Christ. For the process of salvaging our lives makes demands upon us; demands with which we are not fully willing to comply. We hear the Gospel message promising a pleasant eternity and as these lepers in Jesus day, we say, "Why not give it a try? What do we have to lose?" Ours is hardly an attitude of commitment.

Ten lepers got together one day and finding their opportunity, called out to Him, "Jesus, Master, have mercy on us." One of them was not an Israelite but, hiding among the nine he calculated that he would get in on the deal. The Jewish Master would not notice, he schemed, or ask for pedigrees and he would blend in and get a blessing just these Jews. Much to their surprise and amazement, the Teacher granted their request.

Jesus, knowing the Law, said to them to go to the priest for pronouncement of cleanliness and as they went, the record says, they were cleansed. The Samaritan watched wide-eyed as the white scales fell from under his robe and out of his sleeves and his arms were clean and beautiful for the first time in years. This leper returned running. He thanked Jesus for cleansing him. Jesus looked at him and saw that it was not one of the Israelites to whom He was sent, but a man of a bastard culture, a land that worshiped a god named YHVH, but whose worship was far from true, and whose understanding was far from pure. He had but a vague idea what Jesus wanted him to do when he was asked to go to the priest. He was not allowed to even approach a priest. He just did as he was told. Now, overwhelmed with gratitude, he returned and thanked Jesus.

Jesus looked at his disciples and asked, were there not ten cleansed? But where are the nine? There are not found that returned to give glory to God, save this stranger. And he said unto him, Arise, go thy way: thy faith hath made thee whole." (Luke 17:17-19)

Merely Healed

Here is a question for us, what made the others whole? Were they made whole, or were they merely healed? It is when we return and give thanks, it is when we realize our before and after condition, that our faith makes us whole. There are many who have bowed at an altar, many who have made professions of faith, prayed a prayer, even repented of sin, but few have fully realized our wonderful blessing and returned in humility to give thanks. This quality of gratitude is a missing ingredient in the soul salvaging process. We cannot teach thankfulness, we cannot put it into a tract as a step to salvation. We cannot demand appreciation, as it would become an act of compliance instead of a spontaneous act of love.

However elusive unprompted gratitude may be, it is the point that our unworthiness occurs to us that becomes the point of our salvation and wholeness – not the time of our cleansing. The return to show gratitude is the visible indicator that a man has been adopted into the family of God – and that point is out of our control.

Many have been touched by Christ, many have been forgiven of Him, but few have been made whole. When it comes down to words on paper, it cannot be better said than, "Many are called, but few are chosen."

There is a special message here to we who are Gentiles in the flesh. Do we fully realize that we have received cleansing by "hiding" among ungrateful Jews? Paul's comments on this matter are worthy of note.

"I say then, Have they [the Jews] stumbled that they should fall? God forbid: but rather through their fall salvation is come unto the Gentiles… For I would not, brethren, that ye should be ignorant of this mystery, lest ye should be wise in your own conceits; that blindness in part is happened to Israel, until the fulness of the Gentiles be come in… ye in times past have not believed God, yet have now obtained mercy through their [the Jews] unbelief." (Romans 11:11-30)

We have been called now to the feast that we did not, and yet do not deserve only because those who were called spurned their opportunity. If we have been called we must seek to be worthy of acceptance – at the very least we can be grateful. "For many are called, but few are chosen."

Jesus used this phrase again when describing a man, invited to a wedding feast, who, when given a garment to wear, refused it for his own clothes. Here was a man invited in the place of ingrates, though unworthy, a man called, a man who answered the call, but he accepted the favor on his own terms. He wanted to participate in the festivities and food and wine at the expense of the wedding family, but he did not want to do it if cost him his identity to do so. In short, he was very ungrateful. "And he saith unto him, Friend, how camest thou in hither not having a wedding garment? And he was speechless." He was promptly thrown out. For many are called, but few are chosen. (Matthew 22)

Another example was the story of the greedy workers who, after they worked all day wanted more than what they were hired to receive only because they saw others being paid the same for less work. Complaining to the husbandmen, they accused him of being unfair, though they received exactly what they agreed. They showed themselves ungrateful. Their wages were paid, but the last came before them. "So the last shall be first, and the first last: for many be called, but few chosen." (Matthew 20:16)

We need not only be called; we need to be chosen for our gratitude and our lack of complaint. We need to be faithful and thankful. Do we ever consider the sacrifice made for us, the invitation we have been given, or the miracle that has been bestowed on our behalf? Have we counted the price paid by Christ for us as dear, precious and undeserved? Do we wear, without complaint, the beautiful garment we have been given, to appear to the world as one of His own? Do we try to hold to our own way, or withhold faithful service until benefits equal our idea of fairness?

If we want to be counted with Him, there is only one way. The verse in Revelation lists the attributes of those who are with Christ, "... for he is Lord of lords, and King of kings: and they that are with him are called, AND chosen, AND faithful." (Revelation 17:14)

If as many who were cleansed were grateful enough to serve, our efforts of evangelism may reveal better statistics. Many people have professed faith in Christ because He once touched them. Most of our country, as well as a large portion of the world, has been to Christ and asked for cleansing, but only one in, perchance, ten have returned to thank Him, to serve Him, to honor Him... but... "Where are the nine?"

93. *Who says to his servant, "Go and sit down to meat?"*

Luke 17:7, "But which of you, having a servant plowing or feeding cattle, will say unto him by and by, when he is come from the field, Go and sit down to meat?"

Here Jesus was teaching on forgiveness. He said that offenses would inevitably come and cause some to stumble. He added, "Woe to that one by whom the offense comes," and later He said that we must be very careful to rebuke and to forgive so that we tolerate nothing less than what is right, but forgive any offense from which a brother repents. "Take heed to yourselves: If thy brother trespass against thee, rebuke him; and if he repent, forgive him." (Luke 17:3)

This was, to say the least, a tall order. The disciples said, after hearing such an impossible command, "Increase our faith," supposing that the task required more than they were able to do. Jesus' answer was clear that the amount of faith was not a factor. "And the Lord said, If ye had faith as [small as][133] a grain of mustard seed, ye might say unto this sycamine tree, Be thou plucked up by the root, and be thou planted in the sea; and it should obey you." (Luke 17:6) This was clearly a matter of a man's will, of matter of servitude, of obedience. He adds that we need not think that when we forgive it is a great matter as if it makes a man worthy of praise, for, as servants, it is simply our duty.

Mankind has many characteristics of God in his psychological make-up. Though we were made in His image, we were not to own His attributes. Certain traits are left over from the fall. Remember that Satan said that with knowledge we would be as gods, knowing good and evil? He was right to the extent that we now have an overdeveloped desire for power. This takes form in a propensity to judge others as though we were God; to make decisions or maintain control as though we were God; to be praised, to create, and to be worshipped by others as though we are God.

These are only a few of the attributes of God commandeered by fallen mankind. These have been a source of trouble for us and need to be watched closely and held in check. The desire to be thanked appears from time to time, especially when we have done something that we did not want to do, or the act required much effort. The statement, "They didn't even thank me" is heard only when there is pride in the task or gift given. The action for which gratitude is sought, is, in the mind of the giver, above and beyond what was fair, or it was done with reluctance or was done only out of a sense of duty.

---

[133] NIV

If we wonder just what our position is in this Kingdom, Jesus made it clear. When the disciples inferred that thanks would be due anyone who maintained their life in this way that He described, Jesus asked them,

"But which of you, having a servant plowing or feeding cattle, will say unto him by and by, when he is come from the field, Go and sit down to meat? And will not rather say unto him, Make ready wherewith I may sup, and gird thyself, and serve me, till I have eaten and drunken; and afterward thou shalt eat and drink? Doth he thank that servant because he did the things that were commanded him? I trow not. So likewise ye, when ye shall have done all those things which are commanded you, say, We are unprofitable servants: we have done that which was our duty to do." (Luke 17:7-10)

Take Heed to Yourselves

"If thy brother trespass against thee, rebuke him; and if he repent, forgive him." (Luke 17:3) This counsel is probably the most valuable advice for living a peaceable and stress-free life that we will ever hear from anyone. If we can only learn what to rebuke and what to forgive we would all be better off. Stress and pressure builds up in our life when we do not speak up when offenses come. We need to love folks enough to rebuke them when they wrong or offend us.

We also need to forgive and not hold grudges when we are offended. We need not think that we are undeserving of such treatment or insist that we be honored in some way, but we should take wrong and suffer and forgive. What is the duty outlined here if it is not to rebuke when we should and forgive when we should? Here it is made plain that we are required to forgive, expected to have faith, obligated to rebuke all offenses committed and forgive every sin regretted and forsaken.

We may think this will please the Lord so much that He will surely thank us or treat us as special if we accomplish some great and difficult feat of selflessness. Jesus would answer, "I think not. Who says to his servant, 'Go and sit down to meat?'" Jesus warns us not to think of the servant as greater than his Lord.

We must keep in mind our servitude class; we must maintain the form of a servant[134] to have the mind of Christ. Contrary to what we hear from the modern theologian, we are not to prance though the world with the best of everything because we are "King's kids," nor are we to expect thanks for doing our work. What we think of as "our" ministry is actually His ministry. Our "accomplishments" are merely our duty, our position of eminence we fancifully enjoy as being His "right hand man" is, in reality, no more than that of a lowly servant.

Remember, when we have done all...when we have accomplished everything we have been commissioned to do...when we have dotted every "i"

---

[134] Philippians 2:7, "But made himself of no reputation, and took upon him the form of a servant, and was made in the likeness of men:"

and crossed every "t"...say, "We are unprofitable servants, we have only done that which was our DUTY to do.

Humbling thought, is it not? We need to fix this at the root of the cause. We expect thanks when we have done something that we did not want to do. If you become a slave of love and a servant of no mind but to serve, your desire for thanks, appreciation, recognition or reward will subside.

You should not elevate yourself to a level not offered to you. Just as you become a son of God (at His desire)[135] so also you become a friend[136] of God – only when He says so. If you are young in Christ, inexperienced, and ignorant you should not expect to occupy a place of authority or familiarity. It will come – in His time. Paul says, "That the heir, as long as he is a child, differeth nothing from a servant..."(Galatians 4:1-2)

You should not expect power beyond your means, wisdom beyond your understanding, fellowship inappropriate to your station, or reward for accomplishment of your mere duty. After all, who says to his servant, "Go and sit down to meat?"

---

[135] Galatians 4:7, "Wherefore thou art no more a servant, but a son; and if a son, then an heir of God through Christ."
[136] John 15:14, "Ye are my friends, if ye do whatsoever I command you."

94. *Who do you say that I am?*

Matthew 16:13-16, "When Jesus came into the coasts of Caesarea Philippi, he asked his disciples, saying, Whom do men say that I the Son of man am? And they said, Some say that thou art John the Baptist: some, Elias; and others, Jeremias, or one of the prophets. He saith unto them, But whom say ye that I am? And Simon Peter answered and said, Thou art the Christ, the Son of the living God."

Now nearing the end, Jesus asks a question to check the effectiveness of His ministry. The question was put to all and they answer, "Some say John the Baptist or another prophet risen from the dead." When we attempt to define Christianity or wonder about the apprehension of such a mystery, it is sometimes difficult to put into words. Believing in Christ can mean various things to different people. But, when Christ wanted to know how his ministry was affecting the world, He asked, "Who do they say that I am?" This, if we think about it, is a very good way of determining conversion, salvation, and the general effectiveness of ministry.

It is always interesting to look at what was not said as well as what was. Note that Jesus did not ask how many turned out last time we had a meeting. He did not ask about offering amounts, how many claimed to be converted, how many have been healed, how many have prayed to accept the Lord Jesus Christ as their personal Savior. He asked, "Who do they think I am."

Any of us can think back to a time when we had just met the man we work for, or the person we married, or our best friend. All of these relationships, now comfortable, were at one time strained and unsure, stiff and halting. As time went by we got to know them better and became better aquatinted and comfortable. Sometimes, as familiarity grows, respect becomes scarce, we say things we should not, we find privilege where precaution used to be, greed replaces grace, and (if carried to extremes) the relationship is ruined by "getting to know" someone to well. If we have experienced this we know that we are fully capable of such social degradation simply by becoming too familiar.

We can see this familiarity and lack of respect in employee/employer relationships that have gone bad – where one takes advantage of the other because they have become so intimate in their day to day dealing that rank and protocol have long since been abandoned. A boss, however, that has kept personal things to himself, and an employee who has kept all conversation on a business level usually enjoy a respect for each other and, in business, a high level of efficiency.

Marriage is different in structure and purpose, but in the area of respect and decency, it has needs that far surpass any business arrangement. When familiarity overtakes a marriage, advantage starts being taken over the spouse who is lesser respected. There may even be split and complex allegiances that would take years to untangle, that could have been avoided simply by treating spouses with little more respect than would be given a stranger.

There are words we would not use in front of a stranger that we would think nothing of using in our spouse's presence. Men hold doors open for women they do not know and let their wives do it for themselves.

Women can answer a phone with a sweet tone in her voice after just having scolded her husband in the harshest manner. We answer a door with a kind face to house guest that only seconds before was twisted in contempt toward those with whom we live everyday. We often treat strangers better than those we love.

Familiarity Breeds Contempt.

It is the familiarity that becomes the problem. Respect, honor, protocol, are something we give to people we do not know. As we get to know them we become less impressed, and become lax in our approach, test our bounds, take advantage, and soon the relationship is destroyed. But, it need not be.

There are some (few, but nonetheless, some) with whom our respect continues, from fear and unfamiliarity in the beginning to the present, for the very fact that respect is due. Honor is due this person because they are indeed honorable. We cannot always count on this characteristic among ourselves to make our marriages and working relationships work, because few of us are truly honorable; we must therefore honor the position that is held for the sake of respect of those we love and for efficiency in our work, respectively.

However, it is familiarity with Christ that is our concern here. We have all seen the relationship so "familiar" with Jesus that the respect due to a King is absent. We have all witnessed the fast and loose "Christian" who has a relationship with "the man upstairs" or the "the big guy", or those having fingers pointed heavenward and addressing our Creator as "somebody up there".

These make those of us who really know the awesome God we serve tremble and quake. If Christ were to ask today, "Who do men say that I am," we would hear some strange answers. Do you think that the general populace is versed well enough in the Scriptures to answer like they did? Who do you know that could call out Elijah as one of the possibilities as Messiah? Who would have mistaken Christ for Jeremiah? No, I'm afraid our culture would say that He was a space alien, because that is all we know in our society.

Then perhaps, if the question was asked of the common religious man we would hear a "good and wise teacher" a Prophet, a miracle worker, etc., and granted, some might even say the Son of God. I submit that our confession of Christ as the Son of God is only verified by our obedience to Him. How can we say that He is the Son of God and not live as He asked us to?

Have we become so familiar with Him that our respect for Him has waned? Have His words become like singsong in our ears, like the same old story we have heard over and over a thousand times? Do we figuratively roll our eyes, deafen our ears, and begin to hum pleasantly to ourselves as we hear the same words repeated to us even when those words are Commandment from the lips of Christ Jesus?

I further submit that if you have become familiar with Christ, to the point of contempt or disrespect, you have not truly met the Christ of the Bible. The real Jesus will be found worthy of respect and fear far after the fear of unfamiliarity has vanished. His worthiness of respect, His depth of being, and the respect that is due His goodness is more than enough to keep someone from calling Him "the man upstairs."

The power and majesty accorded Him of God His Father is sufficient to carry Him through the millennia with praise and adoration. His accomplishments on earth alone set Him far above us and certainly far above the station of a pageboy employed to answer our bell to do as we say. Shame should be upon those who come before Him.

Humility should be the cloak of those who worship Him. All should fear, bow the knee, and hide their face before Him. A look at Him as He was revealed to John confirms this. His description is awesome and John's response... "And when I saw him, I fell at his feet as dead." (Revelation 1:13-18) You see, He is the Son of the Living God.

Jesus asked long ago, "Who do men say that I am," He asks you today, "Who do you say that I am?"

95. Why does this generation seek after a sign?

Mark 8:12, Matthew 16:4 (Combined) "And he sighed deeply in his spirit, and saith, Why doth this generation seek after a sign? Verily I say unto you, There shall no sign be given unto this generation... but the sign of the prophet Jonas."

What was "the sign of the Prophet Jonas?" Jesus had said before (Matthew 12) that the sign of the prophet was that as Jonah was three days and three nights in the whale's belly so must the Son of Man be three days and nights in the grave. Jesus made it clear that this was the ONLY sign that would be given; the only sign that Jesus was who He said He was. If this sign does not come to pass then we have no obligation but to deem Jesus of Nazareth as a false Christ, ignore Him and wait for the true Messiah. All we have to do is count the days and nights Jesus was in the grave between His death and resurrection and we will own proof that He is the long-awaited Messiah.

This should be easy right? Wrong! Try as you might there are not three days and three nights to be found in the traditional story of His death burial and resurrection. Now we are faced with a choice, either there is no truth to what Jesus said, He did not say it, or the story we arbitrarily attach to the Scriptural account is indeed false. We must find a way for three real 12-hour days and three real 12-hour nights to fit into this written account of His burial and resurrection.

Excerpt from "On Truth"[137]:

When I proposed this problem to men better trained than I they told me that in Jerusalem they don't number days like we do. Over there any part of a day is considered a day, and any part of a night is considered a night. Therefore, Jesus could have been in the grave three parts of three days and it would have been considered three days in total. (Note to myself: When in Jerusalem, don't rent a car by the day.) Yet something was wrong here. Though they may be able to show you three parts of three days between Friday night and Sunday morning, three parts of three nights simply does not exist.

Jesus specifically said, "Three days AND three nights." However, I was out of answers. This feeble attempt was all that theology had to offer me. I was faced with the alternative that Jesus' sign was a failure. He was not in the earth three days and three nights and what is more, no one seemed to care. Did they have more faith than I did? They would say to me, "Well, I may not know when He rose but I know that he did." That may sound good but He said the only sign in which you can be sure, was the length of time. "JUST AS Jonas was . . . SO SHALL the son of man be." If he exaggerated about one He could have exaggerated the other. Could Jesus have died for fifteen minutes and have accomplished the same thing? Or maybe fifteen years? If the time in the grave

---

[137] "On Truth," a booklet and CD audio Bible teaching by Don Harris.

was unimportant it should not be a factor at all. Or, maybe the word "died" was an exaggeration too. As far as I was concerned a miss was as good as a mile.

Was I to believe that the God who created the days of the week; the God who says all of our hairs are numbered,[138] was incapable of properly counting and recording the days of His Son's death in an accurate manner? Should we all blindly go our way saying the Bible is a trustworthy book if God can't count to three?[139]

The story of my quest to find the truth about the three days and nights ended, of course, finding God and His Bible both trustworthy and accurate to within minutes. It was discovered that Jesus was buried on the fourth day of the week (the day called Wednesday) at minutes before sundown, and rose on Sabbath evening exactly 72 hours (three days and three nights) later, just as He said. The Sabbath mentioned as the next day[140] (the day following the crucifixion) was a High Sabbath, the first day of the Feast of Unleavened Bread, *not* the weekly Sabbath. You will find that Passover occurred on the fourth day of the week in the year Jesus died – 30 AD. The sixth day of the week was unavailable to the women to anoint Christ's body because there were soldiers there until First-day morning. The account was true; the sign was true. Men lie to us, we lie to ourselves, but God cannot lie.

Very few things that Jesus said and taught could be considered contemporary only to His day and inapplicable for us, but sadly one such statement is this, "Why doth this generation seek after a sign?" Well, the fact is that our generation seeks after no sign, generally we seek after no truth, most do not care what they believe, and most would rather belong than be right. The words of Jeremiah 5:1 come to mind, "Run ye to and fro through the streets… and seek in the broad places thereof, if ye can find a man… that seeketh the truth…"

It's Greek To Me

Our culture has evolved from our roots in Judaism to a thoroughly Greek philosophy. Our God is deemed far off, inexplicable, illogical and uncaring. The words and ways of Jesus are strange to us. What is essential to Him is hardly important to us. The ONLY sign He gave us has gone uninvestigated. Though adulterated we accepted it – though polluted we embraced it – though illogical we ignored the irrationality of it.

I would to God that we would seek after the sign that He promised and stop our pagan rituals and so-called holidays. All denominations are polluted with the falsehood of holidays based on irrational and arbitrary acceptance of fictional history. Even Quakers, persecuted in the past for non-compliance and

---

[138]Matthew 10:30 But the very hairs of your head are all numbered.
[139] For the facts and details discovered in this fascinating search for the truth of the resurrection, read the essay "On Truth" by this author.
[140] John 19:31

nonparticipation in Pagan holidays, no longer carry the testimony of being "Friends of Truth." They can be found enveloped in and clinging to the false Holy Days and doctrines of Catholic origin and forsaking their own inner witness and the Scriptures.

The very Scriptures we use to justify and celebrate Christmas, Easter, and Good Friday, upon honest evaluation, condemns those days as recycled paganism, lies and presumption. There are hosts of other days and doctrines we celebrate that hang on false assumption, bad theology, false prophecy, Papal decrees, and doctrines of antichrist.

Have we gone so far that we don't even invest an hour or two examining the only sign Jesus gave us? Do you accept Jesus as truly the Son of God because you know His sign to be true, experientially (by discovery and logic) or do you accept the story as truth by ignoring the contradictions, senseless arithmetic, and blatant discrepancies you find in it? Do you hold to Christ in desperation? Or because, as the disciples said when asked if they too would forsake Him, "...we believe and are sure that thou art that Christ, the Son of the living God." (John 6:67-69) May God have mercy on us all.

"Why doth this generation seek after a sign?" We must answer, "We're sorry Lord, but we don't seek after signs, nor do we investigate prophecy, we just believe what we are told by men in whom we have placed our trust."

96. *What question ye with them?*

Mark 9:16, "And he asked the scribes, What question ye with them?"

This event is different than most, in that its question is one that goes unanswered. An answer given in the text will verify the communicated thought; and without an answer recorded, we may only speculate Christ's purpose in asking.

Jesus had just returned from the transfiguration. The event's purpose, that was about to be misapplied and misunderstood by the disciples, has also been skewed in modern theology. When they saw the two men, Moses and Elijah, stand with the Savior, their first reaction was to build a booth (altar) in worship to them. Moses, who symbolized and indeed embodied the Law of God, was known to all Israelites as a man most holy and certainly deserving of reverence. Elijah, the man who was known as a mighty prophet was also there giving testimony to Joshua (Jesus) as Messiah.

We find these two men (Moses and Elijah) as symbols and figureheads of judgment and leadership, direction and guidance, proclamation and prophecy throughout the Old Testament and now, again in the New Testament. We find them here at the transfiguration and in the Revelation as the two witnesses (or at least the two are described). "These have power to shut heaven, that it rain not in the days of their prophecy [Elijah]: and have power over waters to turn them to blood, and to smite the earth with all plagues, as often as they will [Moses]." (Revelation 11:6) Some theologians think this could only describe Moses and Elijah.

Nevertheless, these two men are pivotal as men who have heard from God and are able and uniquely qualified to transfer orders, Laws, Commandments, Scripture, and prophecy to us as mere subjects in this Kingdom. Herein lies the problem with the next event. Herein lies the problem today.

The Bible is an immediate help and source of guidance for millions of Christians. It has become the mouthpiece of God for many people and therefore revered as much as Moses and Elijah were in the time of Christ. In the days of Samuel, God's "word" became precious but it was not to be heard from any prophet, no one was hearing or being given God's vision.[141] In the day we live, we can see the Bible gaining as a source and authority because (as we are told) "God does not speak to us anymore." "What more can He say, than to you He has said?" The old hymn[142] declares that the Bible is now the only source because there is nothing more to be said. But is that true? Is the Bible our only reliable source from which we may gain direction and comfort? Are Moses and

---

[141] 1 Samuel 3:1, "And the child Samuel ministered unto the LORD before Eli. And the word of the LORD was precious in those days; there was no open vision."
[142] How Firm a Foundation

309

Elijah (the Law and the Prophets) to be heeded and revered as the only sources of God's voice?

Listen as the Father, overhearing the intentions of Peter, James, and John, speaks to them in thunderous Commandment. **"This is my beloved son... hear Him."** And when the scene clears, Jesus was standing there alone as the ONLY Law, the ONLY Prophet, the ONLY source. Not Moses, not Elijah, just Jesus only. The writer of Hebrews confirms this as He says, "God, who at sundry times and in divers manners spake in time past unto the fathers by the prophets, Hath in these last days spoken unto us by his Son..." (Hebrews 1:1-2)

The scribes were quizzing the disciples about the Messiah and the preceding events. They obviously put into their minds that the Messiah cannot come until Elijah comes first. They worried over this, thinking that perhaps they were following an imposter who was somehow capable of miracles or trickery. They put forth a pretty good argument because the Scriptures say that the disciples asked Jesus, "Why say the scribes that Elias must first come?" (Mark 9:11) Their concern was that the scribes had Scripture on their side. They could "prove" that Jesus was not the Messiah with the Scriptures.

Now they just returned from an event where **Jehovah Himself** commanded them to listen to His Son, removing Moses and Elijah as supreme oracles. Now the disciples want clarification. Jesus gave them explanation of the prophecy knowing from where their doubts came – the Pharisees and Scribes. He knew that some religious leader somewhere, making a writing into a god, is offering "proof texts" and showing "by Scripture" that the truth is a lie and a lie is truth. So finding the scribes grilling and questioning His disciples again he asks them, "What are you making them doubt now?" He asked, "What question ye with them?"

This Problem Continues Today.

If we cannot hear from God; if God does not, in these last days speak unto us by His son; if Jesus is dead, or mute, or incommunicado, what hope do we have of properly interpreting the Scripture to gain eternal life?

The scribes who studied all of their life – who not only have read the Scripture through several times but probably will copy it by hand two or three times in their life – were far better acquainted with the Scriptures than we are. They missed the Messiah, they were SURE Jesus was NOT the Messiah. What hope do you have? How much of your understanding comes from some man somewhere, or book, or denomination, catechism, or doctrine? How many times have you received, not from Moses or Elijah, not from the words of God, but from the "Word of God"[143] Himself, from the Messiah, from the beloved Son from whom we are commissioned to hear?

Teachers of today secure for themselves a place of authority by teaching the "difficult" Scriptures and diverting focus away from the Living

---

[143] The Word of God being Jesus Christ (John 1)

Christ and toward themselves as interpreters. Jesus would ask our modern-day teachers of doctrine, "What are you making my disciples doubt and question now?" Christ taught that His sheep knew His voice and a stranger they would not follow.[144] It grieves Christ to see the scribes huddled around His sheep confusing them and making them question and doubt what He has taught them in silence and in private.

You can walk in full understanding and faith, clearly hearing the voice of the shepherd. You need not cumber yourself with esoteric questions that have no answers, nor need you arm yourself with answers for questions that no one is asking. You need only live and listen and obey the living Christ, the Seed of God Himself, in us. As the Scriptures witness to your walk with Christ, the world will see that you follow Him in truth. They will see that the Spirit who wrote the Scriptures lives within you and gives you direction.

As for the teachers who assume we are all lost without their guidance – as for those who are the mediator of truth and verity – as for the miscreants who think that we need their input and viewpoint, who take Jesus' disciples off to the side and whisper questions or deceptive doctrines in their ears, Jesus has a question for you, "What are you confusing them about now...What question ye with them?"

---

[144] John 10:5

97. *What was it that ye discussed among yourselves?*

Mark 9:33, "And he came to Capernaum: and being in the house he asked them, What was it that ye disputed among yourselves by the way?"

When we get a little time to ourselves our thoughts can go in directions that we are not proud of, though we may pursue them enthusiastically. It was just such a time for the disciples of Christ. The Lord Jesus noticed a dispute among them. We can only surmise that Jesus was not near enough to hear but was close enough to see that the discussion was lively and emotional.

This must have been a high time of the ministry. The disciples were convinced that the Kingdom, which Jesus had come to establish, was near at hand. They thought it would only be a matter of days or weeks now and the Messiah would reign! "Who will be His right hand man, who will be second in command?" they wondered, and soon began to claim for themselves these positions and powers that would soon be bestowed. The discussion turned lively and then became a debate. The debate soon escalated into a dispute and as they looked over their shoulder to see who could hear and see them, a glance from the Savior quelled the furor.

Later that evening the Lord asked, "What was it that ye disputed [discussed] among yourselves by the way?" They were ashamed to answer because the subject of the argument was power and its fuel was selfishness. It was about to be made clear that seats and power in this Kingdom are not seized by the ambitious nor grabbed up by the greedy. The disciples must have been astonished to hear that even the Lord Jesus Himself did not have the authority to grant their desires. Instead they heard the paradoxical advice to put down ambition, to strive to be less in order to be more, to seek servitude in order to mastery.

We only become self-centered when we spend time away from the Savior. Apart from Him we become convinced of our worth and value to the Kingdom. We wonder how God got along without us before we were born. Sometimes we become very much as Elijah was when he claimed to be the only one who was serving God,[145] after which, God made it clear that there were many who had not bowed their knees to Baal. Nevertheless, it was when he ran from Jezebel and hid in the cave that he felt sorry for himself, and it is when we withdraw from the battle that we nurse our wounds and dream of the medals we deserve.

The worker in the vineyard[146] wondered if they should receive more than they agreed because their plight and toil was even harder to bear when compared to the latecomers that were paid the same wage. Pity, comparisons,

---

[145] 1 Kings 19:10, "... for the children of Israel have forsaken thy covenant, thrown down thine altars, and slain thy prophets with the sword; and I, even I only, am left; and they seek my life, to take it away."
[146] Matthew 20:1

312

distractions, and selfishness will conjure thoughts and evoke conversation of which you will be ashamed upon revisiting the Lord that evening.

One of the great objections that people who try meditative or silent worship have is the initial discomfort, the racing of the mind to defocus from the objective. This initial clearing or centering is a time of inquisition from the Lord. As we approach Him after having gone our own way for a time, He quizzes us on our recent thoughts and wonders, "What was it that ye discussed among yourselves?" We may hear within us His voice saying, "Catch me up on your thoughts and discussions." Ashamed of our recent worries and selfish desires of the day, we may choose rather to be quiet and take what is coming.

"It's Different Today"

We excuse our busy-ness by virtue of the fact that we are living in the 21st century. We complain about life being so hurried. We complain so that we can hide the truth – that we really appreciate the fact that we cannot stop long enough to hear the Lord ask us questions that we do not want to answer.

In many cases we, and no other, have made our lives so cluttered, so busy, so noisy that we fall into bed at night and wake to an alarm the next day. No time for quiet, no time for thought, no time to listen. We deceive ourselves into thinking that our schedules are not of our own making. We deceive ourselves into believing that we are alright, that we are in no need of repentance. We have forgotten the true condition of the man in the mirror and deceived ourselves.

James 1:22-24, "But be ye doers of the word, and not hearers only, deceiving your own selves. For if any be a hearer of the word, and not a doer, he is like unto a man beholding his natural face in a glass: For he beholdeth himself, and goeth his way, and straightway forgetteth what manner of man he was."

Our lives of desperation call us away from our Master. We tend to seek out a comfortable level of devotion that demands nothing of us. We engage only meditations that offer no comparison to perfection, and conversations with Christ that make no case for conformity to any standards of Law. Entertainment, mindless hobbies, reading of novels and time wasting endeavors are employed to take our mind away from the convicting Spirit who haunts us to make changes, to forgive grudges, to cleanse our way and become more like Christ.

We grow tired of correction, weary of conviction and seek out other methods, new and exciting ways, or altogether take a "vacation" from Christ by laying down our studies, meditation or Bible reading. When we stay to ourselves, we come up with silly ideas, dubious doctrines, and we get off track. We argue and dispute our position with others who are backsliders as well. We confuse others and ourselves and eventually, after disaster has been firmly established, we find we need to return to the Christ who has the words of life.

When you return to Christ after spending time "away" from Him, you will find Him fully aware of your diversion and stupidity. Wondering again what silly thing you and your companions have amused yourselves with, He asks, "What was it that ye discussed among yourselves?"

98. *What did Moses command you?*

Mark 10:3, "And he answered and said unto them, What did Moses command you?"

The new Rabbi in town is teaching something novel. He is tearing down the old ways and making new ways to travel. He is replacing the Law of Moses! He is setting aside the Commandments! These must have been the remarks heard on the streets by those discussing Jesus' ministry. There are many today who think the same way. There are those who think Jesus came to destroy, do away with, and set aside, the Law of Moses.

The Pharisees of Jesus' day had forced onto their society a set of by-laws to live by so that life could be lived to the edge of sin without stepping over the bounds. These guidelines were not done under the direction of God however, and spiritual disaster occurred. These were the things Jesus brought up when chiding them about "omitting the weightier matters of the Law," thereby straining out gnats and swallowing camels whole. (Matthew 23) Their plan actually was causing sin, instead of avoiding it. Not sin in ignorance, but sin with a sense of righteousness.

These by-laws were a constant source of discussion and debate. Could a man divorce his wife for any cause or did it have to be a serious one? The Scripture in Deuteronomy 24:1 is vague about the cause and subsequently led to liberal interpretations, "When a man hath taken a wife, and married her, and it come to pass that she find no favour in his eyes, because he hath found some uncleanness in her: then let him write her a bill of divorcement, and give it in her hand, and send her out of his house." So this became a topic for debate.

Here is the complete picture. Matthew writes, "The Pharisees also came unto him, tempting him, and saying unto him, Is it lawful for a man to put away his wife for every cause? And he answered and said unto them, Have ye not read, that he which made them at the beginning made them male and female, And said, For this cause shall a man leave father and mother, and shall cleave to his wife: and they twain shall be one flesh? Wherefore they are no more twain, but one flesh. What therefore God hath joined together, let not man put asunder."[147]

When they saw that Jesus was taking the conservative stance, they were more determined to defend their position and they said to him, "Why then did Moses command to give a writing of divorcement to put her away?" Jesus did not miss a beat and referred to the time before sin entered the equation. He said, "Moses, because of the hardness of your hearts, suffered [allowed] you to put away your wives, but from the beginning it was not so."[148]

---

[147] Matthew 19:3-8
[148] Ibid. -- Genesis 1:27, "So God created man in his own image, in the image of God created he him; male and female created he them."

The Bible is a rich source of guidance when we are in a condition that hinders or hampers our hearing. When we cannot (for reasons of grievous behavior, sin, or rebellion) hear the voice of God within us, we are treading dangerous ground. We are primed and ready to accept error and need a line of demarcation to turn us around. When we find ourselves violating the Scripture we should summarily repent and not try to justify what we are doing. When we are at crossed purposes with the Scriptures we are stemming tides that are flowing God's direction. These are the times to turn about and admit we were wrong and change our behavior. Otherwise known as old-fashioned repentance.

Jesus asked them then, and He asks you now "What did Moses command you?" You will not find a Commandment that is useless to a true Christian. Nor will you will find a true Christian who finds the Commandments of his God useless. As a matter of fact, the Scriptures are as close as a person can get to the voice of God in the earth without a relationship of repentant faith in Christ. The Scriptures are to be respected. Some of them were written in rock with His own finger!

You Can Never Go Wrong Living By The Scriptures.

Questions that plague our modern society could be easily answered, simply by considering the question, "What did Moses command you?" What are the answers to questions like: What can be done about aids, about world hunger, about the homeless, about the family, about crime, and every other illness of society?

Now consider: "What did Moses command you?" But, what should be our attitude about the world around us, how should we conduct ourselves, how should we dress, and speak, and act? What should we give to the poor, what should we give to the work of the Lord? What should we give to our families? Well, "what did Moses command you?" But, how do we counsel others, how do we lend money, how do train our children, how do we provide for our parents? – "What did Moses command you?"

The Old Testament has been set aside for no good reason. There are few who can read the questions listed above and give Old Testament references that provide answers. We have forsaken the Old Testament and found our "New Testament Christian" men and women worse for it. We struggle with questions that have plain answers. We discuss and test doctrines and ideas that would be straightway rejected if subjected to Old Testament scrutiny. We accept more readily bias, tainted and so-called science,[149] even if it negates the scriptures. Our Meetings are crippled and stagnant because we do not have the courage to say, "Thus saith the Lord."

Genesis 2:24, "Therefore shall a man leave his father and his mother, and shall cleave unto his wife: and they shall be one flesh."

[149] 1 Timothy 6:20-21, "O Timothy, keep that which is committed to thy trust, avoiding profane and vain babblings, and oppositions of science falsely so called: Which some professing have erred concerning the faith…"

Quakers have always taught that the same Spirit who put forth the Scriptures resides within the believer. We, who know the voice of God within, know that He makes the Scriptures come alive – more so than merely reading it could ever do.

Jesus was able to lend insight to the Law and Prophets not previously considered, such as, "from the beginning it was not so" or "ye have heard it said… but I say to you…" These depths were available to Him because of the Spirit within Him. He knew personally the Spirit who wrote the Scriptures, just as we who have been baptized in the Spirit also know.

We who are instructed under the Kingdom of heaven can provide for ourselves new dimensions. Dimensions not known heretofore are available to those who read with the Spirit the Testaments, both New and Old.[150]

When you struggle with new insights that controvert your Meeting's ideas, overturn the traditions in the minds of friends and contradict modern "New Testament Christians," it is always appropriate to ask yourself, "What did Moses command you?" Therefore everyone who is instructed in the Kingdom of Heaven is like a man who bringeth forth out of his treasure things *NEW* **and** *OLD*. "What did Moses command you?"

---

[150] Matthew 13:52, "Then said he unto them, Therefore every scribe which is instructed unto the kingdom of heaven is like unto a man that is an householder, which bringeth forth out of his treasure things new and old."

99. *What is the kingdom of God like?*

Luke 13:18, "Then said he, Unto what is the kingdom of God like? and whereunto shall I resemble it?"

Mark 4:30, "And he said, Whereunto shall we liken the kingdom of God? or with what comparison shall we compare it?"

The great Communicator, the great Orator, the most famous Preacher in the world, is at a loss for words. A red letter day indeed! (Pun intended) We would think that Jesus would never be at a loss for words. He matched with the best by retort and rebuttal, debate and discourse, but on this day He has a little problem, He can't seem to put into words an accurate description of the Kingdom of God.

There is a story by Edwin A. Abbott that tells of a place called Flatland. Flatland is a two dimensional world that exists in a plane infinitely flat that is fully aware of left and right but does not have any idea what up and down mean. (To them, any penetration of their flat world by three-dimensional objects is magical, and mystically appears and disappears as it passes through. What is "magic" to them is merely logic to us.) His book is a most interesting excursion into dimensional thinking and relates the story of Christ entering our world and being hindered by lack of dimension.

We could also suppose that it was very difficult for Jesus in many other ways. In the same way as the three dimensional interloper in Flatland had to describe up and down, thick and thin, fat and skinny to folks that knew only two dimensions, Christ finds Himself at a loss to explain to us what the Kingdom of God is like!

The Kingdom, to which we have been invited, likely is a city within another dimension. Cities that descend down from God out of Heaven[151] are not cities, as we now know them. Cities that have streets made of transparent gold[152] are not cites with which we are now familiar. The twelve gates of this new city will each be made of pearl. Not "pearly" as we have been told, but made of one pearl. Solid pearl! Think of the oysters that must be there!

Now it has become Jesus' goal to describe this Kingdom to us. Do we find it odd that He chooses to describe our attitude and us in this Kingdom rather than a physical description of its beauty and its tangible contents? The first glimpse of its beauty comes from John in The Revelation. Jesus Himself never said a word about what it *looks* like. Why did He omit this?

One of the misconceptions of the church at large is their understanding of their rewards. Many speak of "going to heaven" when they die, but the Scripture makes no such a promise. This may shock some (and hopefully

---

[151] Revelation 21:2, "And I John saw the holy city, new Jerusalem, coming down from God out of heaven, prepared as a bride adorned for her husband."
[152] ibid

provoke some to search out for themselves the truth concerning our reward.) The promise was made for us to be with Christ where He is. Where is He to be?

We see in The Revelation that the city of God (the bride of Christ) descends out of Heaven from God and sits upon the earth. The New Jerusalem is set upon the earth and within it dwells the Lord Jesus Christ. According to the Scriptures, we are not going to heaven... heaven is coming to us. (This is, of course, a colloquial use of the word "heaven" I use to describe the splendor and glory of the city.)

The exciting thing is now that Christ has come; the Kingdom of God is not something to wait for, to aspire to, or to strive within our self to attain. It is something that is a continuation of our life here on this earth, an everlasting life that starts here... not there. When Jesus spoke of the Kingdom of God He spoke of a state of being within a person, a state of mind, or an outlook upon life in general. He spoke of the Kingdom being within us and not coming with observation, he spoke of it growing from a small thing into an exceedingly large thing.

When We All Get ... To Heaven?

It is not a new life "over there," it is a continuation of life started here from the second of conception by the Holy Ghost[153] until we come to the fullness of Christ in us, until we finally wake from our long sleep[154] unto the resurrection of the dead in Christ. This is why Jesus said in John 11:26, "And whosoever liveth and believeth in me shall never die," and again in John 8:51, "Verily, verily, I say unto you, If a man keep my saying, he shall never see death." The life in Christ is a continuing life, a life that is not ended by death but only interrupted by sleep, to awake again to everlasting life.

The reward of eternity, as is known by the present day church, is a sorry one. Thoughts of going up, going to heaven, playing harps, becoming angels, going to a place totally unfamiliar, totally unknown, cannot be considered a pleasurable thing to do. Most people who hold this idea are so thrilled about missing the fiery alternative that they do not really care about how boring it all sounds.

The truth is that according to your Bible, our eternity will be a life like we live today – minus the evil influence. Satan will be bound for a thousand years as we dwell with Christ on this earth! Isn't it exciting to think that the very soil under your feet is the soil of "heaven" for a thousand years! If "heaven" were nothing more than these thousand years, it would be

---

[153] Matthew 1:20, "But while he thought on these things, behold, the angel of the Lord appeared unto him in a dream, saying, Joseph, thou son of David, fear not to take unto thee Mary thy wife: for that which is conceived in her is of the Holy Ghost."

[154] 1 Thessalonians 4:13-16, "But I would not have you to be ignorant, brethren, concerning them which are asleep, that ye sorrow not, even as others which have no hope. For if we believe that Jesus died and rose again, even so them also which sleep in Jesus will God bring with him. For this we say unto you by the word of the Lord, that we which are alive and remain unto the coming of the Lord shall not prevent them which are asleep. For the Lord himself shall descend from heaven with a shout, with the voice of the archangel, and with the trump of God: and the dead in Christ shall rise first:"

worthwhile, but it is to continue yet again. After that, the Scriptures say, God will make a new Heaven and a new Earth! Really, not much is said about our existence then. We are not told about life there, what it will be like, or much of anything. Most of what we know is made up "Sunday School" stuff.

Most important is that we need to know that the life for which we strive is NOW, not later. We must shun the escapist's ideas of missing Hell, and we must forget the idealist's ideas of utopia located in the clouds. Even the term "heaven" should be replaced with something closer to the idea found in Scripture.

If reference were to be made to our eternal home it would correctly be referred to as the "Kingdom." (The Kingdom of God, the Kingdom of Heaven, where our Father dwells now in heaven and where Christ is preparing the New Jerusalem for us as a habitation all define this Kingdom.) Also, it is important to realize that the perfection that awaits us there is to be strived for while we are here.

The eternal life we anticipate, is not something we are rewarded with in the by and by, it is the same life that was implanted in us by the Holy Spirit; the same life power in which we live and move and have our being TODAY![155] As we have heard Paul say, "...Christ liveth in me: and the life which I now live in the flesh I live by the faith of the Son of God, who loved me, and gave himself for me."[156]

We call this life in us the Kingdom of God. For that is what it is. It is the very life of Christ in you continuing, progressing, and helping you become more like Him. Jesus said, "...for behold, the kingdom of God is within you."[157]

Your reward starts now and never ends. Jesus said, "...whosoever liveth and believeth in me shall never die"[158] Like within an acorn there is an oak tree, there is Eternal Life bound within this small and miserable one.

The Kingdom is like a mustard seed. It is like leaven hidden in a loaf of bread. It is as seed cast into the ground. It is at hand. What do you think? "What is the kingdom of God like?"

---

[155] Acts 17:28, "For in him we live, and move, and have our being; as certain also of your own poets have said, For we are also his offspring."
[156] Galatians 2:20
[157] Luke 17:21
[158] John 11:26

100. Shall not God avenge his own elect?

Luke 18:7, "And shall not God avenge his own elect, which cry day and night unto him, though he bear long with them?"

When women do it, we call it nagging, when children do it, we call it whining, when we do it in our prayers we call it importunity, persistence, or tenacity.

Jesus was trying to give us an understanding of God's view of our prayers. He made it clear that our Father was unimpressed with long prayers,[159] unmoved by repetition,[160] repulsed by the proud and boastful one,[161] and prayers that tell him what He already knows.[162]

The place of prayer was also important enough for Jesus to mention it. He said that it is to be private, secret, and heard by our Father only.[163] If we take all these points literally (avoiding the things that Jesus said were repulsive to God, like public prayer, boastfulness, repetition, verbose and unnatural petitions) and we replace our previous understanding of prayer with the things Christ said we should do when we pray, what would our prayers be like? Would our prayers resemble anything we are accustomed to now?

For the most part, prayer has become, among the convention of Christianity, a sham. Men in pulpits cannot stand there, preach or sing a song, take up an offering or do anything without it beginning and ending in some pathetic perfunctory prayer. "Well it's time to pray." Then they launch into a paltry diatribe using the obligatory Elizabethan thees and thous making their requests, more to their audience than to God, and then seal it all into a neat little package by adding, "In Jesus' name... Amen." We can almost see them smacking their hands together as if wiping toast crumbs from them and hear, "There! ...That should do it." There has to be something more to prayer than that.

If you were to remove from the common public prayer that which is said for the sake of those standing by, what is said for tradition's sake, what is said by habit, what is said to comply with the denomination or theological understanding of the listeners, and erased all that was not prayed in the attitude of "thy will be done," there would be little left to say. If we further apply to what was left, the fact that it was prayed in public and thereby tainted with pride and arrogance, (or at the very least, self-consciousness) it makes a wash of the whole affair and renders the entire prayer totally useless. In other words,

---

[159] Mark 12:40, "... and for a pretence make long prayers: these shall receive greater damnation."

[160] Matthew 6:7, "But when ye pray, use not vain repetitions, as the heathen do: for they think that they shall be heard for their much speaking."

[161] Luke 18:10-14 ...for every one that exalteth himself shall be abased; and he that humbleth himself shall be exalted."

[162] Matthew 6:8, "... for your Father knoweth what things ye have need of, before ye ask him."

[163] Matthew 6:5-6, "And when thou prayest, thou shalt not be as the hypocrites ...But when thou prayest, enter into thy closet, and when thou hast shut thy door, pray to thy Father which is in secret...."

if we applied what Jesus taught, it would either change our prayers drastically or eliminate them entirely.

Teach Us to Pray

The disciples asked Jesus to teach them to pray. John the Baptist also taught his disciples to pray. Who taught the Pharisees how to pray? They made long prayers and were considered by many to be very spiritual; who taught them to pray? More importantly – who taught you?

In the question, "Shall not God avenge His own elect," we can feel a bite of frustration in Christ's voice. His message is, "…though He bear long with them, I say to you He will avenge them, He has not forgotten them." Jesus just finished a parable about a widow who was persistently nagging the judge to avenge her of someone who had defrauded her previously. The judge said that he did not care because he did not care about her or her cause and that he did not fear God.

Was Jesus comparing His Father to this unjust judge? No, but when we persistently tell God what He is already aware of, we put Him in the same place of a contemptibly unjust judge. We are, in effect, saying that if He were just, He would avenge us; if He were just He would answer our prayer. Jesus wanted us to know that He is not unjust and that He does regard man and will do what is right. We will be avenged, He will answer that which is in His will, though He bear long with us, it will happen.

When we pray in this repetitive importunate way, we should recognize that we are likely doing so out of weariness, and doubt. But, what is worse is that we doubt not ourselves, but God – and we become fainthearted. This story started out by saying, "And he spake a parable unto them to this end, that men ought always to pray, and not to faint."[164] We should pray, not beg.

A similar parable is found in Luke 11:5-10, "Which of you shall have a friend, and shall go unto him at midnight, and say unto him, Friend, lend me three loaves?" The man inside the house makes the excuse that it is not convenient to get out of bed and supply his friend's need and later does so because his friend would not leave his door. "I say unto you, Though he will not rise and give him, because he is his friend, yet because of his importunity he will rise and give him as many as he needeth."

Would you want to receive from God because you aggravated Him? The phrase, "…though he will not rise and give him, because he is his friend" haunts me. Do I want what the Lord does not want? What if He gives me that which He does not want me to have only because I have wearied Him? But here Jesus is saying that we need not pound at the door and beg, we need only ask in His will and wait patiently. "And I say unto you, Ask, and it shall be given you; seek, and ye shall find; knock, and it shall be opened unto you. For every one

---

[164] Luke 18:1

that asketh receiveth; and he that seeketh findeth; and to him that knocketh it shall be opened."[165]

Yet these very Scriptures are taken and used daily to teach importunity as a virtue; as if God is only moved to action by those who are willing to ask, ask, and ask again ...as long as it takes. When we read that message into these Scriptures, we (though inadvertently perhaps) make our loving God out to be equivalent to the unjust judge or the uncaring friend in our midnight crisis. Both portrayals are unacceptable.

Our prayers need to change; we need to change our outlook and view of God as a heartless and unjust judge whom we are expected to convince or coerce.

When you consider God as uncaring you need to ask yourself, "Shall not God avenge his own elect?" You need to ask yourself, "Do I care more than God does?" "Is this situation more important to me than it is to God?" It may be that it is. In that case you need to shift your priorities. In most cases you will find that God is fully aware, is willing to act on your behalf, and will do so when the situation allows Him to realize the full execution of His will. You need only rest in God and quietly think to yourself when doubts arise, "Shall not God avenge his own elect?"

---

[165] Matthew 7:8

101. Where are those thine accusers?

John 8:10, "When Jesus had lifted up himself, and saw none but the woman, he said unto her, Woman, where are those thine accusers? hath no man condemned thee?"

This could easily be the sweetest representation of Christ's compassion found in the New Testament. Its message is plain, its point obvious, its story line compelling, and its hero – flawless. It has all the right ingredients for a memorable and touching story bearing an inescapable moral. The question that Christ asked, however, is deeper still. The story behind His question teaches yet another bit of theology.

Recently I heard a radio broadcast of a famous Bible teacher who is known worldwide and heard by millions. He was preaching a sermon called, "When Jesus broke the Sabbath." Now, I know without a doubt that this man, (though he is now dead) if he were asked if he believed that Jesus was sinless while here on earth in bodily form, he would answer, "Most assuredly!"

Many would answer the same way. It is a point of fact essential for redemption that the Messiah would suffer for sins not His own to effect salvation for us all. How then could He have broken the fourth Commandment? (He in fact never broke the Commandment, He did, however, shatter the man-made laws surrounding Sabbath.) But, in this story of the woman caught in adultery, consider if perhaps we have caught Jesus disobeying one of God's expressed Commandments.

Deuteronomy 17:5, *"Then shalt thou bring forth that man or that woman, which have committed that wicked thing, unto thy gates, even that man or that woman, and shalt stone them with stones, till they die."*

This Commandment is very explicit. All that is required to condemn this woman who was caught in the very act was to bring her to the gate with witnesses and stone her. *"They say unto him, Master, this woman was taken in adultery, in the very act. Now Moses in the law commanded us, that such should be stoned: but what sayest thou? This they said, tempting him, that they might have to accuse him."* Why did they wonder what Jesus might do? It was because they knew within themselves that He would not condone what they had always done, or what they thought should be done, but rather they knew **His answer would be different**. They were right.

The law said plainly that this woman must die and Jesus let her off. He forgave her and sent her on her way. The Law did not specify that if you felt sorry for the accused you may let her go and forgo punishment. The Law made no such provision. Did Jesus break the Law of Moses? The Law states (in other places) that pity will not enter in to the decision at all (as in Deuteronomy 19:21, "And thine eye shall not pity; but life shall go for life, eye for eye, tooth for tooth, hand for hand, foot for foot.") And again in a case where a woman put her hand where she ought not, they were commanded to cut off the hand

324

that disobeyed. A gory task indeed but again He said, "Then thou shalt cut off her hand, thine eye shall not pity her." (Deuteronomy 25:12) So, pity was no reason to spare judgment. The question remains; did Christ break the Law of Moses?

Jesus knew that they caught her "in the very act" and therefore no attorney could cloud or skew the facts to help her appear to be innocent. He knew the Law and therefore no lawyer could twist the law to accommodate her. Jesus also knew men, "for he knew what was in man."

As Though He Heard Them Not

Jesus stooped down, and with his finger wrote on the ground, as though he heard them not." Many have speculated what Jesus wrote. I don't think He wrote anything important; He was just doodling "as though He heard them not." He was pretending not to care, being cool and collected, exercising an exasperating defense from accusation; and when He had everyone's attention and the quiet fell on the crowd so that no one would have to ask, "What did He say?" He stood and said, "He that is without sin among you, let him first cast a stone at her."

And again he stooped down, and wrote on the ground." The woman braced for the worst. She knew within herself that everyone in the crowd that day was better than she; none who stood to condemn her had the weaknesses she had. Those who stood over her were the very ones she envied in her life, those who she, in the secret thoughts of her idle hours, aspired to be, and now she lay face first in the dust before them to receive the just stones of death at their hands. Her breath halted, she awaited the rain of blows.

As the hush fell on the crowd and His proposition to the sinless coursed through their minds and the blood rushed to their faces, their hearts pounded as the convicting power of the words of Jesus rang in their ears. The deafness of their preoccupation was punctuated only by the thud...thud...thud of stones once held by the self-righteous now are being released to the ground as faces turn away and the backs of the convicted are shown to the accused. "And they which heard it, being convicted by their own conscience, went out one by one, beginning at the eldest, even unto the last: and Jesus was left alone, and the woman standing in the midst. When Jesus had lifted up himself, and saw none but the woman, he said unto her, 'Woman, where are those thine accusers? Hath no man condemned thee?' She said, 'No man, Lord.'"

But there was one there that day who could accuse. There was a sinless one. One who was entitled, even by the new criterion Christ laid out, to cast the first stone – Jesus Himself. He had that right. He could have accused her and condemned her, "And Jesus said unto her, Neither do I condemn thee: go, and sin no more." Did He break the Law of Moses?

Over a thousand years earlier, God placed a provision in the Law requiring that two or more accusers condemn this woman, and alas, as if by design, there was only one. No law was broken, no Commandment circumnavigated by clever lawyers, no facts twisted, but paradoxically, the

Law, perfectly executed, gave this woman another chance. Jesus, the only one able to accuse, simply chose not to.

What a wonderful representation this is of His love and perfection toward those who repent and look to Him. Though the law in the hands of sinful men accuses, you need only stand near Christ and let Him find a way to emerge with a second chance. Had Jesus not been there, there would have been one more body thrown into Gehenna. When He is on the scene He will mercifully deal with those who trust Him.

There is only one who can accuse you. There is only one who may exercise the power of condemnation. The accusers in this world will have difficulties of their own to deal with on that great and notable day of the Lord.

On the day that you who love Him are condemned by the Law and dropped at the feet of the Judge of all the earth, look up and you will find yourself with Him alone when He asks, "Where are those thine accusers?"

102. Dost thou believe on the Son of God?

John 9:35, "Jesus heard that they had cast him out; and when he had found him, he said unto him, Dost thou believe on the Son of God?"

The story in John 9 starts out simply, "And as Jesus passed by, he saw a man which was blind from his birth." Who could know the ramifications that were to follow? Interrogations, excommunications, families split, traditions challenged, men of high esteem publicly held in jaundiced scrutiny and one soul's destiny changed from eternal separation from God to the very life of God Himself springing up within him.

The items of interest that day were many, but one is of particular advantage to investigate. "Do you believe on the Son of God?" Here, Jesus cuts through all the hoopla of the day, and asks a simple question.

We can learn a great deal from reading what is written in Scripture, and we can learn from what's missing as well. Is it not interesting that Jesus did not go into the same discussions with this man, or give him the answers to the questions that the Pharisees asked him? He did not ask how he felt about working or worshipping on Sabbath. He did not try to prepare him for his future by stuffing his head full of church language and doctrine. He did not tell him to rush out and purchase a copy of the Scriptures so to arm himself against all the power of the enemy. He just needed to know one thing, *"Do you believe on the Son of God?"*

It is obvious at every turn that the "religion" of Jesus is not the religion that is practiced in mainstream Christianity. Why is that? Could anyone stretch their understanding of what they read in Scriptures to think that the apostle Paul was a Southern Baptist? Or that there was any similarity in the apostle Peter and the Pope? Though many try to claim that the authority of their faith or denomination goes back to the apostles, there are few who would grant admission to someone who preaches like Paul into their ranks (much less make him a minister among them.)

If Jesus taught so vehemently against tradition, why do we insist on propagating it?

If Jesus taught against costumes to impress people, why do we continue to dress our pastors and priests in showy garb as if they were magicians or sorcerers? Even the denominations that do not robe their pastors are not at all free from this accusation, as they dress them in the finest and would be appalled to see them wear simple or even sensible attire to preach.

If Jesus taught against making long, public prayers why do we do it? If he condemned repeating ourselves, and asking for things that God already knows we need, why do we continue this practice? I contend it is because we do not truly and simply believe on the Son of God.

Where Is Your Faith?

If we place our faith in church, we will go *there* to make inquiry as to how we should live, and there we will receive our guidance. If we "believe in" church we will do what pleases the church. If we place our faith in the pastors, it is *there* that we will go for guidance and leadership – because it is those men we seek to please. Similarly, if we place our faith in or believe on the Son of God, we will do what **He** says. If we do what He says, He will love us and the Father will love us[166] and He can reveal the Father to us.[167]

If the Father has been revealed to us, we are far from the worry of being led astray, or being led about by every wind of doctrine. We are far from being oppressed by the church's rules and governments, or being lorded over by its leaders. We have nothing to fear if we place our faith in Jesus Christ alone and seek to worship Him in Spirit and in Truth.

Jesus found this blind man who would not let go of what he knew to be true, thrown out of the traditional place of worship, and by himself alone; however, still rejoicing over his newfound sight. Jesus asks, "Do you believe on the Son of God?" The man responds, "Who is He so that I may believe on Him?" Jesus answers all his questions and tells him that He is the one on whom to believe. So He does …and worships Him.

If we hold to what has been revealed to us, rather than just what has been taught to us by others, we will be as this man was – sure and believing, strong and of convincing testimony, able to stand before interrogating men of great religious stature and able to say, "… one thing I know, that, whereas I was blind, now I see."

When we hold to the revelation of Christ within us, we will invariably find that it goes against the structures and institutions man has made to understand God. Operating and living under our own revelations will fly in the face of those who make themselves to be the purveyors of all things religious.

If we hold to the faith revealed to us we will find we share with this blind man more than an encounter with Christ. We may find ourselves ostracized as well. With the exception of Quakers, I know of no other faith that will let a man go on his own journey, giving guidance where needed and requested, yet letting him find his own way with God. When this ideal works as intended it is the way all Christian community should be.

Everywhere I go, I meet those who feel they are being called away from the folly and irrelevance of modern "churchianity." Even the youngest in the Lord feel that there is something drastically wrong with this institution. Unfortunately, by the time the problem can be discovered, relationships are made, fears implanted, and our respects and allegiances altered and the traditions have taken full hold. These new in Christ, over time, become the elders, lured away from their original and simple faith in Christ, and are fully

---

[166] John 14:21, "He that hath my commandments, and keepeth them, he it is that loveth me: and he that loveth me shall be loved of my Father, and I will love him, and will manifest myself to him."

[167] Matthew 11:27, "All things are delivered unto me of my Father: and no man knoweth the Son, but the Father; neither knoweth any man the Father, save the Son, and he to whomsoever the Son will reveal him."

engaged in the convincement of others new to the faith. Weaned from the Savior as source, these fledglings will soon look to men and the church as source and the problem continues.

The Christian life is as simple as, "Do you believe on the Son of God" and simultaneously as complex as, "Do you believe on the Son of God?" Well, what about it friend, is your faith in men? Is your faith in your church? Is your faith in a strict obedience to laws of man's making, rules of organizations, codes of conduct, traditions of your denomination – or do you believe on the Son of God? Is He real enough to you to tell you what is missing in your life or what needs to be added? Is He all you need for a peaceable and fruitful life? Do you seek or need the approval of men and the acceptance of large groups to have confidence in your relationship with God, or can you have the kind of faith that can withstand being all alone? What about it? "Do you believe on the Son of God?"

"Jesus heard that they had cast him out; and when he had found him, he said unto him, Dost thou believe on the Son of God?" You see, Jesus went searching for him! You may be one who has given up on religion. You may be one who has had your hope of reaching out and finding God, crushed by the merciless and hypocritical leadership of the modern church.

Never stop seeking Christ, for, if you are His, He is seeking you. If Jesus indeed has touched you and your understanding of who He is has caused the demise of your fellowship with the traditional church, I have good news for you... Jesus is looking for you. He wants to ask you a question. He wants to ask you, "Do you believe on the Son of God?"

103. Are there not twelve hours in the day?

John 11:9, "Jesus answered, Are there not twelve hours in the day? If any man walk in the day, he stumbleth not, because he seeth the light of this world."

Sometimes the context of a verse demands that it be reinterpreted. In this case it almost seems that Jesus is cowering before persecution. When the disciples say, "Master, the Jews of late sought to stone thee; and goest thou thither again? Jesus answered, Are there not twelve hours in the day?" This answer is as if Jesus intends to avoid them by darkness, which is not the case.

Just prior to this event Jesus made the statement, "I must work the works of him that sent me, while it is day: the night cometh, when no man can work." (John 9:4) The clearer understanding of this verse would be rendered, Are there not [only] twelve hours in a day? Jesus was saying to them that danger or threatening situations could not hinder the work. At this point, Jesus found himself to be on a timetable, or schedule. He was concerned that certain work that required His presence was carried out. "For night cometh, when no man can work."

Many things in life take precedence or priority over other things by virtue of the lone fact that they are present. Busy-ness is an enemy of things eternal. Impending, imminent things take precedence over important things because our shortsightedness, laziness, or lack of diligence has created an emergency. An emergency is defined as, a serious situation or occurrence that happens unexpectedly and demands immediate action.[168]

Most of our tired lives are lived from one emergency to another, but it need not be that way. We take on too many things. We do not finish what we start. We do not count the cost of projects and endeavors beforehand and we wrap ourselves tightly in our time and finances and social obligations. Living from one emergency to another, we never find time to deal with important issues. How else could we ignore eternal life? How else could we put off fellowship with Christ? How could we be so inconsiderate of our neighbor?

You are driving down a highway and all is well. The traffic is unusually light today and the weather is nice. Suddenly you notice in your rear view mirror a crazy driver weaving in and out of traffic. You see that he is gaining speed and heading your way, so you decide to pull over. As you negotiate an opening in the traffic on your right, a blaze goes by your left, cuts right in front of your fender and weaves its way through the traffic in front of you and is soon out of sight. "WOW! What was that? That crazy driver could have killed someone!"

---

[168] Excerpted from *The American Heritage® Dictionary of the English Language, Third Edition* © 1996 by Houghton Mifflin Company. All rights reserved.

We have nothing good to say about someone who has no consideration for others or their life or property and sets their concerns above everyone else's. As you get further down the road you see that it was a paramedic on His way to work and had obviously heard on his radio about an accident just two miles from where he was. He rushed to the scene and saved a life. All is well, all is forgiven. The man, who was labeled a lunatic just moments before, is now a hometown hero.

What excused all of the lack of concern for person and property? What excused the reckless driving and jeopardy of life and limb? An emergency. Just an emergency and all is forgiven.

What a Great Excuse!

We subconsciously create our excuses for failure to deal with important issues and things eternal by "creating" emergencies in our life. Who of us has not been secretly pleased when a situation that was "out of our control" provided a perfect excuse not to deal with something or someone unpleasant?

Those who live from emergency to emergency could very well be in a situation of their own making and design. It provides excuses for failure, slothfulness, sickness, injury, lack of concern, lack of finances and ineffectiveness. Nearly all of the undesirable and selfish motives in the heart of man can be excused, and in some cases even praised, due to emergencies.

The worst effect, and indeed the most costly, is the effect this kind of living has on the soul. If a man or woman never deals with the eternal verities, the imminent return of Christ, the judgment of their lives by God, simply because they are too busy, they have let their self-woven web of "emergencies" cost them eternal life. Are there not only twelve hours in a day? If certain work must be done in the day, and it MUST be done, and there are only twelve hours of daylight. Could we not therefore reason that some things are more important than even our emergencies?

We must not live our lives only doing what we have to do; we should live our lives doing what is right. Our stomachs are in knots and our blood pressure is up. Our finances are irreparable and our children are strangers to us and we will gladly deal with all of these problems as soon as our present emergency is over. What a pity! For we know that as soon as this present problem is solved another will take its place.

Satan will take opportunity here. We will eventually use up all of our years chasing an ideal, avoiding things eternal, trying to become, trying to attain, and forsake the really important matters. We welcome any diversion, any interruption that takes us away from the judgment we feel in silence. If we seek stillness, devoid of emergencies, we will find our life spent, having never done anything worthwhile. What makes matters worse is that in doing so we rob ourselves of the pleasures with which our God wants to reward us. We are too busy to stop to receive instruction of the Lord OR His blessings.

C.S. Lewis, in his <u>Screwtape Letters</u>,[169] proposes such a scenario when he wrote, (Screwtape speaking of one of Wormwood's patients) *"You can keep him up late at night, not roistering, but staring at a dead fire in cold room. All the healthy and outgoing activities which we want him to avoid can be inhibited and nothing given in return, so that he may say as one of my patients said upon his arrival down here [in hell], 'I now see that I spent most of my life in doing neither what I ought nor what I liked.'"*

Are there not only twelve hours in a day? We must work while it is day, for night cometh when no man can work. You must prioritize properly and not discount the eternal as though it is in the far future. The stress under which you place yourself shortens your time here and makes the day you put off and ignore even closer than you realize. It is not that there is little time or much time, a good time or a bad time, it is that there is only a certain amount of time. You must live as though the statement is true, "night cometh – when no man can work." Soon there will be none. You must work while it is day ... "Are there not only twelve hours in a day?"

---

[169] The Screwtape Letters – C. S. Lewis Copyright Simon and Schuster, New York. (A book putting forth a fictional scenario of a senior devil teaching a junior devil the finer points on how to ruin his "patient's" life.)

IV Last Days

"A man who was completely innocent, offered himself as a sacrifice for the good of others, including his enemies, and became the ransom of the world. It was a perfect act."

Mohandas K. Gandhi
(1869–1948), Indian political and spiritual leader. Non-Violence in Peace and War, vol. 2, ch. 166 (1949), referring to Jesus.

104. What think ye?

Matthew 21:28, "But what think ye? A certain man had two sons; and he came to the first, and said, Son, go work to day in my vineyard."

There are many errors in man's thinking when it comes to doctrine, apologetics, and theology. We have taken simple Christianity and created a maze of hermeneutics, ontology, exegesis (and six other words we cannot use in a sentence). We have made a philosophy out of a lifestyle, and a lifestyle of philosophy.

We would greatly improve our own understanding (not to mention pertinence and effectiveness in the world) if we brought our "knowledge" back down to a ground level "knowing" and not this "painted on," or "crammed in" type, that is necessary to pass muster as an "educated" Christian. Many do not realize that education's true definition is to draw out, or to bring out from within.[170] Today we put knowledge into a student, or attempt to paint it onto him, but true education is to bring out what is known from within.

Jesus was continually using this "drawing out" method when He taught. He would ask, "What do you think," and then He would tell a story. Knowing what was in man, namely, the light that lighteth every man that cometh into the world, He knew that it was enough (if unhindered by "isms" and "ologies") to bring us to a right knowing, a ground of being, or soundness.

We all know within us what makes solid sense, what is right, what is good, what is evil or what is illogical, or what is nonsensical, against nature and false. In some these senses are more developed than others, and they are masked or hindered more so in some than in others. Some people have ignored their conscience so long that it is virtually silent on small infractions and barely speaks above a whisper even when a soul is in danger of eternal punishment. But all of us have it and, if heeded, it will bring us to our eternal home. If ignored, it will remain silent until the day we stand before the Judge of all the Earth, and then it will speak loudly to condemn us and render us without an excuse.[171]

Sometimes, when we hear doctrines or ideas about God or the Bible, we "know" within ourselves that they are nonsense or at least severely flawed. If we raise the question of their validity or ask for clarification we are lambasted with a flurry of pet answers, trite sayings, clichés, using words of no clear definition.

---

[170] From *educere* -- Latin to draw forth

[171] Romans 1:18-32, "For the wrath of God is revealed from heaven against all ungodliness and unrighteousness of men, who hold the truth in unrighteousness; Because that which may be known of God is manifest in them; for God hath shewed it unto them. For the invisible things of him from the creation of the world are clearly seen, being understood by the things that are made, even his eternal power and Godhead; so that they are without excuse: Because that, when they knew God, they glorified him not as God, neither were thankful; but became vain in their imaginations, and their foolish heart was darkened. Professing themselves to be wise, they became fools..."

The seeker is made to feel that "everyone in the world understands this but he alone." With this kind of pressure we succumb and concede that we must be mistaken or ignorant, or perhaps we lack education. It is even suggested that we may be rebellious, and possess a "bad spirit." Adjectives like boat-rocker are bandied and we, in shame, give up and fall in line, choosing rather to be a team-player.

It behooves us to hold to the understanding we find within ourselves. It would benefit us to use the Guide that God put within us to understand rather than quiet God's voice and turn up the volume of education. When we succumb to the masses, we quiet that voice, the only true Guide that we have. How dangerous it is to ignore our Guide!

Flight Lessons Are Not Faith Lessons

As an instrument pilot, I learned to forget how I feel and "believe the instruments" to arrive safely. As a Christian I have learned to forget the instructors and believe my internal Guidance. We all should exercise this gift and learn from God. The Scripture speaks to this. The mark of the New Covenant Christian will be that he will not need a teacher to bring him along but will "know" within.

Jeremiah 31:31-34, "Behold, the days come, saith the LORD, that I will make a new covenant with the house of Israel, and with the house of Judah: ... I will put my law in their inward parts, and write it in their hearts; and will be their God, and they shall be my people. And they shall teach no more every man his neighbour, and every man his brother, saying, Know the LORD: for they shall all know me, from the least of them unto the greatest of them, saith the LORD: for I will forgive their iniquity, and I will remember their sin no more."

We rejoice that the forgiveness of sin was a part of this but we need to read again, "they all shall know me."

You can easily find good examples of Christians rejecting false doctrines -- simply go to any church and listen to the questions of the average Christian. Many are plagued with understanding the Trinity, the inerrancy of Scripture and doctrines of predestination, election, and foreordination. There are disputes about the (so-called) Sacraments, church membership, and what the essentials for salvation are. God's requirements of holiness, and "once saved always saved" doctrines are ever disputed. And these arguments go all the way back to the origin of the doctrines themselves. Why? Because the truly regenerate Christian rejects these man-made doctrines in the very core of his being. Within us we develop spiritual indigestion by swallowing these man-made doctrines and our teachers constantly have to pass out "medications" to alleviate the symptoms. The cause (the spoiled spiritual meat) is ignored.

If you want to find a false doctrine, look for the ones that are preached and taught constantly. They need to be taught over and over because they are regurgitated by the Spirit in man and must be re-introduced and ingested weekly.

The people of Christ's day had their own "once saved always saved" idea going. They assumed that because they were the children of Abraham that they were surely a part of the Kingdom of God. Jesus caught them off guard by telling them a story and simply asking their opinion of right and wrong. He did not ask them if they expected to be included in the Kingdom to come, He asked them to judge this story with the light He knew was in them.

"But what think ye? A certain man had two sons; and he came to the first, and said, Son, go work to day in my vineyard. He answered and said, I will not: but afterward he repented, and went. And he came to the second, and said likewise. And he answered and said, I go, sir: and went not. Whether of them twain did the will of his father? They say unto him, The first." (Matthew 21:28-31)

It becomes clear that, when they answered according to what they were *taught* or answered according to what they *knew within* there were two different outcomes to the same story.

When you hear doctrines that are hard to swallow, doctrines that go against the very Spirit within you, you need to listen to the Spirit within.

If they are too illogical, too ridiculous, if it requires that you make concessions in your character or in your logic to believe these doctrines, they are better rejected until the Spirit of God reveals them to you as true or false. You need to be practical and use your innate ability to reason. It is your gift from God. Believe it or not, you have the ability to understand. So… "What think ye?"

105. Did ye never read in the Scriptures?

Matthew 21:16, "And said unto him, Hearest thou what these say? And Jesus saith unto them, Yea; have ye never read, Out of the mouth of babes and sucklings thou hast perfected praise?"

Matthew 21:42, "Jesus saith unto them, Did ye never read in the scriptures, The stone which the builders rejected, the same is become the head of the corner: this is the Lord's doing, and it is marvellous in our eyes?"

Our Lord's question here asks more than is written. If we listen with the Spirit, we can hear more than we read. Here are two examples of the same question. "Did you never read in the Scriptures?" He is trying to call to our remembrance a text, a prophecy, a parallel, or metaphor. It is as though recalling it in our memory will create a resultant connection.

This is the way that prophecy is supposed to be interpreted. The common way it was done then (and is done yet today) is based in our morbid human fascination for future (fortune) telling. (Not much different than tarot cards or crystal balls.) These folks already had in mind an idea of Messiah that Jesus had to dispel before room in their understanding could be made for Truth. What is occupying the place of truth in your heart? Perhaps the true understanding of prophecy cannot be realized until a false one is removed.

Jesus did these people a great favor by giving them insight into their error of Scriptural interpretation. We should appreciate that He gave us these examples of their omissions and misinterpretations to show us the possibility of such occurrences in our thinking.

The church in our world has such errors in their interpretations as well. Not that certain examples may be pointed out in this writing, or any other, it just stands to reason that where cloudy prophecy and selfish men meet, there will be error. Men are constantly citing and repeating Scripture to prove a point, make a case, justify their doctrine, or vilify another's. When asked questions about future events or things they do not know, they speculate by interpreting and applying some vague prophecy. In so doing, hoops and hurdles, if you will, are set up for the future events to jump through and over to prove it is a fulfillment of the prophecy. True prophecy and fulfillments overcome such foolishness.

The Pharisees and their following were convinced that this man (Christ) could not be who He claimed to be, simply because He did not fulfill their understanding of who Messiah would be. Even today the second coming has a whole set of hoops and hurdles in its path that modern theology has set out for the returning Christ. The Day of the Lord is not even "allowed" to come until a list of prophecies laid out for it is fulfilled to the satisfaction of some theologian. We can hear said, "Judgment cannot come today because (such and such) prophecy has not been fulfilled." Or they may have even several criteria set up in their mind that HAS to happen first, and so on. An early example of this occurs in John 7:27, the Pharisees said that He could not be Christ because they knew where He came from... "Howbeit we know this man whence he is: but when Christ cometh, no man knoweth whence he is." Jesus, frustrated, cries out, "Ye both know me, and ye know whence I am: [it is my Father] whom ye know not."

Anyone can see the danger in this kind of thinking. If Jesus Christ does to the modern theologians what He did to those in the past, His coming may not be anything like we expect...AT ALL! But when it does come, it will PERFECTLY fulfill ALL prophecies. Not one jot or tittle[172] will lack or be left over unfulfilled. What would the modern church do if the return of Christ was not as we have been taught? They of old were not expecting a baby in a manger, though it fulfilled every prophecy perfectly. His coming could be (and probably will be) TOTALLY different that we are expecting. And He could ask, as we puzzle over how all these things happened without our prior knowledge, "Did ye never read in the Scriptures..."

The Pharisees had, in their mind, a course of events, an agenda, a lineage of ancestry, and a conduct that the Messiah would fulfill. They were in the Christ's own presence and did not know it. When they became aware of it, by signs and wonders and irrefutable prophecy, they refused to accept it because their preconceived ideas held greater sway than did even their own internal witness of the heart.

How Can These Things Be?

Nicodemus was a great example of a religious man struggling with his heart telling him one thing while his religion was saying another. He visited under cover of darkness and intended to plead with Christ to help him accept His teachings without destroying his position in the synagogue. (John 3) Jesus quickly cut to the heart of the matter. He offered him no hope of continuing as he was presently by telling him that he has to start over again – from the beginning. He must be born again. We can hear in the Pharisee's answer, the desperation of a man about to lose his status as a "teacher of all Israel." "Nicodemus answered and said unto him, 'How can these things be?'" (John 3:9)

There will come a time that those who are sure of their prophetic understanding, and those who have the future all mapped for us, that they will cry out, "How can these things be?" Consider, how many times and dates have been set? How many books have been written? How many names have been given as antichrist's name? How many more will be? We all (those who tell as well as those who listen) have improperly used prophecy.

"Why are prophecies given then," you may ask, "How should they be utilized?" Prophecies should be read, learned and known, perhaps even memorized, so that when they are fulfilled the prophecy confirms that

_____

172

fulfillment and helps us to recognize it as such at the moment they occur. They are not given to predict the future, neither to cause panic or repentance. They are certainly not to stimulate the already overdeveloped fascination with future events or to sell such books or seminars. Their unique quality is that they are signposts in the road ahead of us that are visible from where we are. You can see them in your future and although they are fuzzy to read from a distance, as you approach they come more and more into focus and as you pass them by they enlighten and inform and guide and identify.

The problem of Scripture familiarity presents itself. Are you as familiar with the Bible as you could be? ...or should be? It should alarm you when you hear unfamiliar passages of Scripture read. Whether Old Testament, New Testament, Apocrypha or the Dead Sea scrolls, you should be aware of what was revealed and written in the past by those who worshiped and served our God YHVH and His Son Joshua Messiah.

One day this doubting, this "seeing through a glass darkly" will come to an end. One day you will see all things clearly, but until then you must search diligently the Scriptures. One day, when the eternal plan is revealed, you may ask, "how did all this avoid my understanding? Why was I caught off guard? How did this happen?" Or, "Why was not this prophesied?" Think of the shame you may feel when Christ asks you, "Did you never read in the Scriptures...?"

106. Which is greater, our gold and gifts or the Temple and its altar?

Matthew 23:17-19, "Ye fools and blind: for whether is greater, the gold, or the temple that sanctifieth the gold?... the gift, or the altar that sanctifieth the gift?"

It is a shame when we find clear doctrines or principles in the Scriptures that have eluded the repertoire of our teachers. Such is the principle of the Temple.

Exodus 25:8 gives a concise and clear reason for the creation of the first Temple (the Tabernacle),

"And let them make me a sanctuary; that I may dwell among them."

God's desire was to live among us, but He could not because of our sinful state. He decided to build a sanctuary, a sanctified place, a place set apart, so that He might live there. Upon approaching, there was a wall of curtains that surrounded the Tabernacle. Inside was a holy area and further in was the Holiest of Holies the very place where God met with the Priest. Many priests would do the work in the holy place but only one High Priest could enter the Holiest of Holies.

"Know ye not that ye are the temple of God, and that the Spirit of God dwelleth in you?"[173] It takes little imagination to transfer this structure onto the New Covenant believer's heart. The Temple of today and eternity[174] is clearly the objective God had in mind when He designed the first Tabernacle.

The fact that the inside of the Tabernacle was not in plain view, but obstructed by curtains, and later, walls, illustrates that it may not be entered by whimsy or capriciously. It must be entered purposefully and with effort. That none but the High Priest may enter the Holiest of Holies shows the ministry of Christ as our High Priest, "...we have a great high priest... Jesus the Son of God..." (Hebrews 4:14) The parallels are many and wondrously deep and meaningful. As you would place mirror to mirror and see endless depths, you will gain, (if you open the Scriptures, and God graciously opens them to you) the understanding that the roughly constructed Tabernacle in the wilderness, the Tent of Meeting in the Camps of Israel, and the glorious Temple of Solomon were all planned and constructed in anticipation of the Temple in human flesh. God with us. The story is an interesting one that covers thousands of years and because the plan was conceived in the heart of God, its breadth is yet untold and its depths are past finding out.

---

[173] Ref. 1 Corinthians 3:16 – 1 Corinthians 6:19, "What? know ye not that your body is the temple of the Holy Ghost which is in you...?"

[174] Revelation 21:3, "...Behold, the tabernacle of God is with men, and he will dwell with them, and they shall be his people, and God himself shall be with them, and be their God."

Alas, Man Muddles The Plan.

Man seemingly said to himself, "Surely there is something in all this I can worship other than God. Ah yes, I can worship the building itself; I can add my work to God's, or I can honor the gifts I bring. I can fascinate myself with the price of all these things; surely I can worship something *other* than God."

Maybe man was not so blatant about his intentions, but it seems that every time there is some beautiful aspect of the plan of redemption, man enters and pollutes it somehow.

The cross has great significance in the life of many Christians; yet, because man has reduced it to symbolism, its true meaning and the revelation of that meaning have been lost and made difficult. It has become a symbol of God Himself, a symbol of holiness, a piece of jewelry to hang around someone's neck, a bumper sticker, or a sign in a churchyard. Because we have attached the cross to everything we consider holy we must suffer seeing it used and abused by the fakes and phonies, we must see it used by the charlatans as they lead away many in error, all led under a banner bearing the symbol we propagate as a symbol of God.

We see it on the literature of the cults and on the doors of the palm readers. It is attached to merchandise and used to exorcise demons in movies. In the newspaper it is scrawled by the insane on the walls of the burned and bombed and burglarized. Finally it is blazoned across national TV as a tattoo in the forehead of Charles Manson.

We need not mourn; we have reaped what we have sowed. True Christians have no business playing with signs and symbols. We should reject them on the grounds of idolatry and only do what we are commanded to do conceding that God knows best what we need to make our lives rich and keep us safe from harm, both physically and Spiritually. Have we been commanded to take to ourselves any symbol? Have we been told to take up the sign of the crucifixion or rather take to ourselves crucifixion itself? Does the word "Nehushtan" mean anything to you?

Man has always gone after rocks and stones, wood and glass, gold and silver, to worship in the place of the invisible God. Our history tells a condemning account of our propensity for signs, symbols, and idols. In the days of Moses, the people murmured against the Lord and therefore He sent among them "fiery serpents." Many died from the bites, so God told Moses to make a brazen serpent to cure the bites. Numbers 21:9, "And Moses made a serpent of brass, and put it upon a pole, and it came to pass, that if a serpent had bitten any man, when he beheld the serpent of brass, he lived."

This is great story of forgiveness, grace, and redemption. A story that even Jesus cited as an example of His own ministry and fate upon a pale.[175] How will man pollute this wonderful act of God? We read in 2 Kings 18:4 that Hezekiah was ridding the land of idols and cutting down the groves where men

---

[175] John 3:14, "And as Moses lifted up the serpent in the wilderness, even so must the Son of man be lifted up:"

worshiped Baal and he "brake in pieces the brasen serpent that Moses had made: for unto those days the children of Israel did burn incense to it: and he called it Nehushtan."

The people worshiped the brass serpent on the pole. Instead of worshiping the God whose power saved them, they attached themselves and their affection to the instrument used by God. Which would you say is greater the pole and serpent, or the God who empowers them? Man appears pitiful and nearly hopeless in this area for he never seems to learn.

History Repeats

We have not come very far from our ancestors. We now have hundreds of signs, symbols, "holy" objects, "holy" places, and even "holy" people. We set things apart (sanctify them) from the ordinary and would argue that we do not worship these things and people, but admit that we do consider them to be different than the rest. Great care needs to be taken here. When we do this, we walk along the border of idolatry. The I CON is squarely between the I AM and the I DOL. We are now on a spiritual journey. When we find our worship attaching to the tangible elements of this world we are moving away from God and toward carnality, spiritualism, witchcraft, sensuality, idolatry, man and icon-centered worship.

The Temple of God has moved into the unreachable heart of man. No longer can we feel and touch the instruments of worship; they are to be handled only by our High Priest, Christ Jesus. Outward signs, symbols, and places are to be esteemed as valuable only as their intrinsic value allows and not a bit more.

Many of our ideas of crosses[176] and icons are flawed by paganism and selectively remembered history; our ritual ceremonies are influenced by sinful and selfish men. None of these signs, symbols, or ceremonies, were ordained by God. Did Christ command us to wear crosses, place portraits or statues of Christ in our home, put plastic fish on our cars, or call our buildings "Houses of God?" Who told us to advertise we are Christians by printing crosses on our stationery or business cards? Do the Scriptures advise us to treat our Bibles as if they were intrinsically different than any other book? These are Nehushtan.

The inordinate attention given to these things is superimposing power or holiness to objects that rot and decay. We are to worship God, not things. These temporal and tangible things can be a trap to capture the attention, worship, respect, and fear that is due to God alone. They are Nehushtan.

The "cross" was only a wooden pole, not a symbol of worship. Our places of worship are nothing more than real estate; the residence of the Holy Spirit of God is wherever obedient Christians happen to be. The Holy Spirit is in the unreachable heart of man.

We cannot point a finger at others. It seems that none of us are clean in this matter. We all have our Nehushtan. If it is not YHVH, there is little

---

[176] It is well known that the word "cross" in the Bible is more perfectly translated "stake." It is far more likely that Christ was nailed, hands over head, to a singular, vertical torture stake.

difference what we worship. Protestants condemn Catholics for feeling toward statues or icons the way the Protestants feel toward their Bibles and steeplehouses![177] The objects we bring into worship, (the gold and gifts) the part that is tangible, must be left out completely if we are to be safe from idolatry. You have a Temple not made with hands[178] in which you can worship and meet with your God.

The gold and gifts made and brought to an external alter are nothing. Your Spiritual Temple is tended by Christ within you. Your life is given upon the altar within and your High Priest, Christ Jesus accepts it from you.

With all these facts in mind, Christ's question carries yet more weight, "Which is greater, the gold and gifts or the Temple and its altar?"

---

[177] A descriptive term for church buildings used by early Quakers. It was distasteful to call a building "Church."

[178] 2 Corinthians 5:1, "… we have a building of God…not made with hands…in the heavens."
Hebrews 9:11, "But Christ being come an high priest …by a greater and more perfect tabernacle, not made with hands…"

107. How can you escape damnation?

Matthew 23:33, "Ye serpents, ye generation of vipers, how can ye escape the damnation of hell?"

When the Savior asks, "How can you escape the damnation of Hell?" the question wreaks of hopelessness and despair. It is as if all means of help and hope are exhausted and damnation awaits inevitably.

The Pharisees bear a bad reputation, mainly because of the stories contained in the New Testament. If we had lived in the days of Christ and considered ourselves as decent and upright persons who sought good and peace, we probably would have sided with these men of dedication and religion rather than with the 13 zealot upstarts from Galilee. Their notoriety was that they roamed the countryside preaching about how wrong it was to strive for the righteousness of these good Pharisees and how it is wrong to give alms publicly and pray in the streets as the Pharisees did.

To the average Jew, the Pharisees were a sect of devout men who loved God and knew His Scriptures. The scribes, so often chided by Jesus, were simply men dedicated to copy the Scriptures correctly so that His written word would be available to more people and later generations. We owe our own Bibles to some of the men who Jesus condemned and criticized!

The Sadducees were also a sect of religious men who only had a different slant on theology and politics. They believed it was okay to involve oneself with the political structure and were left in charge of, or at least had some authority during the Roman occupation. But these were all men of dedication, men due respect by anyone's standards, anyone, that is, except Christ's.

We need not think that we would be a friend of Christ if we lived in His day. As a matter of fact, many of us have been blessed not to live in the days of Christ as we would likely have been in the crowd that cried, "Crucify Him!" Is this hard to believe? Can you believe there were people in the crowd that day that had been at one time blessed by the teaching and preaching of Christ?

I believe there were people there who were part of the thousands who were fed from the five loaves and two fishes. No doubt there were folks there who were cured of leprosy from the touch of this man of Galilee, and I even suppose there were in the crowd that day some of the seventy ministers sent forth by Jesus Himself with power to heal and cast out devils, who now scream out, "Crucify Him!" Just days before, those who cried "Hosanna" are now among these minions of the Sanhedrin crying out, "Give us Barabbas!"[179] I do not know that if I had been there in those days that I would have gone against all I ever knew to be right and just and holy and pious and followed a man who taught against everything my father and his father and his father before him

---

[179] Mark 15:11, "But the chief priests moved the people, that he should rather release Barabbas unto them."

believed. I doubt I would have followed a man who opposed the only "Church" I'd ever known. A man who no one stood beside and declared, "I am with Him!" Not even His own disciples came alongside to declare their allegiance! I must admit I, too, may have joined my voice with the angry crowd and said, "Crucify Him."

We Face The Same Dilemma Today.

As in those days, we now are part of a huge "church" (or at least a religious framework) and when someone declares something to be true that Mom and Pop did not believe... well, that has to be heresy! After all, could someone come against church tradition and be right? Could someone say that the whole church is wrong? Yes, someone could, but they would likely stand alone as Jesus did.

Is there a difference in the Pharisee of Capernaum and the pastor of the First Whatever Church downtown USA? Is there a difference in the seminary student of today and the scribe of yesteryear? Perhaps a better question is, are there any similarities in the religion of today and the religion of Jesus' day?

Really, not much has changed. As in those days, Jesus still condemns hypocrisy, unrighteous living, condemnation of our fellow man, outward practices that replace inward experiences, signs, symbols and traditions.

Whether in the days of the Pharisees or in the 21st century, these practices are wrong. The hypocrisy of a pastor is as repulsive as any Pharisee that plotted the death of Christ. Our suits and dresses, hats and ties have become as the phylacteries and broad borders. The gold and silver steeples that loom over the doors of expensive churches are as near a cause for the Saviors tears as the Temple of Herod ever was.

We are guilty of the same errors as our predecessors. We have made temples to worship in and forgotten the Temple of the heart. We have dressed the outside of ourselves and left the inside to rot and ruin and decay. We have turned our Spiritual well-being over to pastors and teachers and turned away from the voice of Christ within. How shall we escape damnation?

Jesus could see the problem was not so much what they were doing, as it was that they were so caught and entangled in why they were doing it. It was tradition. It was their way of life. It was the way they always did it. It was the way their father and mother did it... it was NORMAL! This is why He said, "How can ye escape the damnation of hell?" Our chances are slim, our likelihood of turning around and walking a different direction than the way of our ancestors is remote. The pressure of family, of friends, of political influences, and of our culture, is so strong we may never escape. How can we?

If you follow Christ you will likely be given a road that is divergent to the familiar one. Christ often calls for a difference to be made. Whether it is that you no longer frequent the same parties as your old friends do[180] or that

---

[180] 1 Peter 4:3-4, "For the time past of our life may suffice us to have wrought the will of the Gentiles, when we walked in lasciviousness, lusts, excess of wine, revellings, banquetings, and abominable idolatries: Wherein they think it strange that ye run not with them to the same excess of riot, speaking evil of you:"

Christ compels you to dress differently[181] or that your schedule of importance and priority changes drastically, you **_will_** suffer persecution. This must be taken in stride and overlooked as of little weight in your decisions for life.

We cannot give in to the pressure of family or friends. If we do, we become entangled and soon find ourselves managed by them. Religion, too, offers a family of sorts; a family that tolerates no changes toward betterment of ourselves if that betterment leaves the majority behind. The Pharisees loved the system, the benefits of being "somebody" and belonging to a reputable group. This is a trap that, once sprung, will hold your pride hostage and your ego for ransom.

The system we find today is the same as that in Jesus' day. Once we are in the system, and the system is in us, we can scarcely find our way out. The trouble is, that system itself is a false god, an idol, a condemned and corrupt replica of the Grace, the power of God, which is given to us inwardly.

If we do not reject the system, it will take us to a point of no return, and our own pride will hold us there. As the Pharisees would not change for "fear of the people," we often reject change as soon as it is discovered that the change will cost us our reputation, or that we may have to stand alone. The operation of our deliverance by Christ is much like breaking someone out of a prison that they do not want to leave. Listen as the Lord pleads.

Isaiah 30:15, "...In returning and rest shall ye be saved; in quietness and in confidence shall be your strength: and ye would not."

Matthew 23:37, Luke 13:34,"O Jerusalem, Jerusalem... how often would I have gathered thy children together, even as a hen gathereth her chickens under her wings, and ye would not!"

The Pharisees *would* not... and *would* not...they finally found that they **could** not. Jesus asks them, "How *can* you escape the damnation of Hell?"

---

[181] 1 Peter 3:3-4, "Whose adorning let it not be that outward adorning of plaiting the hair, and of wearing of gold, or of putting on of apparel; But let it be the hidden man of the heart, in that which is not corruptible, even the ornament of a meek and quiet spirit, which is in the sight of God of great price."

108. *Which of you convinceth me of sin?*

John 8:46, "Which of you convinceth me of sin?

Why did Jesus think that the people of His day did not believe Him? When He warned them, they feared as if it were so. When He blessed them they felt comfort as if it were so, and when He pointed out their impending condemnation they were troubled as if what He said were true to the letter. Why then did He think that they did not believe Him?

The faith, for which Jesus searched the hearts of the people to find, was a faith in who He was. Many who heard Him believed that what He said was true. His logic was impeccable. His stories were compelling and informative, and His delivery was with authority. But, as many today, they did not believe He was who He said He was. They thought he was a very intelligent man, but not the Son of God. Or perhaps He was a very holy man, but they could not believe He was the Messiah. They could not believe He was who He said He was.

WE must also believe He was who He said He was to claim a true faith in Christ. We cannot claim to believe on Him without believing He was indeed the very Son of God, the Messiah. We cannot accept His words if we do not accept the source. The authority of the source is crucial to the authority of the statement.

We may adopt Christ's sayings as our own and live by them and we could say that we are better for doing so (thereby glorifying our own accomplishment) but if we believe that they are indeed the words of God, our actions become mere obedience and the glory becomes God's own. Yes, the source of authority is critical, as we may be willing to act in certain ways, fulfill certain expectations, even deny ourselves certain things as long as it is OUR own course we follow.

We may psychologically or mentally remove His authority over us by equating Him with ourselves. This is done by raising ourselves to His level (the divinity of man) or by lowering Him to ours (the humanity of Christ). This equalization enfeebles the authority of Christ, yet allows us to "believe" in Him. Then we my find ourselves declining His will, even though we may be acting very "Christian." We are following our own will, and though it is very similar to His – it is definitely *ours*, for we have never surrendered to Him as Messiah. We do not believe He is who He said He was. Our actions may be the same as the most obedient Christian, but we balk at His commands and buck His authority. We need to examine our own understanding of Christ.

Is He Who He Claims To Be?

In Matthew 21:33 we read a story of a man who left his vineyard in the hand of men who despised and killed his son. Note that when the husbandman left, the work continued but under another's command. The work did not change, the authority did. Just because a task looks like it fulfills the orders of the boss, does not mean it is done under his authority.

These men continued to grow grapes and harvest them, all the while despising the owner of the ground upon which they toiled. Though our life, work, and even our ministry may resemble the work, and fulfill the orders of our superior, it does not confirm our allegiance to Him. Many men work, and perform well for a man they despise. Do we believe that Jesus is who He says He is?

Jesus asks a question to settle in the minds of people that He is who He says He is. He asks, "Which of you convinceth me of sin?" Today, as Christ is examined for authenticity it is commonly done by the crediting or discrediting His miracles. It is thought that, if we can prove He did miracles we may know He *is* whom He says He is, or if we can prove His miracles never occurred we can prove He was not Messiah.

This is not a test of authority. This is only a test of God's witness. God witnessed to Jesus' ministry by miracles just as He witnessed to the apostles ministry and to the prophets of old. These miracles at the hand of the prophets and apostles did not prove they were Messiahs; it showed God's hand in their work and thereby lent credence to the ministry and authority to their words as the word of God. The sign of Messiah was that He would never displease the Father in sin. Therefore He asks, "Which of you finds a sin in me?"

The sign of the Son of God is not miracles, but sinlessness. Jesus told His disciples that He and His Father were one. He said, that if they saw Him they saw the Father, and that it was not He that did the works that they saw, it was the Father. Jesus was so much a part of His Father that He lived and moved and had His being in the Father, rendering sin as only a moot possibility.

Many have tried, and as many have failed, to show Jesus a sinner. Though He has been accused of everything from being a Sabbath breaker by His contemporaries, to being a homosexual in the days in which we live, He has been vindicated by lack of evidence and bias motives on the part of His accusers.

In all cases, the motivation to expose Jesus as a sinner is merely to discover an excuse for the accuser by indicting the icon of all virtue. The inability to fix sin upon Christ means far more than just finding Him virtuous, or simply more righteous than we are. Its significance goes to His nature more than His will or resolve. It was His nature not to displease God. Sin was not a matter of decision for Him; it was not a struggle within as it is with us, but does that make Him less valuable as an example to us?

No, on the contrary, we have been offered that very nature. We can nurture the seed of Christ planted in us and grow up into Him with a natural desire to please God the Father as He had. His example was not that He was sinless, but that He suffered in spite of His sinlessness. And through that suffering we learn obedience. Does this seem far-fetched? Look at these Scriptures:

2 Peter 1:4, "Whereby are given unto us exceeding great and precious promises: that by these ye might be partakers of the divine nature, having escaped the corruption that is in the world through lust."

Ephesians 4:15, "But speaking the truth in love, may grow up into him in all things, which is the head, even Christ."

John 8:29, "... for I do always those things that please him [the Father]."

1 Peter 2:21, "For even hereunto were ye called: because Christ also suffered for us, leaving us an example, that ye should follow his steps:"

Hebrews 5:8, "Though he were a Son, yet learned he obedience by the things which he suffered..."

All this said we must, after we have found Christ to be sinless, face His next question, "And if I say the truth, why do ye not believe me?"

We must at this point believe or reject Christ; the middle ground is removed as an option. We can no longer consider His sayings acceptable to us, His ways useful, or His manner beneficial, and take it on as our own way as if they originated within us. If we recognize Him as Lord, the relationship must change as well.

He is no longer just a teacher with good ideas, or a philosopher with ideas that clarify life; He now, as Messiah, speaks for God and demands that we subject ourselves to him. With Jesus as your Messiah, you must now honor Him as your Lord, obey Him as your Master, relinquish your will to Him as your Savior, for He is who He claimed to be – Messiah, Son of God.

You must answer His questions, and surrender empty-handed when He asks, "Which of you convinceth me of sin?"

109. If I say the truth, why do ye not believe me?

John 8:46b, "...And if I say the truth, why do ye not believe me?"

The full impact of this discourse is to be understood by reading the entire context, verses 28 through 59. Jesus was assisting the Pharisees in discovering a fact about their Spiritual nature, bondage, family, truth, and about who can and cannot understand. All of which are discoveries that could reveal things about our loved ones and us and could prove to be very frightening.

For the first time these Pharisees were being told that they were not who they thought they were, that they were not from the family they claimed, that they were not even a free people but were slaves and servants to the kingdom of the damned. Wow, a lot to swallow in an afternoon!

He asked, "If I say the truth, why do you not believe me?" Let us examine this for a moment. Let us say that I told you something, reported a fact, expounded a doctrine, or denounced a doctrine held in high esteem, or made any statement at all, with which you did not agree, and, after I did this, you made it clear that you did not believe me. I say to you, "If I say the truth, why do you not believe me?" Would not your answer be something like, "But you have not told me the truth!" The argument becomes circular and unfruitful. If a person cannot see truth... they simply cannot see truth. So the question, "Why do you not believe me?" becomes a question of self-examination. That person must ask himself, "Why do I not believe Him?"

There is a story of a man in military service who wanted to be discharged under section eight. In order to prove that he qualified for this mentally incompetent status, he went around picking up pieces of paper. And after looking at each piece with a glazed look in his eyes, he promptly said, "That's not it!" and returned to frantically searching for his "imaginary" piece of paper. He pulled down posted bulletins, look at them, threw them aside and invariably said, "That's not it!" before moving on to find another. As his condition worsened he was brought to the infirmary, tested, and found indeed to be insane. Then the doctor handed him his recommendation for discharge and told him to take it to his commander. The man looked at the paper and said, "That's it!"

The life of the dedicated Christian eventually becomes a quest to find Truth, but will you know it when you see it? Is it possible to find something you have never encountered? I am convinced there are several kinds of persons that do not recognize Truth. There are those from whom the Father withholds understanding.[182] If these have no guide to lead them to Truth, how will they find it? Can they recognize that which they have never seen? Therefore the question, "...And if I say the truth, why do ye not believe me?" If a man does

---

[182] Matthew 13:11, "He answered and said unto them, Because it is given unto you to know the mysteries of the kingdom of heaven, but to them it is not given."

not believe the Truth when it is told him, could it be because he has no light, no guide, or as Jesus said, "He that is of God heareth God's words: ye therefore hear them not, because ye are not of God." (John 8:47) What horrible words to hear from the Savior of all mankind.

How much of a part does deception have here? It is hard to believe that a person is willingly deceived, but if God has given a man the ability to recognize Truth when he hears it, does it not follow that he will have to willingly ignore what he knows to be true in order to be deceived? Why would anyone do that? Unless it is to gain some advantage offered by the deception or the deceiver? This deception is subtle at first and later becomes a foundation upon which is built larger and larger error until the starting point of the diversion from Truth is difficult to discover.

Are you one who closes your eyes to truth? Are even the simple, everyday bits of reality difficult for you to accept? If you are prone to ignore reality, you may be going down a path of deception leading to your own destruction. One of the best questions you can ask yourself (if you are willing to answer honestly) is this: If what you believe is not correct, do you want to know it? Is your answer yes...or no? Which are you? Assuming your answer is "yes," How much do you want to know it – enough to continually test it by the Spirit within you, try it by the Scriptures, and examine it in the light of solid reason?

Just as there are those who ignore natural facts that are plain and obvious, there are also those who refuse to obey the truth that they clearly see. This may have been the case with some of the Pharisees. Often, it is not the "facts" that are resisted but the implications and consequences that they carry in their wake that cause them to be ignored. The Pharisees were frightened when they realized that the acceptation or condoning of the ideas that Jesus was purporting, would be detrimental and ultimately destructive to their religion. Oddly enough, as ridiculous as it may sound, many times even the Truth of God is rejected on *religious* grounds.

The Danger of Truth Rejection

The rejection of truth (any truth) leads to more deception. The next deception carries yet a heavier load of doubt (and subsequently fear) that mystifies the sufferer under its cruel reign. Sometimes the one who suffers with questions of "Why me, God?" or "Why do bad things happen to good people?" or someone who struggles with understanding the meaning of life may find in their past they have rejected truth and chosen rather to go their own way.

To erase this cloud of confusion, nothing short of repentance will suffice for such an act of rebellion. A faith that has its foundation in man's philosophy, judged and deemed worthy and true, based only on selfishness and how it may be found beneficial, easily becomes nothing more than a tangled web of deceit and tissue of lies that are of no comfort in the time of need. This kind of unsure stuttering, and unclear faith, (a faith that requires less than an honest inquirer to maintain the façade) is a far cry from the house on a rock promised to those who hear and obey the words of Christ.[183]

We must take great care to remain sensitive to the Spirit of God within us. It is so easy to let our inner life become outwardly controlled. We must receive our knowledge and inspiration from God alone. We must repel the idea to do things the easy, popular, or politically correct way and strive to hear the sweet voice of our God within us, the precious Holy Spirit of God, leading and encouraging and prompting us.

We must move with unction, anointing, and grace, rejecting that which satisfies us and our lusts; and when finished, only carries us farther from our Father. The words of Jesus: "Ye are of your father the devil, and the lusts of your father ye will do. ... I tell you the truth, ye believe me not... why do ye not believe me? Because ye are not of God, He that is of God heareth God's words." (John 8)

It would not take many minutes of meditation for a person well versed in the Scriptures to call to mind a saying of Jesus or a Commandment of His that is hard to ascribe to or obey. We must remember that He is Truth. When truth is rejected on any level, He is rejected as well. Why does anyone have difficulty with His sayings? Why do we not believe what He says? It would do us good to examine this question. Perhaps we have a long history of small disobediences. Maybe we never were able to really cross the threshold of submission to Christ as our boss, relinquishing all rule to Him.

Whatever the reason, if you wonder why you have resistance to Truth, or any repulsion toward the virtuous Commandments of Christ, or any rebellion to the clear and distinct written words of God, it is likely that you are lacking light, resisting light, or just trying to bend it to your will and understanding. Forget the smoke and mirrors. Just answer Jesus' question, "If I say the truth, why do ye not believe me?

---

[183] Matthew 7:24-25, "Therefore whosoever heareth these sayings of mine, and doeth them, I will liken him unto a wise man, which built his house upon a rock: And the rain descended, and the floods came, and the winds blew, and beat upon that house; and it fell not: for it was founded upon a rock."

110. Why trouble ye the woman?

Matthew 26:10, "When Jesus understood it, he said unto them, Why trouble ye the woman? for she hath wrought a good work upon me."

Mark 14:6, "And Jesus said, Let her alone; why trouble ye her? she hath wrought a good work on me."

It is said that the army of the Lord is the only one that shoots their own soldiers. The lines behind, shoot those in front. This commentary is well deserved. We do have a tendency to criticize and condemn each other, some on an impersonal level, speaking only in generalities and others more specifically, naming names, or inclusively indicting whole camps or denominations.

We all do this to one degree or another and we all should cease. Solid reproof is beneficial; however, a line should be drawn at personal revelation. Quakers excel at discerning the line over which a mentor (or critic) should not cross. The freedom found among Quakers to worship as led and to live as led is unparalleled in Christendom. Folks are free to find their own way and to "work out their own salvation."[184]

Personal revelation is a marvelous thing. Much like the rich young ruler that came to Jesus and asked, "What good thing must I do to inherit eternal life?" Jesus answered in general terms, as He would say to anyone who came to Him, "Keep the Commandments and you will enter into life." But the young man said to Him, "What lack I yet?" It was then that the Lord gave Him personal guidance that was to help him attain His personal goal, "Go and sell all that thee has and give it to the poor." Probably not what he wanted to hear, but none the less, a personal revelation. This is the point at which all who travel this road of salvaging one's own soul eventually arrives. There is a perfecting, a honing of our lives and a commitment that starts as a question like, "What do I lack?"

Let's pretend for a moment that he did not go away "sorrowful" but heeded the Lord's advice and obeyed. Can you hear the scuttlebutt in the barbershop and at the market? "There goes that man who was rich and gave away everything he had, and now begs." Can you hear the gossip at the dinner table? "Does he think that the town will feed him after he did such a foolish thing?" The conversations overheard at family gatherings would be contending that he has gone insane, cheated his children out of their inheritance, and brought reproach upon the family name. But the talk among those who follow Christ would be totally different. Their gossip would have a different tone. They, who know Christ, know also that Jesus spoke fondly of those who were unselfish and giving. They who know Jesus' doctrine reason, "Christ calls

---

[184] Philippians 2:12, "Wherefore, my beloved, as ye have always obeyed, not as in my presence only, but now much more in my absence, work out your own salvation with fear and trembling."

attention to those who give all they have and it need be only two mites![185] What must Jesus think of this man who gave away a fortune? He must be very pleased." Sadly, their next thought may be, "Does this upstart think that he is better than I am?"

And so it goes, the vitriol begins at church. The unregenerate can be depended upon to show fear, the family will show some selfish concern, but the religious will be bitter and judgmental if someone rises from the pack with a personal revelation (especially when followed by obedience and dedication.) Their motto being, "Do they think they're better than me?" Oh, they may not say it out loud, but that is their thought.

How many of us have taken on a job we were excited about and entered with enthusiasm only to be taken aside and told that we were making the old-timers look bad by working so hard? This is very similar, there are "climbers" in every field, and they all have a specific goal, to work less and be great.

Such was the situation at the house of Simon. On that day a woman (some believe to be Mary of Magdala) broke open the alabaster box of perfume to anoint the head of Jesus. The accusations started to fly. They thought the purposes for this sycophantic expression of feigned care and sorrow were outrageous! "What a waste this is!" they said. What they were really thinking was, "Why didn't I think of that?" or "Why am I not broken-hearted about His imminent death? Why should this woman gain such a place with the Savior? She is no better than I am."

Mary's personal revelation was a real one. She saw the upcoming event and felt deep sorrow in her heart. She had no proud ideas of being embarrassed. She thought no expense of ointment was too great. She cared not what anyone thought; she expressed her love and compassion for Christ by doing what she felt she must do. She knew that next week the oil in her box (worth likely a year's wages) would be worthless by comparison whenever her thoughts would inevitably turn to the death of her Savior and best friend.

Mary Was Compelled To Act

With fear and trembling she made her way to Him and broke the box over Him and massaged the oil into His hair. Jesus realized what she was doing as He, too, was thinking of nothing less that His upcoming passion. He knew that she was anointing Him for His death. Alas, He could not even enjoy the moment, for above the sensations and fragrance His mind was broken in upon by the murmuring of the disgruntled self-righteous as they made their accusations and proclamations of better uses for the oil. As she looks from the corners of her wet eyes and hears the murmurings, panic strikes through her. She wonders in fear whether she would be cast out, Jesus turns to them and asks with sorrow, "Why trouble ye the woman?"

---

[185] Mite: the very smallest bronze of copper coin (Luke 12:59; 21:2). Two mites made one quadrans, i.e., the fourth part of a Roman "as," which was in value nearly a halfpenny.

354

When we see someone working out their salvation with fear and trembling, when a child of God, grateful for Christ's forgiveness, realizes the ransom that was paid for him, what was forgiven and what was given in exchange, sells out, makes sacrifices, gives his all, should we stand in criticism?

Someone may choose to wear a certain hat or not wear one, wear their dress an unfashionable length or their hair in an unfashionable style. We may choose poverty, or fasting. We may give up meat in our diets, or choose to honor certain days. We do not know what was said to these whom, seeking perfection, asked their Savior, "What lack I yet?" We do not know the demands placed upon such a person by the Lord. We should not consider these who seek the Lord with more fervor or dedication, as a threat to us or feel ill will toward them, but rather honor them as living proof that Christ has come to teach His people Himself![186] We should be careful not to regard them as being foolish or unbalanced for simply doing what their Lord has told them to do.

The apostle Paul said,

"...Let not him that eateth despise him that eateth not; and let not him which eateth not judge him that eateth: for God hath received him. Who art thou that judgest another man's servant? ...One man esteemeth one day above another: another esteemeth every day alike. Let every man be fully persuaded in his own mind. He that regardeth the day, regardeth it unto the Lord; and he that regardeth not the day, to the Lord he doth not regard it. He that eateth, eateth to the Lord, for he giveth God thanks; and he that eateth not, to the Lord he eateth not, and giveth God thanks. For none of us liveth to himself, and no man dieth to himself... But why dost thou judge thy brother? or why dost thou set at nought thy brother? ...Let us not therefore judge one another any more: ... Let us therefore follow after the things which make for peace." (Romans 14:2-19)

No one wants to be guilty of troubling those who are following the path upon which God has placed them. It may not be your path, but if it is the same Guide, rest assured, it is the same destination. Perhaps you lack the vision for your own revelation. Therefore, jealousy may be a factor in your intolerance of those who seem to hear a different drummer. These are avenues of meditation you can consider when you hear Christ's question, "Why trouble ye the woman?"

---

[186] A revelation of George Fox, founder of the Religious Society of Friends (Quakers).

111. For which good work do ye stone me?

John 10:32, "Jesus answered them, Many good works have I shewed you from my Father; for which of those works do ye stone me?"

As you read through the New Testament you may run upon ideas or passages that stand out from the rest as axiomatic or key. Such a pivotal Truth will be found in all other stories, and as you continue to search, it becomes foundational. Such is the suffering of Christ. His passion was foretold as early as Genesis 3:15, and with few exceptions can be found in every Scripture dealing with sacrifice, atonement and redemption. It becomes apparent that Christ's sacrifice was an irreplaceable and necessary event, without which none of the plan of redemption is valid or viable.

With just a little reading, you will find another pivotal truth pertaining to our triumph in this world and beyond. There are those, while searching for this abundant life, seek power from God to surmount wickedness. There are some who feel that blessings of worldly goods will bring about every victory and there are those who feel that to be educationally or doctrinally capable will provide the elusive answers to life. While all of these things have merit within themselves we must admit that sadly, they are not within our control.

If a sharp mind is necessary to be spiritually victorious I fear for myself. I have great difficulty remembering Scripture references. I do not consider myself educationally equipped to ward off testing and temptation by quoting Scripture. Some people have great gaps in theology and doctrine yet seem to get along just fine in life, meeting every trial with faith, endurance, and humility. The power of God certainly is not within our ability to use at will, as is the case with His blessings of health, wealth, and prosperity. These are things He chooses to bestow or withhold. We need to know what we can do to effect our state while living here, and what is totally within our power to do.

Jesus went through the land doing good, but more importantly, He did NO sin. 2 Corinthians 5:21 shows us, "For he [Jesus]... knew no sin..." Some say that Jesus was compelled to go through life sinless in order to effect our salvation, but was fully capable of sin.

Some say that it was impossible for Him to sin because He was the Son of God. Though we have to wonder why Satan would bother to subject Him to temptation if it was *impossible* for Him to succumb. It is entirely likely that He did not labor through the temptation at all, just barely emerging victoriously, but happily preferred His father's will and favor over any offer of Satan. Yes, Jesus had a conscience toward God; He had another mission in life – to suffer wrongfully.

"For this is thankworthy, if a man for conscience toward God endure grief, suffering wrongfully. For what glory is it, if, when ye be buffeted for your faults, ye shall take it patiently? but if, when ye do well, and suffer for it, ye take it patiently, this is acceptable with God. For even hereunto were ye

356

called: because Christ also suffered for us, leaving us an example, that ye should follow his steps: Who did no sin, neither was guile [deceit] found in his mouth: Who, when he was reviled, reviled not again; when he suffered, he threatened not; but committed himself to him that judgeth righteously: Who his own self bare our sins in his own body on the tree, that we, being dead to sins, should live unto righteousness: by whose stripes ye were healed." (1 Peter 2:19-24)

In this Scripture we find that pivotal principle of endurance and triumph. In this remark by Peter, we find that we all will suffer, we all may be given up, turned in, persecuted, and treated shamefully, and, if the will of God be so, there is nothing that can be done about it. There is only one thing we can do to make it count on our behalf. We can make sure that when we do suffer, it is for no good reason. If we are brought before the council and harassed for violations we did not commit, actions we did not take, words we did not say, rules we did not break, we are likely suffering as Christians. But, if you *did* violate the rules, if you *did* lash out and revenge, if you *did* take violent actions against your enemy, you are suffering for your own wrongdoing. Do not deceive yourself by believing you are suffering as a Christian. You may indeed be suffering because you are a Christian, but the power of your testimony is lost because you are guilty of the charges brought against you.

What a waste! This is why we are to avoid sin and deceit. This is why we are to be harmless as doves. "For it is better, if the will of God be so, that ye suffer for well doing, than for evil doing." (1 Peter 3:17)

News from Death Row

It is believed that this epistle was written as Peter received the news of Paul's torture and subsequent death. Peter is giving us the secret to a happy and blessed life. On any scale, whether verbal persecution by a close friend or relative, or being burned at the stake as Polycarp was, we are to be blameless in our lives and never deserve any malice or ill treatment.

We are not to seek vengeance, retaliation, retribution, or reward. We are not to break any laws that can be obeyed in a good conscience toward God. We are not to speak evil against our enemies, leaders, or propagate stories that do so. We are to be blameless. With no deceit in anything we say, so that when we suffer (and we will) we will be blameless.

Pay your bills, obey the laws, do what you are asked, comply, subject yourself, humble yourself, pay your taxes, let yourself be defrauded, do not retaliate when lied to, stolen from or cheated, do no ill to your neighbor.

Let nothing be done through strife or vanity, but in lowliness of mind let each esteem others as better than themselves.[187] Love your enemies, bless them that curse you, do good to them that hate you, and pray for them which despitefully use you, and persecute you; That ye may be the children of your

---

[187] Philippians 2:3

Father which is in heaven.[188] Avoid legal wrangling, lawsuits, and arbitration. If someone must lose in a deal, let it be the one whose Father is YHVH. Forgive, forget, forego.

> *"And who is he that will harm you, if ye be followers of that which is good? But and if ye suffer for righteousness' sake, happy are ye: and be not afraid of their terror, neither be troubled; But sanctify the Lord God in your hearts: and be ready always to give an answer to every man that asketh you a reason of the hope that is in you with meekness and fear: Having a good conscience; that, whereas they speak evil of you, as of evildoers, they may be ashamed that falsely accuse your good conversation in Christ. For it is better, if the will of God be so, that ye suffer for well doing, than for evil doing." (1 Peter 3:13-17)*

Christ asked, "For which good work do you stone me?" There is only one reason why this question of Jesus had power – because the basis of His goodness was based in truth. Living above reproach – every day – is the only way to have such power in temptation and comfort in tribulation. The apostles found this power in their own martyr's deaths. Job found it his source of power in his temptation. You will find it too. This power is yours only if your life is truly above reproach – only if you indeed suffer wrongfully.

Think of the power, think of the convicting Spirit in the words said to accusers and persecutors, when you can look your oppressor in the eye and ask as Jesus did, "For which good work do ye stone me?"

---

[188] Matthew 5:44-45

112. Is it not written in your law, I said, Ye are gods?

John 10:34-36, "Jesus answered them, Is it not written in your law, I said, Ye are gods? If he called them gods, unto whom the word of God came, and the scripture cannot be broken; Say ye of him, whom the Father hath sanctified, and sent into the world, Thou blasphemest; because I said, I am the Son of God?"

Here is an occasion where the term "Word of God" is used in a manner inconsistent with conventional understanding of the words. As a matter of fact, nowhere does the term appear in Scripture consistent with conventional usage because ever since the reformation, men have incorrectly attached the name and title "Word of God" to a book that would be more properly referred to as the Scriptures.

The term "Word of God" above does not refer to the Bible, and for future reference, neither does any other. We must, before we attempt to discuss this dialogue in Scripture, settle to whom the appellation rightly belongs. For if we believe that it is a book to which this title should be rightly attached, the message is strained at best, and meaningless at worst. Jesus Christ is the Word of God; He always has been, according to our record, and always will be according to the same.

"In the beginning was the Word, and the Word was with God, and the Word was God." (John 1:1) For centuries past, the Lord has visited man and placed within him an understanding of God's way. This way is foreign yet familiar, unknown yet well known, an enigmatic paradox that makes sense of what we clearly see and do not understand. This understanding was communicated to man by words. Sometimes these words were to a lone man and sometimes the communication was for all people. The one who heard would then relay the words from God to the people. He would give words that make sense to some, providing comfort, but would sound foolish to others and cause rage. Whether they were mystery or medicine, ringing or ridiculous, these words were God's gift – God's plan – they were God's Word.

When we consider the ministry of the words of God that were given to man, it is hard to find any differences between them and the ministry of Jesus Christ. It is not a big leap to understand why He would be called "The Word of God."

God chose to take the form (or more perfectly no form) of words to minister to His people – to communicate to us His way. Ideas we were not capable of formulating were given to us and given authority by virtue of their source alone. With these ideas and their authority we become changed men, capable of righteous judgment and good deeds, vindicators of evil and pursuers of righteousness! The Word of God has come to us, empowering us, giving light and understanding, effecting judgment, and guiding us in a way that we did not know heretofore. We have been commissioned therefore, "Defend the poor and fatherless: do justice to the afflicted and needy. Deliver the poor and needy: rid them out of the hand of the wicked. ... I have said, Ye are gods; and all of you are children of the most High." (Psalms 82:3-6)

Us?...Gods?... Really?

In the above reference, from which Jesus quoted, we see that judgment was turned over to the people to bring about God's will in the earth. This particular Scripture is rebuking them for not doing what they were commissioned to do. Here, Jesus takes this Scripture and expands it, for He tells us more than what is written there. He tells us why God said, "Ye are gods." He said that they were considered gods "unto whom the word of God came." The Word given to us, as far as our God is concerned, makes us gods. The communicative power of God – the transmission of God's way to us – God with us, makes us gods. His truth communicated – His very life given to us makes us gods! ... "I have said, Ye are gods; and all of you are children of the most High."

Now before you go out and begin your own planet or start your own religion, there are some things to consider. All that we are, that is good and desirable, we were made to be, and although we may be *titular* "gods," in *reality* we fall far short of just being decent humans. What needs to be focused upon is the gift.

God gave the men of the Old Testament a wonderful gift when He visited them and spoke to them (whether through Moses or the Prophets or a jackass.) It is a wonderful thing when the creator of heaven and earth gives a word or two to help us along. He has longed for the days of walking with Adam in the cool of the day ever since that pleasure was deprived Him. He sent His Word to men to reestablish communications with His man ever since.

He sent words to Cain; He sent word by Noah, Abraham, and Moses. He put His word in tablets of stone, on scrolls, in the hearts and upon the tongues of prophets. He sent His word and by it He showed His way, His truth, and His life. He said that man should not live by bread alone, but by every word that proceeds out of the mouth of God. The word that proceeds from Him is the bread of life. He sent word after word after word. These formless words of God, these verbal pictures of the ideal, finally took on human form. The communicative power of God – His Word took the form of you and me through a young virgin girl named Mary. Words came to her from God proposing the plan of the salvation of all mankind, "And the Word was made flesh, and dwelt among us, (and we beheld his glory, the glory as of the only begotten of the Father) full of grace and truth." (John 1:14)

Has the Word of God come to you? By the question I do not ask if you have heard God speaking to you, but I ask has God communicated with you His plan, His way, His Son? Are you empowered with God's understanding of life here on earth? Do you know the Way, the Truth, and the Life? God's gift to the men of old was His word. It was ever considered a gift when the Lord spoke to His people.

Even in our day God's gift to us is His Word; no, not the book we all hear referred to as the "Word of God", but the Word of God in truth – Jesus Christ. Although the Scriptures are a wonderful gift, they cannot claim the glorious title of the "Word" nor interpose themselves into John 1, for they merely record the words that were a shadow and echo of the Word that was in God's mind all along to give us. They are a corruptible inscription of the incorruptible words written in our heart, where resides the Author Himself.

When the Author takes residence in a man of faith, out of his belly (his inmost being) shall flow rivers of living water.[189] This flow of knowledge and Spirit is the Word of God. It is the communication of His grace and power to you. Teaching you, guiding you, and enabling you to live righteously, to judge justly, and to understand all things. It is no wonder that He called them gods unto whom the Word of God came!

With a well-spring of knowledge beyond your means, understanding beyond your grasp, and mercy beyond your own compassion, you are indeed SUPER-human. You have stepped onto a rung of the ladder that is, by any other means unseen and intangible. You have finally been empowered to do God's will, given the ability to please your Creator, and enabled to fulfill the destiny meant for you from the foundation of the world. Not to please yourself as some hedonistic Greco-Roman god of mythology, but as a child of the most high God, finally, apportioned the strength to do good!

The Word of God has come to you in the form of Jesus Christ – and "… he called them gods, unto whom the word of God came… I have said, 'Ye are gods; and all of you are children of the most High.' Is it not written in your law, I said, 'Ye are gods'?"

---

[189] John 7:38-39, "He that believeth on me, as the scripture hath said, out of his belly shall flow rivers of living water. But this spake he of the Spirit, which they that believe on him should receive:"

113. Believest thou this?

John 11:26, "And whosoever liveth and believeth in me shall never die. Believest thou this?"

The house of Mary and Martha in Bethany was believed to be Jesus' second home and Lazarus, their brother was as Christ's own. Josephus tells us that Jesus may not have enjoyed the fellowship of His own brothers while He was alive as they too had their doubts as to who He was. When it was reported that Lazarus was sick Jesus waited two days to come to him. Mary and Martha both, (at separate times) declared to Jesus, "If you had been here, my brother would not have died." (It was obviously a remark repeated many times prior to Christ's arrival)

The mood somber, the motions slow and quiet, they were into their fourth day of mourning. The paid mourners left yesterday, only family remained, and concern had turned from Lazarus to his sisters left to carry the burdens of life. When Mary turned and ran out of the house all eyes were fastened on her and they surmised she was going once more to the tomb to weep. She had gone to meet Jesus.

Sometimes when death grips a home it is very difficult to see past it. Death is the sure visitor to every man on earth yet it is least acknowledged and least expected. It is more sure than any plans you have. It is more certain than any of the "one day" scenarios you toy with in your mind. Your grandchildren, your retirement, your fishing trip, your big vacation, all these we speak of with confidence as if they will happen for sure, but the event that is inevitable, we never give it more than one half hour of our thought at a time. Why is this? Because we consider it to be the last thing we do, the last hour we live, the last thought we think, the last everything. We consider it the end.

Jesus said, "... whosoever liveth and believeth in me shall never die." What a promise! This cannot mean what it says! We have known many who lived and believed in Christ and they are dead! How can this be so? This requires faith and likely a new understanding of life and death. Obviously, we will not be able to reason this one out.

We also have to answer the Lord's question that He posed immediately after the statement, "... whosoever liveth and believeth in me shall never die." He asked, "Believest thou this?" Before we answer we must realize that what we say carries little weight. If we go by our actions, if we go by what we do, if we answer according to the incredible amount of effort we go through, the money we expend, and the time and resources we waste trying to stay alive... we must answer, "No, we don't believe this."

Listen to Martha's answer, "Yes Lord, I believe thou art the Christ, the Son of God..." That is a marvelous answer and a wonderful statement of her faith, but it is an answer to some other question, not the one our Lord asked her. He asked, "Do you believe this?" "Oh Yes, I believe all things are possible."

362

"Yes, but do you believe that you will never die?" "I believe in Jesus Christ as my personal savior..." "Yes, but do you believe that you will never die?" "I believe all things work together for good to those who ..." "Yes, but do you believe you will never die?

It seems this question will be evaded if we don't approach from another angle. Some approach from the angle of definition. They may attempt to redefine "death" and "life," "never" and "die," to see if they can make this absurdity fit logically into their experience. But, would you really want to filter the words of Christ through your experience? Some try to approach from a spiritual standpoint. They propose that this dissertation was all prophet doublespeak and therefore paradoxical or metaphorical or at least not understandable this side of death. But, what good does it do to know this truth after the event for which the statement was designed to prepare you?

We are brought to a place of surrender. We must stand guilty of being earthy, sensual and creaturely, and absorbed with the life that passes away. We are too much entangled with the heartbeat, the respiring lungs, and brainwaves; we grasp essentially nothing of the life in God. Know this: There was life before heartbeats; there will be life afterwards. Our duty is to nurture the seed of Christ in us, to grow up in Him. We must let His life (the life of God Himself) overtake ours. We must pull away from our pitiful umbilicals of life here and reattach ourselves to the life that is eternal! We must strive to understand what is the hope in Jesus' declaration, "I give unto them eternal life; and they shall never perish..." (John 10:28)

"That the God of our Lord Jesus Christ, the Father of glory, may give unto you the spirit of wisdom and revelation in the knowledge of him: The eyes of your understanding being enlightened; that ye may know what is the hope of his calling, and what the riches of the glory of his inheritance in the saints, And what is the exceeding greatness of his power to us-ward who believe... Which he wrought in Christ, when he raised him from the dead, and set him at his own right hand in the heavenly places, Far above all principality, and power, and might, and dominion, and every name that is named, not only in this world, but also in that which is to come: And hath put all things under his feet, and gave him to be the head over all things to the church, Which is his body, the fulness of him that filleth all in all." (Ephesians 1:17-23)

The apostle Paul was so sure that his physical life was intertwined with God's that he did not even claim to have any life outside Christ. He said, "I am [dead] crucified with Christ: nevertheless I live; yet not I, but Christ liveth in me: and the life which I now live in the flesh I live by the faith of the Son of God, who loved me, and gave himself for me." (Galatians 2:20) The life that you now live, is it by the faith of the Son of God, or is it by food, clothing, and shelter?

Does Your Life Have A Beginning?

The life in you, is it Christ that lives in you, or is it the same breath you drew from birth? Ye must...We all must be born again! If we are to claim eternal life we must HAVE eternal life. Many seem fascinated with the fact that eternal life has no end, but it has no beginning as well. If the life in us had a beginning, it has an end. A tragic one.

We must be grafted into the life of God. We must become the sons of God. Those who have received Christ as Lord (chief, boss, superior, supervisor) have been given the power to become the sons of God.[190] Jesus has been given authority to bestow that life upon all the Father gives Him.[191]

This disparity must be settled in us. We cannot continue our love affair with our bodies and our lives here on this earth while professing a faith in Christ, claiming His gift of eternal life. We cannot continue to see death as a hopeless, helpless state where all is at an end if we are to be known as those who profess to know Christ in truth. We cannot continue to expend all of our resources to keep our bodies alive, our lungs breathing, and our hearts beating so that we can continue in our selfish way, while we misleadingly profess a faith in a coming Kingdom where we will supposedly live forever. We portray to the world an incongruous person who desires to live forever in fellowship with our King in his world – but only after we have exhausted every possibility of living in our world without Him. We must march to our fate with integrity. We would be lunatic to run to death's door but we, as Christians, should be ashamed to be dragged through it.

We must see physical death as a commencement of life, not as a cessation. We expose ourselves as fraudulent and insincere when we yearn for our lives to continue in spite of the well-known fact that they will end. For when it is our life that we seek, it is His life we forfeit. [192] Could this be what Jesus meant by, "If any man come to me, and hate not his father, and mother, and wife, and children, and brethren, and sisters, yea, and his own life also, he cannot be my disciple."? (Luke 14:26)

You must not flinch when you hear that those who believe in Christ will never die. You should stand firm as the apostle did, and be able to say that the life in you is by the faith of the Son of God.

You should be able to answer in faith and not doubt. You should be able to answer with a resounding "Yes!" when you are asked of the Lord, "Believest thou this?"

---

[190] John 1:12, "But as many as received him, to them gave he power to become the sons of God, even to them that believe on his name:"

[191] John 17:1-3, "These words spake Jesus, and lifted up his eyes to heaven, and said, Father, the hour is come; glorify thy Son, that thy Son also may glorify thee: As thou hast given him power over all flesh, that he should give eternal life to as many as thou hast given him. And this is life eternal, that they might know thee the only true God, and Jesus Christ, whom thou hast sent."

[192] Matthew 16:25, "For whosoever will save his life shall lose it: and whosoever will lose his life for my sake shall find it."

114. Didn't I tell you that if you believe, you will see the glory of God?

John 11:40, "Jesus saith unto her, Said I not unto thee, that, if thou wouldest believe, thou shouldest see the glory of God?"

Mary was distraught. She was, all at once, worried and hurt, afraid and sad, tired and confused. Although many were kind, none could offer her pleasantness or beauty. She may never see beauty again, or so it seemed. Though her family was understanding and helpful they could not make her comfortable. Her mind reeled in contradictions and inconsistency. She wanted everyone to go away and yet she did not want to be alone. Everything was dulled – everything was amplified. She was in a fog of illusion where the only reality presented to her senses was the loss of her brother. Lazarus is dead. She rejected the thought; then she accepted it only to reject it again.

Only those who experience a loss such as this can know how the mind whirls, the heart aches, and the body sickens as it longs to touch and hold someone who can be at hand no more. As the flesh seeks its lost companion the spirit seeks its own kind as well, all to no avail. Nothing is to be done but to invite the awful, inevitable truth into one's mind and cry, "Alas! My poor brother!"

Jesus witnessed the pain that Mary felt and succumbed to it when He contagiously wept at the very sight of her grief. It was not only hers but the grief of those in the scene of tragedy that cut to His heart of compassion; and in this sadness, now His own, Jesus wept.

When we are emotional many points of logic elude us. Many things we would normally do, almost instinctively, are hard to accomplish or difficult to perform. Sometimes the normal or mundane are nearly aggravating and are done reluctantly, questioning within "What difference does this make now that I am immersed in my tragic loss?" But there is a time of shaking back to reality that comes and presents itself to you and tells you that it is time to get back to work, time to rise and be about life again. The question Jesus asked Mary was just such a question. "You are slipping back into your grief, Mary, wake up, and let's get back to work."

With her heart broken she was having a hard time remembering the words of the Savior, even the ones recently spoken to her. "If you had been here my brother had not died," she said when Jesus arrived. I am sure He had the same conversation with her as He had with her sister, Martha, moments before. Jesus told her that, her brother would rise again and she answered automatically, "I know that in the resurrection he will rise again." She and her sister had probably consoled each other with this promise for the past few days.

Then, Jesus reminded her that He was the Resurrection and the Life. She blinked, as if she had received the first of several shakes to awaken her from sleep. We can only assume from the text that Jesus went on to tell her that

365

if she would believe, that she would – on that very day – see the power of God. She blinked and stared into His eyes, and wondered again to herself, "Is He saying that death is not a barrier even now?"

Jesus asked to go where Lazarus was buried. Upon arrival at the tomb He asked to have the stone removed from the grave. Mary suddenly realized that she and Christ were at crossed purposes! Surely He knows that He cannot visit Lazarus in the grave! The body has surely begun to deteriorate by now! She warned Him not to enter. Jesus, realizing by her remarks that she was reentering her new found reality of mourning and separation from her beloved brother asked her, Said I not unto thee, that, if thou wouldest believe, thou shouldest see the glory of God? The third shake to wake her was given and now she started to realize that Jesus had come to do something great.

Emotion Impaired

We become dull and hinder ourselves when our emotions thicken our ears, impairing our hearing by which we receive the Word of God. Emotion, like wine, is not a bad thing; it is a dangerous thing. Too much of either, or an unhealthy indulgence of either at the wrong place and time, or for the wrong reason, can damage the understanding and even dependencies can form.

There comes a time when sobriety and logic are to be reinstated and utilized as an act of our will. Anything that deprives them of their rightful seat in our intellect for an inordinate amount of time becomes a hindrance to our growth and betterment.

Emotion can enhance any situation. It can also mask truth and reality. It is the duty of the aware Christian to identify and clarify the truth in any circumstance. Truth is the only atmosphere in which God can act, operate and communicate. A God who is the embodiment of Truth can only work in an environment of truth. Clouds of emotion can obscure facts and hinder positive movements, and even cause us to work against the very power of our imminent deliverance.

As Mary stepped in front of Jesus and warned Him not to open the tomb, she was working against the power that was working on her behalf. If she could just see... if she could just hear... if she could just understand – alas she could not surmount her grief.

Emotion can hide Christ deep within and hinder His words from being recalled when we need to hear them most. Our bodily comfort and five physical senses can shout out demands that drown out the still small voice that guides us. It is tough to think in spiritual terms when we physically hurt. It is nearly impossible to think of Him who knows no three dimensional boundaries, while being beaten upon three-dimensional rocks. It is hard to consider the miraculous while we are living in the miracle-less. It is difficult to know our lives are hidden in Christ, when Christ is hidden in our lives.

Whether it comes from wine or song, emotion or grief, we must shake off the drunkenness that insulates us from the unpleasant and remember the promises of God. Can we not hear the Savior calling us to remember His words in the midst of our grief and pain, "Come unto me all ye that labor…I will give you rest?" Have we so deeply indulged ourselves in grief that we forget the promises of Christ, "If a man believe in me, he will never die and though he were dead yet shall he live?"[193]

You must hear and you must remember the words of Christ. Even in your pain and suffering, even when you hurt and grieve you must consider His words as promises and not try to think in ways that only salve your current heartaches and soothe your present pains.

When Mary was grieved, her thinking was obscured, her reactions were earthy, and her mind was bound to the three-dimensional world. When you give free reign to your emotions and make no provision for the power of Christ to make needed changes, you need to listen to Christ's question to Mary, as if He were talking to you. Stop, call upon the Savior to help you see things they way they really are. Determine to believe the words of Christ.

In your grief, in your pain will you keep reality in sight? Will your ears be open – will you hear Him say to you; "Didn't I tell you that if you believe, you will see the glory of God?"

---

[193] John 11:25

115. *Where have ye laid him?*

John 11:34, "And said, Where have ye laid him? They said unto him, Lord, come and see."

I understand that to train fleas for a flea circus you put fleas into a glass jar and affix the lid. As the fleas attempt to jump out they bang their little heads on the lid until they become "trained" to jump just below their new ceiling. Afterwards they can be removed and they will remain within the rings of the tiny circus because they think the lid is just above them hindering their distance.

There are highly educated men who stand and teach theology and fools, envy their abilities and knowledge. We should be ashamed to prize so highly the institution that has erected such an impenetrable wall between the simple Gospel message and mankind for whom it was intended. Theology has not helped in the cause of redemption; it has only helped to separate the redeemer from the common man in need. The thinking man, who considers mainstream religion today, hits illogical barriers that cannot be reconciled within the pale of mainstream theology. We have within our vocabulary terms like "Trinity" that confuse people from the outset.

When the average man (the one for whom the simple Gospel message came) says he does not understand how the Trinity works, they may be shamed (by those who defend such a doctrine) for even trying to understand the complexity of "God!" For to them who love the Trinity so, the Trinity IS God. "It is impossible understand the Trinity!" say they, "It is far beyond comprehension." No, it is not that God is beyond you, it is the term that MEN made up and placed into religion that is beyond comprehension.

Today, the term and the concept are so ingrained, that it has become a criterion by which mainstream Christianity decides whether a faith or denomination is valid. They ask, "Do you believe in the Trinity?" They may as well ask, "Don't you believe in the word that was invented by mere men? …that is found nowhere in the Bible… a word that has never been uttered by any of the prophets, apostles, or even Christ Himself? You must be a heretic! But I would ask, is it wise to teach and hold to a doctrine that was never taught by Christ as essential to the faith? Is it wise to "invent" a word or concept about the nature of God (something NONE of us understand) and demand that all who worship Him accept it? It has always amazed me when discussing Quakerism, how often the question is put to me, "Do you believe in the Trinity?"

Omnipotent?

Revelation 19:6 describes God as omnipotent, or at least uses that term to in relation to God. Theologians, however, teach that the term means that God can do anything. This simplistic view causes some problems if taught in this way. A man who thinks about this concept will soon come to formulate the question, in one form or another, "If God is all-powerful can He make a stone so great that He cannot move it?" This view of God causes paradoxes and mental absurdities like these to occur. A better term is "all-mighty."

To consider God as all-mighty shows Him to need no one, to be all-sufficient, to be fully able and unhindered by any weakness, to be capable. This is a concept that is understandable indeed. But whence did the other idea come? It was used to explain the perplexing Trinity! When some poor soul dared to express his confusion about how one God is really three Gods and yet one God or one God in three persons – well, two persons and one "personage of Spirit" – or is it two Spirits and one person? Well, anyway, it is all rolled into a nice illogical package and excused as… "God can do anything!" To which the confused, "less spiritual" person is supposed to reply, "Oh… I see" and then walk away quietly.

Omnipresent?

Another term we attached to God is "omnipresent." This is another word not found in Scripture. When we talk of the concept of Father, Son, and Holy Ghost we can at least find reference made to it, or when using the term omnipotent there is Scriptural usage of the word. But in the case of omnipresence, neither the word nor the concept is there. This one is straight out of the seminary.

Sure, we can wring from the pages an idea that God is everywhere, but why? And why everywhere at one time? Why do we have to believe such a concept? Why is it important? Should we not rather let God speak for Himself on these matters? Are we to believe the immediacy of God is necessary to effect salvation? Where did this idea come from and why do we teach it? Let God show Himself or hide Himself, let Him appear or withdraw, let God be God in our understanding and stop holding His behavior to long, useless words born in the idle minds of theologians.

Omniscient?

Omniscience is the next pretentious word with which we arbitrarily label God. The concept that God "knows everything" is another theological tenet all believers are expected to accept. We even build doctrines upon this faulty premise of fallen man's effort to understand a God he has never met. What is worse, we expect God to jump through these hoops of our creation so that our doctrines make sense. The premise that "God knows everything" is essential to many ideas about God. It is laid out as a solid and irrefutable idea, upon which hope and trust can be placed. But, this premise is a stepping stone to which we have no Scriptural right to tread upon, much less build doctrines upon. We set ourselves and others up for disappointment when we do so. The Scriptures teach that God is wise, God is knowledgeable but where does He claim, "I am God, I know everything"?

This term might have come about to explain the mainstream thinking on the doctrines of election and predestination. "God knows everything so He knows who will cling to Him and who will reject Him in the end." This idea is useless. For the very same concept of an all-knowing God that is used to vindicate Him, showing Him kind in His choices of who to save, indicts Him as cruel for the same reason. Why do we not rather let God be God? Why does He have to be omniscient for us to trust Him? Why does He have to be omnipotent for us to rely on Him, or omnipresent for us to worship Him?

Terms of Clarification?

These concepts confuse, they do not clarify. They *create* problems, they do not solve them. When we add man's codes and rules to God we make a crate for Him to live within, we put a chain around His neck to keep Him within our understanding.

Unfortunately, in our creation of boundaries for God (or ignoring real ones) we make it difficult for Him to speak to us, to guide us, and to communicate His will and way to us. There are many reasons to refrain from codifying or reducing God to terms. The greatest reason I can think of is our fallen nature that renders us so stupid and dull.

We have built a flea circus ring for Him to perform within and yet, we call out in our grief and pain for Him to answer and deliver us. We reason within the borders we created and wonder, If God KNEW all along that this tragedy would happen, why did He let me go this way? And, if He is all-powerful He must have CHOSEN not to help me, perhaps He does not love me. And, if He is everywhere at once why is He so far from me now? All of these unfair accusations and suppositions are based in words and ideas not found in Scripture.

The claim that Jesus knew everything, that He could read minds, and knew the future, creates myriads of theological difficulties. It leaves people questioning His motives and reasoning, and in some cases His love. Perhaps God would be closer and more understandable if we did not make Him who He is not, and let Him be who He is, and who He claims to be. Perhaps if we did not outline and underline, emphasize or de-emphasize, add to or take away from His words, we could receive from them the guidance and comfort for which they were given.

If we understand that God lives with us everyday and that He is not just sitting at the end of time drumming His fingers, waiting for everything to turn out just as He knew it would, life would make more sense. Perhaps if we accept that there are things that we don't know about God, His power and limitations, His presence and absence and what He knows and what He will discover today, that we will become more humble and thankful for His ministry to us. You do not need a predictable God whom you understand, nor do you need a God who only jumps as high as you have trained Him to. You don't need to have a God who knows everything. You need a God who loves you, and that, you do have.

There is something…I can't quite place it…but something wonderful, some blessedness, some comfort in knowing that when Jesus asked Mary, "Where have ye laid him?"… He really didn't know.

116. Is it not written, "My house will be called the house of prayer"?

Luke 19:46, Matthew 21:13, Mark 11:17, John 2:13-17, "And he taught, saying unto them, Is it not written, My house shall be called of all nations the house of prayer? but ye have made it a den of thieves. And the Jews' Passover was at hand, and Jesus went up to Jerusalem, And found in the temple those who sold oxen and sheep and doves, and the changers of money sitting: And when he had made a scourge of small cords, he drove them all out of the temple, and the sheep, and the oxen; and poured out the changers' money, and overthrew the tables; And said unto them that sold doves, Take these things hence; make not my Father's house an house of merchandise. And his disciples remembered that it was written, The zeal of thine house hath eaten me up."

With Passover approaching, Jesus went to Jerusalem. Activity was at a yearly high and people were milling about and preparing for Passover. The monumental task of ridding the city and suburbs of leaven was nearing an end and on the tenth day of the month, the selection of lambs was to occur. Choosing the required sacrifice was not as difficult as it was in days before; many of the people simply went to the Temple and purchased the animal they wished to offer from a man well qualified to select and provide a proper sacrifice.

Those who traveled from great distances were given special provision as well. They need not bring their offerings on the hoof the long journey; they could sell their livestock and their tithe of corn and wine, then carry the money to Jerusalem and purchase their sacrificial animals there.[194]

This had become a great business, but again, wherever the provision and kindness of the Lord meets the slothfulness and greed of man, compassion would be abused. The option of selling and repurchasing was used for gain and the worshipful aspect was gone. Man was involved and he was sure to make money on the deal. The buying and selling had turned the steps of the Temple into a noisy, cluttered barnyard filled with tables of cages and boxes of money. There were men clamoring for the business of the stranger in town, all claiming to have the best deal. It had become a circus.

The temple's outer court was the only place this commerce could be carried out. To do business IN the Temple was an abomination. The Jews did not mind doing it here because this particular court was called "the court of the Gentiles." Jesus saw the disparity and prejudice. As He approached the scene, the Scripture in Isaiah 56:7 repeated in His mind, "Even them will I bring to my holy mountain, and make them joyful in my house of prayer: their burnt offerings and their sacrifices shall be accepted upon mine altar; for mine house shall be called an house of prayer for all people." ALL people! Then

---

[194] Deuteronomy 14:23-29

immediately the reference in Jeremiah 7:11, "Is this house, which is called by my name, become a den of robbers in your eyes? Behold, even I have seen it, saith the LORD." With these two thoughts wrestling in His mind and with the zeal[195] for God's Temple burning within, Jesus went and sat down with some small cords and began to tie them into knots. Surely the disciples asked, "What are you doing? Where are you going?" We have no way of knowing the actions, conversations or thoughts beforehand, but time was taken to construct or purchase a weapon and plan an assault.

We are now nearing the end of the life of Jesus. These, as well as other actions, will prove to be His undoing. As He approached the crucifixion, His preaching became harder toward the established religion and its leadership. On the last Sabbath day before His death He lambasted the hypocritical Pharisees like never before and on this day He went so far as to arm Himself and perform destruction upon the merchandisers of forgiveness.

What Was The Problem?

Were not these "merchandisers" simply helping people do the right thing? They did not create sacrifices, they only supplied them. It was God who commanded that the sacrifices be given and He made provision for them to be bought and sold. What was the problem? Perhaps it was the location. Maybe it was the price. The lack of sincerity could have been a factor. If we cannot determine the problem, perhaps there is a problem with us. Selling sacrifices, marketing forgiveness, merchandising the Gospel, providing at a cost the free relationship between God and His people— is disgusting.

Can we see Jesus going through and overturning the book tables and cassette tape racks dumping boxes of money, unplugging credit card machines and cash registers in the foyer of our conventional churches? Can we hear Him condemn the merchandising, the selling of sermons, the solicitation of "offerings," and the Evangelist for hire? Who has not been offended by these practices? Who has not felt the twinge of guilt, embarrassment or had to dampen pride while being viewed by everyone when an offering plate has been passed beneath their nose?

Why are all these negative sentiments ignored and the practice continued? The answer is simply this, the churches cannot continue in their present state of luxury and growth if people are not asked, compelled, coerced, embarrassed, and (for all intents) forced to give. There is one reason why we ignore the plain truth expressed in Matthew 6:1-4,[196] to give in secret, and one reason only; we cannot build great churches that way. If the people are left to do what they are led to do, nothing will be done. Whether this is because they

---

[195] Psalms 69:9, "For the zeal of thine house hath eaten me up; and the reproaches of them that reproached thee are fallen upon me."

[196] "Take heed that ye do not your alms before men, to be seen of them: otherwise ye have no reward of your Father which is in heaven. Therefore when thou doest thine alms, do not sound a trumpet before thee, as the hypocrites do in the synagogues and in the streets, that they may have glory of men. Verily I say unto you, They have their reward. But when thou doest alms, let not thy left hand know what thy right hand doeth: That thine alms may be in secret: and thy Father which seeth in secret himself shall reward thee openly."

are not listening to God or not led to give to these merchandising churches is not known, but we suspect it is both reasons.

Money is the "fly in the ointment," the evil sufficient for the day,[197] the leaven that overtakes the lump.[198] We have become so used to paying for everything and charging for everything, that we, without a qualm, invite this practice into spiritual things where it does not belong. Let us work toward removing it from our programs and events. Let us treat money as if it carried the potential to destroy everyone it touches – because it does. What element of our society has it not touched and destroyed, what man is there among us who has not struggled under its power?

Whether we have a lot of it or little, whether we use it or it uses us, few of us can say we have enough. Jesus taught that what is sufficient for today is all we can handle. Paul said, "For the love of money is the root of all evil: which while some coveted after, they have erred from the faith, and pierced themselves through with many sorrows." He goes on to say that we need to flee these things and follow after righteousness as though the two (money and righteousness) are mutually exclusive. (1 Timothy 6:10-11)

Foremost, it must be removed from places of worship. Jesus called those who merchandise ministry, thieves. What had they stolen? Jeremiah used the term "robbers." Who had they robbed? Were they not merely exchanging at prices agreed upon by sellers and buyers? Were they not selling merchandise that properly belonged to them? What they had stolen was the worship, the quiet; the silent invitation had become an item for barter. The only place near the Temple where Gentiles could approach was occupied with enterprise. "Ho, every one that thirsteth, come ye to the waters, and he that hath no money; come ye, buy, and eat; yea, come, buy wine and milk without money and without price." (Isaiah 55:1)

The actions and events at the Temple that day were profoundly offensive on many levels – God's sacrifice despised, His Temple desecrated, prejudice, impiety and insincerity to the highest level of the priesthood.

Even though the Law was carried out to the letter, it was the personal communion of the sacrifice that was compromised; it was sincere prayer that was now missing; and because of all this commerce, there was found no room for the Gentiles.

It was no longer "Whosoever will, let him come"[199] it had become "whoever can afford" or "Whoever is accepted among our own kind." Is it not written, "My house shall be called of all people the house of prayer?"

---

[197] Matthew 6:34, "Take therefore no thought for the morrow: for the morrow shall take thought for the things of itself. Sufficient unto the day is the evil thereof."
[198] Galatians 5:9, "A little leaven leaveneth the whole lump."
[199] Revelation 22:17

117. See ye not all these things?

Mark 13:1-2, "And as he went out of the temple, one of his disciples saith unto him, Master, see what manner of stones and what buildings are here! And Jesus answering said unto him, Seest thou these great buildings? there shall not be left one stone upon another, that shall not be thrown down."

Matthew 24:2, "And Jesus said unto them, See ye not all these things? verily I say unto you, There shall not be left here one stone upon another, that shall not be thrown down."

While traveling the country you can see skyline after skyline and wonder at the marvel of man's handiwork. It is difficult not to be impressed by the accomplishments of modern man. We have made great strides in workmanship and in the fight against nature's oppositions. There is a beauty in the skylines and in the individual buildings. It is a beauty that tends to glorify man. We are carried in thought to the creator/designer, or the construction worker, or the owner of such edifices, but seldom are we turned to thoughts of God, and His part in the project.

One of the disciples was fascinated with the beauty of the Temple and all its magnificence and proclaimed, "Master, see what manner of stones and what buildings are here!" It is clear from the text that Jesus was not to be impressed by it. It was as if He saw something they did not see or saw it in a different light. Was He warning us about something? Why did He not just go along with the conversation and be nice and cordial, and say, "My, my yes, they are spectacular aren't they?" Why did He have to be so solemn and decline to participate with their enthusiasm? Are we witnessing a sullen Christ preoccupied with His impending death (as it is only days away at this point) or is there a dire warning to us in His question?

If Jesus walked the modern streets of our world with us we would not act differently than the disciples did and would probably seek to engage His enthusiasm about the "miracles" of modern man. Setting aside for a moment the fact that He is well aware of all things man has accomplished over the centuries, we would likely try to show Him around as we would any stranger who visits us. We might take Him to Cape Kennedy and show Him the Space Center and the accomplishments in our past. We may boast of the strides in modern building construction, the technological leaps made in semiconductors and electronics, satellites and telecommunications. Perhaps we would brag about our medical and pharmaceutical progresses. We would have Him to be impressed with man and his accomplishments by gorging Him on the best of the best in every area of our modern civilization. (Can you imagine what He would think of the Internet?) Imagine us, walking around with the Son of God, showing Him who we are, rather than sitting at His feet and learning who He is. It becomes a foolish endeavor to impress God with man, when man is so unimpressed with God.

A Selective Tour

We would be inclined to show Him the best of our accomplishments and neglect to show Him the darker side of our world. As we may flaunt our amber waves of grain, but hide from Him the world's homeless and hungry who have little of it. We would show Him our beautiful buildings, but not our alleys behind them, our highways but not the gutters. We would likely try to impress Him with our most recent medical breakthroughs but not our psychological failures, with our rising standard of living but not the disintegrating family.

We would show Him our worldwide network of satellite television broadcasts but would be ashamed for him to see any of its content. Would we tell Him that our marvelous internet is now the major conveyance of the world's pornography? We need not wonder whether Jesus was overly solemn as He was shown the wonderful accomplishments of man. It would be difficult to overlook what we know is wrong to admire any rightness in it. I remember a sports car in the 70's that everyone wanted to own, everyone that is, except auto mechanics, because they knew what was under its shiny skin. When we know the inner workings of something are severely flawed, it is difficult to get excited about its appearance.

Truer words are hard to find than, "All that glitters is not gold." The disciples asked, "Do you see all these great buildings?" Jesus responded, "See ye NOT all these things?" When we are impressed with the world and all its glory we are succumbing to the "glitz" and "hype." Madison Avenue, the advertising Mecca of the world, requires that people do not see the whole picture in order to peddle their wares. If you are impressed with the world, it is likely that your eyes are closed. Whether by choice or by hypnosis of the media, if you are enchanted by what the world has to offer you are likely far from sober. If you find yourself seeking the newest and the fashionable, you may want to reevaluate your relationship with truth, reality, and love. For it is hard to sell the world's goods to a person fixed upon the important and real. Those who shun that which will entrap their souls, or those who have the love of the Father within them can hardly see past the danger, or the cost, to thrill at the thought of possessing it. The ads convince us of what we "want," when what we daily need is all that is safe for us. Nothing sharpens a man like pursuing what he needs, and nothing dulls a man like pursuing what he wants. What is sufficient for the day at hand is all the evil we can bear.[200]

How do you feel when you read this?

"Love not the world, neither the things that are in the world. If any man love the world, the love of the Father is not in him. For all that is in the world, the lust of the flesh, and the lust of the eyes, and the pride of life, is not of the Father, but is of the world. And the world passeth away, and the

---

[200] Matthew 6:34, "Take therefore no thought for the morrow: for the morrow shall take thought for the things of itself. Sufficient unto the day is the evil thereof."

lust thereof: but he that doeth the will of God abideth for ever." (1 John 2:15-17)

If you feel dread and anxiety, guilt or even anger when you hear the message in these words, it is likely that you are too deeply entangled in the world. Has your judgment been altered or your priorities shifted by shiny stones of temporary beauty? Are you led by what you see, what your flesh craves, or what fulfils your pride?

The enemy says, "Don't you see all that the world has to offer?" Christ would ask, "Do you NOT see it for what it really is?" Our friends, our co-workers, and even our family may say, "Get with the program! – You can't live in a shell all your life!" We are constantly encouraged, whether subconsciously or overtly, by friends, by family, by advertisements to look and admire, to be amazed and dazzled, to yearn and desire for that which the world offers. We are told what is pretty, we are told what is acceptable; we are told what is gauche and ridiculous. We are enticed by the media, we are lured by the ads and told what is new and improved and what we need and "cannot afford to be without!" We are led to believe what is modern, we are told what is right, and good, what is pretty and useful. We are persuaded to believe what is fundamental to a happy life and told what should be considered basic necessity. It will take wisdom beyond our years, and discernment beyond our capabilities to know what is the truth. We must not yield our attention to the loudest debater nor only look in the direction of glittering sequins, but rather listen to the still small voice.

Jesus was well aware of the exquisite stones that graced the Temple. He knew also the ugly side – He knew Herod, whose money and political motivations propelled the project. He also knew the brevity of this beauty and foretold its imminent destruction. There are many particulars, details and specifics known to God that, if they were known to you, would change for the better the way you look at things. Jesus was confused that his disciples were taken in by the beauty of the stones used in the Temple. A disciple of Christ must not be so superficial and selfish. The world you live in screams in your ear, "Do you see all these things?" While Jesus calmly inquires, "See ye not all these things?"

118. Do ye enquire among yourselves of that I said?

John 16:16-19, "A little while, and ye shall not see me: and again, a little while, and ye shall see me, because I go to the Father. Then said some of his disciples among themselves, What is this that he saith unto us, A little while, and ye shall not see me: and again, a little while, and ye shall see me: and, Because I go to the Father? They said therefore, What is this that he saith, A little while? we cannot tell what he saith. Now Jesus knew that they were desirous to ask him, and said unto them, Do ye enquire among yourselves of that I said, A little while, and ye shall not see me: and again, a little while, and ye shall see me?"

Why do we ask among ourselves when the One who knows is standing in front of us? Shyness, fear of reprisal, or worse yet, fear of being wrong, are all barriers to our understanding. If we could overcome these, we may avail ourselves of sources yet unknown. Perhaps this reluctance to ask the Lord what He meant was from the same male ego that prohibits a man from asking directions even when it is clear to everyone that he is lost.

Unfortunately, the directions the disciples were afraid to ask for were the most important directions they would ever receive. There was no room for ego here. Jesus was presenting a discourse on His death, burial, resurrection, and ascension and told His friends that they would one day follow Him. They wanted to ask Him what He meant by His words but none dared. Why? We do not know, but it is easy to speculate that they were afraid.

Whatever the reason, Jesus was eagerly awaiting the questions that He anticipated would come from His statements. It would not be hard to believe that the question was formed in such an enticing way for the purpose of creating curiosity. Yet all feared to ask. In John 16:16, Jesus said, "A little while, and ye shall not see me: and again, a little while, and ye shall see me, because I go to the Father." He paused – no response from His hearers.

In your mind's eye you may see Him lean forward a little waiting for the inevitable query, but it does not come. His disciples were curious but they did not ask. He sees curiosity cover their faces, brows wrinkle, ears are tugged and beards stroked, but no questions come. They take an alternate route. *"Then said some of his disciples among themselves, What is this that he saith unto us, A little while, and ye shall not see me: and again, a little while, and ye shall see me: and, Because I go to the Father? ...What is this that he saith, A little while? We cannot tell what he saith."* (They turned to each other for answers.)

Many times we may hear some word from God in our spirit or read some passage of the Bible and wonder within ourselves, "What is meant by that?" If we cannot (for reasons unknown) understand the concept or even the sentence and we are puzzled and wonder, "What is this that He saith?" we then look between and among ourselves for answers. We ask each other or look to books. We ask those whom we respect, or check sources or commentaries. All the while Jesus waits, anticipating our asking Him.

He spoke purposefully, and in such a way to spark our curiosity, engage our wonder, and create an interest. His words accomplished that all right, but why are we looking to others to explain it? Are we fearful of an encounter with the One who originated the thought? Why do we fear learning from the very One who is trying to teach us? Our Messiah must puzzle over our behavior. Again, just as He did with His disciples, He must wonder why we do not ask Him.

The Scripture passage continues, "Now Jesus knew that they were desirous to ask him, and said unto them, Do ye enquire among yourselves of that I said, A little while, and ye shall not see me: and again, a little while, and ye shall see me?"

Here, we see our Savior restating His words and in doing so we can hear Him nearly begging, "Don't you want to know what this means?" To which, (if He had asked out loud) the disciples would have answered, "Yes!" Had the conversation gone this direction it would be easy to imagine Jesus then asking, "Well why didn't you ask me? I want to tell you this…it is very good news!"

He goes on to tell them that the explanation of His words is not morbid or fearful, but joyous and exciting! He continues, "Verily, verily, I say unto you, That ye shall weep and lament… but your sorrow shall be turned into joy. …And ye now therefore have sorrow: but I will see you again, and your heart shall rejoice, and your joy no man taketh from you."[201]

They dreaded the answer, as any of us would, when the outlook is bleak. The words were heavy, they reasoned that the prognosis would likely be depressing, but had they only asked they would have heard the good news. When Jesus spoke to them in proverbs and obscure sayings they would frustrate themselves trying to interpret them. They would struggle with the words of Christ much as we do today when we read the Scriptures or hear difficult messages.

We Should Go To Him.

We should have no fear of making Him our teacher and ask Him for clarification or explanation. Why do we go to the professors or other so-called experts? If we but ask, He can make it plain to us. It is His desire to do so. When He explained His comments the disciples exclaimed, "Lo, now speakest thou plainly, and speakest no proverb. Now are we sure that thou knowest all things…"

Revelation from the Most High is probably one of the greatest experiences of the Christian's life. It forms a bond, a communicative bond, between God and us. After all, the main difference between our God and the gods of stone is that our God speaks! The Scriptures are replete with examples:

Jeremiah 33:2-3, "Thus saith the LORD the maker thereof, the LORD that formed it, to establish it; the LORD is his name; Call unto me, and I will

---

[201] John 16

answer thee, and shew thee great and mighty things, which thou knowest not."

*John 5:39-41, "Search the scriptures; for in them ye think ye have eternal life: and they are they which testify of me. And ye will not come to me, that ye might have life. **I receive not honour from men.**"*

*Deuteronomy 29:29, "The secret things belong unto the LORD our God: but those things which are revealed belong **unto us and to our children for ever**, that we may do all the words of this law."*

Mark 4:22, "For there is nothing hid, which shall not be manifested; neither was any thing kept secret, but that it should come abroad."

1 Corinthians 2:10, "But God hath revealed them unto us by his Spirit: for the Spirit searcheth all things, yea, the deep things of God."

When you do not understand, when the sayings are obscure, when you are not clear on a point, a doctrine, a concept, you are to go to Christ and not one another. He can make it clear, expand upon it, or dispense with it altogether. He is the teacher, He is the revealer, and He is puzzled by your lack of confidence in Him when you go to man and his narrow understanding for answers.

When you are perplexed about something that He is trying to teach and you forsake Him for the wisdom of man, or when He finds your nose in books on Greek and Latin,[202] or He discovers that the concept, idea or mystery that He has been trying to reveal to you being bandied about in discussion groups, He asks, "Do ye enquire among yourselves of that I said?"

---

[202] Your author does not disparage the use of books or language studies for the clarification of words and their meanings. It is the use of strained or unintended definitions to *redefine* original intent that causes false doctrines to become "founded upon Scripture." Remember the same Spirit that brought forth the Scripture resides in you.

119. Do ye now believe?

John 16:30-32, "Now ... we believe that thou camest forth from God. Jesus answered them, Do ye now believe? Behold, the hour cometh, yea, is now come, that ye shall be scattered, every man to his own, and shall leave me alone..."

There are a few doctrines circulating within the Christian faith that, eventually, each of us will have to face and evaluate for ourselves. One of these is the doctrine of the security of the believer.

This doctrine, depending on which side of it you encounter, deals with the question, "Once a man repents and becomes at peace with God (and He with him), can he then lose his state of salvation and revert to his old condition?"

There are both those who say the Bible clearly says, "No" emphatically, and others who say it states that this possibility does indeed exist. One side of this argument seems to rely on strained perspectives and definitions of words. Clever arguments and empathetic reasoning are used to give assurance to the lukewarm and backslidden, and the other, more stringent position is in plain view to the common man and becomes apparent to the average reader immediately upon presentation of the Scripture. Unless you are willing to do a lot of mental calisthenics and redefinition of common everyday words, what other conclusion can you come to when you read 2 Peter 2:20-22?

"For if after they have escaped the pollutions of the world through the knowledge of the Lord and Saviour Jesus Christ, they are again entangled therein, and overcome, the latter end is worse with them than the beginning. For it had been better for them not to have known the way of righteousness, than, after they have known it, to turn from the holy commandment delivered unto them. But it is happened unto them according to the true proverb, The dog is turned to his own vomit again; and the sow that was washed to her wallowing in the mire."

The question then becomes, what hope is there for those who do become entangled and overcome again? Can a person again, repent and live in hope of salvation? Here is a great Scripture from the prophet Ezekiel sharing with us the words of the Lord Himself dealing with this subject.

"... When I say unto the wicked, O wicked man, thou shalt surely die ... if he does not turn from his way, he shall die in his iniquity... As I live, saith the Lord GOD, I have no pleasure in the death of the wicked; but that the wicked turn from his way and live... The righteousness of the righteous shall not deliver him in the day of his transgression: as for the wickedness of the wicked, he shall not fall thereby in the day that he turneth from his wickedness; neither shall the righteous be able to live for his righteousness in the day that he sinneth. When I shall say to the righteous, that he shall surely live; if he trust to his own righteousness, and commit iniquity, all his

righteousnesses shall not be remembered; but for his iniquity that he hath committed, he shall die for it. Again, when I say unto the wicked, Thou shalt surely die; if he turn from his sin, and do that which is lawful and right... he shall surely live, he shall not die. None of his sins that he hath committed shall be mentioned unto him: he hath done that which is lawful and right; he shall surely live." (Ezekiel 33:1-16 abridged)

What Have You Done For Me Lately?

These and many other Scriptures show that it is the PRESENT condition of a man that is most important. What you were is of little moment, whether you are a sinner who was a saint or a saint that was a sinner, according to the Prophet Ezekiel, it is what you are NOW that counts.

With that background laid, read again Christ's words, "Do ye NOW believe?" What was the concern of the Savior at this point? He was remembering that there was a time when He was doubted even by His own disciples, and NOW they believed. Then His mind leapt forward to the Prophecy that He would be left alone, and He said, "Behold, the hour cometh, yea, is now come, that ye shall be scattered, every man to his own, and shall leave me alone..." (John 16:32)

Jesus was well aware that these disciples, NOW faithful, will later depart and forsake Him. Poor Peter gets the bad reputation of being weak and a deserter but the Scriptures indicate that Peter was not the only one to promise and renege. "Peter said unto him, Though I should die with thee, yet will I not deny thee. Likewise also said all the disciples." (Matthew 26:35) And later in verse 56 we read, "...Then ALL the disciples forsook him, and fled." Knowing this, Jesus asked, "Do ye now believe?"

There is likely a time coming in our own Christian experiences when we will be called upon to take a stand that will be uncomfortable. We will then find that our stand will be one we will have to take alone, or for no reason readily apparent to those around us and will be based in our faith only. Or, there will come a time when a quiet denial of Christ will be a convenience or not being so straight-laced will gain us an advantage that we would not otherwise have.

Will we have what it takes to take that stand? Don't answer too quickly. For likewise said all the disciples and ALL the disciples forsook him, and fled. When we face the possibility of failure and couple that with the knowledge that we may lose all we have gained to this point in life, we should be humbled, and respectful of the kindness of the Lord heretofore. Although 1 Corinthians 10:13 says we need not fear unbearable temptation, we must know also that we have succumbed to bearable temptation in the past.

Could Christ become an outdated and irrelevant motivation in your life? Could the same Jesus apprehended in the days your youth become impertinent or inapplicable to your present manner of life? Could "mammon" exercise its influence on you and your family until the benefits of being a sophisticated and up-to-date man of the world far outweigh the illusive and intangible benefits of being a dedicated Christian? Don't answer too quickly, for "likewise also said all the disciples."

This is not intended to cast doubts upon the power of faith nor should it cause doubt where God's faithfulness is concerned, but we need not think that we have in our hands, paid, first class tickets. Where there is exposure to sin, there is the possibility becoming corrupted. Paul said in 1 Corinthians 9:27,

"But I keep under my body, and bring it into subjection: lest that by any means, when I have preached to others, I myself should be a castaway."

Just because we believe NOW is no assurance we will believe tomorrow. We must strive to enter in the straight and narrow gate. We must work while it is day. We must run the race. The New Testament is replete with examples requiring us to press forward, strive, work, follow, and hold fast.

We spend too much time worrying over past sins and too little time concerned about present and future ones. Paul shares his heart,

"That I may know him, and ... by any means I might attain unto the resurrection of the dead. Not as though I had already attained, either were already perfect: but I follow after, if that I may apprehend ... Brethren, I count not myself to have apprehended: but this one thing I do, forgetting those things which are behind, and reaching forth unto those things which are before, I press toward the mark for the prize of the high calling of God in Christ Jesus." (Philippians 3:10-14 Abridged).

There may come a day when you, dear reader, may look back upon today as a day you would trade everything you have, to get back. Many will believe the "strong delusion,"[203] many will fall away in the apostasy;[204] many will say to Christ, "Lord, Lord, open unto us, did we not do many works in thy name?"[205]

Why does the Bible give us these scenarios? Why are we even speaking of these things? Because nothing is more dangerous to any achievement than the fantasy of having already attained it. There are no crowns on our heads, there are no medals around our necks, we have not finished our course yet. We could cast off our faith, we could fall from grace, and we could fall back to our lives without God. He that endureth to the END shall be saved.[206]

Jesus knew that in only a few days all would forsake Him. THEN they would run. THEN they would fear. THEN they would doubt. He also knows how you will respond in the time of your temptation and therefore His question pierces your heart, "Do you NOW believe?"

---

[203] 2 Thessalonians 2
[204] Ibid.
[205] Luke 13:25 - Matthew 7:22
[206] Matthew 10

120. *Where is the guestchamber?*

Luke 22:11, Mark 14:14, "And ye shall say unto the goodman of the house, The Master saith unto thee, Where is the guestchamber, where I shall eat the Passover with my disciples?"

The rituals and traditions of some faiths are a fascinating study. I once heard a story of a young girl learning from her mother how to cook the holiday roast. "You must cut it like this before you put it in the pan" mother said with conviction as she removed four full inches from the end of the roast. "Why?" the young lady asked. "I don't know," the mother answered with a look of confusion, "but I've always done it – perhaps we'll ask Grandma tonight. After all, she told me to do it" That night at dinner, the matriarch of the family was finally asked by the granddaughter, "Why did you teach Mom that the end of a roast should be removed?" She answered, "Back in those days... we had a very small oven!" So it is with rituals and traditions. The actions last long after the reasons are forgotten.

In order to look at traditions we need to stand back to consider them. Objectivity and reason must rule the deliberation. We also must realize that while all ordinances may be ritual all ritual may not be ordinance. The Church has found itself involved in liturgies and observances that have done much harm and little good over the years. People, otherwise civilized and kind, tear apart congregations and families with questions of rituals and all the intricacies of their observance. Are they required? How often? So on and so on, ad infinitum.

Let us examine Christ's question, "Where is the guestchamber?" What a wonderful question to ask those who think it compulsory to prepare and participate in the Eucharist. What a question for those who feel it is essential to place common bread in their mouth and call it the body of Christ and those who pretend to drink His blood by drinking wine or juice.

They may find themselves in debates about how and why and with whom it is to be done. Churches split, families quarrel, while theologians (Catholic and Protestant alike) bark out Scriptures to "prove" their points. Should the wine be fermented? Is the bread allowed to be leavened? Should we serve the cup first or the bread? Should we use individual cups or share one? What should the cup be made of? Who is qualified to serve? Who is qualified to partake? Is this service essential for salvation? Does the bread actually become the flesh of Christ? (Transubstantiation) How often should we do this each year...each month... each week? The questions go on indefinitely. One question, however, about this night that is never asked is the one Jesus asked, "Where is the guestchamber?"

Bread is easily purchased at the market or from church supply stores – perfectly round (if you are into Sun worship) or square if you like matzos or broken into tiny pieces, whatever is your tradition. We can find certified leaven free, kosher, salted or unsalted, crackers, or matzos.

The wine can be bought at the same places and may be from California or Israel, it may be fermented or unfermented, red or rosé (never white). Some see nothing wrong with using water in its place and to others that is sacrilege. Are all these concerns valid or can we participate in the Lord's supper with a coffee and doughnut? (This is not said to offend but to provoke thought.) What is important and unimportant about the way this communion with Christ is carried out?

Another Idea

Quakers did not hold to the conventional idea of the "Lord's Supper." The Quakers (as indeed we all should) focus more on the *communion* and less on the *supper*. As a matter of fact, the supper becomes a symbol that complicates and obscures the Truth of this service.

You may meet an old friend and you say, "Let's have dinner." Don't you assume that your intention is, not to eat, but to fellowship with your friend? When a gentleman asks a lady out for dinner, should we assume he is hungry for food? The symbolic gesture is just as much apparent in the Lord's supper. The Lord is not hungry, nor does He care what is served. He comes for the fellowship, the communion, and the company. He does not ask, "Where is the unleavened bread I require?" Nor does He ask for pedigrees on participants. He asks, "Where is the guestchamber that I may eat the Passover with my disciples?"

The fellowship that Jesus requires is the communion of the heart. The company He desires is the humble disciple, eagerly awaiting words from the lips of his Lord – awaiting orders, awaiting corrections, awaiting encouragement. This is the fellowship He desires "as oft ye do this" (as often as you eat) to meet with Him and fellowship. As often as you raise a glass to quench your thirst, consider the blood with which you were purchased. As often as you place food in your mouth to give yourself strength, gain strength from the body that was broken for you as well.

This fellowship is carried on in the heart. This is the guestchamber where resides the Savior, the lover of our soul. It is the guestchamber that is swept and garnished, where the door is opened to receive the Savior whenever He knocks. "Behold, I stand at the door, and knock: if any man hear my voice, and open the door, I will come in to him, and will SUP with him, and he with me." (Revelation 3:20) Herein lies the fellowship, the communion, the company, it is the Lord's SUPper that He desires. There is no fussing about who is invited, no worries about condition, color or location of the bread and wine, no silly debates, no presumptuous priesthood to serve these "holy elements," just the pure fellowship of the heart. This is the true communion in the true guestchamber with the true bread.

The Guestchamber Is Key.

If it is a room, then the furnishings of the room become important. If it is a place we are to go, then when we go and where we go and who goes becomes very important. If the table of the Lord is a tangible table, then even its composition may be of some importance. But if the table, and the bread, and the wine, and the room are only a symbols of a greater spiritual existence, then it all becomes totally unimportant and diverting, dividing and distracting, illusory and bothersome. Where is the guestchamber? It is within us!

Most of the problems we encounter are problems that could have been avoided with ease if we had been fresh from fellowship with the Captain of our Salvation. The communion we need is daily communion, not a yearly or a monthly or even a weekly eating and drinking of "holy" bread and grape juice. The symbols mean nothing compared to the fellowship they represent. Paul, teaching on this very thing says,

> *"For the kingdom of God is not meat and drink; but righteousness, and peace, and joy in the Holy Ghost. For he that in these things serveth Christ is acceptable to God, and approved of men. Let us therefore follow after the things which make for peace, and things wherewith one may edify another." (Romans 14:17-19)*

But is anything wrong with an actual guestchamber and a tangible table and physical bread and wine? Yes, they are to be rejected. These items are to be rejected because they occupy a place in our minds that only the real and true articles should occupy. For example if I asked you, "When was the last time you had communion?" You may think back to the last time you sat with others in a service and participated in the Eucharist (or Lord's Supper if you prefer).

If you asked me the same question I would answer, "This morning." If we participate in "communion" at church, do we feel a need to do so at home? If a person partakes of the Lord's Supper in church to satisfy the Scripture's request to do so, is there a desire to continue that supper throughout the day? No, unfortunately the satisfaction of the pure Commandment cannot come from two sources – one source real, the other merely a symbol.

To live in truth, we must choose – let us choose the substance over the symbol. The question that settles the issue is "Where is the guestchamber?"

121. *What shall I say?*

John 12:27, "Now is my soul troubled; and what shall I say? Father, save me from this hour: but for this cause came I unto this hour."

It is in adversity, troubles, and trials that life teaches us. Rarely, if ever, do we learn from the care free, safe, or comfortable experiences.

I once heard a pastor praying for a group of teens that were going to some foreign field on a mission. He went on and on praying for their "safe" journey. He asked God to let their trip be without incident, and he covered the gamut from lost luggage to reckless cab drivers. He prayed "That their plane would not be delayed, that the weather would be perfect allowing all things to go according to schedule." He went on and on until, perhaps even their toothbrushes were mentioned. If it is indeed true that we learn from adversity, then he very well could have asked the Lord to make sure that these teens go and return and learn nothing at all from their trip, he could have as easily prayed, "Let their character and faith be as though they never went at all!"

We should be less eager to avoid problems in our life. We learn and develop when we have our comforts removed for a time. It is pride that causes us to fear this deprivation of comfort, control, and self-reliance. It is because we know deep within us that our lives of righteousness are balanced delicately upon good circumstances.

We are not as Job was. We are like the more common man that Satan thought Job was. Satan described the common man's character when he said to God, "Do you think he loves you for no reason? You have made a hedge of protection around him, and you bless everything he does. But if you remove all he has, he will curse you to your face." (Job 1:9-11) Maybe secretly, we think this may be true of ourselves.

We feel this hedge of protection and fear its being removed. We fear it being invaded by trouble and testing, but we need not fear *IF* our goal is to move toward perfection. When we pray for God to protect us, are we not admitting our fear that our faith cannot stand testing? Jesus instructed us to pray for God to deliver us from evil. Deliverance from evil is not avoidance of evil. The Psalm says, "Many are the afflictions of the righteous: but the LORD delivereth him out of them all." (Psalms 34:19) Jesus, when praying for us (John 17:15) said, "I pray not that thou shouldest take them out of the world, but that thou shouldest keep them from the evil."

His prayer was not that we should be untouched, but His desire was that we would not succumb to, or be overtaken by the evil in the world. This is on the same line of thought as "lead them not into temptation." This is the temptation to sin James spoke of, "Let no man say when he is tempted, I am tempted of God: for God cannot be tempted with evil, neither tempteth he any man:" (James 1:13)

We must not confuse the trying of our faith with the temptation to sin. We should avoid the temptation to sin and earnestly pray for God to lead us away from it. We are promised an escape from the temptations that are above our ability to resist,[207] but the trial of faith is a different thing altogether. "Knowing this, that the trying of your faith worketh patience. But let patience have her perfect work, that ye may be perfect and entire, wanting [lacking] nothing." (James 1:2-4)

This perfection and entirety is what we forfeit when we escape the trials of faith. Jesus, when facing the ultimate trial, when facing His own crucifixion and death, asked, "... *what shall I say? Father, save me from this hour? ... but for this cause came I unto this hour*." His question was, **why should I seek to avoid the very reason I was born**?

Basic Questions

Some have said that there are three basic questions within all men. They are: Where did I come from? Why am I here? And, where am I going when I die? Many mystics, monks, and holy men have spent countless hours contemplating these questions. The Bible offers answers to these and many other questions if we consider the whole story found within.

Some have gleaned from the Scriptures that we are here to help, feed and clothe each other. Some say that our main task is to preach the Gospel to each other. I contend that good economic times and even slightly motivated persons can accomplish either to some degree.

YHVH could feed the world with a stroke of His hand (He has done it before) and angels could come from heaven and preach the everlasting Gospel to mankind thereby forcing men to repent or perish. But there remains yet a task that even the *Almighty* cannot do. It is not a matter of economics or social order. It is a job only you can accomplish while here on earth. A job so important it is surpassed by none other in priority or consequence. Its weight and solemnity is supported in both the questions, "Where did I come from?" and "Where am I going when I die?" The full realization of which answers in toto the question that plagues all of mankind, "Why am I here?" It is summed up very well in Matthew 5:48, "Be ye therefore perfect, even as your Father which is in heaven is perfect."

Don't let this throw you. To achieve perfection is our destiny and we are to strive to accomplish it here. (It will be impossible to accomplish elsewhere.) This perfection is not hard to define; simply put, it is what you should be, that you are not.

We must accept problems and "the trying of our faith" that exercise us as rare opportunities to hone our character. We must press on, "Till we all come in the unity of the faith, and of the knowledge of the Son of God, unto a perfect man, unto the measure of the stature of the fullness of Christ:" (Ephesians 4:13)

---

[207] 1 Corinthians 10:13, "There hath no temptation taken you but such as is common to man: but God is faithful, who will not suffer you to be tempted above that ye are able; but will with the temptation also make a way to escape, that ye may be able to bear it."

"Whom we preach, warning every man, and teaching every man in all wisdom; that we may present every man perfect in Christ Jesus:" (Colossians 1:28)

Paul taught Timothy to use the Scriptures to this end, "That the man of God may be perfect, throughly furnished unto all good works." (2 Timothy 3:17) This is our admonition as well.

When we encounter trials in life, we must consider them as opportunities to prove that the last failure of faith was not a permanent part of our character. We must seek Christ's word and search the Scriptures on matters of life. We must not make it our goal to eliminate all trouble, to avoid every bit of unpleasantness, to sidestep every stumbling block, to live behind a supernatural hedge of protection, but we must face it with resolve, assurance, and the armor of God. Shall we say, "Father save me from this hour?" But for this cause we came to this hour...to be perfected... to face trial... to work out our own salvation. No, let us go on ... unto perfection...[208] When troubles rear their head, brace yourself, and thank God for the opportunity to perfect yourself. Trust in God...with or without a hedge. A hedge is no sign that God loves you; rather the lack of one shows He trusts you.

When we face the awful, the terrifying, or the unimaginable, you may be facing the very trial that will perfect you. It may be the hour for which you were born – to emerge perfected. When you face your most feared and dreaded undertaking, pray for strength to endure, pray for power to hold steadfast to the end. If praying for escape and avoidance of trouble is a temptation for you listen to the resolute determination in the words of Jesus.

When your only desire is to be what the Father wants you to be, it sounds ridiculous to ask for twelve legions of angels. Why would someone seeking perfection want to escape the hour for which they were born? This comes through loud and clear when Jesus asks, "What shall I say...save me from this hour?"

---

[208] Hebrews 6:1

122. *Know ye what I have done to you?*

John 13:12, "So after he had washed their feet, and had taken his garments, and was set down again, he said unto them, Know ye what I have done to you?"

The government of the coming New Kingdom was a matter of concern for Christ. Mankind has a tendency to set one man above another and form hierarchy that eventually is better described as a food chain. Look at any endeavor of man on any level and you will immediately notice that there are those who seek to be in charge and those who seek someone to be in charge.

We look for leadership and we usually find it. The job usually goes to those who seek it, for there are a few who will accept the heaviness of responsibility for the fleeting reward of leadership and notoriety. For all this we have no lack of volunteers. There is always someone seeking to be above another, someone who gains a sense of worth from leadership. There is always someone who finds the profit in being a leader more enticing than the load of responsibility. But we must ask, are these the people we want to lead us?

Jesus was not uncertain when it came to choosing leaders. He had a plan to find and choose leaders and He had a plan for those wishing to be chief to follow. The plan is so unpopular that it is seldom read, and much less is it used.

*"But Jesus called them unto him, and said, Ye know that the princes of the Gentiles exercise dominion over them, and they that are great exercise authority upon them. **But it shall not be so among you**: but whosoever will be great among you, let him be your minister; And whosoever will be chief among you, let him be your servant: Even as the Son of man came not to be ministered unto, but to minister, and to give his life a ransom for many." (Matthew 20:25-28)*

Here Jesus makes it plain that the path to greatness is not what we may have thought. The Gentiles' political system placed men over other men and they exercise their authority over each other, but above them is yet another authority (the one who placed them there) who exercises their power over their subordinates.

What is the difference in the system Jesus criticizes, and the politics of most any church you will find on Main Street, USA? How did we get under the control of men in our Christian faith? How did we come to totally ignore the direct command of our Lord, "It shall not be so among you"?

If you were to visit the average church to find the pastor whom you did not know, would we be able to find him by the description laid out in Scripture? The portrayal in Scripture of the One we seek would lead us on a reverse course in most cases – away from the prominent, the best dressed, the center of attention. The pastor we would find who fits the sketch Jesus drew for us would not be the man whose feet are washed, but the man who washes feet.

As He taught them this hard lesson, He asks, "Know ye what I have done unto you?" Even by example and demonstration Jesus, acting out the humility necessary for a man to enter the service of God, He was not sure that His disciples understood. "Know ye what I have done unto you?"

They Did Not Understand. *We* Do Not Understand.

Looking around ourselves at the hierarchy and exaltation of men in our churches we have no good answer for the Savior. He asks, "Know ye what I have done unto you?" To which we must answer, "No we must not understand, for we have not followed your example at all." The truth is that if we went into First (Whatever) Church, Main Street Downtown, USA, and followed the Bible definition of a leader we would likely identify the janitor as pastor and not the hair-do and suit that stands each Sunday to pontificate.

We have missed entirely the political structure of the church. We cannot find our system of organization described anywhere but in condemning words of Christ in Scripture. We toy with words and create offices and positions for men and women never intended by Christ. Do we really think that Jesus Christ intended to leave us in the hands of men to teach us and guide us to our eternal home or to lead us toward the righteousness with which they themselves struggle and never attain? Jesus never intended to be an absentee friend who used men as mouthpieces to convey His message to His brethren.

His intention was to fill us with the fully capable Holy Spirit to guide us to perfection and holiness. Instead we sought out men who were willing to forego God's plan of writing the Law in our inward parts and were willing to teach us and we let them do so. We gave them the title of "pastor" from a remote and obscure word that appears once in the New Testament, the very definition of which in our modern day is "one having spiritual charge over a congregation or spiritual overseer". We set him above the rest, and look to him as we should look only to the Living Christ. Our modern definition is flawed. The office is corrupted, and the meaning of the word has migrated and mutated to describe a man who is in diametric opposition to its original meaning.

Jesus told us to seek to be servants in order to find prominence; we found the prominent who seek to be served. These "leaders" ironically, preach to us about, "What's wrong with the church today." When the entire structure of guidance, leadership, and oracle has been handed to fallible men. It is no great wonder what is wrong with the church today.

Jesus taught plainly, verbally, by symbol and by example that He was to be the head of the Church. There is to be no intermediary, no arbiter, no mediator, no intercessor. Those who find a place of eldership or honor are to find it only through service to the brethren. They are to take the lowest seat and be called higher. They are to be servants, they are to wash feet.

As Jesus was about to leave this world, He stood and girded Himself with a towel. Then He made His way around the table with basin of water washing feet, just as the lowest of servants would do. Peter even balked at His idea. For it put Christ in such a humiliating position. Jesus moves along the table on His knees. In our minds, we can see Christ on His knees after having washed the very feet that would in a few moments carry this man to receive thirty silver coins from the enemies of Christ, even knowing this, He humbled Himself, He served, He washed. We can see Him sitting back on the floor with His hands still moist, wiping them with the towel, and looking into His friends' faces asking, "Do you know what I have done to you? I have shown you the way to the top."

We prefer our own way though. We know that we prefer our way, because, for the most part, it is the way we have gone. We would never make the janitor our pastor. Nor would we desire to hear his lowly opinion. We want men to whom we can aspire. We want men who are achievers, intelligent, and sure. By and large pastors of our choosing are not "less" than we are (as they are instructed to be), they are greater. They are not servants – they are served. While the janitor, the parking lot attendant, or the woman who cleans the building during the week is, by Christ's standard, more qualified to lead us, we honor the one who has a personal parking place.

Considering and answering Jesus' question, sadly many of us must say, "No, we _do not_ know what He did when He washed the disciple's feet." Although He showed us a way to eliminate multiple problems in our Meetings and churches, although He laid out a flawless plan of determination and recognition of elders, we missed His message. Just as Israel did when they chose a King to rule them instead of God,[209] the modern church has chosen rather the way of the nations around them and rejected God's plan to be our Pastor Himself.

We must say that we do not understand His example, for we have not implemented His plan for leadership or for organization. We must answer, "No Lord," when He asks, "Do you know what I have done to you?"

---

[209] 1 Samuel 8:4-7, "…for they have not rejected thee, but they have rejected me, that I should not reign over them."

123. When I sent you with nothing, did you lack anything?

Luke 22:35, "And he said unto them, When I sent you without purse, and scrip, and shoes, lacked ye any thing? And they said, 'Nothing.'" Reference Luke 10:1-4, Mark 6:8-9

Waiting on the Lord's provision is probably one of the most difficult areas for the "responsible" Christian. If we take seriously our duty to provide for our house to avoid being labeled by the Scriptures as "worse than an infidel,"[210] then we want to exercise some control over our daily needs. How does this effort of providing for our families balance with the Lord's admonition to seek the Lord and all these things (what we eat, drink, and wear for clothing) will be added to us.

If we heard of a man who would not work to supply his family with food but instead said to them, "Seek the Lord and all these things will be added to you," we would know within ourselves that this man has much to learn about Christian living. Yet the other extreme of being sole provider soon robs God of His rightful place of providence and guidance.

The Bible gives us no clear dividing line as to what is our responsibility and what is our Father's. (It is in situations like these that I feel sorry for those who look to their Bibles for the guidance promised to us through the Holy Spirit.)

In times like these, the Spirit of God can lead us to perfectly balance our lives to please God in every way. As we start to take too much control, the voice of the Spirit speaks to our heart and tells us so; and if we obey, we find ourselves curbing our ambition, perhaps not seeking, or even turning down that promotion. Or, we may find that we are not adding to our possessions, but sometimes, going in the opposite direction all together, we give away our "nest egg" to someone in need.

As we listen and obey, we may find that God has only blessed us hitherto to hold in store for someone else. What we hold, we hold in an open hand. What we earn, we earn with an ear open to our Father's call to come aside awhile and rest in His provision. It is life in this balance; it is life under the direction of God who will keep us in perfect harmony with His divine plan for us. We need not fear living in offense of His command to provide. Nor need we fear offending the equal and opposite command to avoid anxiously asking, "What shall we eat or wear?" His provision is forthcoming to those who give without reservation and live responsibly, and His peace abounds to those who look to Him for guidance. His will may take forms unrecognizable to us at first. His provision may well be the promotion, but it may be as well the financial

---

[210] 1 Timothy 5:8, "But if any provide not for his own, and specially for those of his own house, he hath denied the faith, and is worse than an infidel."

reversal or the loss. As He leads, where He leads, we follow. (To hear some talk, you would think that their God follows them.)

Still it is difficult for the responsible man to expect from God what he could easily provide for himself. We have a tendency to only expect God to intervene or act when we have done all we know to do. We even have a cliché to express such a sentiment. "God only helps those who help themselves" – when in fact the Bible says that God sends rain and sun on the just and unjust.

The Scripture tells us that God helps those who trust Him and commit their way unto Him and do not say, "My hand hath gotten me this wealth.[211] The "Christians" who "help themselves" have a tendency to trust in their own might and only thank God for the power to do so. This, I fear, is only a play on words to assuage their faithlessness as if their act of fear was somehow ordained of God.

A balance must be found. However, without a daily communion with God, that balance is impossible. A comfort of living in, and doing God's will is necessary for this communion to take place and without God's hand upon what we do, we cannot expect His blessing and guidance on the finances attained from such actions.

He will guide any who seek Him. Step by step we will discover that His protection is sufficient, His guidance becomes clearer, and His provision is abundant and timely.

Many of us have also seen the other side. The providence of God can take negative forms as well. All of us nod in agreement when we read Haggai 1:6 "Ye have sown much, and bring in little; ye eat, but ye have not enough; ye drink, but ye are not filled with drink; ye clothe you, but there is none warm; and he that earneth wages earneth wages to put it into a bag with holes." If our lives were just free from accident and breakage, mishap and abnormal wear, many of us could be on top in a couple of months. As it is, we are chasing our troubles and convinced that a little more income will do the trick. When in fact, if we had a little less *problems*, a little less *sickness*, a little less *unexpected calamity*, we could make it. But, we have left God on the outside of our finances. Our thinking has become backward. We call people who do not carry insurance "irresponsible" and those who do not tithe "living under grace." We spend money for that which is not bread, but when money runs low, we complain that we cannot "feed our families." The world's answer (and regretfully some of the church's as well) is cash! That is why everyone lights up when they think about winning the lottery, gaining a large inheritance or winning a large lawsuit or insurance settlement. May God have mercy on us all!

The Bible has much to say about money. Money has much to say about the Christian. Your checkbook will tell you where your priorities are, where your loyalties lay, and where your heart is.[212] Perhaps that is why the Bible has so much to say about money.

---

[211] Deuteronomy 8:17-18, "And thou say in thine heart, My power and the might of mine hand hath gotten me this wealth. But thou shalt remember the LORD thy God: for it is he that giveth thee power to get wealth..."
[212] Matthew 6:21, "For where your treasure is, there will your heart be also."

Most Of Our Hesitation Comes From Fear.

We are afraid to give over our control to an invisible, incommunicative, irrational God. None of us would have any reservation turning our finances over to an all-wise, honorable, just and holy God, with whom we were in constant communication and with whom we were living in totally obedient surrender. It is our idea of God that is unreliable. We must admit that it is our end of the bargain that is lacking. It is our side of this equation that sags with unresponsive prayer and less than enthusiastic obedience. God has proven Himself faithful to everyone who ever trusted Him. We should trust Him as well.

Although this situation was different[213] from ours, the Lord's comments are still powerful and useful. It will do you good to look back at the times that you walked in faith. It can only help to recall that when we were commissioned of God and walked in His way, our needs were provided.

As your record of trusting Him grows over years, it should become easier to trust Him. When you doubt the goodness and provision of God, Jesus may give a little recent history quiz to make His point. "When I sent you without purse, and scrip, and shoes, lacked ye any thing?"

---

[213] The disciples were being told about the impending torture and death that was awaiting their Lord and possibly them. In this particular situation, the Lord was warning them to make provision for them selves because He would be caught, captured and rendered powerless (albeit by His own choosing) to help them. Our situation is different today. He now lives forever to make intercession for us.

124. Have I been so long time with you, and yet hast thou not known me?

John 14:9-10, "Jesus saith unto him, Have I been so long time with you, and yet hast thou not known me, Philip? he that hath seen me hath seen the Father; and how sayest thou then, Shew us the Father?"

Meeting God would be a very different proposition for everyone. For, according to our relationship or understanding, we all have differing ideas about who God is. We have all known people who felt that God was an awesome and terrifying being and others who felt He was somewhat of a kind old man with a white beard, with the personality of a teddy bear, and we have heard every variation in between.

Some even hold that God is anything and everything to all people and that we can call Him what we want or believe Him to be anything we want Him to be. But, of all the things we believe God to be, if we hold to the revelation of Jehovah by the Scriptures, the latter is probably the most incorrect. Regardless of our understanding, regardless of our relationship, regardless of our experiences, God is who He is. He is not a bit more, nor is He less, He is not more liberal or conservative, He is not gentler or more tyrannical than He is indeed. He is who He is. We must remember, when He identified Himself to Moses, the name He took to Himself was YHVH – I Am. He said, "Tell them, I am – Who I am."

He has been a mystery, even to those who worship Him. Phillip asked Jesus, "Show us the Father and it will do us good!" Jesus, very disappointed, asked them, *"Have I been so long time with you, and yet hast thou not known me, Philip? he that hath seen me hath seen the Father; and how sayest thou then, Shew us the Father?"* (John 14:9) Some students of the Bible have taken this to mean that Jesus was claiming here to *be* the Father. Some say that Jesus was claiming to be the same as God the Father in form and power and authority, endeavoring, by this Scripture, to support the Trinitarian theories that Jesus and His Father are equal in these and other ways. But simply read and understood as written, we can see that Christ was lamenting that the mission on which He was sent was so blatantly misunderstood. He was sent to reveal the Father to mankind. His mission was to perfectly represent the Father to mankind. Christ's presence should have enabled man to meet and know God fully and thereby enabling us to serve Him faithfully. This is why we can hear disappointment in Jesus' voice when He says, "Have you not known me? Why would you ask to see the Father?" Sometimes when we ask for things we have already been given, it insults those who offered it.

Getting To Know Him

How long have you known Christ? How long have you known about Him? We have friends whom we have only known a year or so, that we know better than we know our Savior whom we claim to have known and served for years.

There are those among us who are better aquatinted with the founders of their faith or denomination, than they are with Jesus Christ. They can quote Calvin, Knox, Luther, and Fox, but they cannot quote Christ correctly. In reality they do not know Jesus at all; they only know what other men said about Him.

Many people have a second, third, or fourth-hand knowledge of Christ. Many only know what they learned from their parents, some never learned past their primary years as a child in church. To them, Jesus is a figure holding a lamb under one arm and a staff in the other in some dusty portrait in their past; a tradition, a portrait, a statue, or a historical character. "Have I been so long time with you, and yet hast thou not known me?"

Many of us learn of Christ only within a denominational framework. If we read that Jesus said something that contradicts our founders or denominational understanding we ignore it or reinterpret it to comply with our faith. If Jesus steps outside the circle drawn by our denominational forebears we give full allegiance to the traditional ideas that keep us in step with our faith community and friends. We should be ashamed as cowards and traitors if we forsake Christ for such an unworthy and selfish institution as structured religion. If we deny our personal revelation of Christ in order to keep our standing in our fellowship we have denied Christ Himself. We will suffer Christ's denial of us in eternity if we deny Him before men.[214]

We don't know the living Christ because we have not sought Christ outside of our denominational boundaries. Are we so silly to believe that Jesus Christ was a Baptist? Or a Lutheran? Or a Quaker? Are we so ridiculous to think that the Son of God could fall within any of the senseless denominational boundaries we have created?

We have wasted many years by never traveling farther with Christ than our family did, never learning more from Jesus than our denominational Fathers did, never searching past common, and traditional understanding. Jesus asks you again, "Have I been so long time with you, and yet hast thou not known me?"

We must answer this question honestly ourselves, but we cannot stop there. We must repent of the failure by not repeating it. We must learn of Christ. We must learn with Christ. We must not place barriers in our path and demand that guidelines not be violated. We cannot believe that any man or woman, any denomination or religion, has had full comprehension of Christ. We must know that no faith on earth is correct in every area, why then do we hold back from advancing past these lines of ignorance? Is it fear of people, fear of failure, or fear of being alone? We must go on to perfection.

---

[214] Matthew 10:33, "But whosoever shall deny me before men, him will I also deny before my Father which is in heaven."

Christ has a plan for you that includes ideas that may not be found among the people and places and ideas you frequent. He has fresh viewpoints to show you that He cannot, because as He attempted to take you off of your denominational path, you balked and returned to your borders where your friends are, where your family is, where you are comfortable. There is a knowing of the Father that is available only to those who reach beyond what they presently understand and are not tied to ideas that maintain comfortable relationships.

YHVH cannot "fit" into only one man's thinking, nor can He fit into man's denominations. He chose instead to "fit" Himself into a man – Christ Jesus. He is indeed, God with us.[215] We will know Him no other way than to know Him in person. You will never know Him through someone else's experience, or testimony, or doctrine.

Your main purpose should be as Paul's was. "That I may know him…" (Philippians 3:10) What better reward of study, what better benefit of dedication, what better gift to the faithful, but to know Him? To know Christ is to know the Father, the creator of the world. To know Him is to gain from Him the knowledge intended by His incarnation from the beginning of the world. To miss this intimate knowledge is to miss the purpose of His birth, the purpose of His life, the purpose of His death, the purpose of His resurrection, the purpose of His sitting at the right hand of the Father on high. To miss the intimate knowledge of Jesus Christ is to miss the purpose of your life as well.

We all have plenty of ground to regain. We all must admit that we do not know Him as we should. It is time to set upon a quest to know Him. You must not be found wanting when days no longer avail you of opportunities to know Him better. Today, it is time to pray, it is time to study, and it is time to be brave. When you ask to know Him, prepare for the stabbing pain of conviction when He asks, "Have I been so long time with you, and yet hast thou not known me?"

---

[215] Matthew 1:23, "Behold, a virgin shall be with child, and shall bring forth a son, and they shall call his name Emmanuel, which being interpreted is, God with us."

125. *Believest thou not that I am in the Father, and the Father in me?*

John 14:10, "Believest thou not that I am in the Father, and the Father in me? the words that I speak unto you I speak not of myself: but the Father that dwelleth in me, he doeth the works."

Have you ever heard of the uninspired part of the Bible? Yes, there appears to be an entire page that does not belong among the Scriptures. It is the page after Malachi and before Matthew. It says, The New Testament.

There is a divide, in the minds of some, between the Old and New Testament. Some feel the God of the Old Testament was a cruel and exacting God who "visited the iniquities of the fathers upon the children to three or four generations." They further believe that now, in the New Testament, we enjoy life under the regime of Christ who is much kinder, gentler and more tolerating of sin and iniquity. Is this true? Has the plan changed? Have we experienced a change of management, so to speak?

As you read and study the Old Testament you will find that the personality of God was much kinder than some have reputed Him to be. There are several occasions when His tender heart was broken and many times the love that He had for man was displayed. From His first pleadings with Cain to choose the righteous path, to His voice through the Prophet Malachi, we can easily hear His love and concern. Although Cain was banished and cursed for his choice to kill, we should not forget the meeting pertaining to the rejected offering that was held beforehand with God. God came to Cain when his offering was rejected and pled with him as a friend, warning him to be careful that he not resent Abel. That same acceptance awaits all of us who do well.[216]

In the Old Testament, the judgment of God often included death. This was sometimes done by harsh means such like stoning. If we consider, though, that these whose lives were taken away were infecting the minds and souls of those in their influence, or setting examples of disobedience that would be the ultimate demise of hundreds of thousands of God's people, the action made good sense. Our viewpoints are deficient.

Albeit cruel and harsh to inflict further pain upon a sick man, no one would resent or despise a doctor for causing pain on an operating table if he was extracting a cancer. We need not make excuses for the actions of God in the Old Testament. We need only realize that we do not know everything and concede to God's infinite wisdom.

What of the thousands of people in the Promised Land that He gave orders to slaughter? Sometimes He ordered women, children, and cattle to be killed. Can we concede to God's wisdom in this as well? We must admit that

---

[216] Genesis 4:6-7

death does not carry the same weight in the mind of God as it does in the mind of man. With helpless man – death always means loss.

We cannot say that about God. Whether it is because of our God's immense power to resurrect or simply because our deficient vantage point will not allow it, we cannot say that about God. With us who are mortal, life is everything. Our reasoning therefore cannot be matched with God's. Whether death is more or less important, where that importance lies, and death's value balanced with the value of life, are all areas in which will find ourselves severely lacking in understanding, perspective, and ability to determine.

One and the Same

Just as we have a tendency to generalize the disposition of God in the Old Testament, we do the same with Jesus' attitude toward judgment in the New Testament. They are, however, theologically inseparable. Absolutely nothing has changed about the God of the Old Testament and Jesus is a perfect representative of YHVH in the New Testament. If this is true, we have certainly misjudged God and may have misjudged Christ as well.

Jehovah was every bit as kind as Christ was. We find God displaying Christ's attitude toward sin in the Old Testament in this passage in Ezekiel 18:21-23,

*"But if the wicked will turn from all his sins that he hath committed, and keep all my statutes, and do that which is lawful and right, he shall surely live, he shall not die. All his transgressions that he hath committed, they shall not be mentioned unto him: in his righteousness that he hath done he shall live. **Have I any pleasure at all that the wicked should die?** saith the Lord GOD: and not that he should return from his ways, and live?"*

This is indistinguishable from the manner of Jesus. His most familiar and clarion message, given after precluding a just punishment, was "Go and sin no more."

Does Jesus display God's unrelenting attitude toward righteousness? Yes, He does! Jesus, being tolerant and forgiving, is mistakenly credited for removing worldwide condemnation. Though He is famous for saying, "For God sent not his Son into the world to condemn the world," The next verse is much harder to read, "…he that believeth not is condemned already, because he hath not believed in the name of the only begotten Son of God." (John 3:17-18) He actually confirmed the condemnation of the world in this statement. Also, Jesus made demands to believe in Him and Him alone to gain salvation. He was intolerant of any who attempted righteousness without Him, calling them "thieves and robbers," later consigning them to everlasting destruction. He spoke of death and punishment of the wicked and by His words shows us that He was and is very much like His Father.[217]

---

[217] John 5:18-19, "Therefore the Jews sought the more to kill him, because he not only had broken the sabbath, but said also that God was his Father, making himself equal with God. Then answered Jesus and said

It is a futile argument to propose that the government of the Kingdom of God has changed hands, or even changed policies. Jesus and His Father are one. One in policy, one in government, one in direction and goal, they are one in Spirit. When you see Jesus, you have seen the Father. As a matter of fact, we only came to Christ because the Father drew us to Him.[218]

It is a dangerous idea to fear the God of the Old Testament and not fear Christ as your judge. The judgment of Jesus Christ will fully satisfy God and will not vary "one jot or tittle" from the judgment of YHVH Himself. If you have fearful respect toward your "Old Testament God" that you do not have toward your "New Testament Christ" your view of one or both of these members of the Godhead is not a Scriptural one. If you have the impression that Christ is more merciful than His Father, the Scriptures will prove this feeling to be illusory.

If you think that the God of the old covenant waits, desirous to destroy you, and only the grace of Jesus stands between you and annihilation, you have misunderstood Jehovah, or Jesus, or both. It would behoove you to find the truth about these two figures who balance, not each other, but perfectly within themselves, grace and judgment, mercy and justice, compassion and unyielding demand for righteousness. The Scriptures will guide you to a complete knowledge of what is required of you to stand under their inseparable judgment.

If you fear God, but not His son you may be surprised. If you love Christ, but the God of the Old Testament escapes your adoration as a merciful and loving God; if the similarities of Christ and His Father are not apparent to you, you likely have missed a great revelation from the Scriptures of truth.

Jesus wants us to be under no such delusion. His words made it clear, over and over again, that He revealed the Father to us by His life and actions. Our misconception of God is part of the reason Christ came. We need to realize that the Father God of the Old Testament and Jesus the Messiah are two with the same intent, mind, and Spirit.

When you doubt and fear the God of the Old Testament, but hold to Christ as a different judge, operating under different rules, you confuse the issue (not to mention render the greater portion of Scriptures useless and ambiguous).

When was it decided that there was a different God in the days of Abraham and Moses than in the days in which you live? Jesus would ask you, "Believest thou not that I am in the Father, and the Father in me?"

---

unto them, Verily, verily, I say unto you, The Son can do nothing of himself, but what he seeth the Father do: for what things soever he doeth, these also doeth the Son likewise."
[218] John 6:44-45, "No man can come to me, except the Father which hath sent me draw him: and I will raise him up at the last day. It is written in the prophets, And they shall be all taught of God. Every man therefore that hath heard, and hath learned of the Father, cometh unto me."

126. Wilt thou lay down thy life for my sake?

John 13:38, "Jesus answered him, Wilt thou lay down thy life for my sake?
Verily, verily, I say unto thee, The cock shall not crow, till thou hast denied me
thrice."

Heady and impetuous, Peter makes claims of allegiance and loyalty to Christ much like we do when we first take up our new life in Him. Peter wants Jesus to know that he will go to the death for Him if it is necessary. When we first find that this way of life may cause us to be persecuted, the brave among us stick out their chin and the determined brace themselves and pledge that they too will never give in.

The story goes on to prove that Peter was mistaken about his own character. How did he prove that he would not lay down his life? By denying Jesus when his own comfort was at risk. This is the precise point at which our own constitution may bend. We could therefore, gain insight into our condition by answering the question of Jesus, "Will you lay down your life for my sake?"

Perhaps you remember the massacre that occurred in a Colorado High School that was later referred to as the "Columbine Tragedy." It is told that one of the murderous boys, choosing his next victim, asked Cassie Burnell, a girl in the school, well known to have a Christian testimony, to deny Christ to save herself. She would not and lost her life for her stand. Maybe we imagine ourselves proving our allegiance to Christ as godless communist hoards overrun the city in which we live and demanding that all deny Christ or die. We may gain satisfaction in thinking and saying to our friends that we would never deny our Savior, even if threatened with death. Though we have settled on the fact that we would remain allied to Christ, and we are sure that we would never deny Him, He still asks, "Will you lay down your life for my sake?"

When the drama and movie-like scripts in our mind are discarded and "cameras" we envision are no longer recording our heroism, the real world mammon and hard-core temptations take their full effect. What we do when we find ourselves under the scrutiny of our peers, and what we do when those peers are nowhere to be found will be quite different.

Here we do not discuss suffering torture, nor are we debating whether we will die for Christ. Here we consider *living* for Him, for the opportunity to deny Christ in our life rarely comes at gunpoint. It most often comes in darkness, in obscurity, and well beyond the view of those we would impress with a stance of bravery and self-denial. Yes, the real test is not out in the open with everyone watching. It is not a trial whose end result will bring fame and honor to the exonerated party. It is the small tests of allegiance, done in private; choices between our way and His way, choices between comfort and commitment, between conviction and convenience, between the sensible and sensual.

402

These are the tests we fail. These are the ones that cost us our eternal life, not the blatant and public denial of Christ, but the private denials, choices made in offices and homes, directions taken in conversations and lifestyles. In these everyday circumstances we deny that we know Him. These are the times we falter and take up our life (and lay His down). You see, many are willing to die for Christ, but few are willing to live for Him.

"Wilt thou lay down thy life for my sake?" It is our life that is the problem. Our life is the one that we seek to save when we attempt to preserve our comfort and our pleasure. Jesus gave no great hope to those who sought to save their own lives and preserve their reputations. When Jesus asks you to lose your life He speaks, not of death (although it may lead to that), but of the denial of your life, your choice, your direction. "Then said Jesus unto his disciples, If any man will come after me, let him deny himself, and take up his cross, and follow me. For whosoever will save his life shall lose it: and whosoever will lose his life for my sake shall find it." (Matthew 16:24-26)

What does He mean by "lose his life?" What does He mean by "save his life?" We lose our life by laying it aside. We save our life by living it without denial, in pleasure and self-satisfaction. What is a sign of a life without denial? What fruit can be seen in the life lived for yourself? Profit, full barns, gain of the world's goods, are all evidence a life lived without denial. For Jesus goes on to ask those who choose to save life, "For what is a man profited, if he shall gain the whole world, and lose his own soul or what shall a man give in exchange for his soul?"

There are some who live every minute to gain more and more. Their lives are comfort upon comfort, gift upon gift, and feast upon feast. Some give God all the glory for their wealth. Some would be willing to give their lives in death rather than deny Christ. They live in a state of limbo not wishing to blatantly deny Christ but never denying themselves anything they want. Is there such a state? Is there a place in true faith where you can deny neither Christ nor yourself? Is there a way for you to lay down your life and keep it, or to gain the whole world and not lose your own soul?

This question must be answered honestly within ourselves not once – but once a day – perhaps even many times a day. We who gain hope because we are willing to die for Jesus Christ must be willing rather to live for Him in order to fulfill His desire for us. Christ seeks, not those willing to die for Him, but those willing to live for Him.

A Living Sacrifice

The apostle Paul even mentions this concept in Romans 5:7-8, "For scarcely for a righteous man will one die: yet peradventure [maybe] for a good man some would even dare to die. But God commendeth his love toward us, in that, while we were yet sinners, Christ died for us." Who would not be willing to die for as good a man as Jesus? After all, He died for us. At the very least it is an exchange. But to live for Him – that is a sacrifice acceptable unto God.

Our sacrifice is to be a living one, not a dead one. We are to give our lives for Christ while we live everyday, not just die for Him in the end.

Though it is a worthy sentiment, and God holds highly the death of martyrs, we should focus on living for Him. The quality of a martyr's death is giving a life that has previously lived in service to God. The true martyr finds death to be, not a monumental leap towards righteousness, but just another small step in the life of Christ lived everyday. It is your life laid down and His taken up that Jesus wishes for us when He asks, "Wilt thou lay down thy life for my sake?" Again in Romans 12:1, Paul writes of our lives as living sacrifices, "I beseech you therefore, brethren, by the mercies of God, that ye present your bodies a living sacrifice, holy, acceptable unto God, which is your reasonable service."

As you face the everyday choice of comfort or confrontation, acceptance or rejection by your peers or even the simple choice to indulge or deny yourself, you must realize that you have arrived at the crucial point of living for Jesus Christ. Even though we may be willing by lip service to deny all and follow Him, though we may be quick to claim that our life means nothing to us and we will gladly give it in death, we must consider, will we give it as a living sacrifice? To lay down a life when we are finished with it is one thing, but to lay down a perfectly good and usable one...?

You must hear His question and answer honestly. "Wilt thou lay down thy life for my sake?"

127. Why sleep ye?

Luke 22:46, "And said unto them, Why sleep ye? rise and pray, lest ye enter into temptation."

There are several "Christian drugs" that are acceptable to the modern church. While they condemn out-of-hand the use of illegal narcotics, and frown heavily upon the use of some legal substances, conventional Christianity has a plethora of replacement stimulants available to the churchgoer who wishes not to offend. These "legal" substances are only allowed because they do not offend the members of a particular congregation, these rules and regulations are not universally applicable to all churches. I will attempt to rank them according to my experience.

A person who smokes is usually unwelcome in all religious circles. (Although I have visited churches where smoking was only allowed out front, the pastor still complained about his members who would not use the ashtray provided and just flicked the butts on the grounds.) For the most part smoking is unacceptable. As an ex-smoker myself I was disappointed to find that there was no replacement for this forbidden habit. Non-smokers suggested chewing gum, but as any smoker will tell you, there are not interchangeable.

Drinking alcohol ranges from, "What? Are you kidding?" to "As long as it is done in moderation..." to a certain denomination of whom it is said, "Where two or three are gathered... there'll be a fifth."

Another area that is dangerous, though silent, is the area of prescription drugs. I am convinced that there are millions of people who are slaves to these chemicals. They, who would be the first to condemn an alcoholic or drug addict for his recreational use of narcotics, are oblivious to the fact that they are similarly incapable of dealing with life clean and sober. Psychologists and psychiatrist across the country (and indeed around the world) are resorting to drugs to calm the tortured consciences and excite the lethargic, and generally bring people's minds and lives into control.

While driving through Kentucky I heard a commercial on a "Christian" radio station for a "Christian psychologist" offering its service to new clients. It went something like, "Are you depressed? Do you have trouble concentrating? Is your health affected by loss of sleep, anxiety, worry, and fear?" "Are you overweight?" The ad goes on and on asking questions that describe 99% of the population. I find myself screaming at the radio, "If you have these symptoms, go to Christ, my friend! You are under conviction!" Alas, they cannot hear me, but they *will* hear this commercial and they *will* respond. There's will probably be a long and confusing world of psychological doubletalk, getting in touch with feelings, dredging up their past, searching desperately for a reason for their dysfunctional behavior. A little Prozac a little Valium, just to help them deal with their lives, just to help them back on track, and they will soon be just fine. Or will they?

"Gimme That Ol' Time Religion"

The "old time religion" has its strategies and programs for the one suffering from sin as well. Though a little different, it seems to solve the problem for many comers. The old time Pentecostal preachers used to say, "I never quit drinkin'… I just changed wells! I never quit dancin'… I just changed partners! I never quit fightin'… I just quit fightin' God!" All of which may be a very lively and entertaining idea of regeneration but, is it true reflection of a man who has changed or a man who has changed habits?

If I smoke because it fills a void in my Spiritual make-up, am I made better if I choose rather to eat a hamburger or two to fulfill the same purpose? The problem within remains, does it not?

If I need to go to places that are loud and boisterous to quell the torture in my soul, or I need to add alcohol to my bloodstream to dampen the thoughts of enmity with God, or I need to involve myself in ego-satisfying barroom brawls to feel a sense of worth, am I really making myself better or getting closer to the man God wants me to be when I get the same level of stimulus from "religious" (acceptable) sources? Freedom from all bonds (even those we willingly place upon ourselves) is the freedom Christ has in mind for us. Not to need stimulus is far better than any satisfaction of that need.

The conventional church has put coffee cups in hands that once held beer glasses, but the need for stimulus remains. They have made their sermons exciting for those who once went downtown for exhilaration, but the need for stimulus remains. They have provided a full program to keep everyone happy and busy and just slightly defocused so that depression will not creep in, and fear will not take hold. Twenty minutes of silence would devastate most modern Christians. With silence would come thought, with thought would come evaluation, with that, our lives would not stand under the scrutiny God exacts upon us. We know that. However instead of dealing with it and the making necessary changes, we make noise so we cannot hear.

The excitement carries us to the end of the day, but what then? We must sleep. We either take some drug to bring sleep or we work ourselves down to the point that we collapse. We wake to an alarm and then do it all again. Is this the life of a Christian? Before you answer, look around, ask some questions, you will be surprised how many seek refuge in busy-ness, chemical induced dullness (prescription or otherwise), or in just sleep. For the most part, the calm, cool and collected individual is a rare item. What a shame! The standard lifestyle for the man at peace with God is a scarcity.

We must wake up! We must be aware and be afraid of nothing! If we are at peace with God why would we desire to escape? Envision if we were now, living in the Kingdom of God, with Satan bound, and the whole earth was "full of the knowledge of the LORD, as the waters cover the sea."[219] In this beautiful setting can you imagine wanting to be inebriated? Can you conceive

---

[219] Isaiah 11:9

of wanting to be dull, less aware, or blurred in you thinking? Why does any one desire it now? Because their awareness of God brings them less comfort, not more. Awareness of Truth causes pain. Why is Truth NOT the liberator promised by Christ? It does not set us free, it binds us to the knowledge that we are less than we should be. The more we know, the more we need to escape.

We Are A Sin Sick Society.

The words of Deuteronomy 28:66-67 perfectly depict the soul in distress from living a life outside the Law and will of God. They sound much like and ad for a Christian Psychologist. "And thy life shall hang in doubt before thee; and thou shalt fear day and night, and shalt have none assurance of thy life: In the morning thou shalt say, Would God it were even! and at even thou shalt say, Would God it were morning! for the fear of thine heart wherewith thou shalt fear, and for the sight of thine eyes which thou shalt see." This verse describes a man or woman who wishes things were not as they are, a dangerous set-up for depression. Is that you? You are under conviction, my friend.

The word that was not heard in the radio ad in Kentucky, which is likely not heard from the pulpit of the First Church of Unconsciousness, the word that is increasingly unpopular among Christians is "repentance." Repentance will clear the fearful fog between you and God. Truth will prevail in life, leaving freshness to everything it touches. No more desire to close your eyes, no more will you wish for another day, but live in the Way of Light and Truth, honesty and freedom. Turn from your way. You don't need to get busy. Quite the contrary! You need to spend time before God, let Him break your heart, your will, and once surrender is made, the blinders come off. Sobriety will be a way of life. The chains of addiction are broken – because the very reason for them has disappeared!

"Awake to righteousness, and sin not..." (1 Corinthians 15:34) When you are awake yet repentant, you may see your faults ... but you have His mercy, "Why sleep ye?"

128. Could ye not watch with me one hour?

Matthew 26:40-41, "And he cometh unto the disciples, and findeth them asleep, and saith unto Peter, What, could ye not watch with me one hour? Watch and pray, that ye enter not into temptation: the spirit indeed is willing, but the flesh is weak."

Watching is a lost concept. Today in our silly spoiled society, watching pertains to only one pastime, and we all know what it is. Yes, television has assumed command of and consumed every available hour and is marketed to take more and more of our time in our future. So today, we are well practiced to watch one hour. We can watch several hours at a time! If duration is the essential ingredient, all that needs to be done is make the watching entertaining, beneficial, or stimulating enough and we all can, and will, watch for hours. Sadly, many churches and ministries have gone this same entertainment route.

The watching Christ calls us to is much different. Though it is tedious, it is not a matter of will. Though it is mysterious, it is not a matter of intrigue. It is a matter of being called, commissioned, or commanded to do it. There must be an unction that springs from within a person, and the cause for which one is called to watch is not always apparent to the one called.

We see great advantage when we see a sign that says: "No Waiting." No matter why we came, no waiting is better than waiting, but only if the reason we came was to receive. Sometimes we are simply called to wait.

The kind of preaching that rings the triangle dinner bell and hollers, "Come and get it" attempts to place a "no waiting" sign in the church's window as well. In conventional Christianity, we are told that God is sitting on the edge of His seat waiting for us! We are told He waits in anticipation for a petitioner to open his mouth so that He can respond to him.

This concept, however, is not evidenced in Scripture. God was sought for audience. No one presumed that God automatically and immediately heard their prayer whenever they arbitrarily prayed to Him for any reason. Today, we pray whenever we want, for whatever we want, with little concern for God's will and with an attitude that He owes us. If we are not so bold as to think that He owes us an answer, we at least think He is obligated to listen to our petition.

Where did we get such an idea? All of the promises pertaining to God's hearing us are conditionally rendered. *IF* we repent, *IF* we turn, *IF* we depart from evil, *THEN* He will hear. How are we to depart from evil hidden by the noise in our life if we never spend the time silently seeking Him and waiting and watching?

We fly into prayer as if God is a pageboy. We pray for people to be blessed and healthy. We pray for good weather for little league games, pray that God will cover our mistakes in business, or our missteps with relationships, and pray for Him to generally bless our slothfulness. We pray for safety, that God will give us a safe journey back and forth from Las Vegas, or we ask for His protection as we go hang gliding, rock climbing, or sky diving. We ask for His mercies of health and cram ourselves with junk food, carry excess weight, and expect Him to override our surfeiting lifestyles. Messages we hear from today's churches are as carnival barkers calling "step right up" to "whosoever will."

You should feel challenged at this point to find examples of this capricious and thoughtless praying in the Scriptures of truth. The salvation event, blessings, miracles, and the intervention of God's power on our behalf (grace) were done at His will, and those who sought it, sought it with tears and much humility and waiting. We are not called to bark orders to God, nor are we to ask God for miracles of weather, or the healing of our wretchedly abused and over-fed bodies, or to atone for our willful sin, we are called to watch and pray. Watching exposes this selfishness and, undoubtedly, this is the reason for its removal from the life of the Christian.

Be Still and Know

There is a call for us to seek God, to wait for Him, and just to be still and know. Waiting worship[220] perfectly fulfills such a call. Waiting worship is devoid of jovial commotion and excitement, and it frees one from the foolishness that is propagated by the forward motion of life. We are less apt to silliness and selfishness when we slow down and consider the gravity of the present moment. However, this concentration is difficult and uncomfortable. We squirm to be released. This same discomfort has led to activities being included in worship like singing and verbose prayers and exciting sermons to hold the interest of "worshipers." Now, the worshiper may walk out of a world of entertainment into a church full of entertainment to capture their attention. This has led to the church considering itself to be in competition with the world! Our mission is clear; to come out and be separate from the world and we naïvely look to it as a pattern for our worship.

The world's foolishness and noise that is designed to hold our attention everyday has been given a new face and is found in worship services under the guise of keeping folks active in church. In reality, all it really accomplishes is diversion from the reality of our condition. If all that was designed for excitement and diversion were removed from the modern church, the average attendee would fall asleep inside the hour.

Any modern "Christian" would find themselves in the same situation as the disciples that night when they were asked to watch with Christ. He would return and find them sleeping as He did them. "Could ye not watch with me one hour?" No, Master, we cannot. We need excitement because what you call us to do is boring. We need entertainment, because what interests and motivates you does not interest us at all. No, Master, we have no cause other than our own, no interests other than ours and we are so tired... Jesus answers, "Sleep on now,

---

[220] Quaker worship has been primarily waiting or silent worship. All worshippers sat silently waiting until moved upon to speak a word form the Lord. A Meeting *could* pass in total silence. Until recent years, all traditional Quaker Meetings practiced waiting on God in silence – a near perfect fulfillment the command to watch. This is still practiced today in a few Conservative Meetings.

and take your rest: behold, the hour is at hand, and the Son of man is betrayed into the hands of sinners."[221]

The biggest event in Messianic history was about to take place and the disciples were asleep. Without our stimulus package we receive from the world around us (and from our churches) we would be asleep as well. Have you become dependant upon a caffeinated cup of praise and alarm clock preaching? As much as any drug addict who seeks a fix, without it many who insist that they know the Savior are asleep while they walk about, neither knowing what they do while they are awake, nor do they rest while they sleep. We all must come off the fix. We all must come aside and be still. In the quiet the Lord will instruct, cleanse, soothe and prepare us. We must wait and watch. "Could ye not watch with me one hour?"

What kept Christ awake at the place of prayer? What stimulated Him? Can't you watch one hour? The feet of those who carried Christ away to His mock trial and torture came in the same night that they slept. The time in which we live is even more pregnant. Could we not watch one hour? Remember, there were two men in the group of thirteen that night who saw no sleep; Christ, and Judas Iscariot were wide awake. Both had missions, both had stimulus to remain awake. What's yours? "Could ye not watch with me one hour?"

---

[221] Matthew 26:45

129. *Whom seek ye?*

John 18:4, "Jesus therefore, knowing all things that should come upon him, went forth, and said unto them, Whom seek ye?"

We don't hear much about bravery today. Although we can easily find movies and novels that portray men and women who "go against all odds" and risk death, these "fearless" are a poor substitute for the brave. Fearlessness can be a product of ignorance as well as anything else. As a matter of fact, bravery requires fear to be pure bravery. To be brave is to be fully aware of fear, and, in spite of it, walk toward a situation that is unfriendly or dangerous on the basis of principle when it would be just as easy to walk the other way. "Jesus therefore, knowing all things that should come upon Him, went forth..." This example is not an example of fearlessness nor ignorance. This is an example of pure bravery.

Generally speaking, the world is not a friendly place. This is especially true if we profess a faith in Christ. I am sure there are lots of psychological reasons that may be given for such unfriendly behavior, but Jesus, in His inimitably simple style said it this way, "They hated me...they will hate you."[222] The fact is, the more you resemble Christ, the more they will hate you. There are those who are loved by the world and who have a testimony of being a Christian, but even a cursory investigation shows them to be less than forthright about their faith, less than faithful about the Commandments of Jesus, and less than accountable in the judgment of sin.

If Jesus is our example, we have no choice but to take and defend our stand on righteousness with no tomfoolery mixed with it – no mincing of words, no politically correct additions or exclusions, but an honest and forthright answer to all. We need not be unkind or antagonistic, but always true and accurate in our dealings and opinions. Whether toward king or peasant, rich or poor, someone who offers little advantage for ourselves or one who could turn our life for the better upon a single word, we must maintain a testimony consistent with the witness of the Lord Jesus Christ. This will require bravery.

We marvel when we read of the men of the past who looked magistrates in the eye and would not waver from their convictions. We Quakers have such brave men decorating our history. Alas, they are but few today. Some have embraced *concession*, mistaking it for unity.

Some have laid down doctrines considered "divisive" fearing controversy and said nothing as it was replaced by the anti-Christian doctrine of "anything goes." We have foregone "details" in doctrine for the sake of peace only to later find false doctrine firmly ensconced in its place.

When we sow to the wind of compromise we reap the whirlwind of error; when we sow to human reason, we reap humanism. Now, after many

---

[222] John 15:18, "If the world hate you, ye know that it hated me before it hated you."

years of this non-controversial existence, the fellowship of Quakers at large is a mere shadow of its former self when it reflected sharply the Lord Jesus and His Scriptures of Truth.

Undeserving of the name, the majority of modern Quakers no longer quake and tremble before the Lord, but suffer the vanity of pride and self preservation and cower for the sake of "unity." Proud we are of our past and the character of our founding fathers. Yet we are, by great character or bravery, making no path for our own offspring to follow. We could spend long hours reading about the great men who were their forebears and yet witness the children in these Meetings swallowed up by mammon for lack of any greatness in their parents.

Where are those who would stand for "Thus saith the Lord", where are the brave souls who could stand in the town square, facing gallows, and never budge from the revelation written in their hearts by the Holy Spirit? Where are the men who read and knew their Bibles and based their lives upon it? In short, we are suffering from cowardice. In fine, we are suffering from lack of relationship to God.

Love Not Your Lives unto Death

After three years of living with and working with the Savior, Peter denied the reality within himself and denied even knowing Jesus. His is a pertinent example of the kind of bravery that is lacking today. Peter was saving his own skin. We all know that when we find ourselves in public conversation it is prudent to avoid two subjects – politics and religion.

Why are the most important things a person could discuss, avoided? Is it because we don't want to confront, cause arguments, or cause any offense. As Peter did, we avoid unpleasantness. We deny that we know Him by our silence. We cower and avoid instead of standing tall and taking what comes as our example Christ Jesus did. How different Peter's next few days would have been if He asked, "Are you looking for me?" then said, "Here I am!"

This silence is also found in our own homes. We deny that we know God when we leave Him out of the equation of right and wrong. If a mother tells a child not to steal because "You could go to jail if you get caught," we would say that is the basest form of training. A better answer would be, "Because it is against the Commandments of God." Yet when our children ask why something is considered wrong, they are given humanistic reasons like "It offends or hurts others" as if that was the highest priority. Anytime that we leave the divine Truth of God out of any question of right and wrong we deny that we know Him by what we do not say. We make our truth supreme, and God's Truth secondary, our commandments law, and His, simply reference material. "Not giving heed to Jewish fables, and commandments of men, that turn from the truth…They profess that they know God; but in works they deny him…." (Titus 1:14-16)

Today, our faith in God is denied exposure in the secular world and our homes because our hearts fail us. We faint and we are afraid of being laughed at, impugned or penalized somehow. We are cowards. We need to stand before God as such and repent.

There may come a day when we will have to lay all before the world and take a stand for what we believe. The day has already come for us to lay all before our family, our friends and co-workers about our faith in God. You may have to be brave and face the controversy that you have avoided for years. The time has come to walk toward your persecution and perhaps, if you are faithful, you will gain the strength to walk toward your crucifixion if that time were to come as well. It is time to be brave. It is time to stop masking your faith lifestyle as "the right thing to do" or as "good common sense" and call it like it is – the Commandment of God. You must stop acting like it is just a good idea to do right and say out loud, "Thus saith the Lord."

Jesus was in the Garden of Gethsemane, well aware that He had been betrayed, and awaiting the hour that Satan would have free reign. In His mind He could see them organizing the party to go into Gethsemane to fetch Him. He could see them prepare for the crucifixion and even though He knew all that would befall Him, He still had the courage to stay there and wait.

As he heard distant sounds of them approaching, His heart undoubtedly raced as the realization of the end was upon Him. Knowing in Himself that He could call out for twelve legions of angels, He determinedly shook off thoughts of escape because He considered the beneficial effect His death would have for you and me. His brave heart leaped again hearing a twig snap from a tree branch as the armed party of thugs made their way through the garden.

Shhhhh!... Whispers— then silence. As he heard the noise of their feet come to a stop in the circle of His disciples, He stood erect, resolutely walked toward them, and shattering the silence He bravely asked, as if He did not know, "Whom seek ye?"

130. Friend, why have you come?

Matthew 26:50, "And Jesus said unto him, Friend, wherefore art thou come? Then came they, and laid hands on Jesus, and took him."

During the life of Jesus He had many acquaintances and associations. He considered some to be friendly and some associations He considered to be dangerous. He did not invite or entertain compliments, nor did He take heed to threats and ultimatums. Once, when warned by the Pharisees about Herod, (the most powerful and influential man of the area) He scorned the threat and even used a negative epithet to counter the warning. "The same day there came certain of the Pharisees, saying unto him, Get thee out, and depart hence: for Herod will kill thee. And he said unto them, Go ye, and tell that fox, Behold, I cast out devils, and I do cures to day and to morrow, and the third day I shall be perfected." (Luke 13:31-32)

On another occasion, Jesus warned of the doctrine of Herod calling it hypocrisy. As a matter of fact, we can find several examples of Jesus using the appellation "hypocrite" to refer to those who are not the "good" people they appear to be. Why did Jesus not refer to Judas as a hypocrite? Was he not worthy of such a title? Did he not pretend to be a part of the group, all the while plotting the betrayal of Jesus?

Nowhere can we find Jesus using names or titles or even epithets loosely or without reason. If he called someone a descriptive name, it was for a reason. In our society we use terms all the time that we do not mean. Usually, we call people "buddy," "brother," or such, when in fact, they are neither. The Quaker testimony excludes the usage of such idle words and certainly flattering titles[223] that do not apply in reality and truth. It is a testimony that would behoove us all to adopt. We should never assume that that the Lord used words indiscriminately just because we do not say what we really mean. When Jesus called a man a viper, we can be sure that the true heart of that man had the characteristics of a serpent, deadly poison, stealth and likely an incurable bite.

On one occasion, Jesus, in calling a woman a dog, facilitated a miracle for her daughter. The woman watched Jesus healing the sick and lame among His own people; and as a hungry little puppy, begged at the table of the Master for scraps. Jesus said, "It is not meet to take the children's bread, and to cast it to dogs." To which she replied, "Truth Lord, but the puppies get what the children reject." (Matthew 15:26 Paraphrased) She could see that His own people were not accepting His ministry and said so, continuing and extending the analogy that Christ had begun. He was impressed. So much so that He granted her request.

Jesus used many descriptive terms for us while He was here. Foxes, stones, dogs, vipers, hypocrites, slaves, spoiled children, sheep, and goats – the

---

[223] Job 32:21-22, "Let me not, I pray you, accept any man's person, neither let me give flattering titles unto man. For I know not to give flattering titles; in so doing my maker would soon take me away."

list is long and colorful to the imagination. Now let us turn our eyes to a more definitive Scripture. John 15:15, "Henceforth I call you not servants; for the servant knoweth not what his lord doeth: but I have called you friends; for all things that I have heard of my Father I have made known unto you."

By this, Jesus makes it clear that He knows the difference between servants and friends and He chooses to call them friends. Why does He do this? Because, He has revealed everything to them and they are no longer on the outside; they are in the inner circle, if you will. The mind of Christ is revealed to His friends. (Keep in mind that all this is being said by Christ, who knows that there is soon coming a day that all these "inner circle" friends will leave Him to die alone.)

How Jesus, knowing what He knew about His associates, was able to evaluate them in Truth and yet maintain a level of comfort with them is an amazing thing. Another factor in the equation is that Jesus was not unaware about His betrayal, His trial, or crucifixion. He knew who and when. Can not we also assume He knew why Judas had come? How could Jesus ignore what Judas was plotting against Him and still wash his feet that very night in the upper room?

How could Jesus look Peter in the eye and commission him to be the elder to strengthen His brethren while knowing that Peter was, even at that moment, teetering on denying that he even knew Christ at all? Here we witness a quality in Christ that we need for ourselves. Here is an attribute of unselfishness, of seeing the whole picture, of looking through the eyes of God Here is an ability to overlook the weaknesses in others; this attribute, we need for ourselves. Do we have what it takes be "on the inside" and know who is true and who is false and yet love them all? Can we be "inner circle" friends who are fully aware of the weaknesses and inevitable failings, betrayals, and lies perpetrated against us and still wash their feet, be their servant and love them as our own soul?

Most of us must be ignorant of the faults of others in order to love them. If we knew their secrets, we would probably reject them and never claim them as friends. We need what Jesus had. We need the love of God shed abroad in our hearts by the Holy Ghost.[224] His love can empower us in the face of suspicion, (or even clear facts) to ignore the weakness and frailty (and in some cases blatant betrayal) of our brethren and serve them anyway, commission them, entrust them, depend upon them, forgive them, and love them – anyway. What a gift. What a wonderful power His love would be in us.

A Different Principle

Most of us, who feel that we "forgive and forget" or do not hold grudges or get along well with people, do so out of ignorance. We simply do not know the depraved nature of our friends, nor do we want to know their

---

[224] Romans 5:5, "And hope maketh not ashamed; because the love of God is shed abroad in our hearts by the Holy Ghost which is given unto us."

secret habits, their secret wishes, or the sin with which they struggle. If we were aware of these as facts, we would not be able to be friends. Most of us would reject them as acquaintances if we found that they voted a certain political party. Ignorance of differences is essential for those who cannot truly love as Christ.

Most of us require that people love us, agree with us, and even hold our views in some areas before we will consider them friends. But, the kind of love spoken of here is not as far off as you might think. For when the offender is family, we switch to wholly different criteria. They can hold different views, yet you will still accept and love them. They can be politically different, yet they are still family. Some can even hold destructive habits and even harm other persons, yet you care and take them in, and try to help. If you aspire to live with Christ, this is the kind of love you are to have for those called to be in YHVH's Kingdom.

Would Jesus have been justified if He had said to Judas, "So, hypocrite, you come to take me away!" Or "Well, here comes the phony that has sold us to the authorities!"? He could have called Judas many names that would have made us cheer. We would have accepted it because of *our* potential of giving such a response.

Jesus had a different principle working within Him. A principle we would do well to emulate. Jesus was not only willing to let Judas approach, but willing to let Judas take Him, kiss Him, and then turn Him over to the authorities that paid the betrayer for this treachery. Knowing all this and what was about to take place, Jesus kindly calls him "friend." Soon, Judas would hang by his own hands. He had witnessed God incarnate and saw fit to betray him. Even in betrayal the Son of God called him friend; not idle words of ignorance, but knowing his faults, He called him friend. That kind of love would be a hard thing to forget. As his life went silent, I can imagine the love on the face of Jesus was indelibly imprinted upon his vision; and the last words exchanged between himself and the Savior echoed in his ears, "Friend, why have you come?"

131. *Betrayest thou the son of man with a kiss?*

Luke 22:48, "But Jesus said unto him, Judas, betrayest thou the Son of man with a kiss?"

Deceptions, perfidy, treachery and betrayals, in order to be most effective, depend upon a certain amount of intimacy. The closer the deceiver gets the deeper and more effective becomes the subterfuge. Also, the closer the relationship between the betrayer and the betrayed, the harder it is to believe in the possibility of the treason. It is impossible to know what Judas was thinking when he betrayed Christ. But as an insider, his betrayal was most effective.

Through this, you may learn a lesson about human nature and about betrayal and deception. Although enemies from without may be threatening, it is common to find the real nemeses nestled under the wing of their target of betrayal. If deception comes, if treachery is underway, it is likely not sniper fire from a remote location. Whether it is a business or a church, a ministry, or friendly fellowship, any campaign where there is a true enemy fixated upon the demise and ruin of that endeavor; if true betrayal or destruction is to come to an institution, look for that undoing to come from within. Efforts to topple these operations, which come from without, only serve to strengthen them. Efforts from within to destroy, are sure and most effective.

As you consider these things, paranoia may result, but that is not my intention. To be forewarned, however, is to be forearmed. It is also difficult to think about treachery and treason without thinking in military terms. The apostle Paul used many military terms and descriptions when speaking of the Christian's journey and battle with the influence of the world. It is a legitimate analogy between our fight of faith and the commonly understood characteristics of war. It is easy to understand that there is an enemy who has declared war on us and considers our soul as the prize of conquest. When speaking in Spiritual terms and someone refers to "the enemy" we know that it is the enemy of our soul, and is the same tempter who appeared to Eve in the garden and the same who tempted Christ upon the mountains of Jerusalem.

Let us consider for a moment the effort of this enemy to topple the faith of Christians, to render them ineffective or useless. Let us look at the very real threat of Satan to destroy the soul of the Christian by subterfuge. Taking into account that which we have learned, let us consider that although attacks from without may be very real, as was said before, it is more likely to find the real nemeses nearer their target of betrayal. We would do well to look at those we consider friends if we are to be diligent and realistic in searching out deception.

The apostle Jude describes the military action of infiltration as men who "crept in unawares."[225] Here, these men are described as among the

---

[225] Jude 1:3-4, "Beloved, when I gave all diligence to write unto you of the common salvation, it was needful for me to write unto you, and exhort you that ye should earnestly contend for the faith which was once delivered unto the saints. For there are certain men crept in unawares, who were before of old ordained to this

brethren, teaching that sin was covered by prevenient grace and thereby damning the souls of those who believed the lie. Dangerous teaching rarely comes from outside the church.

Deception and treachery are not pleasant subjects but they are a necessary part of a diligent defense. The most poorly defended Christian is he who focuses his eyes upon the adversary that is outside his camp and gives no heed to the enemy inside.

The enemy within may take the form of the trusted one among us, or the eldest leader, or perhaps even the youngest in Christ. Sometimes the host of these thoughts or ideas, which take us away from truth and righteousness, are unaware that they are even suggesting such a departure. As in the case of Peter, Jesus had no qualm about referring to the would-be apostle as "Satan."

As Jesus approached the day of His crucifixion, He told Peter of His upcoming torture. Peter said what would be considered by most as a very brave statement, "Be it far from thee, Lord: this shall not be unto thee." He was telling the Lord that He need not die, but that they could find alternatives. They would even fight to save Him! But Jesus turned, and said to Peter, "Get thee behind me, Satan: thou art an offense unto me: for thou savourest not the things that be of God, but those that be of men." (Matthew 16:22-23) (Notice how the source of the advice Peter gave was determined. Jesus attributed the advice to Satan because it turned men away from what God desires for them, and toward what is safe and desirable to man's flesh.)

The Holy Spirit Will Help Us

We must, through the power of the Spirit and the advice and counsel of the Scriptures, determine what is good and sound advice and doctrine. We must not accept everything that sounds reasonable because we, as men, will tend toward the comfortable and that which "scratches our itch." This itching will undoubtedly be offered a scratch by the deceiving teacher, the well-meaning zealot, the traditionalist among the elders, or anyone WITHIN our fortifications. We must be on guard against such deception. "For the time will come when they will not endure sound doctrine; but after their own lusts shall they heap to themselves teachers, having itching ears; And they shall turn away their ears from the truth, and shall be turned unto fables. But watch thou in all things…" (2 Timothy 4:3-5)

The betrayer will probably not be one who stands and proclaims that Jesus is not the Son of God. The deceiver most likely will not be the one who openly denies the deity of Christ, or claims a false Messiah. Nor is he apt to be one who promotes sin and rebellion against God. He will likely be one who comes as a friend to Christ and "kisses" Him. He will be one who says, "Hail Master!" The most effective deception will be the one least expected from the least expected source, using the least offensive speech. Perhaps a well-

---

condemnation, ungodly men, turning the grace of our God into lasciviousness, and denying the only Lord God, and our Lord Jesus Christ."

respected person with good intentions – like Peter, will speak the pretext. Whose advice (if followed) would have been disastrous to the eternal plan of the salvation of mankind. His advice sounded good and acceptable only to ears not trained to hear error. But ears trained to hear diversion from the will of God, heard the treachery in the advice immediately – even though it was veiled in good intentions, love, concern, bravery and virtue the mind set to God's desires discovered it immediately.

This pivotal event was a grand opportunity for Jesus to teach His disciples this principle of betrayal and treachery (and we of the future as well). So as Jesus heard the rustling of the Temple militia moving through the tender garden foliage in the silence of the night He stood up and watched His friend Judas advance with the soldiers in tow. Judas came closer still until he is face to face with Christ. "Hail Master" he weakly attempts, turning his head on the last syllable glancing behind himself to make sure the soldiers can see his signal to them.

Then, in the light of the near full moon, he kissed Messiah tasting the salty tears of His long Gethsemane prayer still cooling on His cheeks. The soldiers, having received their sign, began to approach; Jesus asked His friend, as if to record this fact for our first lesson in betrayal, "Judas… betrayest thou the Son of man with a kiss?"

132. Are ye come out, as against a thief, with swords and staves?

Mark 14:48, "And Jesus answered and said unto them, Are ye come out, as against a thief, with swords and with staves to take me?"

Luke 22:52, "Then Jesus said unto the chief priests, and captains of the temple, and the elders, which were come to him, Be ye come out, as against a thief, with swords and staves?"

Jesus was probably the gentlest man who ever lived. The prophecies concerning Him bore witness to that fact as well as do the Gospels.
"He shall not cry, nor lift up, nor cause his voice to be heard in the street. A bruised reed shall he not break, and the smoking flax shall he not quench: he shall bring forth judgment unto truth." (Isaiah 42:2-3)

His gentle manner and kindness toward others is apparent in every story about Him. Sometimes this is mistakenly portrayed in modern stories or sermons as weakness or starry-eyed piety, but as we get to know Him by the reading of the Scriptures and by the Spirit of God, we can see that it is nothing less than meekness.

The meekness displayed by Christ and expected to be found in Christians is best defined as the character necessary to have the advantage over someone and not take it. Submission by volition is a perfect balance of righteous and humble character. It is what we witness in Jesus when we watch Him interact with others in the Gospels. It is a goal for which we should strive as followers, and it would serve as a strong witness that we too, have been with Jesus.

Jesus' life was lived in such quiet, such humility, and such submission, He was amazed that those who came to take Him came with weapons. It is often incorrectly said that these were soldiers who came to take Jesus, but they were not soldiers at all they were religious folk, servants of the High Priest, officers under the scribes and elders of the local congregation. Yes, this armed regimen who we commonly think of as soldiers was, in fact, a trembling, rag tag bunch of church members setting out to do "God's work!" This is why Peter looks to Jesus and suggests that they fight them with swords. They never would have tried to take on trained Roman soldiers. No, these were men commissioned by the church of that day, a visitation committee of sorts, sent out to deal with the wayward preacher who did not sidle up to their doctrines and organization. They came to bring Him in or kill Him.

Jesus wanted them to observe their unfounded fears. Their fear of physical harm was apparent by the show of weapons; their fear of public reprisal was apparent by the late hour and darkness; operating under orders of the High Priest assuaged their fear of acting alone. So armed with swords, equipped with lanterns, and commissioned by the religious leaders they were ready for anything. Anything, that is, except meekness.

Jesus went with them willingly. They must have been taken by surprise when He answered, "I am He" to their inquiry as to the whereabouts of Jesus. They had to be surprised when He restored the ear to Malchus the High Priest's servant, which Peter removed with a sword stroke. They had to be amazed when all His disciples fled in every direction and Jesus stood alone silently, meekly waiting to be apprehended. We can see, in the mind's eye, the puzzled faces, the swords slowly lowering and the simultaneously elevating lanterns as the mission quickly came to a quieter conclusion than anyone imagined.

Not Taking Our Advantage

The average man is not ready, or equipped to handle meekness. To them, it is a mystery to have the advantage over an adversary and not take it. For someone to be so capable of winning, yet choose to lose is an incomprehensible concept to the mind of those determined to win. But in the Kingdom of God, these are principles that should be basic to our understanding. Paradoxical axioms are not foreign to the reader of the Bible, nor were they to the followers of Jesus. Who among us has not looked twice at verses such as, Matthew 10:39? "He that findeth his life shall lose it: and he that loseth his life for my sake shall find it." It should not be strange to us that we are to "suffer" and submit to wrong-doers to gain the Spiritual advantage. Knowing two things by the power of the Spirit of God discovers the attribute of true meekness:

That we indeed do have an advantage in the very fact that YHVH has chosen us to be His. It is by the grace of God (the willingness of God to use His power on our behalf) that we are counted worthy of saving.

That salvation is ours only by our attitude of submission to our God as King and that it is in His will we live and move and have our being, that we are "not our own", and that "we are bought with a price."[226] We therefore have no agenda of our own and have no point to press, no axe to grind, no reputation to defend, no cause for which to fight other than the causes of our heavenly Father. We do not march to our own orders or in our own interests, but to His.

We would do well to consider these facts in meditative prayer and seek a revelation from God about the discovery and implementation of meekness. Our enemies should fall backward as we make ourselves available without a fight. They should feel surprise when we willingly give ourselves to them as if they are powerless to do anything without the ability given to them by our Father. Our defense should emulate the defense Christ offered to those who crucified Him. Any speeches of defense should sound like His. Our attitude should be one of meekness.

Listen to the words of the apostle,

---

[226] 1 Corinthians 6:19-20, "What? know ye not that your body is the temple of the Holy Ghost which is in you, which ye have of God, and ye are not your own? For ye are bought with a price: therefore glorify God in your body, and in your spirit, which are God's."

"But we have this treasure in earthen vessels, that the excellency of the power may be of God, and not of us. We are troubled on every side, yet not distressed; we are perplexed, but not in despair; Persecuted, but not forsaken; cast down, but not destroyed; Always bearing about in the body the dying of the Lord Jesus, that the life also of Jesus might be made manifest in our body. For we which live are alway delivered unto death for Jesus' sake, that the life also of Jesus might be made manifest in our mortal flesh." (2 Corinthians 4:7-11)

When we take Christ's attitude of meekness we may well be perceived as someone who knows something that our malefactors do not know. We may be considered as someone with unknown power. Your actions may become mysterious to your enemies, and they become fearful of you and do not even know why. It is when you fight and defend yourself that they are assured that your power lies only within yourself – because it is indeed. It is when you resort to the sword that they are able to evaluate and judge your defense as inadequate. But, when you depend upon God to carry out vengeance, they become mystified. When they are not sure, they fortify themselves. When they are convinced that their enemy knows something that they do not, they approach only by stealth. When they think God is on your side, they worry, they fret, and they panic. It is then that they turn out, under the cover of darkness, armed to the teeth to take a lowly carpenter's boy to jail.

Jesus wanted them to take account of what they were doing and why. He wanted them to see their fears and analyze why they had them. Perhaps they could save themselves if they would just think for an instant and ask themselves why they were so afraid. Jesus said, "When I was daily with you in the temple, ye stretched forth no hands against me," and then He asked, "Are ye come out, as against a thief, with swords and staves to take me?"

133. Do you know I can have an army of angels?

Matthew 26:53, "Thinkest thou that I cannot now pray to my Father, and he shall presently give me more than twelve legions of angels?"

One of the richest statements made in the New Testament is this,

*"Therefore being justified by faith, we have peace with God through our Lord Jesus Christ... For when we were yet without strength, in due time Christ died for the ungodly. For scarcely for a righteous man will one die: yet peradventure for a good man some would even dare to die. But God commendeth his love toward us, in that, **while we were yet sinners**, Christ died for us." (Romans 5:1-8)*

While we were yet sinners... Christ died for us. His death was a profound event with endless implication and inference to anyone who examines the facts surrounding it. The most profound mystery in this event is the fact that it was not murder as some say, nor was it simply a Roman crucifixion of a criminal. This was a voluntary lying down of a life; an example of perfect submission, motivated by the true love of the truly good, to the deepest hatred of the truly evil. It was not only the submission of Jesus Christ, but the allowance of His Father as well, that staggers our reason. The suggestion that twelve legions of angels would be provided at Christ's beck and call, likely came from His Father in reply to Jesus' Gethsemane prayer. God desired to deliver Jesus from this torture at the hands of wicked sinners as much as it was His Son's desire. But for a particular reason, they both allowed it to happen – the joy of winning the ransom.

"Looking unto Jesus ... who for the joy that was set before him [He] endured the cross, despising the shame, and is set down at the right hand of the throne of God." (Hebrews 12:2)

"... remember how he spake unto you when he was yet in Galilee, Saying, The Son of man must be delivered into the hands of sinful men, and be crucified, and the third day rise again. And they remembered his words." (Luke 24:6-8)

"But we speak the wisdom of God in a mystery, even the hidden wisdom, which God ordained before the world unto our glory: Which none of the princes of this world knew: for had they known it, they would not have crucified the Lord of glory." (1 Corinthians 2:7-8)

The redemption of man was a mystery that was hidden in ages past and has yet to be fully revealed. Oh, yes, we who have been made able to be partakers in it have an idea of what it is and we may understand it somewhat, but its fullness and scope will not be – cannot be made real to our unregenerate minds until we come to the day of our own redemption. But, the facet of the crucifixion that is the most mysterious is the aspect of His tortuous death being voluntary.

There is a fine line of distinction between being subject and making oneself subject. Many of us would easily find ourselves being subject to those who are more powerful than we are, more in number than we are, or higher in authority, but can we imagine having power against all those who would withstand us, having power to protect ourselves against any who would harm us, yet not utilize that ability to keep ourselves from any harm, discomfort, or loss?

Lesson from Lilliput

Remember the story of Gulliver's travels? As a man with a weapon or a man of greater physical strength can easily take command of us, *numbers* can provide a clear advantage as well. Gulliver found himself bound fast by Lilliputians much weaker than he, much smaller than he, *but many in number* which crept upon him as he slept.

Just so, some find themselves subjugated by *many* people of *little* stature to whom they have voluntarily given power. The list of oppressors may include their own small children or a boss of little stature who could never physically force submission, but because we assign them authority we subject ourselves to them. This voluntary subjugation must not be confused with the voluntary submission of Christ, however. We subject ourselves when we perceive that the one over us is stronger than we are, whether that is true or not. There may be a clear reason or a just a vague excuse for our subjective behavior, but in most every case it is, at least, perceived that we have no other choice; but imagine for a moment subjection by volition, for there was no such perception of superiority in the mind of Christ about His oppressors.

Jesus was in a world that He made. (John 1:3, Hebrews 11:3) When it came to authority, He had it all. There was no thing or any person who had authority over Him. Although the church of that day attempted to exercise some authority over Him, they had none. Even when Pilate offered Him freedom from crucifixion He never said a word. It surprised Pilate that Jesus would not answer him, seeing that he had full authority over His situation.

> *"Then saith Pilate unto him, Speakest thou not unto me? knowest thou not that I have power to crucify thee, and have power to release thee? Jesus answered, Thou couldest have no power at all against me, except it were given thee from above..." (John 19:10-11)* So much for authority.

The writings of Paul state this of Christ, that He,

> *"... made himself of no reputation, and took upon him the form of a servant, and was made in the likeness of men: And being found in fashion as a man, he humbled himself, and became obedient unto death, even the death of the cross." (Philippians 2:6-8)*

424

Here we see that Christ took on the limitation of the physical body as a matter of His own will. He was now subject to beating and scourging. His voluntary submission to His enemies would further allow mistreatment by those of lesser stature than He. This left Jesus in a precarious state. His life was in jeopardy on a daily basis, much as ours is. (A fact we are reminded of whenever we receive news of a friend or family member being killed by an accident or mishap or illness.) Jesus was now subject to these as well.

His subjection to death has led many to the wrong conclusion that Jesus was murdered. We can hear it said even from the pulpit that "they killed Jesus" but I submit that it was not murder. It was subjection by volition. Some may pose that if Jesus could have stopped His death and did not do so, was it not suicide? No. With suicide, the desire for death is within the person who dies. The Garden of Gethsemane prayer should relieve all doubt that death was the desire of Jesus.

Somewhere between our feeble calculations of suicide and murder lies a concept foreign to the unregenerate man – sacrifice. Our Lord Jesus' death was not murder, but a sacrifice. His "obedience unto death" was made a sacrifice by the free exercise of His submission and choice. In order for this event to be a sacrifice, there had to be a choice on the part of the giver. The Father of the Lord Jesus gave Him that choice when He offered to His Son more than twelve legions of angels to aid His escape from death. There was no more imbalance of strength to make the death of Christ a forgone conclusion. There were no calculations to be made of "them" against "us." Poor Peter was so scared, all he could think of were swords and numbers and strength and might. He saw that the whole operation was about to fall, all because they were few in number and weak in strength. His attitude is much like ours when we are in trouble or when the world comes against us to destroy us. With his fear turned to bravery, he lashed out with his sword to begin his deliverance.

After the first blood was spilled and Jesus restored the man who was wounded, He communicated to Peter that this was not a matter of power or strength. This was not a matter of numbers and swords. He said "Put up again thy sword into his place: for all they that take the sword shall perish with the sword." He wanted Peter to know, "I am not helpless in this situation, for power and numbers both are on my side. I am giving my life as a sacrifice. No man can take my life; I give it willingly." "Thinkest thou that I cannot now pray to my Father, and he shall presently give me more than twelve legions of angels?"

134. Shall I not drink it?

John 18:11, "Then said Jesus unto Peter, Put up thy sword into the sheath: the cup which my Father hath given me, shall I not drink it?"

When you hear that Jesus was our example what does that mean to you? What thoughts come into our mind when you consider your pattern to be Christ? It is likely that you think of the kindness that Jesus displayed, or His sinless nature, or His wholeness of perfection. There may even be feelings of hopelessness to attain such a stature of perfection, causing angst or discouragement. But, would Christ ask you to do what was not within your power to accomplish? Would He ask you to be sinless, demand that you walk on water, or calm stormy seas? Would He deny He knows you before the Father because you did not raise the dead or restore withered limbs? Many things He did without exertion, we cannot even approach on our best day. What was the example He expects us to follow, and to which He will hold us accountable to accomplish?

The example of Christ is not an unattainable goal. His example is within the reach and ability of the regenerated man. It may be distasteful, but it not unattainable. Let us read what the apostle says in 1 Peter 2:21-24,

*"For even hereunto were ye called: because **Christ also suffered** for us, **leaving us an example**, that ye should follow his steps: Who did no sin, neither was guile found in his mouth: Who, **when he was reviled, reviled not again; when he suffered, he threatened not**; but committed himself to him that judgeth righteously: Who his own self bare our sins in his own body on the tree, that we, being dead to sins, should live unto righteousness: by whose stripes ye were healed."* Here we see that our example is one of suffering.

The old English word "suffering" takes on a twentieth century meaning that is not helpful. When we think of suffering we think of pain or heartache, misery or grief, but it is better rendered "letting" or "allowing." Letting is taking on whatever comes our way, as an animal of burden would take whatever load is placed upon it. An animal "suffers" a load of bricks as easily as he would a load of gold. It does not care what is in the bags he only feels the weight and carries the load. It "lets" his master load him by not bucking or balking or trying to walk out from under it.

Our duty is to "let." We need to be like the faithful creatures of burden. We are to accept (allow) the load that is placed upon us. We are to let ourselves be reviled, but not to revile anyone for doing so. We are to let ourselves be cursed but not curse those who do so. The apostle Paul writes in 1 Corinthians 6:7, *"Now therefore there is utterly a fault among you, because ye go to law one with another. Why do ye not rather take wrong? why do ye not rather... [let] yourselves be defrauded?"*

426

Here we see an example of "letting" or suffering as Christ did. Why do we feel that we need to be vindicated, exonerated, or avenged? It is only our own high opinion of ourselves and our pride that makes this idea flare within us when we are defrauded, or someone takes an advantage over us. We should rather "let" these things happen. Paul continues this thought in Romans 12:10-20,

> *"Be kindly affectioned one to another with brotherly love; in honour* **preferring one another**... *Bless them which persecute you: bless, and curse not... Mind not high things, but condescend to men of low estate... Recompense to no man evil for evil...If it be possible, as much as lieth in you, live peaceably with all men. Dearly beloved, avenge not yourselves, but rather give place unto wrath: for it is written, Vengeance is mine; I will repay, saith the Lord."*

When your first thought is toward your "rights" or when you surmise that you don't deserve the treatment you are receiving, or you struggle under the load placed upon you, you are not following Christ's example. When you call lawyers to "get what's coming to you," you are not imitating Jesus. When you run toward medication, remuneration, vindication, you are not letting, you are bucking, and balking and refusing the cup poured out to you.

David Was A Good King.

He was known for being a man after the heart of God and had only two sins recorded to his account in the Bible. David was a man who knew where he stood with God. In 2 Samuel 16 a story is told of a man who came out as David was on his way to Bahurim and cursed David and threw stones at him, calling him a murderer and taunted him. Then Abishai the son of Zeruiah said to David, "Why should this dead dog curse my lord the king? Let me go over, I pray thee, and take off his head." This is a good question. Why should this "nobody" curse the King of Israel? We may even ask, in our times of cursing and abuse, "Why should I have to take this abusive epithet or be lied about or be falsely accused?" David's answer to Abishai the son of Zeruiah may surprise you. The king said, "What have I to do with you, ye sons of Zeruiah? so let him curse, because the LORD hath said unto him, Curse David. Who shall then say, Wherefore hast thou done so?"

David's answer is perfect. It is the answer that should be upon our lips at the ready for usage at the first sign of being reviled, cursed or mistreated by others. If the Lord allowed this, who shall say to him, "Why do you do this?" If the Lord allowed this load to be placed upon me, I will let it, allow it, I will suffer it. I will not balk or buck, I will not seek remedy or remuneration, I will not seek vindication or attempt to clear my name, but will let the Lord avenge, for He will do it justly. How do we know that the Lord did not say to this man, sue, curse, accuse, or test His servant? We do not know. When we wiggle out of our tests and trials by pursuing our own vindication, clearing our own name or suing at the law to win recompense we circumnavigate God's plan of making us better and wiser and showing Himself powerful and mighty in our lives.

Jesus was given a bitter cup, but He was worthy to be given such a cup. Not because He deserved it, but because He was capable of drinking it. The Father knows what you are capable of drinking as well. Great comfort can be found in 1 Corinthians 10:13,

"There hath no temptation taken you but such as is common to man: but God is faithful, who will not suffer you to be tempted above that ye are able; but will with the temptation also make a way to escape, that ye may be able to bear it."

The temptation may be custom-made for you. The Father mixes a drink especially for you. Don't spit it out, push it away, or seek other cups easier to drink. Don't reject the one made for you because it is bitter, uncomfortable, humiliating, or painful. You must trust Him and not be so proud and self-concerned. You must be willing to "let" and not be so obsessed with what is "fair" or "getting what you deserve." The one desiring "what they deserve" does not understand what they truly deserve or they would not ask for it.

The Father hands you a bitter cup from time to time, because He knows you can drink it to the dregs. If you could not… He would not give it to you. Jesus had the right attitude. He asked, "The cup which my Father hath given me, shall I not drink it?"

135. How shall the Scripture be fulfilled?

Matthew 26:54, "But how then shall the scriptures be fulfilled, that thus it must be?"

The traditional concept of Scripture is flawed severely. To believe what is told from the pulpits and taught in the seminaries today, we would have to think that the Bible is more like a magic book than a collection of sacred writings. It is called The Word of God, a title held for Christ alone, and a name the Bible does not claim for itself. The modern Bible is considered a finished, monolithic book, a "closed canon." That is a very opportune stance, since man has added all he wants to it and taken away all he wants to remove, now, he claims that it cannot be added to nor may anyone take anything from it.

Even the "good ol' King James" so revered and adored (even worshiped) by many has lost 14 books since 1611. Still, we are told that the Bible is flawless, inerrant, contains no contradictions and is inspired, or "from the breath" of God. Again, all claims that the Bible does not make for itself.

Some may argue that 2 Timothy 3:16 says that the Bible is inspired. "All scripture is given by inspiration of God..." but it is clear, by the previous verse 15, that this is said about "the Scriptures" that were known by Timothy as a child. It is therefore, impossible that Paul would be referring to the collection of books you now have (your Bible) sitting beside you. These men had never heard of a "New Testament" other than the one that they were preaching. Their faith rested in the living Lord Jesus Christ and not in a collection of scrolls. They learned of the promises and fulfillment of this Messiah through the testimony of the Law and Prophets and the Psalms (and some other writings that we do not have.) It would be foolish to claim that the Scriptures of old were not inspired, but it is just as foolish to claim that the King James Bible is "God breathed." Our definition of, and our faith in Scripture should be identical to the apostles. To have any other view is asking for trouble.

So is our Bible trustworthy? Absolutely! Anyone who knows Christ, has a teacher and guide that can lead them into all Truth. The Truth found in the Bible is no exception; it has to be revealed as well. We must learn from our Guide because, if we do not learn from Him, we will end up with hundreds of interpretations, denominations, divisions, strivings, and arguments even though we all carry the same book. Sound familiar? Yes, it is the very situation we have today. The Bible has done nothing to bring the body of Christ together, rather the reverse. Yet it is unfair to blame the Scriptures for the division. The separations came about because we elevated the book (and thereby man's interpretation of the book) to the level of divinity. This is why Jesus did not say, "I will send you a book, an inerrant, inspired book, which will lead you and guide you into all Truth." No, He said, "...when He, the Spirit of Truth, is come, He will guide you into all truth... and He will shew you things to come." (John 16:13) This Spirit of Truth can take you through the Bible and beyond, showing us everything we need to know to meet life with joy and faith, power and grace, and render us fully capable in every situation, as we look to Jesus the only living "Word of God" and hearing from Him wisdom, knowledge and guidance.

All that being said, where does the "magic" of the Bible come in? Does this book have within it the power of prophecy? Is the future foretold in these Scriptures of Truth? Jesus spoke as though He was living in a sealed destiny or under some cosmic "obligation" to fulfill these prophecies. Did He feel that there were certain things that He must do so that the Scriptures would be fulfilled? As the disciples were thinking of rescuing Jesus from the hands of the wicked men who had come to retrieve Him from the garden of Gethsemane, was Jesus telling them not to resist so that the Scriptures would be fulfilled? Why else would He say, "But how then shall the Scriptures be fulfilled, that thus it must be?" Perhaps it is our view on this verse that makes it sound as though the Scriptures are leading and present events (and therefore history) follow. After all, throughout Matthew, we have heard the author say, "This was done to fulfill the Scripture that..." The Gospel narrative repeats this as if to prove to any student of the Scriptures that Jesus was the fulfillment of the Messianic Prophecies. What role do the Scriptures play in prophecy and how are we to fulfill them?

Yea, Than Much Fine Gold...

The Scriptures have an inexplicable value to the reader. They "are written for our admonition, upon whom the ends of the world are come." (1 Corinthians 10:11) We, here at the "end of the world," are to read and gain insight and knowledge from our ancestors' experiences and thereby be prepared for the inevitable end of all things. Who has not shuddered as they read the words of Paul telling, by the Holy Spirit, the condition of the world near the end? (II Timothy 3:4) But should we act out the wickedness we read there, so as to fulfill the Scriptures? No, of course not. By these words given to us, we should be aware, expecting, and not taken by surprise. We should know the Scriptures and be well versed in them and glean from them the knowledge that our Guide wants us to have, weighing all we read there, in the Holy Spirit and sound reason. In doing so, we may develop a sense of future events that will prepare us for the end time. If we are not prepared, we may find ourselves resisting (as the disciples did) the prophesied plan for our lives.

The disciples had the words in their heads. Jesus felt no need to reiterate the Scriptures to them. They knew what He was speaking of when He mentioned "the Scriptures." What Jesus had to remind them of, what they had forgotten, was the application of what they already knew. He had to remind them that the Scriptures had foretold of the day in which they were living and everything they were about to experience. They were still thick and slow in Spirit. They could not seem to make the connection. It was not until after His resurrection that He explained it fully and finally got through to them.

430

*"And he said unto them, These are the words which I spake unto you, while I was yet with you, that all things must be fulfilled, which were written in the law of Moses, and in the prophets, and in the psalms, concerning me. **Then opened he their understanding, that they might understand the scriptures**, And said unto them, Thus it is written, and thus it behoved Christ to suffer, and to rise from the dead the third day." (Luke 24:44-46)*

To avoid resisting God's plan for us we need to have our understandings opened to the Scriptures. When your understanding is opened, the Bible finally becomes the "Word of God." Although its words are the words of God, and although its records are valuable to men who are given understanding, without the Living Christ to open its message to us, it is nothing more than ink and pages and perhaps a nice leather cover. There is no magic, no messages, no codes, no miracle, just ink, and paper. If we look at our Bible as anything more than what it is, we take the glory due only to the "Word of God" (Christ) and attempt to share it with a corruptible creation.

As the disciples began to "hear" Christ and then "see" His prophecy in the Scripture, they began to understand that there was no choice to be made in the garden that night. There was no war to fight, no territory to win, no property to hold, no reason to resist. Had they been able to understand, they could have applied the Scriptures to what was happening around them. That is what hearing the Word of God is all about! It was when He opened their comprehension, giving them understanding of the Scriptures that they "heard" the word of God for the first time – not years before sitting in synagogue, or at their mothers' knee. They heard it. It is the "extra kick" we feel when a Scripture is made alive to us that should tip us off that we are hearing the True Word of God. It is the "Aha!" experience, the light that comes on, the application of Scripture to real life that is going on around you, that shows that you are being guided, you are being shown, you are hearing the Word of God.

When you do not understand, when you try to fight back, when you try to hold your position and not surrender to those who are seen as enemies, it is then that you need to consider the Scriptures. Is the problem or trouble you are experiencing what you are to expect? Is this difficulty what was foretold by prophecy? Perhaps you are resisting God and His plan that was presented to you in clear prophecy by the Scriptures. If that is so, why do you resist? If thus it must be… "Then how shall the Scripture be fulfilled?"

136. Why askest thou me?

John 18:20-21, Jesus answered him, I spake openly to the world; I ever taught in the synagogue, and in the temple, whither the Jews always resort; and in secret have I said nothing. Why askest thou me? ask them which heard me, what I have said unto them: behold, they know what I said.

My God has been good to me. He has saved me from heartache and misery countless times. One time in particular comes to mind as I read the verse above. Many years ago, I was headed down a path that, I am convinced, would have led to my destruction. I was a young pastor who seemed to have the right doctrine and the right faith, and was becoming more and more firmly ensconced in mainstream Protestant religion. Through a series of events, God showed me my future if I had continued down this path. He showed me the inside of another man's ministry.

As I was brought into the inner circle, I was becoming a major part of a nationally known ministry, headed by a man whom I respected and saw no perceptible differences between him and me. By this man's life and ministry God showed me my own future. It was a bright future by anyone's standard, but a dark one to anyone who knew and loved Truth. It would have been a respectable vocation with no real worries, but I was always on guard and defensive for my station in life with paranoia reigning and hanging over every conversation.

I had no genuine power against sin in my life, but I was always equipped with a quote or a verse to justify it; no real inward change, but a "hope" of a better "someday" in the future. Most of all, the part that made me sickest to view, was the deception. The deception toward my fellow man, my colleagues, my family, the deceit required before the television cameras roll, or the radio microphones come on.

The deception required to keep good people giving their hard-earned money to such a ministry. White lies, embellishments and facts omitted made stories interesting and poignant so that they would wring the heart of the contributors. Then came the self-deception. I started to believe that I was special.

I started to believe that I was a "man of God" that required special treatment, special handling, and respect due to a king or dignitary. A man who is revered believes there are things due him, everything from a designated parking place to a summer home. I was far from the boy of fifteen years who surrendered his will to the will of God. I was no longer "Don," nor was I "Mr. Harris," but "*Pastor* Harris." A Reverend. I loved being called, "Master."[227]

---

[227] Matthew 23:6-12, "And [the Pharisees] love the uppermost rooms at feasts, and the chief seats in the synagogues, And greetings in the markets, and to be called of men, Rabbi, Rabbi (Teacher, Teacher). But be not ye called Rabbi (Teacher): for one is your Master (Teacher), even Christ; and all **ye are brethren**. And call no man your father upon the earth: for one is your Father, which is in heaven. Neither be ye called

(All this honor because a man supposedly "surrendered" to a call to preach the Gospel of the Lord Jesus Christ?)

I took my first opportunity to depart and reconsider my calling. I started from the ground up again to discover the life and ministry that my God required of me. During this time of retreat, the PTL scandal hit. Not long afterward, Jimmy Swaggart fell from his pinnacle of ministry. I fell on my face and was still before God. For the first time, I was afraid of the possibilities.

Pattern of Destruction

Why reiterate all this? I noticed a pattern, or at least an attitude, prior to the downfall of these and other ministries. Secrecy became a part of their day-to-day living. Through friends, or by members of my family that were among these famous men, I was made privy to internal meetings of these ministers and by my own experiences with the ministry I mentioned above, the pattern emerged. Before the love for money or the desire for fame and power took over the hearts of these men, secrecy began to be the byword.

There was more than a change of clothes in the dressing rooms of these men, there were two, then three and perhaps more faces worn before the public. The families and close friends of these men hardly recognized the men they became while in front of the cameras. All of their problems were covered with money and the guilt was covered with the self-deceit that they were different, special men called of God for a grandiose purpose, while the truth of their wretchedness was held in secrecy.

In all cases, paranoia reigned over every action and word, and management of information became top priority. Admittedly prejudiced, I now wonder about the secret meetings of every minister I see, especially those who are involved in mass media "ministry." I have heard enough for a lifetime.

Secrecy and information control is a natural outgrowth of wickedness. To hide our actions from anyone puts us and them on different sides. When we hide what we do, we have determined that the thing we do is disagreeable to anyone from whom we hide it. The Gospel has no component that should be hidden.

Secrecy is not a part of evangelization. It never has been. Paul, testifying before King Agrippa, said, "For the king knoweth of these things … for this thing was not done in a corner." (Acts 26:26) According to Paul, even our sins are not to be kept secret. "Them that sin rebuke before all, that others also may fear." (1 Timothy 5:20)And James 5:16a says, "Confess your faults one to another, and pray one for another, that ye may be healed." Secrecy is not a part of our justification either. Secrecy carries a power of "truth evasion" that can devastate the noblest Christian or topple the most sincere ministries.

Jesus was being questioned by the High Priest of His disciples and His doctrine. "Let me in on your secrets" He could have asked. "Tell me what your

---

masters: for one is your Master, even Christ. But he that is greatest among you shall be your servant. And whosoever shall exalt himself shall be abased; and he that shall humble himself shall be exalted."

plan is, where you plan to take this idea of yours, what is the scope of your ministry? Let me on the inside."

If this question were asked and answered by the so-called ministries of today, it would be shocking to hear the honest answers to them. If you could sit in on a strategy meeting or what they call "damage control" when an unpopular press release is printed or televised, you would be aghast at the language and strategy of your favorite TV evangelist. The secrecy becomes a major portion of the ministry. This idea and practice is not something of the 20th century only. It is as old as wickedness itself. From the days of Adam, when he said, "I was afraid...and I hid myself" until the days in which we now live, nothing much has changed.

As Christians, we should not do anything that requires secrecy. We should be as open books to all those inquiring into our purposes, our strategies, our desires, our goals, our finances, and indeed anything about us. We should have a clear and pure motivation for everything we do. We should press to the fore with our missteps and mistakes and even sins over which we stumble. Instead of justifying them or hiding them we should admit them.

The world is ready to receive, not perfect people, but honest ones. The beautiful Gospel story of Jesus Christ suffers from its intemperate envoys. They are either people who think they are perfect and maintain that "perfection" through deceit, or they are foolish enough to believe that they are arbitrarily forgiven for every sin they commit, so their lascivious lives should be overlooked.

The ministry of Christ seems to be littered with "men of God" who expect the best, demand respect, and maintain that status through intimidation and deceit.

When questioned about His ministry the Lord Jesus was able to look the High Priest in the eye and say, "I spake openly to the world; I ever taught in the synagogue, and in the temple, whither the Jews always resort; and in secret have I said nothing." His ministry was clear of any dispersion, deception, or mental manipulation. Can you and those involved in your ministry honestly say that their secret meetings are reflected in the public ones? Can you look at others with whom you consort and tell them to speak freely about what was said in private?

Even your home is victim to private meetings with ulterior motives and strategies. Can you give your children license to speak freely about what and who was discussed at the dinner table? Secrecy is a cloak of maliciousness. You should be wary of its power to mask undesirable conduct and language. What you say in private should be EXACTLY what you say in public. Then we can answer any who ask us of our secrets, "Why askest thou me? Ask them which heard me ... they know what I said."

137. Why smitest thou me?

John 18:22-23, "...one of the officers which stood by struck Jesus with the palm of his hand, saying, Answerest thou the high priest so? Jesus answered him, If I have spoken evil, bear witness of the evil: but if well, why smitest thou me?"

We do not know who the sycophant to the High Priest was who felt the urge and the justification to strike the first blow, but I am sure he thought of it many times afterward. Up until then no one had dared to lay a finger on the Savior. Whether it was fear of God or of reprisal of the people who followed and loved Him, it is not clear, (probably both) but curiously no one had the courage to do the deed that many wanted to do. There were times when the religious leaders wanted to stone Him, push Him from a cliff, scourge Him, or strike Him, but up until this night, no one ventured it.

It was not uncommon to demand and enforce respect to a High Priest. Under a Theocracy, mind you, a High Priest is the highest authority under God Himself. Had the Roman occupation never occurred there would have been no need to take Jesus to any higher court or to anyone else, to put Him to death. The High Priest was the last in the line of authority before God. There had not been a King in Israel since the captivity of Babylon. So, like kings, the High Priest had the "Yes men" and body guards and officers around them at all times including much pomp and ceremony everywhere they went to reinforce the air of authority. This man who struck Jesus acted on compulsion to correct the lack of respect for this "dignitary" of Jewish leadership.

The idea of demanding respect for the High Priest comes from an obscure Law in Exodus 22:28, "Thou shalt not revile the gods, nor curse the ruler of thy people." (The Old Testament usage of the word gods meant judges, rulers, and the like, ordained of Jehovah to rule.)[228] Paul quoted from this when he ran afoul of this rule before the High Priest. All that he did was claim to have lived without violation of the Law and his own conscience, thought to be impossible by the council (and by many today.)

"And Paul, earnestly beholding the council, said, Men and brethren, I have lived in all good conscience before God until this day. And the high priest Ananias commanded them that stood by him to smite him on the mouth. Then said Paul unto him, God shall smite thee, thou whited wall: for sittest thou to judge me after the law, and commandest me to be smitten contrary to the law? And they that stood by said, Revilest thou God's high priest? Then said Paul, I wist not, brethren, that he was the high priest: for it is written, Thou shalt not speak evil of the ruler of thy people." (Acts 23:1-5)

---

[228] Psalms 82:6, "I have said, Ye are gods; and all of you are children of the most High."
John 10:34-35, "Jesus answered them, Is it not written in your law, I said, Ye are gods? If he called them gods, unto whom the word of God came..."

Paul was fully aware of this Law and respected it. It was with this kind of encouragement that the toady of Caiaphas' court took the liberty to strike the face of our Savior. He felt fully justified, but was He? Jesus, knowing the Law as He did, was also well aware why the man thought to strike Him, but knowing that the Law would require "speaking evil of the ruler," asked him, "If I have spoken evil, bear witness of the evil: but if well, why smitest thou me?"

In our mind's eye we can easily envision this man, full of contempt for Jesus standing close to Him in case He opens an opportunity of condemnation. Nervous and fidgety, trembling at times, the coward waits for his opening to strike Jesus. The High Priest asks Jesus about His doctrine and of His disciples and is interested in any secret strategies He may be plotting. Jesus simply answers that He did nothing in secret but what He had said in private, He said also in public. He finishes His statement with, "Ask them," pointing to the all-familiar faces that He saw in synagogue every Sabbath day, "…they know what I said." The bootlicking worm that hates Jesus so much sees his opportunity to slap that precious face and so he does. Jesus stands with His arms tied behind Him as His cheek reddens and starts to sting, turns to the man and asks him a question in order to turn him inward upon himself and examine the hatred that he has for the Son of God. He wants to know why he hates Him so.

Being a Jew and waiting for Messiah, was all this man ever knew. Did he hate Him because Jesus threatened Judaism? Or perhaps it is that Jesus stood there dripping with innocence, condemning their secret sin, motivations and purposes?[229] Maybe He found himself under conviction just being in the presence of One who exudes such perfection. There are many things about Christ that could make the wicked uncomfortable simply by being present. There are many attributes of our Savior that bring about a strong reaction on the part of those who get near Him. These reactions are caused, for the most part, by fear.

The survival instinct that is observable in dogs is evident in man as well. This base, animal nature in us only gives us three options when we encounter fear – two of which preserve us as we are, and one very odd option – submission to, or compliance with that which makes us afraid, opens us to change. This option is a resignation of sorts; a rolling over and accepting what those who make us afraid choose to do to us, a realization that we are helpless and hopeless without His mercy. (This option, by the way, is salvation)

Fight or Flight?

The other two options are fight and flight. Many of us spend our lives running from Christ. It is because He opens our eyes to shortcomings as we have never before been willing to see them, in the light of the holiness of God.

---

[229] This is the true cause for child abuse today. The innocence in children exposes the impure heart of sinful men and women by mere comparison, causing inexplicable hatred toward the child. The anger leads to physical abuse which causes more secret sin, which closes the loop in the circle of ever-increasing abuse. The simple solution's first step is to make peace with God through forgiveness brought about by heartfelt repentance.

He opens our eyes to our flaws and shortcomings, so we flee what we fear by ignoring or affording no time for thoughts of our condition before God. Those who choose the option of flight are usually very busy with "life" and have little time (or so they say) for introspection, although their reasons are the same (to turn from the exposition of their sin). Those, however, who choose to fight, are as this small man who struck Jesus. Trembling, cowering, but nonetheless ready to lash out and hate, defame, or otherwise discredit Christ in any way. Those who choose to fight Jesus wait for their opportunity to do what they so desire to do – strike!

In modern day these who choose to fight take the form of blasphemers. Movies made about the life of Christ, portraying Him as a sinful, selfish man, or the academics who attempt to prove He did not do or say the things that the Bible records are the blasphemers of today. They attempt to take their blows at Him (a man whom they consider to be dead now for 2000 years) and thereby cause insurrection against Christianity altogether. These who stand to fight hate Christ for who He was, and who He is today. They strike out at Him with curses that contain His name, bumper stickers that blaspheme, jokes that abuse, music lyrics that lampoon, and lives that are nothing less than personifications of anti-Christ. Why are they so against God? Why do they hate Christ? These are questions they must answer for themselves, but I think in some cases it is because He and His doctrine threaten the life that they have built for themselves.

"What a Shame"

The church need not cluck their tongue and feel pity for or outrage against these wicked ones who fight the Savior, for the religious are not guiltless in this matter of fighting what exposes their insincerity or tradition. Even the conventional Christian, who sees their way of worship, their churches, their system, or their gods threatened, ventures to take a poke at the Savior from time to time to keep Him at bay.

Remember, the man in our story today that struck Jesus, who started all the uproar and likely started the chain of torturous events, was probably, in his own mind, saving the "faith" that gave him purpose in life. (You may not be able to pinpoint your discontent or disagreement with Christ – but you should.) This petty coward wanted nothing to do with a religion that did not utilize Priests and religion and temples and hierarchy.

The little man was afraid of losing his life to this Galilean carpenter. Perhaps you are afraid of the same? Jesus was so sinless, so childlike, so innocent, so … right! This man hated Him for reasons deeper than he himself could see; and he shook with rage toward Him. Jesus knew this, and asked him to look inside for a moment and consider, "If I am wrong, tell me, but if I am right… 'Why smitest thou me?'"

138. Sayest thou this thing of thyself, or did others tell it thee of me?

John 18:34, "Jesus answered him, Sayest thou this thing of thyself, or did others tell it thee of me?"

What the conventional church calls "witnessing" the world at large calls "aggravation." This is no secret. At nearly every mall or in most neighborhoods you can find these zealous "witnesses" seeking out someone to tell that Jesus is the Christ, in whom, if they believe, their life will be better than it is now. As they explain the "benefits package" to people who have not asked, they prove to be an embarrassment to those who have a true and living faith. (And an irritation to those who don't)

How does this approach differ from Christ's witness to the world? Did He teach that we should "go and tell?" What are we expected to tell? What are we not to tell? Let's look at some examples of instruction given in the Scriptures.

*Matthew 8:4, "And Jesus saith unto him [a man He had just healed of leprosy], **See thou tell no man**; but go thy way, shew thyself to the priest, and offer the gift that Moses commanded, for a testimony unto them."*
*Matthew 16:20, "Then charged he his disciples that they **should tell no man that he was Jesus the Christ**." Mark 7:36, "And he charged them **that they should tell no man**: but the more he charged them, so much the more a great deal they published it;" Mark 8:30, "And he charged them that **they should tell no man** of him." Mark 9:9, "And as they came down from the mountain, he charged them **that they should tell no man what things they had seen**, till the Son of man were risen from the dead." Luke 5:14, "And he charged him to **tell no man**: ..." Luke 8:56, "And [after raising a girl from the dead] her parents were astonished: but he charged them **that they should tell no man what was done**." Luke 9:21, "And he straitly charged them, and **commanded them to tell no man that thing**." [That Jesus was the son of God]*

Then look at this exchange with Peter:
*He saith unto them, But whom say ye that I am? And Simon Peter answered and said, Thou art the Christ, the Son of the living God. And Jesus answered and said unto him, Blessed art thou, Simon Barjona: <u>for flesh and blood hath not revealed it unto thee, but my Father</u> which is in heaven. **Then charged he his disciples that they should tell no man that he was Jesus the Christ.***

The difference becomes obvious. How many of us have ever been instructed in conventional evangelism NOT to tell others that Jesus was the Son of God? Yet, over and over again Jesus said just that. But why?

The key can be found in His statement to Peter, "For flesh and blood hath not revealed it unto thee, but my Father which is in heaven." This revelation is what Jesus came to discover in the heart of a man. He came neither to put this knowledge in man's heart, nor to reveal himself to mankind. He came to discover those to whom the Father had revealed the Truth.

Jesus' Plan of Evangelism

He explains His mission to Pilate in no uncertain terms, "To this end was I born, and for this cause came I into the world, that I should bear witness unto the truth. Every one that is of the truth heareth my voice." Our mission, too, is to bear witness to Truth. We cannot truthfully witness that Jesus Christ is the Son of God, nor are we able to go about trying to prove that "fact" to an unbelieving world, nor are we to bear witness that He is alive and well, (unless you have seen Him in the flesh) but we should bear witness to truth. Bearing witness to Truth is something we CAN do. We should witness to Truth in our speech, in our life, in our doctrine, in our worship, our work, our business, and our family. We should bear witness to what is true and right and LET GOD THE FATHER reveal that Jesus Christ as the Son of God to whomsoever He wills.

When someone is visited by the Father, and He reveals Christ Jesus as Messiah to him; it shows many things to those who understand His plan. It shows God has chosen them to be a part of His Kingdom. We are not to compel folks to "choose Jesus." For Jesus said, "Ye have not chosen me, but I have chosen you..."(John 15:16) Also when the Father reveals Christ, it shows a supernatural link has occurred; not mental ascent, or a fact accepted in evidence, but a spiritual awareness, made real to the recipient of grace by God Himself. When revelation is this deep, (as it should be) it is not soon shaken when harder times come.

"...but the more he charged them, so much the more a great deal they published it." Unfortunately we have all become victim, to one degree or another, of this zealous teaching and arbitrary "revealing" of Christ. Many things we think we "believe," we have only been taught. How many things do we practice, how many things do we believe that have been placed in us by habit, tradition, example, and custom? How many things that we believe can we say we know that flesh and blood did not reveal, but the Father in Heaven. The truth is, if we had not been taught many of the things we believe, we would not believe them; because they were never revealed to us by the Father.

On the other hand there are things you "know" within you that you have never been taught but you cannot shake.[230] No matter how much you are taught otherwise, you cannot seem to reverse the revelation to your heart. These are things that have been revealed to you. They have been made real to you and you know that you know, even though you have never been shown evidence for

---

[230] Hebrews 12:27, "... signifieth the removing of those things that are shaken, as of things that are made, that those things which cannot be shaken may remain."

it, or even after you are shown "evidence" to the contrary. That is the revelation we need to seek for all Spiritual truth, all doctrine, all principles of life and living, and all relationships. As this awareness of God's voice is honed and sharpened to a fine edge, you can look forward to daily revelation to guide you through the maze of life and find victorious living a reality.

Direct revelation from the Father is the most important element in your walk with Christ. To discover and establish whence and what is revealed to you is a great way to evaluate the depth and breadth of your Christian life, respectively. To recognize, identify and eliminate what has not been revealed to you is a great way to avoid heresy, false doctrine and misdirection.

The ministry of the Holy Spirit is to convince the world, and to call the Father's children. Jesus was always looking for someone to whom the Messiah had been revealed. Jesus sought out those to whom this had been revealed. He did not want that plan to be fouled up by over-zealous people going around convincing the world that He was Messiah. If they would keep His secret, only the Father could reveal the truth of Jesus' identity. Remember, Jesus said, "No man can come to me, except the Father which hath sent me draw him..." (John 6:44) His question to Pilate was no different than His question to Peter earlier. "Whom say ye that I am?" He wondered if His Father had revealed this truth to Pilate, so He asks, "Sayest thou this thing of thyself, or did others tell it thee?"

The source of the knowledge is more important than the knowledge itself. Has Christ been revealed to you, or did someone tell you that He was the Messiah? Jesus said, "Every one that is of the truth heareth my voice." Have you heard His voice, or does your revelation of Christ only go back to a human voice? Is your faith one of education or revelation? When you confess (as Peter did) that Jesus is the Son of God, is the conclusion to which you have come a deduction at which you have arrived or is it a revelation from the Father? When you witness to the world that Jesus is indeed the Messiah, "Sayest thou this thing of thyself, or did others tell it thee?"

139. What shall be done in the dry?

Luke 23:31, "For if they do these things in a green tree, what shall be done in the dry?"

In the day we live, we can choose our commentary on society between many sources. If one news story or political forecast seems a little bleak we can turn the page or channel and find a more positive outlook. I am often criticized for having a darker view of the world than perhaps I should as a Christian. "After all," I am told, "read the back of the book…We win!"

That makes a nice sentiment and a witty one, but would be little comfort to the families of Christians in China watching their children die tortuous deaths, or to the confused and lonely masses of people searching for truth and stability in our churches and Meetinghouses who are given a steady diet of mind candy, empty and foundationless promises, and Scriptural lessons by men who seldom even read their Bibles. The back of the book I read prophesies the very things I see around me today. The world is in trouble. The Church is in trouble. Anyone who thinks otherwise is misinformed, deceived, or selling something.

We the Church of Jesus Christ are unholy and unclean. We accept and even teach the breaking of Commandments. We flirt with the world's offerings and we coax our children to seek what it has to offer. We are sitting in a paper room with gossamer curtains while playing with matches. We have confidence in our doctrines and traditions to help us and our children in the time of need and know not that they are fabrications and empty as exhausted fire extinguishers. You may be one who resents those who tests your ideas, questions your doctrine, and shows them to be false. For it is in these traditions and ideas that you have the ability to hold to God with one hand and to mammon with the other.

Am I being bleak? Am I being negative? Jesus walked through a world that was different from ours. Depending on who you ask, the world was better or worse then. I don't pretend to know if living in Christ's day was better or if people were better or not. I do know that Jesus was despised for no good reason. He was rejected as Savior, as Messiah, as a Rabbi, as a Jew, as an Israelite, as an innocent man, and finally, was killed cruelly for a crime He did not commit. Just as He had been released from carrying His load of the cross, He turned His bloody face from which His beard had been pulled by wicked hands – he turned His face swollen with marks of violent blows landed by religious men – as He turned that lovely face toward the women who watched and wept for Him He said,

"Daughters of Jerusalem, weep not for me, but weep for yourselves, and for your children. For, behold, the days are coming, in the which they shall say, Blessed are the barren, and the wombs that never bare, and the paps which never gave suck. Then shall they begin to say to the mountains, Fall

on us; and to the hills, Cover us. For if they do these things in a green tree, what shall be done in the dry?" (Luke 23:28-31)

What did Jesus mean by this statement? He could only mean that things are going to get worse as time goes on. The time of the green tree was during His time among us in bodily form. During His life, the body of Christ (the Church) was alive like a green and fresh tree, a new tree, a sapling. The strength and vitality of this tree was greater in its future than in its past. But there was coming a time when it would be older and although it will be bigger – it will be drier. This great tree representing the Church will not have the resilience of youth or the health and strength of a tree with its whole life ahead of it. It was a tree that, as far as time goes, was far, far away from the acorn that gave it birth.

As time goes by men get worse, not better. 2 Timothy 3:12-13 says, "Yea, and all that will live godly in Christ Jesus shall suffer persecution. But evil men and seducers shall wax worse and worse, deceiving, and being deceived." If you think that Constantine stopped the persecution of Christians, you may know your history but your Bible does not agree.

Today, in the United States of America, we are free from persecution for one reason, not because we are more "civilized," not because we have laws to protect us from persecution, not because of our "first world" mentality of "live and let live," but because we no longer live a godly life in Christ Jesus. The alleviation of persecution in Constantine's day came because the paganized version of Christianity was accepted and adopted by the Christians of that day. Even under the hand of Constantine, true Christians were persecuted for worshipping on Sabbath and not as "Christians" (on the declared "venerable day of the Sun" that he instituted). Compromise, not Constantine, was the deliverer; just the same as it is today.

Our world is getting worse, the Church in getting worse. As we go down together the Church compromises and the world takes more privilege. Now the world hates with a vengeance those who preach or teach righteousness, and if someone dares to live a life of faith and righteousness today, they would crucify him as well.

The Transplanted Kingdom

In the northwest there are trees that will not be found in the southeast. They simply cannot survive there. Many have tried to transplant a pretty tree from one unique geographical location to another with no success. After a while the mineral content of the soil or the length of days, heat, cold, wetness of soil, will finally take its toll and soon the signs of death begin to appear: brownness, dryness, and finally weakness and death. The olive tree planted in the earth into which we were grafted is a transplant from another world. The young "green tree" was a life that was free from accusation, condemnation, fault, blame, sin, and free from any reproach by anyone. It was a new and strong shoot to start this transplant off right. As time went by it grew and

442

flourished. Adding branches and expanding its root system, it began to take hold.

We are all of this same tree, we have the same root. We are all branches of the same vine but the greenness and tenderness and strength began to wane as we took our nourishment from the strange soil earth. The longer we are planted here the more we will take in minerals and water of a world that does us no good – a corrupt world. The slow poison of the soil, the seasons we never can get used to, and the rain that comes at strange and inopportune times, all begin to take their toll.

We, the body of Christ, are not what it used to be. We know the ravages of time. We cry out for adoption and salvation. We are in "the dry" that Jesus spoke of in His warning. We have great need to filter our nourishment, reserve our water, keep our face to the sun and place our faith in the Husbandman to redeem us and take us back to our far away home.

Persecution will come when you dedicate to Christ. Will you be healthy enough to make it through? Deception is coming, false Christs, false teachers, false prophets, and His Church is dry and diseased and unhealthy. Be cautious of the nourishment you get from the world and look to Christ and let come what may. Be ready to live for Him, ready to die for Him, as ready as you can be. Jesus said, "Weep not for me, but weep for yourselves... For if they do these things in a green tree, what shall be done in the dry?"

140. My God, my God, why hast thou forsaken me?

Matthew 27:46, "And about the ninth hour Jesus cried with a loud voice, saying, Eli, Eli, lama sabachthani? that is to say, My God, my God, why hast thou forsaken me?"

Mark 15:34, "And at the ninth hour Jesus cried with a loud voice, saying, Eloi, Eloi, lama sabachthani? which is, being interpreted, My God, my God, why hast thou forsaken me?"

Of all the questions Jesus ever asked, this one must be the most difficult. It is difficult because there is no satisfactory answer, nor is there premise for the question. We have all heard the theories, but we must not be satisfied with speculation that affronts our Spiritual understanding. Are there any of us who have ever been to Sunday School who has not heard the proposal that "God cannot look upon sin, so He momentarily turned away from Christ on the cross?" These kinds of ideas come from those who feel a need to "help" God answer this difficult question, "Why hast thou forsaken me?"

To these well meaning, but misguided theologians I say, "Thanks, but no, thanks." If God did not answer Jesus' question, as He proved well capable of doing, we cannot presume to answer for Him. The explanation, "God cannot look on sin" has become so universally accepted that now, theology is based and doctrines are defended upon that faulty premise as if it were fact. Ask yourself this question, "If God cannot look upon sin, what hope has the sinner of God's grace and visitation?" Where is this idea borne upon Scripture? It is not. It came from the minds of men in our pulpits. Why hast thou forsaken me? We answer, "Because God cannot look upon sin." But it is an unsolicited answer to a question that Jesus likely did not even ask.

This question, placed in the mouth of Christ Jesus in His torture, presupposes two facts that are yet to be in evidence.

1) That God turned away from Christ in His hour of death (something Christ said that His Father would not do[231] even to sparrows.)[232]

2) That Christ was left uninformed as to why He did so. These are very difficult ideas. Are we to believe that God forsook Christ in His deepest hour of physical distress? If this is true, not only are we to believe that God forsook Him, but we are to believe that Christ did not know why He did so. From the age of twelve years we read that Jesus knew He must be about His fathers business.[233] It was so much a part of His conversation at home that He was

---

[231] John 16:32, "Behold, the hour cometh, yea, is now come, that ye shall be scattered, every man to his own, and shall leave me alone: and yet I am not alone, because the Father is with me."
John 8:29, "And he that sent me is with me: the Father hath not left me alone; for I do always those things that please him."
[232] Luke 12:6, "Are not five sparrows sold for two farthings, and not one of them is forgotten before God?"
[233] Luke 2:49, "And he said unto them, How is it that ye sought me? wist ye not that I must be about my Father's business?"

444

astonished His parents did not know it as well. Also, He told His disciples repeatedly that He would be betrayed and slain. His parables pertaining to this always included the son of the lord or husbandman being beaten and murdered.

Are we to believe that Jesus did not understand what was happening nor why? The prophecies of old were as second nature and were indeed first language to our Messiah. He had intimate familiarity with the Prophets and with the Psalms. He was an integral part of the eternal plan of atonement, sacrifice, and temple ritual. He knew that the sacrifice of Abraham was a type and foreshadowing of His own execution. So are we to believe that at the last moment, He did not know why? The long-departed Moses and Elijah visited this man in person for the purpose of discussing His upcoming passion[234] and yet there are those who think that He was unaware of His lone sacrifice.

This Question Of Jesus Simply Does Not Make Sense.

Perhaps I am only saying aloud what no one has had the audacity to say. Perhaps to some, who worship their Bibles as the Word of God, what I am saying is blasphemy, but my faith has never been built upon senseless or useless premises and I have no intention to pretend that this idea makes sense, nor will I present more useless ideas to cover it up. In the past, I put forth the theory that Jesus was simply quoting the Psalm and not asking God a question at all. I knew in my Spirit that God had not forsaken Him nor did He question why. The quotation from the Psalm came just after the people said, "He trusted in God, let God save Him now." In the same psalm from which this question comes it also says with nearly identical words, "He trusted on the LORD that he would deliver him: let him deliver him, seeing he delighted in him." (Psalms 22:8) The striking similarity in the two statements, twenty-eight generations apart, had to be a curiosity even to the newest reader of Torah in those days. Maybe Christ, in His anguish, was simply quoting David from the 22nd psalm.

Upon another inspection of the verses where this is found (as it appears only in Matthew and Mark) is apparent that those who stood by did not know what He said.

"And some of them that stood by, when they heard it, said, Behold, he calleth Elias. "And one ran and filled a spunge full of vinegar, and put it on a reed, and gave him to drink, saying, Let alone; let us see whether Elias will come to take him down." (Mark 15:35-36)

What He said must have been nearly unintelligible because it was obviously so misunderstood. Perhaps the witnesses who recalled and wrote this, only thought they heard Him quote the Psalm. (This idea may anger those who want their Bible to be perfect, but we must not idolize Scripture at the expense of casting dispersions on Jesus Christ that can only be explained by conflicting doctrines and ideas.) Actually He was speaking Aramaic when He said "...Eli, Eli, lama sabachthani." This introduces in an unusual point of interest:

---

[234] Luke 9:30-31, "And, behold, there talked with him two men, which were Moses and Elias: Who appeared in glory, and spake of his decease which he should accomplish at Jerusalem."

In recent years there has been made available to the western world, Scriptures of dubious, but nonetheless interesting, origin, the Aramaic Peshitta. The church from which they originate makes the claim that the Scriptures in their possession were NEVER translated but were handed to their church fathers, by the apostles, in their original language – Aramaic. Aramaic was the language Jesus and His disciples spoke, and it was one of Paul's languages as well. The Peshitta makes for interesting reading and lays claim to settling our subject at hand (among many others.) George Lamsa, the translator into English, says that this confusing question was actually never asked. He contends that it was a misunderstanding of Aramaic and more correctly reads, "My God, my God, for this was I spared." Jesus knew that this was his destiny. I must say as well, these are, without a doubt, the finest words I can think of to place here. If Christ's whole ministry culminated here, impaled upon a stake, as the serpent Moses lifted upon the pole in the wilderness, it would be a true and accurate statement and a fulfillment of all prophecy for Jesus to cry out, "for this was I spared! For this purpose was I held until now. This was my destiny."

Many people struggle with this question of Jesus. It is as if all that Jesus ever was while He was living, is erased in His hour of death. The question, "Why hast thou forsaken me," tears at the very fabric of the persona He presented, His years of ministry, His confidence, His knowledge and wisdom, even His enviable relationship to His Father now hangs in doubt before all who watch Him die this miserable death and hear Him ask in agony, "Why?" As the crowd waited to see "…if God will save Him" His detractors would likely have shouted a cheer if they heard Christ confess that they were right, that God had indeed forsaken Him. Could He have said that? Whether you accept the Peshitta's rendition of these words or my theory that He was merely quoting the psalm, it is difficult to put these anxious and fearful words into the same mouth that said, "I and my Father are one."

The other Gospels make no mention of this question of Christ at all. Theirs is a story of a more honorable death. They record Christ Jesus crying out, "Father, into thy hands I commend my spirit," and "It is finished: and he bowed his head, and gave up the ghost." (Luke 23 - John 19 Combined) The relationship with His Father unbroken, His death accepted, He resigns to the will and care of God, His Spirit, with no doubts, no fears, no questions. It was not long before this that Jesus asked, "What shall I say, 'Father, save me from this hour?' "…but for this cause came I unto this hour." (John 12) Jesus knew why He was there. He knew exactly why and how His death was to occur. There were few surprises in Christ's life. The torture was not one of them. He was never forsaken. He was not left to die alone and forgotten of His Father. No, it was for this He was set aside since the foundation of the world. For this was He spared. This was His destiny.

V   After the Resurrection

"The great business of man's life is to answer the end for which he lives; and that is, to glorify God, and save his own soul: this is the decree of heaven as old as the world. But so it is, that man minds nothing less than what he should mind most; and despises to inquire into his own being, its original duty and end; choosing rather to dedicate his days to gratify the pride, avarice, and luxury of his heart; as if he had been born for himself, or rather given himself being. And so, not subject himself to the reckoning and judgment of a superior power. To this wild and lamentable condition has poor man brought himself, by his disobedience to the law of God in his heart, by doing that which he knows he should not do, and leaving undone what he knows he should do. And as long as this disease continues upon man, he will make his God his enemy and himself incapable of the love and salvation that He has made real to us by His son, Jesus Christ, to the world."

William Penn
(1644-1718), English Quaker and the founder of the colony of Pennsylvania. From the literary work "No Cross, No Crown"

141. Why are you crying?

John 20:15, "Jesus saith unto her, Woman, why weepest thou? whom seekest thou? She, supposing him to be the gardener, saith unto him, Sir, if thou have borne him hence, tell me where thou hast laid him, and I will take him away."

I can remember searching for Jesus. It does not seem so long ago to me that I realized He was not where I thought He was, or where I was told He would be. Religion and empty words from preachers had left me disappointed with God and discouraged in my "Christian life." The lies and misleadings by men who knew no more than me, the books written and meetings held by those who make their living on the Gospel were found to be as empty as that tomb that Mary discovered in the Garden that morning.

The search for Truth really begins with tears. It is the initial discovery that we are lost and undone and hopeless that breaks one's heart. Mary was at the mercy of whoever was behind this desecration of her Master's grave. Mind you, she had not even thought that He had risen; it had not even entered her mind as a possibility. She was not thinking supernaturally; she was only thinking about what was tangible and physically possible. She assumed a caretaker or gardener had carried him away. This is the mistake we continue to make in our search for Christ today.

We would never assume that the search for Christ, who is a transcendent being, would be a physical one. Why do we assume it will be a mental one ...or an intellectual one? Why do we assume it will require reading (though that is a part of it) or that it will require a teacher or preacher (though these can be a part in our search as well) why do we assume it will be us finding Him instead of Him finding us?

Honest examinations of our efforts to find Christ can prove to be embarrassing. No, the search for Christ must be a spiritual one. He is a Spirit and those who worship Him will do so in Spirit. He is a Spirit; those who search for Him must do so in Spirit.

Thoughts of hopelessness devastate those who have no concept of spiritual journey. It may sound as though "you can't get there from here," but in our devastation and hopelessness we may meet someone who speaks the Word of God to us. In the voice of a stranger, we may hear the voice of God. You will know His voice. He will likely ask, "Why weepest thou?"

Mary honestly answered the angels when they asked, "why weepest thou?" She answered, "They have taken away my Lord and I do not know where they have laid Him." But when Jesus appeared, He asked the same question and added, "Whom seekest thou?" Mary was not in the mood for games. She never answered His question because she assumed the gardener knew fully well WHOM she was seeking. She said, "If you have moved Him tell me and I will arrange to take Him elsewhere." We can only imagine her concern that perhaps Joseph of Arimathaea had reconsidered his offer of a tomb, or that he had only loaned it to him in the haste of the emergency and later had Jesus buried elsewhere. Whatever the reason, she was in no mood to deal with sassy gardeners asking impertinent questions.

Sometimes direction comes from offensive sources. Sometimes the very words we need to hear fall from the mouths of the least likely people. It is an ear trained to hear Truth that will find it wherever it appears. Remember, when Jesus was in front of Pilate He said, "To this end was I born, and for this cause came I into the world, that I should bear witness unto the truth. Every one that is of the truth heareth my voice." (John 18)

The Search For Christ Is Not A Physical One.

You would think that this idea would be self-evident, but many people pursue Christ by physical means. They go where they hear His name mentioned; they read what prints His name and promises to draw readers nearer to Him. They change habits, dress, politics, and language. They pursue memberships, fellowships, and identification with people who profess His name, but rarely do they embark on a true spiritual journey. Perhaps it is because they do not understand the spiritual, but it is more likely that it is because they cannot control the spiritual.

The spiritual journey is an enigmatic one. You can easily find yourself pursuing what you do not understand, in a manner that you do not know, in order to gain a result you have not heretofore experienced. This becomes more than you can handle, so you, whether knowingly or unknowingly, change your course.

We set off on a more familiar journey – the one everyone else has taken – the one that leads to familiar and conventional places and teaches orthodox and customary things while surrounded by common and regular people, only to awake one day with a very familiar feeling of being exactly where you started. This can be quite devastating.

As they took Jesus' body from the tree, the high Sabbath day (the first day of the Feast of Unleavened Bread) was approaching. They had to hurry. Mary wanted to prepare the body for burial. Along with the other women, they waited for the men to make arrangements to get Him from the rugged pole and place him somewhere ...anywhere, because as Sabbath drew on, preparations would be impossible!

This was the fourth day of the week, and at sundown the fifth day began, as well as the High Sabbath. Time drug on, and then several disciples appeared with news of Joseph of Arimathaea's offer of the tomb. They hurried, but Sabbath was upon them.

They placed the body in the tomb only hastily wrapping it in linen and frustrated by the ceremonial Law and pressured by the Commandment, they had to leave. "We will come after the Sabbath and finish," they thought. Sometime after twenty-four hours, on the sixth day of the week, they gathered their spices and returned to the grave to finish the preparation and were greeted by soldiers. They were not granted access to the tomb by the armed guards.

Again they were frustrated, this time by the legal structures and politics of the day. They thought, "Perhaps tomorrow." "Perhaps the soldiers will permit us after two days have passed." "We cannot come tomorrow either!" one of them remembered, "Tomorrow is the weekly Sabbath!"

Now, frustrated by the Commandments, they may have wondered when they will ever be permitted to do the right thing for the Savior they loved. Then, early on the first day of the week, Mary appeared at the tomb, with her spices again, ready to prepare the body. To her surprise she found the door open and the soldiers gone and taking this miraculous opportunity she entered, only to find that someone had stolen Him away.

She can't take any more and she begins to weep and cry. Jesus was there, only not in the place she was looking, and not in form she was seeking, and not for the reason she was there. She was so intent on finding Him, she missed Him. She was so determined to find Him in the form she thought He should be, she mistook Him for someone else.

If you find yourself searching frantically, frustrating yourself at every turn, you may accept things as miraculous that are not at all miracles, and miss true miracles calling them commonplace. You may become discouraged and sad, indignant or mad; you may be reduced to tears, but if the search is pure and the heart is right you will not be disappointed. In your tired and weeping condition you will feel all frustration melt away as a bad dream when He appears and asks you, "Why are you crying?"

142. Why are you so sad?

Luke 24:17, "And he said unto them, What manner of communications are these that ye have one to another, as ye walk, and are sad?"

Three days have passed since the death of Christ. Two of His disciples walk toward Emmaus, a town ten or twelve miles west of Jerusalem. Cleopas, one of them, notices a stranger has joined them in their travels. Surely it was not uncommon for travelers to cluster and keep company on long trips and this day would be no different...or so they thought.

It is said that if you talk to someone for five minutes you can easily find what is most important to him or her. We give ourselves away when we speak, for, as the Jesus said, "Out of the abundance of the heart the mouth speaks." I recently met a woman who was excited about gambling. She talked about where she had been and how much she had won, and where she was going next to try her hand at new machines, new casinos, and new games. It was so much a part of her conversation and thought that she despaired to talk even of her children and rather wanted to talk of gambling. If someone told her she had a problem with it she would probably deny it, insisting that it was just a pastime. But, her speech gave her away, did it not? To be in control of our speech would be to analyze everything we say from an objective viewpoint before it was said, to hear it as it will be heard by others. It is a tiresome exercise, but a sure sign of wisdom and prudence.

Proverbs 29:20, "Seest thou a man that is hasty in his words? there is more hope of a fool than of him."

Ecclesiastes 5, "...a fool's voice is known by multitude of words."

Our emotions also give us away. It is with emotion that we are able to say one thing while communicating another, and it is by emotion that we hear another message other than what someone is actually saying. In order to communicate clearly, we have to be in control of our emotions. To be in full control of emotions is, essentially, to fully engage in none. Our emotive behavior comes mainly from feelings of desperation or fear, but there is a sinister aspect as well. To purposefully emote while communicating can be an attempt to project a feeling onto or into the person to whom we are speaking. Emotion is aptly applied to stage actors. Purposeful emotion has no place in Christian witness. Many times emotion and feelings are held as synonyms, but they are not. A person who emotes their feelings may cause those feelings in someone else, but the act of communicating that feeling need not be done through emotion. It can be communicated through a logical, intellectual exchange on many levels. Emotion nearly always demands reaction. Reaction to stimulus is never higher than the level of an animal. Feelings of joy or sadness, hope or fear are high above the understanding of animals and are legitimate and useful feelings for mankind. To attempt to create these feelings in others, we use *our* emotions. To manipulate others to do or think as we wish, we use *their* emotions.

These men on the road to Emmaus were not emotional; they were feeling very sad. The hope of all Israel had been laid to rest three days ago and, with Him, all hope of a better life for them and their children. They felt that He had promised a life that He was unable to deliver because He had been killed and His mission cut short. They wondered how they could ever regain the momentum that His ministry had developed, or even if they wanted to.

They struggled with their hatred of the men who crucified Him and felt defeated in that hatred. They feared for their own lives at this point and, though we are not told so, this may well have been the reason they were traveling to Emmaus. They wondered what had happened, and why, they wondered what would become of them and the life that had been promised them.

They rehearsed the words of Christ over and over, and thought perhaps they had misunderstood something or misapplied His words to mean something else. Maybe Christ *was* the fake the Pharisees said He was, perhaps they were duped into believing something that was not even true. Could Jesus have been insane – but what about the miracles?

As this vine of reason grew in their minds and tangled, the truth became more and more frustrating and distant. They found themselves walking slower and slower as it occurred to them that if Jesus was a phony, if they had been duped, there was no point in continuing, nor was there any point in looking back. Their feet dragged the road now, as it was becoming hard to see any point in living.

It was just then that Jesus appeared on the road as a traveler. Holding His identity from them, He asked "Why are you so sad as you walk?" It was obvious to anyone nearby, that there was sadness about these two men. It would be nearly impossible to hide such crushing sadness. These men had lost their hope, their future, their purpose, and their greatest friend. They were not necessarily emotional, they were sad, and it showed.

The Disciples Only Lacked Revelation

The men on the Emmaus road only lacked a revelation of the Truth. They needed only to see that what they had thought was true, was not, and what they thought was gone, lost, and hopeless was none of those things at all. In fact, Christ was not gone, He was glorified, and they were not lost but on the verge of being saved. Their hopelessness was far from real. Though they did not know it, Christ was beside them, alive and well!

They only lacked an opening into the Spiritual side of their situation. In the most perilous times in your life, the time when all hope has fled away from you, you may very well be in the best of times and only lack a revelation of the Truth to change your countenance from desperate sadness to inexplicable joy.

The burning in your heart, the revelation in your soul writhing to be released, may be nearer than you think. Your release from the pains of death and separation, your bursting into relief and escape from our entombing fear and anxiety is as close as a conversation with the Savior. He waits to comfort you by sharing His point of view, His perspective and His understanding. From the perspective of Christ there are no problems, no defeat, no oppression, and no evil power that has not been put under His feet. He longs to tell you this and make this real to you in ways you have not yet known.

As you walk your own road of Emmaus, your road of discouragement and escape. As you consider all the things that went wrong and calculate the death and destruction to follow, or you are overwhelmed with the fear of continuing without some tangible presence of the Lord, you may become obviously sad to those around you. As this sadness begins to permeate all of your life, and cynicism sets up a home in you, and your life becomes a display of the sadness you feel, you may become emotional and try to transmit that to others through various means. It may look as though you are angry or contrary, but those are emotions that we are only using.

The Lord sees through meanness, cynical attitudes, and negativity. He does not even ask why you are so negative, or emotional. He does not inquire as to the reasons for your lack of enthusiasm, your lack of direction, or lack of purpose. He wonders why you have not consorted with Him, sought new revelation, new understanding, or a new perspective on your faith. He wonders why you have not sought His perspective. Are you ready for your heart to burn within you? It begins when you honestly answer, "Why are you so sad?"

143. What things?

Luke 24:19, "And he said unto them, What things?"

Owners of stores and markets wonder sometimes how their business presents itself to the public. Even after much training and orientation, an unmotivated employee can make an entire multinational company with years of experience look like a band of novices to the public. Fearing this, they send "shoppers" hired by the company to their stores. They are there for the express purpose of reporting how they are doing and how the company appears to the public.

In the story from which our question comes, we see Jesus doing this. We see Him walking along, "shopping" His disciples as if He were a stranger. He held back their recognition of Him facilitating candid responses to His questions.

He asks such a question that the disciples are flabbergasted at the ignorance of this stranger. "Where are you from that you have not heard of the man from Galilee that has turned this whole country upside-down?" "And the one of them, whose name was Cleopas, answering said unto him, Art thou only a stranger in Jerusalem, and hast not known the things which are come to pass there in these days?"

Word of what was done in Jerusalem, the life of Jesus and His subsequent execution, must have rung throughout the countryside. The story must have been on everyone's lips and in everyone's thoughts over the past three days. You can imagine the conversation at the town well and in the market. "Did you hear about the teacher Joshua?" (Jesus' name in Hebrew/Aramaic) "He was crucified by the Romans for treason." Or "…He was crucified for blasphemy!" Everyone probably had his or her own version of the story.

The Pharisees would gladly be giving reasons for His death and spreading stories about how it all came to be. Then there would be pure rumor, having no basis in fact at all, that would spread among the itching ears of Jerusalem. It was a situation ripe for gossip, rumor, and innuendo. But, what was the truth? When, why and how did it all happen?

Even as His discouraged Disciples walked, the Pharisees were plotting a rumor campaign to purport the theft of His body in the night to offset the fact that it was now missing, even under armed guard! How would Jesus check the knowledge and readiness of the disciples with whom He would soon entrust the everlasting Gospel message?

When they asked, "… hast thou not known the things which are come to pass there in these days?" And he said unto them, "What things?" "Tell me what things you are talking about."

*"And they said unto him, **Concerning Jesus of Nazareth**, which was a prophet mighty in deed and word before God and all the people: And how*

*the chief priests and our rulers delivered him to be condemned to death,
and have crucified him. But we trusted that it had been he which should
have redeemed Israel: and beside all this, to day is the third day since these
things were done. Yea, and certain women also of our company made us
astonished, which were early at the sepulchre; And when they found not his
body, they came, saying, that they had also seen a vision of angels, which
said that he was alive. And certain of them which were with us went to the
sepulchre, and found it even so as the women had said: but him they saw
not.*

In searching out their knowledge, Christ found their facts to be
accurate, but they themselves, discouraged. They had their facts straight, but
they were unsure how those facts were to be interpreted. They exposed their
doubts when they confessed, "...we trusted that it had been he which should
have redeemed Israel!" Their voices trailed into mumbles that could be read
clearly as, "...but alas, it was not to be." Christ saw that they were feeling
defeated in their hearts for they thought Christ, the "great and mighty Prophet,"
was dead. It was as if they were apologizing for the fact that He was
unaccounted among them. "...And beside all this, today is the third day since
these things were done."

These words showed that they had discussed the prophetic sign of
Jonah[235] that Jesus had spoken of in earlier days. He had promised that in three
days He would rise from the dead. Then, as if to lend some credibility to Christ,
they added, "Yes well, women of our company, which were early at the
sepulchre, told us an amazing story when they did not find his body, they came
saying that he was alive." But then he adds sadly and reluctantly, "...but we
went there and were not able to confirm their story."

Jesus was unable to take any more of their sadness and lack of faith and
said, "O fools, and slow of heart to believe all that the prophets have spoken:
Ought not Christ to have suffered these things ...to enter into his glory? And
[then,] beginning at Moses and all the prophets, he expounded unto them in all
the scriptures the things concerning himself." At this point He was still
unknown to them. They assumed this stranger was a student of the Scriptures
and happened to know much about Messiah. They gained encouragement from
Him and invited Him to stay with them. He did so. That evening He opened
their eyes to who He was and then departed from their sight.

The disciples did not pass their test but they did not fail either. They
knew the how and the when but, the why was wrapped in emotion and self-
concern and therefore difficult to be fully known. Jesus helped in two ways; He
turned them back to the Scriptures.

---

[235] Matthew 12:39-40, "But he answered and said unto them, An evil and adulterous generation seeketh after
a sign; and there shall no sign be given to it, but the sign of the prophet Jonas: For as Jonas was three days
and three nights in the whale's belly; so shall the Son of man be three days and three nights in the heart of the
earth."

The Scriptures are an invaluable source for the wavering, doubting, or discouraged Christian. They offer stable words from God; promises and immutable prophecies that can place disjointed events and facts into an eternal perspective and paint a mural of understanding in the heart of the believer. Sometimes this understanding is not even one that can be related in word, but an underlying knowing that gives comfort in times of doubt.

The other way Christ helped them with their discouragement was by His physical presence. When they asked Him to stay He "…made as though He would have gone further… but they constrained him." Jesus then changed His plans and stayed with them. Sometimes our presence can be a great encouragement to those who feel left alone. Sometimes with encouragement, the Lord will stay with us a little longer in our time of doubt and fear, or in the time of embarrassment over our performance on our pop quiz.

So, How Would You Do?

If our Savior wanted to check you out as a possessor of the Gospel message, how much of it could you relate accurately? Do you know who Christ was? Why Christ was? Do you know what things transpired in Jerusalem that day and how they affect you and what effect they have on others?

If Jesus gave you a little pop quiz to see how prepared you are to relate the good news to the world, how would you fare? What "things" do you know about God's plan of Redemption? Do you know who was responsible for the death of Christ and why? Do you know why He was raised the third day? Do you know how all of this fits into Scripture and fulfills thousands of years of prophecy? Are you sure that your Savior has risen indeed and is now seated at the right hand of the Father on High? Does He live in your understanding and in your heart? Is your way dedicated to Him? Does your heart burn within you as He opens the Scriptures to you?

If Jesus appeared as a stranger and asked of the hope that is in you, could you tell Him of the events that changed your life? Could you give a clear and understandable story of the things in your life that led you to such hope... if He looked at *you* and asked, "What things?"

144. *Ought not Christ to have suffered these things?*

Luke 24:25-27, "Then he said unto them, O fools, and slow of heart to believe all that the prophets have spoken: Ought not Christ to have suffered these things, and to enter into his glory? And beginning at Moses and all the prophets, he expounded unto them in all the scriptures the things concerning himself."

A prophet is a marvel to consider. In the days before Christ, God would find and commission men (or women) to speak for Him to kings, as well as the common, the word of God. This word may have been good news or bad, it may have been threats or promises, but it was clear to whoever received it that it was to be obeyed. So what kept anyone and everyone from saying "Thus saith the Lord" and making themselves out to be a prophet? The answer is clearly outlined in Deuteronomy 18: 15-22.[236]

The idea of prophets came from the people who feared God that day in Horeb when the fire of God came down and stood on the mountain. For fear, they asked for a man to go between them and God. God then granted them prophets. To prove themselves genuine to the people, they were given power over nature or the ability to see the supernatural dimension and therefore could tell the people future events. By reason of this power they were called "Seers." Reference 1 Samuel 9:9.

The Lord speaking to us by the prophets is an old idea but their prophecies last until today because many prophets spoke of the time in which we live. They proved themselves to the people of their day as genuine; unfortunately it remains a matter of faith for us that they were true prophets because we can only read about them and believe their prophecies as they come to pass. We have no first-hand knowledge of their sincerity or commission. We cannot test or prove them, as God instructed us to do, we must believe them for the fact that to this date they have not been proven false.

This was the case also with the disciples. They had no more proof than we do. Nevertheless, Jesus chided them by saying, "O fools, and slow of heart to believe all that the prophets have spoken." He acted as though they were foolish NOT to believe all the prophets had to say. He even called them fools! Are we, too, foolish not to believe all the prophets had to say? If so, what are we if we do not even read what the prophets had to say?

---

[236] Deuteronomy 18:15-22, "The LORD thy God will raise up unto thee a Prophet from the midst of thee, of thy brethren, like unto me; unto him ye shall hearken... And the LORD said unto me... I will raise them up a Prophet from among their brethren, like unto thee, and will put my words in his mouth; and he shall speak unto them all that I shall command him. And it shall come to pass, that whosoever will not hearken unto my words which he shall speak in my name, I will require it of him. But the prophet, which shall presume to speak a word in my name, which I have not commanded him to speak, or that shall speak in the name of other gods, even that prophet shall die. And if thou say in thine heart, How shall we know the word which the LORD hath not spoken? When a prophet speaketh in the name of the LORD, if the thing follow not, nor come to pass, that is the thing which the LORD hath not spoken, but the prophet hath spoken it presumptuously: thou shalt not be afraid of him."

Pop Quiz

What do you know about the prophets and their writings? What was Obadiah's message to the people of his time? Who was the prophet that Jesus quoted more than any other? What prophet foretold the circumstances and details of Christ death? These are elementary questions that we, as believers in the Christ of the Scriptures, should know. We must admit that we would rather leave the Old Testament with its difficulties and legalism and saunter through the New Testament with grace at one hand and love at the other, but can we really understand the New Covenant in ignorance of our Father's recorded acts and prophecies?

Jesus also used a term here to describe their attitude toward the prophets that is quite condemning to me personally as a skeptical believer. The term "slow of heart" is quite descriptive of the attitude with which I approach spiritual things. I struggle with dubious miracles and wonder with skepticism at what seems to be exaggerations of the Old Testament. When I read of dreams and visions, I am more apt to blame what a person ate the night before rather than credit them with having heard from God. I am convicted and ashamed when Jesus calls me a fool, and "slow of heart to believe all that the prophets have spoken."

How much more prepared we would be if we were better versed in the writings of the prophets. How much less worry and heartache we would suffer if we knew that God was working His plan in our lives and indeed in the whole world. This advance knowledge is available only to those who look to God for revelation of the writings of the prophets. We need not fear the future nor need we face it in blind, foolish mirth, but with an assurance and strength that comes from knowing.

The people of Christ's day were not unfamiliar with the Scriptures. Remember that what they called "the Scriptures" in those days were more like what we now call the "Old Testament." What they knew (and were expected to know) were the words of the prophets and the Law. Their problem was the same we have today – the application of those words to their lives. We may read of history and predictions about the future with great interest but somehow in the human psyche, we have difficulty with the present. We have difficulty applying today what we knew yesterday about the future. And when we look back on our past, we have trouble coinciding events in our memory that most assuredly happened simultaneously. Time and memories of the past seem incongruent.

Time and prophecy, as well as history, are hard to commingle in our mind. Too much time is wasted thinking about tomorrow as well as what happened in the past, until we find today spent. The principles of prophecy demand application to the present time. Too often we find how prophecy pertained in a situation in the past, but as it is happening, it goes unnoticed. These disciples were walking along, thinking about their futures and worrying, and thinking of the past and wondering, while a prophecy was unfolding in the

458

very minute in which they living and they were unaware of it. It seems as though we were created to live in the present. Perhaps that is why Jesus said that what is sufficient for today is all the evil we can handle, so take no thought for tomorrow – until tomorrow. Reference Matthew 6:31-34.

If you live in the present you are able to apply today what you learned yesterday. You will see prophecy unfold before your eyes and not be taken by surprise or be found in despair and worry. you should know what the prophets said so that you will not find yourself working against an inevitable future and thereby be found working against God's will. You need to gather all the information that God deemed valuable enough to preserve for thousands of years and put into our hands (your Bible).

We all should seek God for revelation in these areas and be quick to believe what He reveals. How embarrassing it would be to be found crying over our condition only to have Jesus point to Scripture and show us that it was all told to us in advance, but we did not read it. How will it be to find that in the darkest hour in your life, there was no praise on your lips but instead, complaint; no gratitude to offer God, who was from the beginning and ever shall be, but only crying out, "Where are you God in my time of trouble?" All the while everything you needed to know to give your journey comfort, meaning and the assurance of knowing you were living in the times that was known of God from the beginning, was provided to you, and you did not so much as look at it, or apply it to your life.

These disciples watched the one they thought was the King of the universe given over to the will of the kings of the earth. The one who could spit and open eyes and ears, now dripped with the spit of wicked men. They wondered, they worried, they faltered, and then they ran. They saw their Savior, their friend, and their hope, cruelly impaled on a hill outside Jerusalem.

They saw the one they thought was the light of the world laid in a dark tomb, sealed by the government that they expected *Him* to vanquish. In their most desperate hour they could have known exactly what was happening and taken some comfort in the fact that God was working His marvelous plan. But, they were slow of heart to believe what the prophets. Jesus reminded them of the prophecies. "Why are you worried, why are you surprised?" "Ought not Christ to have suffered these things?"

145. Why are ye troubled?

Luke 24:38, "And he said unto them, Why are ye troubled? and why do thoughts arise in your hearts?"

Fear and control are mutually exclusive. As a pilot, I learned that to be in control of an aircraft at all times (to be aware of direction, speed, location, altitude, and orientation) can nearly eliminate panic in emergencies. It is unlikely that we will fear what we can control, no matter how difficult or disorienting things may be. It is equally unlikely that we will attempt to control what we fear. This is why people, who like having control, avoid the unknown, unfamiliar and sometimes feign control to assuage fear.

They insist that those around them calm down while, internally, they are frantically trying to figure out a way to gain control. However, this sense of control may only have a calming effect to those pretending confidence in their abilities, i.e. a person with no skill for flying may take the controls of an aircraft from a capable pilot and feel confident, but the other passengers will have a different opinion. In life, a person who is fearless feels capable, and a person who is capable feels fearless. A fearless person may feel qualified to handle the ins and outs of life with precision and safety. Nothing could be further from the truth, but nonetheless, it is the way he feels because he has control.

In things spiritual, we make the mistake of taking the controls from a capable Pilot and navigating our way by what we feel is right, ignoring instruments, and indicators, misinterpreting maps and landmarks and we fly along with our head in the clouds, unaware we are off course, inverted, and descending. Just before permanently purchasing a small patch of real estate with our life, some tragedy or mishap distracts us long enough for the capable Pilot to regain control, correct our attitude, regain altitude, plot a new course from where we have misplaced ourselves and change our heading, all while listening to us whine, "Where is God when you need Him?"

Why does any man want control? Simply because *he is the only one he trusts.* Fear of the unknown, the untried, and fear of failure or embarrassment is a big part of our inhibition to relinquish control. To whom (or to what) have you given control of your life? Are you to give control of yourself to a church body? Allowing the church to guide you would require that you relinquish control altogether. Many Christians claim surrender to the words of the Bible, boasting that they follow only the Scriptures. I often find, however, that this plan allows the "follower" much freedom by way of "private interpretation"[237] of the words, to their own liking. This idea usually ends with the "follower" following his own path, believing it is God's path. This plan may provide a very comfortable and convenient life for them, but it is ineffectual as a strategy to please our living Lord.

---

[237] 2 Peter 1:20, "Knowing this first, that no prophecy of the scripture is of any private interpretation."

What We Need Is A Living Guide.

As a Quaker, I am often challenged about the fact that I honor the Spirit of God as the ultimate Guide and final authority and not the church, (as does the Catholic faith) nor the Scriptures (as does the Protestant faith). The argument goes like this, "If you let only the Spirit tell you what is right, it could lead you anyplace, but if you are led by the Bible (Catholics say the church) it will lead everyone to the same faith in Christ." But I must ask, why is the Spirit of God so mistrusted as Guide?

Many feel that unity is only possible if the rules (no matter their source) are laid out and enforced. When the reality is that everyone I know who gives free course to the Spirit of God share a unity in Spirit and faith and doctrine, while the people who have turned their doctrine over to men or printed pages of a Bible are divided on nearly every doctrinal issue! No, if we are honest in our evaluations, we will find that where the Spirit of the Lord is, there is unity. That cannot be said about the greatest and most obedient members of churches, or about those most devoted to Bible study.

What makes people afraid to give the reigns of their lives to Christ? Why do they trust a book or a church full of men more so than they do the Spirit of God? Why will we believe what Jesus said and mistrust what He says? Why is it so difficult to accept a living, Spiritual Christ and readily accept a Christ of 2000 years ago? Why is it easier to believe what Jesus said, written down more than 60 years after he said it? We trust what was mouth to ear, and then copied out untold times in different languages, translated by people we do not know, printed, copied, and edited numerous times by people of questionable character, and yet we will accept that as a standard and not even seek the risen, living Savior for guidance for fear of being misled.

What an abundance of knowledge awaits the honest seeker, the pure of heart, the one who hungers and thirsts for righteousness if only they were directed to the well of Living water, the Spirit of the living God! The ministry of the Holy Spirit is to teach and to guide; yet we go only by what we can understand – words on a page that we can point to and declare ourselves "right" and "just." We gravitate toward the tangible and the controllable. We want only what we can manipulate and use to our advantage. The Holy Spirit is no such a guide. He is not manipulated or controlled and therefore…is not sought.

From early childhood we are anxious of what is beyond our dimension of understanding, and we fear what we cannot control. Whether this fear is learned behavior, a reasoned reaction or an innate response is debatable, but one thing is for sure, we are guilty of not turning seekers of God toward the Spirit. Instead, we send them toward churches and people, books and teachers, memberships, fellowships and rules and doctrines.

We should feel shame for teaching that Jesus is unreachable or only accessible through the intercession and efforts of men. Jesus is alive and well and fully capable of meeting with any and all who seek Him. He can guide and direct a man's life with finer and finer precision. He can pilot our ship through this hostile atmosphere safely and accurately, but He must have the controls. He does not need to know the consensus of others who have flown here, nor does He need the manual read to Him as He flies, just let Him do what He does best – pilot us!

When the disciples thought that they had encountered Jesus as a ghost, they were astonished. They were frozen and wondered what it was that they were seeing. Fear gripped them and they soon were deafened and stricken dumb with thoughts racing through their mind. Thoughts of spirits and ghosts were now taking the place where there were previously only thoughts confined to the tangible, touchable and "real." What caused this fear to grip them? The appearance of Christ had interposed another dimension in their thinking.

Peter and Cleopas had just returned with the news of the risen Savior. *"And as they thus spake, Jesus himself stood in the midst of them, and saith unto them, Peace be unto you. But they were terrified and affrighted, and supposed that they had seen a spirit. And he said unto them, Why are ye troubled? and why do thoughts arise in your hearts? Behold my hands and my feet, that it is I myself: handle me, and see; for a spirit hath not flesh and bones, as ye see me have. And when he had thus spoken, he shewed them his hands and his feet. And while they yet believed not for joy, and wondered, he said unto them, Have ye here any meat? And they gave him a piece of a broiled fish, and of an honeycomb. And he took it, and did eat before them." (Luke 24:36-43)*

It is obvious that Jesus wanted to prove to them that He was not a ghost. He, everything that He ever was, His mind, His body, and His Spirit, had risen to be *Him* again. He was not a spirit; He was exactly as they knew Him to be.

People are still afraid of Spirits

These men, however, were afraid when they thought He was a spirit. Much as we are when we find comfort in the tangible Christ, He who existed two millennia ago. Our fear of the Spirit of God as teacher comes from this fear of what we cannot touch and control. We all know that the Spirit goes where it wants to, and we hope to always end up with plenty of company around us, believing what can be considered orthodox, doing what could be understood as "normal" and living a life not too far from center. Well, forget it! The Spirit of God is not an option as your Teacher; He IS your Teacher. He is not one of several Guides; He IS the Guide promised by the Lord Himself.

Some *think* that the Bible says,
*"Nevertheless I tell you the truth; It is expedient for you that I go away: for if I go not away, the **BIBLE** will not come unto you; but if I depart, I will send **THE BIBLE** unto you. And when **THE BIBLE** is come, **IT** will reprove*

*the world of sin, and of righteousness, and of judgment...Howbeit when **IT**, **THE BIBLE**, is come, **IT** will guide you into all truth..."*

But it does not say that.[238]

So, when the Spirit of God is so ready, willing and able to lead you, "Why are ye troubled and why do thoughts arise in your hearts?"

---

238 John 16:6-29, "But because I have said these things unto you, sorrow hath filled your heart. Nevertheless I tell you the truth; It is expedient for you that I go away: for if I go not away, the Comforter will not come unto you; but if I depart, I will send him unto you. And when he is come, he will reprove the world of sin, and of righteousness, and of judgment... I have yet many things to say unto you, but ye cannot bear them now. Howbeit when he, the Spirit of truth, is come, he will guide you into all truth: for he shall not speak of himself; but whatsoever he shall hear, that shall he speak: and he will shew you things to come. He shall glorify me: for he shall receive of mine, and shall shew it unto you. All things that the Father hath are mine: therefore said I, that he shall take of mine, and shall shew it unto you. ... These things have I spoken unto you in proverbs: but the time cometh, when I shall no more speak unto you in proverbs, but I shall shew you plainly of the Father."

146. *Children, have ye any meat?*

John 21:5, "Then Jesus saith unto them, Children, have ye any meat? They answered him, No."

It may happen that you give up on being Christian. It could happen you know. You would not be the first to throw in the towel. It may seem to you that you are investing more than you get in return. It may be that you consider the price too high. It may be that your faith has you at risk of looking like a fool. Now, perhaps not just your critics, but even you think that you are dealing with impossibilities. You could feel that it is time that you become more realistic and more conventional. You may be toying with terms like "reality," "normal" and "sensible" to describe a responsible person's life. It would be very natural of you to think this way. Many before you have done so.

In the days after the death of Christ, the disciples had such thoughts. After He had been dead for the three days as He promised, the disciples were worried about His death and how it seemed to be the end of all things they had known before.

Then He appeared to them. His resurrection from the dead was no longer a question, it was reality. Their faith was inspired again and they took heart in knowing that their Savior was alive forevermore. In parallel, you may have been through this time of doubt as well, then the time of weeping, and then the time of revelation. The opening to your heart was such, that you may never again doubt that Jesus is alive forever, but you still become despondent about the fact that He is not bodily, physically here with you as He was with the disciples.

You may think (as I am sure each of the disciples thought), "Sure, He is alive, but what do I do now, how do I do it, and how do I live without His presence? Where is God when I need Him? Am I supposed to believe that He is here even though, in every sense within me, I feel that He is not? It will never be the same as having Him here in person… it cannot be… for He is there (wherever 'there' is) and I am here, and that is the fact!"

I warn you dear Christian, these kinds of "facts" rehearsed in the mind, makes melancholy, worldly, and defeated Christians, because the only alternative is the one that Peter took. That is, returning to what you know.

The disciples were gathered and wondering about these same things. "What do we do now? He told us to wait," one of them said. "Wait for what? We have waited long enough," said Peter, "I am going back to fishing." The other disciples, as discouraged as he, said, "We are going with you." So they set off to work in the domain in which they were expert, no faith required, no parables to figure out, no miracles needed, easy, simple, do-able living.

It is a great temptation for the tired, drained and discouraged believer to pare their lives down until they understand it and take on only what they have already proven that they are well equipped to do. With strength and hope gone there can be no more reaching out toward far-off goals of perfection. We welcome suggestions from our own mind like, "Let's just return to real life. Let's not complicate things! Why add failure to life by adding goals that are difficult to reach? Let's just go back to what we knew best and get control again."

These kinds of thoughts often come after a great disappointment with God. A necessity or situation's reversal for which you prayed that did not happen, a person for whom you prayed who showed no sign of recovery, a circumstance that you laid at the feet of Jesus for "His will" to be done that proved to become worse yet. You are left only to believe that He did not hear, or He did not care, or that His will was for your life is to become more and more miserable – not a great list from which to choose.

You are left with the thought, "Maybe I carried it too far, maybe I missed God's mark for my life, or maybe God is dead after all. Maybe it was true when folks that told me this 'faith in God' business was only crutch for weak people. Perhaps all of this faith stuff was only in my mind." The disappointments that inevitably come and the doubts that follow are strong incentives to "go fishing" and leave this faith business behind.

There are some to whom these thoughts of discouragement have never occurred, and there are others this idea has occurred to, but they have no intention to pursue it. But, there are a few who know exactly what went through Peter's mind and have done just what Peter did and are even now back in the boat doing what they "know" and leaving the "faith stuff" to the others.

Jesus has a question for you who have gone back to your previous way of running your own life. "How's it going?" How are you doing now that you are in control again? Are you making any headway? Are you advancing? Are you now in control and answering all your prayers?

John 21, "...They went forth, and entered into a ship immediately; and that night they caught nothing." You should not be surprised when you find that life does not work as it used to. After Jesus comes into a life, things are never the same. You cannot focus as you once could upon the goal of advancement because you know that advancement comes only from God. You cannot make money your goal, now that you have seen riches beyond gold. All that heaven and earth has to offer now pales in your mind since it has envisioned the new heaven and the new earth. You find that the here and now are a poor trade for eternity. The lack of focus, the lack of vision, the pale incentives, and the lackluster gold and silver make for a poor laborer, a preoccupied workman, and an uninspired employee.

Now What?

With the world's best goal removed from view, life just is not what it used to be and everything it offers simply does not compare. You soon find that your labors (even doing what you "know") are not as fruitful as they once were. So you have returned to fishing, have you...how are you doing? Have you caught any fish? It is time that you admit that you are a changed man or woman

– that you are caught in His net and without Him to tell you which side of the boat to throw the net you are helpless. He stands on the shore with fish on the fire. He stands prepared to offer, cooked and ready, what you cannot seem to find, raw, on your own. You are destined to return to Him and dine with Him again. You are not a fisherman any more; you are a fisher of men.

Disappointment with God is real. Whether you pushed further than you should have, or misunderstood your boundaries or purpose, you may become discouraged and take actions that put yourself back in control. God is waiting on the shore for you with explanations over supper.

Pressure from friends and family can overwhelm a person trying to live by faith and make them look silly and foolish. You can become tired and attempt a return to the way things used to be, but if you have ever known Christ, the return will not be a fruitful attempt. He stands on the shore with instructions to make your efforts pay off, but you must do it His way. If he says cast on the right side, that is what you must do. You must relinquish all control to Him.

The calamity and reversals in the life a person who once knew God is a wonderful sign to him that God has not forgotten him. The lack of incentive for riches that used to drive him to excel is not a curse but a blessing. To go back to the life of doing for yourself and caring for yourself may seem like the right thing to do, but more frustration awaits you when all efforts fail to provide success.

You must admit that you are not doing so well. Success and satisfaction eludes you, not because God is holding back blessing to teach you. Nor is Satan is empowered toward you because you are in sin, but because you are different. You have been changed. You are not as you used to be. You have been shown things that have effected change in you forever. Your outlook, your attitude, your demeanor, all has changed. You have been made incompatible with the world.

If you are among the many who have become discouraged with the life of faith for whatever reason and gone back to "reality," look around you, how are you all doing? Look to Jesus standing right where you left Him. Hear His voice echo over the vast expanse *you* put between you and answer His question, "Children, have ye any meat?"

147. Simon, son of Jonas, lovest thou me more than these?

John 21:15, "So when they had dined, Jesus saith to Simon Peter, Simon, son of Jonas, lovest thou me more than these? He saith unto him, Yea, Lord; thou knowest that I love thee. He saith unto him, Feed my lambs."

When life makes its claims upon us we usually respond to its demands with our time or talent. When we are hungry, we resort to our familiar method of food gathering. When financial needs become apparent, we do whatever it is that we do to match the demand with the money necessary to resolve it. When depression looms, we take refuge in what is our most familiar source of comfort; sometimes it is food or drink.

Taken to the extreme it becomes gluttony or drunkenness and is evidenced by large bodies, redness of face, health problems, or habits out of control. For others, it may take the form of busy-ness with everyday life, or the business of everyday work, in the hope that if we simply do not have time to be depressed that depression will sit in our "waiting room" until it finally goes away.

We have our different ways of dealing with all unpleasantness. It would behoove us all to investigate our own way of handling of it, and let that awareness do the wonderful work of making our actions honest ones and keeping our consciences clear of surfeiting and indulgence in whatever forms they may appear. So, when both the monetary demands of life and the depression that follows failure in present occupations are simultaneously present, it is likely that another course is imminent.

"And Jesus, walking by the sea of Galilee, saw two brethren, Simon called Peter, and Andrew his brother, casting a net into the sea: for they were fishers. And he saith unto them, Follow me, and I will make you fishers of men. And they straightway left their nets, and followed him." (Matthew 4:18-20)

Peter was a fisherman the day Jesus found him. Who would have thought that a handful of months from this fateful day, Peter would again appear and find these same nets, and start again where, on this day, he left off? How could this happen?

How can a man who has walked with Christ, in power and divine commission, a man who witnessed the miraculous, assisted in the ministry of the desire of all Israel; how can a man like this find himself in the same place, with the same narrow vision, handling the same stinking fishnets, in the same occupation as he was three years prior to meeting Christ? It happens by discouragement, by fear, and by threat of discomfort. As long as hope reigns and is within his understanding, a bright future is a possibility. Fishing will be the farthest thing from his mind, but the nets he forsakes today, will bring him comfort tomorrow.

Gone Fishin'

Peter, like us, upon finding life taking much and giving little, resorted to his most familiar form of busy-ness. When all the hope in his life had been rendered impotent and all the dreams of greatness (his own and the new Kingdom's) had become doubtful; when life started to take on a new feeling of insecurity and fear, he looked at his fellows and declared, "I go a fishing."

He went straight to the vocation at which he was adept, capable, and equipped. Also, he was likely encouraged by family and friends to give up this idea of a new Kingdom and just running around the countryside with this unorthodox philosopher and "settle down." Not only had it become easy to say "I go a fishing," but it was even a relief. It seemed such a good idea to go and make some money and return to "real life" that all them who were with him said, "We also go with thee."

It may well be that you have never been discouraged in your Christian walk. It may be that you have never ventured out by faith and found yourself having misunderstood the Lord's words to you, or outran His guidance. Maybe you have never fallen flat on your face and felt silly for believing in such things. It may be that you find your faith an easy routine to practice and perfectly sensible and even pedantic or mechanically understandable; you never experience doubt or fear or desire to return to a life within your own control ... but it is unlikely. Most of us are repelled by the life of faith at first, preferring a life of "realities" and choosing rather to feel the rudder within our reach. The life of faith is not a natural one.

When the life of faith turns away from promises of a bright hope of the future, and starts to dole out lessons on pride and disobedience, it is harder to continue the journey with a smile and a song. But, in those situations, we should feel a sense of responsibility to learn the hard lesson. When we are found in disobedience, if we are mature in faith, we accept the chastisement of the Lord knowing that we share the responsibility in our discomfort. When the lean times come, when the dry times, the silent times -- when the times that we feel alone come. When God has withdrawn Himself, these are the times when we may cast the wistful eye toward the life of our past, when we had friends, money, and when we had control. It is in those times, when we consider our situation and think of how we would have handled this present circumstance BEFORE we turned our life over to Christ that we are in danger of doing that very thing.

It is when we long for the control we USED to have that we are dangerously close to exercising it. The old life is still there, like Peter's nets drying in the sun and waiting for us to pick them up and start where we left off. We can have it all back, the friends, the family, the money, the time, all can be ours again to have and to hold till death do us part. But, is that what we want? At what price?

When you consider the lure of these things in your life, you should consider their cost. You may only possess them at the cost of the peace with God you now enjoy. To know Jehovah as a Father, to know Jesus as Lord, is not a grievous proposition, it is a joyful one. The times when the old life has its strongest appeal are only when you are involved in sin, self pity, or when your present situation hangs in doubt of God's loving care. Time itself heals many hearts that struggle with doubt. You should not be so willing or quick to take the wheel from someone as wise as our good Captain, Christ Jesus.

If you examine what your life, when fully within your control, was able to yield as far as comfort was concerned, it was not really as much as you may think in retrospect. Most all of your efforts in the old way of life can be counted in dollars and cents (a poor indicator of happiness if there ever was one).

Money is considered the root of all evil because of the love it inspires toward itself and the way it replaces God's most desired dependence upon Him. Money feigns itself to be a merciful and loving savior from all woes and heartache, but in the end it demands and eventually takes the very life of its servants, not necessarily in death, but minute by minute, day by day. The world eats up people who are dedicated to money's manipulation and multiplication, and soon spits them out more tired and poor than they went in. How many die poor and lonely in a world that makes such promises of friends and riches?

The world about us promises friends to the successful. Few unsuccessful people have what the world calls "friends." Even some in our families demand that we are successful before we may enjoy their company.

Peter was, in the eyes of those who knew him before his life with Jesus began, a failure as a fisherman, because he quit. All that prestige could be regained if he returned and proved that he could still do it. Peter probably had no wealth to speak of, and when he realized that he was poor and in need of money, fishing was a reasonable solution.

Money will often be found at the base of the world's evaluation of what is important, what is respectable, and what is worthy of a man's life pursuit. To these disciples fish meant money again, power again, and control again.

Jesus is waited on shore with supper for the men who had caught none of these elusive representations of hope all night. With no effort at all, Jesus blessed them with a catch.

The one hundred fifty three fishes were miraculously caught in their net and brought to shore. They represent many dollars to these men. Later, over a plate of fishes, Jesus looks at His discouraged disciple, His eyes glancing down to the fishes that lay between them, and then turns to inventory the huge catch in baskets all around them. Then, looking into Peter's eyes, He solicits his return to the work of the Kingdom by asking, "Lovest thou me more than these?"

148. Lovest thou me?

*John 21:16, "He saith to him again the second time, Simon, son of Jonas,
lovest thou me? He saith unto him, Yea, Lord; thou knowest that I love thee.
He saith unto him, Feed my sheep."*

After Jesus found that Peter had determined in his heart to obey God,
dedicate himself to the coming Kingdom, and forsake the baser life of making a
living by his old occupation, He was now interested in his motivation and
purpose in the work at hand. It would be easy to love Christ more than an
occupation. You could easily dedicate your life to a cause higher than the
common purpose in the work-a-day world, i.e., to purchase food and comforts.

Unfortunately, many are in the "ministry" with this aim. They have
mistakenly reasoned that they would rather be working "in the ministry" than to
be working "in the world." They reason that if they must make a living, it
would be better to make it doing God's work than doing some other labor. This
makes for a poor minister. Jesus called these "hirelings," and frankly, if you
minister to the body of Christ for a wage, you must constantly evaluate your
motivation for doing so. In the parable of the unjust steward in Luke 16, the
panic that overcomes the steward is apparent in the line, "What shall I do? for
my lord taketh away from me the stewardship: I cannot dig; to beg I am
ashamed."

It is apparent, even to the casual reader of this story that the man does
his job not only because he makes a living wage, but also because it is the only
thing he can, or is willing to do. This is a poor reason to be (or remain) a
minister. The door to the ministry should be opened from the inside.

When Peter confessed to loving Christ more than fish, more than his
vocation, Jesus commissioned him to feed His lambs. The young in Christ are
in need of the basic milk, they have no need of meat yet:

*"...For when for the time ye ought to be teachers, ye have need that one
teach you again which be the first principles of the oracles of God; and are
become such as have need of milk, and not of strong meat. <u>For every one
that useth milk is unskilful in the word of righteousness</u>: for he is a babe.
But strong meat belongeth to them that are of full age, even those who by
reason of use have their senses exercised to discern both good and evil."
(Hebrews 5:11-14)*

Here it is obvious that there is a basic training for new Christians.
These "lambs" need to be introduced to the Word of God (Christ) and prepared
by this milk to later receive the meat of strength that belongs to those who are
of full age. Those who have understanding and have come into the family of
God are soon overwhelmed by the reality of this spiritual Kingdom into which
they have been introduced. They feel small and as though they are novices and
perhaps a little frightened. But as they learn to hear from God, the way will

become clear and less frightening as the relationship (and indeed they themselves) begin to grow and develop.

Some ministers are equipped to help these that are new to faith. This is a wonderful ministry and should not be considered insignificant or in any wise "less" than any other work. However, there is a level of teaching that carries a higher consequence than does the ministry to babes. There is a ministry that carries with it a higher level of responsibility. "My brethren, be not many masters, knowing that we shall receive the greater condemnation." (James 3:1)

One Is Your Teacher

It should never be forgotten that we are not to take the title "teacher" because, as Jesus said, "ONE is your teacher, even Christ." (Matthew 23:10.) When we heap to ourselves teachers because our ears itch,[239] we place our faith in severe jeopardy. Teachers have the ability to convince of false doctrine, lead into false realities, introduce false practices, exchange priorities, and provide their students with assurance and security and hope to which they may not be rightfully entitled. They deal in logic and reason, letters and words, theories and philosophies that confuse and befuddle those who listen to them.

They can only teach us what they first convince us that we do not know. What was, only moments before, an inner sense of knowing, placed there by the Holy Spirit, has now been replaced by a view, a theory, or a doctrine of man's reason. THIS is why teachers/masters shall receive the greater condemnation. Feeding Christ's sheep is a serious business. Our reference Scripture teaches that it is not to be done by those who have a casual view of their calling or ministry. The feeding of Christ's sheep requires more of a man than does the ministry of guiding lambs to pasture. Christ continued to test Peter to see if he is the man for the job:

"Simon, do you love me? I know you love me more than fishing. I know that you said that you love me more than making a living as a commercial fisherman, but do you love your new job better than your old job ...or ...do you do your new job because you love your new boss? Simon...do you love me?"

Here is an interesting question indeed. Once Jesus looked around Himself and saw followers by the thousands. He accused them that they did not follow because they believed on Him or loved Him, "...but because ye did eat of the loaves, and were filled."[240] Theirs was a faith of convenience. Even today, many are "Christians" simply because they cannot imagine being anything else. They operate by preference rather than conviction. They prefer to be "Christians" rather than nothing, they prefer to be in the ministry rather than lay bricks, they prefer to teach Bible classes rather than American History. A person living amid only preferences is not to feed Christ's sheep. They cause

---

[239] 2 Timothy 4:3-4, "For the time will come when they will not endure sound doctrine; but after their own lusts shall they heap to themselves teachers, having itching ears; And they shall turn away their ears from the truth, and shall be turned unto fables."
[240] John 6:26

terrible mischief, often without knowing it and with good intention they give grief to the body of Christ with their theories and doctrines, adulterating the pure Word of God to the heart of the believer.

Not only Bible teachers, preachers and Christian workers need to assess their motivation and dedication, but we also who only profess a faith in Christ. Do you love the life of Christianity more than the life you had, or do you love the Savior Himself?

Is it that you simply prefer Jesus to fishing, or do you love HIM? Our churches are populated with hireling preachers that never truly fell in love with Christ. Granted, they are dedicated to the long haul, it is true that they are in for life; no doubt they give of their time, talent, and fortune, but is it because they cannot dig, or to beg they are ashamed? Is it because they cannot or will not do anything else? Or is it because they love Christ and are therefore commissioned to feed His Lambs?

Hireling shepherds who do not love Christ will attempt to take His place.[241] They start to consider Christ's sheep as their own. A hireling that refers to the Shepherd's flock as his own is nothing less than a thief. A hireling who calls the flock of God "my people" and himself "the shepherd" is deluded under his own enchantments. He has taken Christ's place as teacher and as guide because he feels no genuine love or loyalty for the ONE Shepherd mentioned in Ezekiel.[242]

You must honestly answer the probing query of Christ. You, who have retired the previous life and can say to Jesus that you have "left all and followed thee," may still have to look within and answer honestly His question again. Even after you have answered once before in ever so clear words, "Yes, I love you Lord Jesus," you may well be asked again, "Lovest thou me?"

---

[241] John 10:16, "… and there shall be one fold, and one shepherd."
[242] Ezekiel 34:23, "And I will set up one shepherd over them, and he shall feed them…and he shall be their shepherd."
Ezekiel 37:24, "… and they all shall have one shepherd: they shall also walk in my judgments, and observe my statutes, and do them."

149. Simon, son of Jonas, lovest thou me?

John 21:17-19, "He saith unto him the third time, Simon, son of Jonas, lovest thou me? Peter was grieved because he said unto him the third time, Lovest thou me? And he said unto him, Lord, thou knowest all things; thou knowest that I love thee. Jesus saith unto him, Feed my sheep. Verily, verily, I say unto thee, When thou wast young, thou girdedst thyself, and walkedst whither thou wouldest: but when thou shalt be old, thou shalt stretch forth thy hands, and another shall gird thee, and carry thee whither thou wouldest not. This spake he, signifying by what death he should glorify God. And when he had spoken this, he saith unto him, Follow me."

The Christian's life is stages of dedication to God punctuated by individual, daily choices to follow Christ and forsake our own will. When we attempt to save our own skin, when we try to have our own way, we halt our advances in faith. Peter's collapse occurred under pressure of persecution. Our breakdown occurs when we choose that which benefits our comfort while denying the Savior's work in us. If we do not advance through the stages of our Christian life, what is waiting for us but stagnation and, ultimately, discouragement and confusion? We must face every opportunity to fail, not with fear or dread, but with the prize of graduation clearly in focus.

There is a clearing of one's self that takes place when a temptation is conquered. If it has been a fault of yours to give in to a certain temptation, and it is your desire to gain victory over that failure, you should not dread the next presentation of that temptation. It is your opportunity to clear yourself, to prove yourself, to atone, and to advance through and beyond. If the temptation is never presented again, you will live in doubt of your victory; but when there is a record, no matter how small, of your overcoming this difficulty, there is a confidence that occupies that place where fear and dread once was.

It is with this principal in mind I present to you the idea that perhaps Jesus was taking Peter on just such a journey. Peter's heart was, no doubt, heavy with the guilt of having denied the Lord publicly three times in that night of Christ's torture. Now, even in his Lord's presence, the weight of shame was coloring every thought, slanting every word of conversation with Jesus, and nagging every promise of loyalty he espoused. Even as the Lord asked him if he loved Him, he felt as though the Lord had no reason to believe such a coward as he. But the Lord kept asking, "Simon, do you love me?" It was not by chance that the Lord asked him three times; for it was three times that Peter denied knowing Him. There was a clearing, a forgiveness, and a cleansing taking place in the third affirmation of Peter's love for Christ.

While Peter professed His love for Christ, affirming that it was his choice to love Him (the first time he answered) and also that it was indeed true that he loved Him (the second time he answered) he was worried when Jesus asked the third time. The Bible records that he was grieved. Maybe he thought that Jesus did not believe him. He may have thought that Jesus was about to tell him that he did not love Him as much as he thought did: "After all," he thought to himself, "I declared my love for Him before... will He tell me that I will deny Him yet again?" His mind reeled as he remembered the pain of his denial. He remembered the days after, and the resolutions he made, the shame he felt. Finally, he came to the conclusion that his love could stand the test, "I do love Him" he thought, "and if anyone would know that to be a fact it would be He from whom nothing may be hidden." He looked at Christ and said, "Lord, thou knowest all things; thou knowest that I love thee." I am sure a smile crossed Peter's face as he realized what was happening. He finally sensed the balanced account and the forgiveness of his friend, Jesus. The Savior, satisfied, reaffirmed his commission to feed the sheep and went on to tell him other things he should know.

A Third Chance?

A new stage in Peter's life and faith was about to take place. His past forgiven, his resolution of dedication, and his impending conversion and infilling of the Holy Spirit was about to make this fisherman, a fisher of men.

After thrice confirming the love of this disciple, Jesus immediately told him that the rest of his life would not be an easy one, "Verily, verily, I say unto thee, When thou wast young, thou girdedst thyself, and walkedst whither thou wouldest: but when thou shalt be old, thou shalt stretch forth thy hands, and another shall gird thee, and carry thee whither thou wouldest not." Jesus outlines to Peter what was to become of him. He does so with ambiguous terms and with a mysterious and prophetic tone. Had the writer of this Gospel (John) not told us what this signified, we may not have figured it out. We may have applied it some other way as a parable or metaphor, but the writer plainly says, "This spake he, signifying by what death he should glorify God." There is no doubt that Jesus was foretelling the martyr's death that Peter was to encounter when he is old. Peter hears the prophecy and as it goes down into his ears, his expression changes. Then Jesus sees him mentally brace himself for the tortuous fate. Over this broken man's face roll waves of doubt, then faith, then fear again. "How will I do it? Will I keep the faith?" Wisps of fear are doggedly chased by determined faith, and love for Messiah, and headstrong Peter determines to do whatever it takes. It is easy to see in our mind, Jesus reaching, patting his arm, and breaking the spell of anxiety – Peter looks up. Jesus wants him to know that it is not the strength of determination that will make the difference. Neither will knowing the future in advance help us. It is living, learning, and loving daily that will determine our final outcome; our final performance will be a culmination of our daily choices, so, looking him in the eyes, He says, "Follow me."

This third affirmation of love is different from the rest. The first was a decision made; the second was an affirmation of truth discovered and possession taken of it. The third demands action and obedience. Many of us have decided to love Christ more than our occupations or manner of life. Some of us have even looked within to find that we do love our Savior personally and

474

our lives take different direction; different decisions are made because of that love shed abroad in our hearts. But, this love of declaration and dedication to follow the Savior takes on a nuance foreign to the casual Christian. It reveals the cost of service, the price of possession, and risk of loss that accompanies those who are fully dedicated to Truth.

The third question is the same question as the second, accompanied by information. Jesus wanted an informed decision from the disciple. How many decisions would be made for Christ and Christian living if the candidates were made fully aware of the cost and consequences? Jesus tells us in the parable of the sower that when these costs are found out later can render the decisions made in ignorance, of no value. He said, "...for when tribulation, temptation or persecution ariseth because of the word, by and by [immediately] they are offended."[243]

Jesus prophetically informs Peter of his death and persecution and insists that he follow Him. Just as He did when he first met Peter at the seaside when He said, "Follow Me," he looks at him again and says the same words. Recovered and re-commissioned, Peter embarked upon a new life and ministry. He went on from there in faith and power to build the Church of Jesus Christ in the earth, a ministry that continues yet today. He led a life of eternal significance, all the while knowing he must pass through the door of martyrdom one day at the hands of wicked men.

Yes, this third question left him feeling worried, and then he felt cleansed. Even after he was informed, he stood firm and was re-commissioned with the command, "Follow Me." You must not be grieved when you feel questioned of the Lord about the genuineness of your love for Him, as if He is not sure of you. It may be that you are about to gain a new height, graduate to a new level of faith, or receive your commission in total. As you survey the new landscape and evaluate the price tag on dedicated living, would to God that you will have what it takes to answer, "YES!" when He asks the third time, "Lovest thou me?"

---

[243] Matthew 13

150. *What is that to thee?*

John 21:20-22, "Then Peter, turning about, seeth [John] ... saith to Jesus, Lord, and what shall this man do? Jesus saith unto him, If I will that he tarry till I come, what is that to thee? follow thou me."

It is human nature to compare oneself with others. It is the pride in us that makes us want to be flanked by our peers. It is the ego in man that desires to be just a little ahead of those who are at his sides. Some say that this attribute we have in common is a good thing, after all, what great achievements would the space race have accomplished without ego, pride, or ambition?

On the other hand what great messages would we hear from those anointed to speak the Word of God if it was devoid of ego, pride and ambition? What great thoughts would we be able to bring to light, with what clarity and confidence would we be able to deal with hard times if we were able to tame the unbridled passion for self? Pride and pursuit of advancement has its place in life, but it takes the wisdom of Solomon to decipher when and where. Ambition is not an ally to the Christian; it is an enemy. It confuses the otherwise clear mind, it makes the simple complex, and it colors every forward action making motivations untrustworthy.

Jesus taught us to be aware of ego and pride in several ways. His teaching was paradoxical and foreign to our thinking. He taught that if you want to go up, seek a lower seat; if you want to find yourself in the lowest seat, seek the highest. In short, if we follow His instructions, we are not to seek upward but downward.

This is not as simple as it is portrayed in Christ's instruction. We still have to deal with our nature that wants to do things the old way. Information is simply insufficient in this matter; we need a change of our nature. If after driving a car in the United States for several years you were asked to drive a British one that utilizes right seat controls on roads that are left side oriented, it would take some getting used to. Its external operations would be different, but internally, controls would be the same. But, imagine for a moment a car that sped up when you pushed the brake, applied brakes when you pressed the accelerator, turned left when the wheel turned right and right when you turned left. Driving this automobile would require much more training and would be a danger to anyone who tried, because this car's *internal* operations are different and against our very nature. This is the case for those who try "fight the good fight of faith" with an unregenerate mind.

Paul taught against "gain" being an indicator of advancement toward godliness thereby rejecting ambition as a virtue. In 1 Timothy 6:5-12, he warned of men "supposing that gain is godliness: from such withdraw thyself." And Paul reminds us that, "Godliness with contentment is great gain. For we brought nothing into this world, and it is certain we can carry nothing out. And having food and raiment let us be therewith content. ...But thou, O man of

476

God, flee these things; and follow after righteousness, godliness, faith, love, patience, meekness. Fight the good fight of faith, lay hold on eternal life..."

Fighting Ambition

Ambition is touted as a virtue that causes us to look ahead and move ahead. I submit, rather, that it causes us to look to either side. The ambitious are rarely concerned about their own position in life, only their relative position to their peers. Who wants things they have never seen? Who wants to be in places about which they have never heard? Who desires to be, to have, to own, to taste, to touch, to do, or to accomplish things and does not do so because he is made aware by the example of his peers that they may be just within reach? Ambition arises when the prideful are made aware that some possession or accomplishment is in the grasp of others with whom he considers himself equal.

Ambition that is driven by necessity and rightness can be a desirable thing and would be more properly defined as stewardship. Looking ahead ambition is nearly tolerable, resembling stewardship. It is when we look around us that ambition becomes a compulsion. Stewardship looks ahead only, not side to side. Stewardship is a natural result of a pure and undefiled desire to be exactly where God wants us to be. Hebrews teaches us to look to Jesus and to the finish line in this race, not to our fellow runners. "... let us lay aside every weight, and the sin which doth so easily beset us, and let us run with patience the race that is set before us, Looking unto Jesus the author and finisher of our faith." (Hebrews 12:1-2)

Our God has perfectly constructed life's plan to teach us what we need to know and perfect us into the person we should be. Your plan is unlike any other. All contain certain additions, subtractions, problems and blessing peculiar to the needs of each individual. We all get tired of the everyday problems, but have you ever seen someone with whom you would trade lives? You may pick and choose blessings in someone's life, or be willing to trade your problems for their "lesser" ones, but life for life, we all have our heartaches and hey-days, our desserts and disasters. Our Father is working out a great plan in your life to make you into a member of His family, someone who can live eternally, someone who is to be called a child of God. The problems of the people around you will not hone you into this person who God wants you to be, nor will the blessings and possessions of your neighbor satisfy your inmost desires. Neither their mishaps nor their miracles befit you. Let God tailor your life's plan, and then let God bless those around us as He sees best for them. Let God hear no complaining from you, but rejoicing with your neighbor in their blessing and never let it be, so much as thought, that you covet their gifts. Bless those who curse you, as if they are instruments of God sent to make you into who you should be. Be attentive to business, enough so to be found as a faithful steward of God's provision, but never let avarice or ambition be your motivation. Let us fulfill the advice of the apostle:

"Be kindly affectioned one to another with brotherly love; in honour preferring one another; Not slothful in business; fervent in spirit; serving the Lord; ...Bless them which persecute you: bless, and curse not. Rejoice with them that do rejoice, and weep with them that weep. Be of the same mind one toward another. Mind not high things, but condescend to men of low estate. ...Recompense to no man evil for evil. Provide things honest in the sight of all men. If it be possible, as much as lieth in you, live peaceably with all men." (Romans 12:10-18)

Peter was to learn this lesson another day. Today, and for some time after this, he had trouble getting his eyes off of others. Perhaps it was his fishing business that made him a competitive man. Arriving at the shore after a long day's work, a man is compelled to look side to side.

Every evening as they would care for the nets at the shore, the conversation would invariably be, "How many fish did you catch today...? How much money did you make?" He was probably conditioned from childhood to look to either side of him and, by comparison, decide how he was doing. Do you look side to side when you evaluate your life?

You may breathe a sigh of relief when you find your station in life somewhere in the "bell" of the bell curve, somewhere in the "normal" range; but if you knew how insignificant the chart was, you would not care where you fell on it. What pride could be felt by being voted "best looking" in a cage full of orangutans? What gratification could be derived from being the richest man in Calcutta, where millions starve? Would you not rather attain what God has for you? Even if you were voted most beautiful among all mankind, or the richest in the world, and yet you fell miserably short of the measure intended for you by God, of what then, would you have to boast?

To measure yourself by another is a pitiful attempt to elevate your accomplishments, or perhaps, to propel yourself forward to do better by competition. Again, Paul weighs in with this statement, "...but they measuring themselves by themselves, and comparing themselves among themselves, are not wise." (2 Corinthians 10:12)

We must stop comparisons and evaluations of each other. Take your orders and let others do as they will. You can advise when you are asked, and provide an example to those who view your life, but other than a passing glance at those with whom you travel, you should not look to the side but ahead, to Christ. When you look at the position of those around you, that are where you think you should be, or you see those who have, what you think you should have, you are thinking, and living foolishly. Sometimes you may try to justify your coveting by contending that it is some sort of righteous desire or "spiritual ambition." You may insist that you only want a greater ministry for Christ or more money so you can give more, or you only want more free time do God's work. Once you have come to your senses you must admit that when you covet stations in life held by others, you are following men. Men who you have determined to be greater than yourself, granted, but not Christ.

When you want to be ahead of others, and find yourself wondering, "Why do they have all the resources and I have none," or "Why don't they have the problems that I have?" you will be answered by a question of Jesus, just as Peter was, "What is that to thee? ...Follow thou me."

Summary

Sacrificing the chronological aspect of this work, I decided to use the following question asked by Jesus out of sequence, as a summary. It has the sound of eternity in it. Its imposing and thoughtful query leaves the mind grasping for an elusive answer – a *comprehensive* answer to which I don't think exists in the minds of modern men.

151. *When the Son of man cometh, shall he find faith on the earth?*

"... Nevertheless when the Son of man cometh, shall he find faith on the earth?" (Luke 18:8)

For many years, I read this question of Christ with great interest. It was indeed the motivation for the creation of this book. The distinctive language in this particular Scripture created curiosity in me. It led me to doubt that the question can be answered affirmatively. It left me fearing the worst. *"Nevertheless when the Son of man cometh, shall he find faith on the earth?"* Will He find men who really *believe* in Him? Perhaps not!

Why would He ask such a question? Doesn't He know that the United States of America, the supreme world power, is a Christian nation? There are more Christians alive today than ever lived before. Doesn't He know better than ninety percent of our population celebrates the birth of His Son every year? How can Christmas be celebrated without the existence of faith? Will He find faith on the earth? Of course He will!

Could it be that the question is misunderstood? Perhaps we do not define "faith" the same way He does? I would say the chances are good that the reason His question sounds strange to us **is that we are so far from the truth of what real faith is.** What is this singularity He calls "faith" that He expects will be so *rare* among the population of the greatest and largest Christian nation since the beginning of all time?

In this book we have dealt with family relationships, work relationships, financial conditions and considerations. We have experienced the promises of the Almighty to aid in the forestalling of sin, deception, and disease. We have spoken of YHVH's Spirit who meets daily needs and shows how to balance duties in proper management of life essentials. We spoke of Messiah's forgiveness of sin and of living a life above violation of His Father's expressed Commandments. We have delighted with the anticipation of His provision during the darkest hours of man's existence on the earth. However, we know these things will come only **to those who live by faith.**

If we are only now learning that *our* concept of faith may be severely flawed – if this incorrect concept is the only faith we know – then what's to become of us? How will we meet Him without having true faith? More importantly, how will He meet us?

In Good Hands?

John and Jane Doe survived the storm although their house did not. They have confidence today that their future is bright because their home is fully insured. What they *do not know* is that the company in whom they have placed their erroneous trust is on the verge of an evening news exposé.

Tomorrow they will learn what they do not know tonight. In the morning, their 100+-year old company will be revealed as having been bankrupt for many months now, though they fraudulently continued to collect premiums. Tomorrow, on the evening news, they will learn of their unprotected estate, fully discover their *unfounded* confidence, and wholly realize their loss.

Tonight, they sleep peacefully. Though the facts are as true tonight as they will be tomorrow – they sleep quietly. What they do not know allows them to sleep.

Do you have confidence in your faith toward God? Could it be that the faith you embrace is less than the true faith Jesus will demand? Is your faith or the faith of your denomination *THE* faith of which He inquired? If so, why was He so pessimistic about the existence of faith when He returns? If Christ yearned to discover true faith in the end time multitudes **of which you are a part**, in the times **in which you now live**, how can you be sure that you have *that* faith? How can you be *so* sure of something of which He is so *unsure*?

We must have communication with the Creator if we profess to live by faith. We need to speak to Him – *AND He needs to speak to us*! How is this possible? By faith – true faith! I submit that faith is **trust** based in *reality*, not an ethereal hope. Faith is **expectation** based in *substance*, not speculation. Faith is **confidence** based in *Truth*, not fables.

How can a person have any worthwhile experience with a god whose divining is little more than a coin flip, whose discernment is remarkably no better than his own and whose compassion is only engaged by his continual crying and begging? When reality, substance and truth are considered integral and essential parts of true faith, we can easily see how the Lord could ask, *"When the Son of man cometh, shall he find faith on the earth?"*

Also, true faith works toward purification.[244] The modern church is rife with false notions and traditions, recycled paganism and laundered ancient abominations. Can true faith have and hold values contradictive to the God they claim to worship? Do you agree that true faith must be a *pure* trust in a living God – a confident expectation rooted in *reality*, *substance* and *truth*? How can we possess such faith?

---

[244] 1 Timothy 3:9, "Holding the mystery of the faith in a pure conscience."
1 John 3:2-3, "… but we know that, when he shall appear… we shall see him …and every man that hath this hope in him purifieth himself, even as he is pure."

Rejecting the Old Way

I was born in Melbourne, Florida. My father was an unrefined and earthy man, but he was highly intelligent and a good provider. He escaped his Appalachian destiny in coal mining, found an electronics career in the aerospace industry, and eventually retired from NASA at Cape Kennedy, Florida. Although his early years began in a country church, most of his life he scoffed at its foolishness. Yet, he held until his death, a fear of God that surpassed many who boldly profess Christianity.

YHVH was good to me. He provided for me the concept of *two fathers* -- one natural, one by choice.

My step-father, Aubrey Sara was the opposite of my biological father – a true minister and a refined gentleman. He was known around the nation by many families he had touched over the years. Though he had normal ambitions to "be someone" (and even enjoyed a certain degree of fame) I always found in him a desire to know his God better and to love God's people truly. He was indeed my aspiration and example. He taught by precedent what a minister was to be, "Give them Jesus... that's all they need."

He came into my life about the time I left home, so his role of "father" was not necessarily forced on me. I desired it. I *pursued* a relationship with him. He intrigued me as a man of God. I once asked Him, "Aubrey, what do you want more than anything?" He answered quickly, but not rashly, with a finger bobbing upward "That I may *know* Him – and the power of His resurrection." He made me want to know Him, too.

With my natural father, I struggled with who I *was*. With my step-father, I struggled with who I was *NOT*! I knew that in me, that is in my flesh, dwelleth no good thing[245]. The flesh I was born into had a love of the baser life. It craved what can be felt, tasted, smelled or smoked. It was determined to acquire, achieve, and advance and had little tolerance for any discomfort or difficulty. I suffer yet today with the crudeness of my roots. I have a taste for the worldly that has, on several occasions, strained my assurance of a true conversion. Yet, my adoption offered me new potential for which I would strive for the rest of my life.

Both fatherly examples have helped *and* hindered along the way. I may hear my father's crude language come from my mouth, *yet* ironically I recognize it *as* crude because of my adoption and exposure to refinement![246] Contrarily, while aspiring to please God in a ministry to advance the Kingdom, as my step-father illustrated by *his* life, I find the earthy quality of my biological father does not allow me to become so pious that the simple promises of the Almighty go unheeded or despised by common men as he was.

---

[245] Romans 7:18, "For I know that in me (that is, in my flesh) dwelleth no good thing: for to will is present with me; but how to perform that which is good I find not."

[246] Galatians 4:3-6, "Even so we, when we were children, were in bondage under the elements of the world... God sent forth his Son ... that we might receive the adoption of sons. And because ye are sons, God hath sent forth the Spirit of his Son into your hearts, crying, Abba, Father."

What better way is there to exemplify spiritual adoption? In your earthy and physical frame you struggle with your incorrigible flesh – who you *ARE*. Simultaneously, your heavenly Father stands as an archetype of seemingly *unattainable* virtue – who you *ARE NOT*.

What can bring these two contradictive persons together into one? You cannot (outside of pure schizophrenia) allow them both. The flesh tugs at you to remain stitched to your three- dimensional world within your five senses. Your Heavenly Father calls from above. How can you know HOW to be what you should be if you do not pursue communion with your Heavenly Father?

The Man in the Mirror

Your flesh (and likely your peers) promises you will realize this faith by pursuit of a spotless church attendance record or by gaining respect as a religious man in your community, by tallying a long roster of good deeds for your eulogy, or even by becoming a dedicated Bible student. Your Spirit will show you that these are red herrings, straw men and diversions designed to keep you **from** true faith.

In reality, church and its proponents are part of the *problem*, not the *solution*. Following the average church's idea of faith, we will end up with a life spent doing really, really good things at the expense of the best things. The church, as your source, can only destroy true faith in God by directing your faith and confidence toward itself.

Sadly, if you continue as you are, you will find the answer to the question we now explore only after it is too late. You must face squarely who you are, and who you are not if you will ever make true and lasting changes. If you turn your face from the mirror[247] and look to someone other than Jesus[248] as your standard, you will ultimately be deceived and *FAIL* in your faith. You will be one whom the Lord Jesus looks straight through and pleads for a better example of "faith on the earth."

To this point you have lived by worldly intellect, the physical accomplishment of life, the foundation of agreeing friends and family, the confirmation of health and continuance of life and fortune. Through these, you have made your decisions. In these confidences you have lived and moved and had your being. Carrying these processes over into Christianity will eventually destroy true faith in you. You will make an admirable presentation in the church world, granted, but you will end by knowing your pastor better than your Savior, your denomination better than your Bible, and your own **good** better than your *God*. After the fire, you will find yourself sleeping soundly with bankrupt insurance.

---

[247] James 1:23-24, "For if any be a hearer of the word, and not a doer, he is like unto a man beholding his natural face in a glass: For he beholdeth himself, and goeth his way, and straightway forgetteth what manner of man he was."
[248] Hebrews 12:1-2, "… Looking unto Jesus the author and finisher of our faith …"

There must be a New Basis.

All who have experienced the invitation of YHVH and have repented are now being led into life and must discover the *new basis* for that new life. That new basis is faith.

Faith is more than believing, more than receiving goodies from God. Faith is a way of life, but what is it? If the just shall live by faith, it would behoove those of us who claim to be justified by faith to know what it is. The question of Jesus continues to haunt us, *"When the Son of man cometh, shall he find faith on the earth?"* If faith is absent (or near absent) what does that say about those of us who claim to have it? Perhaps we don't.

The parable from which this question comes is speaking of *communication* – one way communication. Because it is conventional and it has worked in the past we continue it, but is this best? Remember, Jesus lamented the fact that importunity worked *instead* of faith. Importunity (asking for our own will) eradicates faith.

Changing the Direction of Communication

We must learn to be quiet and alone with our Father. NO! Not pray! (At least not in its conventional sense) but, LISTENING! If you are alone with Him, between the two of you, you are the less qualified to speak and He has very little to learn from you![249]

We need to learn to worship. NO! Not sing and participate in special music and noise on top of noise – But, sit quietly in His presence – worshipping Him.

We need to learn of Him. NO! Not sit under preachers and teachers and Bible studies, but learn from the Holy Spirit that is shared by the Father and Messiah – and by *YOU*! The Spirit was commissioned to do that very job! "He will lead you… into all truth." The sad fact is that many will be discouraged with the prospect of direct communication because they do not *have* a relationship with the Savior *OUTSIDE* of church.

Myriads of Christians will be baffled by the prospect of worship *other* than the "worship service" at church. Precious fewer will ever learn anything more than a man has taught them.

They will be ultimately discouraged at my admonition because they have no *faith* in *Him*, but rather *their* faith is based solely in the *institution,* in the *clergy,* in the *machine* and in the *form*.

Worship, learning, communion, and basic living by faith seem impossible for many modern Christians without being fed by the institutional church. Note that many primitive Christians maintained their faith, even unto their own martyrdom, without so much as a Bible in their hand. How was their soul fed? One of the most common complaints I hear from conventional Christians who are moving from church to church is, "I'm not being *fed* over there!"

---

[249] Matthew 6:32, "… for your heavenly Father knoweth that ye have need of all these things."

Do you feel hungry for more? Our Savior said, "… I am the bread of life: he that cometh to me shall never hunger; and he that believeth on me shall never thirst." (John 6:35) Is **the problem that you have never come to Him? Could this be?** *Why you are yet hungry and thirsty?* Could it be that you have no *real* faith in a *real* Savior, but only have a faith based upon others around you? Friend, if you cannot make it *OUTSIDE* of the conventional church, you will not make it at all. If you *cannot* worship in your closet then you *should not* worship anywhere else!

My experience is that you will NEVER find out that you do not possess the faith Messiah looks for until you come out of the incubator and try it on your own. Compromise and fear of what others think keeps you in the church machine. But if you like being in the majority, then good news, you are indeed! Almost everyone I meet does it this way. You want to be around others who believe like you do. You want to be a part of a group. The truth is, we all do! We *all* want to be right! No one wants to be wrong! But, **most of us** would rather **belong** than **be right**! You can't belong to two churches at the same time! There is only one church where you can belong AND be right! His Church. We all fancy ourselves as members of His great Church, but membership is by faith – faith based in truth – not truth based in faith. Truth is not something you *believe* is true. Do you know the difference in searching for truth in your faith, and struggling to develop faith in your truth?

Alone Again?

Really, outside of your companionship with your Elder Brother and Savior, you have *always been alone* in your faith. Denominations are not saved, church rolls are not called up yonder, families and bloodlines are not elected to faith, *individuals* are. Real faith requires the strength to stand alone. The clergy and the church have subtly, if not forcefully, juxtaposed themselves as mediators.

When you stand in the invisible and universal body of Messiah, THE Church – the TRUE Church – you stand with Him. From the world's viewpoint you are alone. You may even *feel* alone without your support group, but you will never be alone. C'mon, join the **real** Church, with a **real** Pastor, who baptizes with a **true** baptism, who serves **real** bread, and **really** changes **real** men!

Is yours a true faith? Is your experience with Him real enough that you could live for Him – all by yourself? Is He real enough that you don't need to get wet to be baptized? Is He real enough that you don't need grape juice and crackers to have communion with Him? Is He real enough that you don't need a teacher, pastor, seminary, or Bible commentary to hear His voice? Is your faith real enough that you don't need the acceptance of the majority to know that you are on the right track?

To this point you have considered 150 questions of Jesus. Perhaps this one is the most important yet, *"When the Son of man cometh, shall he find faith on the earth?"*

H

Hatriotism, 164
holidays
    pagan, 307
    replacing Holy Days, 211, 308
Holiness, 63, 110, 142, 391
    Christ's, 65
Holy Days, 210
honesty, 432
humility, 34, 52, 420
Humility, 19, 29, 36, 39, 44, 45, 298, 356, 409
    Christ's, 420
hypocrisy, 238, 274, 372

I

icons, 343, 348, *See* Idols
idolatry, 275, 341, *See* Nehustan
idols, 240
    man-made, 206
    of men, 34
introspection, 67, 143, 152, 155, 158, 166, 181, 196, 250, 262, 277, 288, 294, 306, 312, 350, 353, 375, 390, 435, 451, 464, 476

J

Jesus our Pastor, 82, 131, 280, 309
Joshua, 309
    Namesake of Jesus, 203, 454
    Who led Israel, 277, 454
judgement, 98, 193, 226, 344
judging ourselves, 55, 73, 85, 134, 253

K

Kingdom
    Gospel of, 105, 190
    of God, 26, 30, 40, 96, 101, 104, 125, 129, 131, 169, 174, 186, 199, 241, 248, 257, 258, 271, 289, 318, 336, 421
    of Heaven, 96, 98, 138, 200, 207, 317

L

Law of God, 114, 187
    written in heart, 100
leaven, 374
    doctrine, 128, 134, 248
    removing, 372

Yeast, 320
Lewis, C.S., 332

M

mammon, 25, 99, 126, 127, 235, 236, 237, 272, 288, 402, 412, 441
Meditation, 5, 30, 124, 157, 352, 355
ministry, 88, 91, 119, 122, 149, 247, 271, 454

N

Nehushtan, 341, See Symbolism

O

omnipotent, 368, 369, 370
omnipresence, 369
omniscience, 216, 368

P

paganism, 276, 307, 308, 342
patriotism, 10, 164
peace, 162
Peace, 163
Penn, William, 100, 447
persecution, 153, 213, 216, 281, 357, 413, 442, 475
pride, 128
purpose, 470

Q

Quaker, 35, 100, 123, 131, 187, 188, 266, 385, 397, 414, 447, 461

R

rapture, 97
readiness, 441
Repentance, 182
    for conversion, 54, 261
    of sin, 136
    true, 351
reputation, 29, 67, 140, 141, 172, 173, 189, 212, 219, 301, 344, 346, 382, 421, 424
revelation, 18, 95, 235, 241, 244, 268, 303, 438, 448

* * *

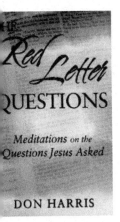

The Red Letter Questions

This book describes the progression of insights and revelation given to Don during the journey that changed his life forever. These are heartfelt thoughts of a man who, through traditional misinterpretation of Scripture, inadvertently disobeyed the God he claimed to love and serve.

On Manna

Do you want to receive the daily guidance that Jesus spoke of? Do you want to know that you daily live and walk in the will of your God?

We must receive the Manna, the Bread from Heaven but, What is it?

On Sabbath

"Is there such a thing as a perfect presentation of Sabbath? Yes! This is it!" MW *(Tennessee)*

For anyone contemplating the Sabbath. This book answers the common questions about the significance of Sabbath to the modern-day Christian. (Also available in Spanish & French.)

Notes:

Contact Information:
Don C. Harris
PO Box 718
Pie Town, New Mexico 87827
www.DonC Harris.com

CPSIA information can be obtained
at www.ICGtesting.com
Printed in the USA
LVOW13s1043290917
550227LV00001B/2/P